ECONOMICS

AN INTRODUCTION TO THE WORLD AROUND YOU
SECOND EDITION

Final Exam
Ques., Dec. 18
3:20-5:20
Armory 106

P9H1295

W9-CKK-168

HC9

ECONOMICS

AN INTRODUCTION TO THE WORLD AROUND YOU
SECOND EDITION

Dennis J. Weidenaar
Emanuel T. Weiler
Purdue University

Addison-Wesley
Publishing Company
Reading, Massachusetts
Menlo Park, California
London · Amsterdam · Don Mills, Ontario · Sydney

Sponsoring Editor: **George M. Abbott**
Production Editor: **Melissa P. Hodgson**
Designer: **Robert A. Rose**
Illustrator: **Reproductions Drawings, Ltd. and ANCO/Boston**
Cover Design: **Robert A. Rose**

This book is in the Addison-Wesley Series in Economics

Library of Congress Cataloging in Publication Data

Weidenaar, Dennis J
    Economics : an introduction to the world around you.

    (Addison-Wesley series in economics)
    Includes index.
    1. Economics.   I. Weiler, Emanuel Thornton, 1914-
joint author. II. Title.
HB171.5.W33 1979   330   78-67942
ISBN 0-201-08517-8

The Blondie cartoon on page 52 is reproduced by permission of © King Features Syndicate, 1975.

Copyright © 1979, 1976 by Addison-Wesley Publishing Company, Inc. Philippines copyright 1979, 1976 by Addison-Wesley Publishing Company, Inc.
All rights reserved. No part of this publication may be reproduced, stored in a retrieval system, or transmitted, in any form or by any means, electronic, mechanical, photocopying, recording, or otherwise, without the prior written permission of the publisher. Printed in the United States of America. Published simultaneously in Canada. Library of Congress Catalog Card No. 78-67942.
ISBN 0-201-08517-8
ABCDEFGHIJ-1-MA-79.

PREFACE FOR TEACHERS

If you were to start from scratch to write a beginning text for both majors and nonmajors, how would you do it? This is the problem we faced in developing a college level first course in economics. We needed an approach that would be analytical enough for prospective economics majors (and for engineering and science students) but would at the same time command the interest of students in the humanities, general business, and home economics.

There are a number of models we might have used.

1. We could have used the *traditional materials* which, with some modifications, have been used during the last thirty years.
2. We could have designed a course emphasizing the *technique of analysis* used in later courses in economics.
3. We could have designed a course around the major social and political *problems* facing the United States.

Because we have taught economics for many years, we have been influenced by each of these models. Parts of this book are no doubt traditional, technique-oriented, and problem solving and indicate our partial acceptance of these models.

None of these models fully satisfied our need, however. We believe that economic theory is the core of economics. At the same time, we are convinced that economic theory need not be as forbidding as the usual techniques of analysis make it appear to be. We believe that typical beginning students want to use economics to interpret and understand what they see happening around them. Sometimes these events involve public policy questions, but many times they involve such mundane questions as "Why is the price of a gallon of gasoline less than the price of a gallon of milk?" or "Why do college students get paid less for doing the same job in a small college town than they would get in a large city?"

We turned, then, to a fourth model. It is this: Select that portion of economic theory and related institutional materials that satisfies two criteria: (1) it has a high probability of being valid and (2) it relates to the life of the student. Economic theory is such a rich lode that unless the textbook writer uses some model to decide what should be included and what should be excluded, a principles text can easily become too long.

Using this model we have omitted some materials usually included in the first course. We have not, for example, included indifference curve analysis. Nor have we placed the usual emphasis on the geometry associated with the theory of the firm.

Our model calls for including some material not usually emphasized in the first course.

1. We have emphasized the impact of relative price changes on output and changes in technology *over the long run*. The theory of the firm relevant for short-run analysis is presented in an appendix to Chapter 5.
2. We have emphasized the linkages between the products and productive services markets. By eliminating the dichotomy between price theory and distribution theory, we have emphasized the unity of a market system for resolving complex economizing problems.
3. In line with recent developments in experimental economics, we have presented a theory of competitive market price that does not

depend on the existence of large numbers and perfect knowledge.

4. Also in line with recent developments in the theory of public goods, we have integrated the government into our model of a market economy.

5. We have included a discussion of the real factors underlying economic growth and changes in employment in a fully developed economy.

6. We have emphasized the role of the interest rate as the bridge between micro and macro economics.

7. We have developed a framework for explaining what is called stagflation.

We think that any part of economic theory that is relevant to the student's life can be taught. We have tried to state economic theory clearly in terms of words and simple supply and demand graphs, leaving the mathematical demonstrations to later courses in economics. We have made generous use of real-life examples as well as teaching aids. We have been gratified that the students who have decided to go on in economics have found themselves prepared for the intermediate theory course. We have also been gratified to find that the students who do not go on have found this course useful.

Finally, a word about the organization of the course. Although by contemporary standards this is a short economics book designed to serve as a one-semester text, it can, if supplemented with problem materials, case studies, and additional readings, also be used as the basic book for a two-semester course. The chapters can be taught in sequence or they can be rearranged in a variety of ways. For example, those teachers who like to teach the macro materials first can teach Unit I and Chapter 3 of Unit II and then skip to Unit IV. Units II, III, and V can be taught as separate blocks. We suspect that many teachers will want to supplement these materials with readings or with some of the many high-quality paperbacks available. Every course is, after all, an individual expression of the teacher's view of life. We hope that you will find these materials as useful to you as they have been to us.

A text such as this is always the product of many people. We are, of course, most indebted to our students who suffered through the four preliminary versions and first edition. We are grateful to James Mak, University of Hawaii, for helping us identify many shortcomings while he taught with us as a visiting professor and to Michael Haynes, Southern Oregon College, for struggling through the first version with us. Our colleagues at Purdue, Peter Harrington, George Horwich, Marianne Talafuse, and Jay Wiley, have improved the book immensely. We of course assume full responsibility for any errors that remain. The text would not have been completed, however, without the skill and patience of Doris Haught, Joan Adams, and Alice Mikesell, our friends, secretaries, and typists. Finally, we apologize to our wives, Kristin and Cathy, for spending more time with the manuscript than with them.

PREFACE FOR STUDENTS

Our goal in the second edition of this book has not changed over the past three years. It is to give you a better understanding of the world around you through a basic understanding of economics.

We believe that you will learn from observing what you see around you from the perspective of modern economic theory. Perhaps an analogy will help clarify this broad objective. If you have just completed a course in geology, the hills, valleys, and ravines around you will no longer simply be hills, valleys, and ravines. Their unique features will reveal information as to how they were formed, when they were formed, and their composition. Similarly, we hope that an understanding of economic theory and economic institutions will help you see the economic landscape around you.

Two basic strategies have been used to help you in achieving this goal. First, as a motivating device we have tried as much as possible to make the material relevant; almost every chapter begins by citing activities or examples that relate to experiences that are familiar to you as a college student. Then, as the chapter proceeds, numerous illustrations are included to maintain this relationship.

Our second strategy was to organize both the book and the individual chapters according to a simple instructional model. This model has three components: (1) specify what we want you the student to understand; (2) design instructional strategies to meet the objectives; and (3) evaluate the degree of success achieved in meeting the objectives.

At the beginning of each chapter, we have specified those objectives we feel will best reflect an important and adequate understanding of the material in that chapter. Given the objectives, each chapter is supplemented with mini-cases and commentaries that offer you various perspectives and provide an opportunity for analysis and criticism. Finally, each chapter concludes with multiple-choice questions that are in most cases analytically oriented. To provide you with immediate feedback, these questions have been answered and the incorrect as well as the correct choices are explained. Each chapter also contains a set of thought-provoking essay questions, most of which, like real-world problems, have no simple answers.

Though our goal and basic strategies have not changed, the economic world around has changed immensely since the first edition was published. The *unemployment-inflation dilemma* of the mid-1970s has not disappeared. If anything, it has worsened, taking a greater toll in terms of unused resources and economic dislocation. The *international economy* is undergoing a major upheaval resulting in the realignment of the strengths of the world's major currencies with a profound effect on life in the United States. The *energy problem* has not disappeared, hard environmental choices persist, and the *role assumed by government* continues to change dramatically. These represent but a sample of the forces that are changing the economic world in which we live.

We have attempted to deal with these changes by including material that provides insight into these events. *The first unit deals with the basic economic problem of scarcity and deals extensively with the nature of resources and the issue of dwindling reserves of minerals, fuels, etc.* Applications of supply and demand have been extended to deal specifically with aspects of the energy problem. An appendix developing *the short-run supply curve has been added using a complete case study as the vehicle for its deri-*

vation. *The explanations of opportunity cost and profit have been expanded and supplemented with more examples.*

The *government chapter is completely new,* reflecting the fact that the United States economy is a mixed market system. *Specific United States tax and expenditure information is put in an appendix.* The "market failure" topics of monopoly, externalities, and income distribution are dealt with in separate chapters much more comprehensively.

Money and banking concepts are followed by a careful comparison of the traditional and monetarist positions. A chapter on the inflation-unemployment dilemma concludes this unit.

International economics is dealt with in the last unit. The concepts of comparative advantage, barriers to trade, and the balance of payments are followed by a discussion of the international monetary system that coordinates international currency flows.

We hope that you will share with us the excitement and satisfaction of understanding the economic world around you.

D. J. W.
Professor of Economics
E. T. W.
Krannert Professor of Economics

West Lafayette, Indiana
January 1979

CONTENTS

STATISTICAL APPENDIX

"Science is built up with facts as a house is with stones. But a collection of facts is no more a science than a heap of stones is a house."

Jules Henri Poincaré
La Science et L'Hypotheses, 1908.

PART I

SCARCITY, RESOURCES, AND THE ECONOMIC SYSTEM

OBJECTIVES

Upon successful completion of this chapter, you will be able to:

1. Cite examples of decisions you have made that reflect the fact that you operate within an economic system. These examples will illustrate how the decisions you make affect this system, and in turn, how you are affected by the decisions others make.

2. Explain the economic concept of scarcity in terms of resources and wants and relate how it underlies all economic decisions.

3. List, and illustrate with examples, the basic questions of every economic system: What will be produced? How will production occur? Who will produce what? and Who will receive what?

4. Identify the common features of all models and explain what an economic model is.

5. Reproduce and explain the relationships among the components of the simple circular-flow model.

6. Identify the products, productive services, and capital markets in the model and list the functions each market plays in answering the basic economic questions.

CHAPTER 1

SCARCITY AND THE ECONOMIC SYSTEM

INTRODUCTION

SCARCITY

A MODEL OF THE ECONOMY

INTRODUCTION

Economics is concerned with the management of scarcity.

How old are you? This may seem a strange, in fact impertinent, question to ask a person who is just beginning a course in economics. We believe, however, that consideration of this question will enable us to focus quickly and sharply on what economics is all about.

Suppose you are 20 years old. We don't know exactly how long *you* will live, but we do know that the life expectancy of the average 20-year-old person in the United States is almost 74 years. In any case, you have a limited amount of time in which to achieve your own personal goals. If in fact you live an additional 54 years, is it long enough to enable you to do all you would like to do? If so, time is not a scarce commodity for you. But if that time period appears inadequate, then the task of managing the next 54 years of your life becomes an *economic* problem. Economics is concerned with the management of *scarcity*, and scarcity exists whenever resources, be they time, food, books, machinery, automobiles, or what have you, are inadequate to meet the wants of a person or a society.

Economics **is the science of managing scarcity.**

Consider in a bit more detail the problem of managing your next 54 years. You will obviously have to make many decisions, and important among them will be: *what* you are going to do, *how* you hope to achieve your goals, *how much* effort you are going to put into your attempts to achieve your goals, and *what rewards* you will receive for your efforts. These decisions are of a kind that everyone must face, and a kind with which every society must cope.

Economic decisions and institutions affect you.

What are you worth? This is the second imperti-nent question that we ask you. You may react immediately by asserting that human life cannot be measured in terms of dollars and cents. The fact remains, however, that we do, and, indeed, we *must* make decisions that affect human life and that implicitly, if not explicitly, provide some judgment about its value.

The point we are making is that the concept of value is very important in economics. You have often heard the adjective "priceless" used to describe something. In economics, however, things are not regarded as having value in and of themselves. Rather, value depends on how much we have of a good or service. In other words, things have value only because someone thinks they have. Even gold has value only because people like to have more of it.

If you continue your college education, it is quite likely that during the 40 or so working years that follow, you will earn a substantial sum. Recently, for example, the projected average lifetime income of a college graduate was $1 million. The amount is smaller for persons with a high-school education and even less for persons without a high-school diploma. But although you may earn $1 million during your lifetime, the answer to the question, What are you worth? is considerably smaller. Much of that $1 million will not be earned in this or even in the next decade, and therefore the value today of the sum of those future earnings is less.

The income you earn during these 40 years will be the most important factor affecting your standard of living. This book deals with the decisions and institutions that are going to influence your earnings during this period. If the economy maintains a sustained growth rate during this 40-year period, your income in all likelihood will rise. If taxes increase substantially, your after-tax income will be less than otherwise. If inflation occurs at a high rate, part of your real income will be chipped away. If the economy falls into periodic fits of depression, your income may be reduced for extended periods of time. The probabilities of all or any of the above events occurring and affecting you directly will also depend on the vocation you pursue during these 40 years. In all cases, many decisions are going to be made in the next 40 years that will have a direct effect on you. You will make some of the decisions individually, you will make some collectively with other members of society, and, in some cases, you will have no hand in the decision; but how you react to the decision will determine its impact on you.

Putting it simply, you have two vital interests in economics. First, you are a participant in a society that uses a particular set of social institutions, and if you are going to be effective in that society, you will have to know how it works. Second, you are a member of the "rules committee." Certainly not everyone will have an equal voice in this "committee." Nevertheless, it is true that in a democracy, more than any other type of governmental organization, you can sit in judgment on your social institutions.

Economic goals are often in conflict.

When you sit on the rules committee, however, you are concerned not only with what will happen if you do something, but also with creating new social institutions that will bring about different outcomes. This introduces the question of social goals. What outcomes do you want?

Consider the goals you have for yourself. Your list might include: freedom to do what you want; a high enough income to enjoy consumption of products; full participation in society; security against the ravages of accident, bad health, and unemployment; and the leisure to fulfill your aspirations to the fullest.

These individual goals are often in conflict. The more you work to obtain a higher income, the less leisure you have. The more you protect yourself with insurance against accidents and bad health, the less you have to use for consumption. These conflicts pose difficult choices, and you will have to choose the set of goals that fits you.

The same thing is true when a society tries to formulate its social goals. Goals of freedom and efficiency may conflict with goals of equality and security. For example, would you favor the adoption of a city income tax in order to finance the day-to-day needs of the unemployed and the dependent in your community? Your freedom to dispose of your income as you see fit is abridged, but at the same time economic security is provided for those who otherwise would suffer severe economic hardship. It is necessary, then, to select that mix of social goals that fits your preconception of what society *ought* to be like.

An important distinction that should be made in economics is between what will happen and what ought to happen.

This statement of what "ought to be" rests on an ethical decision. Economists, as economists, cannot make a decision for you; this is one of the important reasons why economists do not always agree on public policy issues. What "ought to be" is *normative economics*, which contrasts with *positive economics*. *Positive economics* is concerned with what will happen if, given a certain set of economic institutions, you or your government take some action. Knowing positive economics helps you understand the role of the institutions currently being used.

Normative economics deals with how economic issues *ought to be* resolved.
Positive economics deals with how economic issues *are* resolved.

This book attempts to keep *you* in focus as we discuss the economic events and realities that, among other influences, mold your behavior and determine your standard of living. Economics exists as an area of study because (1) your income will surely be too small to satisfy all of your wants, (2) the needs of your community will exceed its capacity to meet them, and (3) the resources at the disposal of your national government simply cannot match all of the wants of society.

This first chapter is designed to achieve two goals: (1) to help you see why economic decisions are an unavoidable part of your life; and (2) to provide you with a means of viewing the overall economy and its many aspects.

SCARCITY

The word *economize* is a key to understanding the concept of scarcity.

"We have got to economize" is a phrase you have heard, perhaps even said, at one time or another. As commonly used, this phrase simply means we have to "tighten our belt a bit" or watch our spending more closely. This use of the word economize opens the door to the basic meaning of scarcity. On a personal level, economizing, as we normally understand it, is necessary if your income is inadequate to sustain your current level of expenditure. This situation could result from a reduction in your income, an increase in your spending, or both. In any case, it becomes necessary to economize when the resources at your disposal do not match your wants. It is precisely this inequality between wants and resources that comprises the basis for scarcity.

Scarcity **is the situation that occurs when resources are inadequate to satisfy wants.**

Scarcity can be viewed from a global or an individual point of view.

Scarcity can be viewed in several ways. Let us consider scarcity first from an overall point of view. At any point in time, there is a limited quantity of resources available. These resources consist of (1) the labor and "skill" embodied in people, (2) the capital equipment accumulated over time, such as machinery, factories, roads, and so on, and (3) the raw materials provided by nature: water, land, and space. In some instances, little modification is necessary to prepare resources for consumption, while in other cases, the activity becomes a very roundabout affair, involving many stages of processing as well as considerable time. The supply of resources and the level of technology primarily determine what is available to satisfy the wants of society. The level of technology—that is, the accumulated knowledge, techniques, and tools used to make goods and services—affects the access to resources and the effectiveness with which we use them.

How real is this concept of scarcity on the individual level? Well, as an example, we will ask you what you are going to do tonight, study for a test to be given tomorrow morning or go to a concert? Should you buy that stereo amplifier you've been eyeing or that programmable calculator? If you've only got $10 left for food for your family and won't be paid for five more days, what should you do—buy bread and potatoes for three meals or splurge the $10 on a Walt Disney movie for the kids?

What do each of these situations have in common? Each one describes a case in which you have to make a choice and by making that choice give up the opportunity to do something else. By taking your children to a movie, you have given up several meals. By choosing to purchase that programmable. calculator, you have also chosen *not* to purchase an amplifier, at least for a while. If you decided to spend the evening enjoying the concert, you know that it will cost you a letter grade on tomorrow's test.

Each choice described above has a real cost. That cost, called the *opportunity cost*, consists of the best alternative choice you gave up. The table below summarizes the three decisions described and the opportunity cost of each one.

Decision	Opportunity cost
1. Go to a concert	A full letter grade on the test
2. Purchase a programmable calculator	A stereo amplifier
3. Attend a movie with the family	Three meals for your family

Why is it necessary to bear these costs? The answer is that our wants—the things that give us satisfaction, such as eating, drinking, listening to music, sleeping, watching a football game, and countless other activities—far exceed our resources, our ability to provide them. This means that we must get along with less than we want. Such a situation in which our wants are greater than the resources at our disposal is called *scar-*

city. This one word describes the basic economic problem confronting all individuals, families, societies, businesses, unions, and governments.

The degree of scarcity varies among individuals.

The fact that both resources and wants are not equally distributed complicates the problem of scarcity when viewed at the individual or family level. If a family's resources are so meager, for example, that the basic requirements of food, clothing, and shelter necessary for survival cannot be met, it is obvious that scarcity exists for that family. The concept of scarcity is less obvious in more affluent societies, where scarcity means not being able to purchase that third automobile or second boat, or not being able to have steak every week.

Does scarcity in fact exist in these latter situations? If the wants referred to in the definition of scarcity are narrowed to encompass only those wants necessary for human survival, then scarcity, as the term is used in everyday language, would not exist in a condition of affluence. Basing their argument on this narrow definition of scarcity, some people today deny the necessity for the existence of scarcity. They assert that a "proper" distribution of the nation's or world's existing resources would virtually erase the problem. The justification given for this narrow interpretation of wants is that most of the wants over and above

the subsistence level are not "natural wants," but rather are socially determined. The fact remains, however, that there are very few people in the world today, even in the United States, who would state that their wants are being satisfactorily met.

The confusion identified above can be clarified if we make a distinction between the terms scarcity and shortage, which are frequently used interchangeably. *Scarcity* describes a situation in which wants are greater than the capacity of existing resources to meet them. Evidence of scarcity in a market economy is the existence of prices. Goods with no prices—free goods, in other words—are not *scarce* goods. It is difficult to find examples of free goods. If you were in a boat in the middle of the ocean, salt water would be a free good.

A *shortage,* on the other hand, exists when at a given price, the quantity demanded of a good or service exceeds the quantity supplied. It is likely that at some higher price, the quantity demanded would not exceed the quantity supplied and a shortage would then, by definition, no longer exist. The good in question still is scarce, however, since it has a price. Only if the price were to fall to zero would the good become a free good and cease to be scarce.

To help clarify your thinking about the concept of scarcity, consider Mini-case 1.1 on p. 8. There may be no correct, or for that matter incorrect, answer. Indeed, you may wish to add another answer that reflects your own interpretation.

The choices necessitated by scarcity are reflected in our daily decisions.

Economics is a social science: It deals with the interactions of individuals as they make the choices dictated by scarcity. In modern industrial societies such as ours, the choices necessitated by scarcity are expressed in many ways. When we buy soap, clothing, or automobiles, we are expressing our economizing choices, or when we decide to work in one place and not another, or to save a larger part of our income rather than spend it on goods and services. Or, when our government decides, presumably with our approval, to collect taxes from us and spend these

---

MINI-CASE 1.1

Scarcity, according to the textbook definition, is all pervasive. It affects everyone. This is incorrect. Human wants, beyond the basic needs of food, clothes, and shelter, are fabricated by persons who see in such synthetic wants the opportunity to enrich themselves materially and politically.

a) The defect in this statement is that it fails to appreciate real human nature, the fact that humans are acquisitive creatures.
b) This statement doesn't really get at the issue, since the textbook definition of scarcity is inadequate. For example, if my salary is $50,000 a year, I can buy all the cokes I will ever want—for me scarcity does not exist for all goods.
c) This statement is basically correct—if the ad-persons of Madison Avenue would quit the nonsense of creating fictitious wants we would all be better off.
d) The statement is inaccurate, since quite frankly I don't care who influences my wants or desires—all I know is that looking at myself and other people, I observe unsatisfied wants and to me that reflects scarcity.

---

tax revenues to provide city recreational facilities, we are joining with others in making economizing decisions. All of these choices involve the balancing of benefits and opportunity costs.

To see how these economizing decisions are linked together in modern economics, we will use a model of the economy.

COMMENTARY

Models are the basis for scientific inquiry. We also use them frequently in everyday life. The following commentary describes some examples of models and identifies three of their common features. Please read the commentary and answer the following questions.

a) How does the use of the word *model* differ when used to describe a model airplane and a model child?
b) List the three common features of models and cite an example that illustrates these features.

WHAT IS A MODEL?

In our day-to-day lives we are constantly using models. Some we do recognize explicitly as such.

A fashion model wears clothes to give other people some idea of how the clothes would look on them. Although the fashion model cannot show exactly how the clothes will look on another person who does not have the same physique, there is usually enough information to deduce this. This kind of model does more than provide information about clothes; he or she is also an ideal—a person to admire and perhaps to envy.

An artist's model is also a real person: an original that is copied by the artist. The copy is

seldom a complete reproduction—the artist omits some details because his purpose is not simply reproduction but is rather the creation of a new work of art.

A model airplane is usually a copy of an existing aircraft. Again it omits details, usually because it is smaller than the original. Many models are of this type: model cars, model soldiers, model ships, and so on. Sometimes such models are built before the originals to help designers test various facets of the design.

The model T was a *type* of automobile rather than a miniature reproduction of one. This usage of the word has continued to apply to varieties of automobiles, televisions, radios, and other kinds of consumer durables.

Like the model airplane, the model of the Indian village is a scale copy that omits some details because of its size. Unlike the model airplane, this model is not a copy of a *particular* Indian village. It picks out and illustrates the important features of most Indian villages. It is, therefore, not a representation of a particular village but a classification system showing the features usually found in Indian villages.

A model child differs the most from the other types of models. From the parent's point of view, a model child is the best possible child. Similarly, a model student is the best possible student from the teacher's point of view. The essential feature of this use of the word is that certain characteristics are picked out as being the most desirable in a certain situation.

These six familiar uses of the word model do differ, but certain common features are beginning to emerge.

First, all models tell us something about another object. The fashion model gives us an idea (though a distorted one) of how we would look in those clothes; the Indian village provides us with a picture of the surroundings in which most Indians lived.

Second, models omit some details of the object they represent. These details are usually irrelevant to the purposes of the model. Thus, the concept of the model student will not include details of the student's hair color (although the concept of the model cheerleader may well include such details!).

This omission means that the model is usually a simplified version of the other object.

Third, some models have the purpose of *recommending* characteristics of the other object.

In this way, we can arrive at a working definition of a model: it is a way of looking at a real-life object by omitting those aspects that are considered irrelevant and outlining the relationships considered important for present purposes.

If this definition is correct, you can see that we often use models without referring to them as such.

A map is a model because it reproduces only some of the features of a certain area. It may, for example, provide only the information necessary to help one find one's way. Similarly, a dress pattern is a model providing enough information for the dressmaker to be able to make a dress. A designer's sketch is also a model that shows roughly what the dress will look like. Note that while these last two may both be models of the same dress, they give different information. A dressmaker cannot use the designer's sketch directly to make the dress, and one cannot know the appearance of the dress just by looking at the pattern.

This is an important point. Since a model is an abstraction—a simplification of reality—it is possible to have different models of the same piece of reality. The type of model will depend on its intended purpose.

Ivy Papps and Willie Henderson, *Models and Economic Theory*. Philadelphia: W. B. Saunders, 1977. Reprinted by permission.

A MODEL OF THE ECONOMY

Economic models can help sort out the many interactions occurring in an economy.

The economic interactions among hundreds of millions of people, the transactions among thousands of business firms, the effects of hundreds of tax laws, and the billions of dollars of government expenditure exemplify the activities occurring in an economic system. The task of sorting out these interactions and interpreting them cannot be accomplished without some means of establishing order in this seemingly chaotic scenario of events.

To achieve some understanding of the complexity of any economic system we will need a way to organize the events occurring in the economic world around us. The rest of this chapter presents such a way.

We intend to achieve this organization through the use of a model, a technique with which you are familiar. The use of models has become an everyday occurrence in your life. For example, a thermometer is a model; it is a device that translates a complex concept, temperature, into a single number. The chief virtue of a model, its ability to simplify, can also be its chief drawback, since simplification means omission of some aspects of reality.

An *economic model* is a simplified representation of reality including only those aspects necessary to observe the essence of the problem under consideration.

Our model of the economy, like a map, should be as broad and encompassing or as narrow and precise as we want it to be, depending on the problem we are considering. If we choose the broad approach, we are taking the *macro* perspective, which examines the way large aggregates fit together; if we select a narrower but more detailed approach, we are using a *micro* perspective, which is concerned with the way the individual entities of the aggregate fit together. A macro map of the United States, for example, would show how the large land masses of the Midwest and South are related by distance and topography to the coastal areas of the East and Far West. Such a map would not show minor rivers, small towns, or county boundaries. It would be useful if we were explaining how one could fly by jet plane from New York City to Chicago, but it would not be useful in organizing a political campaign for the presidency. For that purpose we would need a micro map showing state, county, and township boundaries as well as population densities.

The circular-flow model illuminates the relationships among the basic sectors of the economy.

We will begin our model-building project with a macro representation of the economy. Since our objective is to help you understand the operation of the United States economy, which relies more heavily on free markets than do most economies, we will use a model of a market economy. Examine the simple model of the economy shown in Fig. 1.1. You will see that we have divided the economy into two large parts or sectors, namely, households and businesses; this is an oversimplification, but a useful one. The term *households* refers to the families and individuals who make up the population of the United States. The households consume the goods and services produced by businesses and provide the inputs for production. The term *businesses* refers to the organizations that buy labor and other productive services, convert these productive services into products, and sell the products to households. This model is called a *circular-flow model* since it represents the way money and products flow through the economy in a circular fashion from households to businesses and back again to households.

The two squares on the sides of the circular-flow diagram are labeled "businesses" and "households." They can be regarded as the decision-making centers for these two sectors of the economy. The inside dotted line flowing from households to the circle labeled "productive services market" (arrow 1) represents the services of men and women, and other types of resources owned by households flowing to the market in which they are offered for sale.

A *market* is a medium in which buyers and sellers interact.

In the productive services market, transactions are made that determine the quantities, the amounts of payments for the services, and the destinations of the particular productive services offered by individual households. Once these transactions are completed, the productive services flow into the businesses square where they are converted into products. The dotted line from the productive services market to the businesses square represents this flow (arrow 2).

The dotted line from the businesses square to the "products market" (arrow 3) represents the flow of products, such as automobiles, baby carriages, dry cleaning services, and so on, into the

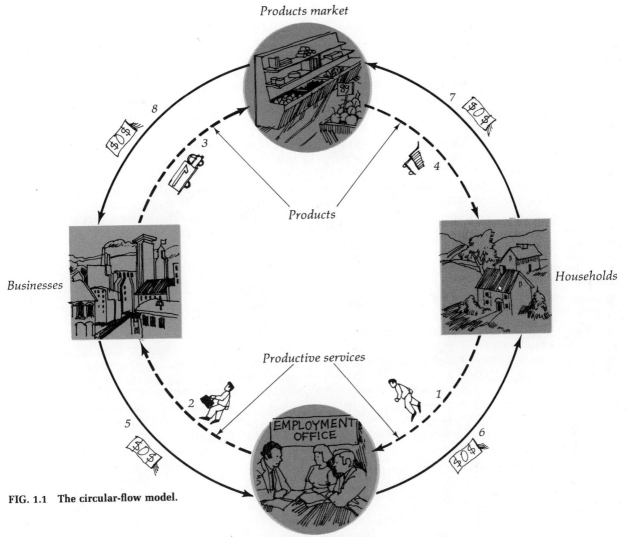

FIG. 1.1 The circular-flow model.

products market, where they are offered for sale. Once they are purchased, the dotted line from the products market to the household square represents the delivery of these products from the market to the ultimate users, the households (arrow 4).

If we were to make a partial list of these flows for a period of time, it might appear as shown at right:

Flow of productive services per year	Flow of products per year
3 billion hours of labor	8 million automobiles
Use of $100 billion of capital	50 million infant diapers
Use of 200 square miles of land	100 million theater admissions

You can imagine how long and detailed the list would be if the quantities of all of the productive services and products flowing between businesses and households were listed.

When one knows the quantities and when the prices of the various types of productive services and products are established in the two markets, the value of the reverse flow of money (as indicated by the outside solid line) can be determined. For example, 3 billion hours of labor priced at $3 per hour yields a flow of money payments equal to $9 billion. Starting with businesses, money would flow into the productive services market to pay for productive services (arrow 5), and from there into households (arrow 6). Households, in turn, spend the income they have received in the products market to buy the goods and services businesses have produced and offered for sale (arrow 7). The money ultimately ends up in the businesses sector (arrow 8). These flows are also shown in Fig. 1.1, represented by solid arrows.

This simple circular-flow model of the economy has a long history in economics. It shows the relationships between the basic producing and consuming sectors of the economy, businesses and households. Businesses sell products to obtain the money to pay households for productive services. Households sell productive services to obtain the money to pay businesses for the products.

Market signals provide guidance for producers and consumers.

In a properly functioning market economy, markets provide a medium for transactions and are the source of price information that helps to guide the flow of inputs and outputs in the economy. The *market for products* guides businesses to produce *what* households demand. If some businesses produce the wrong products, their products will go unsold or, at best, will have to be sold at distress prices. This indicates that the businesses have misinterpreted or ignored the market's signals; as a consequence, they will not have the money income to continue buying productive services.

The *market for productive services* also gives directions to businesses, namely, *how*. If the price of some productive services—say skilled labor—increases, the costs of producing goods that require a substantial amount of skilled labor will rise, and this in turn means that the prices of products relying on skilled labor for their production will rise in the products market. If households buy smaller quantities of the higher-priced products, businesses respond by cutting down on their production of "skilled-labor" products and/or seeking ways to substitute other types of productive services for skilled labor. An economic system guided by markets has many "feedback" relationships. What happens in one market determines what happens in other markets, and vice versa. But the circular-flow model in Fig. 1.1 is too simple to describe fully the economic system.

The financial capital market mobilizes savings.

In Fig. 1.2 you will see that we have included a third market in the circular-flow model, the *financial capital market*. Households not only sell productive services and buy products, they also save and either directly or indirectly buy ownership shares in businesses or lend businesses money, thereby transferring control of real resources to them. When you put part of your paycheck in a savings and loan association, for example, you are really directing your money into the financial capital market.

The functions of the financial capital market can be illustrated simply by the following example. Suppose households do not wish to spend all of their income or, stated differently, do not wish to consume all of the resources to which their money income would entitle them. Indeed, they may place some of their unspent money income in a savings account, in a pension plan, or in one of any number of savings plans. Such actions make money available—actually, resources available—for those who wish to borrow. Suppose that a business seeks funds to invest in apartment houses. To do this, it may sell "securities," which are really offers to borrow in order to obtain the funds. Depending on the type, these securities may carry an interest rate. The interest rate is the price the business will have to pay savers for the use of their funds. The solid horizontal lines in Fig. 1.2 represent the flow of money from house-

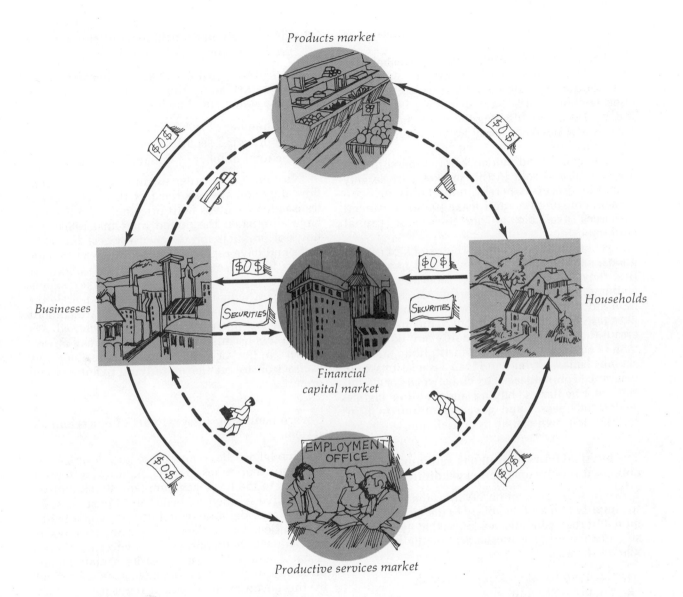

FIG. 1.2 The circular-flow model including a capital market.

holds through the financial capital market, which is the name given to the set of institutions that help mobilize and disperse savings to businesses, in this case to finance the apartment houses. The dotted horizontal line from businesses through the capital market to households represents the flow of securities from businesses to households. Once these securities flow into the households square, they represent ownership certificates or claims.

The financial capital market, as we shall discover later on, has a very important role in any market-directed economy. Most importantly, it allocates households' savings among businesses. It does this by establishing the prices households receive and businesses pay for the use of households' savings.

The claims and evidences of ownership that are bought and sold in this market arise largely from the process whereby households give up present consumption and make the unconsumed resources available to businesses for capital equipment.

When businesses add to their stock of capital goods, such as tools, machinery, and new facilities, they usually have to sell securities, that is, claims or evidences of ownership, such as common stock, to obtain the money to finance their purchase of these capital goods. Thus businesses create the claims that households buy with their money savings. Frequently, institutions such as savings banks, savings and loan associations, and insurance companies act as go-betweens or financial intermediaries, buying and holding claims against businesses and government and in turn selling their own claims to households.

The physical flows of products and inputs can be collapsed into income and expenditure flows.

Now we will make an observation that will help to simplify and add flexibility to the circular-flow model of the economy. We know that every sales slip documenting a transaction in the products market shows:

1. the quantity of each product sold,
2. the price per unit, and
3. the total number of dollars spent.

This last amount is the product of the price and quantity, that is, total expenditure equals price times quantity. Every payroll voucher documenting a transaction in the productive services market also shows:

1. the number of hours worked,
2. the hourly wage rate, and

3. the total amount of the payroll check or the product of the wage rate and hours.

The same price-quantity relationship exists in the capital market. Every time a transaction is made, there is a statement showing:

1. the number of securities,
2. the price per security, and
3. the total number of dollars involved.

In Fig. 1.3, in order to simplify the circular-flow diagram, we use the fact that every dollar transaction involves both price and quantity. We have eliminated the dotted lines that reflect the flows of products, productive services, and securities and have replaced the solid lines with wide arrows to represent both flows at the same time. The wide arrow now represents a money expenditure flow, which, as we have seen, is merely the product of the quantities and prices of the goods and services made available and purchased. We can do this because we know that we can always return to the original documentation for any transaction to get the underlying quantities and prices.

Government is an integral part of our economic system.

The model we have just presented describes an economy that relies purely on markets for the answers to the basic economic questions. But we do not live in such an economy! Consider some of your own day-to-day activities. If you attend a state college or university, most of the costs of your education are borne by the government. If it is not a state school, many of its operations and building construction costs have been subsidized by the government. If you drive a car, you use roads provided by the government. In addition, you receive police protection, are defended by the armed forces, and have access to a judicial system—to mention only a few of the services *not* provided by private producers through the marketplace.

Like any other producing and disbursing agency, the government cannot operate without financial resources flowing into it. If you have a part-time job, you know that your "take-home

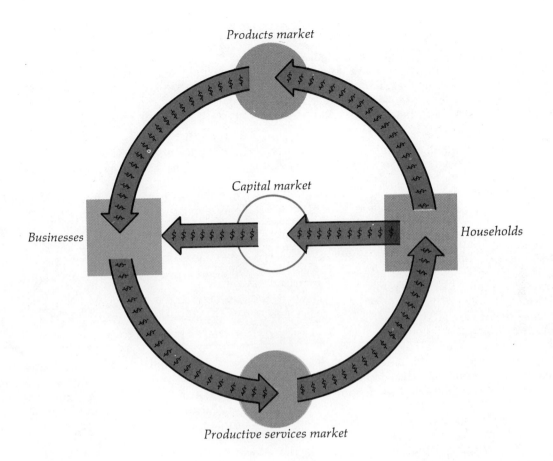

Products market

Capital market

Businesses

Households

Productive services market

FIG. 1.3 The circular-flow model showing money expenditure flows.

pay" is less than your salary. You paid a sales tax on top of the advertised price when you bought that pair of blue jeans last week. The admission price to the show you saw recently included an excise tax.

The government operates in two fundamental ways that compare to the roles assumed by producers and consumers. First, like businesses, government produces goods and services; second, like households, government makes decisions as to how resources will be used. In a sense, govern-ment makes the decision as to what collective or public goods to produce as well as how it wishes to transfer resources among the various groups in the economy. This is why our economy is called a *mixed market economy*. The impact of govern-ment on the economy will be examined in Chap-ter 7. For the present, our analysis will rely heav-ily on the market model.

Consider Mini-case 1.2. Again, as in the pre-vious case, you may not agree with any of the alternatives and may wish to add your own.

MINI-CASE 1.2

The attempt to simplify the real world into neat little compartments made up of consumers, producers, government, and so on is just one more example of the bankruptcy of economics. Instead of enlisting their efforts in attacking real-world problems as they are—such as many sociologists, political scientists, and psychologists do—the economists fritter their lives away playing intellectual games.

a) This assessment of economics is basically correct. It appears that economists are interested only in issues that have quantifiable variables and most real-world problems are not quantifiable.

b) This assessment is basically incorrect, since economists can make generalizations about human behavior that will lend insight into problems even though all aspects of the problem may not be quantifiable.

c) This assessment is incorrect, since it doesn't really recognize that economics deals with choice-making under conditions of scarcity, and that therefore the tools of economic analysis are useful whenever and wherever choices are made.

d) This assessment fails to reflect a real understanding of the scientific method. All sciences worth their salt, social as well as physical, must unravel and simplify the complexities of the real world by simplifying certain aspects of reality, to obtain a clearer picture of "how things work."

Economizing involves decisions concerning what, how, from whom, and for whom.

With this model of the economy in mind, we can add to our understanding of what is meant by *economizing*. Suppose that you were made the absolute dictator of the United States economy. Armed with massive computers and a staff of expert advisers, you would have to make the key decisions that would assist the economy in meeting the needs of the society. What would you have to decide?

You would have to decide, in the first place, *what* should be produced. This would involve knowing what the limits of your output capacity were. You would also have to develop an output plan for the year, consisting of a specific number of automobiles, tons of flour, baby carriages, new factories, miles of new highway, and so forth. As you make these *what* decisions, you would be deciding what portion of your resources you were going to use to produce products for households and what portion for capital equipment, such as machinery and tools. You would decide what portion of total output would go to government.

In the second place, you would have to make thousands of *how* decisions. For example, consider the different ways corn can be produced. Corn can be produced by large inputs of human labor and horse-drawn equipment, as is now the way with the Amish farmers, or it can be produced by massive inputs of capital invested in large tractors and cultivating and harvesting equipment, much as it is done today on large midwestern farms. Between these two extremes, there are hundreds of different ways to produce corn. As an economic planner, you would have to decide which of these technologies to use in each of the thousands of locations where corn is raised. You would have to make the same decisions for each product in the master plan. The task would not be easy. If your choice of technologies were inconsistent with the supplies of each type of resource, for example, you could easily end up with a surplus of labor and a shortage of capital.

In the third place, you would have to generate a set of work assignments so that every worker would know where he or she was supposed to work. This assignment problem could be solved arbitrarily, as it is in wartime military service, or it could take into account the preferences of the workers, which will complicate your problem immensely. These assignment problems we call *from whom* decisions: They involve determining from whom you will get the labor inputs and, if you permit the private ownership of land and capital, from whom you will get the land and capital you assign to particular industries.

Finally, you would have to decide how to distribute the products included in your production plan. There are a variety of ways you can do this. You can use ration tickets to allocate food and other products. Or you can pay out money wages and then set prices in the products market that will ration what you produce. This distribution problem we will call the *to whom* decisions.

Your task of income distribution is complicated by the fact that these decisions are all interrelated. If you strive for absolute equality by seeking to assume that everybody gets the same wage rates, you may have trouble getting the skilled workers to put out as much effort as you would if you gave them a premium wage rate for developing their skills. This would in turn affect the kinds and amounts of goods you can expect to produce in a year.

As we deal with the nature of a mixed, market-directed economy, as we will in the rest of this book, we shall find that the three markets pictured in Fig. 1.3, together with the framework of laws and regulations established by the government, answer these four questions for millions of products and millions of workers every hour.

The *what* question is answered by the products market and the capital market. The prices set in the productive services market, as well as those set in the capital market, serve as guides to producers in choosing technologies compatible with the available quantities of resources and thus answer the *how* question. The prices developed in the productive services markets, taken in conjunction with activity choices of workers and other suppliers of productive services, answer the *from whom* question. Finally, the set of prices called wage rates, rental rates, and interest rates established in the productive services and capital markets determines how much income each household will get to spend on the products being offered in the products markets. In a mixed economy, as we shall see, the government can markedly modify these results by the way it imposes regulations and taxes, and by the way it makes transfer payments.

The important message at this stage is that some type of system will be used to answer these questions in an economy. Many types of systems have been used, ranging from an economy that is basically centrally directed, such as the Soviet Union's, to the early United States economy, which was basically a market-directed economy with very little government involvement. Whenever people, whether in communes or in utopian societies, have tried to live without some system for answering these four questions and for disciplining participants to respond to these answers, their social experiment has failed.

REVIEW QUESTIONS

1. What is meant by the assertion that every economic system faces the fact of scarcity?
   a) All economies have depressions during which scarcities exist.
   b) There are times when some products can be had only by paying high prices.
   c) There are insufficient productive resources to satisfy all wants of a society.
   d) In the beginning, every society faces shortages, but a mature economy overcomes scarcity in time.

2. Scarcity implies:

a) that population growth ought to be reduced.
b) the need for income redistribution.
c) the need for some economic allocative mechanism.
d) capitalism.

3. The economizing problem is essentially one of deciding how to make the best use of:

a) limited resources to satisfy limited wants.
b) unlimited resources to satisfy limited wants.
c) limited resources to satisfy unlimited wants.
d) unlimited resources to satisfy unlimited wants.

4. To a great extent, a market economy solves the basic economizing problem by:

a) making us rich enough to ignore it.
b) having each businessperson plan the consumption of society.
c) having the consumer plan the production of society.
d) allowing businesspeople and consumers to act as their self-interest directs them.

5. The four economic problems of what, how, from whom, and for whom goods shall be produced apply to:

a) centrally planned societies.
b) market or capitalistic societies.
c) underdeveloped societies.
d) all societies.

6. In the circular-flow model of the economy, three distinct markets are shown. These three markets are:

a) government market, business market, household market.
b) financial capital market, productive services market, final products market.
c) profit market, demand market, supply market.
d) resource market, food market, price market.

7. Which of the following best describes the products market?

a) Households offer their services to firms in exchange for money.
b) Goods produced by firms are sold to households for money.
c) Households offer services in exchange for goods.
d) Firms advertise to sell more goods.

8. The use of a circular-flow model:

a) can help us answer the question: What set of social goals should society be maximizing?
b) can shed light on the economic operations within a system of interacting markets but not within a system controlled by a central planning agency.
c) can show us the underlying prices and quantities paid for products and the wages and hours worked.
d) can show how the parts of an economic system fit together.

9. The purpose of a model is:
   a) to simplify a complex system so that events can be organized in a way that is easier to understand.
   b) to include everything that affects a system.
   c) to show how economics can take real problems and turn them into diagrams that explain everything about the problem.
   d) to show how each transaction in the market is made without regard to general principles.

ESSAY QUESTIONS

1. Garrett Hardin, a well-known biologist, has stated what has now become known as Hardin's Law. It is: "You can never do merely one thing." From what the circular-flow model of the economy tells you about the interrelatedness of a money-using economy, give two examples of the application of Hardin's Law in economics.

2. Draw a picture of a circular-flow model. Before you do this exercise take a walk around your campus. Describe the economic events you have seen. Be sure to put each event in the correct flows.

3. It has been stated that with the greater use of computers all goods can be produced by machines. Would this mean that scarcity would be eliminated?

4. Suppose the federal government were to develop a machine that would lend unlimited amounts of newly produced money to anybody who inserted his social security number into the machine. The only restriction to this operation is that the borrower would have to pay a 4 percent interest rate on his loan until he had repaid it. What effect do you think this machine would have on the interest rate in the financial capital market? And what effect do you think this machine would have on the functioning of the economy?

5. Again turn your attention to the simple circular-flow model. Now suppose that all wage rates and other productive service prices were doubled by an act of law. What effect do you think this would have on the products market? Why?

ANSWERS TO REVIEW QUESTIONS

1. Scarcity is defined as the situation that prevails when available resources are insufficient to cope with the wants of society.
   a) This statement means little since scarcity as defined above always exists.
   b) This statement is correct by itself, but does not explain what is meant by scarcity.
   c) This is correct as scarcity is defined above.
   d) This is false. Scarcity is not overcome with maturation of an economy.

2. Scarcity exists when wants exceed the resources available to satisfy those wants. Somehow a system must be developed or emerge to determine what wants will be satisfied.

a) A reduction in population growth implies a reduction in aggregate wants, but it also reduces the output potential of an economy. Scarcity does not necessarily imply pursuit of this strategy.

b) Scarcity means not everyone has as much as he or she wants. It says nothing about how income is distributed among members of an economy.

c) This is correct. Since this is not enough to meet all needs, some mechanism must allocate the existing resources.

d) Scarcity exists in economies of every type.

3. Scarcity is defined as the situation that prevails when wants are greater than the resources available to meet those wants. The economizing problem is the problem of coping with this situation.

a) This is incorrect. Wants are unlimited.

b) This is incorrect. Resources are limited and wants are unlimited.

c) This is correct as explained above.

d) This is incorrect. Wants are limited.

4. A market economy is characterized by the absence of central planning and the presence of individual decisions motivated by self-interests that influence what, how, and for whom commodities will be produced.

a) This is incorrect. Resources will never be sufficient to meet all of our wants.

b) This is incorrect. Letting someone else plan our consumption will neither reduce our real wants nor increase the resources available.

c) This is incorrect for the same reason that (b) is incorrect.

d) This is correct as explained above.

5. Whenever scarcity exists, the problems of what, how, from whom, and for whom exist. Therefore, (d) is correct since it is the only all-inclusive answer.

6. The circular-flow model represents the interactions between the major producing and consuming sectors of the economy. These sectors are businesses and households. The media or arenas in which these interactions occur are represented as markets. The three basic markets are: the final products market, the market for productive services, and the financial capital market. Hence, the answer to this question is (b).

7. The products market is that market in which households buy finished goods and services sold by producers.

a) This is incorrect. It describes the productive services market.

b) This is correct as explained above.

c) This is incorrect. It describes a barter system of exchange incorporating both the products and the productive services markets.

d) This is incorrect. It describes only one aspect of the products market.

8. The circular-flow diagram is a simplified model of our complex economy showing the major sectors and markets and how they interact.

   a) This is incorrect. The model does not prescribe values.
   b) This is incorrect. Even centrally planned systems use markets, albeit frequently modified.
   c) This is incorrect. The model is not that detailed.
   d) This is correct as explained above.

9. The definition of a model is a simplification of reality including only those aspects relevant for understanding the issues at hand.

   a) This is correct as explained above.
   b) This is incorrect. A model does not include everything.
   c) This is incorrect. A model is only an abstraction of parts of reality.
   d) This is incorrect. It is impossible to explain every transaction.

OBJECTIVES

Upon successful completion of this chapter, you will be able to:

1. Identify and define the basic resources of land, labor, and capital as they appear throughout the economy and give examples of combinations of resources.

2. Identify factors that determine the size of the labor force.

3. Explain the process by which capital is accumulated, using the concepts of saving, transfer of resources, and investing.

4. Describe the relationship between prices and technology that complicates the task of measuring resource availability.

5. Explain the fact that specializing, though efficient, "freezes" resources into a fixed form for a given period of time.

6. Cite the implications of "turnover" periods of different lengths.

7. Explain the complications stemming from the fact that some economic resources are not substitutable one for another without a loss in output.

8. Define and give illustrations of the Law of Diminishing Marginal Returns.

9. Explain the relationship between changes in total and marginal output both verbally and graphically.

10. Illustrate the concept of scarcity using a production possibilities curve.

11. Explain the shape of production possibilities curves.

CHAPTER 2

RESOURCES AND THE LAW OF DIMINISHING MARGINAL RETURNS

INTRODUCTION

What kind of image does your college or university bring to mind? Is it a place where persons are prepared for future occupations? Is it a place where people learn to appreciate the aesthetic qualities of reality? Or is it a four-year party school? Few of you probably regard it as an institution that creates human capital, yet this is an important function schools perform in any economy.

How do you view that interstate freeway that passes near your home? Is it a fast, efficient means of getting from home to school or work? Is it a quick way of getting to your favorite recreation area? From an economic viewpoint, the services it yields are inputs in the production process. An apple hanging on a tree in an orchard, for example, is not the same as an apple in your lunch. The roadway plays a role in making that apple available.

This chapter is concerned with resources. As the examples above indicate, they are all around

you, although up until now you have probably not viewed them as inputs in the process of production. Resources, however, must usually be combined to produce the goods and services we want. Furthermore, they cannot be combined effectively without considering a basic economic law that governs the relationship between inputs and outputs. This is the *Law of Diminishing Marginal Returns*.

Resources are scarce. If steel is used for producing automobiles, it cannot be used for metal office furniture. Oil used to generate electricity is not available to heat homes. If you are being educated for a career in social work, you will not be prepared to teach economics. The hard decisions created by the existence of scarcity are represented forcefully in schedules and curves of production possibilities.

This chapter, then, deals with resources, the Law of Diminishing Marginal Returns, and production possibilities.

RESOURCES

Economic resources are divided into three classes—labor, land, and capital—but usually appear as some combination of the three.

You don't have to look far to see economic resources. Factories, machinery, tools, and equipment are easily recognized as specialized kinds of resources, but the park or parking lot outside of your window and the dormitory or house in which you live are also resources. It is traditional to divide economic resources into three types: *labor, land,* and *capital*. But sometimes it is more convenient to divide resources into even more types. The services performed by entrepreneurs, the risk-taking managers of businesses, are sometimes grouped under a separate category called entrepreneurial skills. The services provided by government can also be regarded as sufficiently unique to be called a separate resource or factor of production. For our purposes, however, we will use simply the three categories of land, labor, and capital.

Each of these types of resources yields a flow of productive inputs; hence they are called *productive services*. Labor provides a flow of human services; land provides a flow of raw materials (such as oil, coal, and other nonhuman energy sources), fertility, and space; and capital provides a flow of services from buildings, machinery, equipment, inventories, roads, bridges, and other resources made by humans.

We are using the term *capital* here not in the sense of money or financial resources, but in the sense of equipment—tools, machinery, and factories.

To classify resources in these three distinct forms is a somewhat artificial convenience; in reality, economic resources often appear in some combination of labor, land, or capital. Highly trained neurosurgeons, for example, are obviously a labor resource, but they also embody a good deal of human capital consisting of an enormous accumulation of knowledge and hard-won clinical skills. By far the largest share of their income is payment for their prior investment in human capital, in the time and resources used in developing their special skills, rather than for their labor skills. If, for example, a neurosurgeon's annual salary is $100,000, 80 percent of that salary, or $80,000, could be viewed as the return for the human capital resources, whereas 20 percent, or $20,000, might reflect the value of the labor skills if offered in the market.

Another example illustrating the combined forms in which resources appear is the agricultural land along the lower Mississippi. It is partly *land* (in the economic sense) and partly the capital invested in the dikes that makes it useful for agricultural purposes.

Nonetheless, it is useful to divide economic resources into distinct classes because each of these classes of resources comes into being in a different way. In considering what determines the total quantity of resources available to a nation and therefore its output capabilities, it is helpful to examine the source of each kind of resource. We will now consider what determines the quantity of labor, land, and capital available to an economy.

Labor is the term used to identify human resources.

Labor, when analyzed as an economic resource, is the services provided by the labor force. The size of a nation's labor force is determined by a variety of factors. These include: (1) the size of the population; (2) the legal system, which in the United States effectively bars both young and old people from full participation in the labor force; (3) social practices and prejudices that limit the full participation of females and minority groups in the labor force; and (4) the availability, cost, and payoff from continued education.

While the population places an upper limit on the availability of *labor services* (flowing from the labor force), the actual quantity of labor services is largely determined by work-versus-leisure decisions made by the millions of working people. The kinds of jobs people select reflect these decisions. Members of the working population decide in a variety of ways how many hours they will work each week. Sometimes they decide through participation in union negotiations with employers; sometimes through decisions to

"moonlight"; and sometimes through individual decisions not to work.

Land is the general term used for natural resources.

The term *land,* as used in economics, refers to the natural resources available from nature. These resources include: (1) the natural fertility of the soils; (2) deposits of coal, oil, natural gas, and other minerals; (3) lakes, streams, and other sources of water, including the assimilative capacity of water and air to deal with pollutants; (4) the hills, mountains, plateaus, and other topographical features; and, finally, (5) space, which may ultimately turn out to be more scarce than any other resource.

Over a period of time, the natural resource base of a country is determined not only by what was originally available from nature, but also by the results of resource-management practices and technology.

You have often heard it said that we are running out of oil, or natural gas, or natural resources in general. Such a statement appears to be very sensible—after all, there is a finite limit to what is available on this planet. Much confusion, however, can be eliminated if we make clear the distinction between reserves and resources, two words often used interchangeably.

Consider resources from the perspective of a camera—viewing the earth as though a snapshot were taken identifying all of its resources at a given point in time. Table 2.1 illustrates this static view of the earth's resources and classifies them in terms of discovered and undiscovered resources.

TABLE 2.1
THE INVENTORY OF RESOURCES AT A GIVEN POINT IN TIME*

Discovered	Undiscovered
Developed reserves	
Subeconomic resources	Resources
Mineral occurrences	

* This schematic representation of the resources base appears in *Government and the Nation's Resources: Report of the National Commission on Supplies and Shortages,* Washington, D.C.: U.S. Government Printing Office, 1976, p. 11.

At any point in time, there is a stock or inventory of resources contained in mines, wells, and so on, currently used as inputs for mills, smelters, and refineries. This stock comprises what is known as the *developed reserves* of the world. It includes those resources that are already discovered and exploitable at prevailing prices with existing technology but that are not being used currently. These resources require only further production to make them available as inputs.

Developed reserves can be viewed both as the sources for current production pipelines and as buffers allowing production to occur while the discovery and development of new mines, wells, and so on, go on. These reserves can be compared to the water in a holding reservoir. The water in this reservoir is not the ultimate source, but rather a feeder supply. The amount in the reservoir fluctuates as usage varies and as new water from rivers and rainfall flows in. The ratio between the water in the reservoir and usage in outflow is one index of the supply of water. It may be misleading, however. Over time, one cannot expect this ratio to grow constantly. And indeed, when it falls, as it will from time to time, it becomes serious only when the ratio of reserves to production approaches the amount of time required to develop new reserves.

The next tier of discovered resources contains those that currently cost too much to be developed at existing prices. Examples are coal shale reserves and oil in deep wells. These subeconomic resources will become developed reserves when and if prices rise sufficiently to make their development attractive or technological innovations lower their development costs.

Then there are those resources that are known to exist but are unlikely to be exploited since no price rise of sufficient magnitude nor technological breakthroughs that would make their exploitation feasible appear likely in the foreseeable future. These discovered reserves are called *mineral occurrences*.

Finally there is the large area on the right side of Table 2.1, which represents *undiscovered resources*. As the name implies, these resources are presumed to exist but have not been found. Therefore, the size of the rectangle on the right has little meaning.

This detailed description of resources highlights the problem of identifying the resource base of a country in simple terms. Prices, technology, and substitute resources all influence the magnitude of a given resource base.

Capital consists of resources created by humans.

Capital consists of resources created by humans, whether embodied in tools, machinery, and structures, or in human skills useful in the production of goods and services.

The concept of capital is not limited to machinery, plants, and tools, however. The skills and expertise that people acquire as a result of formal education, on-the-job training, or self-teaching also can be viewed as a form of capital. This human capital takes time to accumulate and entails a real cost.

Capital is formed through saving, transfer of title, and investing.

The unique characteristic of this third economic resource, capital, is that, unlike labor and land, it is created by humans. Before capital can be made, however, someone must give up goods and services that would otherwise be available to be enjoyed. This act of giving up current consumption is *saving*. In addition to saving, someone must be prepared to commit to the production of new capital goods and skills the resources freed by the act of saving. This is called investing.

In addition to the acts of saving and investing, an intermediate step must be taken in modern, money-using economies in order to create capital. The title to the resources released by saving must be transferred from the saver to the person who wants to invest these resources. Every society has developed a set of economic institutions to accomplish this creation of capital. In the Soviet Union, for example, the saving is largely accomplished through the pricing of consumption goods; the transfer of these savings is accomplished through the banking system; and the investment decisions are made by the central planning agency. In the United States, an intricate system of banks, savings and loan associations, and insurance companies are employed, but the investment decisions are made by individuals or groups of individuals.

It is not our intention at this point, however, to describe in detail the way these three steps are accomplished. What we do want to emphasize is that the capital goods you see around you were obtained only because somebody gave up something. There is a real cost for every piece of capital equipment and every educated human being in your environment. Capital, whether invested in equipment or people, is not free; therefore, the quantity of capital can be expanded only through the painful process of sacrificing present consumption for the future.

Perhaps an illustration would be useful in helping you understand how capital is created.

TABLE 2.2

AVERAGE NUMBER OF CARTONS OF BERRIES AND NUTS GATHERED PER HOUR AND PER DAY

Hour	Day						
	1	2	3	4	5	6	7
1	1	1	1	1	1	1	1
2	1	1	1	2	2	1	1
3	2	3	2	2	3	3	1
4	3	2	3	3	2	3	2
5	2	2	3	3	2	1	1
6	1	1	2	2	1	1	1
7	1	1	1	1	1	0	1
8	0	1	1	0	0	0	1
Total	11	12	14	14	12	10	9

You and several young children are the only survivors of an airplane crash on an island in a remote area of the South Atlantic. Once you have recovered from the shock, you realize that you will have to provide for the survival of your party until help arrives.

You painfully discover that by spending eight hours a day picking wild berries and gathering nuts, you can live—even though the fare is not quite what you're used to. After you've lived off the land for several weeks in a haphazard fashion, you decide that there must be some way to reduce the efforts necessary to survive. You organize your "picking and gathering" efforts more systematically, covering the entire island every seven days. This ensures that you can start gathering afresh every seven days without overpicking some areas.

To amuse yourself and maintain your sanity, let us suppose you return to a centrally located spot on the island after each hour of working to check on the children and at the same time to dump the berries and nuts into a number of one-half pint cartons left in the wreckage of your plane. At the end of each hour, you dutifully record the amount of food you have accumulated.

Table 2.2 shows the average number of half-pint cartons of berries and nuts that you gathered every hour, every day during the first several weeks of systematic food gathering.

Examination of your records reveals that the number of cartons collected the third and fourth hours is usually greater than the number gathered at the beginning and end of each eight-hour day. This is not surprising to you, however, since by late afternoon your

efforts diminish as you tire. Also, the quantities collected early in the week are greater than toward the end of the week, as you are forced to search for food on the rocky, barren land, having already covered the more productive areas.

One evening, while sitting on the seashore eating your berries and nuts, you notice that fish swim in on the incoming tide and feed in pools along the shore before returning to sea with the outgoing tide. After existing for several weeks on nuts and berries, the prospect of adding fish to your diet is delightful, so you eagerly try to catch the fish in your hands. After consistently failing to catch any fish, you decide to attempt to weave a crude net out of vines and roots. For a whole week, you spend four hours every afternoon searching for vines and weaving them into a net. This reduces your food-gathering time from eight to four hours a day.

At the end of seven afternoons of working on the net, somewhat hungrier than usual, you spend the first afternoon of the next week stretching your crude net across the entrance to the pools on the shore after the tide has rolled in.

After a number of false starts, you finally succeed in keeping the net in place while the tide goes out, and to your satisfaction you find that you have captured some fish.

As you fish the same pools over a period of several afternoons and record your catch each time the tide recedes, you note that your average catch diminishes. In addition, your net is good only for about two weeks of constant use before it deteriorates to the point where it has to be replaced. As in the case of food gathering,

TABLE 2.3
AVERAGE NUMBER OF FISH
CAUGHT PER AFTERNOON

Day	Number of Fish Caught
1	7
2	9
3	12
4	10
5	10
6	8
7	7

you record regularly the results of your efforts. Table 2.3 shows the average number of fish caught during the first few weeks of fishing.

To use this technique you had to stop gathering berries and nuts long enough to: (1) produce and install the net, and (2) develop the skills necessary to use the new capital equipment. In the process you: (1) gave up current consumption; and (2) committed time and effort to building a new tool and to developing a new skill. From that time on, the fish caught represented the return on the new capital created. You were no longer dependent for your total income on the use of labor and land. You began to use capital equipment to add to and vary your food supply.

When capital is combined with other resources, the result is usually a specialized resource with its own turnover period.

The fact that almost all resources are generously mixed with capital introduces two important complications. The first is that if a resource has been mixed with capital, it is very likely to be *specialized*. What we might otherwise have classified as labor, then, will consist of lawyers, plumbers, carpenters, machinists, and so on. What we might have classified as land will consist of grazing land, wheat land, urban sites, and so on. Thus, in place of having simply three types of economic resources, a modern economy may have thousands of specialized types.

The second complication of the mixed nature of resources is that each type of resource has its own *turnover period*. Once capital is committed

to a particular type of equipment, it normally must wear out before the capital invested in it can be recovered and invested in another specialized form. If you decide to become a dentist, you will have to forgo during your years of training the income you could have received by working. When your dental education is completed, you will receive a return on that lengthy investment only if you practice dentistry, since the skills you acquired may not be highly transferable.

The normal turnover period for capital invested in most human skills is a generation—20 to 30 years. The people in these skills tend to stay with their skills even though their employment opportunities shrink. Their children, however, move on to other skills. As a result of this turnover of the generations, farmers become chemists, glass blowers become lawyers, machinists become engineers, and college professors become garage mechanics.

Turnover is also a characteristic of capital invested in pieces of equipment. The normal turnover period for capital invested in inventories may be six months, but the capital invested in a large punch press has a useful life as a metal former of 15 to 20 years before it is worn out and must be replaced. A heavy overland truck may be considered to have a useful life of 500,000 miles, or four years. In contrast, the capital invested in some of the Roman aqueducts has proved to have a turnover time of about 2000 years. Some cathedrals appear to have at least a 1000 years' turnover time, and who knows, the dormitory in which you are living may still be around in the year 2100.

We can visualize the capital stock of a nation—whether invested in human skills, in adjuncts to land, or in capital equipment—as being potentially a huge pool of water. The existing capital—and additions to the pool—is constantly being frozen into fixed shapes. It stays in these shapes until it slowly melts. As it melts, the water is returned to the pool, and after being allocated to different industries and different skills, is again frozen into various useful shapes. Thus, in place of having three types of homogeneous resources, a modern industrial economy has thousands of types.

THE LAW OF DIMINISHING MARGINAL RETURNS

Let us consider further some of the complications stemming from the fact that some of the economic resources you see around you are fixed in quantity and cannot be increased through savings and investment in new capital equipment. There is, for example, only a certain amount of top soil in the agricultural sections of our country or a given number of acres on Manhattan Island. Similarly, there is only a limited amount of easily accessible fossil fuels. Since outputs can be produced from different combinations of inputs, you would expect that variable resources—capital and labor—could and would be substituted for the limited resource. But complications arise due to the limited substitutability of one resource for another.

This phenomenon has a long history in economics and has been discussed under the heading of the Law of Diminishing Marginal Returns. As is true of many of the so-called laws in economics, the Law of Diminishing Marginal Returns is something you already know largely as a matter of common sense. Before we formalize the law and enshrine it in academic language, however, let us consider several examples of it.

Recall the example in which you were stranded on an island and met your bodily needs by gathering berries and nuts and fishing. Toward the end of the week, your efforts yielded less food than early in the week even though you provided as much labor input. Examine Tables 2.2 and 2.3 in that illustration.

Or consider the fact that urban land is limited in quantity. Suppose, however, that we could substitute capital in the form of infinitely high buildings for scarce central-city land. Skyscrapers would be built with three or four hundred floors or maybe even a thousand floors so that all of the offices in a major city could be included within a four-block area. You know, however, that this would not work. The elevators—as the buildings got taller—would take up more and more of the usable space. Problems of fire prevention would become unmanageable. The problems of transporting large masses of people to and from such buildings would be unsolvable with today's technology. Hence the usefulness of the building

when capital is substituted for land beyond a certain point decreases sharply. This relationship between inputs and outputs has assumed a pattern that is repeated over and over again in nature and, hence, has been formulated into a basic economic law.

The formal statement of the Law of Diminishing Marginal Returns goes back to the economists writing in the eighteenth and nineteenth centuries.

This relationship that exists between inputs and outputs was first observed in agriculture. Since agriculture was the dominant industry several centuries ago, it is not surprising that the economists writing in the eighteenth and nineteenth centuries made the Law of Diminishing Marginal Returns a keystone in their theories.

We can show what these economists were saying by using the bar diagram in Fig. 2.1, which illustrates the relationship between the output of corn and the variable input of labor with land and capital fixed.

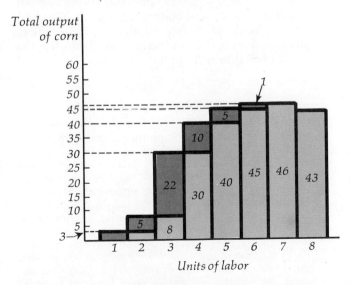

FIG. 2.1   **The relationship between total output and variable labor input when all other inputs are constant.**

The height of each bar represents the total output of corn from a given-sized field using a fixed amount of capital equipment after applying the specified amount of labor shown on the horizontal axis. The shaded section of each bar represents the added or marginal output stemming from each input. You will see, as you examine Fig. 2.1, that with the first few increases in input units, total output increases proportionately more than the increase in the labor input. For example, when the input is doubled from 1 to 2 units, output increases from 3 to 8 units, more than doubling. As more and more of the labor input is used, however, beyond a point each successive increase in the total output becomes smaller until finally a maximum total ouput is reached. In fact, if you keep on attempting to squeeze more output from a given field by adding more of the variable input while other resources are held constant, in time the total output will actually decrease.

The extra, or marginal output, stemming from each unit shown in the shaded top portion of each bar at first increases, reaches a maximum (at 22 in Fig. 2.1), and then declines, ultimately reaching zero at the point where the total output reaches 46.

This example illustrates something we all know as a matter of common sense. It might be useful, however, to cite another example where the outputs are not as clearly identifiable, yet the same principle still applies.

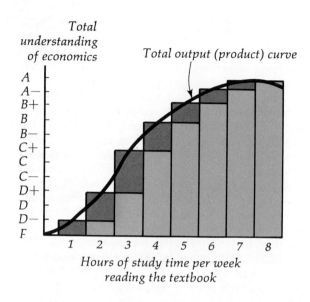

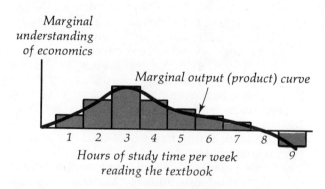

FIG. 2.2   Total and marginal product curves.

Consider the efforts you spend in the study of some subject, say, economics. Suppose the grades in a class accurately reflected understanding and were reported as one of the following: F, D−, D, D+, C−, C, C+, and so on, all the way up to A, and that they are measured by the height of the bars in the upper half of Fig. 2.2. The amount of study time you put in reading your textbook per week is indicated along the horizontal axis. Assume that the hours per week you spend attending class, reading your notes, and so on, are fixed. As in the case of the agriculture example, you can see the operation of the Law of Diminishing Marginal Returns. At first, as you devote more hours to learning economics by studying your textbook, other inputs being held constant, the marginal return (shown by the shaded portion of the bar on the total understanding

graph) increases. For example, the third hour of study per week increases your grade from a D+ to a C+. Then, the more you study, the smaller the marginal reward becomes, until finally, the maximum understanding would be reached. For some people the curve might peak at a level below A, for others it might not peak until far above A. After that, additional study, by increasing fatigue, and so on, would reduce the grade you would earn.

To generalize this Law of Diminishing Marginal Returns, we are going to make another assumption. We are going to assume that infinitely small adjustments in the input of resources can be made, whether the adjustment is in labor applied to a given piece of land and fixed amount of capital equipment, or in hours of study for a particular student. As a consequence, there will be small adjustments in the output stemming from these small input changes. Hence, the number of bars could be increased and each could be made so narrow that a smooth curve line could be drawn connecting the top of each one. Such a curve is represented in the top half of Fig. 2.2 as the total output curve. It is this curve that reflects the fundamental relationship expressed in the Law of Diminishing Marginal Returns.

The Law of Diminishing Marginal Returns expresses the behavior of output in a production process when all inputs are held constant except one. As this one input is increased, the *rate* of output increases slowly at first, then speeds up, and then, beyond a certain point (the point of diminishing returns), begins to diminish. Ultimately the level of total output will reach a maximum and begin to decrease absolutely.

The shaded portions of the total output bars are of interest in themselves. The lower half of Fig. 2.2 consists of a series of bars, each of which is equivalent to the increment to each of the total output bars in the upper half of Fig. 2.2. These bars can also be represented by a smooth curve if they are made numerous and narrow enough. Such a smooth curved line is shown in the lower half of Fig. 2.2 and it is called the marginal output curve.

Marginal output is the addition to total output stemming from a one-unit increase in a variable input.

Since the marginal output curve reflects the rate at which the total output is changing, a unique relationship exists between the total output and marginal output curves. As we move from left to right, the curve representing the marginal output initially rises, then peaks at a level of input use

equal to that where the total output curve becomes less steep. This point identifies the beginning of diminishing marginal returns, for after this level of input, the marginal curve decreases and continues dropping until the total output curve reaches its maximum, after which the marginal curve becomes negative.

Not only are resources specialized, with relatively fixed turnover periods, but they are not freely substitutable for each other without a reduction in output. This makes the problem of economic production more difficult. It means that even in the long run, when resources can be shifted from one form to another, the mix of resources available to a nation may be crucial in determining how effectively it can cope with scarcity. Thus, the Law of Diminishing Marginal Returns may severely penalize economies with large amounts of labor relative to land or other nonaugmentable resources.

Real events appear to have contradicted the Law of Diminishing Marginal Returns.

Now that you know how the Law of Diminishing Marginal Returns works, we will use it to think about hunger and its role in your future.

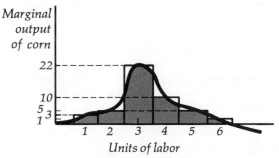

FIG. 2.3   Marginal output curve for corn.

Figure 2.3 is derived from Fig. 2.1 and shows the marginal output curve for corn. We will now modify this graph. In place of a stair-step diagram,

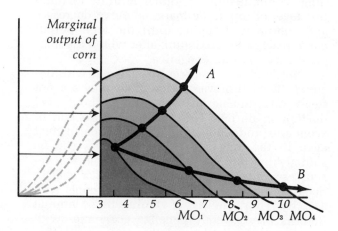

FIG. 2.4   Marginal output curves over time.

been developed for cultivating and harvesting agricultural land. Each of these developments has shifted the *MO* curve outward. Since at any point in time we must be located at a single point on one of the *MO* curves, we can represent these developments by connecting typical points on each of the marginal output curves. This yields line *A*, moving outward and to the right.

We can now use this diagram to pose an important question. If you live in an economy in which these lines have moved outward very rapidly—such as Canada and the United States—then despite a substantial population increase, you will have procured more food from a given amount of land. You will have the impression that the Law of Diminishing Marginal Returns has been repealed. But this is illusory; you have simply moved out from one curve to the next, rather than down a single curve.

On the other hand, if you live in a society in which the increase in population has been more rapid than the gains from technology, you will be painfully aware of the Law of Diminishing Marginal Returns. As more and more people work the land, the extra output will fall. Where the population increase outraces the technological changes, hunger and starvation will become commonplace (see line *B* in Fig. 2.4).

Possibly Thomas Malthus was right when he argued over 175 years ago that population increases combined with a fixed amount of land will inevitably depress the standard of living to the point that poverty and hunger will serve as checks on further population growth.

Why do we raise this depressing problem in connection with the Law of Diminishing Marginal Returns? The answer is that it is this law that makes this prognosis creditable. If it weren't for the Law of Diminishing Marginal Returns, then it would always be possible to substitute capital—a created resource—for land. But as we have seen, there are limits to the substitution of one resource for another. It is this limitation—expressed as the Law of Diminishing Marginal Returns—that raises the ugly specter of widespread hunger in the world.

To clarify your understanding of the Law of Diminishing Marginal Returns, consider Mini-case 2.1.

indicating what happens when large changes in the application of labor to land are made, we will use a smooth line that shows what the marginal output will be when very small additions to labor are made to a given amount of land. We will also move the vertical axis over to the maximum point on the marginal product line (see Fig. 2.4). When we do this we intentionally ignore the increasing-returns portion of input-output relationship because most of the nations of the world are past the region of increasing returns in their use of labor on land. Therefore, other things being equal, any addition to the agricultural labor supply will reduce marginal output. Keep in mind that the curve MO_1 reflects what happens to output when successive additions of labor are made to fixed amounts of land and other inputs.

Over the last 175 years, however, the marginal output lines have been shifting outward and to the right (see MO_2, MO_3, and MO_4 in Fig. 2.4). Why? New technologies have been discovered that have made the land more productive. Commercial fertilizers have been developed. Plant breeding has developed new types of corn, wheat, rice, and other cereals that add to the productivity of the land. New types of capital equipment have

MINI-CASE 2.1

Suppose by some magic the Law of Diminishing Marginal Returns were replaced by the Law of Constant Marginal Returns; that is, beyond some point, returns would not diminish but would remain constant. Which of the following statements would be false?

a) There would be no shortage of good farmland.
b) Trade among areas of the world would be reduced.
c) Real capital—machines, buildings, human skills, and so on—would necessarily be abundant.
d) Urban buildings would be so high that downtown land would not sell for high prices.

PRODUCTION POSSIBILITIES

The relationships among scarcity, resources, and the law of diminishing returns can be shown through the production possibilities model.

Imagine a very simple economy in which all of the resources are fixed in supply and only two commodities are produced: food and recreational services. Also assume that the economy is using fully its human and nonhuman resources and that for the time period being analyzed there are no changes in technology. If, on the one hand, all of the nation's resources, its land, labor, and capital, are devoted to the production of food, assume that one million units can be produced per year. The units could be bushels or tons or whatever. But if, on the other hand, all of the nation's resources were devoted to the production of the alternative commodity, recreation, assume that 1000 units of recreational services could be produced; again, the kinds of units are not important for our illustration. In between these two extreme cases of completely specialized production there are many combinations of food and recreational units that could be produced if the nation's limited resources were devoted to both food and recreational pursuits in different combinations. Table 2.4 lists some of these possible combinations.

This schedule of production possibilities is represented graphically in Fig. 2.5.

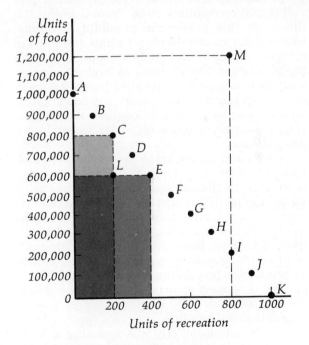

FIG. 2.5 Production possibilities curve.

Table 2.4 indicates that it is possible to produce any one of 11 alternative combinations of outputs. If it chooses to produce 800,000 food

TABLE 2.4
ALTERNATIVE PRODUCTION POSSIBILITIES

Production possibility	Percentage of available resources devoted to		Number of units of output	
	Food	Recreation	Food	Recreation
A	100%	0%	1,000,000	0
B	90	10	900,000	100
C	80	20	800,000	200
D	70	30	700,000	300
E	60	40	600,000	400
F	50	50	500,000	500
G	40	60	400,000	600
H	30	70	300,000	700
I	20	80	200,000	800
J	10	90	100,000	900
K	0	100	0	1000

units, the resources left over are capable of providing 200 recreational units. Point C in Fig. 2.5 illustrates this production possibility. Alternatively, if the society decides it wants 400 units of recreation, then it has enough resources remaining to produce 600,000 units of food. This possibility is represented by point E. In reality, however, let us assume it can choose any combination of inputs; hence, all of the possible combinations would generate a series of points resembling a straight line.

Any point on the graph below the hypothetical line created by joining all the points also represents an attainable combination, but such a point implies either that all of the available resources are not being used or that they are being used inefficiently. Point L is such a point. 600,000 units of food are being produced while 200 units of recreation are being generated. Although only 11 production possibilities are shown in Table 2.4 and Fig. 2.5, many more combinations could have been introduced. They would appear as a series of points defining a line.

If the nation initially was operating at point C and because of the change in tastes, decided to produce the combination represented by point E, it is clear that the result would be an increase in the output of recreation by 200 units—but at a cost of 200,000 fewer food units. The fact that the output of recreation units could be increased *only*

by giving up some food demonstrates the limited nature of the society's resources. If all resources are being used, as initially assumed, the output of one commodity can be increased only by reducing the output of another. Indeed, the only way the output of both commodities can be increased is if more resources were made available or if new ways of combining existing resources more efficiently were discovered. This expansion of resources can and does occur over time as technology changes and the population grows, but in the short run total output cannot increase significantly. (The factors underlying such long-term growth will be discussed in Chapter 11.) Hence, the line defined by all the points is really a production frontier—the outer limit of production possibilities—at any given time.

Let us now ease the assumption that resources are fixed and allow an increase in the resources available for production. In the simplest case, if all resources were doubled, starting from point E, for example, in Fig. 2.5, we can assume that output capabilities would increase and the production possibilities curve would move out to the right. Assuming no change in the wants of people, the problem of scarcity would be eased somewhat; 1.2 million units of food and 800 units of recreation could now be produced instead of only 600,000 and 400 units of food and recreation, respectively (see point M).

If, however, only one kind of input is increased, say labor, while the others remain fixed, what would happen to total output of both products? It is likely that they would both increase somewhat, but certainly less than in the case when all inputs were doubled. As the input of labor continues to increase, however, it is likely that with each succeeding dose, the total output of food and recreation will increase by less and less. Also, it is not likely that both outputs will share in the growth proportionately. Figure 2.6 shows a possible result of first doubling, then tripling, labor. This simple model demonstrates that at some point the added output stemming from increasing the input of one resource decreases. In other words, beyond some level of output, the return to labor begins to decrease with each additional unit of input. The Law of Diminishing Marginal Returns appears.

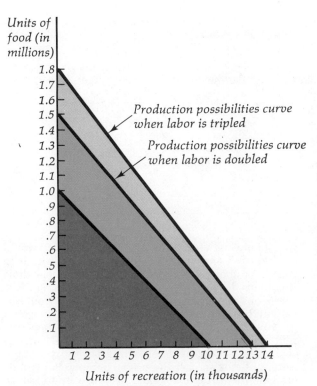

Units of food (in millions)

Production possibilities curve when labor is tripled

Production possibilities curve when labor is doubled

Units of recreation (in thousands)

FIG. 2.6 Production possibilities curves illustrating increasing output from increasing one variable input.

The concept of production possibilities and the nature of choice making that it implies can be seen in the continuation of the nut and berry picking and fishing tale we began earlier in this chapter.

You and several children have survived a plane crash on a remote island. To provide food for survival, you gathered berries and nuts for several weeks. Tiring of that diet, you observed the possibility of catching fish with a net as the tide flows in and out. After spending half of your time weaving and installing the net you finally became successful in catching fish. But now that you've become quite proficient at both food gathering and fishing, you face a new problem. Are you dividing your time between these two activities most effectively? Things have improved, but at the same time become more complicated, since you came to the island. At first, the only alternative to gathering nuts and berries was starving. Now, another alternative is catching fish. During the past several weeks, you've divided your time equally between food gathering and fishing. It is clear that if you increase your fishing time, more fish will be caught, but at the same time the amount of berries and nuts gathered will be reduced. Not being one to make rash decisions, you feel it is important to examine exactly what you gain and lose by varying the way you divide your food gathering and fishing time.

Table 2.5 shows the average number of cartons of food that could be collected and the number of fish that could be caught each afternoon. It reveals that the decision to fish every afternoon for a week would yield 57 fish but would cost you 30 cartons of berries and nuts.

Table 2.6 shows the explicit trade-offs involved between these two activities.

If, for example, you decide to spend four afternoons gathering food and three fishing, production possibility D, you would have 22 cartons of food (in addition to the food gathered each morning) and 28 fish. Alternatively, if you fished five afternoons, you would catch

TABLE 2.5

AVERAGE NUMBER OF CONTAINERS OF FOOD COLLECTED AND NUMBER OF FISH CAUGHT PER HOUR AND PER AFTERNOON

Hour	Day							
	1	2	3	4	5	6	7	
5	2	2	3	3	2	1	1	
6	1	1	2	2	1	1	1	
7	1	1	1	1	1	0	0	
8	0	1	1	0	0	0	0	
Total	4 +	5 +	7 +	6 +	4 +	2 +	2	= 30 Cartons
Fish	7 +	8 +	11 +	10 +	9 +	7 +	5	= 57 Fish

TABLE 2.6
THE TRADE-OFFS BETWEEN GATHERING FOOD AND FISHING

Production possibility	Number of afternoons spent fishing	Number of fish	Cartons of food	Number of afternoons spent gathering food
A	0	0	30	7
B	1	7	29	6
C	2	16	27	5
D	3	28	22	4
E	4	38	16	3
F	5	48	9	2
G	6	54	4	1
H	7	57	0	0

48 fish and gather 9 cartons of food during the remaining two afternoons.

The trade-offs listed in Table 2.6 are illustrated in Fig. 2.7. The number of fish are measured along the horizontal axis and the cartons of food along the vertical axis.

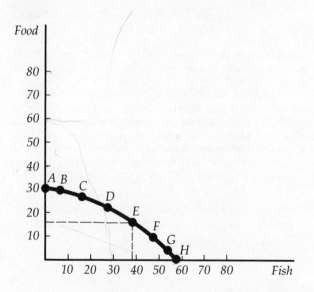

FIG. 2.7   Transformation (production possibilities curve) between food and fish.

You could view this graph as a map of the alternative ways you could use your afternoons. If you spend every afternoon gathering nuts and berries, as you did the first several weeks on the island, you would catch no fish and you wouldn't need a graph to help you think about the problem. But if you spent three afternoons a week gathering nuts and berries and four afternoons making nets and fishing, a graph would be helpful. It would tell you, for example, that you would get 16 cartons of berries and 38 fish, production possibility E on the graph. It would also reveal that to obtain an extra 10 fish, you would have to give up 7 cartons of nuts and berries, production possibility F on the graph. On the other hand, if you were to *reduce* your berry-picking time from three afternoons to one afternoon a week, you would receive 16 extra fish and give up 12 cartons of berries, production possibility G on the graph.

This production possibility curve is sometimes called a *transformation curve* because it illustrates the costs of transforming nuts and berries into fish, or fish into nuts and berries. However, this curve does *not* tell you what combination of fish and berries is best, but only what the alternative possibilities are.

If you move along the curve, increasing the number of afternoons fishing from the first position, possibility A, to the last position, possibility H, you would note that the cost of getting additional fish ultimately increases. After a point, each additional afternoon you devote to fishing will cost you more berries. To answer the question of what combination is best, you would have to consider your tastes. Suppose you really liked fish and no matter how many fish you already had you would always be prepared to give up nuts and berries for additional fish. Then you would always move along the curve until you reached point H.

Most of us, however, do not specialize in consumption. Instead, we vary the goods we consume so as to increase our satisfaction most with the least cost.

Return now to Fig. 2.5. You should find this simple model disturbing. Each successive move from, say, possibility *A* to *B*, from *B* to *C*, from *C* to *D*, and so on entails giving up 100,000 units of food and gaining 100 units of recreation. Is this realistic? Since food and recreation are vastly different commodities, it is unlikely that they would be produced with the same combinations of resources. Hence, as we increase the output of recreational units and decrease food units, would you expect that the resources freed by giving up 100,000 food units would be sufficient to add another 100 units of recreation and that the resources freed by giving up the second 100,000 food units would be sufficient to add still another 100 units of recreation? As we noted earlier in the chapter, resource inputs cannot be perfectly substituted one for the other. This illustrates the fact that as you increase the output of recreational goods, the cost, in terms of food given up, becomes higher and higher.

Most productive processes are flexible enough to allow substitution of resources within a limited range. But the substitution is never complete without some loss of efficiency. This behavior is illustrated in Fig. 2.8, where the production possibilities curve is no longer drawn as a straight line. The move from *E* to *D* will increase the production of food by 100,000 units in exchange for a loss of 100 recreation units. The move from *D* to *C*, adding only 50,000 more units of food, costs another 100 units of recreation. The move from *C* to *B*, adding this time only 30,000 units of food, still costs another 100 units of recreation, and so on. Beyond some point, the resources are virtually no longer substitutable. This decreasing rate of substitutability is reflected in the curvature of the production possibility line.

The problem of combining resources in the production process is enormously complicated by operation of the Law of Diminishing Marginal Returns.

Any system, then, for managing the economy must take into account the limited substitutability of economic resources for each other. The problem of finding the right mix of resources for each level of output is difficult. We will examine this decision process in detail in Chapters 4 and 5.

Another complication arising out of operation of the Law of Diminishing Marginal Returns relates to the questions of what, how, from whom, and to whom. If resources were freely substitutable for each other, each of the areas of the world would not be as likely to specialize in the production of certain products. In the United States, the North could build greenhouses for the production of oranges to substitute for its shortage of the land and climate necessary for citrus fruit growth. The West could fully compensate for its lack of rainfall by using capital for irrigation facilities. But we know that the Law of Diminishing Marginal Returns makes this impossible, and that trade between areas—and between nations—is necessary if the baleful effects of this law on the output per head are to be avoided. Later on, in Chapter 16, we will examine in detail how specialization and trade affect a nation's standard of living.

To clarify your understanding of production possibilities, consider Mini-case 2.2.

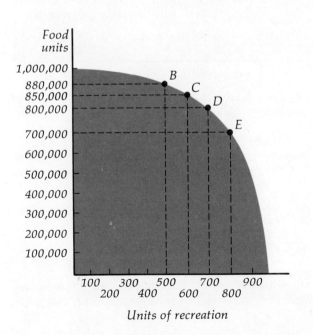

FIG. 2.8 **Production possibilities: imperfect substitutability.**

MINI-CASE 2.2

Suppose the following situation of production possibilities prevails with respect to gasoline and petrochemical fertilizer. If the United States Department of Energy ordered the petrochemical industry to produce 20 percent more gasoline *and* fertilizers than was currently being produced, and if the current combined amount were represented by point *A* on the production possibilities curve, what would you, as spokesperson for the petrochemical industry, tell the FEO?

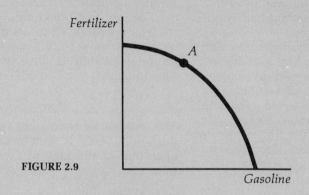

FIGURE 2.9

a) You could not under any conditions produce 20 percent more gasoline.
b) You could not under any conditions produce 20 percent more fertilizer.
c) You could produce 20 percent more gasoline only if you cut back substantially on fertilizer production.
d) You could do both.

The complex problem of production requires control mechanisms.

We have now seen that production in a modern, industrial society is a very complicated process. It involves knowing two basic facts:

1. what resources are available; and

2. how far to carry the substitution of one resource for another.

There is no simple way to organize an economy. A complex mechanism requires a complex control system. We turn now to the role of market and prices as control devices.

REVIEW QUESTIONS

1. The United Coal Company, in an effort to keep up with the growing energy demand, has added crews of 100 persons to its payroll. What crew of 100 workers yields the maximum marginal return? (See Fig. 2.10 on following page.)

    a) 1st   c) 3rd
    b) 2nd   d) 5th

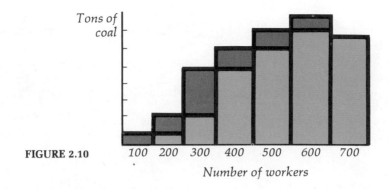

FIGURE 2.10

2. The fact that farm output has increased while the number of acres under tillage has decreased implies:

a) the Law of Diminishing Marginal Returns (LDMR) does not hold for agriculture in the United States.
b) we are operating in the increasing-returns segment of the total output curve.
c) other inputs have increased over time.
d) none of the above.

3. Production possibilities curves tend to be shaped as in Fig. 2.11 because:

a) the more of a product that is produced, the more certain inputs are required.
b) since resources are limited, the output of one product can be increased only with the reduction in the output of the other.
c) all of the nation's resources are being used.
d) resources are not continuously substitutable without loss in efficiency.

FIGURE 2.11

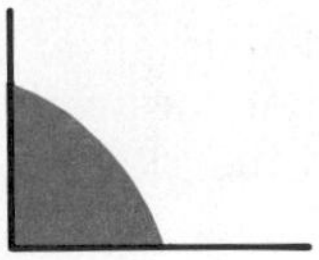

4. Capital is defined as:

a) the natural resources available from nature.
b) any artificial resource used to produce goods and services.
c) money resources.
d) goods and services used for consumption purposes.

5. An economist is told that a punch press has a useful life of 15 to 20 years. What does this fact mean?

a) The press is of high quality.
b) The Law of Diminishing Marginal Returns is true.
c) The press is of low quality.
d) The press is a piece of specialized capital.

6. Your factory produces 300 cars per month using the facilities fairly intensively. Consider yourself in the *short run*. If you want to double your output in response to increases in demand, what will have to happen to the amounts of labor used in your production process if labor is the only variable input?

a) Labor usage would double.
b) Labor usage would more than double.
c) Labor usage would remain the same.
d) Labor usage would decrease slightly.

7. Given a production possibilities curve like Fig. 2.12, what would a movement from point *B* to point *A* exemplify?

a) More production of food with a rate of substitutability that requires giving up more and more recreation in exchange for each unit of food.

b) More production of food with a rate of substitutability requiring giving up less and less recreation exchange for each unit of food.

c) More recreation with perfect substitutability of inputs.

d) More recreation with imperfect substitutability of inputs.

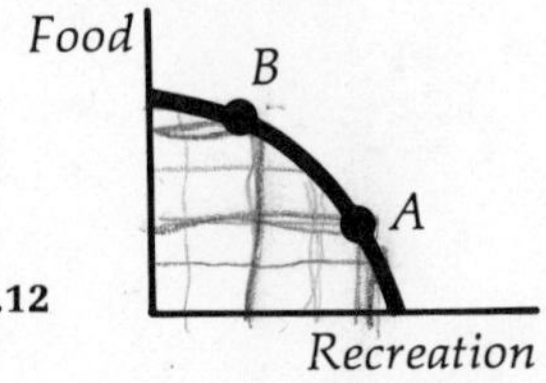

FIGURE 2.12

ESSAY QUESTIONS

1. Explain how the residence hall in which you are now living could be converted into strip-mining equipment.

2. Explain how a farmer who never leaves the farm can, through the turnover of generations, become a physician.

3. Identify three important pieces of social legislation that have affected the quality and quantity of labor as a resource.

4. Suppose society becomes fatalistic about inflation, seeing the value of its savings eroded. What will this do to the production of capital while labor continues to expand? What will happen to the marginal product of labor? What will happen to wage rates corrected for prices?

5. Oil is an exhaustible resource. To compensate for this, more and more capital is used to drill deeper wells, provide land to access oil, and so on. Use the production possibilities curve to illustrate what effect this diversion of capital to oil production will have on the output of a nation.

ANSWERS TO REVIEW QUESTIONS

1. Marginal output is the addition to total output stemming from a one-unit increase in a variable input—in this case workers. In Fig. 2.10 you can see that the shaded rectangles represent the marginal output. The marginal output of the third crew of workers is largest, and diminishes after that level of input. Therefore the answer is (c), the third crew of workers.

2. The Law of Diminishing Marginal Returns describes a situation in which all inputs are fixed except one. If, however, more than one input is allowed to change, the conclusions of the LDMR may not hold.

a) This is incorrect. With the proper assumptions, the LDMR does hold.

b) This is incorrect. It is an irrelevant answer.

c) This is correct as explained above.

d) This is incorrect, of course, since (c) is correct.

3. The production possibilities curve is normally drawn concave to the origin. This is so because under conditions of scarcity, when dealing with the two commodities, more of one product can be produced only by producing less of the other. Furthermore, the rate of substitution between the two goods is not constant since the resources from which the two goods are made are not so efficiently used as specialization increases.

   a) This is incorrect. The statement would also be true for a straight line production possibilities curve.
   b) This is incorrect for the same reason as (a).
   c) This is incorrect. It is irrelevant.
   d) This is correct as explained above.

4. Capital is one of the basic resources and in economics refers to productive equipment made by humans.

   a) This is incorrect. Capital is made by humans.
   b) This is correct as explained above.
   c) This is incorrect. It is the common noneconomic use of the word; it should be called financial capital.
   d) This is incorrect. This refers to consumer goods rather than capital goods.

5. Capital tends to be specialized and have its own turnover period. Machines are designed to do specialized jobs and are not very useful for other activities. Once capital is committed to a particular type of equipment, it is "locked in" that form until it is junked.

   a) This is incorrect. It is irrelevant to the question.
   b) This is incorrect. It is irrelevant.
   c) This is incorrect just as (a) and (b) are incorrect.
   d) This is correct as explained above.

6. To increase output in the short run, producers can increase only the variable inputs, for example, labor usage. But to expand output by increasing only labor brings the Law of Diminishing Marginal Returns into play. Hence to double output in the short run, labor usage will have to more than double since there will be no change in other input usage.

   a) This is incorrect. Since the factory is already operating intensively, it is in the diminishing returns part of its marginal product curve, and therefore labor usage would *more* than double.
   b) This is correct as explained in (a).
   c) This is incorrect as explained above.
   d) This is of course incorrect as explained above.

7. The movement from B to A indicates first of all that less food and more recreational services will be produced. Therefore answers (a) and (b) are incorrect. Since the production possibilities curve is concave to the origin, it is clear that as you move closer and closer to B, you must give up more and more food to get more recreation. Hence the factors of production are not perfectly substitutable between B and A. Therefore, (d) is correct.

PART II

THE MICROECONOMY: PRICES, PRODUCTION, COSTS, AND ALLOCATION

OBJECTIVES

Upon successful completion of this chapter, you will be able to:

1. Explain how the existence of scarcity necessitates a system of rationing, be it price or some other system.
2. Define and illustrate the concept of price.
3. Identify the major factors influencing demand and the nature of the relationship between each of them and demand.
4. Distinguish between demand and quantity demanded.
5. State the Law of Demand.
6. Explain the relationship between changes in price and total revenue in terms of the price elasticity of demand.
7. List and explain the major factors influencing the degree of elasticity.
8. Define supply.
9. Distinguish between quantity supplied and supply.
10. Define and explain price elasticity of supply.
11. Identify the major factors underlying the supply of a good.
12. Define and illustrate equilibrium price.
13. Explain what shortages and surpluses are.
14. Explain, using your own illustrations, how price serves as a rationing device.
15. Identify the allocation and income distribution functions of price.

CHAPTER 3

DEMAND, SUPPLY, AND EQUILIBRIUM PRICE

INTRODUCTION

Whenever wants exceed resources, some form of rationing must be adopted.

Do you want a new stereo set? Why don't you buy one? Would you like a new Datsun sports car? Why not go out and purchase one? If that stereo set you've been eyeing for some time had a price of $20 on it, or that Datsun you've been admiring were available for $500, you probably would indeed go out right now and make your purchase.

Although other factors are certainly involved, price plays an important role in determining what you buy. More generally, price helps to ration existing supplies of products among those who want part of that limited supply. On an even broader scale, prices help allocate resources in market-oriented economies.

Our objectives in this chapter are to help you understand the way prices are determined in a competitive market and see how these prices not only ration the existing supplies of products, but also tell producers (1) how to utilize their productive capacity to produce a continuing flow of products; and (2) how to distribute their supplies geographically and over time. But as you will see, at this point we will be concerned only with what happens in the present and the very near future. In Chapters 4 and 5 we will turn to a more detailed discussion of the way businesses respond over a longer period of time to changes in the prices of products and productive services.

Whenever scarcity exists, that is, when wants exceed the resources available to meet those wants, some means of distributing the resources must be used. Sometimes the means are created through careful planning; in other cases, the means just evolve. Consider the following example.

You are an administrator at your college or university in charge of distributing tickets to a rock concert at which the most popular group in the country is appearing. Unfortunately, the only auditorium available to you will seat just 600 people, yet thousands of students have expressed a strong desire to attend. You obviously have a rationing problem. Here are some of the options available. You undoubtedly could add more.

1. Charge a price so high that only 600 students would be willing and able to attend.
2. Announce a time and day when all the tickets would go on sale at the normal price charged for such rock concerts on campus (say $5) and let "first come, first served" determine who gets the tickets.
3. Allow only music majors to attend, starting with seniors.

4. Allow only students who already own record albums by this rock group to buy tickets.
5. Select 600 names randomly from all those who indicate they want to attend.

The point we are making is that, anytime there is a situation in which wants exceed resources available, some form of rationing *must* be used.

This chapter deals with one kind of rationing—price rationing.

COMMENTARY

The following article is excerpted from the *Lafayette Journal and Courier*. It describes one type of rationing mechanism—first come, first served. Please read the article and answer the following questions.

a) Each successful applicant was to receive $25 per child. What were the costs involved in obtaining that amount?
b) Explain in economic terms why the line was orderly the second day.

WELFARE DRAWS MOTHERS' CRUSH FOR EXTRA GRANT

HARTFORD, Conn. (AP)—First, allocate $1 million to help welfare mothers clothe their children for the winter.

Second, set rules that distribute the money on a first come, first served basis, assuring grants for fewer than half the 93,000 welfare children in the state.

You get one big scramble to be at the head of the line.

On the first day for applications Monday, thousands of welfare mothers stood for hours in the cold and snow to apply for the $25-per-child emergency clothing checks at welfare offices around the state.

Several people fainted in the cold or when crowds surged forward and jammed the doors, trying to get inside to file applications. Six were taken to the hospital in Hartford and at least five were injured in New Haven, where a window also was broken.

"It certainly could have been better organized than this," said Hartford Deputy Police Chief Neil Sullivan as he surveyed the milling crowd on the cordoned-off street.

Roberta Lynch of West Hartford pointed to her 4-year-old daughter, Selena, and said, "She's been crying for the past two hours." Ms. Lynch said that after standing in line more than four hours, she was still 50 feet from the door.

Last month a legislative committee approved rules proposed by the Social Services Department to put the General Assembly program into effect.

At first, the suggestion was for $15 grants. More families would have been helped, but some welfare groups said $15 would not do much good. So the department increased the grants to $25 per child, knowing that more than half the children would lose out.

Later Monday, Gov. Ella Grasso ordered four state buses to be parked outside the Hartford office to serve as waiting areas for applicants forced to wait outside. Coffee and doughnuts were served by the American Red Cross.

By late afternoon the crowd in Hartford had subsided and the lines were orderly. The application process was to continue today.

Associated Press, December 12, 1977. Reprinted by permission. All rights reserved.

A market is a medium in which buyers and sellers interact.

You have heard it said that in a competitive economy prices are set in the market. When we speak of a *market*, we mean a medium in which buyers and sellers interact. Some markets—such as the commodity markets for wheat, corn, and so forth—are highly organized and some—such as the rental market for apartments in a college town—are not very well organized. In some markets, for example the stock market, there are ticker tapes and other communication devices that keep buyers and sellers rapidly and accurately informed about what is happening. In other markets, buyers and sellers must either devote a great deal of time and effort to exploring the market or hire professionals to do it for them. However organized, we shall think of a market as the medium, not necessarily geographic, in which buyers and sellers interact.

A *market* is a medium in which buyers and sellers interact, in which they exchange goods, services, and securities for money or other items of value.

For the present we shall define a *competitive market* as one in which there are many buyers and sellers, each acting independently, and in which there are no restrictions on entry and exit. No restrictive government licenses are required either to enter the market or to leave it. Nor are there privately organized groups that can say who may buy and sell in a given market.

Price means more than the number of dollars required to buy something.

We normally think of the *price* of a product or productive service as the number of dollars it takes to purchase it. Since money is more generally used as one of the goods exchanged, price is expressed in terms of money. This is a narrow definition of price, however.

Price is the ratio of exchange between two commodities.

When we talk about the price of a product, we are talking about the exchange value of one product compared to another. If 10 loaves of bread are exchanged for 1 hour of a specific kind of labor, then bread may be said to sell for 1/10 of an hour's

work. Or if an automobile sells for $8000 and wheat sells for $4 per bushel, then we could say that the "wheat" price of an automobile would be 2000 bushels. For simplicity. though, when we talk about prices, we mean the dollar price of a product—although we could easily express all prices in terms of wheat or hours of work or whatever other unit we chose.

The word *demand*, too, has a very specific meaning in economics and is far more precise than such words as "want" or "need," two terms that are often mistakenly regarded as synonymous. Similarly, *supply* does not simply mean goods available.

To achieve the objectives of this chapter, we will consider in turn the concepts of demand, elasticity, and supply.

DEMAND

Demand means more than the desire for a commodity.

"We demand equal rights." "This is a demand-activated system." "The demand is so great that we can't keep our shelves stocked!" These are all common usages of the word demand. In economics, however, the word demand has a very precise meaning.

Let us begin our discussion of demand by examining a specific question: What influences you or your family's willingness and ability to buy varying amounts of a good or service over a

given time period? For example, most households buy hamburger. How many pounds of hamburger does a typical household purchase per week? What factors underlie its purchase decisions? Some of the factors that certainly are important are:

1. the price of a pound of hamburger,
2. the price of closely related goods (substitutes and complements such as hot dogs and hamburger buns),
3. the family's income,
4. the family's wealth, and
5. the family's tastes.

Other factors could also be cited. In any case, it is clear that the willingness and ability of an individual or a household to buy varying amounts of a commodity are determined by many forces. Given that information, is there any way we can simplify our examination of the factors underlying demand to make it a manageable and useful concept? The answer is yes—by choosing only one of the factors listed above, and by considering the effect of changes in this factor while all other influences are assumed not to change. Generally, economists agree that for most purposes a key influence is price. It is a variable that yields considerable information about quantity demanded when it varies while income, tastes, the prices of substitute goods, wealth, and so forth are held constant.

For example, consider our hamburger illustration. By selecting price as an important factor that determines how many pounds of hamburger a family will purchase per month, and by assuming that no changes will occur in tastes, wealth, income, or the price of related goods, we will discover, by allowing the price of hamburger to vary, the different quantities that the family will purchase at each price level. This information or schedule showing the alternative quantities of hamburger that a family is willing to buy at alternative prices is defined as the *demand* for hamburger. The demand schedule generated in this manner expresses the quantity demanded as a function of price.

Demand **is a schedule of alternative quantities of a good or service that a person (individual demand) or a group of people (market demand) is willing and able to purchase at each alternative price during a specified period of time, other things remaining unchanged.**

COMMENTARY

The following article is excerpted from the *Wall Street Journal*. It describes many of the factors underlying the increase in the consumption of ground beef in the United States. Please read the article and answer the following questions.

a) List the factors that have increased the demand for hamburger.

b) What impact has the increase in demand for hamburger had on the supply and demand for the choice cuts of beef?

c) Is price the chief explanation for the relative reduction in the amount of hot dogs consumed?

GROUND BEEF CONSUMPTION HITS RECORDS AS U.S. BECOMES A "HAMBURGER SOCIETY"

It may have been born in Germany, but it came of age in America.

Hamburger—the ground or chopped beef believed by some to have been eaten first in Hamburg many decades ago—has emerged as the most popular type of meat eaten in the U.S. Changed eating habits, particularly the desire for fast, easy-to-prepare meals and the continuing popularity of fast-food chains, are spurring hamburger consumption to record levels.

Nationally, says William C. Helming, president of Livestock Business Advisory Services, Inc., Kansas City, ground beef will account for at least 40% of this year's expected record beef consumption of 125 pounds a person. That compares with an estimated 25% of beef consumption two years ago and 17% in 1972. Current estimates are that ground beef will account for 50% to 60% of all beef consumed in this country by 1980.

Ground beef comes primarily from cows, which normally sell for considerably less than grain-fed cattle. Last year's expanded cow slaughter made ground beef more plentiful. At the same time, grain-fed cattle, which in preceding years accounted for 70% and more of the U.S. beef supply dropped to about 50% of the total last year. Choice steaks, ribs, roasts and other relatively high-price cuts come from grain-fed cattle.

The increase in the number of working wives is a major impetus to ground beef's rising popularity, meat-industry officials say. Working wives find ground beef is faster and easier to prepare into main dishes than other types of beef, they say.

The skyrocketing growth of fast-food chains in the past 20 years, and the away-from-home eating habits that fueled industry growth, may be equally significant. It's estimated that at least 45% of all beef consumed in the country is eaten at restaurants, school and plant cafeterias and other away-from-home locations. Well over half of that amount is ground beef. It's estimated that patrons

of the three leading hamburger chains alone ate the equivalent of two million head of cattle last year.

"The younger generation has been weaned on hamburgers," one industry executive says. An official at the American Meat Institute, an industry trade association, says that perhaps as many as 50 billion hamburgers will be eaten in U.S. homes and eating places this year, nearly three times the number of hot dogs. At one time, hot dogs, many of which consist largely of pork, out-sold hamburgers.

Reprinted by permission of *The Wall Street Journal,* © Dow Jones & Company, Inc. (October 18, 1976). All rights reserved.

There is an important difference between demand and quantity demanded.

Consider the total market demand for haircuts in a city of 200,000 people where market demand is defined as the sum of all individual demands. If you knew what the demand was, you would know exactly how many haircuts people would be willing and able to buy at all prices in a given period of time. Table 3.1 is a hypothetical representation of demand.

From the demand schedule you can readily identify the quantity demanded at every given price. If the price is $1.50, then the quantity of

haircuts demanded per month will be 45,000. Alternatively, if the price of haircuts is $4.00, then 20,000 is the quantity demanded monthly. You can now see that a change in *quantity demanded* simply means a change from one specific quantity demanded to another specific quantity demanded within the given demand schedule. A change in price causes a change in the quantity demanded.

In contrast, a change in *demand* can be caused by virtually anything *except* a change in the price of the good being considered. For example, if next year people's tastes change drastically so that short hair becomes fashionable, more

TABLE 3.1
A HYPOTHETICAL DEMAND SCHEDULE FOR HAIRCUTS

Price per haircut	Quantity of haircuts that would be purchased monthly
$5.00	10,000
4.50	15,000
4.00	20,000
3.50	25,000
3.00	30,000
2.50	35,000
2.00	40,000
1.50	45,000
1.00	50,000
0.50	55,000

TABLE 3.2
A HYPOTHETICAL DEMAND SCHEDULE FOR HAIRCUTS REFLECTING A CHANGE IN TASTES

Price per haircut	Quantity of haircuts that would be purchased monthly (before the change in tastes)	(after the change in tastes)
$5.00	10,000	20,000
4.50	15,000	30,000
4.00	20,000	40,000
3.50	25,000	50,000
3.00	30,000	60,000
2.50	35,000	70,000
2.00	40,000	80,000
1.50	45,000	90,000
1.00	50,000	100,000
0.50	55,000	110,000

haircuts would be demanded at every price and the entire demand schedule would change. This would be a change in demand. Table 3.2 shows the old and the new demand schedules.

Demand schedules provide the basis for graphing demand curves. By plotting prices on the vertical axis and the corresponding quantities demanded on the horizontal axis, and joining these points, we can draw a demand curve. The demand schedule shown in Table 3.1 is graphed in Fig. 3.1.

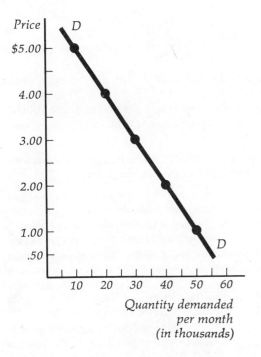

FIG. 3.1 **The demand curve for haircuts.**

Price changes and changes in quantity demanded move in opposite directions.

We now know that demand is a schedule relating quantities demanded with alternative prices. But what more can we say about this relationship? At high prices the quantities demanded are less than at low prices. This inverse relationship between price and quantity demanded exists for virtually every good or service; hence, it is frequently called the *Law of Demand.*

The demand schedules and curves we have illustrated may create the illusion that every change in price elicits a proportional change in the quantity demanded. This is not true. In some cases, price may have to change considerably before the quantity demanded is affected. We are saying, however, that at some point a price change will influence the quantity demanded.

Why do people increase the quantity they demand as the price falls? There are two reasons. First, a reduction in price makes that good relatively cheaper than all other goods and people therefore tend to substitute it for other goods where possible. For example, if the price of Coca Cola falls you would expect people to substitute Coke for Pepsi. Second, the price reduction makes buyers better off. Buyers, if they so desire, can now purchase the same amount of the good as before, and still have some money left over. In a real sense, then, the buyers' income has increased. Whenever income increases you can expect the buyers to purchase more of most goods, including the good whose price has fallen.

Think for a moment of commodities that do not appear to behave according to the Law of Demand. You might cite insulin, a drug necessary for treatment of diabetes, as an example. Further reflection, however, will show you that beyond some point, if the price of insulin continued to be raised, people's willingness or ability to buy it would be reduced, and the quantity demanded would fall. It is true that some people may purchase certain goods—conspicuous consumption goods—simply because they are high priced and that should the price fall enough to make them available to the average consumer, their usefulness as a status symbol would fall and, thus, this class of consumers might buy less. In general, however, there are few exceptions to the Law of Demand.

Although the Law of Demand tells us that if a price rises and other things remain unchanged the quantity demanded will fall, it does not give us any indication of how responsive the quantity demanded is to a change in price. The concept of elasticity will provide this information.

ELASTICITY

The concept of elasticity compares the rate of change of two related variables.

The degree to which people respond to price changes varies widely from commodity to commodity. Two examples illustrate contrasting responses to price change. If the local grocer were to double the price of table salt, would people demand a smaller quantity? The Law of Demand implies that they would, but it is unlikely that the response on the part of buyers would be very noticeable. If the local barbers and beauticians doubled prices, how would people react? Many people would start trimming their own hair.

Elasticity **of demand measures the responsiveness of changes in quantity demanded to changes in price.**

The concept of *elasticity* provides a shorthand way to compare the rates of change of two related variables, such as quantity demanded and price. Elasticity is a ratio between two rates of change. Thus, if you could increase your grade in economics by 25 percent by increasing your study time by 10 percent, we could speak of the elasticity of "grade–study-time" as being 25/10 or 2.5. Or, if a 10 percent increase in the price of soybeans would bring about a 30 percent decrease in the quantity of soybeans demanded, we could say that the elasticity of demand (with respect to price) was 3. This number is called the coefficient of elasticity. The price elasticity of demand could vary along a scale from zero to infinity, being zero

if the quantity demanded did not change even with a very large change in price, and approaching infinity if a very small change in price caused a huge change in quantity demanded.

Price elasticity measures the relative responsiveness of quantity to changes in price.

We will not be overly concerned with the precise, numerical measures of price elasticity of demand. Rather, we will characterize demand as being *elastic* (with respect to price) when the percentage change in quantity demanded is larger than the percentage change in price, that is, when the ratio of the percentage change in quantity demanded to the percentage change in price is larger than one, as is true in the soybean example.

We will say the demand is *inelastic* when the percentage change in quantity demanded is smaller than the percentage change in price, that is, when the ratio is less than one. The demand for table salt, for example, at the price usually

Degree of responsiveness	% change in quantity demanded
	% change in price
Elastic	> 1
Unitary elastic	= 1
Inelastic	< 1

charged for salt is inelastic. Even a fairly large percentage change in the price of table salt would cause little percentage change in the quantity demanded.

Finally, we will note that demand has *unitary elasticity* when the percentage change in quantity demanded is precisely equal to the percentage change in price—and the ratio is equal to one.

These three measures of the responsiveness of quantity *demanded* to a change in price are summarized in Table 3.3.

The total revenue procedure is a useful way of determining elasticity of demand.

A simple method to determine whether demand over a given range of prices is (a) elastic, (b) unitary, or (c) inelastic is the total revenue procedure. Total revenue is the value of the price of a product times the number sold. For example, if a store sells three hand calculators at $50 apiece, the total revenue from calculator sales is $150. If the store sells another calculator, the total revenue increases to $200. The procedure for using the "total revenue approach" is as follows:

1. Reduce the price of a product.
   (The Law of Demand implies that as the price falls, the quantity demanded will rise.)
2. Then measure the change in the total revenue received by the sellers of the product.
   (Since total revenue is the product of price times quantity, and since we assumed the price to fall causing the quantity demanded to rise, whether in fact total revenue rises or falls depends on the relative magnitudes of the changes in price and quantity.)

a) If the total revenue received by the sellers rises, the demand is said to be elastic.
   (In this case, the relative change in quantity demanded is greater than the relative change in price.)
b) If the total revenue received by the sellers remains the same, the demand is said to have a unitary elasticity.
   (In this case, the relative change in quantity demanded is equal to the relative change in price.)
c) If the total revenue received by the sellers falls, then the demand is said to be inelastic.
   (In this case the relative change in quantity demanded is less than the relative change in price).

And, of course, the *reverse would be true.* If the sellers receive less revenue when the price is increased, the demand is elastic. Or, if they receive more revenue when price rises, the demand is inelastic. Table 3.4 summarizes these possible changes.

To apply the total revenue rule for determining the elasticity of demand, suppose that you are running a bookstore and that you have 50 new textbooks left at the end of the school year that initially were sold at $5.00 each. To make the problem simple, also assume that the publisher has announced that a new edition has been published and, therefore, there will be no secondhand market for the books. How should you price these books if your objective is to obtain as large a profit as possible? The answer to this question can be

TABLE 3.4
THE RELATIONSHIP BETWEEN ELASTICITY AND TOTAL REVENUE

If	then	and if		then	and demand is
P↓	Qd↑	TR↑	→	the relative change in quantity demanded is greater than the relative change in price	elastic
P↓	Qd↑	TR↓	→	the relative change in quantity demanded is less than the relative change in price	inelastic
P↑	Qd↓	TR↑	→	the relative change in quantity demanded is less than the related change in price	inelastic
P↑	Qd↓	TR↓	→	the relative change in quantity demanded is greater than the related change in price	elastic

found by finding that price that will give you the largest total revenue. Remember, the cost of the books is not important since you cannot send them back, and your objective is to recover as much of your cost as you can. Suppose that as a result of a small survey, you arrived at an estimate of the demand for the textbooks which is shown in columns (1) and (2) of Table 3.5.

TABLE 3.5

DEMAND AND TOTAL REVENUE SCHEDULES FOR BOOKS

(1) Price	(2) Quantity demanded	(3) Total revenue	
$5.00	0	$ 0	
4.50	5	22.50	Elastic demand
4.00	10	40.00	
3.50	15	52.50	
3.00	20	60.00	
2.50	25	62.50	Unitary elastic demand
2.00	30	60.00	
1.50	35	52.50	Inelastic demand
1.00	40	40.00	
0.50	45	22.50	
0.00	50	0.00	

By examining this table, you will see that the most profitable price for these leftover textbooks is $2.50. *No other price will* yield as large a total revenue. You will be better off selling 25 books at $2.50 and giving the remaining books to a paper drive than you would be if you set the price at any lower level in order to sell more books.

The relationship between demand and elasticity can be shown graphically. Using columns (1) and (2), the demand schedule for books, a demand curve can be drawn (see *DD* in Fig 3.2).

In the range of prices from 0 through $2.50, total revenue rises as the price increases (or total revenue falls as the price decreases). From the information summarized in Table 3.4, you can see that this must be the inelastic portion of the demand schedule (curve). In the range of prices from $2.50 through $5.00, total revenue falls as the

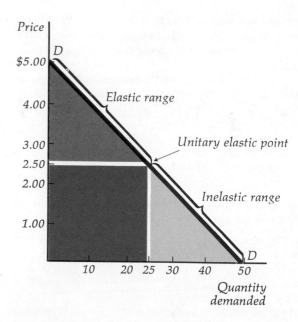

FIG. 3.2   The demand curve for books.

price increases (or total revenue increases as the price decreases). This implies that demand is elastic over this portion of the schedule (curve).

There are many real-world examples of the importance of the concept of price elasticity of demand. For example, the importance of the concept of elasticity has been highlighted by the behavior of the OPEC nations in increasing the price of oil and in the issue of whether natural gas prices should be controlled by the federal government. The OPEC nations raised the price on a barrel of crude oil by 400 percent, knowing that the quantity demanded would not fall by nearly the same percentage; that is, they knew the demand for oil was inelastic.

A number of attempts have been made to measure the elasticity of demand for gasoline. They reveal that in general the demand is inelastic, around −.25. This means that a 40 percent increase in price will cause the quantity demanded to fall by only 10 percent. In the long run, however, as users of this form of energy have the opportunity to change their technology, the degree of elasticity or responsiveness rises.

The degree of elasticity that a good or service reflects depends on many factors. Most important are (1) the availability of good substitutes, (2) the number of ways in which the commodity can be used, and (3) the price of the commodity relative to the buyers' incomes. For the present it is sufficient to know that the total revenue change associated with a price change indicates whether the demand for a product over a given range of prices is elastic, inelastic, or unitary.

SUPPLY

Supply is a schedule of prices and quantities forthcoming at alternative prices per period of time.

The concept of supply is similar to demand in that it relates prices to quantities. Specifically, it refers to the quantities of a commodity that sellers are willing and able to sell at alternative prices during a given period of time.

In a market economy such as ours, the kinds and quantities of goods supplied at alternative prices depend to a great extent on the profit expectations of suppliers. These, in turn, are influenced by many factors, including the price of the good or service being supplied, the prices of the inputs used to produce the good or service, the prices of byproducts, and the technology.

The supply schedule is a list of quantities that will be forthcoming at alternative prices when all of the other factors influencing supply are held constant. Thus a change in quantity supplied can be stimulated by a change in price, whereas a change in supply—that is, in the whole schedule—can be caused by a change in any of the underlying conditions affecting supply except the price of the commobity itself.

Supply **is a schedule of alternative quantities of a good or service that sellers are willing and able to provide at each alternative price during a specified period of time, other things remaining unchanged.**

Table 3.6 shows a hypothetical supply schedule for haircuts. At $0.50 per haircut, only 5000 haircuts will be supplied per month. As the price rises, the quantity supplied increases until at the price of $5.00, barbers are willing and able to provide 50,000 haircuts per month.

Figure 3.3 shows the supply curve derived from the figures in Table 3.6. Normally, when

TABLE 3.6
A HYPOTHETICAL SUPPLY SCHEDULE FOR HAIRCUTS

Price per haircut	Quantity of haircuts that would be supplied monthly
$5.00	50,000
4.50	45,000
4.00	40,000
3.50	35,000
3.00	30,000
2.50	25,000
2.00	20,000
1.50	15,000
1.00	10,000
0.50	5,000

price rises, the quantity of a commodity supplied will be greater, and when price falls, the quantity supplied will decrease. Also, we can speak of the elasticity of supply. Supply is called elastic if the relative change in quantity supplied stemming from a price change is greater than the relative price change. Supply is inelastic if the relative change in quantity supplied is less than the relative change in price.

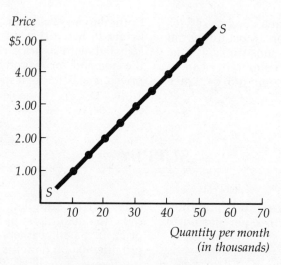

FIG. 3.3   The supply curve for haircuts

EQUILIBRIUM PRICE

The equilibrium price prevails when quantity demanded equals quantity supplied.

Supply consists of a schedule of prices directly related to quantities, that is, when the price increases, the quantity supplied increases. Demand consists of a schedule of prices inversely related to quantities, that is, when the price rises, the quantity demanded decreases. If you compare the demand and supply schedules for haircuts that are shown together in Table 3.7, you will readily see that there is only one price at which *quantity demanded* equals *quantity supplied,* that is, $3.00 per haircut. At this price the equilibrium quantity is 30,000 haircuts.

In Fig. 3.4 these two schedules are graphed, measuring price on the vertical axis and the quantities supplied and demanded per time period on the horizontal axis; *DD* and *SS* are the demand and supply curves, respectively. You will see that the equilibrium price and quantity are identified by the point of intersection of these two curves.

TABLE 3.7
THE SUPPLY AND DEMAND SCHEDULES FOR HAIRCUTS

Price per haircut	Quantity of haircuts that would be purchased monthly	Quantity of haircuts that would be supplied monthly
$5.00	10,000	50,000
4.50	15,000	45,000
4.00	20,000	40,000
3.50	25,000	35,000
3.00	30,000	30,000
2.50	35,000	25,000
2.00	40,000	20,000
1.50	45,000	15,000
1.00	50,000	10,000
0.50	55,000	5,000

Equilibrium price **is the price at which quantity demanded equals quantity supplied.**

The equilibrium price is called the market clearing price since every buyer willing and able to purchase commodities at that price is successful

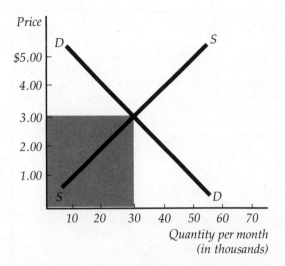

FIG. 3.4   The supply and demand curves for haircuts.

and every seller willing and able to sell at the price is successful; hence, the market is "cleared." In Fig. 3.4, the equilibrium price is $3.00 and the equilibrium quantity is 30,000.

A change in supply or demand brings about an adjustment and a new equilibrium price and quantity under competitive conditions.

Consider now the effect of a change in demand on the equilibrium price. When demand increases, a new equilibrium price and quantity will eventually be determined. This is shown graphically in Fig. 3.5, where the demand curve labeled D_1D_1 reflects the increase in tastes for haircuts shown in Table 3.2. In the first instance when demand increases, a situation develops in which the quantity demanded jumps to 60,000. At the price of $3.00, the quantity demanded is greater than the quantity supplied by 30,000 haircuts per month. Clearly, if price does not change, there is a shortage of haircut services. If the market is competitive, however, two changes occur. Since barbers can no longer serve all the customers, they must use some rationing device. The most lucrative device, to raise the price, is effective because the quantity demanded falls as price

rises. At the same time, the higher price will encourage existing barbers to work overtime, will draw some barbers out of retirement, and will cause new barbers to enter the trade. Over time, assuming a competitive market, a new equilibrium price and quantity will be achieved and the shortage will have disappeared.

If our barbers raised the price to $5.00 per haircut in their attempts to increase their income and resolve the rationing problem, a temporary situation would be created in which the quantity supplied would be greater than the quantity demanded. In place of the shortage, a surplus of haircut services would be created. In time, however, the equilbrium price would be achieved—as long as competition existed.

It is important to remember that the terms shortage, surplus, and equilibrium make sense only in reference to a specific price. There may be a shortage of gas at $0.40 a gallon, but there would be no shortage, as we have defined it, at $2.00 a gallon. Other things being equal, any increase in demand or decrease in supply will create a temporary shortage, while any decrease in demand or increase in supply will generate a temporary surplus.

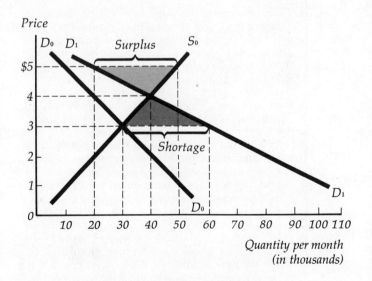

FIG. 3.5   A change in the demand curve for haircuts.

COMMENTARY

The following is an excerpt from an article in *Focus on Economic Issues*. It uses supply and demand analysis to explain the 1973–1974 increase in the price of oil. Please read the excerpt and answer the following questions.

a) The author claims that there are no "economic manifestations" of oil depletion on a global scale. On what does he base that claim?

b) Why was a form of nonprice rationing of gasoline needed in 1973–1974? What form(s) did this rationing take?

c) How does the author suggest that the burden of high gasoline prices on the poor be relieved? Is this a market solution?

ENERGY: THE VIEW FROM THE MARKET

The energy crisis can be viewed from many perspectives: that of the individual consumer or businessperson, the government regulator, the politician, the diplomat, the engineer, the geologist, or many others, including the economist. Each has a unique perspective. This essay will outline the market economy response, as applied to the United States and the world.

The objective of the essay is to introduce the reader to a general supply and demand interpretation of the 1973–74 increase in the world price of oil.

The economic framework

To an economist, "energy" need not be viewed as different from any other scarce commodity. It is subject to the laws of supply and demand: for given costs of production, consumer tastes, and incomes, an increase in price increases the quantity supplied and decreases the quantity demanded both by industry and households. At the equilibrium (market-clearing) price, supply and demand are equal and there are neither shortages nor surpluses in any economic sense.

Particular energy resources do, of course, tend to be exhaustible. But historically, energy supply has been maintained and increased by the continuing advance of technology, which has provided improved extraction techniques and a more or less steady stream of energy substitutes. In economic terms, resource depletion is reflected in rising production costs of energy and hence rising energy prices. These prices in turn stimulate and shape the new technology. Thus variations in the supply of resources may themselves be viewed within the context of an ongoing market process.

Consider some interpretations of the past and present energy scene, using the economist's tools of supply and demand.

The OPEC cartel and the U.S. response

It may come as a surprise that economists do not view the sharp rise of world energy prices, particularly oil, in the last several years as resulting from a worldwide depletion of oil in any physical sense. While fossil fuels are obviously finite, and the U.S. has already used a good deal of its known oil reserves, there are as yet no economic manifestations of depletion on a global scale. For example, the ratio of oil production to reserves worldwide is the same today as it was in 1973. Moreover, the availability of oil in the Middle East, measured by its cost of production, has long been constant in the range of 10¢–40¢ a barrel, averaging about 20¢ or 25¢. When the Organization of Petroleum Exporting Countries (OPEC) raised the price per barrel from about $3 to $12 and above during 1973, it did so by artificially restricting its output of crude oil in what was a pure monopoly or cartel action. This is shown in Fig. 1, where the leftward shifting supply curve in the international oil market reflects the OPEC supply restriction and embargo. Because the demand curve is steep (inelastic), at least in the short run, the relative increase in price following the supply shift is much greater than the relative decrease in quantity. As a result, the revenues going to OPEC countries in 1974, measured by the area of the inscribed rectangles, increased substantially from 30 to 100 billion dollars per year.

The U.S. response to the increase in the world price of oil was to maintain price ceilings, then in

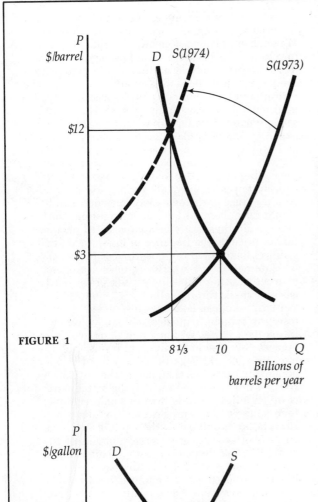

FIGURE 1

Billions of
barrels per year

FIGURE 2

Gallons

force over a good portion of the economy, on crude oil and oil products and on natural gas delivered across state lines. At the same time detailed allocation of crude and refined oil supplies, between and within regions, was undertaken by the Federal Energy Office (FEO). For all practical purposes, the market-price distribution system in oil was suspended and replaced by a centralized command authority.

In the market for gasoline, a refined oil product, the actual prevailing ceiling price was below the equilibrium price, as illustrated in Fig. 2. The equilibrium price is at the intersection of demand and the supply curve remaining after the OPEC restriction and FEO allocations. The ceiling price is the pre-OPEC equilibrium price. The resulting shortage, Q_D–Q_S, was due not only to the shrinkage of supply caused by OPEC, but also because of a reduced share of gasoline among refined oil products. The FEO allocated a smaller portion of crude oil toward gasoline and more toward home heating oil on the assumption that the winter of 1973–74 would be colder than it turned out to be. At the same time, the regional distribution of gasoline was patterned after 1972 use. Even in a year or 18 months, population and resources are highly mobile. Vast areas of the country thus received smaller or larger shares of the smaller total than a constantly adjusting market price-system would have allocated. (The FEO also decided to build up reserve oil stocks during the critical 1973–74 winter, further intensifying the shortage.)

With the ceiling price below the equilibrium and demand quantity greater than supply, some method of rationing (distributing) the supply other than price was needed. Gasoline stations resorted to a variety of tactics: steady customers were given preference, individual sales were limited to 10 or 15 gallons, the stations were closed evenings or on weekends, etc. This way of meeting the shortage led to more frequent visits to stations and to a queuing—a lining up—of cars during prime hours. In effect, time spent in searching for gasoline and in queuing was substituted for the higher equilibrium price as a way of rationing the given supply.

An alternative approach, which the FEO was prepared for but never enacted, was the use of rationing stamps. By this means the unsatisfied or excess demand, Q_D–Q_S in Fig. 2, would have been curtailed by issuing stamps that would limit total purchases at the ceiling price to the quantity Q_S. This would equate demand to supply and eliminate the search and queues. There were several objections to the use of "rationing": (1) The cost of administering a rationing stamp program was substantial, estimated in Treasury Department releases at \$2 billion per year. (2) A rationing stamp program does nothing to encourage the increased supply that the higher equilibrium price eventually brings forth. (3) While some special exceptions can be made, the program in general treats people as equal, giving them equal numbers of stamps. In fact, people's wants vary widely and a rationing stamp program cannot begin to approximate the diverse expression of individual preferences possible under unregulated purchases at an equilibrium price. (A way to meet this objection, as several economists proposed, is to permit those wanting additional stamps to buy them at a freely determined price from those willing to sell them.)

Another consideration in evaluating price controls is the effect they may have on prices in other markets. If all prices are fixed at ceiling levels, then, of course, there are no such effects. But if the prices of some goods are controlled and others are not, as was true in 1973–1974, then the analysis must go a step further. The unsatisfied or excess demand for gasoline, Q_D–Q_S in Fig. 2, will tend to spill over into other markets, where prices are raised proportionately. There are no close substitutes for gasoline, but there are certainly alternative goods on which the resulting excess demand for automobile use can be spent. Unable to buy gasoline and drive their automobiles as much as they would like to at the ceiling price, consumers will tend to travel by other means (air, bus, and rail) or to travel less but perhaps read more, or take up new hobbies. We can only guess at these new expenditures, but we cannot ignore them or assume that the excess demand for gasoline is purely passive and has no inflationary repercussions elsewhere in the economy.

The main argument against simply allowing the price of gasoline to rise to its new equilibrium, at which supply and demand are brought quickly into balance, was that it would be especially costly to the poor. We have seen that holding the price at the lower ceiling level also entails costs insofar as it results in (a) a shortage and reduced supply of gasoline, (b) time lost from work and leisure while searching and queuing, (c) the administrative expenses of a possible rationing-stamp program, and (d) higher prices in uncontrolled substitute markets. Many economists believed that removing the ceiling on gasoline and allowing the higher equilibrium price to equate supply and demand would reduce costs for society far more than it would raise them for low income groups. The latter could thus easily be compensated for the higher price by the issuance of low-priced "fuel stamps" financed out of government revenues.

International comparisons, once again, are instructive. After imposing ceiling prices on the gasoline market in the fall of 1973, almost all Western European countries responded to the resulting shortages, queues, and confusion by lifting the ceilings within a month or two. Prices immediately rose to equilibrium levels and motorists got all the gasoline they wanted (which, predictably, was less than before the OPEC price rise). In this country, in which the actual reduction in oil supplies was less than in some sections of Europe, the ceilings on gasoline, in force since 1971, began to fall below the equilibrium price and create shortages as early as the summers of 1972 and 1973. The shortages continued after the embargo period until the ceilings were finally lifted along with general controls in May 1974. The shortages were thus a result of the ceiling price, not of the OPEC and FEO supply restrictions as such.

GEORGE HORWICH, *Focus on Economic Issues.* Spring, 1977. Reprinted by permission of *The Indiana Council for Economic Education,* © Purdue Research Foundation (1977). All rights reserved.

The adjustment of price and quantity over time

Up until now our analysis of the effects of changes in supply and demand has consisted of: (1) a description of a situation in which a market is in equilibrium; (2) an assumed increase or decrease in supply or demand; and (3) the achievement of a new equilibrium price and quantity. No explicit mention has been made of time, as though it were not important. In fact, however, the element of time is enormously important; hence we must consider briefly how price and quantity adjustments occur over time in a competitive market.

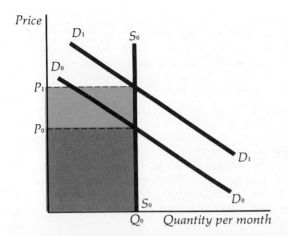

FIG. 3.6 Inelastic supply and the demand for tennis racquets.

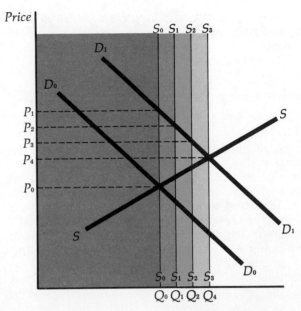

FIG. 3.7 An increase in demand and changes in supply.

We will use as an example an increase in demand for tennis racquets.

There has been a tremendous boom in the sport of tennis in recent years. One reflection of this boom as been a sharp increase in the demand for tennis racquets. How would a competitive market respond to this change? On any given day, the number of tennis racquets available for sale is virtually fixed. In supply curve terms, this means that the supply curve for tennis racquets in the very short run would be vertical. In elasticity terms, the supply is inelastic. See Fig. 3.6, where S_0S_0 is the supply curve of tennis racquets in the very short run and D_0D_0 is the demand curve. The equilibrium price is P_0 and the quantity is Q_0.

Assume that the demand now increases to D_1D_1 per month. If the market functions so that all of those willing and able to buy a racquet at the market price are satisfied, the price must rise to P_1 since that is the only price at which the quantity demanded can be sold and there will be no shortage. This price will prevail as long as the supply coming onto the market each month does not change. In time, however, the supply will change in a competitive market as producers see opportunities for making large profits at the new high price. At first, the added amount coming

onto the market each month may be quite small—generating the supply curve S_1S_1 in Fig. 3.7.

This added supply (S_1S_1 minus S_0S_0) may have been made possible by having workers in tennis racquet factories work "overtime." The price will now fall to P_2. Somewhat later, the supply may increase even further, say to S_2S_2, as plants manufacturing tennis racquets are geared to a second or third shift. The price again will fall—this time to P_3. Finally, after a much longer period, new plants may even be built and the supply curve will shift to S_3S_3 with an equilibrium price of P_4 and quantity of Q_4. If we draw a line joining the initial price and quantity point (P_0,Q_0) to the final price and quantity point (P_4,Q_4), we will have an upward sloping supply curve. This is the kind of curve normally drawn to represent supply. It shows only the "before and after" situation of a change in demand.

The same dynamic approach could be used to analyze the response of demand to a change in supply.

Relative price changes are very important.

The model of supply and demand that we have developed has many fruitful applications. However, we must be careful to remind ourselves constantly that this model is an abstraction from reality that is based on a number of critical assumptions, such as competition and the "other things being equal" assertion. If these conditions hold, then we can go on to say, as we will in the next section, that prices play key roles in rationing and allocating goods and services. But if competition doesn't exist, forces will not be brought into play that will cause prices to adjust as the model suggests. And if other things do change, then the issue of relative and absolute price changes becomes very important. Consider this example. The average level of all prices in the United States increased by about 84 percent from 1967 to 1977. During the same period the price of gasoline increased about 80 percent. A price increase of 80 percent is regarded as impressive by virtually everyone—but when one realizes that at the same time all prices have increased by 84 percent, the impact of this 80 percent price increase diminishes. Hence we must not be misled by the price change experienced by a single good taken out of the context of the behavior of all prices.

Price serves a rationing purpose.

We now know that the equilibrium price of a good is the price at which the quantity demanded equals the quantity supplied. Any buyer willing to pay the equilibrium price will be able to obtain the desired product, but those who are unwilling to pay a price as high as the equilibrium price will simply receive no product. They will be "rationed" out of the market. All suppliers willing to sell their product at the equilibrium price will have no difficulty in disposing of their product, but sellers willing to part with their product only at a price above the equilibrium price will find no buyers. They will be rationed out of the market. This is how the mechanism of price determines who will be able to sell their product and who will be able to buy the desired product. Hence, price is a very useful tool for rationing the available supplies of a product. If 10 million people are willing and able to buy an automobile this year at a price of $3000, but only 5 million cars are produced, then simply raising the price to the equilibrium level—that is, to the price at which quantity demanded equals quantity supplied— will solve the rationing problem. The usefulness of price as a rationing device in centrally planned economies, as well as in market economies, is readily seen from this example.

The allocation and income distribution functions of price.

In Chapter 1 we noted that because of scarcity, every economic system must answer the basic questions of what to produce, how to produce, from whom the inputs will come, and to whom the output should go. The questions of what, how, and from whom can be called the *allocation problem*. In market-oriented economies, resources flow to various productive activities partly in response to price. If consumers demand a good or service, this demand will be reflected in the price they are willing to pay. The relative prices of inputs, in conjunction with output, will determine the product mix and input combinations used in the economy.

The question of "to whom" involves the distribution of income. In a market-oriented economy, the answer to the "to whom" question will be answered in part through prices—the prices for inputs such as labor, land, and the use of capital.

Chapters 4, 5, and 6 will deal with these issues in more detail.

Now that you are familiar with the mechanics by which prices are determined in the market place, you may wish to pause to consider the ramifications of price as an allocating and rationing mechanism. How do you react to Mini-case 3.1?

MINI-CASE 3.1

"Sure, I know that economic systems must develop some means for allocating scarce resources among alternative uses, but the extent to which our economy uses the price mechanism is immoral."

a) This is nonsense since you can't speak about morality without specifying some standards as to what is good and what is bad.

b) There is some truth in the statement since there are circumstances in which reliance on the price mechanism rations out of a market some buyers whose need is generally regarded as greater than some who are not rationed out of the market simply because their income is higher.

c) The statement is false since all systems of rationing are arbitrary in some sense and reflect the biased values of those promulgating their favorite system of resource allocation and rationing.

d) The statement is true, but doesn't at the same time mean that price as a rationing and allocating mechanism should not be used.

REVIEW QUESTIONS

1. If you are able to exchange three shirts for nine TV dinners, then you can correctly say the following about prices.
   a) The price of a TV dinner is three shirts and the price of a shirt is one-third a TV dinner.
   b) You cannot determine the prices unless you know the money value of at least one of the two goods.
   c) The price of a TV dinner is one-third a shirt and the price of a shirt is three TV dinners.
   d) You cannot determine the price unless you know the money value of both goods.

2. Below you will find a series of statements. Pick the one that best illustrates the Law of Demand.
   a) No matter what the price is, people will always demand so much gasoline that there will be a shortage.
   b) If the price of salt went to zero, no more of it would be demanded.
   c) There never is a shortage of any product if the price is high enough.
   d) The higher the price of most products, the more people will want to buy.

3. The reason the Law of Demand usually works is that:
   a) people need products regardless of their price.
   b) most products have at least partial substitutes and people with limited budgets will try to substitute low-priced products for high-priced products.
   c) people can be easily fooled by advertising into believing that it is smart to buy advertised products.
   d) when prices go up, incomes also go up, and this permits people to continue buying products regardless of their relative price.

4. Which of the following would *not* cause a change in the demand curve for football tickets at a local college?

   a) Building an all-weather dome over the stadium, installing padded seats, and lowering the prices of refreshments.
   b) Hiring a very successful "Pro" coach.
   c) Lowering ticket prices by $3.
   d) Adding to the schedule a team ranked in the top ten.

5. Assume that all parking places at a university are of the same quality in terms of location, and so on. Also assume that at the present price for a parking sticker on campus, the market is in equilibrium. What would happen if the Alumni Association successfully applied pressure to force a 10 percent reduction in the price for a parking sticker?

   a) The demand for parking places *off campus* would increase and a new method of rationing off-campus parking places would have to be developed.
   b) The *demand* for parking places on campus would increase and a new method of rationing campus parking places would have to be developed.
   c) The *quantity demanded* of parking places on campus would increase and a new method of rationing campus parking places would have to be developed.
   d) The supply of parking places on campus would increase to compensate for the increase in the quantity of parking places demanded.

6. Recently the Supreme Court made it illegal for the states to prevent abortions in the first trimester (first three months) of pregnancy. If numerous clinics have the capacity to perform abortions, what could we expect to happen to abortions during the first trimester (in the short run)?

   a) All doctors would refuse to perform abortions.
   b) Doctors would now provide abortion services at prices lower than before the Supreme Court ruling.
   c) The price of an abortion would rise due to doctors' high charges for their services.
   d) Nothing would change.

7. If we assume that the short-run elasticity of demand for gasoline is .7, this means that:

   a) a 10 percent increase in the price of gasoline will reduce the quantity demanded for gasoline by 7 percent.
   b) a 7 percent decrease in the price of gasoline will increase the quantity demanded by 10 percent.
   c) a 10 percent increase in the price of gasoline will have little effect on the demand for gasoline.
   d) price cannot be used to ration gasoline. The quantity response is too little to make price rationing effective, regardless of the price changes.

8. Total revenue can be increased by increasing the price of a commodity as long as the demand for that good is:

   a) elastic.
   b) inelastic.
   c) unitary elastic.
   d) Cannot tell from the information given.

9. Recently a hurricane swept through the Mississippi delta region where much of our nation's sugar cane grows. The short-run effect of this will be seen in:

   a) a decrease in demand for sugar.
   b) a decrease in the quantity supplied of sugar.

c) an increase in the quantity demanded of sugar substitutes.
d) a decrease in the supply of sugar.

10. If the price of sugar rises as a consequence of this hurricane, you can expect that the response by consumers will be greater if the demand is:

a) elastic.
b) inelastic.
c) unitary elastic.
d) Cannot tell from the information given.

11. On September 1 of last year, the Local Transit Corporation announced a 5¢ fare increase on bus rides. On October 1, the revenues were exactly the same as the month before. The demand for bus rides is:

a) elastic.
b) inelastic.
c) perfectly elastic.
d) unitary elastic.

12. Which of the following would be totally inelastic in supply?

a) knowledge
b) food
c) clothing
d) land

13. When a regulatory commission (such as the Federal Power Commission) sets a price that is below the equilibrium price for a particular good (such as natural gas), what is likely to result?

a) The demand for the good will increase, creating a shortage.
b) The quantity demanded of the good will increase, creating a shortage.
c) The supply for the good will decrease, creating a shortage.
d) No shortage will develop.

14. Due to the rising cost of sugar, the agriculture department has increased the import quota of raw sugar by 100,000 tons. What economic effects will this have?

a) As the supply increases, the quantity demanded will increase, and if no other changes occur, the price will not change.
b) The demand will increase and the supply curve will move accordingly, in relation to the elasticity of the product.
c) The equilibrium price will decrease according to the Law of Demand.
d) Nothing will happen because the demand for sugar is inelastic.

15. The *Wall Street Journal* reports that there is a domestic surplus of peanuts in the United States, and that the federal government spent about $70 million last year to maintain a price higher than the world price. Which of the following statements is true?

a) There would not be a domestic surplus of peanuts if the price were higher.
b) The surplus of peanuts would disappear if prices of other farm products that could be raised on the same land were to go up enough in price and no increase in price supports would occur.
c) The price of peanut-growing land is too high; if it were lower, farmers would not have to grow as many peanuts.
d) The purchase of peanuts by the federal government is necessary to continue the production of peanuts entirely.

16. In the past several years, the price of gasoline has risen substantially. At the same time, a number of private overnight camping parks have been closed because the costs of maintenance have risen. As a result of these two events,

   a) the price for overnight sites will rise.

   b) the new equilibrium quantity will be lower than before.

   c) the price for overnight sites will fall.

   d) There is not enough evidence to tell.

ESSAY QUESTIONS

1. In your college, there are not enough seats in the basketball arena to take care of all the students who want to see the basketball games. At the same time, there are not enough parking places for student cars. And the small auditorium appropriate for guitar concerts will accommodate only about half of the students who are enthusiastic about classical guitar. You have been given the job of allocating tickets for basketball games and classical guitar concerts, as well as for parking places.

Somebody from your economics class suggested that in order to give each student the choice of what he or she wants the most, you should give each student one hundred ration tickets that could be spent on basketball, classical guitar concerts, or parking places. You would set the ration ticket prices so that the total quantity demanded is equal to the number of tickets or parking places available.

How would your method of rationing compare with other rationing systems, such as: seniors, first; juniors, second; and so on; or, first come, first served. Which do you think would be most fair?

Would you allow students who were not interested in basketball, classical guitar, or parking to sell their ration tickets?

2. There is a shortage of apartments in your college community. What would this shortage do to the price of existing apartments? What would you expect householders to do with easily modifiable space in existing houses? And what, in the long run, do you think would happen to the quantity of apartments available? Now, change the situation. Suppose a price ceiling was placed on all apartments to prevent landlord gouging. How would apartments be rationed? And what would be the short- and long-run response to the apartment shortage if all new apartments had to be rented at prices no higher than the old apartments?

3. Gasoline is selling at $0.70 per gallon. Because of the oil shortage, it is necessary to cut the usage of gasoline by 20 percent. You are told that the elasticity of demand for gasoline in the short run is $-.2$ and that supply of gasoline is perfectly inelastic (in the short run). What price would bring the quantity demanded and quantity supplied into equilibrium?

Now suppose that you were told that a $1.00 price of gasoline would, after a lapse of three years, bring in enough new oil wells and other capacity to make it possible to produce 20 percent more gasoline? What public policy would you recommend? Would you allow the price to rise or would you use some other method of rationing gasoline?

4. Farmers have typically used about 10 billion pounds of nitrogenous fertilizers a year to raise corn and other feed grains. However, because of a large increase in the foreign demand for feed grains produced in the United States, the price of feed grains has almost doubled.

Although there has been no increase in the number of acres devoted to raising feed grains, a shortage of nitrogenous fertilizers has developed. The producers of these fertilizers argue that there has been no reduction in the production of nitrogenous fertilizers. The Department of Agriculture argues that there can be no shortage since no additional acreage is available for feed grains. The fertilizer industry insists that it must be permitted to charge higher prices in order to ration the available fertilizers and to serve as an inducement to build more fertilizer capacity. The Department of Agriculture insists that the shortage is not real and that fertilizer prices should be controlled at last year's level.

How would you resolve this conflict? Which argument is correct?

5. There has been a sudden increase in the demand for small cars as a result of the price rise in gasoline. What would you expect to happen to the costs of producing small cars in the short run? What do you think would happen in the long run? Why the difference, if any?

ANSWERS TO REVIEW QUESTIONS

1. Price is a ratio of exchange between two commodities. If three shirts are exchanged for nine TV dinners, then one shirt can be exchanged for three TV dinners. Hence the price of one shirt is three TV dinners. Similarly, we can say that one TV dinner will exchange for one-third of a shirt. Hence, the price of a TV dinner is one-third of a shirt.
   a) This is incorrect. The price of a TV dinner is one-third of a shirt and the price of a shirt is three TV dinners.
   b) This is incorrect. Price is the ratio of exchange between two commodities and you can use either commodity as the common denominator. It need not be money.
   c) This is correct.
   d) This is incorrect. See explanation (b).

2. The Law of Demand states that price and quantity demanded are inversely related; that is, as price rises, the quantity demanded falls and as price falls, the quantity demanded increases.
   a) This is incorrect. As price rises, the quantity demanded falls.
   b) This is incorrect. As price falls, the quantity demanded increases. New uses for salt will be found at lower prices.
   c) This is correct. At a high-enough price, buyers will be rationed out of the market so that quantity supplied will equal quantity demanded.
   d) This is incorrect. As price rises, the quantity demanded falls.

3. As prices rise, people will tend to substitute other commodities for the one in question. Hence the Law of Demand.
   a) This is incorrect. People can, as the prices rise, do without or with less of some goods by substituting other goods.
   b) This is true as explained above.
   c) This is incorrect. We have little evidence with which to answer this question. Further, it does not address itself to the Law of Demand.
   d) This is incorrect. Incomes do not necessarily rise as prices rise.

4. A change in demand means a change in the entire set of price-quantity-demanded relationships. Virtually anything can cause a change in demand except a change in the price of the commodity in question, since that would cause a change in *quantity demanded*.

   a) This is incorrect. This *would* cause a change in demand. At all prices people would buy more seats.

   b) This is incorrect. Again, at all prices, people would buy more seats—a change in demand.

   c) This is correct. Lowering the price will cause a change in *quantity demanded*, not a change in *demand*.

   d) This is incorrect. This would cause a change in demand.

5. Beginning with an equilibrium situation, a forced reduction in price will cause a shortage of parking spaces since the quantity demanded will now exceed the quantity supplied. See Fig. 3.8.

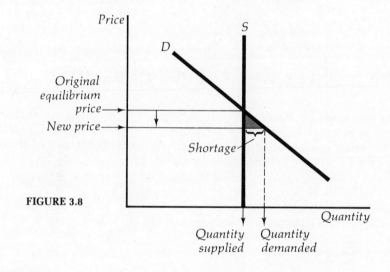

FIGURE 3.8

   a) This is incorrect. The shortage created for on-campus parking places will cause demand for substitutes—off-campus parking places—to increase. Since price is no longer allowed to be the allocating mechanism, at the new lower price, quantity demanded will be greater than quantity supplied. But, we have no evidence indicating a *new* method of rationing off-campus parking places would be required.

   b) This is incorrect. Demand will not increase; quantity demanded will increase.

   c) This is correct. The administered lower price will cause the quantity demanded to rise; since price no longer adjusts quantity demanded and supplied, a new rationing system will be needed.

   d) This is incorrect. We have no evidence for believing new parking places will be provided.

6. By making abortions legal during the first trimester of pregnancy, the real cost of providing this service is decreased and hence the supply can be expected to increase. Other things being equal, the price will fall.

a) This is incorrect. There are some doctors morally opposed and even if the real cost decreases, some doctors will refuse to perform abortions.

b) This is correct. The real cost has decreased substantially; therefore the supply curve will increase and the price will fall.

c) This is incorrect. The price will fall.

d) This is incorrect. The supply and price will both change as will quantity demanded.

7. Elasticity may be defined as the ratio between the percentage change in quantity demanded and a percentage change in price. In this case the ratio is 7 percent over 10 percent, that is, .7. This means a 10 percent change in price will cause a 7 percent change in quantity demanded.

a) This is correct as explained above.

b) This is incorrect. The percentage change in price is 10 percent, not 7 percent, and the percentage change in quantity demanded is 7 percent, not 10 percent.

c) This is incorrect. A 10 percent change in price will have a 7 percent change in quantity demanded.

d) This is incorrect. Price is a rationing mechanism.

8. If the price of a good is increased, the quantity demanded will fall and if total revenue increases, the demand must be inelastic. This is true since total revenue will rise only if the relative effect of the price change (upward) overwhelms the relative effect of the change in quantity demanded (downward).

a) This is incorrect. In this case total revenue will fall.

b) This is correct as explained above.

c) This is incorrect. If unitary elasticity prevails, there will be no change in total revenue.

d) This is incorrect. As explained above, the demand must be inelastic.

9. A hurricane will reduce the supply of sugar cane. Other things being equal, the price will rise and the quantity demanded of sugar cane will fall.

a) This is incorrect. There will be a reduction in *quantity demanded*, not *demand*.

b) This is incorrect. There will be a reduction in *supply*, not *quantity supplied*.

c) This is incorrect. There will be an increase in the *demand* for sugar substitutes.

d) This is correct as explained above.

10. When price rises, quantity demanded falls. If the demand is elastic, the price rise will cause a relatively greater change in quantity demanded than in price.

a) This is correct as explained above.

b) This is incorrect. The relative change in quantity demanded will be less responsive, the more inelastic demand is.

c) This is incorrect. The relative changes will be the same in the case of unitary elasticity.

d) This is incorrect. You *can* tell from the information given as explained above.

11. If the price increased, but revenues did not change, then the relative change in price was just offset by the relative change in quantity demanded, hence, demand is unitary elastic.

a) This is incorrect. In this case, revenues should have increased.

b) This is incorrect. In this case, revenues should have decreased.

c) This is incorrect. In this case, the increase in price would have caused revenues to fall drastically.

d) This is correct as explained above.

12. An inelastic supply situation refers to something absolutely fixed in supply.

    a) This is incorrect. Knowledge is expanding all the time.
    b) This is incorrect. The supply of food has increased and will likely increase over time.
    c) This is incorrect. The supply of clothing can be increased.
    d) This is correct. Land, ultimately, is limited in supply.

13. Whenever a price is set below the equilibrium price, there will be a shortage, that is, the quantity demanded will exceed the quantity supplied at that price. See Fig. 3.9.

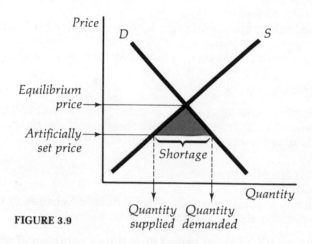

FIGURE 3.9

    a) This is incorrect. Demand will not increase, but quantity demanded will.
    b) This is correct as explained above.
    c) This is incorrect. Supply will not increase, but quantity supplied will decrease.
    d) This is incorrect. A shortage will indeed develop as explained above.

14. An increase in the quota moves the supply curve to the right. With a given demand curve, price will fall.

    a) This is incorrect. True, the quantity demanded will increase as the supply increases, but the price will also fall.
    b) This is incorrect. The increased supply will simply lower the price at which the market is cleared. There will be no shortage if price is allowed to move freely.
    c) This is correct. The increased supply will lower the price.
    d) This is incorrect. Even if the demand for sugar were inelastic, a reduction in price would increase the quantity demanded.

15. If a domestic surplus exists, the price must be fixed at a level above the market or equilibrium price.

    a) This is incorrect. If the price were set even higher, a larger surplus would be created as the quantity demanded would decrease and the quantity supplied would increase.
    b) This is correct. A price increase in crops other than peanuts would stimulate a reduction in the output of peanuts and an increase in the output of these other crops. This reduction in supply would eliminate the surplus if carried out far enough.

c) This is incorrect. This is nonsense. If the return on peanuts is not high enough to pay the "rent," they will not be grown on that land.

d) This is incorrect. If the subsidy were stopped, the price of peanuts would rise and the quantity demanded would fall—but it is unlikely that the quantity demanded would fall to zero.

16. Two events are occurring simultaneously. The price of gasoline has risen, hence we would expect that the demand for overnight camp sites will fall. At the same time, the supply of overnight camp sites has been reduced. A simultaneous reduction in demand and supply will reduce the equilibrium quantity—but will either raise or lower the equilibrium price depending on which change was greatest and on the elasticities involved. See Fig. 3.10.

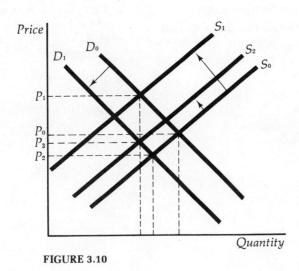

FIGURE 3.10

a) This is incorrect. We cannot tell whether the price will rise or fall.

b) This is correct as explained above.

c) This is incorrect. We cannot tell.

d) This is incorrect. We do know that the quantity demanded will fall.

OBJECTIVES

Upon successful completion of this chapter, you will be able to:

1. Define the process of production.
2. Identify the basic social institutions of centrally planned and decentralized economies.
3. Identify the features of the major types of business organizations.
4. Specify the economic meaning of competition.
5. Explain the role of the decision maker—the entrepreneur—in production.
6. Distinguish between the economic definition of cost and common usage.
7. Define opportunity cost and give examples of it.
8. Distinguish between the accounting and the economic definitions of profit.
9. Explain how prices, costs, and profits provide the information for making production decisions.

CHAPTER 4

PRODUCTION: INSTITUTIONS, COSTS, AND PROFITS

INTRODUCTION

SOCIAL INSTITUTIONS

COST OF PRODUCTION

PROFIT

INTRODUCTION

In this chapter, we want to see how market prices can be used *to direct* the production activities of a society. In the preceding chapter we saw that prices were widely used in many kinds of societies to ration goods and services among buyers. But before goods and services can be rationed, they must be produced; and therefore there must be some method of organizing the production activities of a society.

What is meant by production?

Production is the process of increasing the capacity of goods to satisfy human desires or of rendering services capable of satisfying human desires.

Consider some examples. You are an editor of a school newspaper. Together with the other people in your organization you put together a newspaper that is widely read on your campus. The newspaper is a product and the activities involved in getting the newspaper out each day are production activities.

Or suppose that you have responsibility for distributing the school newspaper to the dormitories and other living units on your campus. Your activities result in the production of a service—the transportation of the newspapers from the printer to the readers. The rendering of this service is a production activity—just as the printing of the newspaper is a production activity. Both goods and services are products that can be supplied only by an organized activity called production.

Any society that is engaged in production activities must constantly answer two questions: What quantities of each product shall be produced? and How shall each product be produced?

In a centrally planned economy, the *way* in which these questions are answered is fairly simple, even though the actual answers selected may not have been easy choices. The planners would first decide what share of their resources should be allocated to consumer goods and what share to capital goods. This first basic decision would be made on the basis of the economic goals agreed upon by the planning body and the the available resources.

In contrast to this, suppose a roulette wheel were used to determine how much of each product should be produced. In one year 12 million autos would be produced and in the succeeding year possibly only 2 million would be produced. In some years, more automobiles would be produced than people really wanted and in other years not enough would be produced.

Suppose, also, that the same roulette wheel were used to pick the production technologies to be used in the production of the indicated goods. If the roulette wheel happened to spin in a certain way, automobiles would be produced by hand methods and this might easily take more labor than is available. Or if the roulette wheel indicated that labor-saving devices should be used in all production activities, it could easily happen that there wouldn't be enough capital equipment and there would be too much labor. Consequently, it is absolutely necessary to have some organized way of deciding how scarce resources should be used—and this involves answering simultaneously the questions of *what* and *how*.

SOCIAL INSTITUTIONS

Every society must devise social institutions to answer the questions of what and how.

Social institutions are established patterns of social interaction, some enacted into law and administered by the courts, and others embedded in custom and tradition.

Consider how a self-sufficient agricultural commune might deal with the questions of *what* and *how.* The members of the commune might vote on what crops to produce—and in this way decide what food and fibres they would have available during the next year. Once they have decided what to produce, they would have to decide how much of their available labor and how much of their available land they would use to produce each crop. The social institution used to make these interlocking decisions might easily be group discussion and consensus. But if it were impossible to reach a consensus about what to produce and how to produce each crop, then it would be necessary—as it has been in many agricultural communes—to appoint a leader to make the decisions. The leader and his acceptance by the group would then constitute the social institution used to organize the production activities.

In communist nations, the major social institutions used to resolve economic problems are the central planning agency and the body of laws empowering it to make decisions.

In the communist nations, there is usually a central planning agency that decides what should be produced—and therefore decides what the people should have. The central planning agency must also decide what technology should be used to produce each good. It must decide, for example, whether to use horses or tractors in wheat production. It must decide whether to use low-pressure or high-pressure technologies in the production of nitrogenous fertilizers. It must decide whether to use coal-fired or diesel railroad engines in the transportation of fertilizers to the farms and crops from the farms to the cities. If successful, it must make these decisions in such a way that it does not have a shortage or surplus of any resources such as land, capital, or labor.

The body of laws creating the central planning agency and empowering it to make these decisions is *the* important social institution of a communist society. Over the years, the people who hold the key offices in a central planning agency have developed ways of resolving their problems. These methods are also social institutions.

In decentralized economies, the competitive market, private property, and enforcement of contracts are dominant social institutions.

If you live in the United States or in one of the other mixed market economies of the world, you also depend on social institutions to organize the production of the goods you use. The competitive market is the dominant social institution in these economies. But competitive markets—where prices are determined—are themselves the result of a unique set of underlying social institutions. Consider two of the most important of these *underlying* social institutions—private property and enforcement of contracts—and the implications they have for business organization.

The existence of privately owned resources is a basic underlying social institution in the United States economy.

If you own property—whether it is a piece of land, a truck, or *even* yourself— your relationships with other people are prescribed by a complex set of rules established by your government. Assume, for example, that you own a city lot. Since it is yours, you have the right to use it, but only within a limited framework. If you use it as a garbage dump, the other people in the community have the right to object and force you to stop dumping garbage on it. Or if you want to build a filling station on a lot zoned for residential use only, you will find that you cannot do it. Or if you sell your lot, and the buyer in payment for the lot agrees to work for you for the rest of his life, you will find that you have broken the law prohibiting "involuntary servitude." Finally, if you sell the lot for twice as much as you paid for it, you will be forced by the tax laws to pay the government a part of your gain. Although there are many restrictions on the use of property, when you acquire a piece of property, you have the right to keep other people from using it without compensation. Your relationship with other people has been changed by your ownership of property.

The complex set of laws establishing your right to the ownership of property is constantly being modified by statute and by judicial decisions. At one time, you could sell your personal services for whatever price was agreed upon. Now you are not permitted to sell them for less than the minimum wage. At one time you could agree to work for 60 hours a week without extra compensation for overtime. Now this is prohibited under certain statutes.

Nonetheless, the laws establishing private property—however restrictive they might be—usually give those who would organize production activities a stake in the outcome of any venture. For example, you decide to buy and sell used books in your dormitory. If you are successful, you will increase your income. If you are unsuccessful, you will lose your original investment. The fact that you can either gain or lose gives you a real interest in how well you organize your production activities.

Enforcement of contracts is a key underlying social institution.

Many economic activities involve making promises about what shall be done in the future. Suppose, for example, you borrow the money to pay your tuition. Your promise to pay in the future is an enforceable contract. If you don't pay, the courts will impose certain penalties upon you.

It is doubtful that markets could be maintained if the government did not, through its judicial system, make arrangements for the enforcement of contracts. The right to make contracts and to expect them to be honored—whether through law enforcement or through tradition—is another

important social institution. These social institutions—the competitive market, private property, and the enforcement of contracts—have given rise to a bewildering array of business organizations. These include proprietorships, of the sort typically used by family farmers; partnerships, widely used by professional persons; limited partnerships, used in real estate ownerships; joint ventures, used in oil exploration; and various types of corporations used to organize manufacturing, financial, and distribution activities. We will characterize three types in more detail. The others you would become acquainted with if you went on to study business organization.

Businesses are organized in a variety of ways.

Proprietorship is the term describing a business operated by and for an individual. The assets of the operation, the land and equipment, belong to the proprietor. The debts incurred to buy the land and equipment are the proprietor's personal debts. If the operation is not profitable and debts multiply, the proprietor has unlimited liability. Creditors are entitled to sue the proprieter, or owner, to collect their debts and if the owner cannot meet his financial obligations, the courts will allow the creditors to take personal assets from him or her, including his or her home. Many small family businesses are proprietorships and most farms have this form of organization.

A *partnership* is a joint proprietorship with two or more partners. Each of the partners has unlimited liability for the debts of the firm and each of the partners can make contracts binding on the other partners. When one of the partners dies or withdraws from the partnership, the partnership is dissolved, and a new one must be formed if the enterprise is to continue engaging in business operations as a partnership.

The *corporation* is the most important social invention in the business organization field, in terms of the value of output. A corporation is a legal entity chartered by the state government and created for the purpose of doing business. It may hold assets, such as inventories, equipment, and land; it may borrow, as it does when it sells short-term notes or long-term bonds; and it can sell stock representing shares of ownership. The own-

The corporation has certain characteristics that have made it the most important form of business organization.

Once in existence, a corporation has advantages. Since it is a legal entity, it can act as a shield for the stockholders, protecting their personal estates from the liabilities of the corporation. Once they have agreed to purchase stock in the corporation, they can be held liable only to the extent of their stock purchase. This characteristic of *limited liability* has made the corporation an important vehicle with a unique capacity to assemble large amounts of capital for business purposes. Few people would be willing to join thousands of other persons in businesses large enough to produce steel, automobiles, telephone systems, and the like were it not for this characteristic of limited liability.

The corporate form of organization can also provide *continuity*. When a stockholder dies, his executor can sell his interests to other persons. Or when a stockholder wishes to terminate his interest in a corporation, he can sell his stock without disturbing the activities of the corporation.

However organized, the privately owned business firm plays an important role in the market-directed economies of the world. It assembles capital. It buys labor and other personal services. It converts productive services into products and sells the products in the appropriate market. This step takes us to the basic social institution in a market economy—competitive markets.

To clarify your understanding of the unique features of the corporation as a form of business organization, consider Mini-case 4.1.

Competition has a special meaning in economics

The word *competition* is a familiar one to you. You have seen competition in practice when you have watched a football game or a basketball game. You have felt it when you have competed for grades in the classroom. Based on your common-sense understanding of competition, you might define it as rivalry between two or more participants under a given set of rules that are intended to prevent violence and cheating.

In the markets you see around you, the government ideally serves as a referee, enforcing

ers are responsible through the board of directors, whom they elect, and who in turn select the persons to manage the corporation.

Proprietorships, partnerships, and corporations are found in every major industry in the United States. Table 4.1 shows the numbers and business receipts of these three types of business organizations.

The impact of the family farm can be seen in the number of proprietorships in the agriculture, forestry, and fishing industry classification. The largest corporations are well represented in manufacturing (for example, General Motors), and wholesale and retail trade (for example, Sears, Roebuck Company).

TABLE 4.1

PROPRIETORSHIPS, PARTNERSHIPS, AND CORPORATIONS, NUMBER AND RECEIPTS, BY INDUSTRY AND SIZE OF BUSINESS RECEIPTS, 1973

(Number in thousands: receipts in millions of dollars)

Item	Proprietorships[1]			Active partnerships			Active corporations		
	Under $50,000	$50,000– $99,999	$100,000 or more	Under $100,000	$100,000– $499,999	$500,000 or more	Under $500,000	$500,000– $999,999	$1,000,000 or more
All industrial divisions:									
Number	9,178	800	670	807	194	38	1,514	166	225
Business receipts	90,453	56,014	164,907	18,313	40,667	62,943	173,553	116,559	2,201,739
Agriculture, forestry, and fishing:									
Number	3,119	193	103	97	23	4	40	4	3
Business receipts	28,917	13,212	23,865	2,481	4,598	5,493	4,419	2,674	15,299
Mining:									
Number	51	3	4	13	1	(z)	10	1	2
Business receipts	463	188	1,263	154	318	1,151	1,031	790	26,971
Construction:									
Number	707	78	71	48	15	3	130	21	25
Business receipts	8,391	5,450	16,996	1,544	3,087	5,477	18,940	14,687	90,191
Manufacturing:									
Number	172	19	20	21	7	2	130	28	52
Business receipts	1,838	1,291	5,332	643	1,467	4,395	20,680	19,570	962,051
Transport and public utilities:									
Number	307	18	16	13	2	1	64	6	8
Business receipts	4,117	1,232	4,068	424	493	1,046	7,296	3,834	169,945
Wholesale and retail trade:									
Number	1,529	273	362	117	68	14	395	78	109
Business receipts	18,439	19,629	95,994	4,132	14,672	21,487	64,741	54,842	655,817
Finance, insurance, real estate:									
Number	700	26	13	369	34	8	400	11	16
Business receipts	6,093	1,774	3,435	5,452	7,070	12,682	20,802	7,782	231,508
Services:									
Number	2,551	189	80	128	43	7	339	18	11
Business receipts	21,918	13,138	13,750	3,459	8,898	11,208	35,493	12,370	49,743

[1] Individually owned businesses and farms.   z Less than 500.

Source: *Statistical Abstract of the U.S.*, 1976, p. 509.

rules to prevent cheating and the outbreak of violence when the rivalry becomes too heated. Thus, there are laws against false advertising, which might give some participants unfair advantage, and there are laws against the use of violence to keep participants from lowering their prices. We cannot list all of these laws—there are many of them—but it is important to see that the maintenance of competitive markets rests to a large extent on legal foundations. Indeed, a market-

---

MINI-CASE 4.1

The courts have tended to treat corporations as legal persons with all the rights and privileges of individuals.

a) This is an inappropriate interpretation because individuals, while having rights, also have feelings as individuals. People care about what others think of them. A corporation, not being an individual person, cannot reflect this concern.
b) This is a correct interpretation. So long as corporations are responsible for their financial obligations they are behaving as responsible citizens.
c) This is a correct interpretation. Corporations have been designed to organize production. So long as they do this efficiently, they have fulfilled satisfactorily their role in society.
d) This is an incorrect interpretation. Corporations are institutions created by society to accomplish certain objectives. Therefore, unlike individuals, they can be regulated as society chooses.

---

directed economy has as much of a governmentally established framework as does a centrally directed economy. The difference lies in the social institutions that governments must maintain.

But when we use the term *competition* in economics we mean much more than "rivalry under refereed conditions." In the section that follows we will define competition as we shall use the term in the rest of this book.

Economic activity is *competitive* if there are no limitations on entry into it and exit from it, apart from the usual requirement that the participants be prepared to pay for the tools and knowledge required to succeed in that activity.

Suppose you are thinking of becoming an accountant. If there are no limitations on your right to be trained—either in a college or a business school—and if once you are trained there are no limitations on the number of people who are permitted to enter the occupation, we can say that the occupation is competitive. You can enter it, compete with the other accountants for business, and leave it if you find it not to your liking.

On the other hand, suppose that the accountants already practicing were to require that you pass an examination before you enter the occupation and suppose that they made the exam so difficult that only a small number of the applicants who were qualified to do the work could pass the exam. Then it is clear that the occupation is not fully competitive. Some people who are qualified to do the work would be excluded. This would restrict the supply of accountants and therefore permit those already practicing to charge higher prices than otherwise.

We can apply the same test to groups of business firms producing the same or similar products. These groups are usually called *industries*. Thus we speak of the typewriter industry, the automobile industry, or the farming industry. An industry, then, is competitive if there are no limitations on entry into it and exit from it, again apart from the usual requirements that the firms considering entry into the industry must be prepared to pay for the knowledge and capital required to succeed in that industry.

Suppose that there are a dozen or so apartment buildings near your campus and that the apartment owners can charge rents high enough to have a larger than normal return on their investment. Without knowing how it came about, each of the apartment owners may be said to be in a position to earn unusually high rents. But will this continue? The answer is no, unless the owners of the existing apartments can find some way to prevent the building of more apartments. Normally, it is impossible to keep information about the profitability of various types of investment secret. When others learn about the profitability of apartments, they too will want to cash in on these opportunities by building additional apartments. Once they do this, the rental rates will fall, and the return on apartment house developments near your campus will fall to the usual rate of return on real estate investment.

This example illustrates another important qualification about our definition of competition. It takes *time* for competitive forces to work themselves out. Few industries, except those with very large numbers of participants selling standardized products—such as farming—give competitive results all of the time. For industries with smaller numbers of participants, competition, like

other economic processes, takes time to work itself out. The "free-entry" definition of competition, which we shall use in this book, really applies, then, to long-run developments. Using this definition, the predictions we make do not always apply in the short run. As we shall find, however, this is not a serious limitation, since very few of the economists' predictions are really applicable to short-run developments.

We have now described the environment in which production decisions are made in a market-oriented economy, but we have not identified the actual ultimate decision maker and the motivation underlying the decisions—whether it be a committee, a person, or some other. We will now consider this issue.

To clarify your understanding of the concept of competition, consider Mini-case 4.2.

MINI-CASE 4.2

In traditional economic analysis, the concept of competition always includes a large number of buyers and sellers, in addition to free entry and exit.

a) This is convenient since we don't have to worry about how long it takes to get from one equilibrium price to another when conditions of demand or supply change. This convenience outweighs the unrealistic nature of the assumption.
b) This is another example of the irrelevance of contemporary economic thought.
c) Given enough time, large number-competition and free entry-competition arrive at the same result. Therefore, you should choose the simpler approach for analysis.
d) Economists are not very good at making short-run predictions. Therefore, it makes sense to deal with long-run analyses, where the free entry definition of competition works as well as the large number definition.

The entrepreneur is a key element in organizing production activity.

In a market-oriented economy, the decision makers, whom we will call *entrepreneurs*, are "operators" who are constantly looking for opportunities to buy in a low-price market and sell in a higher-price market. They may own their own business, they may be hired managers, or in some cases they may be representatives of committees. Consider some examples of entrepreneurial activities.

Suppose the price of gasoline were $0.80 a gallon in Boston and $0.60 a gallon in Chicago. An entrepreneur seeing these price disparities would buy gasoline in Chicago, pay to have the gasoline trucked to New England, and there would sell it for slightly less than $0.80. As long as it cost less than $0.20 a gallon to truck it from Chicago to New England, a return could be earned by shipping gasoline. Eventually, as more entrepreneurs were attracted into the profit-making opportunity, the price of gasoline would rise in Chicago and fall in New England, until the price difference was no greater than, say, the $0.10 it cost to ship it. We can illustrate this with the shifting of supply curves on the twin diagrams in Fig. 4.1. The entrepreneur buys gasoline in the Midwest, shifting the supply curve to the left and increasing the price there. The gasoline purchased is shipped to New England and this shifts the supply curve in New England to the right. The end result is the elimination of price differentials except for the cost of transportation.

A certain type of entrepreneur, sometimes called a speculator, can apply the same reasoning to changes in the price of durable commodities over time. Suppose that the price of corn at harvest time is $2.00 a bushel. Suppose further that at the rate corn is being consumed during the year, it becomes clear that there will be a shortage of corn during the next year. The speculator would buy corn at harvest time, store it, and later sell it for a higher price. When this is done, speculators perform a valuable service. By increasing the price right after harvest they reduce the consumption of corn immediately after harvest and make it available later in the year. This activity of buying corn when it is cheap and selling it when it is dear effectively shifts the supply curves in such a way as to regulate the consumption of corn so that it will last during the whole year.

Entrepreneurs can accomplish the same results when they see disparities between the prices of those productive services required to produce a product and the price of the product itself. Suppose, for example, that a new food product, similar to a pizza, appears on the market. During the novelty period, consumers will find themselves paying a high price for the new product. The persons supplying the new product will find that they are earning a larger than normal return on their investment. The entrepreneurs in the economy will see an opportunity to move in to the higher-profit industry, and in doing so, will re-

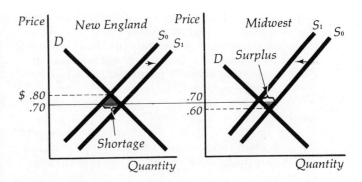

FIG. 4.1 **Price disparities between markets.**

duce the prices of the new product—just as they reduced the prices of small calculators in the five years after their appearance on the market.

Competitive markets are characterized, in the long run, by freedom of entry, as opposed to monopolized markets, which are characterized by limitations on entry. It is clear, then, that *competitive markets* are based largely on governmental laws and regulations. If these laws and regulations are set up largely to prevent free entry, then there are few competitive markets. If the laws are designed to make entry easy, then there will be many competitive markets.

We will now see how competitive markets and the underlying social institutions of *private property* and *enforcement of contracts* can be used to answer the questions: What products shall be produced? and How shall they be produced? To do this we will need to know precisely what is meant by the *costs* and *profits*. We turn now to the definition of costs and the way they influence production.

COST OF PRODUCTION

Cost means different things to different people.

When you read the ads in the newspaper or listen to the sales pitches on TV, you frequently are reminded that the sale items are going at cost—or even below cost! What does this mean?

It is also asserted that the United States Postal Service is charging those who send first-class mail more than it costs to provide the service. At the same time, it is claimed that those who send newspapers and magazines as well as the so-called junk mail addressed to "occupant" are paying less than the cost of providing the service. It is said that the users of the first-class mail services are really subsidizing the delivery of second- and third-class mail. What is meant by "The costs of providing the service"?

To answer these and similar questions, we need to know what is meant by the cost of producing or making available a unit of a product. We also need to know what role costs play in the communications system of a market-directed economy.

The dictionary definition of cost is "that which must be given up or surrendered in order to acquire, produce, accomplish, or maintain something" (*Oxford English Dictionary*, 1971). You will note that this definition can be broken into two parts: the sacrifice (what must be given up) and the objective of the sacrifice (to acquire, produce, accomplish, or maintain something). In economics, the definition of cost is somewhat different.

Cost, in economics, always entails a choice between alternatives.

Suppose you are a farmer and have three one-acre plots, one of which has been planted in wheat, another in corn, and the last in oats. You have only enough fertilizer for one of the three plots and no possibility of obtaining any more. From past experience you know that if you apply the fertilizer to wheat, the dollar value of your yield will increase by $100; if you apply it to corn the yield will increase by $90; and if you apply it to oats, the yield will rise by $50.

What is the cost of this fertilizer to you? If you use it on corn, the cost is $100, that is, what you would be giving up by not applying it to wheat, your best alternative use. If you use the fertilizer on oats, what is your cost? Again the answer is $100, your best alternative use.

The *opportunity cost,* then, is the expense involved in bidding a resource away from its most profitable use. This is equal to what that resource would produce in its best alternative use.

Suppose that the fertilizer could only be used on oats, in other words, there were no alternative uses and you could not sell the fertilizer that you already had on hand. What would be the cost of

using it on oats in this instance? The answer is nothing. You are giving up nothing except the effort in spreading it.

Consider the following examples.

Suppose that you become very interested in the design of hi-fi equipment. This leads you to consider becoming an acoustical engineer. But your aptitude tests indicate that you could also be a successful lawyer. Your father is a lawyer and he indicates that he would like to have you as a partner in his firm and that he is willing to guarantee you an average salary of $20,000 a year. Assuming that your educational costs are going to be covered in any case, what will it cost you to become an acoustical engineer? The answer is that it will cost you $20,000 a year. Even though you cannot expect to make $20,000 a year designing loudspeakers, you may still decide that the extra pleasure you get working with hi-fi equipment will make it worthwhile. But you should realize that when you make this choice, the cost to you of becoming an acoustical engineer is $20,000 a year.

When publishers, in producing economics books, use resources that might otherwise be available for a variety of uses, they incur opportunity costs. These opportunity costs are equal to the extra sales revenue the publishers could generate by using their multiple-use resources to produce other types of books. Note that if the resources had a single use, then economics books would have no opportunity cost. Actually, they do have costs because these resources could be used to produce magazines, newspapers, tradebooks, or other textbooks. If economics books are going to be produced, enough must be sold to keep the resources from being used for these other purposes.

As a generalization, we can say that the *opportunity cost* of producing any good consists of what must be paid to keep that bundle of multiple-use materials and productive services from being used to produce other products. It is useful to see that the "bundle" will include not only the purchased materials and the productive services that producers must buy, but also the value of the multiple-use resources producers already have and could use for other purposes.

When any producer, whether a farmer or an automobile manufacturer, buys intermediate products from other producers, that producer is indirectly buying productive services. A farmer who buys chemical fertilizers is really buying the underlying petrochemicals plus the productive services added by the manufacture of chemical fertilizers. The price of the petrochemicals can in turn be factored into a small amount of purchased materials plus the value added by productive services purchased by the supplier of petrochemicals. Finally, as we will see when we study the national income in Chapter 11, the prices of purchased materials can, if we trace them back far enough through the production chain, be thought of as consisting of the prices paid for the productive services that went into their production.

The cost of any product can then be thought of as the total amount that must be paid for all the productive services that must be obtained either indirectly through purchasing materials or directly through purchasing of resources to produce it.

Why do we labor over this point—that all costs can be thought of as accumulated payments to the suppliers of productive services? The answer is that prices of the productive services have an important story to tell producers. They tell them what technology to use. They play an important role in telling producers how much of a product to produce. But we are getting ahead of our story. For the present, it is enough to see that *the opportunity cost of producing a product is the amount that producers must pay to keep multiple-use resources from being used to produce other products.*

We can put this idea to work in a commonsense way.

Suppose that the public utility commissions that regulate the prices of electricity are unwilling to grant price increases during an inflationary period. As a result, the public utilities cannot increase their wage rates or pay higher interest rates to match those being paid by other industries. This in turn will mean that public utilities will have difficulties bidding for labor and capital. In the end, then, the labor and capital will go to other industries, and the supply of electric power will be diminished. The result will be brown-outs and power failures.

This introduces the question of time. Must the prices of products always be high enough to cover the "costs of production"? Or can there be periods when the prices of products will be lower than their costs of production?

The disparity between short- and long-run costs accounts for the fact that some enterprises continue to operate while showing a loss.

The answer to the question of whether prices must be high enough to cover the costs of production must recognize that in capital-using industries, opportunity costs are usually lower in the short run than they are in the long run. You will recall from our discussion of turnover periods in Chapter 2 that capital invested in factories and in equipment tends to be "frozen" into specialized shapes in the short run. As the capital wears out and depreciation reserves are set aside to replace the old factories and the old pieces of equipment, the capital is again fluid and can be put to multiple uses. But this takes time.

In the short run, the specialized pieces of capital—the punch presses, assembly equipment, the factory buildings—have only one use. They are all designed to produce one type of product. If they are not used to produce that product, they have little value. In a sense they are like a freshwater spring. They are there to be used. If they are not used they will be wasted, as nature takes its toll in rust and decay. In the short run, the only opportunity costs involved in using a specialized piece of equipment are the costs of acquiring the complementary resources—such as materials. Therefore, in the short run—until the specialized capital wears out—the opportunity costs are substantially lower than they will be in the long run.

This explains why some of the railroads in the eastern part of the United States can report large losses and still operate. In the short run they are using up their prior investment in a roadbed and in equipment. In the long run, if they are going to keep their roadbed in passable shape and if they are going to replace their equipment as it wears out, they will have revenues large enough to cover their long-run opportunity costs.

Consider another example.

Suppose that as a means of working your way through college you were to buy a specialized vehicle for transporting canceled checks from your local bank to the nearest Federal Reserve Bank and let us suppose that the bank agreed to pay you a certain amount per pound of canceled checks transported. Initially, you would have to receive enough to: (a) pay your operating expenses for gasoline, oil, tires, taxes, and maintenance; (b) set aside a depreciation allowance on your vehicle so that you could replace it when it wears out; (c) earn a return large enough on your investment in a vehicle that you could afford to take your savings out of a bank and risk it on the purchase of a specialized piece of equipment; and (d) receive compensation that would be large enough for you to give up alternative ways of working your way through college. We might suppose that the bank and you agree that $25.00 a pound is the appropriate price for this service.

Now let us assume that after you have been operating for a few years, an armored truck service offers to do this job for $20.00 per pound. The bank indicates that they will change suppliers for this service unless you can match this price. The question is: Can you do it? You know that your long-run opportunity costs are still $25.00 per pound. But you also know that you will not be able to sell your specialized truck for very much.

You know that you have to cover your operating costs in order to stay in business. You also know that you have to earn enough from this activity to keep you from getting another job. But what about the depreciation reserve for your specialized truck and the rate of return on the money you have already taken out of a savings account to buy the truck? You check around and find that the truck, which originally cost you $10,000, now has a sale price of $1,000. Therefore, you know that in order to stay in business you must earn a competitive return on the $1,000 you could get for your truck if you sold it in the second-hand market. Altogether, then, your short-run opportunity costs would be

a) operating costs $10.00 a pound;
b) compensation for you $7.00 a pound;
c) competitive return on the
   remaining $1,000 investment
   in the truck, including an
   allowance for risk $2.00 a pound.

Therefore, you decide that you can afford to match the price the bank has been offered for this service. You agree to do it for $20.00 per pound. But could you do it for a very long time? The answer is no. Your truck is beginning to wear out and when it goes you know that you will not be able to afford a new one.

Consider Mini-case 4.3, involving interpretation of fixed and variable costs.

This disparity between short-run opportunity costs and long-run opportunity costs accounts for the fact that some enterprises can show losses for

---

MINI-CASE 4.3

Suppose you owned a car, which you use for personal purposes. You are not worried about your car wearing out, since you expect to get a new one as soon as you graduate. You calculate that your fixed costs for taxes, insurance, and licenses would be about $0.10 a mile if you drive 5000 miles a year, and that your gasoline, oil and minimum repair bills are about $0.06 a mile. You are offered a job delivering dry cleaning that will pay you $3.00 per hour plus $0.10 per mile for the use of your car.

a) You should not accept the job, since your employer is unwilling to pay the full cost of driving your car.
b) You should accept the job. The $3.00 per hour is enough to compensate you for the loss of your leisure and $0.10 per mile is enough for the use of your car.
c) You should not accept the job unless your employer will pay a portion of the fixed cost of driving the car.
d) You should not accept the job unless you are willing to treat a $1.00 per hour of your pay as an additional contribution to the use of your car.

a period of time and still survive. It also accounts for the fact that when business is slack, some enterprises—particularly construction companies—will bid on jobs or price their products at below their full accounting costs. As long as the prices producers charge make some contribution toward covering the depreciation of their specialized equipment they are ahead.

In a growing economy, such as we have had in the United States during the last century, the long run is usually not a very long period of time. Many enterprises have had to expand continuously. To do this they have to consider what their opportunity costs would be in a new plant. If prices are not high enough to cover their total costs, they cannot afford to bid for the resources necessary to expand their output.

It is only when enterprises are contracting that the long run tends to be an extended period of time. This is true because it usually takes a decade or so for plants to be worn out and abandoned. But we will discuss more of this in the following chapter, where we will be concerned with the way the production is adjusted in the long run to changes in demand.

To summarize: The cost of production as we will use the term in this book is the amount that would have to be paid to acquire the materials and resources necessary to produce a unit of product. It is a sum large enough to bid the necessary resources (given the optimum technology) away from other activities.

We turn now to the concept of profits. The price of any product can be divided into two parts: the cost of producing the product and the profit, or the amount that is left over after the costs have been paid. What does the term profit mean?

PROFIT

The term *profit* **has generated much confusion because it has several definitions.**

There are few terms that have caused as much confusion as the concept of profit. Businesspersons, for example, frequently quote surveys intimating that Americans are economically illiterate, since they believe that *average* profits run as high as 35 percent. Seldom, however, have the same surveys bothered to identify clearly how profit is defined in the context of the question.

In accounting terminology, profit is a measure of the increase in wealth resulting from the operation of an enterprise. *Gross profit* is used to indicate the difference between the selling price and the cost of materials. *Net profit* or *net income* is determined by deducting the selling and operating expenses from gross profits. Consider the following illustration.

Suppose you decide to go into the business of buying and selling used textbooks. At the end of one year of operation your receipts total $20,000 and your expenditures $18,000. Have you earned a profit? We can't say until we examine your first year's operation in greater detail and clarify what definition of profit we

are using. Receipts from the sale of used books total $20,000 and the used books you purchased from students at the end of the semester cost you $10,000. You hired several students whom you paid a total of $7,000. You operate your business out of your garage and pay utility expenses of $500. You buy cabinets, a cash register, and so on for $1200 from your savings account. Miscellaneous selling expenses amount to $300. One of the students you hired is an accounting major, and he has organized your receipts and expenditures as shown in Table 4.2. In addition to the expenses listed above he informed you that you should make an allowance of $200 a year for the wear and tear on the $1200 worth of equipment you purchased.

It would appear from the net income statement below prepared by your assistant that you have made a *net profit* of $2000. *Gross profit*, you may recall, was defined as the difference between the selling price and the cost of materials. In this example, *gross profit* would be $10,000.

From an *economic viewpoint*, something is wrong with this analysis, however. First, you have put a lot of your time and effort into the operation. You estimate that you have devoted at least 10 hours a week for 50 weeks. The question you must ask is what could you have earned managing a similar operation for someone else. If you could have earned $5 an hour, you should

TABLE 4.2
STUDENT SAVER BOOKSTORE INCOME (PROFIT)
STATEMENT FOR 1979

Revenues		
Sales of used books		$20,000
Less cost of used books		10,000
Gross profit		10,000
Operating expenses		8,000
(Salaries of assistants, utilities, depreciation, and miscellaneous expenses)		
Net Accounting profit		2,000
Implicit Costs		
Competitive salary of owner	$2,500	
Competitive garage rental	240	
Interest (adjusted for risk on investment)	108	2,848
Net economic profit		−$ 848

have included, as part of your expenses, salary payments to yourself of $2,500. This would reduce your net income or profit to a minus $500. Second, that garage you have been using also has a cost. If you could have rented it to someone for $20 a month, you would have to add another $240 to your expenses. Third, the $1200 you withdrew from your savings account would have paid you $60 at the going rate of interest of 5 percent, and indeed, if you had invested that $1200 in a project as risky as your used book operation, you would have required at least a 9 percent rate of return, or $108.00. If you include these opportunity costs, your operation has a negative profit of $848.00.

This example illustrates the different ways the term profit is used. In accounting language, the net profit refers to the difference between the selling price for a product and the expenses involved in producing it; economic profit means what is left over for the organizers of an activity after *all* expenses are paid, including the interest forgone by not investing all financial resources elsewhere.

Profit is defined in economics as what is left over after *all* of the opportunity costs of production have been met, including the interest forgone on the investment of the owner. We shall refer to this definition as *economic profit*.

In some small corporations and in many partnerships and proprietorships, as in our used book operation example, the owners are not only the managers but also do much of the routine work. They usually draw a salary for their effort, but in many cases the salaries are smaller than what they could earn working elsewhere in some equally interesting jobs. As a result, from an economic point of view, profits are overstated.

In both large and small businesses, it is also customary for the owners to provide a large part of the capital. Some of the capital is borrowed. The interest on the borrowed capital is included among the expenses. But the interest that companies would otherwise have to pay to get the capital that the stockholders provide (or the owners of partnerships and proprietorships) is not included among the expenses of the business. Again, accounting profits are larger than economic profits.

Over the long run, if opportunity costs are not met, then such production activities as farming, producing electric power, and transporting finished goods from one part of the country to another cannot be expanded to provide products for a growing population. They are costs, just as the hiring of skilled workers is a cost of sustaining a production activity.

Profits are measured in different ways.

How large are profits in the United States, looked at from an *economic* point of view? There are many ways of measuring profits. During the two decades from 1956 to 1976, accounting profits averaged 11 percent of the value added by corporations and about 5 percent of sales. It is doubtful that economic profits were more than a third of these figures. This means that economic profits averaged less than 4 percent of the value added by manufacturing corporations and about 1.5 percent of the sales. This indicates the fact that the major share of any commodity consists of the opportunity cost of producing it. This will be dealt with in more detail in Chapter 5.

It is probably not the average size of economic profits that activates entrepreneurs, just as it is not the average size of reward at the gaming table that activates gamblers. Rather it is the possibility of some large payoffs for those who are really successful. But this is speculation. It is enough for us to see that economic profit—what is left after taking opportunity costs out of the sales dollar—is an important factor in determining how the questions of *what* and *how* will be answered in a decentrally controlled economy.

In summary: market prices, costs, and profits provide the information for answering the what and how economics question.

To get some ideas as to how market prices, operating through costs and profits, serve as a communications system, we will develop an imaginary case study of how they might guide a young entrepreneur. Then, in the following chapter, we formalize our intuitive understanding of how market prices work and apply our understanding.

MARKET PRICES, COSTS, AND PROFITS: HOW THEY TELL YOU WHAT TO DO IF YOU START YOUR OWN BUSINESS

Suppose that you see an opportunity to make a profit delivering pizzas from a wholesale bakery to the dormitories on a college campus. How would prices, costs, and profits guide you?

After making an informal market survey, you decide that you can charge $0.30 more per pizza than they will cost you when you buy them. You

decide to gamble on setting up a business of your own while you are in college. Accordingly, you pay for some advertising in the school paper, you have some hand-bills printed listing what you have for sale, and you rent an office and put in a telephone to receive orders. Finally, you employ some other students at $2.50 per hour plus $0.10 a mile to use their own cars to pick up the pizzas at the wholesale bakery and deliver them to the student living units. In a sense, the market has told you that you should provide this new pizza delivery service to your campus.

Happily, the enterprise is really successful. In place of earning $200 a month, which you had thought of as a minumum figure to justify your time and effort (including the deterioration of your grade point average), you find that you are making about $400 a month. The additional $200 is economic profit, which you get for making your capital investment supplying a new product.

Unfortunately, one of your employees sees how well you are doing. She decides to duplicate your operation and charge slightly less than you do. This will probably expand the total market, but you soon find that you are barely making the $200 minimum you had set for yourself when you started your business. You do notice, however, that competition makes you very interested in making sure that the deliveries are prompt and that the order takers do not make a mistake in listing the orders to go to the deliverers.

And then, although your market is expanding, disaster suddenly strikes. A paper company in your town sees an opportunity to put on a half shift that will employ college students from 7:00 P.M. to 11:00 P.M. every evening. They pay $4.00 an hour. You realize that you have to raise your wage rate to, say, $3.50 an hour in order to keep the number of delivery persons you need to conduct your business. This will cut into your accounting profits so much that you doubt that it will be worth your while to continue.

But then you learn that you can get a specialized delivery truck with warming trays built into it to replace most of your delivery personnel. You estimate that if you use the truck your total expenses will be only slightly higher than they were when you were paying $3.00 an hour. But a used truck will cost $6000 and you have only $3000 saved from your business.

Finally, after some agonizing, you decide to go ahead with the purchase of the truck. To do this, you decide to borrow the additional $3000 you need from the local bank. At this stage, although you will probably not be aware of it, the market is telling you that you should substitute capital for labor. It is telling you what technology to use.

To your satisfaction, the decision to buy the truck turns out to be a good one. During the next two years you make your $200 a month plus a 10 percent return for your investment in the truck and in some months you make much better—particularly during the mid-term and final exam months. In fact, you do so well that you are able to pay off most of what you owe on the truck.

But then you run into a depression during your senior year in college. The number of students coming to your campus falls off substantially and you find that after making allowances for the depreciation of your truck you are making less than enough to compensate you for the additional investment in the truck and the $200 a month you consider to be a minimum.

What should you do? Again, the market has presented you with a decision point. What is it telling you to do? You examine your expenses very carefully. You find that your truck will bring you only $500 on the used market and that it will be difficult for you to make over $100 a month at any other job you can find during this period. Therefore, your minimum net income will be $100 a month plus enough additional income to give you a 10 percent return on the $500 you could get for the truck in the used market. The market, you decide, is telling you to keep on providing the service, even though your accounting profits for tax purposes are less than what you considered your minimum to be.

Finally, at the beginning of your second semester, the student enrollment falls off so much that you find you cannot earn your new minimum. You decide that you will throw in the sponge and seek some other type of work to finish your college years. Again, although you may not know it, the market has spoken to you. It has told you that the resources you are using to provide a pizza delivery service are more valuable if they are used in other activities.

In the following chapter we will see how these market directives mesh together to provide guidance to millions of independent producers in simultaneously answering the questions: *What* products should be produced and in what quantity, and *How* should they be produced?

COMMENTARY

The following is an excerpt from an article in *Business Review*. It examines the concept of profit from the viewpoint of the individual and society. Please read the excerpt and answer the following questions.

a) List two ways of looking at the size of profit.
b) What are the three functions of profit from the individual's perspective?
c) What role does profit play for society in a capitalist economy?

PROFIT IN A FREE ECONOMY

Profit, like politics and religion, is a subject that evokes strong feelings and hot arguments. At one extreme, profit is said to be the fruit of shameless exploitation that cheats the consumers, pollutes the environment, and oppresses the workers. At the other extreme, profit is said to be the reward for hard work, risky investment, and clever innovation—enterprises that have no undesirable consequences and that in fact are indispensable for social welfare and progress.

Neither of these extreme views is accurate, but each does contain elements of truth. Fundamentally, profit is simply a tool for achieving social goals. However, like a pistol or a scientific discovery, the profit tool can be misused. Thus society's task is to construct safeguards that prevent, or at least discourage, the objectionable uses of the profit mechanism but that still allow society to gain from the beneficial uses.

Profit: what is it and how much is there?

Profit is simply the difference between revenue and cost.[1] In economic terms, it is the return to the

[1] Actually, profit is not a simple concept. Throughout this article, profit will be the difference between *explicit* revenue and cost; this is often called the accounting definition of profit. Explicit costs, for example, are employees' wages, raw materials costs, machine rentals, taxes, and so on. Economists use a more subtle definition of profit—the difference between revenue and costs, both explicit and *implicit*. An implicit cost is, for example, the salary that the owner of a business could have made in his highest paying alternative occupation.

owners of capital—the capitalists. Capital is any product used to produce another product, such as a printing press or an oil refinery. The owners of capital are those having legal claim to the capital equipment; for the most part, they are the stockholders of the nation's companies. Stockholders receive their profit in two forms. Some is received as annual dividends. The rest is reinvested in the company, thus building the value of the company's stock; this profit is eventually captured when the stock is sold.

How much profit do capitalists make? One way to answer this is to look at the profit rate— that is, profits relative to production costs. People generally estimate the profit rate to be quite large. For example, in a recent survey, the average person guessed the *after-tax* profit rate of manufacturing corporations in 1974 to be 33 percent.[2] In fact, however, the after-tax profit rate in manufacturing was 5 percent. A second way to look at the size of profits is to examine the share of

the national income earned as profit. In the United States, after-tax corporate profits have averaged about 6 percent of national income over the last 45 years; even the *before*-tax rate has been only 11.5 percent (see table). Moreover, a recent study argues that profits as a share of national income have been falling since World War II.[3] In short, corporate profit rates, on average, are smaller than many people believe and may not even be growing as fast as national income.

Profit: a valuable social tool

Profit has been defined as the monetary return to the owners of capital. Why should capitalists be rewarded at all? The answer is simple. If a society decides that forcibly coercing individuals to produce certain goods and services is undesirable, then there must be some other incentive to encourage people to commit resources, such as time and money, to production. Presumably, the probability of earning a money return that exceeds the costs of production (that is, of earning a

[2] Estimates of particular profit rates are even more strikingly incorrect. For example, the average person felt the after-tax profit rate of petroleum companies was 61 percent in 1974; in fact, it was 7.2 percent. The survey was conducted by the Opinion Research Corporation of Princeton, New Jersey. It is reprinted in *New Jersey Business*, August 1975, pp. 25–27.

[3] See William D. Nordhaus, ''The Falling Share of Profits,'' *Brookings Papers on Economic Activity*, No. 1 (1974): 169–217. Nordhaus has adjusted the profit data somewhat, so they are not perfectly comparable to those presented in the table.

AFTER-TAX PROFITS HAVE AVERAGED ABOUT 6 PERCENT AS A SHARE OF NATIONAL INCOME

	(A) Net national product (billions of dollars)	(B) Net corporate profits before taxes (billions of dollars)	(C) Net corporate profits after taxes (billions of dollars)	(D) Before-tax corporate profit rate (column B divided by column A × 100%)	(E) After-tax corporate profit rate (column C divided by column A × 100%)
1929	$ 95.2	$ 10.0	$ 8.6	11%	9%
1933	48.6	1.0	0.4	2%	1%
1939	83.2	7.0	5.6	8%	7%
1940	92.2	10.0	7.2	11%	8%
1945	200.7	19.7	9.0	10%	4%
1950	266.4	42.6	24.9	16%	9%
1955	366.5	48.6	27.0	13%	7%
1960	460.3	49.7	26.7	11%	6%
1965	625.1	77.8	46.5	12%	7%
1970	889.8	74.0	39.3	8%	4%
1971	961.2	83.6	46.1	9%	5%
1972	1055.1	99.2	57.7	9%	5%
1973	1184.1	122.7	72.9	10%	6%
1974	1277.2	141.0	85.2	11%	7%

Data from *Economic Report of the President, 1975.*

positive profit) will make production attractive. Thus profit can act as the desired incentive. Furthermore, profit fulfills a broader social function than simply encouraging production. It also serves as a signal of the kinds of goods and services that society deems most valuable.

The individual's view. From an individual capitalist's point of view, profit has three functions. First, some of the profit is a payment for investing his money in capital equipment instead of spending it elsewhere. The capitalist's money is like the laborer's time. A laborer can spend his time either relaxing or working. He will work only if he is paid enough to be compensated for not relaxing. Similarly, a capitalist will buy a factory or a machine only if he earns more that way than by doing something else with his money, such as depositing it in a bank. So, much of what is called profit is merely interest on the capitalist's money.

Second, some of the profit is compensation for the risk a capitalist assumes in investing in uncertain enterprises. Everyone knows that buying stocks is riskier than putting money in a bank account. The firm whose stock you buy may suffer a decline in sales or, worse, go out of business. Either way, the value of the stock falls, possibly to nothing. No such thing happens with a bank account. The money value of a bank deposit cannot decline (except possibly in the case of bankruptcy), and it is possible to earn a guaranteed interest rate. Moreover, deposits in amounts up to $40,000 are insured against default at almost all banks. Obviously, under these conditions, no rational person will buy stock rather than open a bank account unless the expected return on the stock exceeds the expected return on the bank account by enough to make the extra risk worth taking. This extra compensation for risk is another element of what is called profit.

Third, part of profit is a reward for enterprise and invention. Invention usually occurs because the inventor sees it as a means of earning money. So, part of profit is a compensation for the inventor's effort and insight. Profits of this kind usually are temporary, being ultimately competed out of existence as rivals and imitators adopt the technique. But as one source of innovational profit

disappears, another arises somewhere else in the economy so that there is always some innovational profit in existence.

Society's view. The pursuit of profits by individuals also produces gains for society. Profits provide the incentive for capital formation and hence for economic growth. By providing interest on the capitalist's investment, compensation for risk, and reward for inventiveness, profits create incentives to invest money in the machines and factories needed for economic progress. In more general terms, profits signal to producers which goods are most desirable to society.

A timely illustration of this is the development of the energy industry. Before industrialization, fuel production was minimal. Some coal and wood was used for heating purposes and for forging tools, but most other energy demands were met with wind and water power and with the labor of men and their beasts of burden. Petroleum was merely an object of curiosity. With the emergence of industrialization, however, energy demands multiplied enormously. It quickly became *profitable* to extract coal and petroleum in huge quantities and refine them for various uses. People wanted the products offered by industrialization. In response to the profit that those new desires made possible, resources were diverted from other uses to the production of the energy needed to fuel the industrial machine. Thus, it was the lure of profit that organized resources so as to satisfy the desires of society. Now petroleum is becoming scarcer, and petroleum prices are rising. The result? Predictably, new profit opportunities have developed. Oil companies now find it profitable to pump out of the ground petroleum that was formerly too expensive to recover. Research is being devoted to producing petroleum products from nonpetroleum sources, such as coal, and also to finding alternative sources of energy. So profit once again is leading businessmen and entrepreneurs, through their own self-interest, to satisfy some of the desires of society.

JOHN J. SEATER, "Profit in a Free Economy," *Business Review*, May/June 1976. Reprinted by permission of the Federal Reserve Bank of Philadelphia.

REVIEW QUESTIONS

1. All of the following are basic institutions of a market-oriented economic system except:
   a) the private ownership of property.
   b) a central planning agency.
   c) enforcement of contracts.
   d) competitive markets.

2. Mr. Jones owns some stock in a corporation. If the firm runs into financial difficulty and fails, then:
   a) the amount Mr. Jones invested will be returned to him at once.
   b) Mr. Jones will lose his home because of his liabilities.
   c) Mr. Jones should try to make up his "sunk costs."
   d) limited liability makes him liable only to the extent of his stock purchase.

3. From an economic point of view, when does an activity *not* have a cost?
   a) When someone else "foots" the bill.
   b) When the choice involves giving up nothing.
   c) When the return is greater than the cost.
   d) When the government sponsors the activity.

4. When will some firms operate for a period at what clearly appears to be a loss?
   a) When fixed costs exceed variable costs.
   b) When revenues cover fixed costs, but not variable costs.
   c) When variable costs are recovered.
   d) When variable costs exceed fixed costs.

5. The three terms net profit, economic profit, and gross profit have different definitions. In any given business operation, if you were to rank these three definitions of profit in terms of size from smallest to largest, they would appear in the following order:
   a) Gross profit, economic profit, net profit.
   b) Gross profit, net profit, economic profit.
   c) Economic profit, net profit, gross profit.
   d) Net profit, economic profit, gross profit.

6. Which of the following would *not* be included in the accountant's concept of costs for a business operation?
   a) Property taxes, insurance, utility fees.
   b) Wages and salaries of workers.
   c) Normal return on owner's invested financial capital.
   d) Depreciation on buildings and fixtures.

7. A local ice-cream store proprietor wonders whether she should continue to operate her own business. After exploring the job market she finds the best she can do is to obtain a position with a national chain to manage its store in town at $15,000 per year, working the same number of hours. The bank is currently paying 10 percent on savings deposits, the only other investment opportunity open to her. Her record books reveal the following expenditures and revenue.

Raw materials	$10,000	Sales	$66,000
Hired help	16,000		
Utilities, taxes, and other expenses	9,000		
Owner's salary	20,000		
Depreciation	5,000		
	$60,000		$66,000

Assume there are no other explicit costs and the owner has $100,000 of her own money in her operation. What should she do, if income were the only issue?

a) Go out of business since she is earning less from her money invested in her business than she could elsewhere.

b) It makes no difference—she is earning in her business exactly what she would earn if she had invested her money elsewhere.

c) Stay in business since she actually is earning more on her investment from her store than she could in the bank if she adjusts her salary to the appropriate value.

d) You can't tell from the evidence given.

8. Suppose that speculation in feed grains were made illegal and that farmers were required to sell their grain to dealers as soon as it was harvested. This would:

a) assure the public that the grain would be available all year without wide price fluctuations.

b) make prices low at harvest time and very high some time later.

c) cause people to consume too little grain early in the year.

d) prevent speculators from preying on the public.

ESSAY QUESTIONS

1. A corporation is similar to a legal person. It can owe debts and it can accumulate assets. Does this mean that if personal income taxes were reduced and corporation taxes were increased, households in general would have a higher standard of living?

2. "A society based on the social institution of private property is concerned with things and not with people." Criticize this statement.

3. There are only three car rental agencies at most airports and there is no room for additional ones. Does that mean that the car rental business is competitive? Explain your answer.

4. The sanitation workers in New York City receive wages higher than are necessary to attract the number of qualified workers required to do the job. Civil service exams are then given and only those receiving the highest scores get the sought-after jobs. This eliminates many qualified workers who would work for less if given a chance. Would you characterize this occupation as being competitive?

5. Suppose that over the years beauticians' average income was 50 percent higher in Florida than in Virginia. You are asked to explain how this differential could come about. What would you look for?

6. Most of the railroads in the northeastern part of the United States are in bankruptcy and are seeking aid from the government to keep operating. You study the situation and find that if service is discontinued on the feeder lines serving the small towns, the railroads could be rescued from bankruptcy without government aid. You propose that this be done, but governors of the states involved object, arguing that the small towns "need" the service. How would you define "need"? What argument would you give to refute this claim that the small towns "need" the service?

7. The opportunity cost of providing public golf facilities is larger than the amounts people are willing to pay to play on these facilities. What does this mean? How could you justify taxing everybody in a town to pay the golf course deficit? Can you apply the same analysis to a swimming pool constructed in the inner city?

8. The Studebaker Company had large deficits for a number of years before it stopped making automobiles. How could the company continue producing cars in those large-deficit years?

9. Suppose the college or university you are attending were run for profit. And suppose that it has buildings and equipment worth $50 million. Measured in the usual way, your college shows a profit of $1 million. Should you and the other students insist that tuition and fees be reduced because the college is exploiting you?

10. The electric public utilities in your state have aggregate profits of $100 million. This is about 2 percent of the amount that stockholders have contributed to the capital of these public utilities. Should you insist on a rate reduction to eliminate the $100 million of "unjustified" profits?

11. How large a return do you think you will have to get from your investment in a college education before you can say you are showing a "profit" on your investment?

ANSWERS TO REVIEW QUESTIONS

1. Social institutions are established patterns of social interaction, some enacted into law and administered by the courts and others embedded in custom and tradition. Those institutions that characterize a market-oriented or decentralized economic system include profit, ownership of property, enforcement of contracts, and competitive markets. The key institution of a centralized economic system is the central planning agency. Hence, the correct answer is (b), a central planning agency.

2. The corporation is characterized by the fact that it has a "limited liability" provision for its stockholders. Its owners can be held liable only for the value of the stock they own.
  a) This is incorrect. One's investment is not protected in a corporation.
  b) This is incorrect. The stockholder is liable only for the value of his stock holdings, not his personal property.
  c) This is incorrect. It is a nonsense answer.
  d) This is correct as explained above.

3. Cost in economics always refers to a choice between alternatives. Hence the only time a cost does not exist is when there is no alternative or the alternative is valueless.

   a) This is incorrect. Someone will experience a real cost even though it may not be you.
   b) This is correct as explained above.
   c) This is incorrect. A cost still exists.
   d) This is incorrect. Someone will bear the cost through taxes.

4. Specialized pieces of capital equipment have only one use for all practical purposes. In the short run, the only costs involved in using a specialized piece of equipment are the costs of acquiring complementary resources such as labor, electricity, raw materials, and so on. Therefore, the opportunity costs of producing the output that the capital equipment is designed for are substantially lower in the short run.

   a) This is incorrect. The relationship between the amount of fixed costs and variable costs is not at stake here.
   b) This is incorrect. If variable costs are not covered, production will not occur—it will generate short-run losses.
   c) This is correct. As long as variable costs are recovered, any revenue left over will help cover the fixed costs and operations will continue until in the long run the capital equipment is replaced or junked.
   d) This is incorrect for the same reason as (a).

5. Gross profit is defined as the difference between the selling price and the cost of materials. Net profit is determined by deducting the selling costs from gross profit. Economic profit is determined by deducting the implicit costs such as forgone interest, wages of owner, and so on from net profit. Consequently, economic profit is smallest, followed by net profit and economic profit. The correct answer then is (c).

6. In an accounting sense, total profits equal the difference between total costs and revenues. Accountants, however, define total costs differently than do economists. Economists include as part of costs a rate of return on invested financial capital that is equal to what would be received if the capital were invested elsewhere.

   a) This is incorrect. These costs are included in both definitions.
   b) This is incorrect for the same reason as (a).
   c) This is correct as explained above.
   d) This is incorrect for the same reason as (a).

7. The economist's definition of costs includes all of those listed. The owner, however, is paying herself too much—she is worth only $15,000 in the market, hence costs are really only $55,000, not $60,000. Further, since the owner has $100,000 of her own money invested, she is giving up earning $10,000 by not investing it in the local bank. Therefore the real costs are $65,000. Since her gross receipts are $66,000, the owner is making more by operating her own store.

   a) This is incorrect as explained above.
   b) This is incorrect. It would be true if receipts were $65,000, but they are $66,000.
   c) This is correct as explained above.
   d) This is incorrect as explained above.

8. When speculators enter the market, they buy when the price is low. This increases the demand and pushes the price up. They then proceed to sell when prices are high, and this increases supply and lowers the price.

a) This is incorrect as explained above. The price would be low at harvest and high later as reserves dwindled.

b) This is correct. These extremes would not be moderated since the speculator's activity would now be illegal.

c) This is incorrect. The price would not be that low at harvest time because of the speculators.

d) This is incorrect. It assumes speculators prey on the public.

OBJECTIVES

Upon successful completion of this chapter, you will be able to:

1. Define industry, firm, and plant.
2. Explain, using examples, how, under competition, firms will tend to adopt least-cost technologies in the long run.
3. Explain why firms in the same industry tend to use similar technologies.
4. Explain, using examples, why equilibrium prices, under a competitive market system, will tend in the long run to be equal to the firms' opportunity costs.
5. Use supply and demand graphs to illustrate the effects of changes in demand on industries operating under constant cost conditions.
6. Use supply and demand graphs to illustrate the effects of changes in demand on industries operating under increasing cost conditions.
7. Describe the learning curve and use it to explain how firms price products in industries with rapidly changing technologies.
8. Explain the effect of the activity choices of the suppliers of productive inputs on the price and mix of final goods and services.
9. Relate how the price system works as a communications system carrying the messages of suppliers and demanders to decision makers.

CHAPTER 5

PRODUCTION: HOW PRICES GUIDE PRODUCERS

INTRODUCTION

When you look around the economic landscape, you see constant change. The computer industry, with its larger than normal profits, has been growing rapidly. The cattle-feeding industry expands and contracts. New technologies are constantly being introduced. A decade ago the very large and powerful tractor was a rarity, and farms were smaller. Now the large tractor and the large farm is the rule in the agricultural states of the Midwest.

Shortly, you will be participating in this "permanent revolution." You will probably change employers at least four and possibly more times. You may be forced to learn new skills as old skills become obsolete. Or you may choose in midcareer to go back to an educational institution to learn a new set of skills, not because you are forced to do so by the market but because you find yourself growing tired of doing the same thing year after year.

Since you are going to be an active participant in a market-directed economy, it is important that you understand its underlying logic. The changes that occur around you will, for the most part, work themselves out through prices generated in a market. The market will tell you where society would like to have you work and tell you what skills it would like you to learn.

In Chapter 4, we described the major types of business organizations and identified the institutions underlying production in our economy. We defined the opportunity cost of a product as what has to be paid to keep the resources required to produce the product from being used in other forms of production. We then defined and illustrated the concept of profit and concluded with an explanation of how prices, costs, and profits provide information for making production decisions.

Now we will focus on how the business firm operates as it seeks to achieve profits for its owners. Although the United States economy is characterized by millions of different producing firms, certain patterns of behavior do emerge that enable us to make some generalizations about how the firm operates. These patterns reflect the firm's response to cost and price information.

First, however, we will clarify what is meant by a firm, industry, and plant.

A useful way to describe the diverse productive activity of the American economy is to list the major types of industries that produce the economy's output. You will recall in Chapter 4 that we identified the number and size of firms in the eight major industry's classifications: agriculture, forestry, and fishing; mining; construction; manufacturing; transportation and public utilities; wholesale and retail trade; finance, insurance, and real estate; and services. An *industry*, therefore, refers to a subset of the economy's productive enterprises.

A *firm* or a business is an economic enterprise organized for profit. A single firm may be involved in many industries and may have one or more plants.

A *plant* is a production unit designed around a set of relative prices to achieve a given output at a minimum cost. Most plants in a specific industry will be similar in size and design.

In seeking to identify patterns of behavior among the producing units in our economy, one can take both a short-run and a long-run perspective. The long-run view implies that the production decisions made by the plant managers and business executives are not limited simply to using workers on an overtime basis or adding a new shift. Rather, all options are open to them including building a new plant. A reason for taking this long-run view is simply that little happens immediately in economics and we are looking for those changes that help us see what is happening around us.

To provide a complete picture, however, we will from time to time introduce some short-run impacts, and we will conclude this chapter with an appendix dealing specifically with the short-run perspective.

The broad generalizations we can make by observing the *long-run behavior* of firms *under competition* are:

Proposition A: Firms will adopt least-cost technologies; and

Proposition B: The prices of products will equal their opportunity costs.

PROPOSITION A:
FIRMS WILL ADOPT LEAST-COST TECHNOLOGIES

There are many ways to produce goods and services.

The major goal of any business firm is to earn the maximum profit for its owners. It does this by producing the kinds of goods and services in which that firm has special expertise or advantages. In the pursuit of that goal, the firm must use the best or most efficient techniques of production. The old expression "there are many ways to skin a cat" contains an important truth. There are many ways to produce any product, and as we said in the last chapter, one of the important decisions any producer must make is to choose the best combination of resources.

Consider the range of possibilities simply for marketing foods. The old-fashioned grocery store with its barrels of dried beans, crackers, and flour was labor intensive. The ratio of sales clerks to customers in the store was about one to one. At the same time the investment in buildings and equipment was minimized. This type of grocery store could still be used if it were economically

feasible. Indeed, in most parts of the world where labor is cheap this is the preferred method of marketing food products.

At the other extreme we have the large supermarket with electronic sensing devices to read the symbols on each package and a central computer to record the price of each item at the checkout counter. The ratio of workers to customers is very low in this type of store. At the same time the ratio of capital investment per dollar of sales is quite high.

Between these two extremes there are many possible technologies for marketing food. Why, then, you may ask, are so many of the supermarkets alike? Wouldn't it be reasonable to expect these many types of grocery stores to exist side by side in the retail food markets?

Competition forces entrepreneurs to choose least-cost combinations of resources.

The answer to these questions is that competition will drive the entrepreneurs to choose the least-cost combinations of resources. Suppose you wanted to operate an old-fashioned grocery store in direct competition with a modern supermarket. You would have to pay the competitive price for labor—not the price that your grandfather paid when he ran an old-fashioned grocery store. As a result, you would have to charge more for your merchandise and this would drive most of your would-be customers away. It is true that in some locations you might be able to run a high-priced convenience store organized on an old-fashioned basis, but this type of store accounts for a very small percentage of all retail food sales. The fact is that competition has driven food stores to use that technology that will minimize their costs. In other words, the market is telling them which technology is best.

From this and many other examples we could conclude that *competition drives entrepreneurs to adopt least-cost combinations of resources.* When they fail to do so, other sellers can sell for lower prices and take business away from them.

For the most part this means that most firms in the same industry will use the same or similar technologies. Thus, steel companies tend to have very large mills. Chemical companies use similar equipment to produce like products. Family farms tend to be about the same size. Gasoline stations along superhighways look alike.

Even the exceptions to this least-cost rule indicate that prices tell producers what technologies to use.

Even the exceptions to this rule can tell us something about what guides entrepreneurs in choosing production technologies. In the Southwest along the Mexican border, where labor tends to be relatively less expensive, electronic firms tend to use more labor-intensive production technologies than the same firms use in the north-central urban areas, where labor is more expensive. Why does this happen? The answer is that it pays firms to substitute labor-saving devices for labor in the North where labor is expensive. It does not pay to make this substitution in the Southwest where labor is cheaper.

If you are driving along country roads in the Midwest you may see Amish and Mennonite farmers still using horsedrawn equipment to cultivate their fields. Does this mean that competition does not drive them to use least-cost methods of cultivation? Again the answer is no. Because of their religious convictions many of them are reluctant to work in industrial companies. They are, therefore, willing to accept a lower income for their efforts. The opportunity costs of keeping them in the farming business are low enough that they can afford to use horses rather than tractors. In other words, the farmers have a different set of input prices for the resources they are using, and this produces a different technology.

Even after taking account of these exceptions, it is fair to say that competition will drive producers to use least-cost technologies. This means that firms producing similar products will tend to have similar-sized production facilities or plants. And these plants will tend to use the same or similar production processes.

We turn now to the second proposition.

PROPOSITION B:
THE EQUILIBRIUM PRICES OF ALL PRODUCTS WILL BE EQUAL TO THEIR OPPORTUNITY COSTS

You may recall that in Chapter 4 we defined the opportunity cost of an input in the production of a commodity as the value of what that input would produce of any other commodity. We then went on to state that, as a generalization, the opportunity cost of producing any good consists of what must be paid to keep that bundle of multiple-use materials and productive services from being used to produce other products. Consider the following illustration.

If prices are higher than opportunity costs, the output for new plants will reduce prices.

Suppose that an industry—in this case the corrugated-container industry producing shipping containers—has been very profitable. Prices are higher than opportunity costs, and the industry has accounting profits larger than what is required to compensate stockholders for their capital and risk bearing. In short, the industry is showing an *economic profit*. How would a competitive industry respond?

The firms already in the industry would build more optimum-sized plants to capture a larger share of the industry's economic profit. New firms would be organized to build new corrugated-container plants. As a result, the supply of corrugated containers would increase, and this would reduce the price of corrugated containers until they were equal to their opportunity costs. The supply and demand curves in Fig. 5.1 illustrate this result. The output from new plants will drive prices from P_0 to P_1 and will eliminate economic profits.

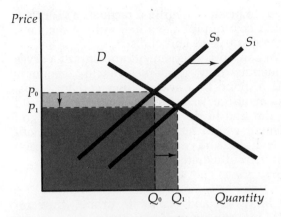

FIG. 5.1 An increase in supply of containers.

If prices are lower than opportunity costs, old plants will not be replaced, resulting in less output and higher prices.

Suppose that the demand for corrugated containers shrinks and their price falls below their opportunity costs. What would happen? The firms would not replace their old, high-cost plants as they wear out. Some firms would fail and their creditors would dismantle their facilities and sell the equipment for junk. In either case, the supply of corrugated containers would decline and their price would rise until it did cover the opportunity costs for the remaining firms.

It is clear, then, that prices higher than opportunity costs cannot persist in the long-run competitive economy. Nor can prices lower than opportunity costs persist. Economic profits bring the entry of new plants, and *economic losses* will force the exit of plants. As a result, the only price

that can persist over time is that price which is equal to the opportunity costs of production.

If some firms have superior resources, the prices they pay for these resources will rise and profits will disappear.

You may object that some firms will have plants in better locations than others or will have better management. As a result, some firms will persist in having economic profits, even after all of the above adjustments have taken place.

The firms that have better locations will, in the long run, have to pay higher rents for their superior locations. Those that have better management will have to pay higher salaries to their managers to keep them from going elsewhere. The prices of their superior productive services will rise and this, in turn, will cause their costs of production to rise. As a result, they too will have prices equal to their costs of production.

We will find these two propositions very useful in explaining what we see around us in the world of change. To make them more real, we will now present three cases that demonstrate how the adjustment processes would occur in a competitive economy.

The first case illustrates an industry's response in which output can expand in the long run without incurring higher per-unit costs. This is called the *constant-cost* case. The second case represents industries operating under *increasing costs*. These industries have long-run supply curves that are upward sloping. Case III focuses explicitly on the pricing policy of a firm experiencing rapid technological progress. It explains the *learning curve* as a phenomenon generating *decreasing cost* in the long run.

CASES

CASE I: AN INCREASE IN THE DEMAND FOR TENNIS EQUIPMENT AND INSTRUCTIONAL SERVICES AND A REDUCTION IN THE DEMAND FOR GOLF EQUIPMENT AND INSTRUCTIONAL SERVICES. THE CONSTANT-COST CASE.

Suppose that tennis becomes very popular with people of all ages and at the same time golf loses

some of its popularity. How would a competitive, market-directed economy respond?

Because the tennis and golf industries are relatively small, we can ignore the effect of these changes in demand on the prices of resources employed in them. It is true that in the short run there could be a shortage of tennis pros and a surplus of golf pros. But in the long run, golf pros or their children can be trained for other occupations, while the shortage of tennis pros would be eliminated by a temporary increase in their wage rates and the resulting increase in their numbers.

If there are no unique resources to become higher priced as output rises, the industry will be a constant-cost industry.

When you stop to think about it, there are no unique resources used in either the tennis or golf industries. A unique resource is a resource so specialized that it cannot be used effectively in other industries—even after enough time has elapsed to convert it into another form or shape. A health-water spring is a unique resource. While it could be used for irrigation, its value for irrigation is so small compared to its value for medical purposes that it might be said to be a resource with only one use.

An industry that is small relative to the total economy and does not employ unique resources is unlikely to have a feedback effect that modifies the prices of productive services. This simplifies our task substantially. We can now represent the long-run supply curves for both the tennis and golf industries as horizontal lines. That is, after an adjustment period it will cost no more (per

racquet) to produce a million racquets a year than it would cost to produce a half million racquets. The same is true of golf clubs.

We can now use demand and supply curves to illustrate how a market-directed economy would respond to a switch from golf to tennis. The demand curve for tennis equipment would move out and to the right. The demand for golf equipment would move inward and to the left. The beginning and concluding situations for each industry are illustrated in Fig. 5.2.

Price increases and economic profits draw resources into the expanding industry.

The first effects of the change in demand would be an increase in the price of tennis racquets and a reduction in the price of golf clubs. Inventories of tennis racquets would become depleted, and retail stores could sell them for higher prices. Inventories of golf clubs would become swollen and the pro shops would lower the price.

With prices higher than opportunity costs, economic profits would appear in the tennis equipment industry. Meanwhile, with prices lower than opportunity costs, economic losses would appear in the golf equipment industry. How would the two industries respond?

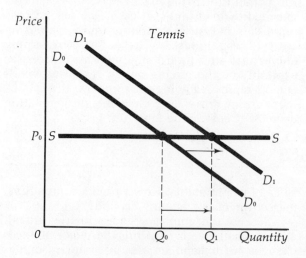 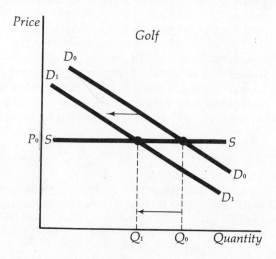

FIG. 5.2   Changes in the demand for tennis and golf equipment: constant-cost case.

The firms in the tennis industry would, as a first response, expand their outputs as best they could within existing facilities in order to get a larger net profit. They might do this by crowding more workers into existing factories or by adding a second shift. Both of these expedients would tend to add to per-unit costs compared to producing tennis racquets with least-cost combinations of resources.

Price decreases and economic losses push resources out of contracting industries.

Meanwhile, the firms in the golf equipment industry would be doing the opposite. They would be using fewer workers than the number for which the factories had been designed. While they would be able to cut their losses by this expedient, they still would be showing losses. They would not be producing golf clubs under least-cost conditions.

It is interesting to note that these two compensating adjustments would be made possible by the transfer of resources from the golf equipment industry to the tennis equipment industry. Most of these transfers would be indirect. Golf equipment workers would find work somewhere in the total economy, and meanwhile the tennis equipment industry would employ additional workers from somewhere in the total economy.

In the end, it is the building of new plants or the closing of old plants that completes the adjustment.

Finally, the tennis equipment industry would build more plants, adding to the quantity supplied and reducing the price of tennis equipment to its previous level, P_0. Meanwhile, some of the plants used by the golf equipment industry would be abandoned. This would reduce the quantity supplied and increase the price of golf equipment to P_0. Both industries would come back into equilibrium, with prices again equal to their opportunity costs. The tennis equipment industry would have more plants and the golf equipment industry would have fewer plants.

When you stop to think about it, this explanation is also in line with your common-sense understanding of the economy you see around you. Profits tend to attract resources. Entrepreneurs see a chance to buy resources cheap and sell the products for more. Losses tend to repel resources. The entrepreneurs experiencing losses cannot afford to compete with the profit-making entrepreneurs in the bidding for resources. Profits and losses are, then, the mechanism by which a market-directed economy responds to the changing demands of households. This type of economy has sometimes been called a "carrot and stick" economy, where profits are used to attract the donkey and losses are the stick that pushes him.

CASE II: AN INCREASE IN THE DEMAND FOR COAL AND A REDUCTION IN THE DEMAND FOR FEED GRAINS. THE INCREASING-COST CASE.

Suppose an import quota is imposed by the United States on crude oil imported from the Middle East—presumably to protect the United States from politically inspired embargoes of oil. Suppose that the quota so reduces the amount of oil imported that foreign countries do not obtain enough dollars to buy the quantity of feed grains—corn and soybeans—they had been buying. Clearly, then, the import quota will have two effects: (1) it will markedly increase the demand for coal as a substitute source of energy; and (2) it will reduce the demand for United States exports of feed grains. Can we trace the effects through the economy of these compensating changes in demands? The answer is yes, but the problem is not as easy as the transfer of demand from golf to tennis.

When there are unique resources, productive service prices change when the output of the industry changes.

Coal-producing land is a unique resource. Its highest value is for coal production and it is worth a great deal less for agriculture or other purposes. Similarly, corn and soybean land is worth a great deal more for the production of feed grains than for grazing land. The demand for coal will directly affect the price of coal-producing land, and the demand for feed grains will directly affect the price (or rent) of the corn- and soybean-producing land. In tracing out the effects of changes in the demand for final products we cannot assume—as we did before—that the prices of resource inputs would be unaffected by the changes.

The increasing-cost case involves upward-sloping supply curves.

Accordingly, the long-run supply curves for both feed grains and coal will be upsloping (and not a horizontal line as before). The reasons for this are somewhat subtle but not too difficult to understand.

When prices of corn and soybeans are high, the price of corn and soybean land rises. Farmers, then, try to use their high-priced land intensively by applying more fertilizers and by cultivating more frequently. In effect they are substituting capital and labor for land, but, as you remember from our discussion of resources in Chapter 2, this substitution is never complete. The further the substitution is carried, the less effective it is. Translated into costs, this means that the larger the total production of corn and soybeans is, the higher will be the opportunity costs of producing them.

The opposite is also true. When the total output of corn and soybeans is smaller, the opportunity cost of producing these two crops will fall, land will be less expensive, and farmers will apply less fertilizer and use fewer cultivations. As a result, opportunity costs are smaller per unit.

The same thing will be true of coal production. As coal-producing land goes up in price, coal producers will use their coal lands more intensively. They will invest in heavier equipment so that they can remove the overburden from deeper deposits of strip-mining coal. They will invest in equipment to exploit their under-the-surface mines more completely. Thus, the larger the industry's output of coal, the higher will be the opportunity cost of producing it. And similarly, the smaller the industry's output of coal, the lower will be the opportunity costs of producing it.

When the long-run supply curves are upsloping—as they are in the case of feed grains and coal—the industries are said to be producing goods under conditions of *increasing costs* (rather than constant costs). Fundamentally, the reasons for the existence of increasing cost industries is that some resources are unique and cannot be transferred from one industry to another. Thus corn and soybean land cannot be converted into coal land. To compensate for the shortage of a unique resource, the firms in the industry substitute other resources for it and this leads, via the Law of Diminishing Marginal Returns, to higher opportunity costs.

Once we recognize that some industries are characterized by increasing cost conditions, it is easy to explain what happens when there is a shift in demand from one product to another, in this case from feed grains to coal.

Higher prices and profits attract resources into expanding industries.

Figure 5.3 shows the situation before and after the changes in demand. The initial effect of an increase in demand for coal will be to create large per-unit profits for coal, and the decrease in the demand for feed grains causes large per-unit losses in the production of feed grains. The prices change, rising sharply for coal and falling for feed grains.

As coal producers add more shifts and add more workers to each shift, the output of coal rises and the price falls. Finally, as more coal mines are opened, the price of coal falls still further, but never comes back to its original price. It is permanently higher because of the increases in the prices of some of the unique or nontransferable inputs.

Lower prices and losses push resources out of contracting industries.

The reverse is true of feed-grain production. Initially, the price would fall to what the farmers would regard as catastrophic levels. In the short run, they would find it impossible to use as much fertilizer or energy or as many cultivations. This would cut the output of feed grains and increase their price, but they would still be showing losses. Eventually, some of the feed-grain land would be taken out of feed-grain cultivation and put into

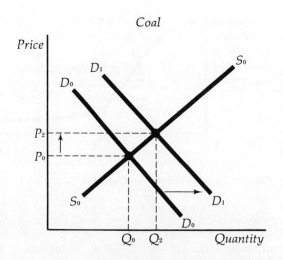

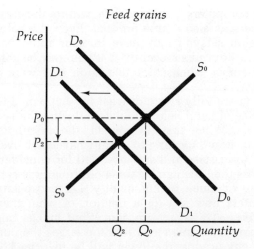

FIG. 5.3   Changes in the demand for feed grains and coal.

grazing land. When that final result occurred, only the best land would be used for feed grains and it would not be cultivated as intensively as before.

As a consequence there will be a shift of resources from farming to the economy in general (as some farmers quit and as all farmers use less equipment and fertilizers). You also will see the shift of resources from the economy in general to coal mining. In effect, then, the profits in coal mining will attract resources out of farming, and the losses sustained in feed-grain production will push resources out of farming into coal production.

In the increasing-cost case prices do not go back to their old levels.

However, compared to the first case, something new has been added. The equilibrium prices of both coal and feed grains have been changed. The increased scarcity of coal lands now reflected in the price of coal will cause the opportunity costs and therefore the prices of such metal products as automobiles, refrigerators, and stoves to rise. Given the Law of Demand, fewer of these products will be purchased than would be if prices were unchanged. What this really means is that the productive-service market is telling households

to purchase fewer coal-using products. The two sets of markets, taken together, comprise a communications system. Even though households would like to buy more automobiles, refrigerators, and the like, they are persuaded by the change in relative prices to buy fewer, and thus they participate in the conservation of coal.

The reverse is also true. The reduction in the cost of producing feed grains tells households via prices in the products market to eat more meat. The reduction in the relative price of wheat and other feed-grain products says "you should expand your consumption of this class of products."

CASE III: THE INTRODUCTION OF A NEW PRODUCT. THE LEARNING CURVE AND THE DECREASING-COST CASE

There is something unique about the way new products are initially supplied that leads us to treat them in a special way.

Consider for a moment some of the items around you that you use daily. Many products were not available 15, 10, or even 5 years ago. The hand-held calculator you probably have on your desk is a prime example. The microprocessor, which underlies the electronic revolution we are now experiencing and which will make sophisticated home computers commonplace within the next ten years, is also a new product. Even the color television set you may have in your room has been introduced so recently that you may be able to remember when color television sets were a novelty.

You are fully aware of what has happened to the price of hand-held calculators during the last 10 years. When first introduced, the calculator you can now buy for $10 would have cost over $100. Solid state hi-fi sets now sell for considerably less than the cumbersome old tube-type sets and are of much higher quality. Large capacity computers now sell for a fraction of what they sold for just a few years ago. What makes this possible? Does this mean that the larger the output of any product the lower will be its price?

The concept of the *learning curve* provides an explanation of the pricing of new products.

When you first start to do something—say play tennis or shoot pool—you put in a lot of effort without appearing to accomplish much. After hours and hours of practice, however, you will find that what was once hard to do has become quite easy. Indeed, when you watch tournament professionals play tennis, you are impressed with how easy they make it look.

The same thing is true when it comes to producing new products. Producers not only have to train people how to do the many skilled jobs associated with producing the product, but they also have to develop new tools and equipment for mechanizing many jobs. New component suppliers have to be induced to enter the industry, and they too must learn the tricks of the trade. Consumers must be convinced that the new products will really work. All things considered, the costs and therefore the prices of new products tend to follow a pattern plotted in what is called a *learning curve*. Each product has its own learning curve, but the curves are similar enough that we can use a generalized curve to represent a typical new product's cost experience (see Fig. 5.4).

We have measured the cumulative output of the industry along the horizontal axis. In the case of hand-held calculators, we would add each

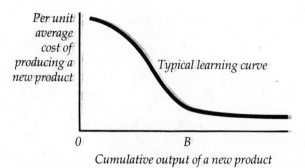

FIG. 5.4 A generalized learning curve.

year's output to the last to find out how many calculators had ever been produced. At first, the number would be in the thousands, then hundreds of thousands, and finally in the millions. To make these numbers manageable, we will use a ratio scale to measure the average price per unit.*

The learning curve we have pictured here shows that the larger the cumulative output of a product, the lower will be its cost until finally at some point, B in this case, the curve becomes parallel to the base line. Put another way, the larger the cumulative output of new products, the lower will be their unit costs, until finally there are no more "learning curve economies" to be achieved.

This may sound complicated, but it is something you have already confronted in many different products. For example, when television sets were first introduced they were very expensive. As they became widely used, their prices were lower. And finally, when all of the learning curve economies were realized, their prices were stabilized.

The learning curve will also play an important part in developing new sources of energy.

Solar energy will no doubt become cheaper as people learn how to store heat efficiently and pro-

---

* When examining a series of statistical data over a period of time, we often wish to know about the ratio of change (not the absolute change) that has occurred between two dates. In this case, we are examining a ratio of decrease. A constant ratio of decrease will plot as a straight line on a ratio chart or semi-logarithmic chart as it is called.

duce panels that convert sunlight into electrical energy.

It is interesting that companies operating in new-product industries have learned how to anticipate learning curve efficiencies in the pricing of their products. Some companies have reduced the prices of their products faster than their costs have declined, expecting that the larger output would bring lower costs. This has introduced a highly dynamic element into the pricing of new products. It has also posed a constant threat to old industries, whose products are always in danger of becoming obsolete.

The *economies of scale (size)* is another reason why the costs (and prices) of some *new* products go down when the output is increased.

If you were operating a repair facility for automobiles, you could run a small operation and still have low costs. Once you have five or six mechanics so that each can specialize in a certain type of repair work you would have realized most of the economies of scale (size). In fact, the larger your establishment is the more you spend on supervisors and the higher your unit costs will be.

We could represent the economies of scale for a repair facility by a shallow curve with a minimum point (see Fig. 5.5). This curve shows that per unit costs will decline slightly until a certain number of automobiles are repaired per month. But once you reach a certain size—as measured by the output of repair jobs—your costs

will rise. This accounts for the multiplicity of small repair garages in every community.

In contrast, some products are produced by technologies that make economies of size or scale very important. The small paperboard mills that characterized the industry during the early part of this century usually had very high per unit costs. Modern mills producing about 1000 to 1200 tons of paperboard a day have much lower per ton costs. In many areas of the country, where trees have to be transported long distances to supply a mill, very large mills have higher per unit costs.

We can represent the economies of size for the paperboard industry by a much deeper curve, such as the one in Fig. 5.6 below.

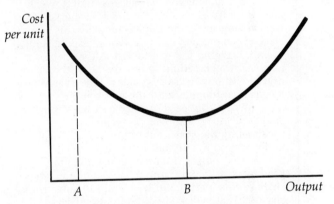

FIG. 5.6 Cost curve for producing paperboard.

These economies of scale also create the impression that some industries are "decreasing cost" industries. At first companies tend to build small plants to serve local markets. Then as a product, such as heavy paper sacks, gains acceptance, there is a rush to see which companies can first exploit the economies of size. This causes costs and prices to fall.

Each industry has its own curve. Some curves are very deep and some are very shallow. When an industry has a deep curve the combination of the "learning curve" and the associated economies of scale can produce marked reductions in per unit costs as the output of new products increases.

We will also be concerned with economies of scale in Chapter 8, when we discuss "natural"

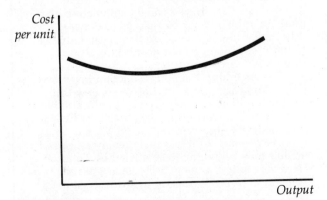

FIG. 5.5 Cost curve for automobile repairs.

monopolies. A natural monopoly occurs when the optimum-sized plant is so large relative to the market that there is only room for one company.

In competitive industries (where the econ- omies of scale will be fully exploited by many producers), the appearance of decreasing product costs is largely due to the technological innovations underlying the learning curve.

COMMENTARY

The following excerpt is from an article that describes the rapid price decreases that have occurred in the digital watch industry. Please read the excerpt and answer the following questions.

a) What factors allowed Texas Instruments Inc. to lower its prices?
b) What has been the impact on domestic and foreign competition of Texas Instrument's pricing strategy?

THE GREAT DIGITAL WATCH SHAKE-OUT

Texas Instruments Inc. has set the digital watch market on its ear again. Roaring after market share with a vengeance, the Dallas company this week slashed the price of one of its most popular models in half, bringing it down to $10. Already the cheapest watch selling in any quantity, the TI digital will now be selling below the price of any mechanical timepiece for the first time.

The dizzying pace of price-cutting—from $2,000 to $10 in just over five years—is accelerating the shake-out of producers already under way in the digital watch market. The pressure is coming from the semiconductor producers, who are trying to carve out a major share of this market and who build the electronic circuitry that makes lower production costs possible.

Casualties. The shake-out started 15 months ago, when TI dropped its first bombshell—a $20 model that industry and retailers alike were not expecting for another year. That move was a dramatic, early gamble by TI to take over the mass market from the traditional watch companies such as Timex Corp. and to block the competition from the host of other companies planning to grab a share of the soaring market. . . .

"The biggest question mark now," [according to William B. Heye, Jr., of TI], "is how far the new price will increase 1977 sales." Before TI decided to cut its prices this month, it anticipated U.S. sales this year to reach 19 million digital models. "This approaches one-third of the total U.S. watch market of an estimated 60 million units," he says. Market penetration by digitals last year was only 25%, he figures.

But the combination of lower LED watch prices and the introduction of cheaper LCD watches in June could blow the market wide open. Half of the watches sold in the U.S. are priced at $20 or less, and Heye believes that these moves could boost 1977 sales by as many as 10 million additional units. The only major stumbling block now is insufficient capacity.

Factory costs. But whatever the final increase in the number of digital watches sold this year, some manufacturers do not see any accompanying rise in factory dollar sales because of the steadily declining prices. "This year will be a fairly modest year in growth—no more than a few percent in dollars," predicts Fairchild's Corrigan.

Lower prices are possible because production costs have dropped as volume has grown. "Our semiconductor approach to cost reduction has helped here," TI's Heye says. By automating its production line, TI has brought labor down to the "absolute minimum level" so that it can reduce its initial production costs by as much as 60% as volume increases, he says.

TI aims to duplicate this reduction in production costs when it brings in its new LCD production line in Lubbock, Tex. It will introduce a line of LCD models in the next month or two, and some industry observers expect the price to be as low as $20—one-third less than the lowest-priced models now beginning to be offered by Timex. Heye says only that he expects some $20 LCD watches to be on the market this year, "but not a lot."

The $5 watch. As fierce as it has been, the price-cutting shows no signs of slackening. Commodore Business Machines Inc. has already started selling a $10 LED watch on a small scale. And by Christmas, predicts Harris Sorchych, "down-and-dirty LED watches, that are assembled in the Far East, will be going for $5."

That might be bad news, not only for many U.S. producers but also for the Swiss watch industry. The electronic watches are dropping too fast for the Swiss to get aboard. TI's new factory selling price means that the digital watch module is now "approaching $3," TI's Heye acknowledges. And a $3 price means that digitals can be turned out as cheaply as any mechanical movements, says Fairchild's Corrigan. He notes that the Swiss have said that 40% of the total worldwide watch market will be digital by 1985 if the production cost drops down to mechanical watch levels. "For the Swiss," Corrigan says, "1985 is here."

Reprinted with permission from *Business Week*, May 2, 1977.

REVIEW QUESTIONS

1. In general, when competitive conditions exist it is true that in the long run:
   a) equilibrium prices of products will exceed the opportunity costs of producing them.
   b) firms will employ a wide variety of technologies for producing the same product.
   c) firms will continue to operate as long as their variable costs are met.
   d) equilibrium prices of products will equal their opportunity costs of production.

2. Dr. Pepper, Coca Cola, and 7-Up companies all reported record sales in a recent year. This encouraged several firms to enter the soft-drink market. Assuming these firms to be competitive and profit seeking, one could conclude that:
   a) soft-drink prices were higher than opportunity costs.
   b) soft-drink prices were lower than the long-run marginal costs.
   c) soft-drink prices will skyrocket in the near future.
   d) soft-drink prices would have to be set by the above-named firms.

3. Suppose that the current increase in interest in tennis goes so far that many people now playing golf stop golf and start playing tennis. The *initial* effects on industry T, the tennis racquet industry, and industry G, the golf club industry, would be that:
   a) prices would tend to rise in industry T.
   b) profits would rise in industry T.
   c) profits would fall and losses might appear in industry G.
   d) All of the above.

4. In the *long run*, when all resources are shiftable from industries G to T, you would expect that:
   a) the prices of tennis racquets would return to their pre-boom levels.
   b) the prices of tennis racquets would be permanently higher than their pre-boom levels.
   c) the prices of tennis racquets would be lower after the boom had run its course.
   d) It is impossible to tell from the information given what would happen to tennis racquet prices.

5. And, in the long run, when all resources are shiftable from industries G to T, you would expect that:
   a) the prices of golf clubs would return to their predepression prices.
   b) the prices of golf clubs would be permanently lower than they were before the depression in the club industry.

c) the prices of golf clubs would be higher after all of the adjustments had occurred. The golf club industry is an "increasing cost" industry and this would force the higher prices.

d) It is impossible to say from the information given what would happen to golf club prices in the long run.

6. Now suppose that golf club makers are so committed to their craft that neither they nor their children are willing to leave the golf club businesses, regardless of their wages. As a result:

a) the prices of golf clubs will be higher than they were before there had been a decrease in the demand for clubs.

b) the prices of golf clubs will be lower than they were before there had been a decrease in the demand for clubs.

c) the prices of golf clubs will be the same—the constant-cost case.

d) It is impossible to say what would happen to the prices of golf clubs after a reduction in the demand for clubs.

7. Suppose there was an increase in the demand for product X and a decrease in the demand for product Y. Pick out the *incorrect* statement.

a) If the resources needed to produce X were different from those needed to produce Y, then resource prices would change.

b) The short-run effect would be an increase in the price of X and a decrease in the price of Y.

c) The production of X would increase while the production of Y would decrease.

d) If the resources needed to produce X were different from those needed to produce Y, then there would be a downsloping supply curve for X.

8. During the 1960s, larger and larger percentages of each high-school graduating class went to college to study for "white-collar jobs." At the same time fewer and fewer high-school graduates entered apprenticeship programs to become plumbers, pipe fitters, and tool makers. As an economist, you would expect that:

a) the price system would break down; it cannot deal with employment and shortages in the labor market.

b) the price system would increase the wage rate in the white-collar fields and reduce them in the unpopular blue-collar fields.

c) the price system would reduce white-collar wage rates and increase blue-collar wage rates.

d) the price system would not change the mix of products being purchased by households; it would merely change the costs of producing goods.

9. During the last two years the producers of oil-well equipment have been showing very, very high profits. In fact, the profits are much higher than are necessary to keep the usual number of plants operating. In the short run this indicates that:

a) the supply curve for oil-well equipment is very elastic.

b) there is necessarily a large measure of monopoly power in the oil-well equipment industry.

c) the society wants the oil-well equipment industry to expand its output.

d) the oil-well equipment industry is in equilibrium.

10. At the present time the "feedlot" industry, which takes beef cattle off the range and feeds them corn and other seed grains in order to produce high-grade beef, is very unprofitable. In fact, more than 80 percent of the feedlots are showing deficits. This indicates that:

a) feedlots are badly managed. If they were well managed, they would be profitable.

b) feedlots are showing the effects of the Law of Diminishing Marginal Returns.

c) feedlots are using resources that the participants in the economy would rather have used in other production activities.

d) although there are about 5000 independent feedlots in the United States, they have monopolistic tendencies and have overpriced their product.

11. In the last several years, microcomputers for home use have been introduced and their price has fallen sharply. The primary reason for this is that:
    a) wages have increased only moderately in recent years.
    b) the growth of transportation facilities has increased the size of the market allowing cost reductions.
    c) firms producing these products have learned how to increase their efficiency and reduce prices.
    d) competition from imports has forced the price down.

ESSAY QUESTIONS

1. You travel in Greece and Spain and note that all of the elevators in the hotels have operators. When you get back to the United States, you note that your hotels have automatic elevators. At the same time you are told that unemployment in the United States is in excess of 6 percent of the labor force. Why don't the hotels in the United States use people who would otherwise be unemployed to run their elevators?

2. Why do most farmers use large tractors rather than horses to pull their ploughs and other farm equipment?

3. Suppose, because of the shortage of fossil fuels, that gasoline prices increase to $5 per gallon. Suppose that the widespread use of solar energy keeps electricity from rising in price. Describe the automobiles you would see on city streets. What would happen to intercity travel by automobiles (assuming no changes in design)?

4. Why are supermarkets widespread in the United States and rather rare in many parts of the underdeveloped world?

5. Why do most factories producing a particular product look alike?

6. Shortly after a substantial price increase farmers seem to be pleased, but after two or three years they tend to complain about farm prices even though prices have continued to be high. Is this because they are habitual complainers, or is there something else involved?

7. Somebody has said that the "picnic never lasts very long in a competitive economy." Explain this statement and demonstrate why profits and losses are short-lived in a competitive economy.

8. In an effort to keep tobacco prices high, the government has restricted the planting of tobacco. It has done this by granting each farm a quota of tobacco-producing land. The quota is tied to the land, so that when land is sold, the new owner gets the quota. After a period of time—long enough so that the land is mostly held by new owners—would the price of tobacco be consistently higher than the opportunity cost of producing it? Explain your answer carefully.

9. American Motors develops a new electric automobile that has a 400-mile range before it needs recharging. The technology is available to foreign companies as well as other automobile companies in the United States. How long do you think American Motors could make high profits from selling the new car?

10. List several industries that you think would have a horizontal supply curve. List several industries that you think would have an upsloping supply curve. How do these two groups of industries differ?

11. Suppose a windfall profits tax is imposed on any industry that has a large increase in profits. Suppose that tax takes 100 percent of all the additional profits over and above the last five years' average. How would that affect the functioning of a market-directed economy?

12. Suppose there are so many college graduates that they can't find jobs. And suppose that there are so few skilled workers that the construction industry can't get enough people to build the houses people want. How would a market-directed economy solve this problem? Can you provide a better alternative solution? What is it?

13. The prices of services have risen rapidly over the last twenty years. What does this show? Would you try to prevent this by using price control measures to keep the cost of living from rising?

ANSWERS TO REVIEW QUESTIONS

1. When competitive conditions exist, firms will be driven into using least-cost technologies (Proposition A) and, in the long run, equilibrium prices will equal opportunity costs (Proposition B).
   a) This is incorrect. Equilibrium prices will equal opportunity costs.
   b) This is incorrect. Since firms are forced into the least-cost technology, most of the firms will employ basically the same techniques.
   c) This is incorrect. Only in the short run will firms continue to operate as long as variable costs are met. In the long run, fixed costs must also be met.
   d) This is correct as explained above.

2. The competitive assumption means no firm is restrained from entering the soft-drink market. Other firms will be tempted to enter if economic profits can be made—that is, a return higher than normal. The existence of economic profits indicates that prices are higher than opportunity costs.
   a) This is correct as explained above.
   b) This is incorrect. Other firms would not enter in this case.
   c) This is incorrect. Prices will probably fall.
   d) This is incorrect. Opportunity costs will determine price.

3. The initial effects of the tennis boom will increase profits in the tennis industry and cause losses in the golf industry.
   a) This is true. The increased demand for tennis racquets, and so on with the supply fixed in the short run will raise prices.
   b) This is correct. The higher price will raise profits.
   c) This is also correct. The lower price will cause losses.
   d) This, then, is the answer to select—all of the above are correct.

4. In the long run, the output of tennis equipment will increase and the golf industry will shrink in size.

a) This is correct. Since resources are shiftable, we can assume that constant costs prevail and that prices of tennis equipment will fall.
b) This is incorrect. Only if increasing costs exist will this occur, and this is not the case.
c) This is incorrect. With constant costs, the prices will return to their original level.
d) This is incorrect. The needed information is supplied as indicated in (a).

5. Since resources are shiftable, we again can assume constant costs.
   a) This is correct because of the above assumption.
   b) This is incorrect because of the constant-cost assumption.
   c) This is incorrect because of the constant-cost assumption.
   d) This is incorrect. See (a).

6. Since golf equipment manufacturers are committed to their trade, the price must be lowered to sell all of their output and the workers will take a lower wage rate than otherwise.
   a) This is incorrect. Prices will be lower for golf clubs.
   b) This is correct as explained above.
   c) This is incorrect. Prices will be lower.
   d) This is incorrect. See (b).

7. This is a generalization of the above series of questions. If resources are easily substituted into the production of X from Y, then constant costs prevail.
   a) This is a correct statement, but not the answer. The resources used for X would increase in price and those used in Y would fall.
   b) This is correct and hence not the answer. The price of X will rise as the demand for it increases and the price of Y will fall as the demand for it falls.
   c) This is correct and therefore not the answer. In response to the increased demand for X and the consequent price rise, producers will manufacture more of X and Y will decrease for the opposite reasons.
   d) This is incorrect and therefore is the answer. If resources needed for X were different from those needed for Y, there would be an upsloping supply curve for X.

8. The reduced supply of plumbers, pipe fitters, and tool makers will increase wages in those areas while the wages of white-collar workers will fall relative to the blue-collar workers.
   a) This is incorrect. Wages, the prices for labor inputs, will change.
   b) This is incorrect as explained above.
   c) This is correct as explained above.
   d) This is incorrect. Consumers do respond to prices.

9. Under competitive conditions, the high profits in the oil-well equipment industry would reflect an increase in demand and a higher price as a response.
   a) This is incorrect. If the supply curve were very elastic, the increase in demand would have little effect on prices and therefore on profits.
   b) This is incorrect. It reflects a short-run phenomenon.
   c) This is correct. The market through price and profits is communicating to the oil-well equipment industry that more equipment should be provided.
   d) This is incorrect. In equilibrium, prices will equal opportunity costs and the very high profits will disappear.

10. The losses being incurred in the feedlot industry reflect overexpansion—at least in the short run. Hence, they should cut back.

   a) This is incorrect. It takes time to adjust to the vagaries of the market.
   b) This is incorrect. It is irrelevant.
   c) This is correct. The communications system is telling the owners to take resources out of the feedlot industry.
   d) This is incorrect. There is no restraint on entry.

11. Wage rates that have increased even moderately would increase the prices, other things being equal. The size of the domestic market is already adequate for firms to exploit the economies of scale. Competition from foreign firms has been minimal in this area. The correct answer then is (d), firms have exploited the learning curve.

APPENDIX TO CHAPTER 5

OBJECTIVES

Upon successful completion of this appendix, you will be able to:

1. Explain how the firms in an industry make short-run adjustments to changes in demand.
2. Describe the relationship among total output, variable costs, and fixed costs.
3. Show graphically that total unit and variable unit costs reach a minimum where they equal marginal unit cost.
4. Show graphically and explain why economic profit is maximized at that level of output where marginal cost equals marginal revenue.
5. Explain why a firm will continue to operate while sustaining a loss as long as variable costs are less than total revenues.
6. Explain that under competition, economic profit will be zero in the long run.
7. Show how the industry short-run supply curve is derived from the marginal cost curves.

THEORY OF THE FIRM AND THE SHORT-RUN SUPPLY CURVE

During periods of economic growth, changes in the population of plants are the dominant response to increased demand.

In Chapter 5, we were concerned about the way a competitive industry responds in the long run to changes in demand. When the demand for a product increases, firms normally build new plants. We also saw that when the demand for a product decreases, firms let some plants wear out and do not replace them. In this way, by building more plants or letting old plants wear out, a competitive industry adjusts to changes in demand.

In a growing economy, such as that of the United States during the last century, these induced changes in the population of plants usually work themselves out in two to three years. Consequently, competitive industries can adjust their output rather quickly to changes in demand during periods of economic growth.

An important part of the theory of the firm deals with short-run adjustments.

There is, however, a well-known body of economic theory that assumes that, in the short run, the population of plants in an industry is given and that adjustments to changes in demand are made by using these plants either more or less intensively. This body of theory is called the *theory of the firm*. In this appendix, we will develop this theory of the individual firm and show how it can be used to explain how the supply of a good or service changes in response to economic events in a competitive industry. In other words, we will explain the derivation of the short-run supply curve. Following this appendix is a case dealing with the oil and gas industry that illustrates the short-run analysis of the firm's behavior.

We will use the electrical switch industry as a model around which the theory of the firm will be constructed. The electrical switch industry is a highly competitive industry that is relatively easy for firms to enter and leave. There are no important trade secrets, and it is not difficult to get a plant operating efficiently once it is built.

To make our problem more interesting we shall assume that you were graduated from college as an electrical engineer 10 years ago and since that time have acquired experience in managing plants in the electrical components industry. You recently inherited $2 million dollars from a long-forgotten uncle and are interested in going into business for yourself.

Many factors enter the decision to buy a plant.

You hear of a recently built plant that is being sold by an estate. The asking price for the plant is $1.5 million. The plant is so new, however, that you cannot base your purchase decision entirely on the past profit record of the plant.

You learn that the plant produced and sold 1.2 million switches last year at $1.25 each for a total sales revenue of $1.5 million. The costs of operating the plant during the past year, includ-

ing a manager's salary comparable to your present salary, were $1,080,000, leaving an unspent net flow of cash into the plant from the manufacturing operations of $420,000. Your question is: Should you pay $1.5 million for a plant that produced a net cash flow to the owner of $420,000?

The calculation of estimated economic profit includes the cost of your forgone investment opportunities.

The offer sounds interesting, but having worked in the industry for a decade, you are well aware of the risks that exist in the electrical switch business. Switch designs change rapidly and market prices fluctuate widely, rising sharply in some years and falling in others, and so you decide to estimate the economic profits of the plant.

To do this you calculate that your annual "fixed costs" (costs that must be paid whether the plant is producing or not and do not change with the level of output) would include the following:

a) Depreciation (the amount
necessary to replace the machinery
and equipment as they wear out),
property taxes, and insurance $150,000
b) A 15 percent return before taxes on
the $1.5 million investment to
compensate you for not putting
your money into some other form
of activity or securities of equal
risk   <u>225,000</u>

Total "fixed costs"   <u>$375,000</u>

You are realistic in putting quotation marks around the term *fixed costs*. Until you make the investment, you can treat these figures as fixed costs in the sense that you will face them year after year. But you also know that once you have put your money into this venture, it will take you at least 10 years to get it out. If something happens to the switch industry that reduces your earnings, there is no way you can include these fixed costs in the prices of switches. After the investment is made you will be stuck. If your net cash flow is $375,000, you will be as well off as if you had not made the investment. If it is less, you will have lost part of your original investment.

If the results of last year are any basis for projecting the coming year, your net cash flow will be $420,000. You would then have an *economic profit* of $45,000 ($420,000 minus $375,000). Now the question is: Should you be venturesome or cautious?

The calculation of fixed and variable costs will help your decision-making process.

Because you are concerned about the safety of your investment, you ask your accountant to look over the operating results and identify the relationship existing between the different levels of output and the *variable costs* of operating the plants. The variable costs include the raw materials (which we shall assume are not very important), labor, energy, and supervision. In order to understand the relationship between variable costs and output, you request your accountant to provide an analysis indicating how much costs would rise as you went from one level of output to another, for example, from an output of 600,000 switches a year to an output of 700,000. These costs are *marginal or incremental costs.*

Marginal cost is whatever the production of one additional unit adds to the total costs of production.

The figures the accountant prepared are shown in Table 5A.1. The variable costs (column 2) increase whenever output (column 1) increases. You would expect this, just as you would expect to use more gasoline on a long trip than on a short trip. But when you examine the marginal cost figures, a different pattern emerges. The marginal costs associated with increasing plant output by each group of 100,000 units fall until the plant produces 800,000 units a year. Thereafter, the marginal costs for each 100,000 units are constant until the plant output increases to 1,200,000 units a year. After that, the marginal costs for each 100,000 units rise rapidly. These figures suggest several things: (1) the plant is not efficient at low levels of output; (2) the plant is not efficient at high levels of output. The plant is cost effective only within a fairly narrow range of outputs.

But you want to know more about your costs, and so you ask to see how the figures look when

TABLE 5A.1

TOTAL OUTPUT, VARIABLE AND MARGINAL COSTS OF PRODUCING ELECTRICAL SWITCHES

(1) Output (in thousands of units)	(2) Variable costs (in thousands of dollars)	(3) Marginal costs (in thousands of dollars)
0	$ 0	—
100	250	$250
200	450	200
300	600	150
400	700	100
500	775	75
600	825	50
700	870	45
800	910	40
900	950	40
1000	990	40
1100	1030	40
1200	1075	45
1300	1143	68
1400	1241	98
1500	1416	175
1600	1716	300

so-called fixed costs are taken into account. To do this, you ask your accountant to prepare a table showing how *per-unit* (or average) costs vary with different levels of output.

Column 1 of Table 5A.2 shows the various output levels and column 2 shows the fixed unit costs at each level. Fixed unit costs are the fixed costs divided by the output. Since fixed costs total $375,000, the fixed unit costs at an output of 100,000 units are $3.75. Fixed unit costs decline with each increase in output. This is reasonable since fixed unit costs are an average, in which the numerator (total output) rises while the denominator (fixed costs) stays the same.

Variable unit costs, column 3, are the variable costs in Table 5A.1, divided by the output of the plant. They fall, reach a minimum at an output of 1,300,000 units, and then rise.

Marginal unit costs, column 4, are the marginal costs for each 100,000 units shown in Table 5.A.1 divided by the *extra or incremental* output. For example, the marginal unit costs of the first 100,000 units of output are $250,000 ÷ 100,000 = $2.50. The marginal unit costs of the second 100,000 units are $200,000 ÷ 100,000 = $2.00,

and so on. For convenience, we have expressed incremental output in units of 100,000. Suppose, for example, that you want to know the marginal unit costs involved in increasing output from 600,000 to 700,000 switches. You would observe that the incremental costs of adding the extra 100,000 switches to the output schedule was $45,000 (see Table 5A.1). Therefore, the marginal unit cost would be $45,000 divided by 100,000 switches, or $0.45 a switch. You will note that marginal unit costs (column 4 in Table 5A.2) are high at low levels of output, decline as output grows until they reach a plateau of $0.40 between 800,000 and 1,200,000 switches, and then rise rather rapidly. The last 100,000 switches would have a marginal unit cost of $3.00.

Total unit costs (column 5) are the sum of the fixed unit costs in column 2 and the variable unit costs in column 3. They represent the costs, including the necessary cash flow to break even, of producing switches at different levels of output. You will see that because of the overriding importance of fixed costs, total unit costs decline until the plant is producing 1.4 million units a year. Thereafter, total unit costs rise.

TABLE 5A.2

TOTAL OUTPUT AND FIXED, VARIABLE, MARGINAL, AND TOTAL UNIT COST DATA
FOR PRODUCING ELECTRICAL SWITCHES

(1) Total Output (in thousands of units)	(2) Fixed unit costs	(3) Variable unit costs	(4) Marginal unit costs	(5) Total unit costs
0	∞	0	0	0
100	$3.75	$2.50	$2.50	$6.25
200	1.88	2.25	2.00	4.13
300	1.25	2.00	1.50	3.25
400	0.94	1.75	1.00	2.59
500	0.75	1.55	0.75	2.30
600	0.63	1.38	0.50	2.01
700	0.54	1.24	0.45	1.78
800	0.47	1.14	0.40	1.61
900	0.42	1.06	0.40	1.48
1000	0.38	0.99	0.40	1.37
1100	0.34	0.94	0.40	1.28
1200	0.31	0.90	0.45	1.21
1300	0.29	0.88	0.75	1.17
1400	0.27	0.89	0.98	1.16
1500	0.25	0.94	1.75	1.19
1600	0.23	1.08	3.00	1.31

Figure 5A.1 shows these three concepts of unit costs graphically: total unit costs, variable unit costs, and marginal unit costs.

Unique relationships exist among the three unit cost curves.

A unique relationship exists between the marginal unit cost curve and the variable and total unit cost curves. The lowest point on the variable unit cost curve is between 1.3 and 1.4 million switches a year and the lowest point on the total unit cost curve is slightly more than 1.4 million switches a year. As long as the marginal unit costs are lower than variable unit costs, the production of more switches pulls the variable unit costs down. Once the marginal costs rise above the variable unit costs, however, variable unit costs increase. Therefore, the minimum point on the variable unit cost curve will necessarily be where the marginal unit cost curve crosses the variable unit cost curve.

Consider the following illustration. Suppose that the people in a class of 10 have an average height of 65 inches. If a new (marginal) person who is 54 inches tall is added to the class, then the average height of the class will be reduced by an inch. Of if the new (marginal) person is 76

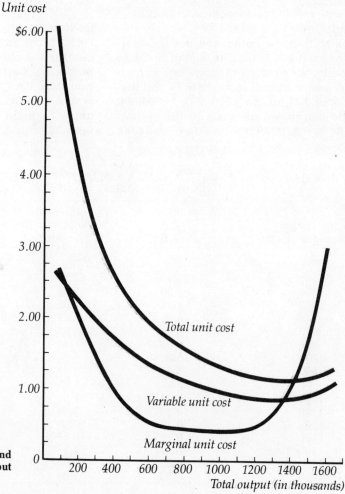

FIG. 5A.1 Total, variable, and marginal unit cost at each output level.

inches tall, the average height will be increased by an inch. Thus, when the marginal unit cost is lower than the average variable costs, it will pull the average cost down. And when the marginal unit costs are higher than average variable costs, it will pull the average up.

Figure 5A.1 shows that the marginal unit cost curve crosses the total unit cost curve at its minimum point—for the same reason. As long as the marginal unit costs are lower than total unit costs, total unit costs will decrease.

You now have a better perspective of your costs. But profit, your ultimate concern, depends on revenues as well as costs, so we will now examine the factors underlying your firm's receipts or revenues. The industry is characterized by numerous electrical switch producers and each firm takes the price of switches as a given. In this case, the market price happens to be at $1.25 per unit. Table 5A.3 shows total output, total revenue, average revenue per unit, and marginal revenue per unit. Total revenue is the product of price and quantity. Average revenue per unit is total revenue divided by total output, and marginal revenue per unit is the change in total revenue divided by the change in total output. In Fig. 5A.2,

marginal revenue is plotted for each level of output. It yields a horizontal line showing that whenever an extra switch is sold at a price of $1.25, the plant receives an extra or marginal sales revenue of $1.25. If the marginal revenue curve were upsloping, each additional unit sold would bring in a larger amount.

Marginal revenue is the amount that the sale of one additional unit of product will add to the total revenue.

Economic profit is maximized at the level of output where marginal cost equals marginal revenues.

After drawing marginal revenue on the graph and comparing it to the cost curves, it may occur to you that the previous owners were not thinking accurately about their costs and revenues. You will recall that they were selling 1.2 million units at $1.25 each, for a net profit, after subtracting fixed costs, of $45,000 (net cash flow of $420,000 less fixed costs of $375,000). Why not increase the output of the plant until marginal unit costs

TABLE 5A.3

TOTAL OUTPUT, UNIT PRICE, AND TOTAL AVERAGE AND MARGINAL REVENUE PER UNIT DATA
FOR PRODUCING ELECTRICAL SWITCHES

(1) Total output (in thousands of units)	(2) Price per unit	(3) Total revenue (in thousands)	(4) Average revenue per unit	(5) Marginal revenue per unit
100	$1.25	$ 1,250	$1.25	—
200	1.25	2,500	1.25	$1.25
300	1.25	3,750	1.25	1.25
400	1.25	5,000	1.25	1.25
500	1.25	6,250	1.25	1.25
600	1.25	7,500	1.25	1.25
700	1.25	8,750	1.25	1.25
800	1.25	10,000	1.25	1.25
900	1.25	11,250	1.25	1.25
1000	1.25	12,500	1.25	1.25
1100	1.25	13,750	1.25	1.25
1200	1.25	15,000	1.25	1.25
1300	1.25	16,250	1.25	1.25
1400	1.25	17,500	1.25	1.25
1500	1.25	18,750	1.25	1.25
1600	1.25	20,000	1.25	1.25

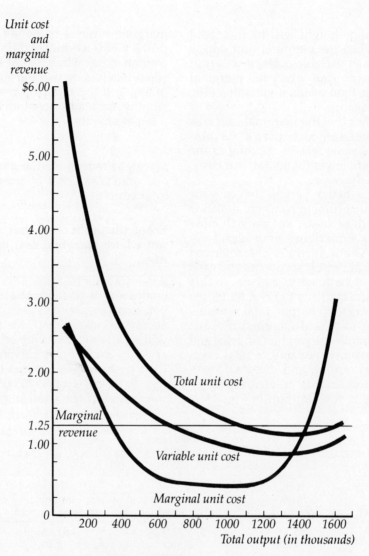

FIG. 5A.2   Total, variable, and marginal unit cost and marginal revenue at each output level.

are equal to the marginal revenue from the sale of the last switch? Whenever the extra output costs less than the extra revenue you get from selling it, you add to the net cash flow and therefore to profits. Or, conversely, whenever extra unit costs are greater than the extra revenue from selling the extra output, you subtract from the net cash flow, therefore reducing profits.

To put this theory to the test, you might ask your accountant to estimate net profits if you were to increase the output to the point where the marginal cost curve crosses the marginal revenue line. By assuming that there was a smooth curve that connected the figures in Table 5.A.2, your accountant would be able to come up with the following net profit estimate:

Sales revenue	
(1,440,000 units at $1.25)	$1,800,000
Variable unit costs	
(1,440,000 units at $0.91)	1,310,000*
Net cash flow	490,000
Less "fixed costs"	375,000
Economic profit	$ 115,000

* For easy calculation, we have rounded off the figure $1,310,400 to $1,310,000.

By applying the rule that output should be increased until marginal unit costs are equal to marginal revenue, you would be able to increase the economic profit of the switch plant from $45,000 to $115,000!

Based on this analysis, you decide to buy the switch plant. But remember, once you pay the $1,500,000 for the plant, you are locked in. You know that your accountant will continue to tell you that your fixed costs are $375,000 a year, but you also are wise enough to know that your so-called fixed costs are not costs any more. If the plant didn't produce $375,000 a year to cover your "fixed costs," nobody else would want to buy the plant and you would be stuck with the $1,500,000 investment in the plant. As a result, you always know that your goal is to maximize the net cash flow from the operation and hope that it will be enough to provide the $375,000 a year needed to break even.

A change in the economic environment will stimulate changes in the operation of a plant.

You are fortunate. Shortly after you bought the plant, there was a sudden increase in the demand for electrical switches. The price went up to $1.75 a switch. Following the profit maximizing, you increased output to 1,500,000 switches a year. Your accountant estimates economic profit at $840,000 as follows:

1,500,000 switches @ $1.75	$2,625,000
Less: 1,500,000 switches @ $0.94	1,410,000
Net cash flow	1,215,000
Less "fixed costs"	375,000
Economic profit	$ 840,000

Figure 5A.3 shows the new demand situation. You will notice that while producing 1.5 million switches a year, you will suffer some average (variable unit) cost penalties. Total unit costs will have risen from their minimum point. Nonetheless, net profits will be largest when you are producing 1.5 million units a year. (To test this, you may want to make some profit calculations at an output less than 1.5 million units.)

After a year of earning these large profits, you suddenly are faced with a crisis. Several companies not in the industry, seeing that the switch business is very profitable, decide to produce switches. After a year or so of building plants and converting old ones to the switch business, they all start producing switches at about the same time. The supply of switches increases so much that the price falls sharply to $1.00 a switch, as is indicated in Fig. 5A.4. Now what should you do?

A firm should continue to produce as long as variable costs are covered.

Your accountant tells you that the full cost of producing switches, even after adjusting output in accordance with the marginal-unit-cost-marginal-revenue rule to 1.4 million switches a year, is $1.16 a switch. But knowing full well that fixed costs are really sunk costs, you ask your accountant to tell you what variable unit costs would be producing 1.4 million units a year. He responds that variable unit costs would be $0.89 a switch. You then reduce output to 1.4 million units a year but, against his advice, continue to operate. Should you have done so?

At the end of the year your accountant brings the following figures:

Sales revenue	
(1.4 million @ $1.00)	$1,400,000
Variable costs	
(1.4 million @ $0.89)	1,245,000*
Cash flow	155,000
Less "fixed costs"	375,000
Net loss	($ 220,000)

* The figure $1,246,000 is rounded off to $1,245,000 for easy calculation.

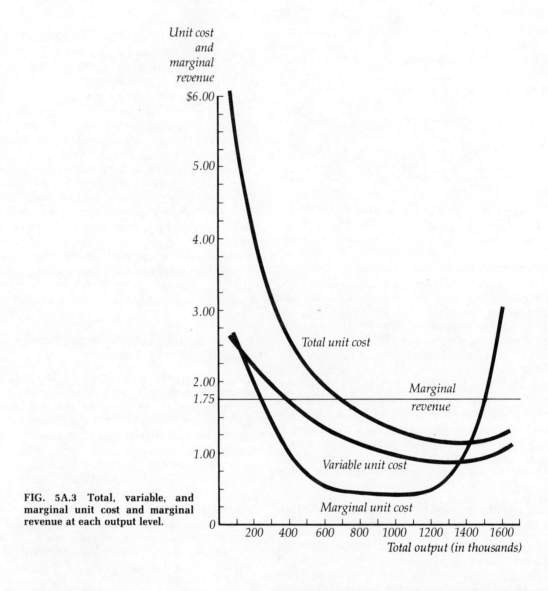

FIG. 5A.3 Total, variable, and marginal unit cost and marginal revenue at each output level.

The loss looks frightening, but when you stop to think about it, it is clear that you were correct. Had you stopped operations completely, cash flow would have been zero and you would have had the same fixed costs. The economic loss would have been $375,000 rather than the actual $220,000. Any positive cash flow will reduce the loss. As long as sales revenues are at least as large as variable costs, you are better off operating. The reason is that fixed costs are really pseudo-costs. Once you bought the plant, your fixed costs ceased to be costs in the usual sense of a forgone alternative. You own the plant and the best you can do is to operate it and obtain whatever you can from it until it wears out.

What would happen if the price went even lower—say to $0.75 a switch as indicated in Fig. 5A.5? Even after you cut back output in accordance with the marginal rules, variable costs would still be higher than the market price. Your accountant brings the bad news shown in the table opposite.

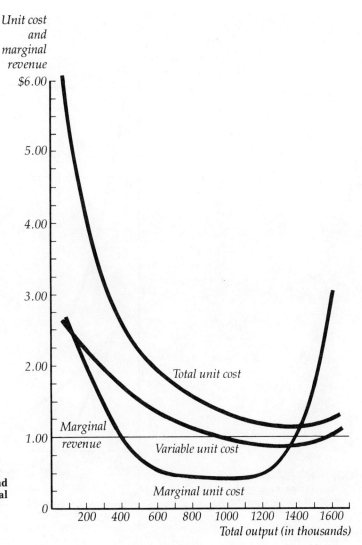

FIG. 5A.4 Total, variable, and marginal unit cost and marginal revenue at each output level.

Sales revenue	
(1,350,000 units @ $0.75)	$1,012,500
Less variable costs	
(1,350,000 units @ $0.89)	1,201,500
Cash loss	(189,000)
Less "fixed costs"	375,000
Net loss	($ 564,000)

You would now clearly be better off closing the plant and laying off the work force. You would lose only $375,000 rather than $564,000. What is more, you would not be reducing the cash balance and therefore your ability to start up again when prices went back up.

You would, of course, have to take account of the possible loss of key workers and material suppliers, and if you thought that the very low price was temporary, you might keep on operating. But as a rule, when prices are less than variable unit costs it usually pays producers to stop producing.

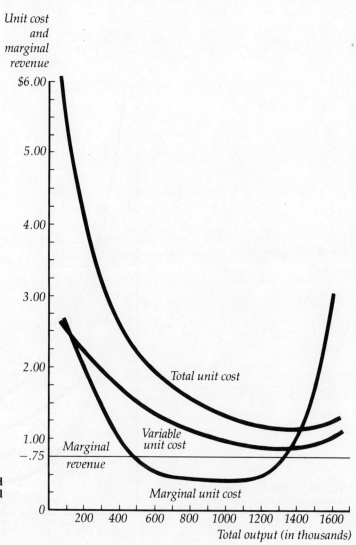

FIG. 5A.5 Total, variable, and marginal unit cost and marginal revenue at each output level.

In the long run, economic profit is zero.

In the long run, you would discover that the price of switches would settle down to about the minimum cost of production, including fixed costs. You would also know that you would produce about 1,425,000 switches a year—enough to achieve the lowest total unit costs.

Expressed in terms of Fig. 5A.6, you would know that the equilibrium price would be that price that was tangent to (just touching) the lowest point on the total unit cost curve. At that output, you would be using your plant most effectively.

Why, you might ask, would one come to this conclusion? We have already seen that when an

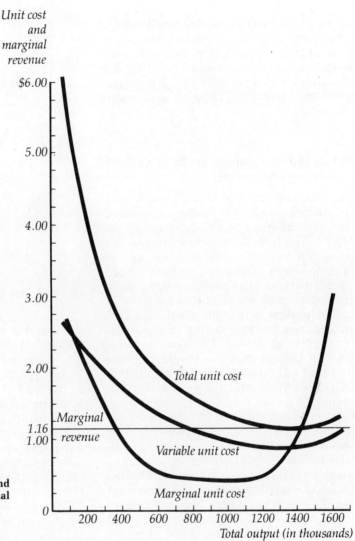

FIG. 5A.6 Total, variable, and marginal unit cost and marginal revenue at each output level.

industry is profitable, and plants have net cash flows larger than necessary to cover their capital costs, companies tend to build more plants. The resulting increases in the supplies of products tend to reduce their price.

The long-run equilibrium price of switches must then be $1.16, which, as we have seen in Table 5A.2, is the lowest total unit cost of pro-ducing switches. If the price were consistently higher than this, more plants would be built and the resulting increase in quantity supplied would reduce the price. Or, if the price of switches were lower than $1.16, then plants that were wearing out would not be replaced, and the resulting de-crease in the quantity supplied would increase the price.

In the long run, then, economic profit would be zero. Net cash flow would replace the plant when it wears out (depreciation expense) and leave enough to keep you, given the risks involved, from taking your capital out of the electrical switch business and putting it into some other investment.

The short-run industry supply curve is derived from the marginal cost curves.

You might also observe that the marginal unit cost curve and those of your competitors have something very important to tell us about an industry. They tell us how the business firms in the electrical switch industry will respond in the short run (before new plants can be built or old plants abandoned) to changes in prices. Your short-run supply curve for electrical switches is precisely that portion of the marginal unit cost curve running from the intersection of the variable unit cost curve to the top. We have shown it in Fig. 5A.7. It tells us that you would produce 1.4 million units at $0.98 a switch, 1.5 million units at $1.75 a switch, and 1.6 million units at $3.00 a switch.

The other producers would have similar marginal unit cost curves. If they were very different, their plants would not be efficient enough to compete in the industry. This tells us how we can derive the short-run supply curve for any industry—the baby carriage industry, the gray castings industry, or the electrical switch industry. All we need to do is to add together these marginal unit cost curves—just as we added the demand curves for individual purchasers to get an industry demand curve. The sum of these marginal unit cost curves is the short-run supply curve for an industry. It tells us how the industry will respond in the very short run—before new plants can be built or old ones closed—to changes in prices.

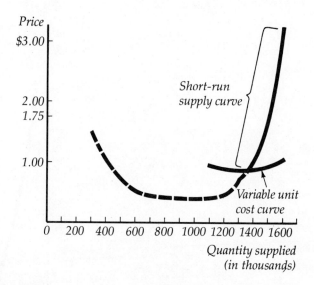

FIG. 5A.7 **The short-run supply curve.**

In the world we actually see around us, it is seldom this simple. New plants are constantly being built and old ones closed. When prices rise, the response is based partly on the sum of the marginal unit cost curves and partly on changes in the rate of plant building. Nonetheless, there is an important element of truth involved in this demonstration: When the technology of the industry is such that relevant positions of the marginal unit cost curves are steep—as they are in most manufacturing industries—the short-run supply curves are quite inelastic. In the short run, then, profits will rise rapidly, when there is a sudden and unexpected increase in demand. And the reverse is true. When there is a sudden and unexpected decrease in demand, profits will fall rapidly. In the long run, however, it is the change in the number of plants that will bring prices back to their long-run equilibrium level and eliminate economic profits.

We turn now to a case illustrating the short-run response of industry to an increase in price.

CASES

CASE I: APPLICATION OF ECONOMY'S RESPONSE TO RELATIVE PRICE CHANGES: A SUDDEN INCREASE IN THE REAL PRICE OF OIL AND NATURAL GAS.

The behavior of business firms in response to sudden changes in the economic environment can be reasonably well predicted.

Suppose, for example, that the oil producing and exporting countries, OPEC, without warning, triple the price of oil and that natural gas prices are allowed to rise simultaneously. How would producers, and consumers in a competitive economy, respond in the absence of government regulations?

In the short run—before additional oil and gas wells could be drilled and before manufacturing processes and factory and home heating systems could be adapted to the higher price of oil and gas—the producers of oil and gas would have substantially higher profits. Their real incomes would rise and the real incomes of consumers would fall. This is because the demand for and supply of oil and gas are quite inelastic in the short run.

It is true, of course, that makeshift means would be found to use less oil and gas. Householders would reset their thermostats to lower temperatures. Businesses would discontinue the use of oil and in most cases energy-wasting plants and equipment. The demand for products other than oil and gas would probably shrink in view of the larger amounts that people would be spending to purchase oil and gas, and this could lead to falling prices and unemployment in many industries.

After a lapse of a year or so, the economy would begin to adapt to the higher relative prices of oil and gas. But in the intermediate period—before factories could be rebuilt and cities redesigned—many changes would occur. Consider a brief and incomplete list of these changes.

1. Householders would install insulation and storm windows in the colder climates.
2. Carpools would be organized to save commuting costs.
3. Producers would divert their engineering departments from other activities to the conservation of energy in their plants.
4. Households would buy fewer of the energy-intensive products such as home appliances, whose relative prices would have risen as a result of the higher costs of producing them.
5. Domestic oil companies would drill additional oil and gas wells in proven fields in order to "cash in" on the higher prices for oil and gas.
6. Coal deposits would be worked more intensively as preparation for the expected increase in the demand for oil and gas substitutes.
7. Investments would be made in nonconventional sources of oil and gas. These would include the exploitation of oil shale, oil-bearing tar sands, and the gasification of coal.

In the intermediate period, the demand for oil and gas would be substantially more elastic. The supply of oil and gas would also become more elastic. But since so large a percentage of the oil comes from foreign sources we can think of the additional domestically produced oil as merely replacing the oil that would otherwise be imported.

In the long run, the higher relative prices of oil and gas would have profound effects on the shape of the economy.

It is impossible to list all effects. But consider a few of them.

1. Coal, uranium, solar energy, and wind power would account for a much larger percentage of the energy used in a nation.
2. Deep oil and gas wells would be economical to drill.
3. Industries would be encouraged to move away from the coasts, where they have been dependent on imported oil, toward the coal fields, oil shale deposits, and sunny deserts

if solar energy becomes competitive in price with fossil fuels.

4. Overland trucks would virtually disappear from the highways in favor of truck piggybacking by railroad trains, which use less energy per ton-mile.

5. Automobiles would be very small and might possibly run on methanol rather than gasoline.

6. Suburbs would be less popular because of the increased cost of commuting. The central cities would again become popular places to live.

7. Manufactured products requiring metal would tend to be miniaturized, leading to completely different types of home appliances.

8. Fewer people would be employed in manufacturing and more people would be employed in the service industry as higher energy costs made manufactured products relatively more expensive.

9. More people would live in apartments and in row houses as architects concentrated on energy-saving designs for housing.

Looking at these stages from the point of view of economics, we can say that the demand for oil and gas will, in the long run, be quite elastic. If OPEC continues to maintain a high price for petroleum, the industrialized countries of Europe and North America will finally adopt their economies to the new set of costs. The supply curves of energy from other sources will also become quite elastic. The price of energy may be higher than it was originally, but as new sources of energy replace oil and gas, the monopoly that OPEC now has will disappear.

This example has three important implications. In the first place, we can see that *changes in relative prices can have a powerful effect on the economy*, after they have had a chance to work themselves out. They can literally change your life-style. They can change the location of industry. They can change the products you buy. They can change the type of employment you will be able to get. They can change the power of labor unions. They can change the pattern of international trade and the way nations relate to each other.

In the second place, the initial change in the distribution of income, with larger incomes flowing to the oil and gas producers and smaller incomes flowing to the rest of us, lasts for a short while. New and more costly oil and gas wells will replace old ones. New sources of energy will replace old sources of energy, assuming that the energy industry is competitive. The prices of energy will, after a lapse of time, again be equal to their opportunity costs. In any market-directed economy, windfall or unexpected profits, even though they appear to be unfair, do serve as a catalyst for bringing about change.

In the third place, this example tells us how interdependent a market-directed economy is. We have seen how a simple change in the price of oil and gas resources in the productive service markets can change the mix of products offered and purchased in the products market. We have also seen how a change in relative price can change the mix of resources being used, with coal, uranium, solar power, and wind power replacing oil and natural gas. And finally, we have seen how a change in relative prices can affect the technologies used to produce the new mix of products.

REVIEW QUESTIONS

1. You are operating a plant that produces widgets. Your accountant insists that you operate your plant at that level of output where your per unit profits are largest. Your sales representative insists that you operate your plant where your total output will be largest. Your manufacturing manager

insists that you should operate your plant where your variable costs are minimized. Which of the following is correct?

a) Your accountant is right. You should aim to maximize your profit per unit of output.
b) Your sales representative is right. The larger your market the larger your profit will be.
c) Your manufacturing manager is right. You should operate your plant where your input of materials and labor is minimized per unit of output.
d) None of these persons is necessarily correct. You should continue to increase the output of your plant until your marginal costs are equal to the price of the product in a competitive industry.

2. When a firm that is maximizing its profit experiences an increase in demand for its product it will respond in the short run by increasing its output. When this occurs you would expect all of the following to occur except:

a) marginal unit costs will fall.
b) variable unit costs will rise.
c) total unit costs will rise.
d) total profits will rise.

3. In a normally functioning market economy you can expect all of the following to be occurring, except:

a) some firms will be earning positive economic profits year after year.
b) some firms will have no economic profits year after year.
c) some firms will be forced to cease operations after years of profitable operation.
d) some firms will become profitable after several years of "negative" economic profits.

4. The short-run supply curve for a product reflects the following:

a) the costs of building new plants.
b) the time it takes to wear out old plants.
c) the technological innovations that could be developed in a growing industry.
d) the sum of the marginal cost curves of the plants that comprise the industry.

ESSAY QUESTIONS

1. Before the eastern railroads were taken over by Conrail, they lost money for years and yet they continued to operate. How can you explain this? What symptoms of "bad health" would you have expected them to show?

2. You figure that including a fair return on your investment and depreciation, it costs you $0.18 a mile to operate your automobile. Your "out-of-pocket" expenses for gasoline, tires, and normal repairs account for $0.10 of the $0.18. A friend of yours offers to pay you $0.15 a mile to use your car for short trips. Should you take it? If you do, how will you justify selling the use of your car for less than your per mile costs?

3. You are a farmer. When you raise 10,000 bushels of corn on a hundred acres, your total unit cost per bushel is $1.50. Your marginal cost of increasing your output from 10,000 to 12,000 bushels is $2.00 per bushel. The price of corn is now $2.01. What should you do?

a) Produce 10,000 bushels so that the profit per bushel will be maximized.

b) Produce 12,000 bushels so that your marginal cost will almost equal the price of corn. Explain your answer in ordinary language.

4. You will notice that when the price of oil rises, the industry produces more oil, even before the companies in the industry have a chance to build new plants. Is this evidence that oil companies were intentionally holding back their production to increase the price of oil?

ANSWER TO REVIEW QUESTIONS

1. The objective is to choose that level of output that will maximize total profits. Output should be increased whenever marginal revenue (the extra income) is larger than marginal cost (the extra cost). When this is done each additional unit of output will contribute to increasing total profits. When output is increased to the point where marginal costs exceed marginal revenues, then the extra output reduces total profits.

   a) The accountant is wrong because she is emphasizing per unit profit. She should be emphasizing total profits.

   b) The sales representative is wrong. It is easy to produce so much that total is reduced (marginal revenue is less than marginal cost).

   c) The manufacturing manager is wrong. Even though you have passed the point of greatest efficiency in using labor and materials, you can still make larger profits by going to the point where marginal costs are equal to marginal revenues.

   d) This answer is correct for the reasons stated above.

2. A firm that maximizes its profit under conditions of competition will operate at the level of output where marginal cost equals marginal revenue. Since the marginal cost curve intersects the total unit and variable unit cost curves at their minimum point, any increase in output will cause marginal, available, and total unit costs to rise and profits will rise. Hence (a) is the correct choice.

3. In the long run, firms operating under conditions of competition will earn zero economic profits. As long as positive economic profits exist, other firms will enter the market and squeeze out the economic profits. Therefore (a) is the correct choice. You cannot expect firms to be earning economic profits year after year. Answers (b), (c), and (d) accurately describe what happens to firms under competition, hence they are not correct.

4. The short-run supply curve is derived from the assumption that the population of plants is given and does not change in the short run.

   a) The cost of building new plants is irrelevant, since the short run assumes that the population of plants is given and does not change.

b) Again, if the population of plants is given, the time it takes to wear out old plants and thus reduce the population is irrelevant.

c) Technological innovations are made through the building of new plants and the redesigning of old ones. The short-run supply curve is based on the assumption of a constant population of plants.

d) This is the correct answer. In the short run, varying output in a given population of firms is the only way industry output can be adjusted. The sum of the marginal cost curves tells you how much more or less will be produced when the price of a product is increased or decreased.

OBJECTIVES

Upon successful completion of this chapter, you will be able to:

1. Define the productive services market, explain the functions it performs, and represent it in the circular-flow model.

2. Explain what is meant by "derived demand" and show how the demand for productive services is a "derived demand."

3. Define the value of marginal product (VMP) and, given a table listing alternative quantities of a variable input, the alternative marginal physical products, and the product price, be able to determine the VMP.

4. Apply the concept of the value of marginal productivity to the demand for labor.

5. Explain differential wage rates in terms of the supply of different types of labor.

6. Explain the Law of Equal Advantage.

7. Identify three functions that wages fulfill in a market-oriented economy.

8. Explain how the demand for loanable funds is determined by the value of the marginal productivity of capital goods.

9. Explain what determines the supply of loanable funds.

10. Use supply and demand curves to illustrate the effect on the interest rate of changes in supply and/or demand.

11. Explain why a "family" of interest rates exists.

12. Explain the process by which the capitalized value of a resource is determined.

13. Explain and give examples of the concept of economic rent.

14. Explain how economic rent serves as a device for rationing and for telling producers which technology to use.

15. List and explain the factors included in the concept of profit.

16. Describe how productive service prices answer the basic economic "from whom" question.

CHAPTER 6

THE PRODUCTIVE SERVICE MARKETS: PRICES AND THEIR ROLE IN THE ECONOMY

INTRODUCTION

Price is a word we most frequently associate with the number of dollars we have to pay to obtain some good or service. But price is really a ratio of exchange, so it does have a broader interpretation. Wages, rents, and interest rates are all prices. If you get a job next summer, you will be paid a specified amount per hour in exchange for the services you provide your employer. This is a price your employer must pay—a price for your productive services. If you open a savings account in a savings and loan association, you expect to receive interest; the interest rate is a productive service price. In this chapter we will be concerned with: (1) the factors determining these prices, with emphasis on the demand for productive services; (2) the four basic productive service prices—wages, interest, rent, and profit—and the tasks these prices perform in the management of a competitive, price-directed economy.

These prices—prices for productive services—are determined in the productive services market. To see where the productive services market fits in the overall economy, see the circular-flow model, Fig. 6.1. The productive services market shows businesses demanding productive services from households. Note the expenditure arrow from the businesses square leading to the demand curve in the productive services market. You can also see that the supply of productive services is largely determined by the decisions of households. Notice the arrow from the households square leading to the supply curve in the productive services market.

THE DEMAND FOR PRODUCTIVE SERVICES

The demand for productive services is determined by the demand for final products.

Consider labor as a service. If you attend a rock concert at your university, your willingness to spend $6 for a ticket reflects your demand for the performers' services. Your purpose in attending the concert was simple and final—you wanted to hear the performing group. Most labor services, however, are not purchased for the final satisfaction they yield. They are demanded only because they are a necessary ingredient in the production of some other final good or service. The demand for auto workers, for example, is derived from the demand for automobiles.

The other productive inputs, land and capital, also are demanded primarily because they contribute to the production of some final good. The demand for cows, for example, is derived from the demand for milk. The demand for circular saws is derived from the demand for residential housing.

The demand for productive services, like the demand for final products, follows the Law of Demand—the higher the price, the smaller the quantity demanded. The Law of Diminishing Marginal Returns sheds light on this aspect of the demand for productive services.

The Law of Diminishing Marginal Returns governs the output response of added units of input.

You will recall from our discussion of the Law of Diminishing Marginal Returns that as the amount of a variable resource increases when combined with fixed resources, beyond some point each successive amount of output created will be smaller, that is, the marginal output will decrease. To refresh your memory, we have reproduced the marginal product chart from Chapter 2 to demonstrate why the demand curve for productive services such as farm labor is downsloping (see Fig. 6.2). As more and more farm labor is combined with capital and land, the physical output attributed to the last unit of labor added will get smaller and smaller beyond a certain point.

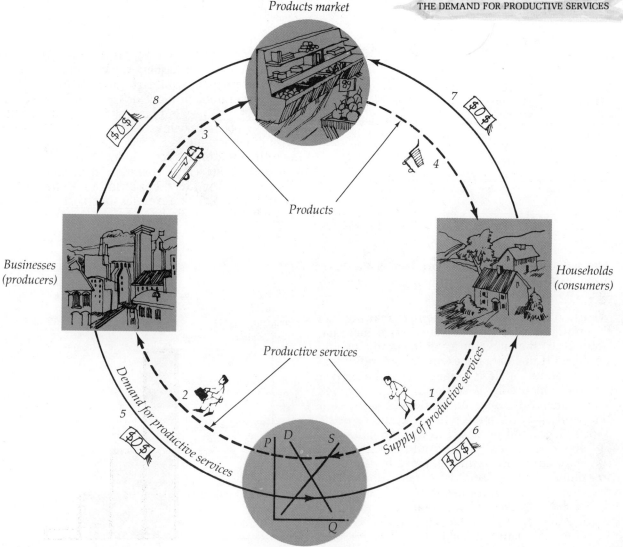

FIG. 6.1   **The productive services market in the circular-flow model.**

The fact that the marginal product curve decreases provides an explanation for the fact that the demand curve for productive services is downsloping. To demonstrate this we will use the marginal product schedule as a basis for determining the demand for labor—a productive service. Please examine Table 6.1. Column 1 shows alternative levels of input use, while column 2 shows the added output or marginal product stemming from each unit of input. (Only the portion of diminishing marginal product is shown.)

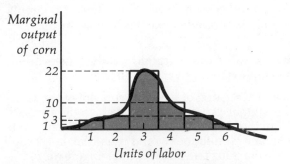

FIG. 6.2   **The marginal product (output) of corn.**

TABLE 6.1

THE VALUE OF THE MARGINAL PRODUCT

(1) Number of units of labor used	(2) Marginal product	(3) Price of product	(4) Value of the marginal product
3	22	$5	$110
4	10	5	50
5	5	5	25
6	1	5	5

ble 6.1, would be 4. Why? If 3 units were used rather than 4, the farmer would reduce costs by $30, but revenue would go down $50 (the value of the marginal product of the fourth worker is $50). Net income would fall by $20. Thus it would pay to go back to using 4 units of labor. The extra unit of labor would cost less than the value of the marginal product. If more than 4 units were used, the extra labor would cost more than the value of the marginal product. For example, a fifth worker would add $25 to revenues but cost $30, thus reducing net income by $5.

The value of the marginal product is the marginal product multiplied by the price of the product.

We can obtain the value of the marginal product by multiplying each of the successive marginal products by the market price of the product being produced. Consider, for example, an individual farmer producing corn. Suppose that the market price at which corn is selling is $5 per bushel. The values of the marginal products, starting at the point of diminishing returns, would be $110, $50, $25, $5, and on down to zero. In column 4 of Table 6.1, the VMP is derived by multiplying the marginal products in column 2 by the price in column 3. The result is a translation of the marginal product quantities into dollar amounts.

A chart representing the value of the marginal product for the individual farm can be derived from the information in Table 6.1. It has the same shape as the marginal product chart we first saw in Chapter 2 (see Fig. 6.3). The vertical axis now, however, measures the *value* of the marginal product rather than marginal product. It is simply the marginal product axis multiplied by $5.

The value of the marginal product determines the employment of variable inputs.

As an illustration of how this concept of the value of marginal productivity influences the demand for productive services, consider how many units of labor a corn farmer would use if the daily wage rate were $30. The answer, referring again to Ta-

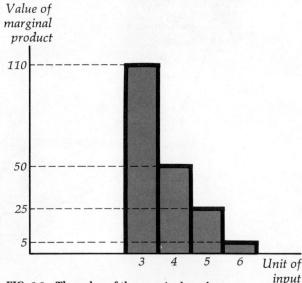

FIG. 6.3   **The value of the marginal product.**

Now suppose that the daily wage rate rose to $60. The corn farmer would no longer wish to use more than 3 units of labor. If more were used, the extra worker would have to be paid more than the value of the marginal product obtained.

The same relationship would hold if our hypothetical farmer were adding capital or land to his operation. The less expensive the extra capital or land, the more would be gained by expanding its use.

This concept, the *value of marginal product*, has given us an important reason why the demand for productive services satisfies the Law of Demand. As more of a productive service is used with fixed quantities of complementary productive services, the smaller would be the value of the marginal product, even if the price of the final product did not fall. This fact, combined with the fact that the price of a product falls as output of the industry increases, explains why the demand curve for productive services is downsloping.

You might say "this is just common sense." Why be so concerned about a downward-sloping productive services demand curve? The answer is that while we know it occurs, we often act as if we don't really believe it. When a minimum wage law succeeds in raising a wage rate of a particular type of labor, we are surprised to learn that firms usually find ways to use less of it. Or, when the interest rate rises, people borrow less and buy fewer new houses.

To make these concepts more realistic, put yourself in the place of the manager of food services for your college or university. Your immediate problem is to decide what wage rate to use in employing student workers. You would probably work through the following short-run scenario.

1. My cafeteria prices cannot be higher than a certain level, or the students in the university will go elsewhere for their food. My food prices must therefore be "competitive."
2. If I employ 100 students, the last student I employ adds about $3.50 per student hour to my gross income after paying for the food and other related costs. (This is the VMP of the 100th student hired.)
3. If I employ 75 students, the last student will add about $4.50 per hour to my gross income, again after paying for food and other related costs. (This is the VMP of the 75th student.)
4. I cannot employ fewer than 75 students and still keep the facilities clean enough to get students and faculty to eat in my cafeteria. So my problem will be to decide on a wage rate between $4.50 and $3.50 per hour.
5. I post a $3.50 per hour wage rate, expecting to hire 100 students.
6. But only 75 show up.
7. I try a $4.00 wage rate for a week. I get 90 students, but I notice that the last 5 students are not worth the $4.00 I am paying them. (Their VMP is less than $4.00.)
8. As a result of quits and no-shows, I drop 5 students.
9. In the end I find that it is most profitable to hire 85 students at $4.00 per hour.
10. Now suppose that during the next year students were less inclined to work or decided to work elsewhere and $4.00 per hour would attract only 65 students. To get the 85 I need, I would post a price of $4.50. And so on.

What can we learn from this simple example? Both supply (the number of students willing to work at each of the series of prices) and demand (the number I would hire at each of a series of prices) are important in determining productive service prices. If the price is too high, more people will show up than can be used profitably. And if the price is too low, not enough people will show. More people could profitably be hired at higher prices.

The above example reflects the short run because it is closer to our everyday living. In the long run, when you as manager of the cafeteria have time to shift resources around, you could go even further in reducing the number of students you would hire at higher wage rates. You could do this by installing "automat" equipment and other devices to cut down on labor.

Productive service prices are an important part of the communications system in a price-directed economy.

Productive service prices, then, are an important part of the communications system in a price-directed economy. They tell producers about the activity (and risk) preferences of the suppliers of productive services. They are instrumental in telling producers what type of technology to use in producing goods and services. In the end, because they influence the prices of final products, they play a role in telling consumers what mix of products to buy.

In the rest of this chapter we will be concerned with particular types of productive service prices, and the part they play in running a price-directed economy.

WAGE RATES: THE PRICE FOR LABOR SERVICES

Suppose you were considering becoming a day laborer, bricklayer, carpenter, college professor, physician specializing in eye surgery, undertaker, professional manager, or engineer. What will determine the wage rate you will receive once you are fully trained, and how will this wage rate influence the functioning of the economy?

To answer these questions we must again think about what determines the demand for and supply of the services of persons in each of these skill groups.

The demand curve for labor, like other productive services, is downsloping.

The demand for any type of labor is determined by the two sets of factors we considered at the beginning of this chapter; namely, the nature of the demand for the final product and the value of the marginal product as more and more of a particular type of labor is combined with complementary resources. We will not repeat this discussion. It is enough at this stage to remember that the demand for any type of labor, including unskilled labor, is downsloping.

The supply of labor in different skill categories is determined by the activity choices of households.

The supply of labor available in each of these skill categories is largely determined by the decisions persons make as they choose one occupation or another. You will remember from our discussion in Chapter 2 about the nature of resources, that labor, like other resources, has a turnover period. People enter an occupation, work at it for years, and then retire. Meanwhile, as other persons enter the labor force, they too will choose an occupation. If they choose not to become glass blowers,

the population of glass blowers will shrink. Or if more people choose to become carpenters than are dying, retiring, or dropping out, the population of carpenters will expand. These occupational decisions (as well as other factors) will create a set of wage rates for different occupations.

The Law of Equal Advantage describes the way households make these decisions.

The answer to the question above, what will determine your wage rate, is to be found in what Professor Kenneth Boulding has called the *Law of Equal Advantage*. Using his words, the law may be stated as follows:

"If the owners of any resources think these can be put to better advantage in some other use than the one in which they are employed, the resources will be transferred from the less advantageous to the more advantageous use.... As long, therefore, as there are people who believe that the resources they own, whether these be their own bodies or some other object, will yield them a greater advantage in an occupation different from that in which they are at present employed, then resources will be transferred from one occupation to another."*

Translated into the vernacular, this law says people can decide to do whatever they want to with resources they have, but normally they will want to use them in such a way as will bring them the maximum benefit. But "benefit" or "advantage," as Boulding puts it, may be defined differently by different people. It all depends on what they wish to obtain from their resources. Consider what people take into account in choosing occupations.

* Kenneth E. Boulding, *Economic Analysis*, Fourth Edition, Vol. 1, New York: Harper and Row, 1966, p. 87.

In considering the advantages and disadvantages of an occupation, people consider many factors.

Many people are concerned with *leisure opportunities* associated with various occupations. The fact that waiters do not work standard hours may be of enormous importance to some people. They may use their resources in such a way as will give them more time off. In contrast, physicians normally work 60- and 70-hour weeks, with few periods in the week when they can put their responsibilities aside.

There are other *nonpecuniary advantages and disadvantages* associated with various occupations. Some people are very conscious of social status. They tend to gravitate to those occupations they think will bring them the admiration of the society in which they are living. College teaching has had a high social status and this, combined with the opportunities for leisure associated with the academic year, has no doubt attracted many people into this occupation. In contrast, septic tank cleaners do not enjoy the same social status, and at times their work can be unpleasant.

People must take into consideration *capital requirements* associated with entering different occupations. Physicians must spend at least ten years in a combination of premed courses in college, medical school, and internships before they are qualified to practice medicine. Carpenters must usually put in an apprenticeship of three or four years' duration and in addition must provide their own tools. During the preparatory years, candidates for an occupation normally give up the chance to earn a higher income in a less skilled occupation. In addition, it is frequently necessary for people to borrow the funds for educational and equipment-buying purposes. Thus the capital requirements for different occupations vary substantially, and the wage rate must be high enough to permit an adequate return on necessary capital investment.

Risks associated with different occupations vary, and people have very different attitudes toward risk bearing. At any one time, more than two-thirds of all the professional actors and actresses seeking roles are unemployed, but when they do find employment, their compensation is normally very high. People who want a steady job with a predictable paycheck would find acting a difficult profession.

The *expected number of years of employment* differ substantially from one occupation to another. Professional football players seldom play more than fifteen years. Judges, on the other hand, continue working until they are in their seventies and eighties.

Finally, there are some *native ability requirements* that make it difficult for some people to enter an occupation. Not everybody, even with access to the capital requirements, could be an eye surgeon. It takes great manual dexterity and steady nerves. The same thing may be true of most professional sports. When native ability requirements play an important role in determining the supply curve for an occupation, we say that the wage rate consists largely of economic rent, a term that will be explained later in this chapter.

These factors, summarized under the heading of the Law of Equal Advantage, are largely responsible for the way people are distributed among occupational groups. People also make decisions about whether they want to use their time for work activities or for leisure.

These activity choices—what shall I do and how many hours shall I work?—jointly determine participation in each occupational category.

The activity choices of individuals taken together create pressure for wage changes.

Consider what would happen if over a 10-year period young people were to decide they would rather have lower-paying white-collar jobs than higher-paying blue-collar jobs, such as carpentry, toolmaking, plumbing, and the like. The arrows in Fig. 6.4 indicate the net flow of persons out of blue-collar skills and into white-collar skills, such as computer programming, teaching, social service jobs, and so forth.

In a competitive economy, the wage rates in the white-collar skills would go down and wage rates in the blue-collar skills would go up. Once the gap between these two wage rates had reached a certain size, the differential would be large enough to prevent a further outflow of people from blue-collar jobs into white-collar jobs. A new equilibrium would have been reached.

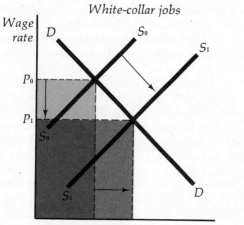

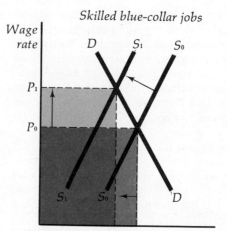

FIG. 6.4 Supply and demand for white-collar and skilled laborer jobs.

The supply curves for various types of labor, together with the resulting wage rates, reflect the activity choices of households. The supply curves for labor in a competitive economy are an expression of the activity choices of people. They tell us what people want to do. Indeed, we could argue that they are as valid an expression of human choice as are the product demand curves we stressed in Chapter 3.

Wages perform several important functions in a market economy.

What, then, is the role of a wage rate in a price-directed economy? In the first place, it is a means of allocating people among different employers and different work activities. Suppose there is a shortage, at existing wage rates, of toolmakers. Those employers who have most critical need for toolmakers will bid up the price of toolmakers, and this will shift toolmakers from one industry to another.

In the second place, wage rates in a competitive economy, reflecting as they do the relative scarcities of different types of work, are a means of telling businesspeople what technologies to adopt. If toolmakers' wage rates rise and computer programmers' wage rates fall, businesspeople are encouraged to adopt computer-designed tools instead of bench-designed tools.

In the third place, wage rates are an important cost of production. When blue-collar wage rates rise, those products containing large amounts of blue-collar labor will rise in price more than other products. This flowthrough effect on product prices will reduce the purchases of those products that have become high priced and increase the purchases of those products that have become less expensive. In effect, the price system rations the consumption of those products that the labor force does not want to make.

Mini-case 6.1 is presented to help you clarify the secondary and tertiary effects of activities affecting the productive service market for labor.

MINI-CASE 6.1

Suppose a federal law is passed increasing the minimum wage to $5 an hour. As a consequence, you can expect that:

a) in the long run, the number of jobs will increase. Low wages do not create additional jobs; rather, they eliminate them by cutting into the purchasing power of the people who must spend all the money they make.
b) unemployment will increase. It is an unavoidable conclusion from supply and demand analysis that when a price (wage) is artificially raised above the equilibrium level, the quantity demanded will decrease and the quantity supplied will increase.
c) little change in current hiring policies will occur. If employers need workers to produce a product, they will hire them and pass the added wage cost on to the consumer.
d) some workers will be better off and some workers will be worse off. The majority of workers will be retained and receive a windfall increase in wage, while a few unproductive workers will be let go.

COMMENTARY

The following is an excerpt from an article entitled "The Declining Value of College Going." It describes how the market for college-educated persons has changed both in terms of supply and demand since the 1960s. Please read the excerpt and answer the following questions.

a) What are the causes underlying the changes in the demand and supply of college-educated workers?
b) How is the market mechanism coping with the excess quantity supplied?

THE DECLINING VALUE OF COLLEGE GOING

For decades the American higher educational system has both provided individuals with training and education promising high earnings and occupational status, and supplied society with skilled specialists and white-collar workers. In the 1950s and 1960s in particular, the job market for college graduates was exceptionally strong; education was a major means to socioeconomic mobility and national economic growth. With a minority of young Americans—albeit an increasingly large one—attending college, and a growing demand for the educated, the financial rewards for the college trained were sizable and stimulated many to extend their education from 12 to 16 or more years of formal schooling. Spurred by the demand for college training, the higher educational system was significantly expanded, and many more millions enrolled than ever before. With a bull market, there was little incentive to examine the value of college education carefully: Whatever it was that was being taught was paying off in good jobs for graduates. The response was simply to expand higher education—to open the door to larger numbers of people, including disadvantaged minorities.

This golden age of higher education came to an abrupt end at the outset of the 1970s, when the 25-year boom in the college job market withered into a major market bust. For the first time in recent history, new bachelor's graduates began to have difficulty obtaining jobs, and the relative income of college workers fell significantly.

Extent of the downturn

It is important to recognize that the market turn-around of the seventies is a far-reaching, unprecedented development of sizable dimensions. By all relevant measures, the economic status of college graduates is deteriorating, with employment prospects for the young declining exceptionally sharply.

From 1969, the last good year in the college job market, to 1975, the starting salaries of male graduates in industry, having increased rapidly in the previous decade, dropped sharply, both in real terms and relative to the earnings of other workers. College Placement council data show a decrease of 23 percent in the real starting pay for men with social science or humanities degrees; a fall of 21 percent in the real pay for beginning BS mathematics majors; and of 17 percent for beginning electrical engineers with doctorates. Declines in real rates of pay of such magnitude have not been experienced by other workers and constitute a sharp break with past patterns of change.

As a result of the decline in relative incomes and starting salaries and in the face of continued increases in tuition and fees, the rate of return on the college investment has fallen significantly. According to one set of estimates, the return dropped from 11–12 percent in 1969 to 7–8 percent in 1974. A decrease of this magnitude is unprecedented.

Temporary, cyclical, or long-run?

Analysis of the causes of the seventies' turn-around suggests that the market developments represent a major break with the past and are not simply cyclical or temporary phenomena. Underlying the collapse of the college job market is what promises to be a long-term change in the supply-demand balance due to several factors. On the demand side, the growth of most sectors of the economy, using a relatively large number of college graduates, has leveled off after two decades or so of rapid growth. While the growth of certain other sectors also employing significant numbers of college graduates (such as finance and professional services) has not declined, it has been insufficient to maintain the pace of employment.

Coincident with the leveling off in demand was an extraordinary increase in the number of new graduates seeking work—the result of the large numbers that were of college age and chose to go to college and graduate school in the 1960s. While the number of students increased rapidly throughout the 1960s, the number actually graduating and seeking work did not increase by as much—largely because many chose to obtain graduate training in the booming market. With the decline of the seventies, the proportion enrolling in graduate schools has fallen, while those who sought graduate degrees four or five years earlier have finally entered the market, with the result that supply has increased sharply. Estimates of the number of new BAs seeking work, obtained by subtracting those going to graduate school (but ignoring the movement of older people into graduate training), suggest that the number of new male BAs "on the job market" increased by 8 percent per annum (relative to the male work force) from 1968 to 1973, compared to a modest 1.75 percent per annum in the sixties. In addition, the flow of new graduates was so much greater throughout the period than the number of retiring BAs that the total supply of college-trained workers increased rapidly as a fraction of the work force—a development almost certain to continue into the 1980s due to the continued small number of college graduates nearing retirement age.

This combination of deceleration of growth in demand and massive increase in supply in the 1970s—not the overall recession or some other relatively short-term development—underlies the remarkable turnaround in the college job market and appears to have caused the decline in the fraction of young males entering college. Some young people considering higher education are responding to the decline in job opportunities and the declining rate of return on the educational investment, Responses to changing incentives have been found in a wide variety of professions—law, physics, engineering, accounting—and for the aggregate of college students. These results do not imply that educational decisions of all people are motivated by economic conditions, only that a large number are sensitive to the job market.

RICHARD FREEMAN and J. HERBERT HOLLOMAN, "The Declining Value of College Going," Reprinted with permission from Vol. 7, #7, *Change* Magazine, September 1975.

INTEREST RATES: THE PRICE FOR THE USE OF FINANCIAL RESOURCES

The interest rate is determined in the financial capital market.

The interest rate as a separate and distinct productive service price is determined by the supply of and demand for loanable funds in the financial capital market. In the circular-flow model in Fig. 6.5, we have shown a supply and demand graph in the financial capital market linking the squares of businesses and households.

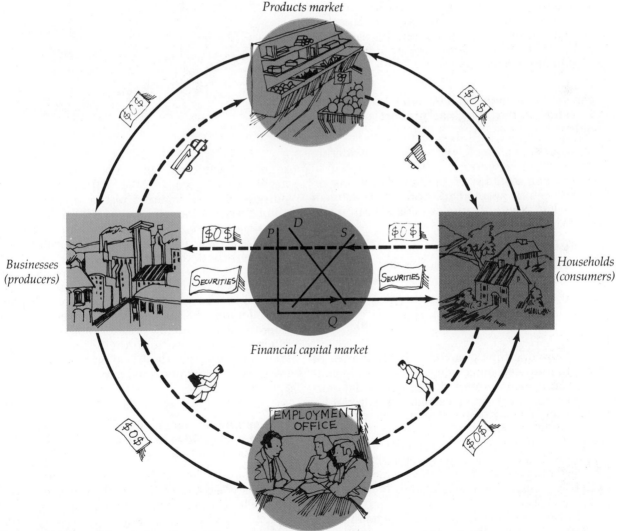

FIG. 6.5 The financial capital market in the circular-flow model.

The supply of financial capital in this market comes from households and businesses who save. The demand stems from the desire on the part of businesspeople and households to borrow money—largely to finance the purchase of buildings, equipment, inventories, dwellings, and other pieces of real capital. Note the arrow from businesses square to the demand curve in the *financial* capital market. (Capital, you will recall from Chapter 2, consists of resources made by humans, including human skills.) The value of the marginal product of capital, just like labor or any other productive input, plays an important role in determining its demand: in this case, how much money borrowers are seeking in the financial capital markets.

Demand for loanable funds stems largely from the value of the marginal product of capital goods.

If you were operating a business and considering purchasing a new truck with a price tag of $30,000, you would want to know the rate of return you could expect to make on this investment of $30,000. Your calculations for a year might look like this:

Original cost of the truck $30,000

Net income after subtracting all costs, including the depreciation of the truck   6,000

Percent return on original cost

$$\frac{\$6,000}{\$30,000} = .20 = 20\%$$

At any one time there are a large number of opportunities for purchasing capital equipment that would earn a return for the potential purchaser. Some of these investments might yield a 20 percent rate of return like the truck. Others might yield 15 percent, 10 percent, and so on. As long as there are capital-equipment investment opportunities yielding a rate of return higher than the current interest rate on borrowed money, there will be a demand for loanable funds to be used in this manner.

If, then, we made a list of all the amounts that borrowers would like to borrow to buy new trucks, new apartment houses, new factories, and

so on, we would see what, in a sense, the capital needs of society were. (We will ignore, for this purpose, the self-financed pieces of capital.) Not all of these capital uses are equally profitable, of course. Suppose, then, that we were to arrange this list according to the percentage return that borrowers think they can earn on their additional investment (value of the marginal product expressed as a percentage of the original cost). Using this list, we could easily construct a demand curve for *loanable funds*—the term we will use to refer to the amounts businesses, households, and other entities want to borrow. The demand for loanable funds is really based on the value of the marginal product of capital expressed in percentage terms.

The supply of loanable funds is determined largely by decisions to save and to buy securities rather than hold money.

To explain in detail what determines the supply of funds is a complicated problem, particularly if we include commercial banks as a supplier of loanable funds. We will simplify the problem by excluding banks because, as we shall see later in Chapter 13, they have the special power to create the money they lend in the financial capital markets.

The supply of loanable funds (excluding commercial banks) is determined largely by the willingness of households and businesses *to save* and to use their savings to buy securities. When persons save, they receive income but do not use it to buy goods and services in the products market; they abstain and forgo their right to enjoy goods and services. But this is only part of the story. Having decided not to spend all of their income, they then must make the second decision to funnel their savings into the financial capital market. They must decide (1) not to use their savings for direct investment in a piece of farm equipment, a truck, or a house, and (2) not to hold their savings in the form of money. Consider the following illustration.

Suppose you are lucky enough to get a summer job that pays you $10 per hour and that you have the chance to work 50 hours a week for 12 weeks. You total income, ignoring taxes and other deductions, would be $6000. Further suppose that you are very frugal and spend only $1000 during the summer, leaving you with $5000 in savings. You could keep the $5000 in your dresser drawer; you could use it to buy a pick-up truck to do odd jobs when you went back to school; or you could take your money to a savings and loan association and exchange it for an interest-bearing claim against the association, or buy a bond issued by a corporation. Only if you put your savings in the savings and loan association or used them to buy a bond would you have added to the supply of loanable funds.

The simple decision chart below shows what your choices are.

Spend $1000 on consumption goods

You receive
$6000

Save
$5000

Spend on capital goods
Hold the money unspent
Buy securities, or deposit funds in bank, that is, *supply loanable funds*

Producers have the same set of choices with the earnings they receive from the sale of products, after meeting costs. They can either spend the money or save it. They then have the same three choices for disposal of the saved portion.

In order to simplify our problem we shall assume—until we deal with the demand for money in Chapters 13 and 14—that households and businesses put all of the money they do not use for direct investment in capital goods into the financial capital market. Under these circumstances the supply of loanable funds is determined largely by the willingness of households and businesses to save.

The interest rate is determined by the supply and demand for loanable funds.

The price at which loanable funds are sold is the *rate of interest*. When there is an increase in demand for loanable funds and the demand curve shifts to the right, the rate of interest rises. Or when households and businesses decide to save more, the rate of interest falls. Figure 6.6 shows a situation in which an increase in demand increases the interest rate and an increase in supply reduces the interest rate.

The loanable funds explanation of the interest rate has many applications to present-day affairs. There are people, for example, who believe that the energy shortage is really symptomatic of a shortage of capital. They argue that the oil, natural gas, and coal industries, together with the public utilities, will have to invest billions of dol-

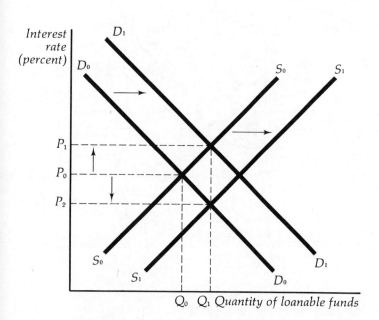

FIG. 6.6   Changes in the supply and demand for loanable funds.

then go on to argue that there are not enough people willing to save and lend the money to provide these trillions of dollars, and that, as a result, the interest rate will be very high during this period.

What would happen if households and businesses are not willing to save enough to finance the construction of these energy-producing capital goods? It is true that the government could create the money to buy these capital goods and thus keep the interest rate from rising, but not without other complications. The act of saving releases the resources from the production of consumption-type products like soda pop, clothing, baby carriages, and what have you. If people do not save and government-created money is used to buy these capital goods, inflation increases and interest rates rise.

The important truth for us to remember about savings is that the act of saving makes it possible for a society to produce capital goods without causing inflation. Thus, when you look around you, every piece of capital you see—the dormitory you may be living in, the road in front of the dormitory, the trucks on the road—represents the soda pop somebody might have drunk, the clothing somebody might have worn, or the lecture somebody might have paid to hear.

lars to provide the energy people will want during the last quarter of the twentieth century. They

---

COMMENTARY

The following is an excerpt from an article entitled "Development of Capital Markets in the United States." It describes the functions of financial capital markets. Please read it and answer the

following questions.
a) Why does a market economy need capital markets?
b) What do the capital markets achieve?

FUNCTIONS OF CAPITAL MARKETS

The quantity of goods and services that an economy can produce, given its endowment of natural resources and state of technology, depends on the size of its capital stock and on available labor services. The current change in an economy's capital stock is defined as its current rate of

investment and is equal to the amount of its current product that is not consumed. The rate at which capital can accumulate is determined by the amount of potential current consumption an economy is willing to forgo—the amount it is willing to save. Savings and investment, therefore, are necessary prerequisites for the maintenance and growth of economic welfare as measured by per capita income.

If all units in an economy always maintained balanced budgets, with savings equal to investment, the economy would have no need for capital markets. The need for capital markets arises when the desired savings of some economic agents differ from their desired investment in real assets. The purpose of capital markets is to allow separation of savings and investment and satisfy the resulting need to transfer resources from net surplus units (those having desired savings that exceed their desired accumulation of real assets) to net deficit units.

Because of the difficulty of carrying out barter through time, such transfers of resources are facilitated by means of financial assets, which represent evidence of debt or ownership. These financial assets may represent claims on other financial assets but ultimately represent claims to real assets. Since the transfer of resources between surplus and deficit units may be for any specified time period, the financial assets accompanying and evidencing such transactions may be for any maturity. Capital markets, therefore, are defined here to include all financial assets and all transactions in such assets *regardless of maturity*.

By allowing individuals to separate their own savings and investment, financial assets and markets in them make it possible, first, to obtain an increase in individual satisfaction for a given level of income and, second, to obtain an increase in the economy's total income for a given rate of saving. Financial assets allow an individual to reallocate his consumption through time, given his total income or wealth, by borrowing or lending and thereby consuming relatively less in one time period and relatively more in another. When individuals differ in their preferences for current relative to future consumption, the choices available to them are expanded and their satisfaction can be increased if they have the opportunity to trade in goods through time, as well as at a given time.

It may also be possible to increase productivity, given the rate of saving and available resources, through a redistribution of savings and investment if individuals have different entrepreneurial opportunities and abilities. With such differences, the total return on capital—and, therefore, society's total income—can be increased by transferring savings from individuals whose investments would yield a relatively low rate of return to individuals whose investments would yield a higher one.

Under such circumstances, there is an incentive to specialize, with some individuals saving more than they invest and others investing more than they save. The gains from the redistribution of investment from low- to high-yield projects can be exploited until the marginal rate of return is equalized on all investment projects.

An additional factor favoring the separation of savings and investment is the possibility that some projects may require investment in amounts larger than the savings available to any one individual. This obstacle can be overcome by pooling the savings of several individuals. Gains may be made from such pooling until the marginal rates of return are equalized on large and small projects.

STEPHEN W. DOBSON, "Development of Capital Markets in the United States," *Business Review*, April 1976, Federal Reserve Bank of Dallas. Reprinted by permission.

The interest rate is an important part of many different productive service prices.

When you rent an apartment, a large part of the rent you pay is used in turn to pay interest to those who have lent money to the owners of the apartment. When you pay an ophthalmologist for personal services—say, eye surgery—part of what you pay consists of the interest return on the investment he has made in his skills and his equipment. When a company reports accounting profits, a part of what is typically called profits really consists of the interest return on the amounts it has invested in buildings and equipment. The interest rate is part of many productive service prices.

The interest rate performs many tasks in a market-directed economy.

In modern industrial economies, the interest rate set in the financial capital market is an extremely important price: (1) it rations savings among those who would use them to acquire capital goods; (2) it serves as a guide to the choice of capital-using technologies within companies; (3) it influences prices of final products and, therefore, rations products among households.

The interest rate rations loanable funds among competing uses.

It is in the financial capital market where the decision is made as to who will get the loanable funds and, therefore, what capital goods should be built. Consider an example.

The electric power company in your town wants to build a new standby power-generating station. It is seeking $5 million to do this. The school system also wants to build a new stadium for the high-school football games. It too is seeking $5 million. The public utility offers to pay the buyers of the securities 9½ percent. Your school board offers to pay only 8 percent (adjusted for any differences in the taxability of the interest). As a result, the public utility gets the funds and, therefore, builds the standby power-generating station. Your school board was, in a sense, rationed out of the market.

In this rationing process, the costs of investigating the credit worthiness of the borrowers and making the loan are important costs. When a financial institution, such as a savings and loan association, lends you money to build a new house, it has to take into account the costs of a credit search to see whether you pay your debts, the cost of making an appraisal of the lot on which you intend to build your new house, and the bookkeeping costs of recording your monthly payments. Small loans will usually carry higher interest rates than large loans because of these costs.

Different borrowers and different types of securities carry different credit risks. The possibility that Exxon Corporation will go into bankruptcy and not be able to pay off its debts is minimal. On the other hand, when a newly organized business borrows to start a book store, the risk of failure is quite high. Therefore, lenders will typically want a fairly high-risk premium added to their interest rates in order to compensate them for the credit risks associated with this type of loan.

The interest rates you see in the market place also reflect the credit risks and the cost of making loans.

All this means that the interest rate is really a family of rates. Some interest rates will normally be higher than others, just as the wage rates in unpleasant places to work usually have to be higher than the wage rates in pleasant places. As a result, in the performance of their rationing function, the financial capital markets also reflect the cost of making loans and the willingness of lenders to accept credit risks. Those borrowers with good credit ratings will be able to borrow money for lower rates of interest than those with poor credit ratings.

The interest rate also tells businesses how to use their capital.

In addition to rationing loanable funds among borrowers, the interest rate is also an important guide to businesses and individuals in the management of their capital assets. When they purchase a piece of capital equipment, they are giving up a lump sum of money for a series of future income payments. To compare the two choices, we have to understand how the interest rate is used to make "present value" calculations. Consider the following illustration.

Suppose that you have inherited a spring that provides water with alleged curative effects. It is expected to supply water for only five years before it will be taken over by the city. We will suppose that during these five years the spring would produce a $10,000 net profit each year and that the profit is available only at the end of every year. What should be the selling price for the spring if the going rate of interest were 10 percent? Your first guess might be that the spring would be worth $50,000 since during the next five years it will produce $50,000 in net profits. But, if prospective buyers were to pay $50,000 for the spring, they would be better off lending their $50,000 to a friend at an interest rate of 10 percent a year. In this way, they would have a net income of $5,000 per year for each of the five years, and in addition they would have their $50,000 back in five years.

The prospective buyers' problem will be to figure out how much they can afford to pay now for the spring and still earn a 10 percent return on their money during the five years.

The interest rate can be used to establish value of a stream of income by discounting future payments.

The interest rate is the key to understanding how to calculate the value of something today that you can't have until next year or five years hence. You've heard the expression, "a bird in the hand is worth two in the bush"; well, it is also true that one thousand dollars in the palm of your hand now is worth more than a thousand dollars due you one year from now.

If you lend someone $1000 at 10 percent for one year, you will receive at the end of one year $1100 (the original $1000 plus $100 interest). Conversely, the *present value* of $1100 due one year from now is $1000. Similarly, if you lend $909 to someone for one year at 10 percent, you will receive $1000 at the end of one year (the original $909 plus $91 interest). You can say in this case that the *present value* of $1000 due one year hence at 10 percent is $909. This $909 is also said to be the *discounted value* of $1000. Now, change the interest rate. If you lend someone $1000 for one year at 6 percent, you will receive only $1060 one year from now, and if you lend someone $943 at 6 percent, you will receive $1000 one year from now; that is, the present value of $1000 is $943 at a 6 percent interest rate.

Note that the present value of $1000 loaned for one year at 10 percent was $909, while it was $943 at the 6 percent interest rate. The higher the interest rate, the lower the present value. Time, too, is an element in calculating present value. If someone owed you $1000, paying a 10 percent interest rate, but it wasn't due for two years, it would be worth only $827. The more distant the time of payment, the lower the value.

We will not go into the mathematics underlying the calculation of present value, or discounting, as it is called. Instead, we will show you a shorthand method of determining the present value of a given amount at various interest rates for various periods of time. Table 6.2 lists these values. To see how it is used, consider the "health-water" example. What is the present value of a spring that will deliver $10,000 net profit a year for five years if the going rate of interest were 10 percent? Table 6.2 tells you that $1.00 to be paid to you at the end of one year at an interest rate of 10 percent is worth $.909 today

TABLE 6.2

THE PRESENT VALUE OF $1 RECEIVED AT THE END OF VARIOUS TIME PERIODS AT 5, 10, 15, and 20 PERCENT INTEREST RATES

(1) Time period in years from now	(2) 5%	(3) 10%	(4) 15%	(5) 20%
1	0.952	0.909	0.870	0.833
2	0.907	0.826	0.756	0.694
3	0.864	0.751	0.658	0.578
4	0.823	0.683	0.572	0.482
5	0.784	0.620	0.497	0.402
6	0.746	0.564	0.432	0.335
7	0.711	0.513	0.376	0.279
8	0.677	0.466	0.326	0.233
9	0.645	0.424	0.284	0.194
10	0.614	0.385	0.247	0.162
15	0.481	0.239	0.122	0.065
20	0.377	0.148	0.061	0.026
25	0.295	0.092	0.030	0.011
50	0.087	0.009	0.001	0.000

(Column 3, Row 1). Similarly, $1.00 to be paid you two years from now at a 10 percent interest rate is worth $.826 today (Column 3, Row 2). So, $1.00 to be paid you at the end of each year for five years, beginning one year from today at a 10 percent interest rate, is worth today: .909 + .826 + .751 + .683 + .620 = $3.79. Hence, the present value of the health-water spring is $3.79 × 10,000 = $37,900, using the 10 percent interest rate. If the rate were 5 percent, the present value would be $43,300, and if the rate were 15 percent, the present value would be $33,530.

Present-value calculations can tell you what to do now to get future benefits.

Using this table and related compound interest tables, decision-makers can translate the value of future events into present values. Thus, the interest rate serves as a bridge between the present, when action has to be taken, and the future, when the benefits will be realized. Suppose you were thinking about buying 100 shares of stock in a company. By discounting the expected dividends from the stock, you can determine what the present value of that stock should be. If it is higher than the market price, you will buy it. If it is lower, you will not.

Or suppose you are considering going into a variety of different occupations. Some of them, such as law or medicine, pay off late in life. Other occupations, such as professional hockey or foot-ball, pay off early in life. Armed with such a table, you could then ask which occupational strategy would give you the highest present value.

Businesses continually use present-value calculations in making decisions about how they will manage their capital funds.

COMMENTARY

The following advertisement appeared in the Sunday Magazine of the *New York Times*. It describes a savings plan in which the depositor receives interest on the first day money is deposited rather than when it is withdrawn. Read the ad and answer the following questions.

a) What is the basis for the $976.81 payment?
b) Is this a good deal for the saver?

Surprise! Only the Chase Savings Center will pay your savings interest in advance.

Get your interest now... not years from now.

Deposit $4,000, for example, in a 4-year savings plan.
Today.
The Chase Savings Center will pay you $976.81 in interest.
Today.
In fact, at the Chase Savings Center you can get up to 10 years* of savings interest to spend the day you deposit your savings in the bank.

With Interest-In-Advance, your savings are safe for the future and you have the interest to enjoy now.

The highest prepaid interest allowed by law.

So take advantage of the Chase Savings Advisor at the Chase Savings Center.

Interest-In-Advance is just one of the surprising new ways our Savings Advisor has to show you how much more your savings can do.

Member FDIC

 CHASE

In accordance with Federal regulation, any withdrawal permitted prior to the contracted maturity will result in a penalty which is a reduction of the rate of interest paid on the amount withdrawn to the maximum permissible passbook rate and a forfeiture of three months' interest on the amount withdrawn. To the extent necessary to effect such forfeiture, interest prepaid to you shall be deducted from the amount withdrawn. In addition, there will be deducted from the amount withdrawn any unearned portion of such prepaid interest. Your prepaid interest is subject to income taxes in the year in which the interest is paid.

The Chase Advantage

Courtesy The Chase
Manhattan Bank

If we did not have an interest rate, we would have to invent a substitute.

Thousands of these present-value calculations must be made every day in the use of capital goods. How much is it worth spending to purchase a punch press to last an extra 10 years? How much thicker should the highways be? How much is it worth spending to make metal rust-proof? How much is it worth spending to treat railroad ties to keep them from rotting? And we could go on. Our objective is not to require you to make all of these present-value calculations, but to point out that if we didn't have an interest rate to guide us in making these decisions, we could not manage our stock of capital goods to get the most benefit from them. If we did not have an interest rate, we would have to invent something to replace it.

If the interest rate is rejected, other devices for allocating capital among industries and among different uses within industries must be used. Some other set of standards to do what the interest rate does for a price-directed economy must be established.

The interest rate as an element of cost also rations products among households.

Finally, the interest rate (considered as a family of rates) has an enormous influence on the prices of products offered for sale to households in the products market. Products that are capital intensive—steel, public utility services, paper, aluminum, and so on—will go up in price when the interest rises. The reverse is true when the interest rate falls. In this way the interest rate serves as a communications device telling households to buy more or less of certain classes of products, depending on the inclination of these same households to save or not to save.

Mini-case 6.2 is provided to help you see the relationship between the interest rate and the capitalization process.

MINI-CASE 6.2

Last month you entered a contest. Today you were informed that you won. The prize consists of either (1) a $20,000 lump sum payment given immediately, or (2) a $1,000 per year payment annually for the next 30 years. You must select one or the other. What should you do?

a) Select the $1,000 a year option because after 30 years you'll have $30,000 and that's better than $20,000 in a lump sum today.
b) Select the $20,000 lump sum—a "bird in the hand is clearly better than two in the bush."
c) You can't tell until you know what the interest rate is, and the *higher* the rate, the greater is the probability that you will accept the lump sum payment of $20,000.
d) You can't tell until you know what the interest rate is, and the *lower* the rate, the greater is the probability that you will accept the lump sum payment of $20,000.

ECONOMIC RENT: THE PRICE OF A PRODUCTIVE SERVICE ABOVE THAT NECESSARY TO OBTAIN ITS USE

When you hear the term *rent*, you probably think of the monthly payment for using the services of an apartment, or the cost of using an automobile owned by Hertz or Avis for a short period of time.

This use of the word rent differs from the way it is used in economics; in fact, the terms *economic rent* and *quasi-rent* have been coined to emphasize a usage different from everyday usage.

The term *rent* had its origin in economics in the analysis of the return to land as a productive resource, so it is not surprising that the everyday usage of rent refers to the use of property for a fee for a given period of time.

The term rent, as used by David Ricardo and other nineteenth-century classical economists, is best illustrated by an example. Assume that one acre of land yields 150 bushels of corn. If corn is selling for $2 a bushel, the value of the corn produced by that acre of land is $300. If *all* costs of production except payment for the use of the land amount to $300, the land would yield no rent or surplus. However, if the price of corn increases to $3 a bushel, the value of that same acre's yield rises to $450. If no increase in production costs occurs, that land yields a rent or surplus of $150. Similarly, if the price of corn rises to $4 a bushel, the rent or surplus increases to $300 for that acre.

Hence, as originally used, rent was not a cost, but a return on land determined by the price of the output of the land. The unique feature of rent, as opposed to other productive service prices, is that it describes the return on an input that is fixed in supply. Rent was first used to describe land, because it is the classic example of an input that is limited in supply. Other productive services, however, are also fixed in supply, at least in the short run, and hence the term *economic rent* was coined to include the surplus, earned by other productive services such as labor. Consider the following examples.

Assume your college or university is about to open a new cafeteria and the manager advertises in the school newspaper for student help. She estimates that she will need 50 student employees. The ad offers to pay $2.50 an hour. In response to this ad, however, only 10 students offer their services. The next week, the manager places another ad in the school paper. This time, she offers to pay $3.00 an hour, but only 10 more students apply for the openings. After several more attempts at advertising, she finds that in order to hire 50 workers she must pay $4.50 an hour.

TABLE 6.3
THE SUPPLY OF WORKERS AT EACH WAGE

Hourly wage offered	Number of students offering their services
$2.50	10
3.00	20
3.50	30
4.00	40
4.50	50

Table 6.3 shows how many students are willing to work at each alternative wage offered by the successive ads in the student newspaper.

If the manager ultimately offers a wage of $4.50 an hour, those workers who were willing to work at lower wages will receive an amount above their acceptable wage. This surplus wage is called *economic rent*. Table 6.4 shows the amount of economic rent each group of workers would receive at each alternative wage. Those workers offering their services at $2.50 an hour receive $0.50 economic rent if the wage paid is $3.00. They receive $1.00 economic rent if the wage paid is $3.50, and so on. Those willing to work only at $4.50 an hour receive no economic rent.

TABLE 6.4
THE AMOUNT OF ECONOMIC RENT RECEIVED BY EACH GROUP OF WORKERS

The hourly wage at which each group of workers is willing to work	Economic rent (hourly) for each group at alternative wages				
	$2.50	$3.00	$3.50	$4.00	$4.50
$2.50	——	$0.50	$1.00	$1.50	$2.00
3.00	——	——	0.50	1.00	1.50
3.50	——	——	——	0.50	1.00
4.00	——	——	——	——	0.50
4.50	——	——	——	——	——

You own a spring that is perceived by many people to have certain curative properties. You find that you can sell health water for $1.50 per gallon and that all of the costs, including packaging, delivery, and so forth, amount to $0.50 per gallon. Since the spring produces 1000 gallons of packageable water per year, your net income from the well is therefore about $1000 per year. How much of this income consists of economic rent? The answer is that *all* of it is economic rent. Economic rent is defined as that portion of a productive service price that is above and beyond that necessary to induce the supplier to supply the service.

The concept of economic rent exists in many less extreme cases. Consider quite a different example. When a heavyweight boxing champion is paid millions of dollars to fight a challenger, most of this productive service price is economic rent. His second-best alternative activity would probably earn less than 1 percent of this amount. The rest—so far as inducing him to give up other activities in favor of being a prizefighter—is pure surplus and not required to get him into the ring. Technically, the term *quasi-rent* is used to refer to a factor temporarily fixed in supply.

Or, when the owner of the land at the corner of 57th Street and Fifth Avenue in New York City leases the land to a company as a site for an office building, virtually all of that income is economic rent. The second-best noncommercial activity for this might be to use it as a home or a private tennis court for the owner, and the income implicit in these activities is so small that we could say that all of the money income from the leasehold is economic rent.

Consider an example closer to home. When dedicated college professors teach classes in economics, the chances are that a portion of their salaries consists of economic rent. What other activity would give a person a chance to be an actor, a creator of ideas, a teacher of values, a manager of his or her own time, and all within the compass of an academic year? If dedicated professors would take a 50 percent cut in pay before they would seek a nonacademic job, then it might be said that half of their money income is economic rent.

You might be tempted to ask, Why should society pay resource owners more than is necessary to get them to provide the productive service flowing from that resource? Why, for example, should the owner of the urban land be paid for the use of it? Why should economics professors be paid more than is necessary to get them to teach? In short, what role does economic rent as a portion of productive service price play in the functioning of a price-directed economy? There are a number of answers to this question.

COMMENTARY

Here is an article written by a newspaper sports editor. He deals with the determination of salaries. After reading it, consider the following.

a) Where does economic rent enter an analysis of this article?

b) Do you see any contradictions in the editor's argument?

c) How would you deal with the issue he is confronting?

JUST HOW MUCH IS TALENT WORTH?

The Secretary of Labor recently told the United Auto Workers that negotiating big pay increases into long-term labor contracts could spell economic suicide for the nation.

Let's kick that astute statement around a bit. In fact, let's kick that right into the sports field, starting with the question:

Just how much is the ability to accurately and consistently hit a baseball, throw a football, or hit 20-foot jump shots really worth? . . .

The President of the United States, be he Republican or Democrat, gets an annual (taxable) salary of $200,000. He also gets annually $50,000 (taxable) for expenses and an additional $40,000 (nontaxable) for travel and entertainment.

Based upon performance and responsibility, can we honestly say that the country's greatest sports figures should be paid as much as the President?

If so, somewhere along the line we have lost our sense of values.

Sure, many persons (me included) would rather watch a quarterback complete a bomb to a receiver than watch the President at a news conference, unless it is to announce a tax cut or end of a war. . . .

But can we *honestly say that our greatest athletes are worth as much as they are being paid?* Many of them work only eight or nine months a year at their trade, and maybe some of them will work only five or six years. But the big-moneyed ones, with some exceptions, are making more on their name outside the sport with investments, endorsements, and in business, than they are making for participating on the field, ice, or floor. Some have gone broke with such outside interests,

but many are making extra thousands. . . .

The great ones draw promoters, advisers, and consultants like gnats around a pickle jar. With these guys pushing for their 15 percent, the price goes higher when contract talks begin. And, like I've said before, it's the sports fan who pays. . . .

I don't advocate that athletes should play for peanuts, but I do feel that as a *nation we have misplaced our sense of values.* . . .

I don't blame the player for getting all he can get, but I do blame the society and system that gives an athlete far more than he is worth, then socks the paying public to make it possible to overcompensate him. . . .

I don't see an end to astronomical salaries, nor do the owners, or players, as long as the crowds keep jamming the stands. But, I still say many of our values are misdirected.

P.T. Barnum had the idea: "There's a sucker born every minute." Is the sucker the paying public or the TV network that makes such high salaries possible with their enormous rights fees?

Bruce Ramey, Sports Editor of Sports Forum. *Lafayette Journal and Courier,* Friday evening, April 24, 1970. Reprinted by permission.

Economic rent is a rationing device.

In the first place, economic rent serves as a rationing device. When there are many competing uses for the corner of 57th Street and Fifth Avenue, some device must be used to decide who will get to use the land. That use that generates the largest income after all other expenses are met will enable the potential renter to outbid the other renters.

If that portion of a productive service price consisting of economic rent were made illegal, and all resource owners could be paid only what is necessary to get them to supply the resource, then some other system would have to be invented to determine the best use of that particular resource.

Suppose that in place of using prices, a system of random numbers were used to allocate the use of scarce resources. Consider the effects:

1. Fifth Avenue in New York City would be a hodgepodge of mom and pop stores, hardware stores, residences, department stores,

and the like—depending on who drew a given random number.

2. College professors whose incomes consisted partly of economic rent would have to be assigned to universities on a random number basis.

3. Effective managers of industrial activities would be divided among large and small businesses on a purely random basis.

If neither price nor random number scheme were used, then some form of central planning would be necessary in order to allocate these scarce resources. A number of people would be required to run the central planning agency, and a different set of goals might be employed to allocate the economy's scarce resources.

Economic rent: a device for telling producers which production technology to use.

In the second place, the economic rent portion of productive service prices is a device for telling the users of these services to adopt technologies that will use these services sparingly. Thus, land in the high-rent areas in cities typically has tall buildings on it. Similarly, high-priced managers are used to manage large operations.

Economic rent flows through to prices of final products and thus causes households to use resource-scarce products sparingly.

In the third place, the prices of final goods and services include economic rent as a part of their costs. Thus, when natural gas is scarce, and the economic rent return on gas wells is high, petrochemicals tend to be high in price. As a consequence, households as buyers of products limit their purchases of petrochemical products. In other words, the rationing effect "flows through" to the purchasers of the final products.

Suppose a law were passed making it mandatory that all products be sold at cost, excluding economic rent as a cost of production. Thus, gasoline prices could not include royalties to the owners of oil wells—whether they be private individuals or oil companies. Then gasoline prices would be too low to ration gasoline among competing users, and some other device, such as rationing stamps, would have to be used to prevent shortages of gasoline from appearing.

The economic rent portion of productive service prices is thus an important ingredient of a price system. But economic rent—defined, as it is, as a surplus—is considered by many social critics as an immoral device for distributing income. It is at this point that the social goals of efficiency and equality diverge. If economic rent were eliminated, something would have to be put in its place.

Mini-case 6.3 is provided to help you clafiry the concept of economic rent.

MINI-CASE 6.3

Which of the following statements best represents the economic rent portion of a productive service price?

a) I love to play tennis, but I have turned down an offer to play professionally because it won't pay me enough to make it worth my while to leave medical school.
b) I love to play tennis and the club owner pays me just enough as a tennis pro to keep me from going into some other line of work.
c) I love to play tennis, but the amount of travel involved in playing professionally as well as the exhausting schedule simply will take too much out of me. I don't want to risk my future health by "wearing myself out" in just a few years.
d) I love tennis and I'm going to play professionally as long as I can regardless of what my other opportunities are. There will still be time left to do other "dull" things after I'm too old to play tennis professionally.

PROFITS

The profit rate can be defined as the ratio of reported profits to stockholders' equity.

In addition to wage rates, interest rates, and rental rates, there is a fourth price which we shall discuss briefly. This is the profit rate. In some developing countries, it is quite common for stockholders to earn a 25 to 30 percent return on their investment in corporations. In other developed countries, such as the United States, it is unusual for corporations to earn more than a 20 percent return on their capital. What determines this profit rate? There are a number of ways in which the profit rate is defined. Here is a common definition.

The *profit rate* is reported profits (sales minus expenses) divided by the amount of capital, called equity, that the stockholders or the owners of a business have contributed to the business.

These contributions include the dollars the stockholders have paid the corporation when they purchased stock and the firm's accumulated profits that were not distributed in dividends. Defined in this way, the median profit rate for the largest five hundred manufacturing corporations in the United States in 1976 was 13.3 percent.

Profit as commonly defined really includes interest, rent, and a return to the stockholders of a corporation.

You will recall from our discussion of profits in Chapter 4 that the term profits as it is usually used in everyday speech most frequently refers to accounting profits. In accounting terminology, profit is a measure of the increase in wealth resulting from the operation of an enterprise. *Gross profit* indicates the difference between the selling price and the cost of materials and *net profit* is determined by deducting the selling and operating expenses from gross profit. It may include interest and other elements of opportunity cost.

Consider interest. In 1977 the interest rate on high-grade corporate bonds was about 8 percent. Had the corporations not obtained the capital from stockholders they would have had to borrow it and pay at least the going rate of return on corporate bonds. Therefore, this portion of the reported profits is not really profits. It is a cost of capital.

Another unspecified portion of reported profits consists of quasi-rents. You will recall that economic rent is a payment to the owners of a resource that is in fixed supply because of limitations of nature.

In a changing, growing economy, some entrepreneurs are fortunate or far-sighted enough to be in the right place at the right time. Suppose that there is a large increase in the demand for paper. The owners of paper mills will find that they can rent their paper-making facilities to others for more than it would cost to replace them. Why? It takes three to four years to design and build a paper factory. When the price of paper rises, the owners of paper-making facilities can temporarily charge more for the use of their facilities than they could in the long run—after additional paper factories have been built. This extra return for being at the right place at the right time is sometimes called *quasi-rent,* meaning a payment very similar to economic rent.

You may ask why, since quasi-rent seems to be a pure surplus, it couldn't be taken away from corporations in some type of excess profits or windfall tax. The answer to this question is that the quasi-rent portion of the profit rate is the inducement that attracts other businesses into an industry where prices are higher than opportunity costs. It is a surplus, but it does have a function in a competitive, price-directed economy.

When there are artificial restraints on entry, as we find in our discussion of monopoly power in the next chapter, then the quasi-rents are not temporary. They represent a return to the owners of the monopoly, and the return they get is called *monopoly rents.* But this gets us ahead of our story.

There is a third type of return to stockholders that is neither interest nor rent. *It is a payment for bearing the uncertainties and risks of the future.* You will recall that we discussed the necessity of risk-bearing in Chapter 4. We pointed out that when a business invests funds in new factories, it usually takes twenty to thirty years to get the funds out of them. During this period, many things can happen. New technologies may make paper-making factories obsolete. New products may replace old ones. New social institutions may reduce the net profitability of privately made investments in plant and equipment.

Suppose, in this connection, that you had invested funds in the transportation industries over the last 150 years. Your investment in pony express would have lasted only a few years. Your investment in the network of canals that carried the bulk of freight during the first two-thirds of the nineteenth century would have been lost because of competition from the railroads. And finally, if you had invested in the railroads in the northeast portion of the United States, you would also have lost your investment because of competition from trucks and airlines. It is not given to normal human beings to foresee the future.

We turn now to the pricing of this third component of the profit rate—the return to stockholders for bearing the risks that losses may occur in the future. Many people are unwilling to bear risks. To them a "bird in the hand is indeed worth two in the bush." If all persons were unwilling to bear risks, then it would be impossible to develop new industries or to commit large amounts of capital to an economy in which the winds of change were blowing gustily. Yet we know that some people are willing to trade a "bird in the hand for two in the bush." We shall call this willingness to trade the certainty of money in hand for an uncertain future gain, *uncertainty bearing*.

Economic profit on the net return to uncertainty bearing can be a positive or negative value, depending on how willing people are to gamble on the future.

During the California Gold Rush of 1848, the economic profit from gold mining was probably a negative figure. The value of the resources devoted to gold mining probably exceeded the value of the gold recovered. People were so willing to gamble on the future, with the hope that they would strike it rich, that in the end the average miner had to accept negative economic profits as his return for gambling on the future.

In contrast, during periods when people are profoundly discouraged about the future of the economy, such as during the Great Depression, the economic profit rate must be positive in order to induce people to commit their funds to the uncertainties of the future.

In the real world, productive service prices appear in complex combinations.

We have now completed our discussion of the four types of productive service prices that play important roles in determining how the nation's income will be distributed. We should alert you to the fact that the prices you see in the market-

place are usually combinations of these four prices.

Suppose, in this connection, that after getting undergraduate degrees in biology and engineering, you go on to law school and then specialize in patent law. And suppose that you become one of the nation's experts in patent law as it applies to microbiology. Your fees after subtracting your office costs amount to $50,000 a year. Does this total consist of wages? Is it interest? Is it economic rent? Or finally, could you call it profit? The answer is that the service you are selling is a combination of all four types of productive services we have been discussing.

You are putting in time and effort, and part of what you are getting will be small payment for your labor. You are also receiving interest on the investment you made in your education, a return on your human capital. In view of your unique preparation in biology, engineering, and law, you will be one of the few persons qualified to practice patent law in the microbiology area. This, together with your legal experience, will give you an element of uniqueness; as a result, part of your income will be economic rent. Finally, you have gambled heavily on the long-run importance of microbiology patent law. Part of what you get will be a payment for the risks you have taken. You have no guarantee that your field of specialization will continue to be important.

Thus, if you were thinking about your income in the future, you would have to think about what is likely to happen to these four sets of prices. You might argue that the wage component should rise with the general level of wages. You could also argue that the interest component of your income would rise or fall with the long-term rate of interest. The rent of your unique abilities would depend on what happened to the demand for lawyers in the microbiology area. Finally, if there are many people who are willing to bear the unusual risks of committing themselves to your field of patent law, the profit component of your income will fall. You are a supplier of a complex combination of productive services and your income will vary with what is happening to the various markets that govern the pricing of your services.

REVIEW QUESTIONS

1. Based on the information below and the fact that the price of labor is $35 per day, how many workers per day should a manufacturer purchase?

	Units of labor input	Marginal produce/day	Product price	
a) 6	1	8	$4	32
b) 5	2	11	4	44
c) 4	3	13	4	52
d) 3	4	15	4	60
	5	14	4	56
	6	8	4	32
	7	5	4	20

2. If the Law of Equal Advantage is assumed to be working in the economy, then:

a) wage rates must be equalized dollar for dollar for all industries.
b) anyone who is willing to work can find a job.
c) people may choose to work in occupations which have relatively low wage rates because there are nonpecuniary advantages involved.
d) any monopolies in the labor market will be declared illegal.

3. Because of the widespread availability of education, people now tend to avoid "servant-type" jobs. On the basis of this fact, you would expect that:

a) relative prices of services would rise.
b) the relative prices of services would stay the same.
c) the relative prices of services would fall.
d) It is impossible to say.

4. Suppose a wage-price freeze was announced that would keep wage rates for skilled workers below their equilibrium level. Which of the following results would you expect?

a) There would be an increase in the number of skilled workers.
b) Skilled workers would be wasted since many firms could afford to use skilled workers for lower-skilled jobs.
c) Skilled workers would be in such short supply that there would be shortages of products produced by skilled workers.
d) Unskilled workers would be laid off.

5. Suppose, all other things remaining equal, that a new minimum wage law is passed that makes it mandatory to pay $5 per hour for all types of labor. You would expect that:

a) there would be a reduction in the quantity of highly paid skilled labor that would be demanded.
b) there would be a reduction in the demand for capital to replace labor.
c) there would be a reduction in the quantity demanded for unskilled labor.
d) there would be no change in the quantity of labor demanded; labor is an essential in the production process and nothing can change the quantity of labor used per unit of output.

6. The competitive rate of interest on consumer loans is 9 percent. The government passes a law making it illegal to charge more than 6 percent. You would expect that:

   a) if lenders obeyed the law, there would be no problem.
   b) if lenders obeyed the law, poor people with doubtful credit ratings could not get credit.
   c) if lenders obeyed the law, prices would ration access to credit.
   d) the number of people who would want to borrow would fall.

7. When the interest rate rises, this automatically:

   a) increases the present value of long-term projects.
   b) decreases the present value of long-term projects.
   c) causes businesses to allocate their capital to long-term projects rather than short-term projects.
   d) increases the price of common stock, since the interest rate is used to discount future dividends.

8. Suppose the price of energy rises substantially. As a result, many energy companies find it profitable to invest in the discovery and development of new energy sources. But it turns out that energy is a very capital-intensive product, so:

   a) the rate of interest will tend to fall because of the resulting depression.
   b) the rate of interest will tend to rise because of the increase in the demand for capital.
   c) the rate of interest will not be affected by the energy shortage since the economy will make a full adjustment to the new set of scarcities.
   d) the rate of interest will fall because the energy shortage will generate additional savings.

9. When the New York Housing Authority sets a maximum price for rent below the equilibrium price for rent what will occur?

   a) A surplus of apartments to rent will result.
   b) Supply of housing facilities is expected to increase.
   c) Quantity demanded of housing will increase, creating a shortage.
   d) The demand for apartments will increase, creating a shortage.

10. Economic rent refers to:

   a) the price Barbra Streisand must pay for her apartment.
   b) the wage Barbra Streisand receives above that amount necessary to keep her in show business.
   c) the opportunity cost Barbra Streisand must pay for being a superstar.
   d) the return on Barbra Streisand's investment in music school.

ESSAY QUESTIONS

1. Suppose that the marginal value product of lettuce workers is $2.50 an hour. Then suppose that a union wage settlement gives them $3.50 per hour. Over a four- or five-year period, what would you expect to happen?

2. At $3.50 per hour the employers realize that there are more workers applying for jobs than there are jobs. What measures would you expect employers to take in sorting through the people who were seeking work? What would these measures do to the "employability" of those who have minimal labor force skills?

3. Once the $3.50 wage has become widespread in the lettuce-growing industry, what would you do to prevent discrimination by race and national origin? Would you have the same problem if the wage rate were $2.50 an hour? What conclusions could you then draw about the relationship of high wage rates to discrimination?

4. Suppose a law is passed making it mandatory that all workers be paid the same wage rate regardless of the nature of the job or the training required for it. What types of labor would be in excess supply and what types of labor would be in short supply? How would you solve the problem of getting the labor to the places that need it?

5. Suppose that unpleasant labor were paid the same wage rate as pleasant labor and suppose that there weren't enough people willing to take the unpleasant jobs. How would you decide who should do these jobs?

6. Suppose that the colleges train too many people to program computers. And suppose, as a result, that computer programmers' wage rates are low. What will this do to prices of products that are produced with the assistance of the computer, compared to prices of products made without using computers? Would you say that the government should take action against the cheap, computer-made products?

7. Interest rates ration loanable funds among competing demanders. Suppose that those who would build new gambling establishments in Las Vegas can pay higher rates of interest than those who would build new homes for poor people. Doesn't this mean that there is something wrong with the system?

8. Suppose you decided to ration loanable funds in the capital market. What criteria would you use to decide what were the most important uses for the nation's capital? Would these criteria represent what you think is best for people? Or, would they represent what the people think is best for themselves?

9. Suppose that because you thought an education was important, you made loanable funds available to colleges and universities at an annual 2 percent rate. What would this do to the way the colleges and universities would use their capital funds in constructing buildings and other equipment?

10. Suppose that because of the energy shortage, you would decide to subsidize the interest rates paid by public utilities by requiring that the government pay any interest in excess of 4 percent. How would this change the way public utilities would design capital equipment? If this low capital charge were to "flow through" to the purchasers of electricity in the form of lower electric rates, what would this do to the demands for capital funds by public utilities?

11. Suppose that you decided to eliminate land rents by passing a law stating that it was illegal to buy or sell land or to rent land. Suppose, too, that you were able to enforce it. What would this law do to the productivity of agriculture?

12. Land rents are very high in Hawaii. Suppose that in an effort to reduce the cost of living in Honolulu, you passed legislation making it illegal to charge more than $50 per acre for the use of land. You justify this because most of the land is owned by a few families who are the descendants

of missionaries who originally came to Hawaii to do good and ended up by doing well. What would this law do to the functioning of the Hawaiian economy?

13. It is generally agreed that profits are very high in illegal activities, such as prostitution, producing and selling illegal drugs, and in the juice rackets where money is lent at usurious rates of interest. Why is this?

14. Would the price of these illegal products be lower if the activities were made legal?

15. What would happen to the quality of the products sold if these illegal activities were made legal?

16. If the profits and prices of illegal activites were lower, what would happen to the quantities of these products that would be purchased? Given all this, where do you stand? Would you make these activities legal?

ANSWERS TO REVIEW QUESTIONS

1. To answer this question you should first calculate a table showing the value of the marginal product at each input level. It should look like the following:

Unit of input	VMP
1st	$32
2nd	44
3rd	52
4th	60
5th	56
6th	32
7th	20

Based on this table, the employer should hire 5 workers. If the 6th worker is hired, costs will rise by $35 and revenues increase by only $32, generating a net loss of $3. If only 4 workers are hired, adding a 5th will generate $56 in revenues and only cost $35, a net gain of $21. Hence the answer must be (b), that is, hire five workers.

2. The Law of Equal Advantage is:

"If the owners of any resources think these can be put to better advantage in some other use than the one in which they are employed, the resources will be transferred from the less advantageous to the more advantageous use. . . . As long, therefore, as there are people who believe that the resources they own, whether these be their own bodies or some other object, will yield them a greater advantage in an occupation different from that in which they are at present employed, then resources will be transferred from one occupation to another."

a) This is incorrect. The law does not say anything about equality of money wage rates.
b) This is incorrect. The law does not say anything about job opportunities.
c) This is correct. The law simply states people will work at that occupation that, all things considered, will yield them the greatest advantage. More is involved than money wage rates.
d) This is incorrect. This response is irrelevant.

3. In the market for "servant-type" jobs, supply has decreased. This will cause the price or wage to rise.

   a) This is correct. The decrease in the supply of servants will cause the price to rise, other things unchanged.

   b) This is incorrect. As noted in (a), the price will rise.

   c) This is incorrect. A decrease in supply will increase, not decrease, price.

   d) This is incorrect. We do know that the price will rise.

4. If wage rates for skilled workers are kept below the equilibrium rate, there will be a shortage of skilled workers—the quantity demanded will exceed the quantity supplied.

   a) This is incorrect. There will be a reduction in the quantity of skilled workers supplied.

   b) This is incorrect. If anything, skilled workers will be used only for skilled jobs since there is a shortage of them.

   c) This is true. The shortage of skilled workers will be transmitted through the economy and emerge as a shortage of the commodities they produce.

   d) This is incorrect. If anything, there may be a greater demand for unskilled workers to do the jobs some skilled workers formerly did.

5. The labor market consists of many submarkets. A wage of $5 an hour is likely to be above the equilibrium wage for unskilled workers and below the equilibrium wage of skilled workers.

   a) This is incorrect. This submarket would probably not be affected much.

   b) This is incorrect. At the new $5-an-hour wage, many unskilled workers will probably be replaced by machines. Hence, there will be a reduction in the quantity demanded of unskilled labor but an increase in demand for capital equipment.

   c) This is correct. The increased price of unskilled labor will reduce the quantity demanded.

   d) This is incorrect. See explanations (b) and (c).

6. A law forcing the interest rate down to 6 percent will cause a shortage of loanable funds since at 6 percent the quantity demanded will exceed the quantity supplied.

   a) This is incorrect. There is a shortage of funds and since price is no longer being used, a new allocating mechanism is necessary.

   b) This is correct. Certain people will be rationed out of the market and the "high-risk" borrower will be one of the first.

   c) This is incorrect. Prices will no longer fulfill their rationing function.

   d) This is incorrect. The new lower legal rate will increase the quantity demanded.

7. A given amount, say $1000 invested for one year at 10 percent, will yield $100 in interest. If the interest rate were only 5 percent, the yield would be $50. Hence the higher the interest rate, the greater the value in the future. By the same token, however, the higher the interest rate, the lower the *present value*.

   a) This is incorrect. A rise in interest rate would *lower* the present value.

   b) This is correct as explained above.

   c) This is incorrect. We really can't say much about this answer without more information. We said nothing about a differential in long- and short-term interest rates.

   d) This is incorrect. It will lower the price, since the present value falls as the interest rates rises.

8. The demand for loanable funds will increase and other things being equal, interest rates will rise.

   a) This is incorrect. Interest rates will rise, not fall.
   b) This is correct as explained above.
   c) This is incorrect. The interest rate will respond to the increased demand.
   d) This is incorrect. Interest rates will rise, not fall.

9. If the legal rent ceiling is below the equilibrium rate, quantity demanded will exceed quantity supplied and a shortage will emerge.

   a) This is incorrect A shortage, not a surplus, will occur.
   b) This is incorrect. At the lower rent, the quantity supplied will fall and there is no reason to expect the supply to increase.
   c) This is correct as explained above.
   d) This is incorrect. Quantity demanded, not demand, will increase.

10. Economic rent is defined as that portion of a productive service payment above the amount necessary to induce a supplier to provide the service.

   a) This is incorrect. This confuses rent with economic rent.
   b) This is correct as explained above.
   c) This is incorrect. The opportunity cost is whatever she is forgoing by being a superstar.
   d) This is incorrect. Economic rent is defined above.

PART III

THE MIXED ECONOMY AND ITS PROBLEMS

OBJECTIVES

Upon successful completion of this chapter, you will be able to:

1. Identify the bases for government's role in the economy

2. Demonstrate, using the circular-flow model, how government fits into the mixed-market economy.

3. Explain how taxation and borrowing modify the mix of goods and services produced and consumed.

4. Explain the criteria for designing a tax system.

5. Explain the difficulties involved in determining the incidence of a tax.

6. Use supply and demand analysis to illustrate the incidence of a per unit tax under specified conditions.

7. Analyze the major taxes in terms of the incidence of taxes under given conditions.

8. Identify transfer payments that appear in the form of "tax deductions."

9. Define a tax in terms of progressiveness, regressiveness, and proportionality.

10. Identify the conflict that occurs between majority and minority choices when governmental decisions are made.

11. Explain how a mixed-market economy answers the basic economic questions.

CHAPTER 7

GOVERNMENT AND THE MIXED MARKET ECONOMY

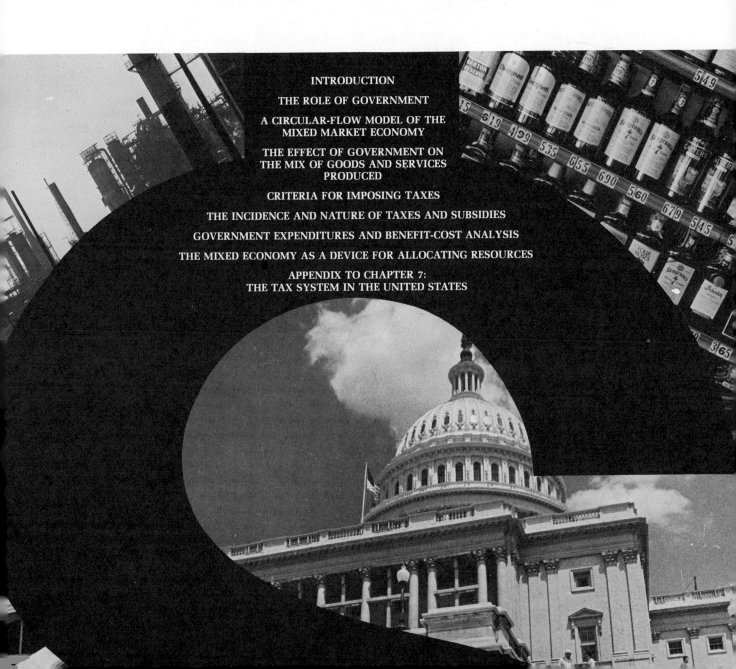

INTRODUCTION

As you look around in your day-to-day activities, you see stores, buildings, establishments, and institutions that are privately owned; among them are supermarkets, car rental agencies, dentists' offices, gas stations, and so on. But intermingled among these privately owned establishments you also see post offices, social security offices, public schools, state universities, federal and state parks, city halls, and many other government institutions that are publicly owned and operated. How do these institutions fit into a market-directed economy?

If you work, examine your check next payday and you will see that a substantial amount has been deducted for payment of social security and income taxes. Although no one likes to pay taxes, we have come to regard them as a necessary facet of the work-a-day world.

Whenever you step into your car and move from your driveway onto the city streets and highways, you expect them to be there and in reasonably good repair. These streets are available for anyone to use. No toll is charged.

When you were younger, it is quite likely that your parents enrolled you in the local public school system. They did not have to pay an explicit tuition fee. It is also very likely that your grandparents are receiving monthly pension checks from the social security administration.

These are just a few reminders of the fact that you do not live in a pure exchange economy of the type we have been describing in the last six chapters. The government takes a substantial part of your income and provides you with a large number of services.

From an examination of the economy as a whole, it is clear that virtually every transaction in the private sector is influenced by the government. We shall use the term *government* to include units at all levels: federal, state, and local. Some idea of the role of government is conveyed by the following facts: (1) there are almost 78,000 governmental units in the United States, (2) the government purchases over 20 percent of the total output of goods and services of the United States; and (3) directly and indirectly, through expenditures and transfer payments, the government redistributes 37 percent of the income generated by production.*

The government directly regulates the prices of public utilities, trucking services, railway and waterway services, milk, oil, gasoline, and many farm products. These price-controlled areas account for a substantial portion of the goods and services purchased in our country. In addition to direct price regulation, the government has a major impact on the rest of the economy's output through such regulatory agencies as the Environmental Protection Agency (EPA), the Federal Trade Commission, the agency authorized to implement the Occupational Health and Safety Act (OSHA) and many others. It is simply incorrect to say that the United States economy is a purely market-directed economy.

The United States economy, like those in Western Europe, is a *mixed economy*. That is, it is an economy based partly on private ownership and free exchange and partly on government regulation and involvement.

In this chapter we will be concerned with the role of government, citing those specific areas in which most persons agree that governmental activity is not only appropriate but necessary. Then we will discuss how the government fits in the flow of economic transactions using the circular-flow model. The effect of government on the mix of goods and services will be considered next, followed by an analysis of the criteria, incidence, and nature of taxes and subsidies. The problems the government faces in selecting projects to undertake will then be examined, and the chapter is concluded with a discussion of the mixed economy as a device for allocating resources. A brief appendix highlights the tax system of the United States.

---

* In 1976, for example, GNP was $1706.5 billion and government *purchases* of goods and services at all levels was $361.4 billion, or 21 percent. Total *expenditures* by governments at all levels was $633.9 billion, or 37 percent.

THE ROLE OF GOVERNMENT

The government provides the legal foundations for economic transactions.

In a democracy, the government is a means whereby citizens can act collectively. If you and others want more police officers to protect you for example, you express your demands to your elected city or county officials, who can then ask the appropriate governmental agency to hire the police officer. The alternative to hire your own night watchmen or bodyguards to protect you—is not feasible for most of us. As a first step in understanding the role of government in our economy, then, it is useful to view it as an entity that we use to register our collective, in contrast to individual, demands for goods and services.

What should be purchased collectively? This is a difficult question to answer because it involves ethical as well as economic considerations. We shall, however, list some considerations that you would take into account in deciding what should be acquired through the government and what should be acquired through direct purchase in the marketplace. These considerations deal with property rights, collective goods, natural monopolies, high-risk ventures, and economic security.

It is basic to realize that a market-oriented economy could not exist unless there were a government to define the property rights of individuals and corporations and to enforce the contracts individuals and corporations make. In other words, a market-directed economy could easily bear the label "made by government."

In our political and economic systems, the ownership of property—whether it is a plot of land or a share of stock—entails the possession of certain rights *with respect to other individuals.* If the land is a corner lot in a city, the owner can keep other people from using it. Depending on the zoning restrictions, the owner can put a tennis court on it for his or her own use but cannot use it as a place to dump garbage or construct a high-rise apartment. The specific bundle of "human rights"—that is, permissible behavior with respect to other people—is defined by law and therefore regulated by government. The point is that *no* market-directed economy can exist in a vacuum. It depends on the body of laws that defines the rights you buy and sell when you enter the marketplace, whether you are selling baby carriages, land, or shares of stock.

The laws establishing the enforceability of contracts are also necessary if a market-directed economy is going to exist.

If an employer tells you that you will be paid $4 an hour and you find yourself unable to collect the $160 at the end of a 40-hour week, you not only will be reluctant to work for an employer in the future, but will most likely seek recourse through the courts. Or if you lend money to a corporation that pledges a piece of land as security for your loan and that corporation is unable to pay you back as specified in the contract, some entity—in this case the government—must be in a position to transfer the land to you. Without a government that can enforce contracts, you will not be able to engage efficiently in personal market transactions with others, and businesses will not be able to produce goods and services efficiently.

As noted in Chapter 4, the bundle of rights and duties associated with the ownership of property is constantly changing. At one time in United States history, if you owned a stretch of riverfront, you could freely dump whatever you wanted into it. Now, of course, you cannot. What is important for the operation of a market-directed economy is that these rights and duties be fairly secure and predictable, not that they be forever immutable. When these rights and duties change unpredictably, people are reluctant to engage in trade, and a market-directed economy cannot function well.

Now that we have considered how government provides the environment for a market-directed economy, we will discuss those areas of economic activity that most people agree are the appropriate domain of government. First, however, we will examine means by which most people are directly affected by government.

Taxes, subsidies, and transfer payments are vehicles of government interaction with the rest of the economy.

The changes created by introducing government into a market economy are felt by the individual most directly through the effects of taxes, subsidies, and transfer payments. Since they are so important to an understanding of a mixed market economy, we will define each of these terms.

A *tax* is a payment imposed by a government. This levy may be made in payment for a service provided, but usually the conditions for tax collection do not require that a service first be performed.

There are many kinds of taxes, but two broad categories are revenue taxes and sumptuary taxes. *Revenue taxes* are designed to raise revenue to finance government operations, for example, personal income tax. *Sumptuary taxes* are imposed to control consumption, for example, alcoholic beverage taxes. Most taxes have both revenue and sumptuary elements, however.

A *subsidy* is the governmental provision of economic assistance to the private sector producers or consumers of a particular good, service, or productive input. In some respects a subsidy is a negative tax. The government receives no equivalent compensation in return for the subsidy, but the recipient must meet certain conditions for assistance. The effect of a subsidy is to alter the price of certain goods or services and thereby change its output, supply, or use.

A *transfer payment* is any income flow that represents a change in the distribution of income but not a compensation for a current contribution to production. There are both government and private transfer payments. Social security benefits and veterans' pensions are important government transfer payments, while bad debt writeoffs, charitable contributions, and contest prizes represent private transfer payments.

Governments supply collective or public goods.

Many of the activities you engage in as an individual have effects that only you and perhaps your family are aware of. When you buy a new TV set, for example, you and your family are the primary beneficiaries. You pay the bill and you reap the benefits. But there are other activities that you engage in that may affect others. if you own a motorcycle with a muffler system that doesn't muffle, the thrill you receive as you rev up the motor and rapidly accelerate may be viewed as a curse by your more placid neighbors.

The point we are making is much broader than these personal examples, however. All goods, services, and factors of production can be viewed in terms of what is called the *exclusion principle*. A good, service, or factor of production that meets the exclusion principle is one in which only the buyer receives the benefits and bears the costs of the transaction—others are excluded. If a good does not conform to the *exclusion principle* such as the use of your motorcycle, then we say it has spillover, or third-party effects. You receive the benefits of riding your motorcycle but your neighbors bear some of the "costs."

Now, *public* or *collective goods* are those goods that by their nature are not subject to the exclusion principle. Their spillover effects are so great that they must be dealt with in a special way. *Public goods* have several characteristics— their effects are indivisible and so broadly distributed that certain individuals who do not want them cannot be isolated from them without incurring great expense, and indeed, in some cases cannot be isolated at all. By the same token, public goods cannot be provided efficiently on a volunteer basis.

If public goods were sold in the marketplace, the buyers would receive benefits. But persons who did not buy the goods would also receive benefits—in a sense, those who also received benefits would be said to be "free loaders" because they are getting benefits without paying for them. When the costs of identifying "free loaders" and charging them for the benefits they are receiving is so high as to make it infeasible to do so, then the market system by itself will not lead to the production of an optimum quantity of public goods.

There are many examples of goods whose services are not easily divisible, and where the costs of forming voluntary groups to supply them are high. These costs, called *transaction costs*, are the costs of getting people together to conclude a transaction. National defense is one of the best examples. Federal government funds for national defense pay for military services that are for all practical purposes indivisible and available to everybody. A private organization could conceivably supply these services and charge everybody according to the amount of "protection" each person felt he or she was getting, but this would involve constantly interviewing people—or possibly working out some new technology for peering into peoples' minds. In either case, the cost of collecting from wouldbe free riders would be too high. National defense, then, is a collective good. The only way we can get the appropriate amount of it is to have the government produce or purchase it and levy taxes to pay for it.

Other common examples of collective goods are police protection and a court system. Police protection presumably provides all citizens with protection from violence, and yet there is no inexpensive way to sell the benefits of domestic peace to those who benefit. We all benefit from a court system, and yet it would be difficult to sell the benefits that flow from the fair resolution of domestic conflicts on an individual basis. A complete listing of all of these collective goods is impossible. Were it not for government, however, the supply of these types of goods and services would be inadequate.

There is no distinct line separating collective goods and those that have some but not all, of the characteristics of collective goods. An example of a quasi-collective service is education. Not only do the persons who receive the education benefit, but third parties also benefit. Both the purchasers of educational services and third parties are able to live in a society where people can communicate with each other more effectively, thus creating an environment in which all of us are clearly better off. How should these third parties pay for the benefits they are receiving if the business of education were entirely left to the market system? Conceivably, as in the case of public television, some means could be found to encourage them to make a voluntary payment for the benefits they are receiving, but the transaction costs of doing so are high.

Public roads are another example of a quasi-collective good. In this case, the service from the good is divisible; the persons who receive the benefits can be identified. Automobile owners use the streets and highways, but the transaction costs of having toll stations along every city block or every exit ramp would be too high. It is more efficient to have the government levy a fuel tax and in this way charge for the use of the publicly provided streets and highways.

As noted above, in addition to quasi-collective goods that *benefit* third parties; there are also products that produce *damages*. Automobile-caused pollution is an example. Persons who buy the gasoline for their automobiles receive the benefits of transportation along a highway. At the same time, however, their automobiles emit pollutants that impair the health and environment of others. Just as the government can logically be involved in supplementing the availability of education, so too can it be involved in restricting the production of those products that involve damages to third parties. We will deal with such issues in Chapter 9, which discusses pollution and other third-party effects at some length.

Government is also involved in regulating and supplying products produced by natural monopolies.

The markets for some products are simply too small to allow many producers to use the most efficient scale of production. If, for example, there were three producers of electric power in a given city, no single producer could use the most efficient technology. In an effort to achieve the share of the market that would enable a producer to use the most efficient scale of production, a producer would be likely to reduce the price until the other producers were driven out of the business, leaving one producer. This kind of situation is labeled a *natural monopoly*.

It is widely recognized that there are natural monopolies in some areas of transportation, communication, and electric power generation and that, as a result, governments grant monopoly franchises to firms, such as public utilities, and in turn regulate their prices. Or, as in the case of European railroads and electric power utilities, governments may own and operate these natural monopolies themselves.

Governments subsidize high-risk ventures where private capital hesitates to make commitments.

All investment expenditures involve risk. The owners of a business are never absolutely sure when they build a factory or power generator whether the technology or price of fuels will change so radically that the installation will be obsolete. Nonetheless, businesses do build new facilities and in doing so depend on a return large enough to cover the cost of their capital and the risks they incur.

There are, however, some kinds of risks that are so unpredictable that it is impossible to establish a reasonable risk premium to be added to the cost of capital.

Consider the following examples. No public utility has yet demonstrated that a breeder reactor will work in the generation of electric power. The cost of an experimental facility is in excess of $1 billion—a figure so high that an individual utility company could easily face bankruptcy if it failed to make a breeder reactor work. In cases such as this, it can be argued that the government, because it can spread the risk of failure over all of the taxpayers, should build or subsidize a demonstration breeder reactor.

The extraction of oil from oil shale is an unproven process, but one that at present appears to be expensive given the alternatives. If oil were to sell for $17 to $23 dollars a barrel, however, the extraction of oil from shale could become economically feasible. The future price of oil, then, introduces a major uncertainty—and partly because the domestic price of oil is determined by government regulations. Consequently, it can be argued that these price uncertainties are simply too great to justify a major commitment of capital by a privately owned company to the extraction and sale of oil from shale. And again, it can also be argued that the government should play a role by guaranteeing a high enough price for oil from shale that a private company would be justified in making a major investment in shale oil technology.

The same type of reasoning can be used to justify the government's support of basic research. Knowledge about how the physical universe functions is available to everybody and it is therefore unlikely that private organizations will finance it since they cannot capture the returns on such investments. While the return for such an investment is not favorable for a private company, it may be very favorable for society as a whole com-

bined. In a sense, then, the fruits of basic research may be said to be a collective good.

Governments provide security for their citizens against event-caused losses of income.

During the decade from 1965 to 1975, government expenditures for social welfare programs increased from $77 billion to $287 billion (from $104 billion to $226 billion in dollars adjusted for inflation using 1972 as the base year). In a sense, this protection against loss of income due to adverse events is a collective good that voters have asked their government to provide for them. Table 7.1 shows how the major areas of social welfare expenditures have grown since 1929.

It is, of course, true that there are many private devices for achieving the protection against some event-caused losses of income. People can save for their old age—and there are many private pension funds. People can purchase their own health insurance and not depend on Medicare and Medicaid. People can put money in savings accounts to tide them over periods of unemployment. But only a small fraction of the population will use private devices to protect themselves against event-caused poverty. In the past, the extended family—where uncles, aunts, brothers, sisters, and grown children all lived in the same community—the church, and other private charities helped to protect those who did not protect themselves. However, with the demise of the extended family and the decline of the church as the center of the community's social life, these old bulwarks against insecurity have crumbled. Instead, people have delegated these protective activities to the government. One of the reasons for this may be that people prefer to live in an environment in which all the basic wants of society are being reasonably well met; in that sense, social insurance takes on a characteristic of a public good.

There are some who believe that these social insurance programs are really expressions of a widespread desire to equalize incomes, arguing that the rich have high incomes partly because of good luck and consequently they should pay higher taxes to help take care of the poor. They also argue that the poor have low incomes partly because of bad luck and deserve to have income

TABLE 7.1

SOCIAL WELFARE EXPENDITURES UNDER PUBLIC PROGRAMS BY GOVERNMENT AT ALL LEVELS IN SELECTED FISCAL YEARS IN BILLIONS OF DOLLARS

(In current dollars)

Year	1929	1950	1960	1965	1970	1975
Total expenditures	$3.9	$23.5	$52.3	$77.2	$145.8	$286.5
Social insurance	0.3	4.9	19.3	28.1	54.7	123.4
Public aid	0.1	2.5	4.1	6.3	16.5	40.5
Health and medical programs	0.4	2.1	4.5	6.2	9.8	16.6
Veterans' programs	0.7	6.9	5.5	6.0	9.1	16.7
Education	2.4	6.7	17.6	28.1	50.9	78.4
Housing	—	—	0.2	0.3	0.7	3.0
Other social welfare	0.1	0.4	1.1	2.1	4.1	7.9

Source: *Facts and Figures on Government Finance,* 19th Biennial Edition, (Washington, D.C.: Tax Foundation, Inc., 1977), Table 18, p. 31.

transferred to them. These people see the maintenance of a minimum income as a collective good that a wealthy society should undertake.

Whatever the reason (and it is not yet clear whether these are primarily social insurance programs or income equalization programs), it is clear that governments in the mixed economies of Western Europe and North America are committed to helping those who would otherwise be poor because of age, health, or unemployment.

Because of the importance of collective goods, governments have an important part to play in any market-directed economy.

A price-directed economy will not automatically produce the optimum quantity of collective goods. Depending on the criteria used, for example, an economy can have too many privately owned automobiles for the amount of publicly owned roads. It can be rich in housing and poor in sewers and police protection. In the United States we use political direction (voting by ballot) and market direction (voting with dollars) to secure the combination of private and collective goods we have. We turn now to the way the public economy (largely a command economy in which people respond to orders given by a government) and a market economy (in which people respond to the incentives created in the marketplace) interact to create a new type of economy, which we shall call the *mixed economy.*

A CIRCULAR-FLOW MODEL OF THE MIXED MARKET ECONOMY

You will recall that we used the circular-flow model in Chapter 1 to represent the way the three markets (products, productive services, and financial capital markets) and the two sets of decision makers (producers and consumers) interacted. This model showing the money flows is in Fig. 7.1. In the model of a market economy the answer to the basic economic questions of what will be produced, how, from whom, and for whom are determined by the interaction of the "purchase" decision of households (the demand for goods and services) on the one hand and the "activity" decisions of households (the supply of productive services) on the other.

As shown in Fig. 7.1, however, this model is an incomplete representation of the real economy in which you and I live. There is no place for the expression of collective demands for public

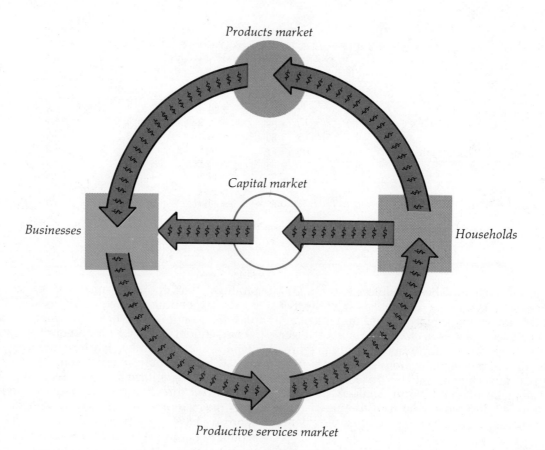

Products market

Capital market

Businesses

Households

Productive services market

FIG. 7.1   The circular-flow model showing money expenditure flows.

goods, except, of course, as people join together voluntarily to purchase goods and services. But you will remember that voluntarily joining together to buy collective goods entails the problem of what to do about free riders and the transaction costs of bringing them into the group.

To visualize how government, with its emphasis on collective goods, fits into an otherwise market-directed economy, examine Fig. 7.2. You will see that the circular-flow diagram has been modified to include government.

First, we have divided the households square into two boxes: one labeled "individual decisions" and the other labeled "collective decisions." The individual decision box represents the choices of families as described earlier, except

now the spending and saving decisions are based on after-tax incomes. The new collective decision box represents all of the decisions made by governmental officials, who determine how tax payments and monies loaned to the government will be spent. We will regard this box as reflecting the decisions of elected officials and their appointed assistants acting in their official capacity and not as members of families.

To be specific, let us suppose that you live in a small town. You, of course, determine the routine expenditures you make for bread, rent, gasoline, and so on. But part of your expenditures—the collective part—is delegated to the town council members. Where do the members of the town council obtain their resources? They obtain them

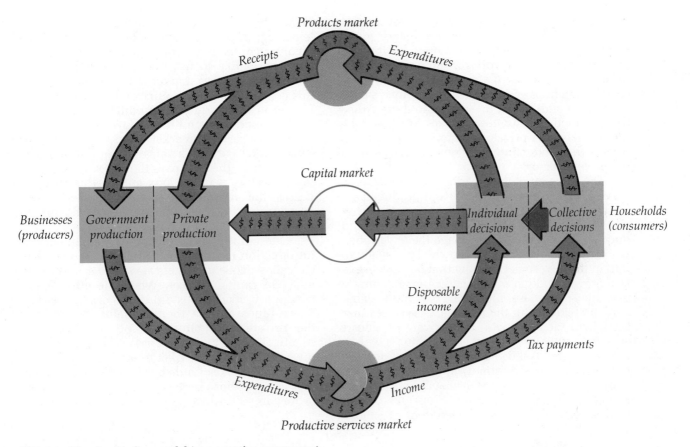

FIG. 7.2   The circular-flow model incorporating government.

by taxing your income and your property and by borrowing from you. The fork in the income stream running from the productive services market to the household squares indicates the division of income between disposable (after-tax) income and payments to governments at all levels.

With this division in mind, we can think more realistically of the collective decision box as containing not only town council member decisions but also the decisions of state legislators, governors, representatives, senators, and the president of the United States—the whole complex of persons who determine how public monies will be spent.

The expenditure streams flowing from the households boxes toward the products market

represent the individual expenditure decisions of households (for example, the purchase of food, clothes, appliances, and so on, from private producers) and the collective (governmental) expenditure decisions (for example, the purchase of sanitation services by the government from a privately owned firm). All of the individual decision expenditures and some of the collective decision expenditures flow to the products market. Part of the collective decision stream expenditures bypass the products market, however. This stream represents expenditures for services actually produced by government. Examples are educational services, police and fire protection, and judicial services. We will view these government production services as being created in the left-hand side of the producers square, labeled "government production." This side of the producers square represents the production activities of the millions of people who work for the government at all levels as well as the services of its physical capital, such as government buildings, roads, equipment, and parks. In contrast to these collective production activities adjacent to it, we have the box labeled "private production," which represents the production decisions and activities of the private sector.

The division of the government into decision makers (on the consumer side) and producers (on the producers side) is a useful concept since government consists of both decision makers and producers. The persons who manage the government workers (and the government-owned physical capital) in the government production box are similar to other production managers in the economy in that they purchase productive services—labor, land, and so on—in the productive services market where they compete with private producers. Note the arrow representing expenditures by both the government and the private sectors for productive services. Their motivation is different, of course, since government managers are not motivated by profit expectations. Consider the following example. The superintendent of schools in your home town has to hire teachers and maintenance people to operate the public schools. This involves competing with private businesses who also would like to use the same resources. The productive services market is the arena in which this competition for resources takes place.

As in the case of the products market, some of the money expenditures flowing toward the productive services market bypass it. When your supermarket collects a sales tax on the products you purchase there, it pays these taxes directly to the collective decision box and in this way bypasses the productive services market. These taxes are included with the other taxes flowing to the collective decision box.

One additional comment will complete our introduction of government into the model. The collective decision makers also have access to the financial capital market. When the government borrows, it takes funds out of the capital market. These funds are not then available to flow into the private production box of the businesses square. Thus, when your local school board borrows in the capital market to build a new basketball arena, it takes funds out of the capital market that would otherwise be available to build a new factory in your town.

THE EFFECT OF GOVERNMENT ON THE MIX OF GOODS AND SERVICES PRODUCED

When the government taxes, and to some extent when it borrows, it reduces private demands for products.

When the government taxes, it diverts funds from individual households to *collective decisions*, and thereby *reduces private demands*. In this way, it releases resources that would otherwise be used to produce automobiles, vacations, and so on. The government, then, with its tax dollars, purchases the services of these released resources to produce collective goods.

As we will see in Chapters 13 and 14, we must be cautious about stating the effects of government borrowing in the capital market. If the government borrows money that would otherwise have been used by private businesses to construct houses, apartments, and factories, then government borrowing, like taxes, serves to reduce private demands. But when the government uses its revenues to make transfer payments, it doesn't reduce private demands except for the administration costs involved. Instead it shifts these demands from taxpayers to transfer payment recipients.

Social security taxes are collected from workers and are therefore diverted from entering the individual to the collective decision making box (see Fig. 7.2). Once received, they are then transferred directly to groups such as retired people in the form of social security benefits. The families who receive these benefits spend them in turn on rent, food, clothes, and so on. What, then, does a transfer payment achieve? The answer is that it serves to transfer command over resources from taxpayers (or lenders, if the government borrows to finance them) to those receiving social security benefits.

To be more specific, in 1975, government at all levels paid over $168 billion in transfer payments to retired people, old soldiers, poor people, people with health problems, students, and many other categories. These transfer payments served to redirect income, and thus command over resources, from taxpayers to those entitled by law to receive these payments. Taxes plus transfer payments do not reduce private demands—they merely shift these demands from one set of families to another.

Taxes and transfer payments change not only the mix of products produced by the economy but also their prices.

The mix of products produced by a mixed economy is markedly different from that produced in a pure market economy. Not only do taxes and government expenditures shift resources to meet public demands, they also change relative prices. If the government is demanding large quantities of cement to build roads, then cement will be expensive for private users. This will have a feedback effect on the prices of products produced in the private economy. A mixed economy is not just a market economy with an added ingredient. It is a qualitatively different type of economy.

Taxes change the after-tax prices of productive services as they are perceived by workers and other suppliers of productive services.

Taxes not only divert income from taxpayers, but also change their perceptions of the prices established in the productive services markets. Suppose, for example, you are asked to clean an irrigation ditch in the heat of the summer. Your would-be employer offers to pay you $5.00 an hour for this unpleasant job. It sounds like a good wage, but if taxes take 25 percent of $5.00, leaving $3.75, you may view the job differently. In making the decision as to how you are going to use your time, you would normally consider the $3.75 as the wage you receive for doing the job. It is this price and not the $5.00 wage that determines your behavior.

Sometimes economists are tempted to treat a mixed economy as behaving like a slightly modified exchange economy. This is a mistake because the mixed economy responds to different stimuli, and has a different set of relative prices, a different distribution of income, and different answers to the questions of what, how, to whom, and from whom, as we shall see in the next section of this chapter.

CRITERIA FOR IMPOSING TAXES

In an approximate sense, taxes are the prices people are willing to pay in a democracy for the services they obtain from the government. Persons who give up individual choices over products in favor of those purchased or produced by the government as an instrument of collective choice do, in a sense, make a trade. They say, "we will give up the income if you give us the services." As we have seen, this generalization is more accurate for some types of collective goods than others.

When the government operates a business, such as the post office or the Tennessee Valley Authority, the payments it receives for the services it is selling are clearly for value received. If sending a letter is not worth as much as the cost of the postage, people would not use the postal system. What, however, should be the criteria by which the appropriateness of a tax is judged? Equity (fairness) and efficiency are both involved, and consequently one's values greatly influence the criteria used to judge a tax. This section discusses the most important criteria.

The *benefit theory* of taxation regards taxes as a price for collective goods.

When the government uses the *benefit theory of taxation*, as it does when it levies a per-gallon fuel tax for the building and maintenance of highways, then taxes are, in essence, a price. Whenever persons use the highways, they pay for the use in gasoline taxes. The same thing is true when cities collect water taxes to pay for sewerage treatment. The social security taxes are perceived by many citizens as being levied on a "benefit basis." People pay social security taxes and in return get social security benefits, although the linkage between social security taxes and benefits is not as close as many people think.

When governments use general revenue taxes that are not linked to the delivery of specific services, however, the concept of a tax as a part of an exchange transaction is more tenuous. Taxes are compulsory payments to the government. A person who makes a tax payment may receive few if any benefits from the governmental services being rendered, while others who pay no taxes do indeed receive benefits. Only in the sense that the individual taxpayer is a member of a society that receives benefits can the tax be said to be a part of an exchange transaction. Because the linkage between the payment of taxes and the receipt of benefits is so loose, alternative bases of taxation are necessary if a good tax system is to be designed.

The *ability to pay* is another criterion used to justify taxation.

The belief that families with higher incomes should pay a larger percentage of their incomes to the government in taxes than lower-income families simply as a matter of equity or ability to pay is known as the *vertical equity* or *ability to pay* theory of taxation. The personal income tax,

with progressively higher rates on each income bracket as income rises, is an example of a tax based on the "ability to pay" principle. Is there a basis for relying on the "ability to pay" principle? It is clearly an ethical issue rather than one of economics. Although the argument that the last $1,000 earned by a millionaire is of much less value to the millionaire than the last $1,000 earned by a $10,000-a-year person appears logical, it is difficult if not impossible to prove this from a purely *economic* point of view.

Horizontal equity requires that persons with the same income pay the same taxes.

Another principle frequently cited by designers of tax systems, known as *horizontal equity*, is that people with the same incomes should pay the same taxes. This works as a principle so long as the tax system is not used to accomplish goals other than raising revenue. If the government rebates taxes to people who insulate their homes, or to businesses that invest in pollution-abating equipment, for example, then the principle of horizontal equity is violated since people who insulate their homes in effect pay fewer taxes than do others at the same level of income.

Efficiency is a criterion that implies that taxes should not be costly to collect.

Certain types of taxes, such as sales taxes, involve very few administrative expenses. Businesses do not have to hire experts to calculate them and state and local authorities can collect them without heavy auditing expenses. Personal income and corporation income taxes, on the other hand, are very complicated. Taxpayers frequently use experts to calculate their taxes, and the federal government maintains a large staff to check on tax returns. Does this mean sales taxes should be increased and personal income taxes reduced? Not necessarily. Many principles have to be applied in designing a tax system, and efficiency is only one of them. But other things being equal, the smaller the ratio of administrative costs to revenues received, the better a tax is.

Fiscal neutrality should be observed.

Another way of analyzing a tax is to assess its impact on the allocation of resources. If sales taxes are levied on all products alike, they do not encourage the purchase of one product at the expense of another. Excise taxes, however, such as those levied on long distance telephone calls, tend to discourage the use of the telephone and therefore, according to this principle, are not fiscally neutral. We should, however, remind you that the tax system is used for many purposes. A case in point is the the tax on alcoholic beverages or tobacco. This is an excise tax that is used in-tentionally to discourage the purchase of such products; in this instance, therefore, the rule of fiscal neutrality is not appropriate.

Taxes can also be used as a stabilizing device.

Later on, in Chapters 12 and 15, we will discuss the role of taxes and government expenditures in stabilizing the economy and preventing unemployment and inflation. We will delay this discussion until after we discuss the factors underlying the growth of the economy and the problems of unemployment and inflation.

THE INCIDENCE AND NATURE OF TAXES AND SUBSIDIES

In a mixed economy, there are many different types of taxes and subsidies. Consider for a moment the taxes you pay; payroll taxes for social security, personal income taxes, property taxes, sales taxes, excise taxes on theater tickets, and gaoline taxes, to mention only a few. Although not as well known, there are at least as many different types of subsidies. Subsidies, however, are either explicit or implicit in nature. An explicit subsidy is one in which the government makes a direct cash payment to recipients who have satisfied certain conditions, for example, a payment to a business to pay for the installation of pollution-abating equipment. Implicit subsidies involve no direct payment. They are made in a variety of ways: reduction of specific tax liabilities (for example, deduction of mortgage interest for personal income tax calculations); government loans at preferential interest or loan guaranties (for example, student loans); provisions of goods and services at prices or fees below market value (for example, school lunch programs); or govern-ment purchases of goods and services above market prices (for example, price support programs for farmers), to name only a few.

The question of *incidence* is concerned with who really bears the tax or who really receives the benefits from a subsidy, whether it is explicit or implicit. The person who bears the tax is the one whose income is lower as a result. This may be a different person from the one who pays the tax. For example, the department store pays the sales tax, but the consumer is the one who bears the tax. Or if the government grants an exclusive franchise to an airline to fly a profitable route on the condition that it provide service to a small community, it in effect is subsidizing the service to that community even though it is not making a direct payment to the airline to provide the service. The residents in the small community benefit from the implicit subsidy to the airline. Their real incomes are larger than they otherwise would have been had they been required to pay the full cost of airline service themselves.

COMMENTARY

The following is taken from an article entitled "The Federal Subsidy Picture: A Blurred Image." It cites the long tradition that subsidies have experienced in this country. Please read the excerpt and answer the following questions.
a) One of the first industries to be subsidized was

the domestic merchant fleet. Have you any information about the nature and magnitude of the subsidies (if any) currently received by the United States merchant fleet?

b) What forms of subsidies did the early railways receive?

c) What are the key elements of a subsidy?

THE FEDERAL SUBSIDY PICTURE: A BLURRED IMAGE

If there is a negative overtone or stigma surrounding the word "subsidy" for many people today, it is interesting to reflect that such a negative attachment has not always been the case. In fact, the concept of the subsidy is almost as old as our nation itself. When the First Congress convened in 1789, its initial action was to devise a system for administering oaths of office. However, the next item of business was the enactment of a tariff law to protect and promote the new nation's agricultural and industrial development. Included in the legislation was a special subsidy feature designed to encourage the growth of an American merchant fleet. All goods imported into the United States in American vessels were to have their customs duties reduced by 10 percent, and a tonnage tax favorable to American shipping interests was also made part of the law.

From this early beginning, the government has used the subsidy time and again, not only to influence the pace and direction of economic development, but for diverse other purposes, including the promotion of science and the arts, and to mitigate the normal workings of market demand and supply forces when deemed desirable. Not only have their purposes varied over time, but subsidies have taken a number of different forms. For example, from 1827 to 1866, private interests were granted well over 6 million acres of public lands to stimulate the building of canals and the improvement of rivers. In addition, these same interests received right-of-way grants and public funds by means of direct governmental contributions, stock subscriptions, and loans. Between 1850 and 1871, the railroads were granted more than 180 million acres of Federal and state lands to spur their development. Significant sums of public monies have been used to subsidize the building of ships on American ways as well as the crews that manned them. Although complaints about the U.S. Postal Service are legion, it is, nonetheless, worth noting that the first mail subsidy was paid by the Government in 1845— more than 130 years ago—and the tradition still remains in force. Indeed, the Committee on

Agriculture of the U.S. House of Representatives observed more than 20 years ago:

While originally the subsidy mechanism was employed to expand transportation, to encourage foreign trade, and to foster domestic industrial development, more recently subsidy and subsidylike programs have multiplied to such an extent that their impact is felt by virtually all elements in the Nation's economic structure.[1] . . .

The staff of the Joint Economic Committee of the U.S. Congress (JEC) is to be applauded for their efforts in attempting to develop an analytically clear and operationally useful definition as a first and necessary step in the assessment of Federal subsidy programs. Their work, entitled "The Economics of Federal Subsidy Programs," was published in January 1972. . . .

On defining a subsidy

The Office of Management and Budget (OMB) defines subsidy as "a monetary grant to a unit engaged in commercial activities." . . .

The definition used by the OMB and cited earlier is far too restrictive. The proposal of the JEC appears to represent a far better alternative:

. . . a subsidy is defined as the provision of Federal economic assistance, at the expense of others in the economy, to the private sector producers or consumers of a particular good, service or factor of production. The Government receives no equivalent compensation in return, but conditions the assistance on a particular performance by the recipient—a quid pro quo—that has the effect of altering the price or costs of the particular good, service, or factor to the subsidy recipient, so as to encourage or discourage the output, supply, or use of these items and the related economic behavior. . . .

[1] U.S. Congress, House, Committee on Agriculture, "Government Subsidy Historical Review," 86th Congress, 2nd Sess., Committee Print, June 3, 1954, revised May 10, 1960, p. 1.
[2] See Joint Committee Print, January 11, 1972, p. 18.

The efforts of the JEC bore fruit in the form of estimates of Federal subsidy costs more in keeping with its expanded definition of the subsidy concept. These data are shown in the table for the fiscal years 1970 and 1975. . . .

Direct cash subsidies represent cash payments from the Government to a firm or individual in the private sector engaged in a market activity as specified in the subsidy legislation. Among these activities are housing construction, school attendance, and production of certain crops, to name just a few. . . .

Credit subsidies arise whenever the Government enters into a loan transaction with the effect of lowering the rate of interest below that which the borrower would otherwise have to pay. They may take the form of a straight cash payment to offset part of the interest cost of the loan; they may involve a direct loan from the Government at lower interest rates than the borrower could obtain in the private market; or they can utilize a Government guarantee or insurance of a loan to effectively lower the risk of default and thereby the rate of interest obtainable by the borrower. . . .

When the Government sells to the private sector a good or service at a price below the prevailing market price or below its actual cost in the case where a private market may not exist, a benefit-in-kind subsidy arises. One of the most notable examples is the food stamp program. . . .

The type of subsidy showing the largest absolute increase in the table is tax subsidies. A tax subsidy is generated when a special provision in the law allows an individual or a firm engaged in a specific market activity to make a smaller tax payment to the Government than would have otherwise been the case. The estimates in the table measure the reduction in revenues to the Government resulting from these special provisions. . . .

A concluding observation

The foregoing analysis demonstrates that subsidies do exert a pervasive influence on our economy. Their scope of application, their diverse forms, and the significant sums of money involved are all persuasive reasons for ongoing public concern. . . .

For by their nature, subsidies represent the conferring of benefits on special groups in our society, rather than on the general public. In a society which stresses the dominant role of free competitive markets, and, at a time when there is so much concern over the appropriate role and size of Government, both fiscal prudence and simple equity demand that objective and appropriate

SUMMARY OF FEDERAL SUBSIDY COSTS (In Billions of Dollars)

	Fiscal Year									
	Direct cash subsidies		Tax subsidies		Credit subsidies		Benefit-in-kind subsidies		Total order of magnitude	
	1970	1975	1970	1975	1970	1975	1970	1975	1970	1975
Agriculture	4.4	.6	.9	1.1	.4	.7	—	—	5.7	2.5
Food	—	—	—	—	—	—	1.5	5.9	1.5	5.9
Health	.8	.6	3.2	5.8	—	—	4.6	10.2	8.6	16.6
Manpower	2.0	3.3	.6	.7	—	—	.1	.1	2.6	4.1
Education	1.9	5.0	.8	1.0	.1	.1	.4	.4	3.2	6.5
International	.1	—	.3	1.5	.6	.9	—	—	1.0	2.4
Housing	.1	1.7	8.7	12.9	3.0	1.1	—	—	11.7	15.7
Natural resources	.1	.1	2.0	4.1	—	—	.1	.1	2.1	4.4
Transportation	.3	.6	—	.1	—	—	.2	1.7	.5	2.3
Commerce	2.0	.3	14.1	19.3	.1	—	1.8	1.9	18.0	21.5
Other	—	—	9.4	13.1	.1	.1	—	—	9.5	13.2
Total order of magnitude	11.6	12.3	39.9	59.7	4.1	2.9	8.8	20.2	64.4	95.1

Note: Individual items may not add to totals due to rounding.
Source: Federal Subsidy Programs, Joint Economic Committee (Washington: U.S. Government Printing Office, 1974), p. 5.

standards be applied where the public purse is involved. To that end, there should be no flagging in the effort to sharpen and to clarify what for many still remains a blurred image of the subsidy picture.

SHELDON W. STAHL, "The Federal Subsidy Picture: A Blurred Image," *Monthly Review*, September-October 1976, Federal Reserve Bank of Kansas City. Reprinted by permission.

Institutions do not bear taxes: only indidivuals do.

The determination of the incidence of taxes or subsidies is difficult to pinpoint in all cases, but there are certain situations in which we can analyze the incidence of specific taxes or subsidies. Our concern will be with the incidence of taxes and subsidies among persons. A business—whether organized as a corporation or as a partnership—deals with different groups of persons. The stockholders comprise one group; the executives are a second group; the workers, apart from the executives, are a third group; and the customers are a fourth. Whenever a tax is levied on a business, one or more of the persons in these groups ultimately bear the tax. It is important to recognize that corporations, or any businesses for that matter, do not bear taxes. Only persons can bear taxes or receive benefits from subsidies. When a business pays a tax, some group of individuals will bear the tax. From an economic policy point of view, it is important to ascertain who these groups of individuals are.

Mobility of resources influences who bear the taxes or reaps the benefits of subsidies.

If an activity is taxed and if people who supply the resources used in that activity can use them equally well in some other untaxed activity, then the tax will be passed on to the purchasers of the product. This is the *escape theory* of tax incidence. Similarly, if an activity is subsidized and if people are free to move their resources into the subsidized activity, then the subsidy will be passed on to the buyers of the product. We will call this the *capture theory* of subsidy incidence. Consider some examples of a per-unit tax.

If a $1000 tax were levied on "gas guzzling" cars, defined as those getting less than 15 miles per gallon, then the buyers of these cars would pay the tax. The resource owners—in this case the workers and the stockholders in automobile companies—would see no reason to accept a lower rate of return for the resources used to produce such cars since these resources could easily be moved to small-car production. As long as the resources could "escape," the tax would be passed on to the buyers of the product. This can be shown graphically in Fig. 7.3 below. The supply curve for large cars is represented as a horizontal line reflecting constant costs of production. Regardless of the slope of the demand curve, the tax would be passed on to the buyers of the large cars, raising the price from P_0 to P_1. The owners of the resources used in this activity could escape without penalty.

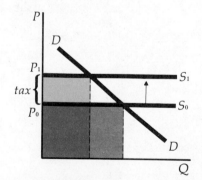

FIG. 7.3   A tax passed on to the buyer of a product.

Consider another example. Suppose that sparkling health water was produced by 1000 producers, all with wells that flowed at the same rate regardless of the

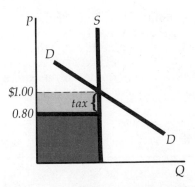

FIG. 7.4 A tax borne by the supplier of a product.

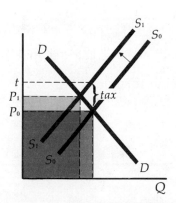

FIG. 7.5 A tax borne by both demand and supplier of a product.

price, and that the market price of health water was $1.00 per gallon. The second best use for this water would be as regular drinking water, which would sell for $0.25 a gallon, or the cost of producing and bottling it. Now suppose that a tax of $0.20 a gallon is placed on the production and sale of health water. Who would bear the tax? The answer is that the owners of the health water springs would bear the tax. If they tried to pass the tax on, the buyers would buy less. Some of the health water producers would lose the difference between the $0.25—the cost of bottling it—and the selling price. Rather than waste their water, they would offer to sell for less. The after-tax price would finally settle down to $0.80. The resource owners would be stuck with the tax. Why? They had only one use for their resource and they couldn't escape. Figure 7.4 illustrates this example.

If all resources can escape without penalty from a taxed activity, then the tax will be passed on. Otherwise, it will be borne by resource owners.

What can we learn from these two examples? If resources have multiple uses and can escape from the taxed activity, then purchasers will bear the tax. If resources have only one use and they cannot escape, then resource owners will bear the tax. Incorporating our earlier analysis of productive services prices, we can say that a tax on opportunity costs will be shifted to purchasers and a tax on rent will be borne by resource owners.

When only some of the resources can escape, the division of the burden will be determined by the elasticities of the supply and demand curves, as is illustrated in Fig. 7.5.

The reverse is true of subsidized activities. If there are no restrictions on entry, a competitive industry that has just received a subsidy—such as the right to take depletion allowances on the value of trees used to make paper—will have a larger return on capital than other industries.

The companies in the subsidized industry, in this case the paper industry, would expand, hoping to increase their output and therefore their profits. This expansion of capacity in a competitive economy would reduce the price until all of the subsidy would be passed on to the purchasers of paper. If there are no restrictions on entry, the drive to capture the subsidy will drive product prices down until they are equal to per-unit opportunity costs less the per-unit subsidy.

When one of the resources is limited in supply and cannot move into the subsidized industry, then the owners of that resource, and not the producers, will capture the subsidy. Consider farming. From time to time, the federal government subsidizes wheat farmers by entering the market and buying enough wheat to increase its price. Initially, those farm operators who also own their own farms will benefit from this subsidy: Their prices will rise relative to their costs. Over time, however, the price of wheat land will rise, reflecting the economic rent to be made by raising wheat. The young farmers replacing the ones who are retiring will have to pay more for their land, and they will find that they are no better off than farm operators were before wheat farmers were subsidized. The subsidy implicit in the higher prices of wheat will have already been captured by the present landowners.

Unfortunately, the "escape" and "capture" theories of the incidence of taxes and subsidies have limited application. They can be used to explain who will bear excise on specific commod-ities or reap the benefits of specific subsidies. They are, however, difficult to apply to such general taxes as the personal income tax and the corporation income tax. Unless a taxpayer regards leaving the country as a viable alternative, there are very few escapes from taxes of this type.

MINI-CASE 7.1

Suppose that all college educational services are sold by competitive profit-making firms. Now suppose that a large percentage of the college teachers love their work so much that they would work for half of their current wage rates. Other employees would not take a reduction in their pay. If a large excise tax is levied on higher education, then:

a) The tax would be passed on by the profit-making firms to the students who were paying for their education.
b) Part of the tax would be borne by the professors and part would be passed on to students.
c) All of the tax would be borne by the professors. There would be no reduction in the quantity of education supplied, and there would be no increase in the price of education.
d) Education is so vital to the nation that such a tax would have no effect on the quantity of education purchased and therefore would be passed on in its entirety to the students.

Who ultimately pays the tax is important, but so is the nature of the tax in terms of its impact on persons in different income levels. Therefore, we will now discuss taxes and subsidies from this perspective.

Taxes and subsidies are classified as being progressive, regressive, or proportional.

A complication in managing the public sector of a mixed economy involves appraising the impact of government taxes, transfer payments, and expenditures on the distribution of income. Economists have used the terms progressive, proportional, and regressive to refer to the effect of a tax or subsidy on the distribution of income.

A tax is *progressive* if it takes a larger percentage of higher incomes than it does of lower incomes.

A tax is *proportional* if it takes the same percentage of incomes regardless of the size of the income.

A tax is *regressive* if it takes a larger percentage of lower incomes than it does of higher incomes.

Thus an income tax that takes 25 percent of a $20,000 income and only 15 percent of a $10,000 income is said to be progressive. If the percentages were reversed, then the tax would be said to be regressive.

These same terms can also be used in describing the effects of transfer payments or expenditure programs on the distribution of income. Transfer payments, such as social security benefits, which add a larger percentage to the incomes of the poor than to the incomes of the rich, are said to be progressive. Those that do the reverse are said to be regressive.

GOVERNMENT EXPENDITURES AND BENEFIT-COST ANALYSIS

Early in this chapter we identified the provision of collective goods as one of the basic functions of government. But government, like the private sector, is constrained by scarcity. What collective goods should government provide—more dams and waterways, more regulation of business, or more health services? This section contrasts the behavior of the private sector and that of government in determining its priorities.

Benefit-cost analysis is built into the private sector.

In the private sector the questions of what, how, and so on, are answered by the marketplace. Suppose you are thinking about buying a car and have decided that it will be one made by General Motors. You would have many choices—all the way from the Chevette to the Cadillac Seville. How would you go about making this choice?

You might consider the advantages or benefits of moving up one step in the GM line compared to the extra costs of doing so. In other words, you would apply an implicit form of what is called *benefit-cost analysis*. In reflecting on the extra pleasures you would anticipate from a luxury car, you would probably reduce your evaluation of these pleasures by some appropriate amount to account for the fact that they would not come immediately when the car is purchased, but over time. You might also take into account the extra costs of owning and driving a large car. In this way you would obtain a crude estimate of the value of the car to you today. You can then compare this value with its cost. If the benefit-cost ratio is positive, you would buy the car.

Why can't you do the same thing when you, with other people in a democracy, choose the

appropriate level of government expenditures on a project? The answer is that you can, but it is much more difficult. Whereas the market economy gives you many chances to say you want a "little more or a little less" of something—all the way from automobiles to movies—public decisions cannot be made that way. Consider the following example.

You must choose whether you want a new waterway connecting the Tennessee river system and the Gulf of Mexico. In so doing you must think not only about whether the project as a whole makes sense, but also about whether it should be constructed with top-quality materials, beautifully landscaped and having wide and deep waterways, or with average quality materials for small barges. Your calculations might look like those in the table below (although they are only fictitious examples).

The minimum plan with small locks and no landscaping would cost $1.6 billion. If you discount the net revenues after costs of operation at 6 percent, you have a project with a present value of $1.7 billion. This generates the following benefit-cost ratio, in which the benefits are expressed as the present value of the project and the costs as the present cost:

$$\frac{\text{Present value}}{\text{Present cost}} = \frac{\$1.7 \text{ billion}}{\$1.6 \text{ billion}} = 1.06.$$

The ratio for Plan A looks favorable, but should you go further? Consider Plan B. The benefit-cost ratio is:

$$\frac{\$2 \text{ billion}}{\$1.85 \text{ billion}} = 1.08.$$

The extra present value of the project is larger than the extra costs; therefore, the benefit-cost ratio for Plan B is higher than for Plan A. You will get 1.08 of present value of the $1.00 that you spend. The opposite is true

Plan	Cost of project	Marginal cost	Present value of net revenues (6% discount note)	Extra present value
A. Canal: small locks	$1.6 billion	$1.6 billion	$1.7 billion	—
B. Canal: large locks	$1.85 billion	$250 million	$2 billion	$300 million
C. Canal: large locks plus landscaping	$2.10 billion	$250 million	$2.05 billion	$ 50 million

of Plan C. When you compare the extra present value of Plan C with the extra cost, you find that it wouldn't be worth doing.

$$\left(\frac{\$2.05}{\$2.10} = 0.98\right).$$

Now all of this sounds very exact, but in reality it seldom works out so neatly. The estimates of future net revenues are very difficult to obtain and define. Should you include the value to the southern states of the canal as an attraction for industry from the north? The answer is no, unless you also subtract the loss to the northern states. Would there be a net gain in national productivity from this shift of industry? That is hard to measure. What discount rate is appropriate? Is it the interest rate on government debt, or a higher interest rate because there are significant risks that the canal may not serve as many businesses as had been assumed?

But of even more importance, these projects are seldom considered individually by the population of voters. the projects are usually imbedded in a budget with many items in it, and it is difficult for voters to express their wishes on individual projects of this kind. As a consequence, many public projects become bargaining weapons. The president or a senator will in essence say: "You support my pet project and I will support yours."

The public economy, with its reliance on voting, does not have an effective substitute for the market system as a device for making the "little more or the little less" decisions so important in the efficient allocation of resources. Nevertheless, there must be some way of combining private and collective decision making, which raises the question of how the mixed economy can best be used.

Mini-case 7.2 is provided to help you clarify your thinking as to the criteria that should be used in evaluating government spending programs.

MINI-CASE 7.2

In selecting the appropriate projects to be included in the federal government's budget, the following consideration should be *most* important:

a) Which projects will show the highest profit return when goods produced by the government projects are sold in open market.
b) Which projects will have the largest marginal social benefits compared to the marginal social costs.
c) Which projects will best solve the "free rider" problem.
d) Which project is most progressive in its effect on the distribution of income.

THE MIXED ECONOMY AS A DEVICE FOR ALLOCATING RESOURCES

Every society, whether a group of students operating an isolated summer camp or a nation of 220 million persons, must answer the basic economic questions: what, how, from whom, and to whom. How does a mixed economy differ from a pure exchange economy in answering these questions? A mixed economy has a wider range of social devices available to resolve these questions and may serve a different set of social goals.

The mixed economy can use the market with its unique characteristics.

A mixed economy can use the market to answer these questions, and the market has several unique characteristics.

First, since people buy and sell only when they believe it will be to their advantage, the market, unlike a political system, operates by unani mous consent. It is unnecessary to get a majority of those involved to approve a project. Only those persons who like Beethoven records, for example, will buy them.

Second, the information required to run the economy does not have to be assembled at one point. Decisions are made in a decentralized fashion. Managers of businesses and consumers can focus all of their efforts on acquiring the knowledge they need to produce and purchase, say, recreational services, and then make their decisions.

Third, the market economy rewards people for being innovative in finding new ways to produce products and in so doing encourages people to develop new knowledge. The producers of, say, hi-fi sets, who use the new knowledge can sell their products for less or give you a better hi-fi set, which forces competitors to follow suit.

Fourth, the market is less sensitive than a political democracy to the objections people raise when a new technology is introduced. When somebody discovers how to use less labor to produce glass bottles, private industry will go ahead and do it, even though some people lose their jobs. When, however, somebody discovers how to substitute equipment for people in the defense of the nation, it is extremely difficult for the government to close a naval base. Local politicians usually object, even though it can be demonstrated that the naval base is no longer necessary.

A mixed economy can use taxes and subsidies to enhance or detract from the market solution.

In addition to the market mechanisms at its disposal, a mixed economy can use its power to *tax* and *grant subsidies,* both explicit and implicit, to influence the way the market answers the basic economic questions. When the market economy does not distribute income the way society wants it to, society, collectively, can levy taxes on workers and redistribute the proceeds.

When a government taxes and grants subsidies, it helps the market shift resources from one place to another. Public schools and state universities, for example, have helped excess labor move away from the farms. Sometimes, however, taxes and subsidies thwart the market. Price sup-

ports for peanut growers, for example, have kept resources from moving out of the peanut growing industry.

A mixed economy can use its power of regulation and thus alter the market solution.

In addition to taxes and subsidies, the government can also use its power to regulate economic activity. When a government uses its regulatory powers, it prohibits certain activities (for example, you will not market a certain type of drug), or it mandates specific activities (for example, the use of emission control equipment on automobiles). Usually the penalties for disobeying these rules are severe enough that they cannot be treated as hidden prices. For example, if you dispense unapproved drugs, the fine or jail term is usually high enough that you cannot treat the fine as the price you have to pay to engage in that activity.

There are the three sets of social institutions available to a mixed economy to accomplish the allocation of resources: the use of the market, the imposition of taxes and subsidies, and the creation and enforcement of regulations. What combination of these three social institutions should be used to answer the economizing questions? The answer depends on the goals society, operating both through the market and its government, is trying to achieve. Consider the following illustration of how the energy problem could be faced by a mixed economy.

The market economy has a solution for the energy crisis.

In the first place, a mixed economy could resolve this problem with the market solution. We have already seen in Chapter 5 that higher prices for energy will change relative prices in such a way as to allocate the available energy among alternative uses. There would be no apparent shortage as defined in economics. Higher prices will also spread the use of exhaustible resources over time. Owners with natural gas and oil in the ground would hold it back in reserve if prices were expected to be enough higher in the future to make it worthwhile to do so. Prospective shortages of fossil fuels together with their high prices would induce people to seek other sources of energy. In other words, if left alone, the market could provide a solution to the energy problem.

Energy taxes and subsidies can speed or slow down the market solution.

In the second place, the government could help the market allocate and conserve oil and natural gas by the use of taxes and subsidies. It could place a high tax on the use of gasoline, creating, for example a price of $2 a gallon, as in fact many European countries have done. Or the government might impose a tax proportional to the weight of cars, as West Germany has done. Higher gasoline prices and higher prices for large cars would encourage automobile producers to concentrate on designing gas-conserving cars, commuters to use car pools, and encourage people to move back to the cities.

The government could also make subsidies available to producers of substitute fuels. These subsidies could take many forms. They could guarantee minimum prices for substitute fuels, or they could grant coal producers the right of eminent domain in the purchase of new coal-bearing land. The government could also subsidize research on the development of fusion and nonfossil sources of energy, as well as making subsidies available to encourage the insulation of homes and apartment houses.

A mixed economy can use selective taxes and subsidies to enhance the effects of relative price changes in the market. West Germany adopted market-enhancement policies and has successfully reduced its dependence on oil and natural gas. These same policies are available to other mixed economies.

A criticism of both market and market-enhanced policies is that they do not take into account the special problems of the poor. When gasoline prices rise, the poor, unlike the middle- and upper-income groups, do not have the financial resources to buy new, gas-conserving, cars, nor can they afford to move closer to their work.

A concerned majority in a democracy can use its government to help poor people make the adjustment to a new set of relative prices. It can grant fuel stamps (and possibly heating oil stamps) to poor people. These fuel stamps, like food stamps, could cover, say, half of the cost of the gasoline required for work and necessary shopping. The fuel stamps could be a temporary expedient that would be phased out over a two- or three-year period. While such a program would limit for a period of time the conservation effects of higher relative prices for gasoline and heating oil, it could achieve a different mix of social goals.

When a government uses regulatory powers to resolve the energy crises, it requires a centralized information system.

In the third place, the government can use its regulatory powers to resolve the energy problem. When it does this it substitutes central direction for a decentrally controlled market system.

In place of relying on business managers and consumers to obtain the knowledge they need, government officials must have the knowledge about how to conserve energy in literally thousands of different situations in the economy. In place of relying on consumers to make their own trade-offs between paying high energy prices and buying other products, the government officials would make the decision for them.

Consider some of the regulatory programs that could be or have been proposed to produce and conserve energy.

1. Motorists may not exceed a 55 mile-per-hour speed limit. Drivers exceeding this limit are subject to a fine.
2. Automobile producers shall redesign automobiles in order to achieve a specified number of miles per gallon of gasoline.
3. After a certain date the production of cars emitting amounts of pollution above specified amounts shall be banned.
4. Maximum prices shall be maintained for oil and natural gas produced in the economy.
5. Public utilities will be required to use coal in place of oil and natural gas, unless the regulatory bodies think that it is not feasible to do so. This determination will be made by government officials on a plant-by-plant basis.

6. No industrial company may use natural gas or oil unless the regulatory body approves it. A company that persists in using oil or natural gas will pay a special tax based on usage.

This is a partial list of the regulations that have been proposed or used to resolve the energy problem. We do not propose to say which combination of (1) the market, (2) market-enhancing taxes and subsidies, and (3) regulations is best. In deciding this, the trade-off between different social goals must be considered. For example, if people value the freedom to make their own decision about how they will use energy, they will choose the market or some combination of the market and market-enhancing taxes and subsidies. If they want to treat energy as a collective good to be allocated by the government, they will then turn the problem over to the government and let the government acquire the knowledge it needs to solve the problem for them.

REVIEW QUESTIONS

1. In the mixed market economy that characterizes the United States, government plays an important role in all of the following activities *except*:
    a) defining and enforcing the contracts essential to market exchange.
    b) specifying explicitly what and for whom goods shall be produced.
    c) modifying the mix of goods and services produced through its tax and spending policies.
    d) providing goods and services not subject to the "exclusion principle."

2. Governments differ from private businesses in the following ways. Select the *incorrect* statement.
    a) Governmental units do not typically rely on the profit motive.
    b) Governmental units have the power to coerce while businesses usually do not have this power.
    c) Governmental units do not combine economic resources to produce goods and services while private businesses do combine resources to produce goods and services.
    d) Governmental units, because of their power to tax, can make massive transfer payments to specified groups of individuals, whereas businesses cannot usually do this.

3. Which of the following statements is representative of a regressive tax?
    a) A citizen earns $25,000 and pays $5,000 in taxes; another citizen earns $6,000 and pays $1,200 in taxes.
    b) A citizen earns $20,000 and pays $2,000 in taxes; another citizen earns $8,000 and pays $1,600 in taxes.
    c) A citizen earns $20,000 and pays $2,000 in taxes; another citizen earns $5,000 and pays $500 in taxes.
    d) A citizen earns $25,000 and pays $5,000 in taxes; another citizen earns $5,000 and pays $500 in taxes.

4. Suppose no taxes are levied on annual family incomes under $10,000, and that a 10 percent tax is levied on that part of all family incomes above $10,000. In considering the effect of this tax on the distribution of income, it can be said that above $10,000, this tax is:
    a) proportional.
    b) progressive.
    c) regressive.
    d) impossible to tell from the data provided.

5. The major *economic* effect of taxes is to:

a) provide money to the government so it can subsidize industries producing public goods.
b) obtain control of resources from private uses.
c) obtain control of resources so the Federal Reserve can increase the discount rate.
d) increase the productivity of resources by reallocating resources away from the public sectors toward the private sectors.

6. A number of principles are considered when taxes are levied. The one *least* likely to be considered is the:

a) exclusion principle.   b) costs of collection.   c) ability to pay.   d) benefit received.

7. A mixed economy in which the government takes 25 percent of the personal income in taxes to spend on public goods (national defense, police protection, etc.) differs from a competitive, purely market-directed economy in the following significant way.

a) The government always wastes the money it spends while individuals do not.
b) The market-directed economy responds to the demands of small groups of individuals for out-of-the-way products whereas the government representing the majority can override the wishes of the minorities.
c) The competitive, market-directed economy can solve the free rider problem and a mixed economy cannot.
d) The competitive, market-directed economy can solve the externality problems associated with third-party costs and benefits while a mixed economy cannot.

8. Suppose an excise tax is levied on production of bonded whiskey. The industry is competitive and it produces many types of alcoholic drinks. No tax is levied on other alcoholic beverages. In the long run,

a) the tax would be paid by the distilleries and borne by the distilleries.
b) the tax would be paid by the distilleries but passed on to purchasers.
c) the tax would be paid by the consumers and then passed back to the distilleries in the form of reduced revenues.
d) the tax would be paid by the distilleries but because including it in the price of whiskey would so restrict the market, the distilleries would tend to absorb a large portion of the tax on bonded whiskey.

ESSAY QUESTIONS

1. Assume the railroads east of the Mississippi finally go into bankruptcy. The federal government takes them over and contributes $10 billion a year toward their operation. How does this $10 billion differ from $10 billion that the railroads might have received if they were operated as private corporations?

2. Discuss the implications of this railroad take-over for you as a person who never uses the railroads. What would it mean for you if you were a confirmed railroad buff and used the railroads whenever you could?

3. Now suppose that a new Amtrack system is proposed that will restore railway passenger service to all communities that were served by the railroads in the 1920's. It will cost $25 billion a year in addition to the expected revenues from the new passenger service. How would you make a cost-benefit analysis of this proposal? Be specific.

4. A friend of yours argues that medical services in the United States are too expensive for the average family. To remedy this he proposes that the federal government take over all of the costs of providing medical services. Does this mean that medical services will *cost* less? Who will pay for the services? What would this government provision mean for the person who despite the availability of governmentally supported clinics insists on a private physician? Discuss the ways such a program could be financed.

5. Suppose a friend of yours tells you that there is no reason why the government, since it runs the United States mint, should tax everybody to pay for government services. The government can print the money it needs for everyday operations. Discuss and indicate the economic purpose of taxation.

6. How does government borrowing differ from government taxation? Assuming that if people did not buy government bonds they would buy corporate bonds, what will be the effect of the government's borrowing the funds it needs for operations?

7. How does a transfer payment differ from a government purchase of a productive service? List five programs of transfer payments you see in operation around you.

8. A friend argues that the United States should adopt the value-added tax which has been used so successfully in Europe. Specifically, he argues that a 20 percent tax should be levied on the difference between what a corporation pays for materials and what it receives for selling its products. He is convinced that if this tax is used, the government could afford to reduce everybody's income taxes by a third. Who would pay this value-added tax? What effect would it have on the distribution of income? Would it be progressive or regressive?

9. How does the corporation income tax differ from the value-added tax? Who do you think actually bears the corporation income tax?

10. As a means of redistributing income, a presidential candidate proposes that all income in excess of the average family income be taxed at a flat 75 percent rate (no exemptions and no deductions). Assuming that the mechanics of collecting this tax could be worked out satisfactorily, who would bear the tax? In what cases do you think the tax would be passed on in increased costs of products and in what cases would the tax be borne by the taxpayers? Be specific. Give examples.

11. The welfare system of the United States is a transfer payments program. It is designed to help certain classes of low-income people. Appraise the economic impact of this program. How would you improve it? What effect does this program have on the real income of the working poor?

12. Interest income from the ownership of municipal bonds is exempt from federal income taxation. What effect will this exemption have on the cost of providing governmental services in the United States? This exemption is a form of transfer payment to the rich. Can you think of alternative programs which would make it easier for the cities and states to borrow without transferring income from low- to high-income groups?

13. Suppose that as a means of increasing food production in the United States the federal government pays the farmer a subsidy amounting to a dollar a bushel for all feed grains. In this way the farmer can sell his grain at the market price and collect in addition a dollar a bushel from the government. Appraise the effect of this program on: (1) families considered as consumers of food; (2) families considered as taxpayers; (3) farmers who rent their lands; and (4) the landowners. What effect do you think this program would have on the distribution of income in the United States?

14. As a means of conserving oil the federal government proposes to levy a $1.00 a gallon tax on gasoline. Discuss the economic impact of this tax. Suppose that the government increases the exemption level on the personal income tax enough so that a family that drives 10,000 miles a year will be no worse off than before the tax. What effect will this tax reduction have? Now put the two together. Would this program succeed in conserving oil? List the other alternatives for conserving oil and compare the economic impact of each.

15. Discuss the major differences between a mixed economy and a pure market-directed economy. Indicate the criteria you would use in deciding to use the government or the market to get goods produced.

ANSWERS TO REVIEW QUESTIONS

1. In the mixed market economy that describes the United States we find that a key role played by government is that of ensuring an environment in which economic transactions can be made with a legal system to guarantee their enforcement. Since the government purchases over 20 percent of the goods and services produced and directly by its taxing and spending policies affects over 35 percent of national output, it certainly changes the mix of goods and services produced. The kinds of goods that government provides are collective goods, or goods that by their nature are difficult to provide privately without spillover effects. These goods are not subject to the exclusion principle. The one area that the government does not play a dominant role in is telling producers what and for whom goods should be produced. The market answers this question in most instances. Hence the correct answer is (b).

2. The government differs from the private sector according to the nature of its transactions in several ways. The government has the power to tax and taxes are compulsory payments. In the United States, the government does very little actual producing of goods but does produce significant amounts of services. The government spends in several different ways. It purchases goods and services from the private sector and it also makes transfer payments. While the private sector in general has fairly clear-cut criteria for making expenditures, the government sector does not. Many of the activities engaged in by the public sector have no market price by which the benefits and, in some cases, the costs can be evaluated.

a) This is not the proper choice. This statement is correct. Profit is not a criterion for governmental expenditure.

b) This is not the proper choice. This statement is correct as noted above. Taxation is a form of coercion.

c) This is the proper choice. The statement is incorrect. Government does purchase labor, capital, and land resources to produce services such as national defense, police protection, and in the case of the TVA, electric power.

d) This is not the proper choice. The statement is correct. The government has both the resources and the power to make such transfers.

3. A regressive tax is one levied so that the percentage of income paid in taxes decreases as the income rises.

a) This is an incorrect answer. In this case the citizen earning $25,000 is paying a 20 percent tax and the person earning $6,000 is also paying a 20 percent tax. This is a situation in which the tax is proportional.

b) This is the correct answer. The citizen earning $20,000 pays only a 10 percent tax while the lower-income person earning $8,000 is paying a 20 percent tax.
c) This is incorrect. Both citizens are paying a 10 percent tax.
d) This is incorrect. The citizen earning $25,000 is paying a 20 percent tax and the person with the lower income is paying a 10 percent tax. This tax is progressive, not regressive.

4. If one family earns $20,000, it will pay, according to the plan outlined in this question, a 10 percent tax only on the last $10,000 earned. Hence, it will pay $1,000 on a total income of $20,000, or 5 percent. If another family earns $30,000, it will pay a 10 percent tax on $20,000, or $2,000. Note that in this case the tax paid as a percentage of the family's total income is 6⅔ percent. As incomes rise, the percentage of income paid in taxes also rises. Hence, this is a progressive tax scheme. The correct answer is (b).

5. The imposition of taxes releases resources from the private sector and places them at the disposal of the government.
a) This is incorrect. Taxes do provide money for the government, but to subsidize industries certainly is not the major effect of taxes. They may not even be used in this way.
b) This is correct as explained above.
c) This is incorrect. The Federal Reserve is not involved in this question.
d) This is incorrect. It may or may not happen, but in any case it is not the major economic effect of taxation.

6. The exclusion principle is a term that describes the nature of certain goods that have spillover effects. The cost of collecting taxes, consideration of the benefits received, and ability to pay are all principles that are likely to be examined when a tax is levied. The correct answer then is (a).

7. A mixed economy in which the government plays a significant role will differ from a purely market-dominated economy in that the mix of goods and services produced and the kind of inputs used will reflect the expenditure choices of the government as well as the private sector.
a) This is incorrect. There is no basis for assuming that the government *always* wastes the money it spends while the private sector does not. One would run into serious difficulty even trying to define the word waste in this context.
b) This is correct. If a small group of people want to buy buggy whips and the demand is sufficient, a small number of buggy whips will be provided. If, however, the decisions as to what to produce depend upon majority vote, no buggy whips will be provided.
c) This is incorrect. The free rider problem exists when the benefits of certain expenditures or actions cannot be withheld from those who don't pay them.
d) This is incorrect. This is the same answer as (c), but cloaked in different terminology.

8. The key to answering this question lies in the ability of resources to be transferred from the production of one good to another in the long run. If a tax is levied on just one product of the liquor industry, say bonded whiskey, the producers will bear part of the cost in the short run. But in the long run, they will withdraw resources from the production of bonded whiskey and use them for liquor without the excise tax. A smaller amount of bonded whiskey will be produced and the price will be higher, transferring the tax to those willing to pay the additional amount.
a) This is incorrect as explained above.
b) This is correct as explained above.
c) This is incorrect. In the long run the consumer will pay the tax.
d) This is incorrect. As long as resources can be shifted, the distillery will do so, ultimately forcing the remaining consumers to pay the tax.

APPENDIX TO CHAPTER 7: THE TAX SYSTEM OF THE UNITED STATES

OBJECTIVES

Upon successful completion of this chapter, you will be able to:

1. List the major types of taxes and their relative importance in federal and state and local finance.

2. List the major types of government expenditures by function.

3. Illustrate how the spending and taxing policies of the government would be reflected in the budget of a typical family in the United States.

4. Analyze the major taxes in terms of their incidence.

5. Cite a number of implications stemming from the existence of the personal income tax.

6. Cite evidence concerning the income equalizing effect of the tax system in the United States.

GOVERNMENTAL EXPENDITURES AND TAXES

Only a few taxes account for the bulk of governmental revenue.

When governments at all levels collect taxes amounting to 40 percent of the nation's total personal income, it is difficult to rely on only one type of tax.* The top half of Fig. 7A.1 shows the source of the federal government's revenues by major types of taxes. The federal government depends largely on three revenue sources. In 1975–1976, for example, individual income taxes accounted for 40.5 percent of revenue; the insurance trust revenue, including social security taxes, amounted to 26.4 percent; and corporate income taxes made up 12.8 percent of the revenue. As can be seen in the bottom half of Fig. 7A.1, state and local governments depend largely

on property taxes (18.7 percent); sales taxes (17.9 percent); and individual income taxes (8.1 percent). Grants from the federal government also comprise a substantial share of revenues, however, amounting to 18.2 percent. Table 7A.1 summarizes the combined tax receipts of government at all levels in 1975.

Three kinds of expenditures comprise almost 70 percent of federal government spending.

The expenditures of government at the various levels in 1975–1976 are represented in Fig. 7A.2. At the federal level, insurance trust expenditures comprise the largest single category of expenditures, accounting for 25.9 percent of the total. Close behind were national defense and international relations at 25.7 percent, while 17.7 percent of the federal government expenditures went to state and local governments. The remaining 30.7

* In 1975, for example, total tax revenues of all levels of government were $507 billion, and total personal income for the United States was $1257 billion.

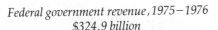

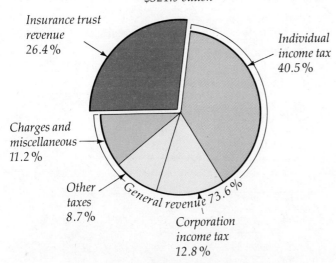

Federal government revenue, 1975–1976
$324.9 billion

Insurance trust revenue 26.4%

Individual income tax 40.5%

Charges and miscellaneous 11.2%

Other taxes 8.7%

General revenue 73.6%

Corporation income tax 12.8%

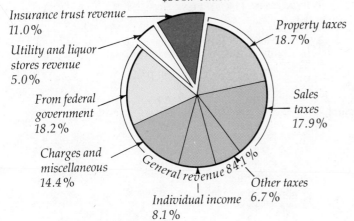

State and local government revenue, 1975–1976
$304.7 billion

Insurance trust revenue 11.0%

Utility and liquor stores revenue 5.0%

From federal government 18.2%

Charges and miscellaneous 14.4%

General revenue 84.1%

Individual income 8.1%

Other taxes 6.7%

Property taxes 18.7%

Sales taxes 17.9%

FIG. 7A.1 Total revenue by major financial sectors for the federal government and for state and local governments: 1975–1976. Source: *Governmental Finances in 1975–76*, **Bureau of the Census, September 1977, p. 2.**

percent of expenditures were distributed among education, public welfare, interest on the debt, health and hospitals, highways, natural resources, and miscellaneous other categories.

State and local expenditures are dominated by education (31.8 percent); public welfare (10.7 percent); insurance trust (9.5 percent); and highways (7.8 percent). Table 7A.2 lists the combined amounts and percentage shares of the major governmental expenditures at all levels.

These tax and revenue figures are more meaningful when translated into the budget of the typical family.

The expenditure and revenue figures cited in the previous section are so large that they have little

TABLE 7A.1

TAX REVENUE, 1975–1976 AT ALL LEVELS OF GOVERNMENT

Item	Amount (millions of dollars)	Percentage of total
Total taxes	$499.9	100.0%
Individual Income Tax	143.8	28.8
Insurance Trust	100.6	20.1
Sales and gross receipts	70.9	14.2
Charges and miscellaneous	67.6	13.5
Property	51.5	10.3
Corporation Income Tax	47.3	9.5
Death and gift	6.0	1.2
Motor vehicle and operator's license	4.2	0.8
Other	8.0	1.6

Source: *Facts and Figures On Government Finance: 1977* (New York: Tax Foundation, Inc., 1978), Table 7, p. 19.

TABLE 7A.2

GOVERNMENTAL EXPENDITURE BY FUNCTION, FISCAL YEAR 1975
(all levels)

Item	Amount (millions of dollars)	Percentage
Total expenditures	$539.1	100.0%
Insurance trust and social insurance administration	109.7	20.3
National defense and international relations	95.8	17.8
Education	95.0	17.6
Public welfare, hospitals, health	64.3	11.9
Interest on general debt	33.0	6.1
Highways	22.8	4.2
Natural resources	16.2	3.0
Financial administration	11.9	2.2
Police protection	9.5	1.8
Transportation	5.3	1.0
Other functions	75.5	14.0

meaning for the average American. Hence we have calculated what the impact of government taxation, borrowing, and expenditure programs is for you.

Suppose that after you have finished your college education you get married and you and your spouse find jobs providing a joint income of about $300 a week. At this rate, your family income would be about 20 percent higher than the median family income in the United States in 1975. If you paid your proportionate share of the taxes, you would pay about $6,250, or 40 percent of

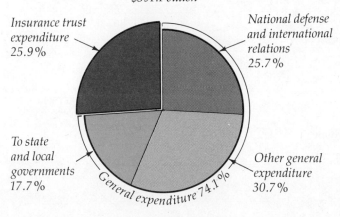

Federal government expenditure , 1975–1976
$391.1 billion

Insurance trust
expenditure
25.9%

National defense
and international
relations
25.7%

To state
and local
governments
17.7%

Other general
expenditure
30.7%

General expenditure 74.1%

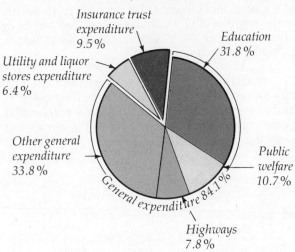

State and local government expenditure , 1975–1976
$305.3 billion

Insurance trust
expenditure
9.5%

Education
31.8%

Utility and liquor
stores expenditure
6.4%

Other general
expenditure
33.8%

Public
welfare
10.7%

General expenditure 84.1%

Highways
7.8%

**FIG. 7A.2 Expenditure by major financial sectors for the
federal government and for state and local governments:
1975–1976. Source:** *Governmental Finances in 1975–76,* Bureau of the Census, September 1977, p. 3.

your annual income, to governments at all levels.
If you bought your share of the government debt
that was issued in 1975, you would pay about
another $550 to the government.

   Some of the taxes you pay would be taxes
you pay knowingly, such as income taxes, social
security taxes, property taxes, and sales taxes.

Other taxes are hidden in the prices of the products you buy. These would include property taxes
paid by businesses on their capital investment,
excise taxes, tariffs on imported products, and
possibly the income taxes that corporations pay
on their profits. Your proportionate share of the
major taxes is shown in Table 7A.3.

TABLE 7A.3
YOUR TAX BILL

Individual income taxes	$1750
Property taxes	625
Sales and gross receipts	975
Corporate income taxes	575
Social security, unemployment compensation, etc.	1185
Other	1240
Total taxes	$6250
Plus purchases of government debt	550
Total payments to government	$6800

The $550 we assumed that you would use to buy government bonds is your share of the total government debt issued by *all* levels of government. These bonds are purchased through a variety of channels. You might choose to participate in your employers' payroll saving plan to buy government bonds, your insurance company may use some of the money you pay it to buy government bonds, or your savings and loan association may put some of your current savings into government bonds. Whether it is done directly or indirectly, we shall assume that you have purchased your share of the government bonds issued by government.

What did you, through your government, buy with your money? Table 7A.4 shows how the government spent your money. We have classified government spending according to the purpose of spending.

TABLE 7A.4
HOW THE GOVERNMENT SPENT YOUR MONEY

	Total government spending
Social security	$1400
Education	1150
National defense	1100
Welfare and social service	825
Interest on debt	425
Highway and transportation	275
Natural resources	175
Financial administration	125
Housing and urban renewal	75
Other	1250
Total	$6800

COMMENTARY

The following is an excerpt from the *Business & Financial Letter* of the Federal Reserve Bank of San Francisco. It describes the changing nature of governmental spending at all levels. Please read the article and answer the following questions.

a) What is the difference between final government demand for goods and services and demands by government enterprises?

b) How important are government enterprises in the United States economy?

c) What has been the cause of the change in the mix of federal and state and local government expenditures?

HOW GOVERNMENT SPENDS

American governments at all levels have become very conscious of their outlays. The word "crisis" has been widely used, especially in the wake of the New York debacle, as citizens have felt compelled to reduce expenditures even for the worthiest of purposes. This growing concern suggests the need to determine how Federal, state and local governments have been exercising their spending powers—either to demand resources or to transfer funds from one group in the economy to another.

Final and enterprise demand

Most of the overall government demand for resources represents final demand for goods and services, for such purposes as defense, education and public safety. But a significant proportion represents demands by government enterprises— that is, institutions which sell their output and whose products are thus a final demand for someone outside government. The difference, sometimes a narrow one, depends on whether or not the price reflects a reasonable value of the product. Thus the postal service and municipal power, water and transit systems are government enterprises, whereas public universities are not because tuition typically bears little relation to the cost of operation. (Highlighting the difference, national-income statisticians exclude government enterprises from the government-expenditures category of the GNP accounts.)

Government enterprises constitute a fairly large portion of the economy in most countries. In Great Britain, for example, the Government controls all the "commanding heights" of the economy, such as coal, steel, transportation and utilities. In this country, the opposite is true; in 1975, government enterprises accounted for only 1.5 percent of GNP with a value added of $22 billion. And judging from the experience of such government enterprises as the postal service, expansion in other fields seems unlikely.

Resource demand trendless . . .

In contrast, government's final demand for goods and services in 1975 amounted to 22.4 percent of GNP, or $339 billion. Just over half of this was the government's wage bill, but the rest represented a range of purchases, from paper clips to schoolrooms to guided-missile cruisers. On the average, final government purchases amounted to 25.0 percent of real GNP in the 1951–55 period, fluctuated narrowly during the next 20 years, and then fell to 21.5 percent of real GNP in the 1971–75 period. This downtrend does not show up when current-dollar figures are used instead of real-GNP figures—but by either standard, government has not increased its relative share of the demand for resources in the past quarter-century.

Nonetheless, a radical shift has occurred in the mix of spending by level of government. Between 1951–55 and 1971–75, the mix shifted from 63 percent Federal to 61 percent state and local, largely because of a secular decline in (Federal) defense spending coupled with a similar increase in (state-local) education spending. These are the two dominant spending categories, defense accounting for 68 percent of Federal demand for goods and services, and education for 41 percent of state-local demand. The shift in the mix of spending may be slowed by the recent increase in defense expenditures and the slowdown in education spending, but a reversal of the trend seems unlikely.

. . . but transfer share up

As noted at the outset, government may exercise its powers either to demand resources or to transfer funds from one group to another. Over time, spending has increased somewhat faster in the latter category than in the former. Thus, between the first half of the '50s and the first half of the '70s, total government spending rose from 26.0 to 32.5 percent of GNP—almost entirely because of the rise in the transfer share from 5.6 to 10.9 percent of GNP.

The term "transfer" might suggest a conscious government reallocation of income to the poor, but this is only a partial truth. Aside from some $20 billion (1975) in subsidies to business and net interest on government debt, the $172 billion in transfers to persons is split in a number of ways— 48 percent for social security (OASDI) and related programs, 13 percent for government employees' retirement, 12 percent for direct welfare relief, 11 percent for unemployment compensation and workmen's compensation, 9 percent for veterans' programs, and so on. The large bulk of these transfers thus represents a major part of the nation's pension system, with payments going to individuals at all income levels.

The rapid growth of transfer payments has been almost entirely a Federal phenomenon. This reflects the broadened coverage of the social-security program after 1966, reinforced in recent years by growing Federal administration of direct relief programs. The principal milestones include the advent of food stamps in the 1960's and the start in 1974 of the supplementary security-income program (SSI), which replaced the locally administered programs of aid to the elderly, blind, and totally disabled. State-local transfers now consist largely of employee pensions and aid to dependent children (a Federally funded but locally administered program).

Result: more government

Altogether, the major trends over the past quarter-century have included a sharp increase in the share of GNP going to state-local spending for goods and services, offsetting a declining share of Federal spending for such purposes, along with a sharp rise in the relative importance of Federally centered transfer programs, especially social security. The result (as noted) is a quarter-century of expansion in total government spending from 26.0 to 32.5 percent of GNP. But because of the offsetting movements in goods-and-services and transfer spending, the Federal-spending share of GNP has fluctuated around a fairly flat trend during this quarter-century. The rise in the overall spending burden has been concentrated at the state-local level, which helps explain the hard-pressed situation of many state and municipal governments today. . . .

LARRY BUTLER, *Business & Financial Letter,* January 21, 1977. Reprinted by permission of the Federal Reserve Bank of San Francisco.

ANALYSIS OF MAJOR TAXES

Taxes are calculated in terms of a base and a rate.

In the 1975–1976 fiscal year, government at all levels collected almost $360 billion dollars in taxes. All taxes are expressed in terms of a base and a rate. The tax *base* is the unit of value on which the tax is levied, and the *rate* is the proportion of the appraised monetary value of the base that the government collects as a tax. For example, the base of the personal income tax is adjusted gross income, while the base of a sales tax is the value of goods purchased on which the sales tax is levied. The rate of the personal income tax increases with the base. The rate of a sales tax is a specified percentage of the value of the taxable goods purchased, for example, 4 percent or 5 percent.

The incidence of corporate profits taxes is difficult to determine.

In 1975–1976, the federal government collected almost $50 billions from corporate profits taxes. You will recall that we assigned $575 of the corporate profits taxes to you as part of your tax bill. Who bears the corporate profits tax?

The corporate profits tax is levied on the accounting profits of the firm. The tax is 22 percent of all profits plus 26 percent surtax of all profits in excess of $25,000, making a total of about 48 percent for all sizeable corporations. Frequently, corporate profits taxes are also levied by states, so that roughly half of corporate profits are taxed away by government. Is the corporate profits tax a tax on the big corporations and on wealthy people? Is it passed on to purchasers, or absorbed by the corporations as a reduction of their profits?

To think about this we shall suppose that initially corporations had not been paying this tax and that corporate profits had reached an equilibrium level. (You may want, in this connection, to review our discussion of opportunity costs and profits in Chapter 4). Now suppose that a 50 percent tax is levied on corporate profits.

Initially, corporate profits would be reduced and the owners of the corporation would really bear the tax. If the total output in the economy was stationary or declining, and if corporations were not permitted to invest outside the country, it is possible that the owners of the corporations would continue to bear the tax.

Over the long run, however, two things would happen. First, corporations would move capital overseas, where it would be taxed at a lower rate. Second, in an expanding economy, corporations would have to go to the capital markets for additional equity capital. The prospective stockholders would be unwilling to accept a lower rate of return on a corporate investment than they could get on overseas investments or on noncorporate investments, for example, government securities, partnership investments in apartment houses, ships, and so on.

As a result of the shortage of capital, the supply of goods produced by corporations would shrink, or at least would not rise as rapidly as demand would rise. The prices of corporate products would rise, and this would make corporate profits *after taxes* high enough so that stockholders would receive (1) the competitive interest rate on their investment and (2) the appropriate risk premium. Thus, the corporate profits tax would be passed on to the purchasers of products.

At this point, however, we have to introduce some ambiguity into the analysis. You will recall from our discussion of profits in Chapters 4 and 6 that some of the corporate profits consist of quasi-rents due to monopoly positions or to short-term shifts in demand. This portion of the total profits could be taken by the corporate profits taxes without in the end causing prices to rise. They are not part of the opportunity costs of corporations.

Because of this ambiguity we cannot say precisely how much of the corporate profits tax will be passed on to the purchasers of products and how much will be borne by the owners of the corporation. If you believe that most industries in which corporations function are characterized by workable competition, then the bulk of the corporate profits tax will be passed on to the buyers of their products. If, on the other hand, you believe that most corporations have substantial monopoly positions, then only a portion of the corporate profits tax will be passed on to the buyers of the products. If low-income people spend a larger percentage of their incomes on products produced by corporations than do wealthy people, the corporate profits tax can easily be a regressive tax. There is no simple answer to this problem.

Using the same type of reasoning we could think about the other common taxes in the United States tax system.

Property taxes, levied as they are as a percentage of the assessed valuation of land, buildings, equipment, and inventories, are largely embedded in the prices of the products you buy. Only the taxes levied on the land itself—probably a small portion of the total—would be absorbed by the landowners. Thus, the property tax tends to be a regressive tax.

Sales taxes of the type you pay when you buy any product in a retail store also tend to be regressive, since low-income people spend a larger percentage of their income on products sold in retail stores than do high-income people. Sales taxes are clearly added to the prices of the products you buy. Only when certain necessities, such as groceries and drugs, are exempted from the sales tax does the tax become less regressive.

Social security taxes are withheld from your paychecks to finance the social security system. They are also regressive since they are imposed as a 6.05 percent of the first $17,700 of an employee's wages.* Thus, persons earning more than $17,700 pay a smaller percentage of their total income into the government for social security than do poor people. (Their expected benefits upon retirement are also a smaller percentage of their average lifetime income.)

Employers are also required to pay social security taxes for employees. While these are paid by businesses, they are probably treated as one of the costs of doing business and are included in the prices of the products companies sell.

Excise taxes, such as taxes on cigarettes, beer, distilled spirits, long distance telephone calls, and customs duties paid on imported products such as oil are included in the prices of products sold by business. These taxes are probably regressive since they are included as part of the prices of products, although the case is not entirely clear since many of these products are luxuries purchased largely by the upper-income groups.

Some interesting problems are associated with the personal income tax.

The individual income tax is so important, accounting for almost 60 percent of the revenues generated at all levels of government, that we will focus on it. It is natural to think that personal income tax applies to all income received. But this is not true. Of the total personal income received in the United states, only about half is treated as taxable income. Many items are excluded from the base of the personal income tax;

* Both the base and the rate will increase until by 1990, the rate will be 7.65 percent and the base will be $42,600.

for example, social security benefits and other government pensions; deductions such as interest on home mortgages and consumer loans; taxes paid to state and local governments; contributions to charity; a portion of medical expenses and other allowable deductions; and personal exemptions, including earned income credits. The federal government collected a little over 21 percent of this reduced base in 1976. Had the tax base been broadened to include all personal income, the average tax rate could have been cut in half.

The interesting question to ask about the personal income tax is why the government does not reduce the number of deductions (sometimes called "loopholes") and thus expand the tax base.

The personal income tax is intended to achieve many objectives in addition to raising revenue.

An important reason why tax loopholes are not simply closed is that the raising of revenues is just one of the objectives that the income tax is intended to achieve. Consider, for example, some of the provisions built into the income tax to achieve these objectives:

1. Interest from the bonds issued by state and local governments is exempt from taxation. This is a subsidy intended to reduce the cost to state and local governments of building schools, streets, and other public amenities. People who buy these tax-free bonds receive what is in essence a subsidy from the federal government. This creates a demand for these securities, enabling the states and local governments to borrow money at a lower interest rate.
2. Social security benefits are not taxable. This is a direct subsidy to older persons and others who qualify for such benefits.
3. Interest payments on home mortgages are deductible for tax purposes. This is a subsidy to encourage home ownership. A portion of this no doubt flows through to the home building industry, since their market is expanded because of this subsidy.
4. Contributions to churches, charities, and schools are not taxable. The family that

makes the contributions deducts them from its tax base. In effect, the taxpayers who support these private charities receive a subsidy to encourage them to do so. Because of the subsidy, contributions to nonprofit educational and charitable institutions are higher than they otherwise would be.

5. The internal revenue service permits the rapid depreciation of new rental properties, thus creating accounting losses that can be offset against a taxpayer's other taxable income. This is called a tax shelter, and is a subsidy granted to taxpayers who invest in apartments and other rental property. Who benefits from this subsidy? The answer is that renters probably benefit. The subsidy has increased the supply of housing and thus kept the rents down. It has also, of course, reduced the taxes of those who have invested in rental property.

It is clear from this list of subsidies that the personal income tax is intended to accomplish many goals, among which the raising of revenue is only one. The so-called loopholes are in fact subsidies intended to achieve specific objectives.

Should loopholes be abolished?

Should these implicit subsidies be abolished and the tax base increased? If the tax base were increased until it approximated the total personal income of the United States, the tax rates could be cut in half. Why are the tax *rates* important?

The higher the marginal tax rates, the more likely people are to emphasize untaxed activities, such as "do it yourself activities," over taxed activities. Consider some examples:

1. You can work overtime and receive $10 an hour or stay at home and raise vegetables in your garden. If your marginal tax rate is 50 percent, you get only $5 an hour (even though your employer pays you $10). The higher the marginal rate, the larger will be your tendency to work in your garden.

2. Assume you are a good manager and you live in a small town. You are 45 years old and your children are in high school. The opportunity to move to a better job in a large city presents itself. It will pay you $10,000 more a year, but your children object. Furthermore, you and your wife enjoy the town you live in. Should you take the job? No. If the tax rate is very high, it won't pay you to give up the nontaxable satisfactions of living in a small town for the extra after-tax income. Result: the economy is deprived of having your managerial services applied to a larger factory.

Marginal tax rates are important in the allocation of resources. As marginal tax rates rise, they reach a boundary point where people will choose "do-it-yourself" and barter activities over the taxed benefits of the money exchange economy. Economists do not know where this boundary point is and it may differ substantially from individual to individual.

COMMENTARY

The following is taken from an article entitled "Taxes, Revenues and the Laffer Curve." It shows through the use of a single diagram how people react to different tax rates and the implications of these reactions for raising revenue. Please read the excerpt and answer the following questions:

a) At what point on the "Laffer curve" is government revenue at a maximum?
b) What kinds of events cause the curve to shift over time?
c) How have politicians reacted to the "Laffer curve?"

TAXES, REVENUES, AND THE LAFFER CURVE

As Arthur Laffer has noted, "There are always two tax rates that yield the same revenues." When an aide to President Gerald Ford asked him once to elaborate, Laffer (who is Professor of Business Economics at the University of Southern California) drew a simple curve, shown on the next page, to illustrate his point. The point, too, is simple enough—though, like so many simple points, it is also powerful in its implications.

When the tax rate is 100 percent, all production ceases in the money economy (as distinct from the barter economy, which exists largely to escape taxation). People will not work in the money economy if all the fruits of their labors are confiscated by the government. And because production ceases, there is nothing for the 100-percent rate to confiscate, so government revenues are zero.

On the other hand, if the tax rate is zero, people can keep 100 percent of what they produce in the money economy. There is no governmental "wedge" between earnings and after-tax income, and thus no governmental barrier to production. Production is therefore maximized, and the output of the money economy is limited only by the desire of workers for leisure. But because the tax rate is zero, government revenues are again zero, and there can be no government. So at a 0-percent tax rate the economy is in a state of anarchy, and at a 100-percent tax rate the economy is functioning entirely through barter.

In between lies the curve. If the government reduces its rate to something less than 100 percent, say to point A, some segment of the barter economy will be able to gain so many efficiencies by being in the money economy that, even with near-confiscatory tax rates, after-tax production would still exceed that of the barter economy. Production will start up, and revenues will flow into the government treasury. By lowering the tax rate, we find an increase in revenues.

On the bottom end of the curve, the same thing is happening. If people feel that they need a minimal government and thus institute a low tax rate, some segment of the economy, finding that the marginal loss of income exceeds the efficiencies gained in the money economy, is shifted into either barter or leisure. But with that tax rate, revenues do flow into the government treasury. This is the situation at point B. Point A

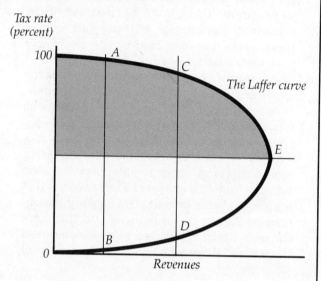

represents a very high tax rate and very low production. Point B represents a very low tax rate and very high production. Yet they both yield the same revenue to the government.

The same is true of points C and D. The government finds that by a further lowering of the tax rate, say from point A to point C, revenues increase with the further expansion of output. And by raising the tax rate, say from point B to point D, revenues also increase, by the same amount.

Revenues and production are maximized at point E. If, at point E, the government lowers the tax rate again, output will increase, but revenues will fall. And if, at point E, the tax rate is raised, both output and revenue will decline. The shaded area is *the prohibitive range for government*, where rates are unnecessarily high and can be reduced with gains in *both* output and revenue.

Tax Rates and Tax Revenues

The next important thing to observe is that, except for the 0-percent and 100-percent rates, there are no numbers along the "Laffer curve." Point E is not 50 percent, although it may be, but rather a variable number: *It is the point at which the electorate desires to be taxed.* At points B and D, the electorate desires more government goods and services and is willing—without reducing its productivity—to pay the higher rates consistent with the revenues at point E. And at points A and C, the electorate desires more private goods and services in the money economy, and wishes to pay the lower rates consistent with the revenues at point E. It is the task of the statesman to determine the location of point E, and follow its variations as closely as possible.

This is true whether the political leader heads a nation or a family. The father who disciplines his son at point A, imposing harsh penalties for violating both major and minor rules, only invites sullen rebellion, stealth, and lying (tax evasion, on the national level). The permissive father who disciplines casually at point B invites open, reckless rebellion: His son's independence and relatively unfettered growth comes at the expense of the rest of the family. The wise parent seeks point E, which will probably vary from one child to another, from son to daughter.

For the political leader on the national level, point E can represent a very low or a very high number. When the nation is at war, point E can approach 100 percent. At the siege of Leningrad in World War II, for example, the people of the city produced for 900 days at tax rates approaching 100 percent. Russian soldiers and civilians worked to their physical limits, receiving as "pay" only the barest of rations. Had the citizens of Leningrad not wished to be taxed at that high rate, which was required to hold off the Nazi army, the city would have fallen.

The number represented by point E will change abruptly if the nation is at war one day and at peace the next. The electorate's demand for military goods and services from the government will fall sharply; the electorate will therefore desire to be taxed at a lower rate. If rates are not lowered consistent with this new lower level of demand, output will fall to some level consistent with a point along the prohibitive side of the "Laffer curve." . . .

The easiest way for a political leader to determine whether an increase in rates will produce more rather than less revenues is to put the proposition to the electorate. It is not enough for the politician to propose an increase from, say, point B to point D on the curve. He must also specify how the anticipated revenues will be spent. When voters approve a bond issue for schools, highways, or bridges, they are explicitly telling the politician that they are willing to pay the high tax rates required to finance the bonds. In rejecting a bond issue, however, the electorate is not necessarily telling the politician that taxes are already high enough, or that point E (or beyond) has been reached. The only message is that the proposed tax rates are too high a price to pay for the specific goods and services offered by the government.

Only a tiny fraction of all government expenditures are determined in this fashion, to be sure. Most judgments regarding tax rates and expenditures are made by individual politicians. Andrew Mellon became a national hero for engineering the rate reductions of the 1920's, and was called "the greatest Treasury Secretary since Alexander Hamilton." The financial policies of Ludwig Erhard were responsible for what was hailed as "an economic miracle"—the post-war recovery of Germany. Throughout history, however, it has been the exception rather than the rule that politicians, by accident or design, have sought to increase revenues by lowering rates.

Adapted from JUDE WANNISKI, *The Way the World Works: How Economies Fail—And Succeed*, Harper & Row, 1978. Reprinted with permission of the author from THE PUBLIC INTEREST, No. 50 (Winter 1978), p. xx. © 1978 by National Affairs, Inc.

There are many interesting questions, although largely unanswered, connected with the personal income tax. What is the best trade-off between the size of the tax base (and therefore the level of tax rates) and the granting of subsidies through deductions and other devices? To what extent do people think in terms of their after-tax income (and therefore after-tax prices) before they accept difficult or unpleasant tasks? To what extent does a personal income tax discriminate against people living in large northern cities or in Alaska, where it takes more money income to live comfortably than it does in smaller towns in the Sun Belt?

The tax system in the United States does not appear to have made the distribution of income more equal.

Attempts have been made to appraise the net effect of all forms of taxation in the United States on the distribution of income. The latest, and perhaps the most comprehensive, study of the effects of taxation on the distribution of income has been made by Joseph A. Pechman and Benjamin A. Okner for the Brookings Institution.* Using a sample of 72,000 individuals and families, and rea-

* Joseph A. Pechman and Benjamin A. Okner, *Who Bears the Burden?* Washington, D.C., The Brookings Institution, 1974.

soning from eight sets of assumptions about tax incidence, the authors found that the tax system of the United States did not markedly change the distribution of income in this country. They found the after-tax distribution of income to be very close to the before-tax distribution of income, even when the corporate income tax is assumed to be borne half by stockholders and half by property owners in general.

REVIEW QUESTIONS

1. The federal government depends primarily on the following taxes for its revenues:
   a) individual income tax, property tax, and corporate income tax.
   b) insurance trust tax, individual income tax, and corporate income tax.
   c) property tax, individual income tax, and sales tax.
   d) sales tax, property tax, and individual income tax.

2. When all levels of government are combined (federal, state, and local), the two largest classifications of expenditures are:
   a) national defense and highways.
   b) national defense and insurance trust.
   c) national defense and public welfare.
   d) insurance trust and education.

3. Assuming that you and your spouse get about $15,000 a year in income and pay about $6,000 a year in taxes to all levels of government, which of the following taxes is *least* regressive?
   a) personal income taxes of $1750 per year.
   b) social security and unemployment compensation taxes combined of $1200 a year.
   c) sales taxes of $1000 a year.
   d) property taxes of $600 per year.

4. Assuming that the economy is workably competitive, that unusual profits due to shifts in demand have been eliminated by firms changing their production rates, and that there are many opportunities to use financial capital in noncorporate activities, then:
   a) the corporation income tax is actually borne by corporations considered as persons.
   b) the corporation income tax is borne entirely by the stockholders in corporations.
   c) the corporation income tax is shifted back and comes out of the workers' pay.
   d) the corporation income tax is largely shifted forward and paid by the persons who purchase products produced by the corporate sector.

5. The tax base for the individual income tax is about half of the total personal income received by individuals. The rest of the tax base is exempt from taxation. If the tax base were increased to include all income received by individuals, the personal income tax rates could be cut almost in half. The failure to increase the tax base (and therefore cut income tax rates) is largely the result of:

a) constitutional limitations that make it impossible to levy taxes on social security benefits, interest paid on home mortgages, and the like.

b) administrative problems that would arise if personal income taxes were levied on income used to make charitable contributions, unemployment benefits, and other forms of income not included in the tax base.

c) the efforts on the part of rich people to avoid paying income taxes by insisting that there be many loopholes that they can use to shelter their income from taxation.

d) the government's use of the personal income tax to accomplish many objectives, such as the encouragement of home ownership and charitable activities, the subsidizing of state and local government borrowing, and the maintenance of retirement incomes.

6. With respect to the personal income tax, some believe that there exists a tax rate beyond which increases in tax rates will decrease rather than increase total tax revenues. Thus, if they are correct it is possible that a 90 percent rate would lead to the collection of smaller tax revenues than a 40 percent rate. All of the following statements would be true except:

a) people will resort to barter and other nontaxed activities rather than pay such a high rate of taxation.

b) people will increase their "do-it-yourself" and other nonspecialized activities. This will reduce the productivity of the economy, and thus limit the size of the tax base.

c) the higher the tax rate the greater is the temptation to cheat in making out income tax returns.

d) at higher tax rates, it becomes more difficult to shift the incidence of taxes and therefore revenues fall.

7. Considering the entire tax system of the United States, including the taxes levied by state and local as well as by the federal government, it is probably true that:

a) the tax system of the United States is regressive.

b) the tax system of the United States is proportional.

c) the tax system of the United States is progressive.

d) the tax system is progressive at low income levels and regressive at high income levels.

8. At the present time, the tax system of the United States:

a) is designed chiefly to stabilize the economy.

b) has caused income to be distributed considerably more equally.

c) is based largely on the benefit principle and therefore is geared to take taxes from people in accordance with their use of the government.

d) has had little effect on income equality.

ESSAY QUESTIONS

1. Suppose that the personal income tax were the only form of taxation in the United States and that it was necessary to collect about 40 percent of the tax base in order to pay for government expenditures. Suppose further that you wanted the personal income tax to be progressive in its impact on personal income. Discuss the problems that you think would arise.

2. Is the corporate income tax really a tax on corporations considered as a separate class of person?

3. Who do you think actually bears the following taxes and what effect will the taxes have on the distribution of income? (1) the sales tax; (2) the portion of the social security tax paid by the employer; (3) the excise tax on long distance telephone calls; and (4) the tariff on imported oil.

4. If food, drugs, and services are exempt from state sales taxes, are those taxes necessarily regressive?

5. If government expenditures are largely regressive—that is, they benefit the poor more than the rich—would a proportional tax system make the distribution of income more or less equal?

6. If Pechman and Okner are correct and the tax system of the United States does not change the distribution of income, why should we not levy a comprehensive sales tax on all activities? Discuss the problems that would arise. Do you think that the gains in administrative simplicity would be worth the disadvantages of such a tax system?

7. Suppose you were given the task of designing a tax system for the United States. What factors would you take into account? What taxes would you use?

ANSWERS TO REVIEW QUESTIONS

1. In 1975–1976, the individual income tax accounted for 40.5 percent of the federal government's revenue, the insurance trust (social security) taxes accounted for 26.4 percent, and the corporation income tax accounted for 12.8 percent of the revenue. Hence (b) is the correct answer.

2. When you examine Table 7A.2 you will see that insurance trust expenditures (social security, unemployment benefits, and other transfer programs) and national defense are the two largest expenditure classifications. Education is in third place and public welfare is fourth.

a) This is incorrect since highway expenditure is far down the list.
b) This is correct as explained above.
c) This is incorrect. Public welfare is fourth on the list.
d) This is incorrect since these comprise the second and third largest expenditures.

3. Personal income tax is probably the least regressive. As your income rises, the marginal tax rate rises. On the average, the higher income families pay in personal income taxes a larger percentage to all levels of government.

a) This is correct for the reason given above.
b) This is incorrect since social security taxes are proportional and are not levied on that portion of an individual's income above a given level.
c) Sales taxes are regressive. They are not levied on that portion of the income that is saved. Rich people save more than poor people. Therefore rich people pay a smaller percentage of their income in sales taxes than do poor people.
d) Property taxes are passed on and included in rents and in the prices of ordinary products. As a result, poor people, who spend a larger portion of their incomes on rents and the purchase of products, probably pay a larger percentage of their incomes for property taxes than do rich persons.

4. The "escape" theory of taxation tells us that investors will not put additional capital in corporations unless the rate of return is at least as large as they could earn in noncorporate activities—such as building apartment houses and so on. In order to get capital, corporations must then earn as much after taxes for their stockholders as the stockholders could receive from noncorporate uses of their capital. Under these conditions, corporation income taxes will be passed on like any other expense to the purchasers of their products. It follows that:

a) This is incorrect since corporations do not bear taxes, they only pay them. The taxes must be borne by people.
b) This is incorrect. Stockholders will receive as much from corporate activities as they would from noncorporate activities.
c) This is incorrect. Corporations will have to pay the going rate to workers.
d) This is correct for the reasons given above.

5. The answer is that the personal income tax has traditionally been used to accomplish many objectives.

a) There is no constitutional reason why the income tax could not be levied on social security benefits, interest on home mortgages, and the like.
b) There are no additional administrative problems involved in expanding the tax base. Indeed, there would be fewer administrative problems, since excludable income would not have to be defined.
c) Rich people do like to have devices to shelter their income from taxation, but they are not the principal beneficiaries of most of the exclusions from the tax base.
d) This is correct as explained above.

6. Answers (a), (b), and (c) are true. They accurately describe the responses of taxpayers to high and increasing tax rates. Answer (d) is a nonsense statement. Therefore the correct choice is (d).

7. According to Pechman and Okner of the Brookings Institution, the after-tax distribution of income in the United States is about the same as the before-tax distribution of income. Therefore the tax system of the United States is proportional in its total impact on the bulk of personal incomes of the United States. Therefore (b) is the only correct answer.

8. Based on the evidence we have, the tax system does little to affect the distribution of income.

a) This is incorrect. Certainly there is concern about the effect of taxes on economic stability, but it is not the only or even chief concern.
b) This is incorrect. The study of Pechman and Okner does not support this.
c) This is incorrect. The benefit principle is only one consideration in designing a tax system.
d) This is correct as noted in the Pechman-Okner study.

OBJECTIVES

Upon successful completion of this chapter, you will be able to:

1. Cite statistics indicating the concentration ratios in manufacturing in the United States.
2. Cite the conditions that are necessary for monopoly power to exist.
3. Explain how monopoly power can be identified.
4. Identify major sources of monopoly power and give examples of monopolies created by these sources.
5. Identify factors that limit monopoly power.
6. Use the concepts of marginal revenue and marginal cost to explain the pricing strategy of a profit-maximizing monopolist.
7. Explain the effects of monopoly in terms of allocation and distribution.
8. Cite the results of empirical attempts to measure the effect of monopoly.

CHAPTER 8

MONOPOLY

INTRODUCTION

If you decide to purchase a new American-made automobile, you can be quite certain that it will be made by one of four manufacturers, and if you purchase a box of breakfast cereal, you will likely find it is produced by one of four manufacturers. But if you purchase a man's or woman's coat, it is likely to have been manufactured by one of a large number of firms.

These are common indications of something you already know—that the markets in which products and productive services are sold in the United States are tremendously varied. Consequently, it should not surprise you that attempts to explain how goods and services are produced in the United States economy must incorporate the fact that in some industries, such as agriculture, there are many producers, while in other industries, such as the manufacture of automobiles, there are only a few producers, and in still others, such as communications and electric power, there is only one producer.

Public concern about the effects of concentration of economic power or monopolistic tendencies is not new. A call for governmental action to deal with such concentration arose in the United States during the period of economic growth after the Civil War. More recently, the United States Senate has held extensive hearings on the nature and effects of monopoly power.

The term monopoly refers technically to a market with a single seller. More broadly, it implies the absence of competition.

Monopoly power exists when there is a single seller or a small number of sellers and when there are restrictions of one type or another on entry into an industry or occupation.

This chapter will cite the historical events that led to today's market organization and will discuss the relationship between economic concentration and market power. Then it will identify examples of monopolies in the United States economy and consider the sources of monopoly power and its effects on the overall economy.

THE DEVELOPMENT OF MARKET STRUCTURE IN THE UNITED STATES

The industrial structure of the United States has undergone vast changes.

The industrial structure of the United States today is vastly different from that prevailing barely more than 100 years ago in the pre-Civil War era. At that time, agriculture was the dominant industry, employing fully two-thirds of the labor force, and the family farm was the most common form of "industrial" organization.

During the 1850s, there were no major utilities, the railroads that existed were small and diverse, and manufacturing was conducted in small local plants or shops. The invention of the sewing machine was just bringing the manufacture of clothing into the factory, and shoes were still handsewn, mainly in the home.

The Bessemer steel furnace was not yet widely used, and the technology of open-hearth furnaces did not exist. Ironmasters were just beginning to shift from hammering out bar iron in a forge to new methods of rolling.

The United States economy was, indeed, characterized by small-scale enterprise operating in relatively small markets. It is not surprising, then, that the prevailing body of economic theory emerging from that period was based on the existence of many independent, small-scale producers. Changes were in store, however.

Agriculture showed the most dramatic change. The share of workers in agriculture dropped precipitously from 67 percent in the pre-Civil War era to 20 percent in 1929, and today accounts for only 3 percent of the civilian labor force.

Dramatic changes also occurred in the manufacturing, transportation, and utility industries. Mergers and growth increased economic concentration to the point that in 1929, the 200 largest corporations controlled almost 50 percent of the assets of nonfinancial corporations.

It is not surprising, then, that this period also generated a reaction to the increased concentration of economic power in the form of antitrust legislation.

Federal government antitrust actions began in the late 1800s.

The first attempts to counter the growing economic importance of the trusts created through merger and growth came in the form of state laws. They were ineffectual, however, and the federal government moved into the arena with the Sherman Antitrust Act of 1890. This act prohibited combinations or conspiracies—especially trusts—in restraint of interstate trade, and forbade monopoly or the attempt to monopolize. Under this act, the Standard Oil Trust was dissolved in 1911. The Sherman Antitrust Act, however, proved to be weaker in effect than its designers had planned, and in 1914 the Clayton Antitrust Act was passed. It specifically prohibits price discrimination and the holding of the stock of one corporation by another when doing so lessens competition. Labor organizations are explicitly exempted from the antitrust laws since labor, according to the act, is not a commodity.

Over the years, a number of laws have been passed to strengthen antitrust legislation. The Federal Trade Commission Act (1914), The Robinson-Patman Act (1936), and The Miller-Tydings Act (1937) are examples.

The economic reasoning underlying this legislation is to restore or create the conditions of competition perceived necessary for a market-oriented economy. These conditions, many buyers and sellers, and free entry and exit of producers are basic assumptions underlying the model of supply and demand described in Chapter 3 and the theory of the firm under competition explained in Chapters 4 and 5.

The competitive model of the economy does not describe the real world accurately.

Since the nature of production prior to the Civil War was characterized by many small firms, the competitive model provided a reasonably good analysis of the United States economy at that time. That period was short-lived, however, and by the turn of the century most firms were operating under conditions that could not be clearly identified as either competitive or monopolistic. Clearly, a theory focusing exclusively on competitive conditions or on the other extreme, monopoly, was inadequate. In response to this gap, the theory of *monopolistic competition* was introduced in the 1930s.*

The theory of monopolistic competition describes a situation in which the elements of competition and monopoly both prevail. These conditions change the nature of the equilibrium solution that would occur in either situation and provide an "in-between" outcome. Although this theory has never been a completely satisfactory analysis of our market structure, it openly recognized the problems not faced by the existing theories.

The key idea in the monopolistic competition model of markets is *product differentiation*. A class of products is described as being differentiated as long as there is any basis, real or imagined, for consumers to believe one seller's product is different from another.

The implication of this is that to the extent that sellers can differentiate their product, they have some power to raise prices without losing customers to other close substitutes. Examples of such differentiated products are soaps, toothpastes, patent medicines, and so on.

* Edward H. Chamberlin and Joan Robinson authored distinct but related works addressing the same issue: Edward H. Chamberlin, *The Theory of Monopolistic Competition*, (Harvard University Press, Cambridge, Mass.: 1932). Joan Robinson, *The Economics of Imperfect Competition*, London: Macmillan, 1933.

Oligopolies exist when very few firms hold market power.

Various theories of market structure have also been created to explain the case in which there are very few, say two or three, producers in any given market. The term used here is *oligopoly*.

The key concept in the analysis of oligopolies is the mutual interdependence among the firms in the market. An oligopolistic firm is influenced by the behavior of its rivals, and its own behavior in turn influences those rivals. As a consequence, each firm must consider what its opponents are doing and the way its opponents may respond to its own actions. Examples of oligopolistic industries are those of steel, aluminum, and automobiles.

Since the key descriptor in market organization has historically been the number of sellers, much of the research conducted to measure the magnitude and effect of imperfect markets has consisted of attempts to measure the economic concentration of the various industries in the economy.

Economic concentration is used as a measure of monopoly power.

Although the terms monopoly and competition are relatively easy to define, the actual task of measuring the degree of monopoly power or competitiveness in a given market is beset with problems. Ideally, we would like to measure the power that a firm or group of firms exercises over price. This, however, would involve specific knowledge about the firms' demand curves—knowledge terribly difficult to obtain. We might also seek to measure the performance of firms in the market, but this is also difficult since so many factors in addition to market power may be active. The easiest approach is to measure market structure in terms of the percentage of the market held by the top 4 or 8 or 20 firms. It provides a simple statement about the condition of "fewness" of an industry but is subject to a fundamental criticism; namely, does economic concentration imply monopoly power and inefficiency?

An overall picture of economic concentration in manufacturing in the United States can be seen in Table 8.1. It uses several measures—value added, payroll, value of shipments, and capital expenditures—to express the impact of the largest firms in 1967 and 1972. For example, it shows that the 50 largest firms accounted for 25 percent of the value added, 17 percent of employees, and 26 percent of the capital expenditures made by manufacturing companies. Table 8.2 shows industry concentration ratios (the percentage of output accounted for by the largest firms), and reveals that many industries appear to be dominated by relatively few producers.

Although it is obvious that American manufacturing industries are highly concentrated, does it follow that they are therefore neither competitive nor efficient? Numerous studies have attempted to identify whether any relationship exists between industry concentration, as a measure of monopoly, and profit rates.

The conclusions of these studies have been summarized by Peter Asch as follows:

> It is important to realize that the statistical findings of past studies have varied rather widely, and that there is no such thing as a universal, or even a consensus, conclusion as to the precise significance of concentration in explaining profitability. No one has concluded that concentration in any sense completely explains profit performance, and no such conclusion would be supported by economic theory. Even when the condition of entry is also considered, there obviously exist other factors that must be expected to influence profit levels. The degree of risk and behavior of demand are two obviously influential elements that vary from industry to industry. Moreover, a number of writers have suggested that characteristics of the firm—such as absolute size—may affect profit levels apart from the influence of industry-wide characteristics.[*]

Obviously monopoly power is a complex phenomenon influenced by many factors. We can, however, make some generalizations about the sources and effects of monopoly. The remainder of this chapter deals with those issues.

[*] Asch, Peter, *Economic Theory and the Antitrust Dilemma,* John Wiley and Sons, New York, 1970, p. 186.

TABLE 8.1

SHARE OF VALUE ADDED, EMPLOYMENT, PAYROLL, VALUE OF SHIPMENTS, AND CAPITAL EXPENDITURES ACCOUNTED FOR BY THE 200 LARGEST COMPANIES: 1972 and 1967

(Percent)

Company rank group based on value added by manufacture		Value added by manufacture	All employees[1]		Production workers			Value of shipments[2]	Capital expenditures, new
			Number	Payroll	Number	Worker hours	Wages		
50 largest	1972	25	17	22	17	18	24	24	26
	1967	25	20	25	18	18	23	25	27
51st to 100th largest	1972	9	6	6	6	6	7	8	9
	1967	8	6	7	5	6	6	8	13
101st to 150th largest	1972	6	5	5	5	5	6	6	6
	1967	5	4	5	4	4	4	6	6
151st to 200th largest	1972	4	3	3	3	3	4	5	5
	1967	4	4	3	3	3	3	4	4
200 largest	1972	43	31	37	32	32	40	43	46
	1967	42	34	40	30	31	37	43	51

Note: All percentages are independently rounded and do not necessarily add to totals.
[1] Includes employees in central administrative offices and auxiliaries serving manufacturing establishments.
[2] Includes a substantial, but unmeasurable, amount of duplication because of shipments of materials and products among manufacturing establishments for further processing.
Source: Concentration Ratios in Manufacturing, Special Report Series, 1972 Census of Manufactures, U.S. Department of Commerce, Bureau of the Census, October 1975.

TABLE 8.2

PERCENTAGE OF SHIPMENTS ACCOUNTED FOR BY THE 4, 8, AND 20 LARGEST COMPANIES IN SELECTED MANUFACTURING INDUSTRIES, 1972

	4 largest companies	8 largest companies	20 largest companies
1 Motor vehicles and car bodies	93%	99%	99%
2 Cereal breakfast foods	90	98	99
3 Chewing gum	87	98	100
4 Tires and inner tubes	73	90	98
5 Papermills	59	83	99
6 Soap and other detergents	62	74	85
7 Distilled liquor	47	73	91
8 Radio and TV	49	71	86
9 Metal office furniture	42	54	76
10 Bread, cake, and related products	29	37	50
11 Meatpacking plants	22	37	51
12 Mobile homes	26	37	56
13 Book publishing	19	31	56
14 Hosiery	19	29	46
15 Men's and boys' clothing	20	27	41
16 Steel metalworks	9	15	24

Source: Concentration Ratios in Manufacturing, Special Report Series, 1972 Census of Manufactures, U.S. Department of Commerce, Bureau of the Census, October 1975.

There are many examples of the exercise of monopoly power in the product and productive services markets.

You will recall that we defined a competitive market as one in which there are either a large number of buyers and sellers, each acting independently, or, in the long run, a market in which there are no restrictions on entry and exit. Some economists would call this workable competition in contrast to pure competition. But for simplicity's sake we have called this type of market rivalry *competition*.

You don't have to look far to see examples of monopoly in the products market. The United States Postal Service has a monopoly in the service of first-class mail delivery. It has the right by law to prevent the use of the mailboxes for the delivery of mail by any other organization. A relatively small number of oil-producing nations may also be said to have monopoly power in the pricing of crude oil. These nations control enough of the world's oil resources so that by withholding oil from the world market they can increase its price.

In the productive service markets there are also many examples of monopoly power. Some banks, particularly those in small towns, have monopoly powers. They can pay lower interest rates to depositors than if they were operating in a truly competitive market; and since the government normally restricts the number of banks in a community, they can do so without fear that other banks will move in to eliminate their extra profits. Similarly, some labor unions have monopoly power; they have been designated as the sole seller of certain types of labor. The buyers of that labor are prevented by contract from paying less than a particular wage rate, even though there are willing sellers at lower prices.

The key to identifying a monopoly is the relationship between the price it charges and its opportunity cost.

How do you know whether a seller is exercising monopoly power? Does the fact that a seller is very large compared to other producers indicate the existence of monopoly? Unfortunately, it is not that simple. We can say, however, that if the price of a product is higher than its opportunity cost over an extended period of time, there must be some type of restriction that prevents businesses and people from moving in to take advantage of the higher prices.

Suppose a university charges students $3000 a year to live in its dormitories. Further, assume that a private organization offers to provide comparable facilities and food services for $2000. We will assume that to protect its dormitory business the university requires that all undergraduate students live in university dormitories. This restriction, which really denies other businesses open entry into the student-dormitory business, gives the university monopoly power in establishing dormitory rates.

Or suppose that the graduate students working as teaching assistants decide to organize a union. In place of being paid $4000 a year as a teaching assistant, they might, as members of the union, negotiate a $7500 a year stipend. The teaching assistants who keep their jobs would be happier, but the university, faced with these higher costs, would no doubt reduce the number of teaching assistantships available. If year after year there were more highly qualified applicants for these assistantships than assistantships available, it would be clear that the new wage rate for teaching assistants was a monopoly rate. It is higher than is necessary to recruit the graduate students to do the job.

Monopoly power can be achieved and maintained by restricting the entry of would-be competitors.

Businesses or persons can obtain monopoly power by finding a way to keep other businesses or persons from entering the monopoly-priced activity. In the examples we have just considered, the university used its power over students to keep other businesses from entering the dormitory business. The teaching assistants' union was able to use its power to keep the university from hiring qualified persons at less than the union wage rate. In effect, the union could prevent the entry of qualified teaching assistants who would work for less if the university were permitted to hire them.

COMMENTARY

The following is taken from an article entitled "Antitrust: The Coming Battlefield." It summarizes the contents of a book by Robert Bork, a Yale University law professor who served a brief stint as Acting Attorney General during the Nixon administration. Please read the excerpt and answer the following questions:

a) Bork asserts that the original goal of antitrust has been twisted. Does this interpretation merely reflect his values? How can you tell?

b) What is his basis for defending bigness?

c) The author of the article claims Bork is not anti-antitrust. Do you agree with the author based on the information in the article. Why or why not?

ANTITRUST: THE COMING BATTLEFIELD

A nationally prominent attorney, who later became an Associate Justice of the Supreme Court, once told several hundred lawyers at a meeting of the American Bar Association that there was no sense worrying too much about the complexity of the antitrust laws. Antitrust, the attorney said, is in the good old American tradition of the frontier sheriff; he didn't sift evidence, distinguish between suspects and solve crimes, but merely walked the main street and every so often pistol-whipped a few people.

Robert H. Bork tells that anecdote in the opening pages of his brilliant new book, *The Antitrust Paradox: A Policy at War With Itself* (Basic Books, 388 pages, $18). Even if the story is apocryphal it's an apt description of the state of the antitrust laws these days.

Antitrust shows signs of becoming the economic battleground of the late 1970s and 1980s. Americans traditionally have distrusted bigness, and any major corporation that says it isn't looking nervously over its shoulder at the trustbusters— both elected and self-appointed—either fails to comprehend or is unwilling to acknowledge a frightening reality.

The last few years, after all, have seen a major new federal law extending the scope and authority of the antitrust laws, a nearly successful effort to bust up the oil companies, a pending suit to force AT&T to divest itself of Western Electric and government investigations of everything from "price signaling" in the steel industry to "product competition" among cereal makers. The government's zeal has been matched by businessmen using civil antitrust suits to gain a toehold on larger competitors.

Ominous turns

In the welter of legislation and litigation, antitrust law has taken some ominous turns. The original goal of antitrust was to maximize consumer welfare. The law now is being twisted into protecting inefficient firms and penalizing efficient ones. The ideological basis of antitrust has shifted from economic efficiency to the objective of social and political equality. Never mind the contradictions in all of this; an occasional pistol-whipping is bound to be good for the greedy corporate soul, isn't it? . . .

The message is straightforward: ". . . modern antitrust has so decayed that the policy is no longer intellectually respectable. Some of it is not respectable as law; more of it is not respectable as economics; and . . . because it pretends to one objective while frequently accomplishing its opposite, and because it too often forwards trends dangerous to our form of government and society, a great deal of antitrust is not even respectable as politics."

The irony is, of course, that antitrust law in its early days was seen as a means of deflecting calls for socialist reform. But, as Mr. Bork notes, "that was not without cost, because the process tended to make antitrust more interventionist in order to show that other reforms were not needed, and so the ideas that propelled statist philosophies gradually edged into antitrust and lodged themselves there." . . .

He argues that mergers which increase efficiency should not be prevented; there is nothing inherently wrong about bigness. To the argument that such efficiencies could be achieved by internal expansion, Bork replies that if merger is the preferred route, it must be because it involves lower costs. If at least two firms of comparable efficiency survive, the ability to restrict output and increase price hasn't been increased significantly. And if the two firms attempt to manipulate prices so that consumer interests aren't efficiently served, they will become vulnerable to newcomers to the business.

Bork also demolishes the notion that in concentrated industries product competition has somehow been substituted for price competition. He notes that conventional oligopoly theory ought to predict a lessening of product competition if its basis for predicting a lessening of price competition makes any sense. He also points out that product competition introduces so many variables that tacit collusion becomes impossible and that product rivalry can erode profits just as surely as price rivalry.

Bork's conclusions receive support from recent research by others. Most studies show that price increases in the most concentrated industries have in fact been smaller than in the less concentrated

industries. The "shared monopoly" theory holds that the largest firms collude to achieve high profits. If that's true, it follows that the profits of the smaller firms in the industry would be higher as well—a prediction also not supported by the evidence.

Much of the popular interest in antitrust doubtless is a result of inflation. Politicians and self-appointed public interest advocates find it easy to blame inflation on industry's "obscene" profits, which are in turn explained by mushy theories about shared monopolies and other antitrust conspiracies.

Concentration unchanged

But consider: From 1958 to 1965, the wholesale price index rose less than 2% a year. In the past 12 years, we've sometimes had inflation of more than 10% in a given year. Yet, throughout both periods, the amount of concentration in industry (and the strength of unions, it might be added) remained virtually unchanged. Yet if the general hostility toward big business can be fanned into breaking up the largest firms, the result is likely to be higher prices, slower productivity increases, aggravation of the balance of payments and increased government intervention as Congress seeks a way to increase incomes.

Mr. Bork observes that a policy of free markets is not in any sense narrowly pro-business. A policy of free markets is a policy for free competition and consumer welfare. Business sometimes seeks government policies that lessen the rigors of competition, so it is particularly the role of government that is dangerous in interfering with the processes of free markets.

Nor is Mr. Bork anti-antitrust. He recommends that antitrust policy be shaped to strike at three classes of behavior: outright price-fixing; horizontal mergers that create very large market shares and leave fewer than three significant rivals and deliberate predation designed to drive rivals from a market. He is hopeful that antitrust excesses can be reined in, yet in his *Final Thoughts* he confesses some foreboding:

"To study antitrust at length, to wonder at the manifold errors of economics and logic displayed, to see that the errors move the law always in one direction, is to begin to suspect that a process much deeper than mere mistaken reasoning is at work. It seems as though the intellectual terrain is regarded as important not in and for itself but as a field of action upon which the political order moves against the private order."

From J. FRED WESTON, "Antitrust: The Coming Battlefield." Reprinted with permission of *The Wall Street Journal*, © Dow Jones & Company, Inc. (April 14, 1978). All rights reserved.

SOURCES OF MONOPOLY POWER

Governments have traditionally been a source of monopoly power.

Governments have been a major source of monopoly power throughout recorded history. To raise money to fight wars and to meet other governmental costs, sovereigns have sold the right to favored individuals to be the sole seller of products like salt and tea. The English government made major grants of monopoly power to the East India Company. Indeed, the Boston Tea Party grew out of the attempt by the King of England to limit the number of sellers who could do business in the colonies.

Governments typically grant *patents* to the inventors of new products or processes on the assumption that the granting of exclusive rights will encourage the invention of new products. A patent gives patent holders the sole right to use the new knowledge they have created for a period of seventeen years, and many times for more years if there is a series of patents; thus, producers selling patented products have the right to keep others from using the new knowledge they have created. Polaroid cameras, most proprietary drugs, and many other newly invented products are priced in markets protected by patents from would-be competitors.

Many *tariffs* and *import quotas* are intended as barriers to keep foreign-made products from competing with domestically produced products. In recent years the United Auto Workers has favored higher tariffs on foreign-made automobiles as a means of protecting their union members from the competition of lower wage rates abroad.

During the late 1960s and early 1970s, the steel companies sought to restrict the entry of foreign steel into the United States. More recently, at the industry's behest, the federal government has moved to set minimum acceptable prices on steel imports.

Over thirty years ago the city of New York established the number of taxicabs legally permitted to be on the streets. As a result, a cab fare in New York City is a monopoly price—a price substantially higher than it would be if any person who wanted to could operate a cab.

Monopolies have also been granted unintentionally by governments.

Not only are there many examples of intentional grants of monopoly powers to individuals and businesses by government, but there are also many unintentional grants of monopoly power. Most of the unintentional grants of monopoly power have been made initially to protect the public from unscrupulous sellers of products and services.

Also for protection, the state occupational licensing laws are presumably intended to prevent unwary buyers from employing incompetent physicians or lawyers. These laws usually require that the licensee have a minimum education and pass some type of examination. Originally, licensing was limited to a few professions; but in recent years, licensing is required of beauticians, barbers, embalmers, bartenders, television aerial erectors, television repairmen, chiropractors, and many other workers. When licensing is required, there is always a temptation to set the requirements at a higher level than is required to protect the public. By restricting the supply, those already in an occupational group find that they can charge a higher price for their services. Whether licensing laws are used primarily to protect the public or to permit monopoly pricing of services is an open question. Probably some of both occurs.

The regulatory agencies created to protect the public from monopolistic practices have, in fact, created many artificial barriers to entry. Under the guise of maintaining competition in the transportation industry, the Interstate Commerce Commission has prevented the railroads from lowering their rates and has refused to license new interstate trucking companies. Only recently, the Civil Aeronautics Board has eased entry to firms seeking to enter the air transportation industry. State liquor control boards have limited the number of firms that can sell liquor in many communities. Some state pharmacy boards have denied the right of nonpharmacists to start a drug store and hire pharmacists. These examples illustrate some of the many ways that governments may intentionally or unintentionally create barriers to entry into an industry or occupation.

There are also nongovernmental sources of monopoly power.

Nongovernmental sources of monopoly power include the limited size of the market relative to the optimum-sized plant, ownership of key resources, and, under some circumstances, price maintenance agreements and advertising. Consider the so-called natural monopoly case first.

A *natural monopoly* exists when the market is small relative to the optimum-sized production facility.

You will recall from our discussion in Chapter 4 that there tends to be an optimum-sized plant in each industry. Efficient steel-making plants are large. So too are modern breweries. But size by itself does not create a natural monopoly. If the market is so small that there is room for only one or possibly two or three firms operating efficient plants, then those firms may be said to have monopoly power based on the natural limitations on entry.

Public utilities are usually cited as natural monopolies. If three or four electric-power companies were to serve the same community, each company's unit costs would be higher than if there were only one company. All the companies—and their customers—would have to pay the costs of maintaining duplicate distribution facilities. To avoid this duplication and to achieve the lower costs, the states usually grant franchises to a single company, thus giving it the sole right to serve a community. In return for this protection from competition, the public utility must submit to price regulation by the state.

In addition to the classic case of natural monopoly, there are many manufacturing industries or parts of industries where there are elements of natural monopoly. The knowledge and start-up costs associated with the production of many scientific and medical instruments are so high, *relative* to the potential size of the market, that there is room for only two or three firms. The market for very large computers may also be too small to support many efficient firms. In effect, then, a small market relative to the costs of entry may constitute a *de facto* barrier to entry.

The ownership of key resources is another nongovernmental source of monopoly power.

If you happened to own the land on both sides of the Grand Canyon, you could set your own price for the right to see the canyon. Or if you were the sole owner of all of the commercial timberland in the United States, you would have a great deal to say about the price of paper and lumber.

The ownership of key resources is an important source of monopoly power in the pricing of crude oil, bauxite, and possibly copper. It may become more important as some of the developing countries supplying these and other resources take a more active role in their pricing. Perhaps the best example of monopoly power stemming from this source is the pricing of crude oil from the Oil Producing Export Countries (OPEC); together, these countries have over 50 percent of the known reserves of low-cost crude oil. By restricting the production of oil from their fields they were able to triple the price of oil during 1973 and 1974. Whether the resulting high price of oil will bring about more drilling and a large enough output from other fields to threaten the control of the present producers is yet to be determined. What is clear is that, in the short run, the ownership of this key resource has given the oil-producing countries monopoly control over the world price of crude oil.

Cartel agreements not to engage in price cutting is another potential source of monopoly power.

In some countries, contractual agreements between competitors not to engage in price competition are legal and can be enforced. In the United States these agreements are said to be against the public interest and they cannot be enforced in a court of law. In fact, under the Sherman Antitrust Act, every contract, combination in the forms of trusts or otherwise, or conspiracy in restraint of trade or commerce among the states is illegal, and those who participate are subject to substantial penalties—even jail terms. As a result, the cartel agreements—as these are called—are probably not an important source of monopoly power in the United States.

During periods of price weakness in an industry characterized by excess capacity, business-people will frequently give speeches to their trade associations calling for "statesmanship" in the pricing of their product. They may even engage in some illegal and covert discussions aimed at controlling pricing. But the history of these informal agreements is that they do not work. The temptation to cut prices in order to use excess capacity is too great, and since any agreement is unenforceable, the other participants to the agreement can seldom discipline the price-cutters.

However, in countries where *cartels* are legal, they have played a major role in the pricing of many products. Even in these countries, the cartels have had a great deal of difficulty controlling the entry of new firms and the building of additional capacity. As more firms take advantage of the cartel pricing of an industry's products, the advantages to each of the firms of maintaining monopoly prices are diminished.

In the United States, most of the cartels that do exist are sponsored by the government. The government has organized a cartel that requires milk producers to sell all fluid milk at government-determined prices. The government has also helped the farmers restrict the output of feed grain in order to increase their prices. Some state governments have required that all bottled alcoholic beverages be sold at manufacturers' suggested retail prices, thus restricting price competition among the sellers of liquor.

Advertising is sometimes cited as another potential source of monopoly power.

Economists disagree about the economic effects of advertising. Some would say that most of the advertising directed at consumers is intended to appeal to their emotions. The consumers are supposed to believe that if they use Ultra Brite, Right Guard, and Listerine, their love life will be measurably improved. Advertising of this type, it is argued, gives the seller monopoly power.

Once buyers believe that these products have some mysterious ability to improve their lives, they will buy them even at prices higher than those charged for other equally effective products. Looked at in this way, advertising consists of building an image for a product that makes it appear unique and in this way bestows monopoly power on the seller of that highly advertised product.

However, advertising is also a means of informing buyers about products. Information, as we have seen, is not a free good. Therefore, when informational advertising is included in the price of the product, the consumer is merely paying one of the normal costs of producing goods in a modern industrial economy.

Much of the advertising directed at businesses consists of information considered to be useful to purchasing agents. It is intended to acquaint them with the range and specifications of alternative products. Even some advertising directed at the consumer has a substantial informational content. Consumers, for example, have probably learned about the advantages and disadvantages of many foreign-made cars from magazine and newspaper advertising.

The informational content of advertising probably reduces the cost for a new producer to enter a market. The Japanese maker of the Mazda automobile would probably have had to spend a great deal more to introduce the rotary engine to the United States market if advertising were not possible.

On balance, it is difficult to say what the net effect of advertising is on the competitiveness of an economy. It probably does build favorable emotional images around some products. At the same time, it is an effective way of conveying information and thus makes it less expensive to introduce new products that will compete with existing products.

The need to acquire knowledge is not necessarily a barrier to entry.

Every activity, whether it is selling books in a university book store, teaching economics, producing computers, or building skyscrapers, requires knowledge. You have to learn the related skills before you can participate in the business or occupation.

Knowledge is not a free good like air in the wide-open spaces of the desert or water in the middle of Lake Michigan. Knowledge is a commodity for which people use resources to produce and income to buy. When you get training in a skill or a profession, you are really buying knowledge.

Therefore, the need to acquire the knowledge necessary to produce a computer or to become a physician is not necessarily a barrier to entry. It is something you have to pay for in order to enter an activity just as you have to pay for tools and other specialized pieces of capital equipment.

Inevitably, then, a firm that first produces a new product has an advantage over those who would enter the industry later. The Xerox Corporation, for example, learned a great deal about its production and marketing as the first producer of photographic copying equipment. Those who would enter the industry later must also expect to have start-up costs during their learning periods. These start-up costs are not contrived barriers to entry but are part of the normal costs of assembling the capital and labor necessary to produce the goods.

It is only if would-be competitors are prevented through patents and other devices from acquiring the knowledge necessary to enter an industry that a head start will tend to create a monopoly position. Knowledge, unless protected by patents, is not a unique input that is unavailable to other firms. It is an input, like other resource inputs, acquirable at a cost.

Nor is the necessity of acquiring the knowledge associated with a skill or a profession a monopoly-creating barrier to entry, unless contrived devices are used to limit the number of persons who can acquire the necessary knowledge. Some unions have control over the number of persons who can become apprentices, and in this way they can limit the number who will be able to acquire the knowledge necessary to become plumbers or electricians. In the absence of these special regulations, the need to acquire knowledge is not a true barrier to entry.

However, the cost of knowledge can appear to be a barrier, as we saw when we discussed the concept of a natural monopoly. When the size of the market is limited relative to start-up costs and the cost of building an optimum-sized plant, then it may not pay many firms or workers to acquire the knowledge to enter the industry or occupation. This kind of limitation may leave an industry or an occupation with too few firms or workers to make the activity really competitive. At the present time portions of the microelectronic industry are characterized by high knowledge and start-up costs relative to the size of the market. During the early part of the nineteenth century, the isolated rural areas typically did not have many highly skilled furriers and cabinet makers. The markets were too limited to justify many persons learning these trades. But it is not the cost of the knowledge *per se* that is the barrier. It is the size of the market *relative* to the cost of the knowledge. Knowledge, like capital, is just another resource that would-be producers must assemble if they are going to enter an industry or occupation.

Technological change can destroy monopoly power.

The development of new products and new technologies has substantially limited the monopoly power of firms in competing industries. The late Joseph A. Schumpeter* has called this the *process*

* *Capitalism, Socialism, and Democracy*, 3d edition. New York: Harper & Row, 1950.

of creative destruction. The air transportation and long-distance trucking industries, both developed during the last fifty years, have substantially reduced the monopoly powers of the railroads as carriers of people and high-value products. The long-distance telephone has largely replaced Western Union Company as the dominant seller of message services. The companies in the aluminum industry, together with the producers of other nonferrous metals, have affected the power of the United States Steel Company and other large steel companies in the pricing of their product. Creative use of plastics in furniture has affected the long-held unique role of wood. The development of low-cost oceanshipping and communications systems has converted the automobile market into a world market. And we could go on with a long list of the monopoly-destroying effects of new technologies in various areas.

Technological change, based as it is on the development of new knowledge, has probably destroyed more monopoly positions than it has created. But this, too, is difficult to establish definitively until economists have done a great deal more empirical work on the relationship between the structure of industry and technological change.

We return then to a simple proposition. Whenever you think a firm or a labor union has monopoly power, ask yourself this question. Are there any barriers that will keep others from entering the monopoly-priced industry or occupation? If there are, you probably have a monopoly. These barriers could be based on governmental rules, a limited market compared to efficiently sized plants, the ownership of key resources, or possibly cartel agreements and advertising. If there are no barriers, you will probably find that in the long run the prices of the products will be equal to their opportunity costs.

EFFECTS OF MONOPOLY: PRICING

Concern over monopolies stems from the effects that they may have on the economy. These effects take several forms. Monopolists are likely to charge a higher price than would be charged under competitive conditions. The scarce resources of the nation will be allocated differently when monopoly power is exercised. Incomes are likely to be redistributed and profits of the firm exploiting its monopoly position are likely to be larger than those under competition. Each of these effects will be considered in turn.

A monopolist will seldom charge the highest possible price.

Would a monopolist automatically charge the highest possible price? Or is there some price between the highest possible price and the competitive price that would be most profitable?

To see how monopoly and competitive prices differ, we shall suppose that initially the dry-cleaning industry in New York City is competitive. We shall also

suppose that the dry-cleaning industry is characterized by constant costs. Thus, if there is an increase in demand for dry-cleaning services, additional plants will be built and more dry-cleaning services will be provided with no increase in price over the long run. If there is a decrease in demand, some dry-cleaning plants will be abandoned. Under these conditions, dry-cleaning services will sell at prices equal to their opportunity costs at price P_0 in Fig. 8.1. The horizontal supply curve reflects the long-run constant cost assumption.

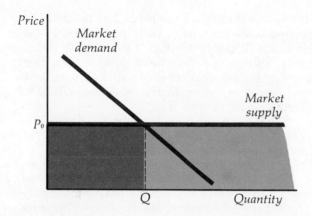

FIG. 8.1 Dry-cleaning prices under competitive conditions and constant cost.

Now suppose that the mafia moves in and forces all of the owners of dry-cleaning establishments to sell their businesses to Dry Clean, Inc. Using their extra-legal powers, the mafia could also prevent entry of new firms into the New York City dry-cleaning market. In short, Dry Clean, Inc. would have an airtight monopoly. How would Dry Clean, Inc. price dry-cleaning services?

The chances are that the mafia, as the real owners of Dry Clean, Inc. would use a trial-and-error method of searching for that price that would give them the highest net income. But suppose that somebody in the "family" had taken economics and suggested that an economist be employed to estimate the demand curve for dry cleaning in New York City?

Once the demand curve for dry-cleaning services has been estimated, the owners would want to know what would happen to receipts and costs if they changed the price they charged. An increase in price would, according to the Law of Demand, decrease the quantity demanded—but whether it would increase or decrease receipts would depend on the elasticity of demand. The change in quantity demanded brought about by the price change would also have an effect on costs as the owners adjusted the supply of dry-cleaning services.

These two changes (the change in total receipts and the change in total costs), occurring simultaneously as price changes, provide the key to understanding the pricing behavior of the monopolist. To discuss this, we will need two concepts: marginal revenue and marginal costs.

The concept of marginal revenue can be illustrated graphically along with the demand

curve. Table 8.3 shows a hypothetical demand and marginal revenue schedule for the services of having a suit dry cleaned. Columns 1 and 2 represent the demand schedule. Column 3, total revenue, is calculated by multiplying price (column 1) by quantity demanded (column 2). Column 4 shows the change in total revenue stemming from a 100-unit change in sales. For example, when the quantity demanded increases from 200 to 300, total revenue increases by $600. Column 5 shows the change in quantity demanded when price falls by $1. Column 6 is the marginal revenue schedule. Column 6 is derived by dividing column 4 by column 5, the ratio of the change in total revenue to the change in quantity demanded.

Marginal revenue **refers to the amount by which total receipts change when sales change by one unit.**

The demand and marginal revenue schedules are graphed in Fig. 8.2.

We still cannot determine the monopolist's pricing strategy until we know something about the monopolist's costs.

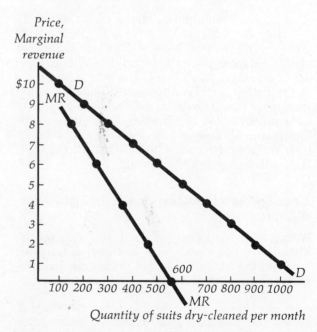

FIG. 8.2 Demand and marginal revenue curves.

Marginal cost **refers to the amount by which total costs change when output changes by one unit.**

If we assume the monopolist's unit costs are constant, we are really assuming that marginal costs do not change as output is varied (see Table 8.4). The total costs double as the quantity supplied doubles, but the increment to total costs stays the same. For example, whether you increase output from 100 to 200, or from 700 to 800, costs increase by the same $4 per unit.

Figure 8.3 combines the demand schedule, marginal revenue schedule, and marginal cost schedule. From Tables 8.3 and 8.4, it can be seen that marginal cost equals marginal revenue at an output of 300 suits dry cleaned. The demand curve reveals that 300 units of dry-cleaning services can be sold at $8.

If the mafia were to pick a price higher than the $8, the marginal revenue curve would tell them that they could do better. By reducing their price to $8, they could add more to their total revenue than they would add to their costs—thus increasing their profits.

Or if the mafia were to pick a price lower than the $8 price, the reverse would be true. By increasing the price to $8, they would subtract from their costs more than they subtracted from their total revenue—thus increasing their net profits.

Therefore, by comparing marginal revenue and marginal cost, the mafia or any other monopolist can always pick a profit-maximizing price. This price is always higher than the competitive

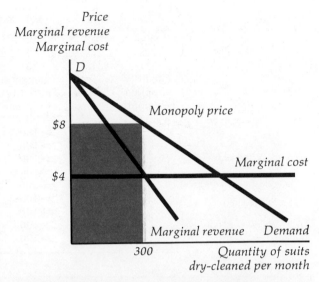

FIG. 8.3 Determination of monopoly price given the demand, marginal revenue, and marginal cost curve.

price, although it need not be the highest possible price. The difference between the monopoly price and the competitive price—in this case $4—is a form of tax that the monopolist can charge because of the restrictions on entry. Since 300 units are sold, the producer earns a "monopoly" or economic profit of $1200 per month. You will recall from Chapter 4 that economic profit, which is identical to monopoly profit, is defined as what remains after all the opportunity costs of production have been met.

TABLE 8.3
DEMAND, TOTAL REVENUE, AND MARGINAL REVENUE FOR DRY CLEANING SUITS

(1) Price	(2) Quantity demanded per month	(3) Total revenue	(4) Changes in total revenue	(5) Changes in quantity demanded	(6) Marginal revenue: col. 4 ÷ col. 5
$10	100	$1000	$800	100	$8
9	200	1800	600	100	6
8	300	2400	400	100	4
7	400	2800	200	100	2
6	500	3000	0	100	0
5	600	3000	−200	100	−2
4	700	2800	−400	100	−4
3	800	2400	−600	100	−6
2	900	1800	−800	100	−8
1	1000	1000			

TABLE 8.4

HYPOTHETICAL CONSTANT COST SCHEDULE FOR DRY CLEANING SUITS

(1) Quantity supplied per month	(2) Total cost	(3) Change in quantity supplied	(4) Changes in total cost	(5) Marginal cost: col. 2 ÷ col. 1
100	$ 400	100	$400	$4
200	800	100	400	4
300	1200	100	400	4
400	1600	100	400	4
500	2000	100	400	4
600	2400	100	400	4
700	2800	100	400	4
800	3200	100	400	4
900	3600	100	400	4
1000	4000	100	400	4

MINI-CASE 8.1

Monopoly power appears to exist in many industries. Whether in fact, however, monopoly power is being exerted is not easy to document. Nevertheless, we can be quite sure that monopoly power is being wielded whenever:

a) an industry is dominated by four or less giant producers,
b) the prices of the goods and services of suspected monopolies increase suddenly with no apparent justification,
c) the prices of the output are higher than the opportunity costs of producing them, or
d) the profits of the suspect firm are much higher than the average profits for the industry.

EFFECTS OF MONOPOLY: RESOURCE ALLOCATION AND INCOME DISTRIBUTION

The intrusion of monopoly into an otherwise competitive economy changes the allocation of resources and the distribution of income.

Let us imagine that one company, which we might call Gargantua, Inc., was allowed to purchase 95 percent of all the commercial timberlands in the nation. Gargantua, Inc. would clearly have monopoly power over the pricing of forest products, such as dimensional lumber, plywood, particle board, and paper. The owners of the other 5 percent of the timberlands would sell their forest products at whatever price Gargantua, Inc. set for its products.

Assuming that before Gargantua, Inc. got control of the timberlands the industry was workably competitive, how would the emergence of this monopoly change the allocation of resources and the distribution of income? There are two certain answers and one possible answer.

In the first place, it is certain that forest products would be selling at higher prices and the quantity supplied would be less than that under competition. The management of Gargantua, Inc. would no doubt price their products so as to maximize their profit. To do this, they would choose that output that would make their long-run marginal costs equal to their marginal revenue. As a result, the prices of forest products would be higher and the quantity purchased would be lower than before. In turn, the forest products industry would use a smaller quantity of productive services than it had before Gargantua, Inc. took over.

The owners of the productive services released from the forest products industry would have to seek employment for their services elsewhere. As a result, the competitive sectors of the economy would respond to the low price of the newly available productive services and expand their output to offset the contraction in the output of the forest products industry. In this way, monopolies have an *allocation effect* on the economy. Too few of the monopoly-priced products are produced and too many of the competitively priced products are produced—compared to what

would happen if all industries were competitive. Figures 8.4(a) and 8.4(b) show how the allocation effect will work itself out.

In Fig. 8.4(a) the prices of forest products rise because of monopolist price setting. As a result, people will buy fewer new houses, paper, and other forest products. The quantity demanded falls from Q_0 to Q_1 and the price rises from P_0 to P_1. The resources released from the forest products industry (as indicated by the arrow) when employed will add to the supply of products in other industries and therefore, if nothing else changes, reduce the price of these products. In Fig. 8.4(b), the increase in supply, given the demand curve DD, causes the price to fall from P_0 to P_1 and the quantity demanded to increase from Q_0 to Q_1. However, the picture is not quite this simple. Since the prices of forest products rise, there is likely to be an impact on the demand for other goods and services. Hence you would expect that the demand curve in Fig. 8.4(b) would change—it might increase and indeed it might decrease. In these cases, it is hard to predict the impact on price and output.

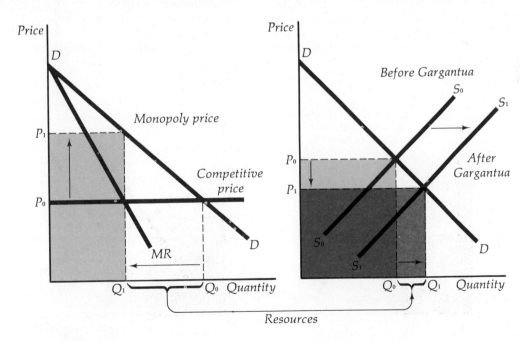

FIG. 8.4   a) Forest products.   **b) Competitive products.**

In the second place, it is also certain that there will be a *redistribution of income*, with more going to the owners of Gargantua, Inc. and less going to the owners of the resources employed in the competitive sectors of the economy. In a real sense, owners of Gargantua, Inc. may be said to exploit the rest of the economy.

Finally, resources may be used less efficiently in Gargantua, Inc. than they otherwise might have been. The owners of Gargantua, Inc. are not forced by competitive pressures to use the lowest-cost technologies. They may choose to use higher-cost technologies just because it is easier to do or because they may be reluctant to release people who would otherwise be pushed out of the monopolistic industry. If resources are used less efficiently, then the total output of the economy will fall. But this last conclusion is a speculative one; it may or may not happen.

Monopolistic pricing of *productive services* also has effects on the allocation of resources and the distribution of income.

Let us suppose that the antitrust division of the federal government was successful in splitting up Gargantua, Inc. into a fully competitive forest products industry. But this time, let us suppose

that the Forest Products Workers Union (FPWU) was organized to represent all the workers of the forest products industry. Further assume that after a successful strike, no employer was permitted to buy labor except at union wage rates. To make the case complete, we will suppose that the union-negotiated wage rate was set at $10 per hour, which is $5 higher than the "competitive" rate of $5 per hour. What would the increase of $5 per hour do to the way the economy would function?

Again, we will get an *allocative* and *distributive* effect. Obviously, the costs of forest products will rise, even after employers have adopted new technologies to minimize their input of labor. This increased cost will cause forest products to sell for higher prices—just as the takeover of the industry by Gargantua, Inc. caused the same result.

The reduced output of forest products—together with those savings of labor caused by the adoption of labor-saving technologies—will cause resources to be released to seek employment in the "competitive" sectors. As a result, the competitive portion of the economy will be expanded, but at lower wage rates than before it was asked to absorb the additional labor released from the forest products industry. Result: wage rates are

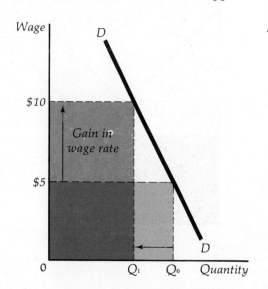

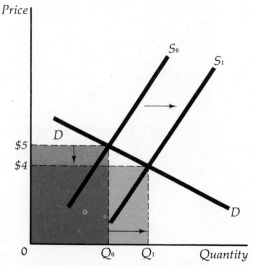

FIG. 8.5   a) Forest products industry.

b) Nonunion sectors.

higher in the unionized portion of the economy and lower in the competitive portions of the economy.

Again, a pair of supply and demand diagrams will illustrate these results. You will see in Fig. 8.5(a) that the increase in wage from $5 to $10 in the unionized industries reduces the quantity demanded of workers from Q_0 to Q_1. As workers become unemployed in the forest products industry and seek work elsewhere, they will increase the supply of workers and tend to drive wage rates down in the competitive sectors of the economy. In Fig. 8.5(b), the increase in the supply of workers from Q_0 to Q_1 reduces wages from $5 to $4.

We should hasten to say that not all unions fully exploit their monopolistic position, and the analysis we have just considered should not be considered to be a description of the way all unions operate. Some unions negotiate wage rates in such a way as merely to offset the bargaining power of businesses in rural areas where there are few employers. Our point is that unions and all other combinations of productive service sellers can have the same effect on the operation of an otherwise competitive economy as do the monopolistic sellers of products. They can make a market economy less responsive to the product and activity choices of households than it would otherwise be.

MONOPOLY POWER: AN ASSESSMENT

How important is monopoly power?

Economists are not agreed on how important monopoly power is in the economy we see around us. There is dispute among economists about how many firms are required in a market, along with open entry, to make an industry workably competitive. Indeed, there is dispute about what constitutes freedom of entry into a market.

Rather than get involved in these disputes, we will be content to say that monopoly can easily infect any part of a market-directed economy. Adam Smith, one of the early economists, writing in 1776, stated:

> "*People of the same trade seldom meet together, even for merriment and diversion, but the conversation ends in a conspiracy against the public, or in some contrivance to raise prices. It is impossible indeed to prevent such meetings, by any law which could be executed or would be consistent with liberty and justice. But, though the law cannot hinder people in the same trade from sometimes assembling together, it ought to do nothing to facilitate such assemblies, much less render them necessary.*" *

* Adam Smith, *The Wealth of Nations*, New York: The Modern Library, 1937, p. 423.

It would be to the advantage of each of us, if we could manage it, to sell our services or products at monopolistic prices and buy services and products at competitive prices. It is natural, then, that we should try to use the government or other means to stifle competition when we are selling things and at the same time encourage competition among those who are selling things to us.

Fortunately, technological change, along with the natural greed of people, has tended to make monopoly somewhat self-limiting. Railroads have lost a great deal of their monopoly power as airlines and trucks have taken a large share of their business. The development of a world market for automobiles has limited the monopoly powers of labor unions and automobile companies. The rise of the service and recreational industries has provided many product alternatives to older and sometimes monopolistically priced manufactured products.

The growth of the economy, which we will study in Chapter 11, has also tended to make the economy more competitive. Markets have widened as more nations are included in the world market. New products become increasingly important. Price rivalry for leadership in some new industries, such as the small computer industry, has become particularly intense.

We come back to the questions: In the long run, how effective has the competitive market been as a social institution? Has the competitive market protected consumers from the exercise of monopoly power?

What are the effects of market power, the ability of a market participant to influence price, quantity, and the nature of the product in the market? To answer this question we must rely on empirical studies by economists.

William G. Shepherd has summarized the studies that have been undertaken to assess the effect of market power in his book, *Market Power and Economic Welfare.** His conclusions are as follows:

1. With respect to the *allocation effect*—a reasonable estimate of the pure allocation effect would yield a loss of 1 to 2 percent of national income.
2. With respect to the *distribution effect*—a conservative estimate would be that in any year at least 3 percent of national income is distributed mainly toward inequality, because of market power.
3. With respect to the *inefficiency effect*—a con-

---

* William G. Shepherd, *Market Power and Economic Welfare,* New York: Random House, 1970.

servative estimate of the average effect on efficiency would be 5 percent of costs where market power is high and 3 percent where it is moderate.

To express these figures, which are crude estimates at best, in meaningful terms, we would like to point out that the GNP grows 3 to 4 percent per year. The misallocated loss due to monopoly is somewhat less than one year's growth in GNP.

Wherever there is monopoly, the effectiveness of the price system as a device for communicating product and activity choices is impaired. Probably the competitive model, which we considered in the preceding four chapters, can be used as an approximation of the way the United States economy works in the long run—just as the study of human physiology can be used as an approximation of the way the human body works, despite all of the viruses and infections that impair the normal functioning of the body. Competition, like other social institutions, does work imperfectly, but without competition it is possible that the effectiveness of the market economy could be completely destroyed by the unchecked growth of monopoly.

We turn in the next chapter to an examination of some of the problems arising out of our reliance on that other major social institution, private property.

REVIEW QUESTIONS

1. If the price of a product is higher than its opportunity cost over an extended period of time,
   a) the law of diminishing marginal returns has been bypassed.
   b) there is a surplus of the product.
   c) there is possibly some barrier to entry in the market.
   d) marginal revenue is less than marginal cost.

2. Which of the following statements is *not* true of "natural monopoly"?
   a) It arises from governmental grant of monopoly power.
   b) It refers to an industry where competition is too costly and wasteful in terms of economic resources.
   c) It refers to a company that becomes a monopoly after years of "natural" competitive struggle.
   d) An electric power company is an example.

3. Free entry into the competitive market is not universal in the United States. An example of restriction of competition is one of the following:
   a) Burger King is priced out of the competitive market.
   b) The Federal Drug Administration requires that an expenditure of about $4 million be made to prove the safety and efficiency of a new drug to replace existing drugs.
   c) General Electric purchases a new packing machine allowing it to package light bulbs more inexpensively than Westinghouse.
   d) Wheat prices fall due to a blight, and hardship results.

4. A monopolist seeking to maximize his profit will:
   a) set that price at which total receipts are the highest.
   b) set the highest price that he or she can "get away with."
   c) set that price at which the addition to total receipts just matches the addition to total costs.
   d) set that price where costs are at a minimum.

5. Monopolies are usually viewed with concern, from an economic point of view, because:
   a) size is inherently dangerous; the larger the firm, the more likely it is to squeeze out the "little producer."
   b) resources will be allocated in an inefficient manner.
   c) the government may be put at the mercy of several large producers.
   d) the variety of goods available in the marketplace will be limited.

6. Which of the following is *not* an effect of a monopoly in the functioning of a market-directed economy?
   a) The total capacity of the economy to produce goods and services will probably be reduced.
   b) If the demand of the monopolized product is highly elastic, competitors may come out with acceptable substitutes.
   c) If the demand of the monopolized product is highly inelastic, the price of the item could be raised.
   d) The total capacity of the economy to produce goods and services will probably be increased.

ESSAY QUESTIONS

1. Define competition in the long-run sense. Do you believe that there really is free entry into large industries, such as steel and aluminum, or is entry restricted by the size of the investment required? Does competition occur from foreign sources?

2. If the IBM Corporation has consistently had large profits—larger than required to get the capital the company needs—over an extended period of time, does this mean that there are noncompetitive elements in the company's pricing? What are the impediments to entry in this business?

3. In most of the service activities there are not too many suppliers. Does this mean that monopoly pricing will characterize the service industries in your hometown in the long run?

4. How do you account for the many licensing requirements such as those for television aerial erectors, beauticians, chiropractors, accountants, etc.? Is it entirely due to the need to protect the public?

5. In what sense can it be said that labor unions have monopoly powers? What are some of the limitations on these monopoly powers?

6. When industries such as the postal industry are monopolized, why is it possible to charge some customers more than the cost of producing the service and other customers less than the cost of producing the service? Can you apply your answer to the alleged overcharging for first-class mail and the alleged undercharging for third- and fourth-class mail? Can you apply your answer to the maintenance of railroad services to rural areas which do not pay their way?

7. What is your image of a monopolist? Is this a true characterization?

8. Monopolists always charge the highest possible price because we are at their mercy. Comment.

9. When the government helps the farmers charge higher than competitive prices (by output restrictions) for such products as tobacco, cotton, and peanuts, what does it do to the productivity of American agriculture? Be specific. Does it necessarily reduce the total tonnage of crops produced? What, then, is the difficulty?

10. Suppose you were appraising the static fed into the system by monopolies in the United States. Would it be greater than the static fed into the systems of the developing countries where it is common to close the border to foreign competition as soon as there is a domestic producer? Would it be greater than it is in the European countries where cartels are very common? Explain your answer.

11. Would you defend every market-directed system in the world as being responsive to the product and activity demands of the people? What criteria would you use in appraising the different systems of the world?

ANSWERS TO REVIEW QUESTIONS

1. Monopoly power is being exercised when, in the long run, price of the product is higher than the opportunity cost of producing it.
    a) This is incorrect. It is irrelevant.
    b) This is incorrect. It too is irrelevant.
    c) This is correct as explained above.
    d) This is incorrect. Monopolists will seek to operate where marginal revenue equals marginal cost.

2. A natural monopoly exists when the market is small relative to the efficient-sized production facility.
    a) This is correct and therefore is the "wrong" answer. Governments do give natural monopolies license to operate.
    b) This is correct and therefore is the "wrong" answer. See explanation above. Too many producers would be inefficient.
    c) This is incorrect and therefore is the "right" answer. It is for technological and efficiency reasons that natural monopolies exist.
    d) This is correct and therefore is the "wrong" answer. The electric power industry fits the description above.

3. The restrictive practices that enable a monopolist to survive do not include efficiencies gained through technology that allow one firm to produce at a lower cost. If the competitive system is working, in the long run this differential will disappear as some firms adopt a similar or better technology. Some firms, too, will fall by the wayside.

    a) This is incorrect. If Burger King is less efficient, the competitive market will "push them out."
    b) This is correct. It is an example of a regulatory agency creating an artificial barrier to entry.
    c) This is incorrect as explained above.
    d) This is incorrect. It is likely a short-run phenomenon and does not restrict entry.

4. Monopolists will earn the greatest return by establishing a price at which they can sell that quantity where marginal revenue equals marginal cost. That is, they find the level of output at which an increase or decrease in production will lower their profits.

    a) This is incorrect. Costs as well as receipts must be considered.
    b) This is incorrect. As explained above, the price that maximizes profit may not be the highest price, but rather the one where marginal revenue equals marginal cost.
    c) This is correct. This is another way of saying the level of output where marginal revenue equals marginal cost.
    d) This is incorrect. Receipts as well as costs must be considered.

5. From an economic point of view, monopolies disrupt the efficient (from a competitive-market viewpoint) allocation of resources and cause income to be redistributed toward the monopolist.

    a) This is incorrect. Size alone may not be "evil" from an economic point of view.
    b) This is correct as explained above.
    c) This is incorrect. We are concerned with efficiency and income distribution.
    d) This is incorrect. This is not the primary economic concern.

6. Monopolies will normally charge a higher price and produce a smaller quantity of a product than would occur under competition.

    a) This is correct and therefore is a "wrong" answer; monopolies will use resources inefficiently.
    b) This is correct and therefore is a "wrong" answer. If the demand is elastic, a slight price increase will increase the amount supplied and encourage would-be competitors to enter if possible.
    c) This is correct and therefore is a "wrong" answer. The degree of elasticity of demand is not a result of the monopoly.
    d) This is incorrect and therefore is the "right" answer. The monopoly with its allocation of resources will reduce total capacity of the economy.

OBJECTIVES

Upon successful completion of this chapter, you will be able to:

1. Demonstrate that the land, air, and water are environmental resources.

2. Explain the relationship between property rights and third party effects.

3. Distinguish between external effects regarded as "goods" and those regarded as "bads."

4. Demonstrate, using supply and demand curves, the effect of externalities on price and output.

5. Provide a number of remedies for dealing with third-party effects.

6. Use the concept of marginalism in assessing the appropriate level of expenditures for environmental control

7. Identify four approaches to dealing with environmental problems.

CHAPTER 9

ECONOMICS OF THE ENVIRONMENT

INTRODUCTION

PROPERTY RIGHTS

ECONOMIC ANALYSIS

APPROACHES TO ENVIRONMENTAL
PROBLEMS

INTRODUCTION

If you are a nonsmoker, you have undoubtedly noticed that the smoke from a cigarette placed in an ash tray anywhere in your vicinity inevitably curls upward, seeks you out, and quickly envelopes you. If you are the driver of a compact or subcompact automobile, you're likely to be exasperated at the frequency with which combative drivers nonchalantly cut you off.

These pet peeves and many other similar events may appear to have little to do with economic theory. But actually they represent the tiniest tip of an iceberg of economic issues falling under the rubric of *externalities*.

The model of the market economy demonstrates that resources are allocated most efficiently under conditions of pure competition. There are several important exceptions to this generalization, however, one of which obtains when not all costs and benefits are embedded in relative prices.

The 1960s may well be described as the "decade of environmental awareness." No issue in recent history has been so widely recognized as important to survival as that of environmental concern. What once was regarded as the bailiwick of a few fanatical conservationists and the pet concern of an eccentric president named Teddy Roosevelt has broadened into virtually every corner of contemporary life.

Air pollution, water pollution, land pollution, and noise pollution have become terms familiar to children in elementary school. Even kindergarteners do not hesitate to identify careless adults as "litter bugs."

What does economics have to do with pollution and the environment? The programs to reduce pollution are usually described in terms of regulations prohibiting certain kinds of behavior and of the creation and implementation of technologies designed to eliminate the polluting byproducts of our industrial society. Engineers clearly have an important role to play, as do governmental regulators. But where does economics enter?

Economics is vitally involved in issues of the environment for two basic reasons. First, like all resources, environmental resources are inadequate to cope with society's demands on them. Therefore, decisions must be made as to what these resources shall be used for, how they shall be used, and for whom they shall be used. Hence, economic analysis can be applied to environmental problems in the same way that it is applied to any economic issue.

Second, environmental resources differ from traditional resources in a fundamental way that affects their use. The market economy is dependent on the existence of certain conditions if it is to fulfill its role as an efficient allocator of resources. These conditions include competition and the existence of certain rights associated with the ownership of private property. You may recall from Chapter 7 that we discussed the importance of property rights. This chapter will first explain the relationship between property rights and resource use. Then the economic analysis underlying resource uses will be discussed. Finally, several approaches to dealing with environmental problems will be presented.

PROPERTY RIGHTS

Environmental problems are most obvious in production activities.

Economic activity involves production, exchange, consumption or use, and distribution. It is in the process of production that environmental problems first occur. In production, energy is used to transform resources from their natural forms into goods and services useful to people. These basic resources and energy sources include ores, fossil fuels, and other elements. The processes by which the ultimate goods and services are produced range from simple activities such as picking berries to complex processes such as operating a nuclear-fueled power plant. The raw materials and energy used in production do not disappear as they are used. They remain with us at the end of their production and use cycle—but in vastly different forms. The question is where these spent resources go and in what form, and what effect they have on our environment.

The places to which these spent resources go are called *sinks*. There are three kinds of sinks—the air, the land, and the water. It is because of the nature of these sinks, into which energy and materials are discharged, that the issue of property rights arises. Property rights are reasonably well defined for land. Consider the following illustration.

The following event happened recently. Two college students had been partying, and on their way home they became lost and turned onto a street that ended in a cul-de-sac. It was a dark evening, the skies were heavily overcast, and it was raining hard, as it had done all day. The driver was unaware that the road ended in the cul-de-sac and, assuming that the space between two houses located on the cul-de-sac was where the road should have been, continued in that direction. After being slowed down by numerous shrubs, the car came to a halt in the wet grass, stopped by a large tree. The driver attempted to back up, but the wheels simply sank deeper and deeper into the mud. His attempts to rock the car succeeded only in digging the car deeper and deeper until the axle was on the ground.

The spinning of the wheels and the roaring of the engine awakened the home owner, who peered out of his bedroom window and saw the auto stuck in his lawn. Donning rubbers and an umbrella, he confronted the young driver, who was complaining about the quality of the care given the city streets. Ultimately the authorities were called and the car towed away.

The next morning the two red-eyed college students reappeared at the owner's home, apologized, and promised to make restitution for the damage done to the landscaping. Had they not done so, legal means existed for the home owner to recover the damages created by the violation of his private property.

The owner of that home had certain clearly identifiable property rights that accompanied ownership of that home.

Unfortunately, property rights are not so neatly defined in many other areas of economic interaction. For example, what kind of rights do property owners have over the air that lies above their property? Or if I own a lot on a lake, what rights do I have about the cleanliness of the water I face everyday?

Markets are the vehicles by which property rights are voluntarily transferred in our economic system.

If you purchase a new Ford, you pay the dealer whatever it costs and in exchange you receive the automobile. What you really have purchased, however, is the right to do what you want with the automobile—subject, of course, to laws that have been passed to protect the rights of others, such as speed limits, licensing, inspection, and so on. If you run a red light and cause a collision with another auto, you will be held responsible for the damages. But if you ride up and down the street, emitting exhaust that pollutes the air of neighbors, a remedy for the damages you may have imposed on their health is not nearly as easily attained. Your neighbors own the lots on which their homes reside, but the ownership of the air surrounding the house is not clearly defined.

Let us suppose that you purchase a summer cottage on a beautiful, pure-water stream. A short time later, Paper Company A buys 100,000 acres of timberland and a mill site at the headwaters of the stream. When Company A starts producing paper, there may be a barely noticeable color change in the water, and possibly some reduction in the number of fish to be caught. But if Paper Companies B, C, and D, who have also bought timber and mill sites on the river, start producing paper, the effect will be very obvious. The water in the river will quickly become polluted; the color will turn a dark brown, and the fish will disappear.

Consider another example. Assume your grandparents have owned a home in Los Angeles, California, since 1930. During the 1930s and 1940s the air was clear and beautiful. As a result of the increasing concentration of high-horsepower automobiles in the Los Angeles basin during the 1950s and 1960s, however, a serious smog problem has developed.

In both of these examples your private property rights have been infringed upon. Your summer cottage has lost value as a vacation place because the paper mills have, in effect, trespassed on your property. You have suffered real damages. The same is true of your grandparents' home in Los Angeles; their right to breathe the clean air originally associated with the ownership of property has disappeared.

Consider a food-processing plant that generates large amounts of sewage. If that plant constructs a pipe to a nearby river and simply uses the river as a sink, the quality of the river will suffer in the immediate area of the spillway. If that plant is the only major disposer of sewage, the river may be capable of assimilating the sewage reasonably well—indeed, this natural assimilating capacity is a natural resource. But if numerous other firms also decide to use the river as a sewer, that capacity will quickly be exceeded, causing damages to many others who did not contribute to the pollution.

The costs involved in reimbursing the injured property owners are often prohibitive.

How would you get all of the cottage owners along a stream together to assess the damages that all of you had collectively sustained? How would you decide how much each of the mills should pay? Indeed, should the first mill, which has not reduced water quality materially, be charged at all? The costs involved in these questions are called transaction costs.

In the case of the damages arising out of smog, how would you charge the automobile owners for the right to drive a pollution-causing car? How would the revenues from these charges be distributed among property owners? Should the property owners who sold their homes at low prices in order to get out of the Los Angeles basin be reimbursed, or should present property owners—many of whom had bought their homes for low prices because they were smog-bound—also be reimbursed?

These and many other transaction problems make it very difficult for third parties, such as property owners whose rights are infringed upon, to be compensated for their loss. These costs imposed on the property owners are called third-party costs, or external costs. The owners of the paper mill did not include in their costs of production those costs passed on to the downstream cottage owners, the third parties. When the car owner bought the pollution-causing automobile, the costs of operation did not include the costs borne externally by the home owners whose rights to breathe fresh air were infringed upon.

External costs (*third-party costs*) **are those costs of production not borne by the producers or the consumer, but that ultimately fall on a third party who receives no benefit from the activity.**

Price normally restricts the use of a resource.

Environmental problems, then, are directly related to the fact that the market economic system, which is based on exchange between people who have carefully defined property rights, does not work well when these rights are held jointly by everybody, which in most cases means nobody. If air, water, and other commonly held land were privately held, it is much less likely that they would be used to the point that their natural assimilative capacities would be overtaxed. Why? Because a price would be placed on the use of these scarce resources, and as the demand for them increased, the price would rise.

An example of the tendency to "overuse" resources that have low or zero prices can be seen in our national park system. Anyone who regularly camps can testify to the fact that many more people wish to use such national parks as Yosemite and Yellowstone for camping than the parks can adequately accommodate. More specifically, the demand for camping sites is greater than the supply at the existing entrance fee. The park authorities have chosen to use a "first come, first served" method of restricting entry rather than letting the price rise to equate the quantity of sites demanded with the quantity available. The reason for restricting is simply that the park, which is a natural resource, cannot hold or assimilate more than a specified number of campers without causing the park's beauty to deteriorate rapidly.

This problem of common ownership or no ownership is not limited to any given nation. The same issue pertains to such diverse natural resources as whales, space, and the oceans.

COMMENTARY

Read the following newspaper article (italics added) and answer these questions:

a) Are property rights involved in this smoking issue?

b) What approaches do you suggest be used to protect the rights of the nonsmoker?

c) List other "off-beat" examples of external costs.

PROF ADVOCATES RIGHTS OF NONSMOKER

BLOOMINGTON—Is smoking a health hazard to people around the nonsmoker? Should smoking be allowed only in private among consenting adults?

These are more than rhetorical questions.

An Indiana University professor raises them seriously, and Lynton K. Caldwell has the credentials to back up his statements. He has been active in environmental studies, pollution and public policy for 10 years.

Caldwell, professor of public and environmental affairs at I.U., has served on an Environmental Health Panel of the National Institute of Health. *He thinks smoking in public comes under what he calls "biomedical politics and public policy decisions."* "In the seven years since warning labels first appeared on cigarette packages, a major change has occurred in the biopolitics of smoking," Caldwell said. *"As evidence has grown that cigarette smoke is harmful to nonsmokers, first steps have been taken toward treating smoking as a form of air pollution.* Airlines divide their cabins into smoking and nonsmoking sections and they have long since abandoned the practice of giving away cigarettes. The state of Arizona has prohibited smoking in public conveyances and places of assembly."

Last August a British journal, *New Scientist,* carried an article entitled "Should Public Smoking Be Banned?" The article, Caldwell said, reported on a campaign launched by the British Health Education Council to focus attention on the health risks to children breathing air contaminated by tobacco smoke.

"The heavy use of cigarettes and the role of tobacco in public revenues and in employment may suggest that protective action against smoking has gone about as far as it can go without arousing popular resistance," Caldwell said. On the other hand, he lists three factors that continue to work toward restricting use of cigarettes. They are:—An increase in the incidence of lung cancer and emphysema.

—The concept that each individual has a right to a healthful environment, or at least a court-enforceable right against hazards to his health inflicted upon him by other people.

—The proposition (largely theoretical at this point) that ill-health unnecessarily incurred because of individual indulgence or indifference places a burden on all society, and the health hazarding behavior of the individual becomes a matter of public concern. Caldwell said the fluoridation of public water supplies has been a controversial issue in some areas, and added:

"The case against public smoking is far stronger than that against fluoridation because all persons may be adversely affected by inhaling tobacco smoke and no benefit whatever accrues to public health."

According to Caldwell, the case of the cigarette is probably the most simple and direct example of the way in which knowledge may be brought to bear upon political decisions. He cited a consistent advance during the past seven years in establishing public control over what he calls "this health hazard and public nuisance."

"The indications point toward the treatment of cigarette smoking as a taxable private vice,

tolerated among consenting adults but prohibited from infliction upon the nonsmoking public," he said. "Under such circumstances the glamor of the cigarette could sink to the level of snuff."

Journal and Courier, Lafayette, Ind., Saturday, March 16, 1974. Reprinted by permission.

ECONOMIC ANALYSIS

Economic analysis rests on the foundation created by the existence of scarcity. Consequently, the efficient allocation of resources is a key issue in all economic analysis. Economists are trained to ask the question, "What is the effect on the allocation of *resources* of any institutional change in the economic system?" In the context of environmental issues, the logical question to ask is, "What is the impact of the existence of external effects on the allocation of resources?"

When third-party costs are not included in total costs, too much of the products made by pollution-causing technologies may be produced.

What happens to the allocation of resources when these third-party damages are not included in the cost of producing goods? In terms of supply and demand analysis, the existence of third-party costs appears in the form of a supply curve that is located to the right of where it would be if it included *all costs*. Remember that supply represents the alternative quantities of a commodity that producers are willing to provide at alternative prices. Other things being equal, the lower the costs, the larger will be the quantity they will

provide at every price. When third-party costs are excluded and suppliers don't have to pay for using the environment, they will produce a larger quantity at each price than otherwise. This is shown in Fig. 9.1, where the supply and demand curves for paper are drawn. The supply curve of paper will be too far to the right (S_1), the price will be too low (P_2), and too much will be purchased (Q_2). Since other resources are also used in the production of paper, this means that too few of the other nonpolluting products would be produced and sold. In other words, too much of a product will be produced when one of the resources used in its production—in this case the waste-assimilating capacity of the environment—is free.

Third-party costs may also be internalized as additional costs of obtaining complementary resources.

The result described above is not inevitable: Let us suppose that the only reasonable living place for people who work in the paper mill is along the river. If only paper mill workers live along the damaged part of the river, and they are paid

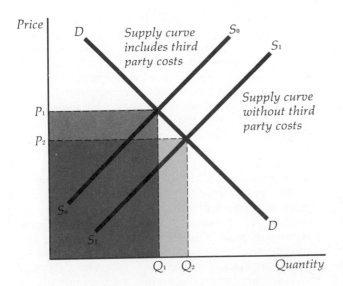

FIG. 9.1   Prices and outputs in the polluting industry.

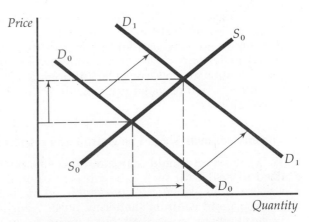

FIG. 9.2   Prices and outputs in an industry with "third-party" benefits.

a higher wage for living there, the third-party costs will show up as additional labor costs. There are several difficulties with this hypothetical solution, however. For example, only rarely are the persons actually bearing the pollution paid for it directly. Also, as a means of reducing their labor costs, the paper mills might decide not to consider a pollution-abatement program.

Third-party effects may also be third-party benefits.

The externalities problem may involve not only third-party costs but third-party benefits as well. Consider a company that builds a plant in an area where there are no other employers with the same skill requirements. This firm would have to teach most of its employees the required skills, presumably at the standard wage rate. Training costs are high, and if some of the newly trained workers leave the area to work elsewhere, their new employers will receive third-party benefits; they will get trained workers without having to pay for the training. The initial company's demand for employees would be larger if it could charge "other" companies for the "free-loader" benefits the other companies were receiving.

Many other activities benefit not only the purchaser of the product but third parties as well.

For example, education is frequently cited as an activity that benefits not only the purchaser but also the entire community. Examine Fig. 9.2, in which the supply and demand for privately provided educational services are represented. Assume for purposes of illustration that no educational services are provided publicly. The supply curve of, say, elementary school services, would be upward sloping, indicating that private producers would supply more at higher prices. The demand curve would reflect the benefit of elementary school education as perceived by the families that purchase the service. In fact, however, the benefits to society as a whole would exceed those perceived solely by the private demanders. Few persons would dispute that we are all better off in a society where the basic skills of reading, writing, and so on are broadly known. This implies, then, that the demand curve that includes both private and social benefits would be further to the right than that incorporating only privately perceived benefits. In Fig. 9.2, D_0D_0 reflects only the private benefits of elementary school education, while D_1D_1 includes the benefits to society as well. The effect of including these societal benefits is reflected in a higher equilibrium price (P_1) and a larger equilibrium quantity (Q_1).

Contour farming is another example. Farmers who prevent rapid run-off water help not only themselves but also the downstream residents, who are thus less threatened by floods.

It is clear, then, that when there are externalities, the social institutions we have been discussing do not necessarily produce the best allocation of resources. However, there is room for the invention of new social institutions and for the introduction of social decisions into the allocative process.

The environment should be viewed as a resource.

To what extent should scarce resources be mobilized to deal with such externalities as polluted streams, smog-laden air, undesirable odors, ugly environs, and eardrum-shattering noises? Earlier in the chapter we described the environment itself as a resource, a resource that provides a flow of services similar in many respects to the flow of services emanating from the more conventional resources of land, labor, and capital. We noted in Chapter 2 that the peculiar combination of resources used in any production process depends partially on the price of the input. As long as

environmental resources remain outside the domain of private property regulations, and are thus available at a zero price, they will be used more intensively than the other resource inputs. It should not be inferred as a consequence that the resources provided by the environment should not be used at all, as is suggested by some environmental groups. Rather, the same rules of marginal behavior followed with respect to other resource inputs should be applied to environmental resources.

Consider the following abstract, but useful, analytical example. A river has many uses. It provides a means of transporting cargo; it can be aesthetically pleasing to watch; it can provide enjoyable recreation in the form of swimming and boating; and, indeed, it can provide an outlet for waste disposal. To "clean up" a given stretch of a river can be accomplished technologically in different ways. In all cases, however, the higher the level of cleanliness desired, the costlier becomes each incremental improvement. For example, tertiary sewage treatment plants discharge a "higher quality" of water into the river than a primary treatment plant, but the cost is considerably higher. This relationship is shown by the upward sloping marginal cost curve in Fig. 9.3. As you move to the right along the horizontal axis labeled environmental quality, the expenditure required to achieve each additional unit of water quality increases. Similarly, the marginal benefit curve is downsloping. Each incremental expenditure to yield a higher environmental quality produces proportionally less improvement.

Hence the value society places on each addition to environmental quality diminishes as the quality improves. The optimal level of environmental expenditure occurs where the marginal benefits equal marginal costs. For example, Q_1 is not an optimal level of environmental quality for our hypothetical river stretch because at Q_1, the benefit of increasing the environmental quality of the river exceeds the cost. Therefore, a net gain can be realized by improving the quality of the river. At point Q_2 the opposite is true. Only at the environmental quality level Q_0 do incremental benefits equal incremental costs.

It can be seen that the concept of marginal analysis introduced in Chapter 2 is a useful tool even in dealing with the topic of pollution.

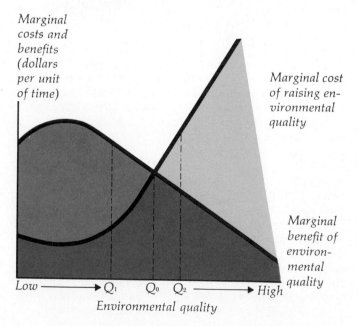

Marginal costs and benefits (dollars per unit of time)

Marginal cost of raising environmental quality

Marginal benefit of environmental quality

Low → Q_1 Q_0 Q_2 → *High*

Environmental quality

FIG. 9.3   Marginal analysis of environmental quality.

APPROACHES TO ENVIRONMENTAL PROBLEMS

What can be done within the framework of a mixed economy to solve the problems whose symptoms are seen as pollution? Four basic approaches can be taken. The first is to do nothing—let things work themselves out. The second is to invoke government regulation. The third is to modify the economic system by providing pseudo-market arrangements to generate price signals where none exist. The fourth is government takeover of the means of production.

The "do-nothing" approach is the least obvious strategy to implement to deal with environmental problems.

Our natural reaction to any problem is to do *something.* The existence of externalities in the environmental sphere has long been recognized even by ardent pro-market supporters as a special case in which the market simply cannot function effectively because the price signals on which it depends do not reflect all aspects of societal costs and benefits. To do nothing in the case of clearly identified external effects is to perpetuate and even exacerbate the inefficient use of resources. If such an approach were nevertheless pursued, its results are predictable. The environment would continue to deteriorate until it would become necessary to pay higher wages and therefore use different production techniques in order to attract workers to contaminated areas. The lower use of pollution-intensive products resulting from the higher prices would partially resolve the problem.

It is also quite likely that private groups would sue in the courts to recover the damages they have sustained as property owners. At some point the prospective benefits of protecting their property from environmental deterioration will be sufficiently large, relative to transaction costs.

The costs of this approach are great. In the process, many species of wildlife and plants might well become extinct. Only isolated areas of pollution-free environments would remain, and these few would command prices so high as to exclude all but those who place a very high value on environmental purity. The life expectancy of humans might well decline. It is clear that many would find the do-nothing approach an unacceptable solution.

Regulation is the most frequently suggested approach to environmental problems.

When problems arise, such as those generated by pollution, the immediate and natural response of most people is that "something ought to be done!" If a firm is pouring chemicals into a river that is killing the fish, it should be enjoined from continuing that activity. If a coal-burning electricity-generating utility is emitting excessive sulfur oxides from its smokestacks, it should be forced to either "clean up its act" technologically or switch to a "cleaner" fuel. Automobiles that spew pollutants out of their exhaust pipes above a specified level should be banned from public roads. Regulation in a mixed economy appears to be a natural response to the threat of pollution. The world, however, is not as simple as the solutions to the above examples presume.

The Environmental Protection Agency (EPA) is the federal government agency directly responsible for regulation in the environmental sphere.

The EPA was created in 1970 after it became obvious that environmental problems were not neatly divided among the areas where existing agencies such as the Interstate Commerce Commission (ICC), Federal Power Commission (FPC), Civil Aeronautics Board (CAB), and so on were already operating.

The primary functions of the EPA and related state and local agencies are to develop standards for air and water quality and to create a system of rules or regulations for achieving the specified standards.

What in fact are the economic consequences of regulatory action, for example, prohibition and setting of standards? Like any institutional change, the impact of a new or modified regulation will be felt beyond the initial point of contact. The following examples illustrate the problem.

Public utilities in the Midwest provide relatively inexpensive electric power by burning the coal that is abundant in southern Illinois, Indiana, and Kentucky. This coal, however, has a very high sulfur content. Let us assume that the EPA has established standards for sulfur oxides that the utilities cannot meet if they continue to use the high sulfur coal and the equipment they now have. There are several options open to them. They might change to an oil-fueled operation, or they might modify the existing equipment if technologically feasible to reduce the sulfur oxide count. Either alternative will raise the cost of producing electricity. The state-appointed agency that regulates the rates and quality of the electric utilities will surely be petitioned by the utilities to allow them to raise their rates, based on the claims of the utilities that their costs have clearly increased. The state regulatory agency knows that if the utilities do not receive "normal" rates of return on their invested capital, the stockholders and bondholders of that company will seek other forms of investment. This will make it very difficult for the utilities to expand or improve their facilities in the future when demands for their services increase.

If the regulated utility does switch to a higher-cost fuel, such as oil, its new demand, if sufficiently larger, will raise the price of oil to all users. High sulfur coal, on the other hand, will fall in price as the demand for it falls. Ultimately, the key question is, What is the impact of regulation on the efficiency with which scarce resources are used? Different firms and industries use different technologies, some of which have wide latitude for substituting inputs while others find it very expensive to modify their input mix. In such cases, across-the-board reductions in specified emissions will impose cost penalties more heavily on some industries than others.

Assume, for example, that the goal of a regulation is to reduce the average emission of a given pollutant by 25 percent. One firm, whose technology is such that no good substitutes exist for the polluting input, might have to be forced out of business while another firm, by substituting a nonpolluting input, might be able to reduce its contribution of pollutants to the atmosphere by 75 percent at very little added cost. Economic efficiency would urge that the latter firm be called on to account for the bulk of the reduction. Yet such programming is very difficult to achieve for several reasons. The information necessary to identify what industries should be given what kind of standards usually either doesn't exist or is costly for a government agency to obtain. Enforcement also would be very difficult.

Earlier in this chapter we indicated how marginal analysis is useful in identifying the goals toward which environmental policies should be designed. The ideal level in any given situation is the level at which the marginal benefit from reducing pollution is equal to the marginal cost. Regulation, however, is a very blunt instrument of control in which differential marginal treatment of different producers is difficult to achieve. We now turn to an approach that can be more finely adjusted to achieve these marginal conditions.

MINI-CASE 9.1

When expensive pollution-abating equipment—such as catalytic converters on automobiles—is required, the manufacturers usually fight the requirement. Nevertheless, it can be demonstrated that under competitive conditions, the costs of this equipment are passed on to the buyers of the product. From an economic point of view, you would say that:

a) They are foolish to fight these requirements since, after a transitional period, they can pass the costs on to the buyers.

b) They are wise to fight these requirements since in the end the cost of the additional equipment will come out of their profits.

c) They should be expected to fight these requirements since the higher prices will limit the size of their markets for specific products.

d) They should fight these requirements since they are inflationary.

The quasi-market approach attempts to create the conditions that could exist when all costs are internalized.

The *quasi-market approach* to remedying environmental problems begins with the premise that because external effects exist, resources are not being used efficiently. Unless external economies are taken into account, too much of some goods and services and too little of others will be produced. The quasi-market approach is designed to correct the inappropriate price signals sent out in these cases through the use of tax and subsidy policies. We will illustrate the imposition of taxes first.

Consider a firm that is piping chemical wastes directly into a river. The first step under this approach is to estimate the cost that the firm imposes on others by its activities. Once the cost has been estimated, the appropriate governmental agency would impose a tax on the firm. The tax would be expressed as so many dollars (or cents) per unit of waste discharged. Ideally, the amount of the tax would equal the costs imposed on others. The tax would be proportional to the volume of waste—or, if it could be shown that the damage increased more rapidly than the increased discharge of the waste, an increasing per-unit charge could be levied.

A variation on this approach would be to determine what level of pollution is consistent with what the nation through the political process perceives to be an acceptable standard of living. The EPA or another appropriate regulatory body could then specify the maximum number of units of each kind of effluent to be discharged in a given time period. Permits to discharge specified fractions of this total amount of pollutant would then be sold at public auctions. The price established in this way, like any other productive service price, such as wages, rents, and interest, would then reflect the cost of using the environment as a sink. The firms that could treat their wastes cheaply would do so. Others would buy the permits. In both cases, the price of protecting the environment would be included in the price of the product. This approach eliminates the EPA's necessity for gathering the detailed information necessary to impose "fair" standards on firms with widely differing production processes.

Such an effluent charge would have the effect of raising the private costs of production to that level at which all costs, including environmental costs, are included. An effluent tax serves to impose a price on the use of the air and water resources that previously had no price because of the difficulty of assigning property rights to them. Thus the incentive for economically efficient use of air and water is restored.

An alternative approach is that of paying subsidies of a given amount for each unit of waste *not* discharged. This is in contrast to the effluent tax, which imposes a charge on each unit of waste discharged. There is an important difference between the tax and the subsidy approaches, however. A tax is paid ultimately by the purchaser of the product, while a subsidy imposes the cost among all taxpayers in general. Consequently, it does not increase the price of pollution-intensive products and therefore does not discourage their use.

Governmental takeover of productive resources is an approach involving a fundamental change in social institutions.

A fourth approach is to have the government take a far more active role than regulation and enforcement, namely, government takeover and operation of the private industrial activities giving rise to pollution. This fundamental institutional change would not eliminate the problem unless the government would at the same time undertake to implement existing technology to reduce pollution. In this case the government would make its pollution abatement decisions on more criteria than profitability and efficiency. This distinction between private sector and governmental decision making was discussed in Chapter 7. Profitability considerations would be combined with value decisions and cost/benefit studies would presumably assume much greater importance. The political process would involve innumerable decisions formerly handled in the decentralized decision process of the market economy.

It is important to remember that this approach entails two steps: government takeover *and the implementation of measures* to reduce pollutants or in some cases cease producing items yielding high emissions of harmful substances). Mere takeover does not ensure that the second step would follow, as the existence of pollution in countries with socialist governments amply testifies.

The existence of externalities is no barrier to the use of the price system. It merely requires that the mixed economy be able to invent new insti-tutions for dealing with these externalities. The question of which institutions are most appropri-ate is a political problem and in the end will involve a trade-off between different social insti-tutions.

REVIEW QUESTIONS

1. When there are third-party benefits, as there are in the case of education, then it is reasonable to:
   a) subsidize some educational expenses.
   b) tax schools more heavily.
   c) levy higher taxes on educated people.
   d) let the market determine how much education should be produced.

2. If a study of a paper mill is conducted because of complaints of water pollution in a neighboring river, and the study shows that the plant hasn't been including external costs in its production costs, then the group study concludes:
   a) the supply curve of the mill is "too far" to the right—too much paper is produced.
   b) the supply curve of the mill is "too far" to the left—too little paper is being produced.
   c) the supply curve of the mill is not affected by external costs.
   d) the demand for paper will continue to decrease as pollution increases.

3. Suppose it is the general practice of the plastics industry to dump its chemical wastes into nearby streams. As a result, the people who live downstream from the plastics plants are unable to use the rivers and streams for recreational purposes. As a result of this general practice, you would expect that the prices of plastic products would be:
   a) about right since they are equal to their opportunity costs.
   b) too low.
   c) too high.
   d) impossible to determine from the material given in the question.

4. Now suppose the Environmental Protection Agency imposes a daily fine larger than the cost of processing the wastes to avoid dumping harmful substances in the rivers and streams. After an adjustment period, assuming that competing products did not face such a tax, you would expect that:
   a) the output of plastics would be reduced.
   b) the output of plastics would be about the same.
   c) the output of plastics would increase since the companies would no longer face the criticism of their downstream neighbors.
   d) the prices of plastics would decline because companies would be able to increase their invest-ment in facilities.

5. From an economic point of view, the existence of pollution in an area is best solved by an approach that will:

   a) return the river to the state that prevailed before the area was settled.
   b) force the polluting company to bear the costs of cleaning up.
   c) require government expenditure.
   d) ensure that the marginal benefits equal the marginal costs of cleaning up.

6. One of the reasons for the continuing contamination of the environment is that:

   a) sufficient taxes could not be imposed to deal with externalities of this type.
   b) no private company has either the profit incentive or power to deal with such external problems as air or water pollution.
   c) private industrial antipollution teams have been unable to make any scientific progress in pollution control.
   d) the climate of the world keeps altering so that we have not been able to diagnose the real sources and types of pollution.

ESSAY QUESTIONS

1. The oceans are being polluted because they do not belong to anybody. Cricicize.

2. Why is it difficult for you to charge for the use of the air over your property or the water in the river along your property? Does this mean that whenever transaction costs are high, a market-system for allocating resources is not practicable?

3. You live in a steel town. It is dirty. Does this automatically mean that steel prices do not include the costs to you and your neighbors of the pollution involved in steel making?

4. What is the appropriate criticism, if any, of the following argument. "Some rivers should be treated as industrial sewers. The people will avoid living along them and this will be reflected in the cost of producing goods in this area. Industries that are pollution intensive will move into these areas because it is cheaper for them to do so than to clean up their processes. In this way: (1) the people who are there get paid for the unpleasantness of the production process; and (2) consumers, in general, tend to get cheaper products than they would if all production processes had to be pollution free."

5. How could you use excise taxes and subsidies to correct the difficulties arising out of the transaction costs of enforcing private property rights to air and water?

6. List all of the activities that you can in which third-party benefits exist. What governmental actions can be taken to encourage the expansion of these activities?

7. No ship owner can afford to pay to maintain a lighthouse. Therefore, the government should install the lighthouse and pay for it from the general tax revenues. After you have thought about this, do you think that there are any voluntary organizations, such as marine insurance companies, that could afford to operate the lighthouse in order to reduce their costs? What are the difficulties of organizing these voluntary organizations to provide governmental services? Are there any half-way houses between the governmental production of these services and the governmental support of them?

ANSWERS TO REVIEW QUESTIONS

1. When third-party benefits exist, persons not directly involved in the transaction receive benefits. These external benefits are not reflected in the benefit calculations of the marketplace, and hence the supply of such goods provided is less than that which would occur if all benefits were accounted for. Consequently, by the market measure—more resources should be channeled to activities providing external benefits. Hence:

   a) This is correct. Education, particularly grade-school and high-school education, is regarded as providing external benefits. Thus it is subsidized so that the resouces allocated to it will approximate what the market would do if all benefits were included.
   b) This is incorrect. This would take even more resources away from the external good.
   c) This is incorrect. It is irrelevant.
   d) This is incorrect as explained above. The market provides too few resources for external goods.

2. When external costs exist, all of the costs are not attributed to the producer or buyer, hence the supply will be greater than under a properly functioning market system. This means that with a given demand, the price will be lower and the quantity demanded too large by this market measure.

   a) This is correct as explained above.
   b) This is incorrect. Supply is too large, not too small.
   c) This is incorrect as explained above.
   d) This is incorrect. We have no basis for making this assertion.

3. External costs exist here, hence the supply will be too large and the price too low—as measured by the market.

   a) This is incorrect. Prices are too low.
   b) This is correct as explained above.
   c) This is incorrect. Prices are too low.
   d) This is incorrect. We do know that when externalities exist, resources will be allocated differently than when the market is functioning properly.

4. A fine will presumably increase the costs of the producers and shift the supply curve to the left, that is, reduce the supply.

   a) This is correct as explained above.
   b) This is incorrect. The supply will be less.
   c) This is incorrect. The supply will fall as costs have risen.
   d) This is incorrect. Costs will not fall, they will rise.

5. The decision as to how to deal with pollution like any other decision involving the use of scarce resources should follow the marginalism rule: clean up to that level where marginal costs equal marginal benefits.

    a) This is incorrect. Marginal costs would exceed marginal benefits.

    b) This is incorrect. This doesn't address the issue.

    c) This is incorrect. This doesn't address the issue.

    d) This is correct as explained above.

6. In a market-oriented economy, the existence of externalities is related to the contamination of the environment.

    a) This answer is incorrect. Technically, there is no limit to the amount of taxes the government could impose, if it so desired, to force externalities to become "internalized."

    b) This is correct. In a market-oriented economy, firms will operate at the lowest cost possible and as long as others are willing to bear some of the external costs, no incentive exists for internalizing the costs.

    c) This is incorrect. Scientific progress is being made in dealing with pollution, technologically.

    d) This is incorrect. The assertion may or may not be true, but it is irrelevant anyway.

OBJECTIVES

Upon successful completion of this chapter, you will be able to:

1. Explain the two approaches used to describe the distribution of income.
2. Cite figures to show how income is distributed among the families in the United States.
3. Interpret a Lorenz curve of income distribution.
4. Describe the factors affecting the Gini index.
5. Explain how the official government poverty level is calculated.
6. List the factors underlying the decline in the number of people below the poverty level.
7. Identify the characteristics of those persons below the poverty level.
8. Identify the characteristics of the "rich."
9. Discuss three approaches to dealing with poverty.

CHAPTER 10

INCOME DISTRIBUTION IN A MIXED ECONOMY

INTRODUCTION

MEASURES OF INEQUALITY

WHO ARE THE POOR AND THE RICH?

REMEDIES FOR INEQUALITY AND
POVERTY

INTRODUCTION

The issue of income inequality—some families receiving large incomes and others small incomes—generates more heated debate than any issue in economics. This is not surprising, since all of us are concerned about the size of our income, and quite frequently about the size of others' incomes. This concern means that income distribution plays an important role in determining what type of economy you will live in. Your great-grandfather lived in a largely capitalistic economy in which government had a low profile. Taxes comprised a smaller share of a worker's income, and there were few government social welfare programs, such as the social security system. You, however, live in a *mixed economy*, in which taxes and social programs play an important role. In this chapter, we will see how income is distributed in the United States, examine who are the rich and the poor, and consider what can be done about the problem of poverty.

Economics deals with the choices involved in production, consumption or utilization, exchange, and distribution. Although all of those activities are important, it is distribution that determines the standard of living that you will personally experience. In a pure, price-directed economy the distribution of income is determined by the quantity and prices of the productive services each family sells. Those families that sell large quantities of high-priced productive services receive large incomes. Those persons who have inherited large estates receive large incomes for the use of the services they own. Those physicians who work long hours and sell their services at high prices receive high incomes. And those families who sell small quantities of low-priced productive services receive low incomes.

It is interesting to note that the price system, whose key function in a market economy is to allocate resources, has never produced a distribution of income that has satisfied people, not even in your great-grandfather's time. People have always found ways to redistribute the income generated by a price-directed economy. During the nineteenth and early twentieth centuries, churches and private charities collected contributions from the rich and redistributed them to the poor.

There are two basic meanings to income distribution—functional income distribution and personal income distribution.

Functional income distribution reflects the claims on the goods and services produced in the economy that rise from the ownership of the resources used to create the output. The income generated from the use of these resources takes the form of wages and salaries, rent, interest, and profit. You will recall these factor payments from Chapter 6. Personal income refers to the way the nation's output is distributed among the different households that comprise the economy.

Figure 10.1 shows how the national income "pie" was divided in 1977. Compensation to em-

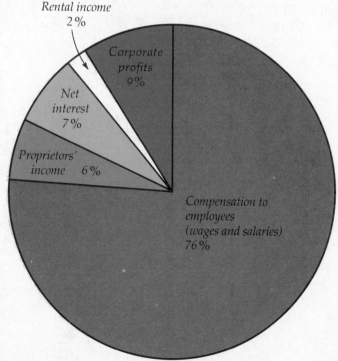

FIG. 10.1   **The national income pie—1977.**

ployees, which consists of wages and salaries plus employer contributions to social security, comprises the lion's share of income earned—76 percent. Corporate profits equal 9 percent, proprietors' income (which includes farm and business and professional income) accounted for 6 percent, net interest for 7 percent and rental income for 2 percent. Table 10.1 shows the distribution of income over time by decade since 1900. The dominant trend is the increase in the share going to employees as wages and salaries and the decline in proprietors' income. This reflects the decline of the family-owned farm and the small "mom and pop" businesses.

The key point that the functional income distribution shows is that the United States is basically a "wage and salary economy."

The personal distribution of income is the measure most frequently cited in the context of income redistribution.

Government is vitally involved in income redistribution.

In recent years, with the development of the mixed economy, the government has played an increasingly important role in determining how income will be distributed. The federal government relies on progressive income taxes to take more taxes proportionately from high-income families than it does from low-income families. The federal government has a social security system in place that redistributes income from working people to retired people.

How, then, is pretax income distributed in the United States? To answer this question, look at Table 10.2. In 1975, about one-eighth (12 percent) of the families in the United States had weekly incomes of less than $100, and 56 percent of the families had weekly incomes of less than $300. The figures in this table also show that at levels of about $500 per week, the percentage of the families receiving larger incomes falls sharply. For example, only 1 percent of the families received incomes in excess of $1000 a week. This 1 percent includes the Rockefellers, professional athletes, and movie stars.

The income distribution tree represents how incomes are distributed among families in the United States.

Perhaps an easier way to think about this is to think of the income distribution profile as being a "tree" (see Fig. 10.2). The bar at the base of the tree diagram represents the 6.8 million families receiving $100 a week or less. Moving up the tree, almost 12 million families, or about 21 percent, received between $100 and $200 a week; and 13 million families, or 23 percent, received between $200 and $300 a week.

TABLE 10.1

DISTRIBUTIVE SHARES (PERCENTAGE) OF TOTAL IN U.S. NATIONAL INCOME, 1900–1970, 1974, 1976 (Decade averages of shares for individual years)

Decade	Employee compensation	Proprietors' income	Corporate profits	Interest	Rent	Total
1900–1909	55.0	23.7	6.8	5.5	9.0	100
1910–1919	53.6	23.8	9.1	5.4	8.1	100
1920–1929	60.0	17.5	7.8	6.2	7.7	100
1930–1939	67.5	14.8	4.0	8.7	5.0	100
1939–1948	64.6	17.2	11.9	3.1	3.3	100
1949–1958	67.3	13.9	12.5	2.9	3.4	100
1954–1963	69.9	11.9	11.2	4.0	3.0	100
1963–1970	71.7	9.6	12.1	3.5	3.2	100
1974	74.9	8.1	9.2	5.4	2.3	100
1976	75.9	6.5	9.4	6.4	1.7	100

Source: Irving Kravis, "Income Distribution: Functional Share," *International Encyclopedia of Social Sciences*, Volume 7, New York: Macmillan and Free Press, 1968, p. 134. The 1974 and 1976 data came from *Economic Indicators, May 1978.* U.S. Government Printing Office, 1978.

TABLE 10.2
DISTRIBUTION OF INCOME BY LEVEL OF INCOME 1975

Weekly income (approximate)	Annual income	Number of families receiving this income (in thousands)	Percentage of families receiving this income
0–$100	0–$4,999	6,766	12.0
$100–199	$5,000– 9,999	11,920	21.2
200–299	10,000–14,999	12,561	22.4
300–399	15,000–19,999	10,584	18.8
400–499	20,000–24,999	6,548	11.7
500–599	25,000–29,999	3,574	6.4
600–699	30,000–34,999	1,787	3.2
700–799	35,000–39,999	857	1.5
800–899	40,000–44,999	572	1.0
900–999	45,000–49,999	357	0.6
1000–1199	50,000–59,999	234	0.4
1200–1399	60,000–69,999	196	0.3
1400–1599	70,000–79,999	157	0.2
1600 and over	80,000 and over	78	0.1

Source: *Consumer Income* Current Population Reports, No. 105, June 1977, p. 36, Table 4 (figures interpolated above $24,999), Office of Management and Budget, Department of Commerce.

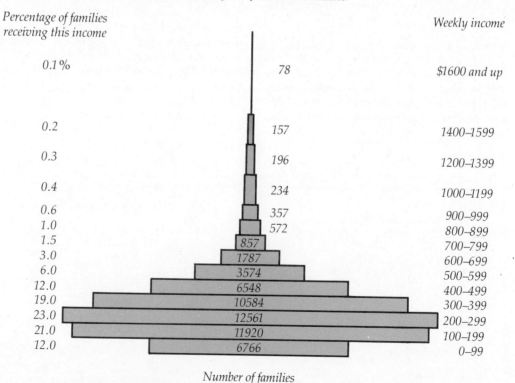

FIG. 10.2   The "tree" of income distribution for the United States, 1975.

The median family income in the United States in 1975 was about $275 a week. Or put another way, if you were to place each family in a long line according to the size of its money income from the lowest to the highest, the median family would be in the middle of the line. Thus, if your family had an annual income in 1975, before taxes, of $13,719, it would be right in the middle of the income distribution.

The average or mean income (total income divided by the number of families) was a little higher in 1975. If the total income flowing to all families had been divided equally, with the Rockefellers receiving exactly what your family was getting, then each family would have received $15,546, or a little more than $300 a week in 1975. Adjusted for inflation, the average family income at the end of 1978 would be about $19,500, or a little less than $400 a week.

Only one-eighth (13 percent) of the families received incomes in excess of $25,000, or about $500 a week, and a little more than 1 percent of the families received incomes of $50,000 or more a year. If the top of the income distribution tree were pruned—that is, if all of the income over $50,000 (about $1000 a week) had been taken in taxes from the 1 percent of the families in this income bracket and divided among the remaining families—the incomes of these remaining families would have been increased on the average of about $286 a year, or a little less than $6 per week.

The fact that the narrow top of the income distribution tree doesn't have much foliage has an implication for tax policies. To collect enough taxes to accomplish the goals of expenditure programs, it is necessary to impose the taxes on the upper middle part of the income-distribution tree, as well as on the top. There is not enough total income in the narrow top part of the income distribution tree to finance large new programs.

We can also use the concept of the income distribution tree to consider alternatives to the existing distribution of income. In Fig. 10.3, the top diagram shows how the complete egalitarians, those who would like the nation's income to be distributed equally among families, would prune the tree. They would have the income distribution tree be one long rectangle with all families earning about $15,600.

The rest of this chapter will be concerned with: (1) measuring equality and inequality in the distribution of income, (2) identifying the rich and the poor, and (3) appraising different methods for modifying the distribution of income to make it conform to the ethically determined standards acceptable to society.

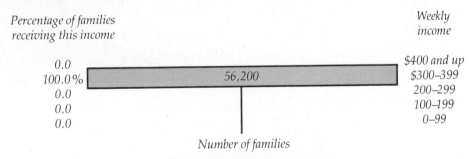

FIG. 10.3   Egalitarian income distribution tree.

MEASURES OF INEQUALITY

The *Lorenz curve* is used to measure income distribution.

Another way of viewing the distribution of income is to plot it on a *Lorenz curve*. The figures underlying a Lorenz curve for the United States are presented in Table 10.3. To understand these figures, imagine all the families and unrelated individuals in the United States lined up according to income size from the lowest to the highest.

TABLE 10.3
PERCENTAGE OF AGGREGATE FAMILY INCOME RECEIVED BY EACH FIFTH OF FAMILIES
AND TOP 5 PERCENT FOR SELECTED YEARS

Year	Lowest fifth	Second fifth	Middle fifth	Fourth fifth	Highest fifth	Top 5 percent
1947	5%	12%	17%	23%	43%	18
1950	4	12	17	23	43	17
1955	5	12	18	24	42	17
1960	5	12	18	24	42	17
1965	5	12	18	24	41	16
1970	6	12	17	23	42	16
1973	6	12	18	24	41	16
1974	6	12	18	24	41	16
1975	5	12	18	24	41	16

Source: Calculated from Table 13, *Consumer Income*, Current Population Reports p. 60; No. 105, June, 1977, p. 58. Office of Management and Budget, Department of Commerce.

We could then mark off the boundaries between each fifth of the income receivers and determine what percentage of the aggregate income of the nation each fifth received.

Table 10.3 shows that there has been little change in the distribution of income over the 28-year period from 1947 to 1975. The lowest fifth received about 5 to 6 percent of the aggregate income and highest fifth received about 41 to 43 percent. The highest 1 percent received about 16 to 18 percent of the aggregate income.

The data from this table are plotted as a Lorenz curve in Fig. 10.4. If the income of the nation were equally distributed, the diagonal line from the Southeast to the Northwest would describe the distribution of income. The first 20 percent of the income receivers would receive 20 percent of the income. Since the next 20 percent of the income receivers would also receive 20 percent of the aggregate income, the first 40 percent of the income receivers would get 40 percent of the income, and so on.

However, when the data from Table 10.3 are plotted, the line joining these points sags from the diagonal. The lowest 20 percent of the income receivers receive only 5 percent of the income. When we add the 12 percent of the income that the next 20 percent get, we find that the lowest 40 percent of the income receivers only get 17 percent of the aggregate income. The highest fifth of the income receivers get about 41 percent of the income, or about eight times as much as the lowest fifth.

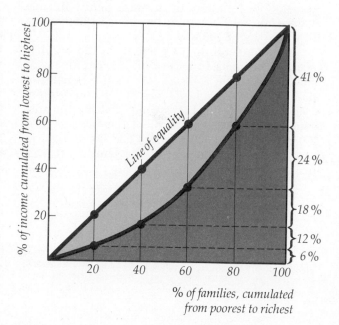

FIG. 10.4   Lorenz curve for the United States—1975.

The sag in the Lorenz curve has been used to measure the inequality in the distribution of income. The ratio of the area between the Lorenz curve and the line of equality to the total area lying below the line of equality is called the *Gini index*. The larger the index, the more unequally the income is distributed.

While there appears to have been little change in the distribution of income in the United States since 1947, there has been an increase in the amount each family has earned.

If we were to plot the Lorenz curve for the years 1947 to the present, using the data from Table 10.3, the curves would lie almost on top of one another. The Gini index did not appear to change significantly during this 28-year period.

Although the relative distribution of the income earned by these families did not appear to change, the average income received increased during these 28 years from about $3,500 to $15,500 (a part of this is inflation and a part of it is real growth). As a result, there was a widening absolute gap between money incomes of the lowest 20 percent and those of the highest 20 percent of the income distribution. In 1947, the highest annual income in the lowest fifth was about $1,500 and the lowest income in the highest fifth was about $5,000, a difference of $3,500. In 1975 this difference had increased to about $15,000, with the lowest family in the highest fifth receiving about $22,000 and the highest family in the lowest fifth receiving about $7,000.

What would you conclude from looking at these figures? Two answers stand out: (1) The income distribution appears to be very stable. (2) The spread in dollar incomes between the poor and the rich seems to be getting wider. Although the Lorenz curve provides a useful way of examining the distribution of income, however, it does not tell the whole story. We need to take account of a number of factors that influence the usefulness of these figures for measuring the inequality of incomes in the United States.

The life cycle is a factor affecting the Gini index.

Consider the economic stages you pass through in your life. If you are in college now and paying your own way, your income is probably in the lowest fifth or quintile. In fact, you may be included in the poverty statistics. Once you are out of college, you will probably be in the middle quintile, earning say, $300 a week. If you marry a person earning what you are you will create a family unit with an income of $30,000 a year. If you both do well in your jobs, you will find that your family unit is in the upper 5 percent of all

families, with an income in excess of $35,000 a year. After a period of time you decide to have a family and one of you stays at home to take care of the children. Your family income drops and you slip back into the middle quintile. After the children are old enough to be in school, and both partners are again working, your family, measured by your income, will be classified as rich. Assume that both of you move into high-paying jobs as you get older and your combined incomes will place you in the upper 1 percent of the income-receiving units. You are now, so far as income statistics are concerned, one of the super-rich. Some 35 to 40 years from now, with some savings in the bank, social security, and a good pension, you both retire to a warm climate. Your money income has suddenly dropped and you fall into a lower quintile, but you don't worry about it because you now own your home and need only take care of it and keep your household equipment and automobiles in good repair.

Were you really poor when you were in college? Were you really rich just before you retired? Did your real income drop when you moved to a warm climate and had more leisure? These are all questions that complicate income distribution statistics. Life-cycle changes in income show up as inequalities of income and affect the Gini index.

It is probably true, although we cannot say for certain, that fluctuations in income due to career changes have probably increased during the last 30 years. People stay in school longer, more wives are working, and more people find it possible to retire early. If this is true, then an unchanging Gini index could easily conceal shifts toward greater equality in life-time incomes.

Changes in family composition influence the Gini index.

A related issue in understanding income distribution is the effect of family size. When the real income per family is low, families tend to stick together. Grandmothers tend to live with their children and share their small pension with the larger family. Children live at home even though they have a beginning job. When family incomes rise, however, the larger families split apart. Grandmother finds it possible to live in her own apartment, grown children move into their own living quarters, and in place of one large family unit, with multiple earners and a fairly large income, you have three family units, of which two may easily be classified as poverty families.

This common response to higher real income affects the income distribution statistics. Affluence appears to produce poverty. The lower-income families created by this splitting away process value their independence more than the higher income and security of a large family.

Geographical differences in income affect the distribution of income.

If you live in Bogalusa, Louisiana, your cost of living is substantially lower than if you live in Anchorage, Alaska, or New York City. A family income in New York City that would place you in the highest quintile in the nation could provide a lower standard of living than a middle quintile figure in a small southern town. Even among major cities, there are substantial differences in the cost of living. Using an index of 100 for the United States, New York City has a cost of living of 116 and Atlanta, Georgia, has a cost of living of 91, or about 78 percent of the New York City figure. This means that an Atlantan family in the fourth quintile of the income distribution could have as high a real income as a fifth quintile family living in New York City.

Leisure versus work decisions distort the Gini index.

People have different tastes for leisure. Some students, when they are graduated from college, would rather have a low-paying 20-hour-a-week job in Hawaii than a 50-hour-a-week high-paying job in Boston, Massachusetts. One student will end up near the bottom of the income distribution and the other in the middle quintile. Is there really a difference in their real incomes? The job-holder in Hawaii enjoys more leisure and a beautiful environment, and yet the income distribution will reflect an inequality of money incomes produced by the occupational choice decision.

Increases in the real income of the nation make it possible for more people to choose leisure over the money income. A poor society demands that everybody work. A rich society can afford to have people opt out.

People also make choices about how much risk they want to take in connection with their jobs. Actors and actresses do very well when they are working and are poor when they are not. Some lawyers earn huge incomes while others hover near the poverty line. At the same time, people who take civil service jobs are generally assured of a steady lifetime income, without much variation. When people choose occupations with wide variations in expected incomes, are they really poor when their incomes are low? Or do they receive some "psychic income" from the possibility that they may strike it rich next year? This is a question that makes it difficult to interpret the income distribution figures—especially since increases in the real income of the nation make it possible for more people to choose risky occupations without fear of destitution.

Government services to the poor as well as taxes distort the income distribution figures.

During the last 10 years there has been a large growth in government expenditures to help the poor. Some transfer payments, such as social security benefits, are already in the income distribution figures, but many are not. Medicare, Medicaid, food stamps, rent subsidies, public housing, training programs, and many other in-kind services to the poor are not included in the income distribution figures. Nor are the various types of educational benefits available to poor and rich alike.

At the same time, the tax programs tend to take a larger share of the money incomes of the rich than they do of the poor. We have to be careful with this generalization. Some taxes, such as sales taxes, are regressive. But they are not included in the distribution of money incomes. Other taxes, such as the corporate income tax, come out of incomes before they are received, and some special provisions in the tax laws relieve the rich from paying their share of the taxes. But on the average, the families in the upper quintile of the income distribution pay a larger share of their money incomes in income taxes than do families in the lowest quintile of the income distribution.

It is difficult to correct for the hidden impact of government on the distribution of incomes. But some economists have attempted to do so.* Tables 10.4 and 10.5 show the income distribution figures for 1952, 1962, and 1972, before and after adjustment for in-kind transfers and other items.

Table 10.4 shows the quintile shares of the aggregate income before adjustment of in-kind government benefits, education, available leisure, capital gains, underreporting, and family size for the period 1952 to 1972. After adjustment for these "corrections" (and this does not include adjustment for life cycle or geographical dispersions of money income), the figures are quite different. These are shown in Table 10.5.

After adjustment, the families in the top quintile received about two and a half times rather than seven or eight times as much income as the families in the lowest quintile in 1972. The figures also show that there is a marked trend toward equality during this 20-year period. The after-tax incomes of the upper quintile, as a percentage of the total, fell from about 35 to 32 percent. At the same time, the share of the lowest quintile increased from about 8 percent to 13 percent.

The various adjustments appear to make the income distribution less uneven.

Which set of figures should you believe? We cannot give you a clear answer to this question. The figures that are usually quoted do not take into account the many "corrections" discussed above. As is true of many aggregative figures, they may easily conceal what is happening. At the same time, it is very difficult to quantify the effects of such corrections as life-cycle changes, the fragmenting of families, geographical differences in incomes, substituting of leisure for work, and the

* Edgar K. Browning, "The Trend Toward Equality in the Distribution of Net Income," *Southern Economic Journal* 43 (1976): 912–923.

TABLE 10.4
FIGURES FOR MONEY INCOME SHOW ONLY SLIGHT CHANGES IN INCOME DISTRIBUTION . . .
Percentage Money Income Shares for Families

	Lowest fifth	Second fifth	Third fifth	Fourth fifth	Highest fifth
1952	4.9	12.2	17.1	23.5	42.2
1962	5.0	12.1	17.6	24.0	41.3
1972	5.4	11.9	17.5	23.9	41.4

Source: U.S. Bureau of the Census, "Money Income in 1972 of Families and Persons in the United States." Current Population Reports Series P-60, No. 90 (Washington: U.S. Government Printing Office, 1973). Adapted from Browning, p. 913.

TABLE 10.5
. . . BUT FIGURES THAT COUNT IN-KIND TRANSFERS AND OTHER ITEMS MAY REVEAL MARKED TREND TOWARD INCOME EQUALITY
Percentage Adjusted Money Income Shares

	Lowest fifth	Second fifth	Third fifth	Fourth fifth	Highest fifth
1952	7.8	14.8	18.8	23.3	35.3
1962	9.0	15.1	19.1	22.9	34.0
1972	12.6	16.1	18.4	20.9	31.9

Source: Browning, p. 919.

provision of in-kind services to the poor. It appears that the distribution of income is not as unequal as the unadjusted figures indicate, and that there has been a shift toward greater equality in the distribution of after-tax income during the last 30 years.

Does this mean that poverty has disappeared in the United States? The answer is no, as you can see when you drive through the inner cities of the United States and rural areas of Appalachia. We turn now to these questions: "Who are the poor?" and "Who are the rich?"

WHO ARE THE POOR AND THE RICH?

Poverty is difficult to define precisely since it has many dimensions.

We need an economic definition of poverty in order to examine how policy makers in the mixed economy approach the elimination of poverty as a goal. Two definitions compete for acceptance. One defines poverty as having too little income to participate in the social life of the nation. This definition arbitrarily asserts that a family lives in poverty if its income is less than half of the median income of the nation. In 1975, a family had to have an annual income of almost $7000 to escape from poverty.

The other definition, now widely accepted as the official government definition, is that a family is in poverty if its income is inadequate to provide for a nutritious diet, adequate housing, and other necessities. Using this general definition, the federal government defines poverty as an income that is less than three times what it takes to buy a nutritious diet. This means that the poverty threshold would be higher for a large family than for a small family. Price-level increases also raise the threshold income for poverty. Table 10.6 shows the average poverty threshold for a family of four for selected years from 1959 to 1976.

TABLE 10.6
THE AVERAGE POVERTY THRESHOLD FOR A NONFARM FAMILY OF FOUR 1959 TO 1976

1959	$2975
1964	3169
1969	3743
1970	3968
1971	4137
1972	4275
1973	4540
1974	5083
1975	5500
1976	5815

The number of families with incomes below the poverty threshold has decreased since 1959.

Using the official definition of poverty, Fig. 10.5 shows that the number of people living in poverty families has declined since 1959, despite an increase in the total population. Nonetheless, in 1976, there were still about 25 million people living in poverty.

This decrease in the number of people living in poverty is largely the result of economic growth. Real GNP per capita increased almost 70 percent during this period. Increases in productivity have enabled unskilled as well as skilled workers to obtain higher real wage rates, and millions of workers were able to rise above the poverty threshold. In addition, economic growth and the availability of time-saving household appliances has made it possible for more women to participate in the labor force. In 1959, almost 15 percent of family heads who worked part-time and about 9 percent of those who worked full-time were in poverty. By 1972, only 3 percent of the family heads who worked full-time could be classified as being in poverty.

In other words, economic growth has enabled those people able to work to rise above the poverty level. Increases in social security benefits and other types of transfer payments, which have been made possible by economic growth, have also taken many people off the poverty roles.

Families most likely to be in poverty are those with a nonworking head.

Who are the 25 million people who were living in poverty in 1976? This is a hard question to answer without going into too much detail. One generalization is that more and more poverty families are headed by a person who does not work

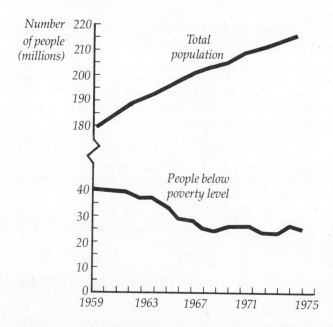

FIG. 10.5   As total population rises, the number beneath the poverty level declines.

Source: Total population, including Armed Forces overseas, is an unadjusted fourth-quarter average for these years based on monthly figures of the U.S. Bureau of the Census. Poverty level figures are taken from *Current Population Reports*, Series P-60, No. 106.

because of disability, age, responsibilities in the home, or perhaps an inability to cope with work. About half of the poverty families are headed by women, many of whom have small children at home. About a sixth of the persons in poverty are in families headed by persons 65 years of age and older. Young people who are unable to find work also represent a portion of the 25 million persons living in poverty.

Poverty, then, is *increasingly* a problem of nonparticipation in the economic system, some of it because people can't find work, some of it because people do not perceive themselves as members of the labor force, and some, the largest portion, because people are unable to work. This represents a marked change from the situation three or four generations ago, when a large portion of the working poor could be classified as living in poverty. Now the problem of poverty is largely a problem of helping those who do not have jobs.

Most of the income of the rich stems from human capital.

When we speak of people being rich, we usually think of the Rockefellers, the Hunts, and other persons living on rent, interest, and dividend receipts. But this ignores the changes in the economy that have marked the last 50 years. Now an increasingly large percentage of the nation's wealth consists of human capital—trained physicians, accountants, professors, computer specialists, and so on. Because of these changes, we will define wealth as the ability to obtain an income from whatever source—whether from physical capital or from human abilities.

With this definition in mind, we could define the rich as those families who receive an income in the upper 5 percent of the income distribution. In 1975, this would include those families who had incomes in excess of about $34,000 a year. Adjusted for changes in the cost of living from 1975 to 1978, this would mean that an annual income of about $42,500, or a weekly income of a little less than $900 a week, would be enough to place a family in the "rich" category.

Who are the rich? Because of data limitations we will have to rephrase the question. Who are the families who earn $50,000 or more per year? Are they the idle rich, who clip coupons and receive dividends, or are they people who, for the most part, work for a living?

The answer is that for the most part they are people who work for a living. The average family earning in excess of $50,000 a year received about 85 percent of its income from wages and salaries or from self-employment. Some families, it is true, do live on interest and dividends, but they make up a small percentage of the rich families. Most rich families are headed by persons who work for a living. These working rich families tend to be headed by well-educated males with four or more years of college. Almost 60 percent of these families have two or more earners, and more than half of the families have four or more members in them.

The average income of rich families was about $70,000, and in the aggregate they received almost $55 billion dollars. If you were to take away all income in excess of $50,000, these families would lose approximately $16 billion dollars, or enough to give every family of four living in poverty about $2500. Should this be done? To answer this equstion, we will have to consider different strategies that a mixed economy might take to produce a more equal distribution of income.

MINI-CASE 10.1

The minimum or poverty level of income in a nation as affluent as the United States should be defined as follows:

a) The minimum income any family gets should be no less than half of the average income received by families in the top 20 percent.
b) An income sufficient to provide every person with adequate diet, clothes, and housing.
c) An income at least as high as the average income received in the United States.
d) Whatever can be earned by a family head willing and able to work at least 40 hours a week.

REMEDIES FOR INEQUALITY AND POVERTY

All countries have developed social institutions for dealing with poverty.

We have already seen that no country is willing to accept the distribution of income generated by the price system without some modification to meet that society's goals. Despite the advice of some nineteenth-century economists that the poor should take care of themselves, The Church of England, as well as the local charities, provided care for people who would otherwise have found themselves in abject poverty. In the United States, where immigrants were struggling to get ahead in a new country, there were many self-help charities sponsored by ethnic social groups. The churches in the cities and small communities raised money to take care of poor families and members of the family, which included the aunts, uncles, and cousins, and those living in rural communities took care of their relatives who were less well off than they. Local governments established "poor farms," or county homes, as they were sometimes called, to take care of older persons who did not have relatives to take care of them.

Every society has developed a set of social institutions for dealing with the problem of poverty. The problem is not a new one. In this section we will consider three sets of social institutions for dealing with the question of poverty and the inequality of incomes. They make up a smorgasbord of social institutions for dealing with this age-old problem. We do not advocate any one of them, but no doubt some combination of these institutions will characterize the economy in which you will live during the rest of this century.

Nineteenth-century capitalism, if reinstituted, would emphasize economic growth as a means of combating poverty.

One set of social institutions can be characterized as *nineteenth-century capitalism*. It relies almost exclusively on the private market economy without major government modification. Consider how it might work if it were reinstituted. The government at the federal level would not take responsibility for changing the distribution of income or alleviating poverty. It would be concerned with encouraging economic growth. To do this, it would design a tax system that would encourage people to save and to invest in new capital equipment. Income taxes, in this system, would be proportional. Corporate taxes would be replaced by a value-added tax to be borne by the purchasers of the products rather than the producers.

The federal government, if this set of social institutions were chosen, would be largely concerned with doing three things. First, it would provide a framework of laws, and a system of enforcement would assure the continuance of property rights and the performance of contracts. People could be sure that undertakings that extended far into the future would not be interrupted by changes in government regulations. Second, it would serve as a police force to make sure that nobody was barred from the marketplace by monopoly practices or by restrictive legislation. Third, it would provide for defense against incursions from abroad.

You might ask, What about such programs as social security and public education? Would they be sponsored by the government? The answer is no—unless there are external economies to be realized. Each family would be responsible for saving enough to provide for its old age. Since education involves some third-party benefits, those who advocate a return to nineteenth-century capitalism argue that the government should support education through tax credits or a voucher system.

How, you might ask, would this type of system make a contribution to the elimination of poverty? Those who advocate these social institutions say "look at the nineteenth century and the early part of the twentieth century." The United States was able to take huge numbers of poverty-stricken people in successive waves from various parts of Europe and the Orient and convert them into middle-class citizens. They argue that the United States economy during the nineteenth century was a machine for reducing poverty. The members of the ethnic groups that came to this country as peasants from agrarian societies were poorer than the poverty classes in the United States at the present time.

The advocates of a return to these social institutions say that *economic growth is the key.* Establish a set of social institutions that will encourage economic growth and the poverty problem will take care of itself. They argue that the last wave of agrarian migrants coming into the cities—in this case black families from the South—are just as competent as the other ethnic groups that came to this country. Just give them a growing economy and time to adjust to urban living and they too will move into the middle class just as members of many immigrant groups have done.

Those who oppose this approach argue that such a "trickle down" method of helping the poor also helps the rich. Indeed, it may help the rich proportionately more than the poor and thereby increase the income gaps between the poor and the wealthy. They argue that poverty is just as much an issue of relative incomes as of absolute incomes and that therefore this approach is unacceptable.

Would economic growth and private charities be adequate in urban society?

Would private charities take care of the problem of poverty? This is very unlikely. Things have changed. With improvements in transportation, the extended family has disappeared. The population of the nation is increasingly crowded into urban communities where there is little sense of community. It is doubtful that people living in suburbs would feel the same sense of responsibility for the people in the inner cities as did the people who lived in the cities in the past.

Would economic growth lift people out of poverty as it did in the past? Again, we have an unanswered question. The poverty families, as we have seen above, are largely headed by people who are not members of the labor force. Economic growth and full employment might pull a small number of them into the labor force, but many, perhaps a larger percentage than in the past, are simply unable to work. Economic growth would not help them.

The negative income tax could be added to the nineteenth century model.

Because of these likely results and a concern for the welfare of others, the *negative income tax* has been proposed as a device for alleviating poverty. The NIT, as it is called, could be joined with the nineteenth-century model and is a device for placing a floor under the incomes of people.

The negative income tax works this way. First, establish the *minimum income* to which every family shall be entitled, whether family members work or not. Suppose the minimum that is chosen is $5000 per year. Then, in place of paying taxes, a family with no income would receive regular payments from the internal revenue service—negative taxes—that would provide the family with a base income of $5000 a year.

Second, establish a *marginal tax rate* for families getting assistance from the government. Suppose the marginal tax rate chosen were 50 percent. Then, when members of the family earn $1000 from part-time jobs, their family assistance checks go down by half of their additional earnings. They would get $4500 from the government. This, added to their $1000 of outside earnings, would give them a family income of $5500. For each additional earned dollar of earned income, the family assistance checks would go down $0.50. Families would then get family assistance checks until their earnings totaled $10,000. After that they would be on their own.

The negative income tax has advantages and disadvantages.

What are the advantages of the negative income tax? First, in place of having the government provide food stamps, public housing, Medicaid, and child care in the proportions that the government decides is best, the NIT allows the low-income family to decide for itself how it will spend its income. Second, the many federal programs require that social workers first determine whether family members *can* work. Only if the answer is no will they receive public assistance. The NIT permits the individual members to decide for themselves whether they can work or not.

What are the disadvantages of the NIT? First, and most important, it is extremely difficult to design a negative income tax that has (1) a high enough minimum income and (2) a low enough marginal tax rate to accomplish the objective of supporting poor families while at the same time giving them adequate incentives to work. Consider examples A and B in Table 10.7. In example A, the minimum income is $5,000 and the marginal tax rate is 50 percent. The minimum income in A is scarcely high enough to support a family of four, and yet with a relatively high marginal tax rate of 50 percent—much higher than many middle-income families pay—family assistance payments would continue until the family income had reached $10,000 per year. To get the marginal tax rate down to a more reasonable figure, such as 25 percent, it is necessary to lower the minimum income—as in example B—to $3,000, and to continue providing family assistance payments until the family's income reaches $12,000 per year. Thus, if the minimum income is high enough to provide a reasonable floor under family incomes, the marginal tax rate must also be high in order to keep the cost of the program within bounds. Or, if the marginal tax rate implicit in

the program is low, then the minimum income must be quite low or the cost of the program will get out of hand. The dilemma then is that either the cost of the program will be high, and many working people will receive supplemental income from the government, or the marginal tax rate imposed on poor families will have to be higher than the marginal tax rate imposed on middle-income families.

Second, to the extent that the poverty problem is a problem of people not being able to work because of disabilities, age, child-care problems, and so on, then the NIT will not solve the poverty problem. Any reasonable minimum income would not be enough to take care of the non-working family. Social workers would then be required to decide which families should receive assistance in addition to the NIT, and this tends to defeat the purpose of the NIT.

Socialism is another suggested alternative.

There are some persons who say that no set of social institutions that involves the private own-

TABLE 10.7
NEGATIVE INCOME TAX: TWO EXAMPLES

	Family Assistance Payments		Total Income	
Earnings	A 50% Marginal tax rate	B 25% Marginal tax rate	A 50% Marginal tax rate	B 25% Marginal tax rate
0	5,000	3,000	5,000	3,000
1,000	4,500	2,750	5,500	3,750
2,000	4,000	2,500	6,000	4,500
3,000	3,500	2,250	6,500	5,250
4,000	3,000	2,000	7,000	6,000
5,000	2,500	1,750	7,500	6,750
6,000	2,000	1,500	8,000	7,500
7,000	1,500	1,250	8,500	8,250
8,000	1,000	1,000	9,000	9,000
9,000	500	750	9,500	9,750
10,000	0	500	10,000	10,500
11,000	0	250	—	11,250
12,000	0	0	—	12,000

A $\begin{cases} \text{\$5,000 minimum income} \\ \text{50\% Marginal tax rate} \end{cases}$

B $\begin{cases} \text{\$3,000 minimum income} \\ \text{25\% Marginal tax rate} \end{cases}$

ership of land and capital will ever solve the problem of inequality. They argue that only socialism—the government ownership of the means of production—can give the workers their full share of the output.

Many nations have partially or fully eliminated private property. Great Britain has nationalized coal, steel, transportation, and many other basic industries. Yugoslavia has transferred the ownership of factories to the workers. Russia and the countries of Eastern Europe under Russian domination have confiscated all land and capital used in the production of goods and services and transferred it to the state. China has done the same. Half of the world's population now lives in countries that have eliminated the private ownership of the means of production.

If a democratic government pays the former owners of the nationalized industries by giving them government bonds for their ownership rights, then there is little to be gained by public ownership. The interest on the government bonds will replace the dividends the former owners had received, and there will be no noticeable change in the distribution of income. If for reasons of low productivity a plant has to be closed, a democratic government, as the new owner, is in a difficult position. When it tries to close low-productivity steel plants, for example, the government now must assume the blame for the loss of jobs in a given location and, if the political pressures are strong enough, it will have to keep the plant open even if it means higher prices for consumers or inefficient operation.

The welfare state is an alternative to socialism or nineteenth-century capitalism.

In addition to nineteenth-century capitalism and socialism as models for dealing with poverty and inequality, there is a third set of social institutions that a mixed economy can use. This third set is sometimes called a *welfare state* and is best exemplified by income distribution policies of Denmark and Sweden.

This set of social institutions contains four essential ingredients: (1) reliance on the price system for allocating resources; (2) the management of aggregate demand to minimize unemployment;

(3) a steeply progressive tax system, which takes a large percentage of any income in excess of the median income; and (4) an all-inclusive social security system that assures a family of protection against the loss of income due to unemployment, health, and old age.

Few countries have gone as far as the Scandinavian countries in adopting this particular set of social institutions, but most countries in Western Europe and North America have some elements of this system. The United States, for example, depends largely although not entirely on the price system to allocate resources. The United States tries to manage its aggregate demand in order to minimize unemployment subject to the strength of inflationary pressures. The United States has moderately high marginal tax rates on personal income and corporate earnings, and the government is now spending over half of its budget on social security transfers and the provision of special services, such as food stamps, Medicare, Medicaid, special education for the young, the poor, and aged, and the disabled.

We cannot discuss each of these programs in detail, but they make up the social institutions that surround you. They provide the grist for much of the debate about how far the United States should go in creating new social institutions to deal with poverty and inequality.

Ultimately, the issue is what goals you think an economic system should achieve.

The fact that high marginal tax rates may limit the rise in productivity and reduce the rate of economic growth is *not* by itself an effective argument against the adoption of income-equalizing policies. There exists a trade-off between the goals of efficiency and growth on the one hand and the goal of equality on the other hand. The more equality the less efficiency, and vice versa.

Arthur Okun has used a very effective analogy to illustrate this trade-off relationship.* He calls it the "leaky bucket" example. Suppose you were using a bucket to transfer water—or, in this

---

* See, Okun, Arthur, *Equality and Efficiency, the Big Tradeoff*, The Brookings Institution, Washington, D.C., 1975.

case, income from the rich to the poor. Some programs, such as public support of education, may not cause any loss of income. Other programs may entail large administrative expenses. Little of the income that is taken from the rich actually goes to the poor. The bucket is leaky. Or suppose that the rich choose lower-income activities rather than paying the higher taxes associated with more effort or greater risk. Again you have a leaky bucket; only a part of the income you intended to get transferred actually gets transferred to the poor.

Some people would favor income-equalizing policies even if the bucket were so leaky that none of the income actually got transferred to the poor. It would be enough to have the rich made poorer. Other persons would only favor income-equalizing transfers from the rich to the poor if the bucket did not leak at all.

The choice between efficiency and equality is an ethical choice. You have to base it on what you want the economy to accomplish. We turn now to the factors underlying economic growth and the management of aggregate demand.

REVIEW QUESTIONS

1. In 1975, the mean family income (total income divided by the number of families) in the United States was about $15,500. From what you know about the distribution of income in the United States, it is clear that:

   a) more than half of the families in the United States received an income above $15,500.
   b) about half of the families in the United States received $15,500.
   c) more than half of the families received an income below $15,500.
   d) it is impossible to say whether more than half or less than half of the families received $15,500.

2. Suppose the distribution of income is determined only by the price system (and not by gifts, taxes, and transfer payments). A family's income will then depend on:

   a) the quantity and price of the services it sells.
   b) the amount that it gets from the government in welfare and other transfer payments.
   c) the degree to which union pressure for higher wage rates works.
   d) the legislated minimum wage.

3. At the present time in the United States, wages and salaries (payments for work performed) account for approximately the following percentage of all income generated by the economic system:

   a) 33 percent.
   b) 50 percent.
   c) 66 percent.
   d) 75 percent.

4. When you examine the income distribution tree, it is clear that:

   a) the rich people (families with incomes of over $50,000 a year) account for about one-third of the families.
   b) more than half of the families receive incomes of less than $200 a week.
   c) more than half of the families in the United States get incomes between $200 and $600 a week.
   d) incomes of $1,000 a week are not common, and yet about 10 percent of the families get this much while 12 percent of the families get less than $100 a week.

5. Given the three Lorenz curves shown, select the correct answer based on your examination of the graph.

   a) Curve C represents a more equal distribution of income than curve A.

   b) Curve B represents a less equal distribution of income than curve C.

   c) In curve B, 50 percent of the families share 50 percent of the income.

   d) In curve A, 70 percent of the families receive about 60 percent of the income.

6. Consider the following two income distributions:

   A. Four people in a room each receive $10,000 and the fifth person receives $60,000 a year.

   B. Four people in a room each receive $20,000 amd the fifth person receives $90,000.

   Now draw the Lorenz curve for these two situations. The Gini index is:

   a) larger for A than for B, indicating that income is more unequally distributed in A than in B.

   b) larger for A than for B, indicating that income is less unequally distributed in A than in B.

   c) larger for B than for A, indicating that income is more unequally distributed in B than in A.

   d) It is impossible to determine from the information how unequally income is distributed.

7. In 1947 the average income of the lowest fifth of the income distribution was $1,500 and that of the highest fifth was $5,000. Because of inflation and economic growth, the dollar gap between the average income of the lowest and highest fifth was increased. In 1975, the lowest fifth had an average income of $22,000. This indicates that:

   a) in 1975 the distribution of income was more unequal than in 1947, with the rich getting more relative to the poor.

   b) in 1975 the distribution of income was more equal, with the poor getting more relative to 1947.

   c) the larger the spread between the money incomes of the poor and the rich, the more unequal the distribution of income.

   d) It is impossible to say what has happened to the distribution of income.

8. Ann took a corporate job after graduation. Her income was low at first, and reached a peak about five times higher than her starting salary. When she retired her pension was equal to her average income during the forty years she worked for the corporation. Joe was not as venturesome. He took a job as a teacher. His starting salary was $10,000 and his ending salary was $20,000, and after the same 40 years of work he retired on a pension equal to his average income. It can be said that:

   a) Ann's life cycle of earnings would make the distribution of income, during her life, more unequal than Joe's.
   b) Joe's variations in income would contribute more to inequality than would Ann's.
   c) life-cycle changes in income do not contribute to the equality or inequality of income as measured by the Gini index, since the Gini index applies to one year only.
   d) it is impossible to tell from the data given which person would contribute more to measures of inequality.

9. Government services to the poor, such as medicare, medicaid, food stamps, rent subsidies, public housing, and occupational training programs:

   a) do not change the distribution of real income.
   b) do change the distribution of real income, but do not change the number of people recorded in official statistics as being poor.
   c) do not benefit the families that receive these services and therefore should not be taken into account in counting the number of poor people.
   d) have increased the incomes of the upper fifth of the income distribution more than they have increased the incomes of the lower fifth.

10. Considering what has happened during the last hundred years, it can be said that the most important factor reducing poverty in the United States has been:

   a) the rise of labor unions.
   b) government programs to provide direct aid to the poor.
   c) the redistribution of income via income taxes and government subsidies of income from the rich to the poor.
   d) economic growth and the availability of public education.

11. At the present time, most of the individuals remaining in poverty are there because:

   a) their wage rates are not high enough for them to earn enough even though they are working full time.
   b) for a variety of reasons they do not work full time.
   c) they are lazy.
   d) they can collect welfare benefits.

ESSAY QUESTIONS

1. Suppose that lifetime incomes were equalized to the point that the only differences that were left were those that represented the work preferences of people—that is, some would prefer to do less difficult jobs and some would prefer to be paid less and work fewer hours. How would the Lorenz curve look under these circumstances? What technical factors, such as part-time work, multiple family workers, early retirement, and so on, would govern the distribution of annual incomes? List all of the technical factors you can that would make the Lorenz curve sag.

2. Most income comes from work. Therefore, if income is to be equalized by taking it from some and giving it to others, most of the redistribution will have to be between workers. Criticize.

3. Suppose all property income were taken in taxes. What effect would this have on the way the economy functions? Would this markedly redistribute income?

4. Why do you think that the distribution of income is so difficult to change in economies that do not make revolutionary changes in their social institutions?

5. Is a sagging Lorenz curve the price an economy pays for private ownership of resources, including human capital? List measures that have tried to redistribute income within the framework of a private-enterprise, market-directed economy. How successful have they been?

6. The negative income tax has many advantages. It would give direct aid to the poor, it would not require an army of welfare workers to administer it, and it would give the poor the right to make their own decisions about how they will use their incomes. Discuss the problems the negative income tax creates. How would you solve these problems?

7. "The rich are well off because their ancestors stole land from the Indians and exploited the poor who came to this country to work in their factories." Give a critique of this statement against the background of the income distribution statistics.

8. Which of the following statements best describes the problem of inequality in the United States?
   a) The distribution of earned income is unequal, which is the major cause of the unequal distribution of money incomes.
   b) The distribution of property income, particularly from inherited wealth, is so unequal that it in turn makes the distribution of the total income of the United States very unequal.

9. If the government were to pay the owners of steel mills, railroads, and automobile factories and take them over, then the distribution of income would be much more equal. Is this correct? Discuss how a price-directed socialistic system would change the distribution of income.

10. The redistribution of income via progressive income taxes and transfer payments can lead to inefficiencies. These inefficiencies are described by Arthur Okun's "Leaky Bucket Analogy." Are these inefficiencies, by themselves, a sufficient justification for not redistributing income? If you were trying to create the "good society," what trade-offs would you take into account?

ANSWERS TO REVIEW QUESTIONS

1. The mean income is equal to total income divided by the number of families in the nation. Median income is that level of income with an equal number of families with both higher and lower income.
   a) This is incorrect. The mean income is higher than median income.
   b) This is incorrect. This is true of median, not mean income.
   c) This is correct as explained above.
   d) This is incorrect. We do know that more than half of the families received less than $15,500.

2. In a pure price system there are two factors that determine a family's income: the quantity of productive services it sells and the prices of these services.

   a) This is correct for the reason given above.
   b) This is incorrect, since in a pure price system the government would not redistribute income through taxes and transfer payments.
   c) Unions may have an effect on the prices of productive services, but they do not control the quantity of services that will be offered for sale or purchased.
   d) This is incorrect, in a pure price system there will be no legislated minimum wage.

3. The answer is that wages and salaries accounted for about 65 percent of the national income in 1977. Self-employment income accounts for another 6 percent. The balance, about 29 percent, goes to the owners of property, including land and securities. Therefore (c) is the correct answer.

4. The United States is primarily a middle-class society. Less than .01 percent of the families get incomes in excess of $50,000 a year or $1,000 a week. More than half of the families receive incomes between $200 and $600 a week.

   a) This is incorrect for the reason given above.
   b) This is incorrect. About 33 percent of the families get less than $200 a week.
   c) This is correct. 60 percent of the families received incomes between $200 and $600 a week in 1976.
   d) This is incorrect as explained above.

5. The Lorenz curve plots the percentage of total income received against the percentage of families receiving this income. The greater the sag, the greater the income inequality.

   a) This is incorrect. Curve C has a lower sag than A, and hence is less equally distributed.
   b) This is incorrect. Curve B has a smaller sag than C, and hence is more equally distributed.
   c) This is incorrect. A straight 45° curve would reflect this.
   d) This is correct. About 70 percent of the families earn 60 percent of the income.

6. After looking at the two diagrams, it is clear that the area between the diagonal line and the Lorenz curve is larger for situation A than B.

   a) This is correct. Situation A is described by Lorenz curve A, which obviously has more sag than B. This indicates that the income is more unequally distributed.
   b) This is incorrect. The larger the sag the more unequal the distribution of income.
   c) This is incorrect. The sag is smaller for B than A.
   d) This is incorrect. Whenever there are two or more persons it is possible to arrange their incomes according to size and draw a Lorenz curve. It is then possible to estimate the Gini index.

7. It is impossible to say what has happened to the distribution of income without comparing the Lorenz curves for the two periods. No data are given above on what happened to the incomes of the second, third, and fourth quintiles.

   a) This is incorrect. As indicated above, it is impossible.
   b) This is incorrect for the same reason.
   c) The size of the spread does not measure the distribution of income. In fact, the unadjusted figures indicated that inequality was approximately unchanged.
   d) This is the correct answer. The data are not adequate to tell you what has happened to the distribution of income.

8. A Gini index measures the inequality of income at a given time. Because some people are just starting their careers, others are in midstream, and still others are retired, the Gini index reflects the differences of income due to the normal life cycle of earnings. Ann's variation in income is larger than Joe's. Therefore, people like Ann would make the Gini index larger than people like Joe. It follows that:

a) This is correct for the reason given.
b) This is incorrect. Joe's income varies less during his lifetime than Ann's.
c) This is incorrect. Life-cycle changes in income are important because there are millions of people at different stages of development in any one year.
d) This is incorrect. The data are sufficient to answer the question.

9. Government services to the poor are not included in measures of the incomes received by the poor. As a result, the statistics make it appear that all of these programs taken together do not lift people out of poverty. In considering the distribution of income it is necessary to take these programs into account: They markedly affect the average real incomes of the lowest fifth of the income distribution.

a) This is incorrect. These programs obviously increase the real incomes of the poor.
b) This is correct. These programs have lifted many people out of the poverty class as measured by official statistics.
c) This is incorrect. Although there may be some waste, these programs do benefit the poor and must be taken into account in counting the number of people living in poverty.
d) This is incorrect. The spread between the incomes of the upper fifth and the lowest fifth is narrowed substantially by the effect of these programs.

10. The rise of productivity and the economic growth flowing from it, together with availability of public education, have been the major factors contributing to the reduction of poverty.

a) This is incorrect. Labor unions may have helped some, but less than 25 percent of the labor force is in labor unions.
b) This is incorrect. Government services to the poor have made a small contribution relative to that made by economic growth.
c) This is incorrect, for the same reason as in (b) above.
d) This is correct for the reasons given above.

11. At the present time, the bulk of the persons who are officially listed as living in poverty are so classified because they could not work at full time jobs even if they wanted to do so.

a) This is incorrect. Less than 3 percent of the family heads who work full time have families living in poverty.
b) This is correct for the reasons given above.
c) This is incorrect. Most of those in poverty are there because they cannot work full time.
d) This is incorrect. While the welfare alternative may keep some people out of the labor market, it would not be possible for mothers with small children, disabled people, and many others in poverty to work full time even if there were no welfare program.

PART IV

THE MACROECONOMY: GOALS, POLICIES, AND PROBLEMS

OBJECTIVES

Upon successful completion of this chapter, you will be able to:

1. Explain why we measure the economy.

2. Explain how total output or GNP can be measured in terms of investment expenditure, government expenditure, consumer expenditure, and net foreign expenditure.

3. List the relative magnitudes of the major components of national income measured as the sum of factor inputs.

4. State the relationships among Gross National Product (GNP), Net National Product (NNP), and National Income (NI).

5. Be able to list and explain the shortcomings of GNP as a measure of the nation's output of goods and services.

6. Define index number and explain the usefulness of the consumers price index, wholesale price index, and implicit price index.

7. Describe how the consumers price index is computed.

8. Describe the general trend of real GNP growth during this century.

9. Explain how output is related to the number of hours worked and productivity.

10. List and explain the factors determining the growth of real income in the United States and indicate their relative importance.

11. Analyze how public policies influence the rate of growth.

12. Analyze the problem of poverty in terms of its relationship to economic growth.

CHAPTER 11

MEASURING THE ECONOMY'S GROWTH

INTRODUCTION

The economy is measured for two basic reasons.

The United States Public Health Service and numerous private nonprofit agencies such as the American Cancer Society and Heart Association constantly remind you of the importance of undergoing periodic health checkups; in other words, you are encouraged to have your health "measured." The criteria against which your health is measured are the normal ranges for pulse rate, blood pressure, blood count, temperature, and so on. In each case a number is given to your body's performance. If your index of health by any of these criteria differs significantly from the norm, a prescription—perhaps medicine, exercise, or some other form of treatment—is immediately made. The goal, of course, is to restore your body to "normal" health.

Economic indicators serve a parallel purpose. Measures such as gross national product, national income, income per capita, disposable income, and so on are used by policy makers to identify the health level of the economy. If it is found ailing, appropriate policy prescriptions should be made to nourish it back to health. Such policy prescriptions and the difficulties involved in their application will be explained in Chapters 12, 13, 14, and 15.

The federal government spends millions of dollars each year simply to measure our economy. The measurement of economic activity is important for two fundamental reasons. First, because of scarcity, we cannot achieve all of our economic goals simultaneously; consequently it is imperative that we have some evidence of "how we are doing" to minimize misuse of scarce resources as we attempt to achieve our goals.

The second reason why the measurement of economic activity is important is the interdependent nature of our economy. In previous centuries, most of the economic activity was undertaken in small, self-sufficient economies. Certainly there was trade among the various parts of a nation, but both transportation and communication systems were too primitive to generate high degrees of interdependence. This is no longer the case. Specialization and division of

labor have contributed more to increased productivity and higher standards of living than any other aspect of economic activity. For example, lettuce from California provides salads for East Coast residents, and lobster flown from the Northeast is served in restaurants all over the country.

The benefits of specialization and division of labor, however, like all events of an economic nature, are not without costs. The most significant cost is precisely this high degree of interdependence that division of labor and specialization entail. Consider, for example, the effects of a strike among steel workers in the United States. Within several weeks the effects would appear in closely related industries such as the automobile and appliance industries. Several weeks later, the effects would reach out to encompass the suppliers of the automotive industry. And in time, the service industries that cater to these suppliers would feel the effect.

It can be seen that the interdependent nature of our economic system no longer grants us the privilege of being unconcerned about the level of activity in other parts of our nation. Your job may very likely be affected by an economic event occurring 2000 miles away and, therefore, the health of the economy affects you directly.

This chapter deals with two major concepts. First it explains how the economy is in fact measured. Second, using the measurement instruments developed, it analyzes the performance of the United States economy and the factors underlying its growth.

HOW TO MEASURE THE ECONOMY

The economy can be measured in terms of stocks and flows.

There are two basic ways we can examine an economy. We can view it at a moment in time by taking, as it were, a snapshot of it and then analyzing the snapshot much the way an aerial photographer might. Such a snapshot taken with an economy-wide-angle lens would reveal a vast number of factories, trucks, homes, highways, and so on, a given size population and labor force, and a given stock of natural resources. This "snapshot approach" is called a *stock,* or fund, approach and measures the wealth of an economy at a given point in time.

We can also view the economy for a given period of time by taking, as it were, a motion picture of it and examining the nature of the changes that occur during the period under study. This movie would reveal assembly lines producing cars, factories being built, land being developed, old buildings being razed, young people entering the labor force, and many other changes too numerous to cite. The "movie approach" is a *flow* approach and measures the output and income of an economy over a given period of time.

Perhaps the following illustration will clarify the two approaches even more. If you were to make a list of all the things you own (assets) and then make a list of what you owe to others (liabilities), you would have prepared what is called a *balance sheet,* which is a record of your wealth position, measuring the *stock* of your assets and liabilities. If, instead, you were to keep a daily record of your purchases and income receipts for a year, you would have prepared an income statement revealing a record of the *flow* of goods and services purchased and the flow of income received.

Our economic goals—sustained economic growth, a low unemployment rate, or security during periods of economic or physical hardship—are defined over periods of time; that is to say, most of the important measures of output are flow measures. Hence, we will focus our attention on those gauges desgined to measure flows rather than stocks, that is, income and output rather than wealth.

During the course of a year, many goods are produced in an economy the size of the United States. One way of measuring this output would be to make a list describing each of the items or services produced. Obviously, this list would be most extensive and detailed; yet, this is exactly what the gross national product (GNP) measures. It does so, however, by measuring goods and services in the common denominator of the dollar, at their market value. This method allows us to express the total value of output in a year in one lump figure, GNP.

Simply to say that the value of output when totaled gives us GNP does not shed much light on how the figure is calculated. Actually, two different approaches are used. One is called the expenditure, or spending, approach and the other is called the income, or factor, approach.

The expenditure approach to GNP consists of adding up consumer, government, business, and net foreign expenditures.

The total value of expenditures for output is achieved by totaling the expenditures of consumers, businesses, government, and foreigners. These four categories encompass all of the expenditures for goods and services.

Consumer expenditures include purchases of goods, both durable and nondurable, and services by households and individuals. Government expenditures include the spending of state, local, and federal governments. This government expenditure recorded in GNP does *not* include transfer payments. Foreign expenditures include only the value of net expenditures, that is, the value of exports minus imports. If exports exceed imports, this value is positive; but if imports exceed exports, it is negative. Business expenditures, called officially gross private domestic investment expenditures, include expenditures for machinery, plant, and equipment, and expenditures for residential construction. The accumulation of inventories is also included in the category of investment expenditure.

If all of the goods and services produced in the economy in a year's time were purchased in that year, the value of expenditures would equal the value of that year's output. The fact that in some years more is produced in the economy than is purchased, while in other years more is purchased than is produced, means that a simple measure of total expenditure will not yield an accurate measure of the economy's output. Hence, unsold inventories are regarded as a kind of investment expenditure. By the same measure, if inventories are reduced in a given year, that component of investment expenditure will be negative.

Gross national product **is the final market value expressed in dollars of all the goods and services produced in the economy over a given period of time, such as a year.**

Table 11.1 shows that in 1977 the total value of GNP equaled $1890 billion. The same table shows the value of expenditures undertaken by each of the four sectors listed above.

The income approach measures GNP from the input side.

The income approach or factor approach measures the economy from the input rather than the expenditure side of the economy. It is important to understand that ultimately every penny of final expenditure finds its way back to some individual

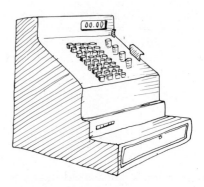

TABLE 11.1
GROSS NATIONAL PRODUCT, 1977

Item		Billions
Gross national product		$1890
Personal consumption expenditures	$1210	
Government purchases of goods and services		395
Gross private domestic investment		294
Net export of goods and services		−9

Source: *Economic Report of the President*, January 1978.

as a form of income or to some level of government as a tax receipt. Since this is true, total expenditure must equal total income plus tax receipts, and therefore GNP as measured from the expenditure approach will equal GNP as measured from the income approach when the appropriate adjustments are made.

Consider the following example as an illustration of the income approach to measuring national output.

Assume that you have just paid $400 for a new stereo player. This purchase would be included in GNP as $400 worth of consumer expenditure if we were measuring GNP from the expenditure approach. How is the purchase measured from the income approach? How will it be distributed among the parties involved in its production? Many steps are involved, and we will trace through several of them to demonstrate how expenditures also comprise income of one form or another.

Step 1: The retail appliance store receives your $400 payment for a stereo set. The store owner distributes it as follows:

Payment to wholesale distributor	$250
Payment for utilities and insurance	10
Reserve for value of equipment worn out	5
Payment for wages and salaries	75
Payment for rent	15
Payment for interest	5
Payment of taxes	20
Return on the owner's investment (profit)	20
Total	$400

You will notice that the first payment can be regarded as payment for raw materials. In other words, a good or service has been purchased from some other producer. One of these producers, the wholesaler in our example, views his receipt of $250 in the same light as the appliance store owner viewed his receipt of $400 for the stereo. The third payment reflects the fact that in the process of doing business, the appliance store's equipment, for example, cash register, fixtures, cabinets, and so on, wear out. The value of the equipment lost through the wear is a real cost of doing business and is regarded as a payment for depreciation. The second payment also represents a form of input. It is a cost of doing business.

The five remaining payments are for various kinds of productive inputs. Wages and salaries are payments for labor. Rent is a payment for the use of land or buildings. Interest is a payment for the use of financial capital. Tax payments can be viewed as a payment to government for services used indirectly in production. The return to the owner for his investment is the payment he receives for risking his financial resources in this operation, yielding a result called profit. Note that we are using the accounting definition of profit in this example.

Now consider step 2, which describes how the appliance wholesaler distributes receipts.

Step 2: The wholesaler receives $250 from the appliance store. It is distributed as follows:

Payment to component manufacturers	$100
Payment for utilities and insurance	20
Reserve for depreciation	5
Payment for wages and salaries	80
Payment for rent	10
Payment for interest	5
Payment for taxes	15
Return on the owner's investment	15
Total	$250

Step 3: The component manufacturer receives $100 from the appliance manufacturer. In this case we will assume that the component manufacturer purchases no parts or raw materials from other producers. The $100 received by the component manufacturer is distributed as follows:

Payment for utilities and insurance	$10
Payment for wages and salaries	50
Reserve for depreciation	5
Payment for rent	5
Payment for interest	10
Payment for taxes	15
Return on owner's investment	5
Total	$100

In each of the three steps described above, payments were made to utility and insurance companies. In return for their services they each receive a payment, which also is distributed as one of several forms of income.

Step 4: This step really occurs simultaneously with the other three steps and incorporates the expenditures made by the firms above for utilities and insurance. You will note that the three firms together spent $35 on insurance and utilities. The insurance and utility companies distribute the receipts as follows:

Reserve for depreciation	$ 5
Payment for wages and salaries	5
Payment for rent	5
Payment for interest	10
Payment for taxes	5
Return on owner's investment	5
Total	$35

Now to demonstrate that all receipts ultimately are income payments, examine Table 11.2 in which the factor payments made in each of the four steps above are totaled by kind of income payment.

The total payments in the form of wages, rent, interest, profit, taxes, and depreciation equal the amount initially spent for the record players (see column 5 in Table 11.2). The same analysis applies to every expenditure for goods and services that occurs in an economy. That expenditure ultimately finds its way to some factor of production.

If we add only the first four rows in column 5, we obtain the sum of income payments. In our example, these payments equal $320. For the nation as a whole this sum is called national income (NI). If we go a step further and include the fifth row, taxes, we obtain the sum $380. For the economy as a whole, this sum is called net national product (NNP). Finally, by including depreciation, we achieve our initial $400 expenditure. For the entire economy this sum is called GNP.

TABLE 11.2
DISTRIBUTION OF FACTOR PAYMENTS

	(1) Appliance retailer	(2) Wholesaler	(3) Component manufacturer	(4) Utility and insurance company	(5) Total
Compensation to employees (wages)	$ 75	$ 80	$50	$ 5	$210
Rent	15	10	5	5	35
Interest	5	5	10	10	30
Profit	20	15	5	5	45
Total income payments	$115	$110	$70	$25	$320
Taxes	20	15	15	10	60
Net product	$135	$125	$85	$35	$380
Depreciation	5	5	5	5	20
Gross product	$140	$130	$90	$40	$400

Earlier we measured GNP by summing the *expenditures* for the goods and services produced in a year, adjusted for differences between what is produced and what is purchased. You have now seen that GNP can also be defined as the sum of *income* payments to the factors of production plus tax payments to government and a depreciation allowance.

Table 11.3 shows that the value of the net national product for the year 1977 was $1693 billion. Since GNP was $1890 billion, the difference between the two, depreciation, was $197 billion.

TABLE 11.3
GROSS NATIONAL PRODUCT: INCOME APPROACH, 1977
(in billions)

Gross national product	$1890
Capital consumption allowance (depreciation)	197
Net national product	1693
Indirect business tax and miscellaneous adjustments	173
National income	1520
Compensation of employees	1156
Proprietors' income	98
Rental income of persons	25
Corporate profits and inventory valuation adjustment	140
Net interest	101

Source: Monthly issues of *Survey of Current Business* published by the Department of Commerce, U.S. Government.

The values of income receipts in the form of wages and salaries, rent, profit, and interest are also shown for the United States in 1977.

Net national product and national income are useful measurements closely related to GNP.

We have identified a number of measures in addition to GNP related to the total output of a nation. We will now summarize them. The first is *net national product* (NNP).

GNP less depreciation, or capital consumption allowance, equals net national product. When equipment is used, it wears out. Accountants normally include an estimate of the depreciation of equipment among the expenses of a company in order to obtain a net profit figure, and it is reasonable to do the same in estimating net output of a nation. The net national product (NNP) is, then, a measure of the net output of a nation after subtracting an allowance for depreciation from GNP.

The difference between GNP and NNP is basically the same as the difference between gross domestic private investment and net domestic private investment. Net national product less indirect business taxes equals national income. Indirect business taxes consist of all taxes paid by businesses except corporate income taxes and employer contributions to social security. The national income, then, is also a measure of the total amount of final products produced, but unlike the GNP, it measures the production after subtracting depreciation and indirect business taxes.

We have seen why gross national product, net national product, and national income are used almost interchangeably by many analysts as measures of the total output of a nation. The GNP and NNP are measures of the output of final products, and the national income measures the *value added* by the inputs of productive services.

One additional useful adjustment to the accounts used to measure the economy that considers the size of the population involves creation of a set of per capita values. Gross national product per capita, national income per capita, and so on can all be calculated simply by dividing the values by the population.

These large aggregate figures are quite remote from the day-to-day activities of the average individual. But there are two aggregate figures that do mean more to you as a consumer and worker. These are personal income and disposable income. Personal income is derived by adjusting national income for income earned but not received, for example, social security tax contributions, and for income received but not earned, for example, transfer payments. Disposable income is the income of all persons remaining after subtracting personal taxes. Disposable income is either spent or saved.

SHORTCOMINGS OF GNP AS AN ECONOMIC MEASURE

Since GNP is measured in terms of dollars, changes in the general level of prices yield a distorted evaluation of output.

An important difficulty in measuring national output arises out of changes in the general level of prices. Since GNP is measured in dollars and the value of the dollar changes, this money measure of output will depart from real output. If all prices doubled, then the GNP would double, even though there was no change in the physical volume of output. Therefore, we must find a way to "correct" for changes in the GNP due to changes in the general level of prices.

Price indexes have been devised to overcome the measurement problem caused by changes in the value of the dollar.

Statisticians have created indexes to adjust for the fact that the dollar as a measure of the value of output varies over time.

An *index number* is a figure that shows the relative change, if any, of prices, costs, or similar statistical phenomena between one period and some other period of time selected as a base period. The base period is usually assigned the index number of 100.

For example, if the price of a pound of a given quality hamburger was $0.80 in 1972 and $1.20 in 1978, then the ratio of the later period price to the base period price is $1.20/0.80 = 1.5, a number free of any measurement unit. Such ratios are calculated for many commodities and an average ratio is computed from them. As an illustration, consider the following collection of products. This hypothetical collection, or "basket of commodities" as it is sometimes called, consists of the following:

```
  10  tons of steel
1000  gallons of milk
   1  ton of aluminum
   5  baby carriages, and so on
```

You may ask why the various quantities of different products are specified. Not all commodities are of equal importance in expenditure plans. For example, the price of pins is not as important in the average consumer's budget as the price of bread. Hence, different quantities of various products have different weights, depending on their relative importance.

Once the basket of commodities has been chosen, the price index shows the percentage relationship between the price level in a given year and the base year. The base year is the year arbitrarily chosen in which the price level is defined as being 100. Thus, when we say that the consumer price index has moved from 100 in 1967 to 190 in 1978, we are in essence saying that the aggregate price of the basket of commodities included in the consumer price index has increased 90 percent over the base year.

Price indexes must be interpreted with care.

Price indexes as measures of general price changes appear to be more accurate than they actually are. A difficulty is that price indexes are based on: (1) an arbitrary basket of commodities, and (2) a basket that must contain the same commodities from that time forward. For example, the widely used consumer price index is measured by prices of the basket of commodities that an urban family of four with a moderate income would purchase. This definition makes the price index apply directly to a fairly small percentage of households; additionally, this basket must be held constant even though this same group of people may change their buying habits over the years.

There are three basic price indexes commonly used in the United States.

The three basic price indexes used in the United States today are the Wholesale Price Index (WPI), the Implicit Price Index (IPI), sometimes referred to as the GNP Deflator, and the Consumer Price Index (CPI).

The *Wholesale Price Index* is the oldest continuous price index in the United States, having been introduced in 1902 as an aid in evaluating the effect of tariff laws on the economy. The WPI measures the general price level of goods (including imports) at their first level of transaction, thereby excluding prices received by middlemen or retailers. No services are included. The WPI includes some 2200 commodities, and the information for constructing the index is collected primarily from questionnaires sent to producers.

The price index that is usually used to "correct" the GNP is called the *Implicit Price Index*. By examining Table 11.4 you will see that the general level of prices as measured by this index has increased from 100 in 1972 to about 141 in 1977.

The *Consumer Price Index* was initially constructed to measure the rapid rise of prices in the post-World War I era. Prices obviously were an important part of wage negotiations, and a measure of inflation was needed. The CPI measures the price change of a constant market basket of goods and services over time. It has three major uses. First, during periods of price rise, it is an index of inflation and therefore measures the success of government policy. Second, it is used to deflate (adjust) statistics such as retail sales, hourly earnings, and personal consumption expenditures for price changes and convert them into "inflation-free" dollars. Third, the CPI is used to "escalate" income payments. Almost nine million workers are now covered by collective bargaining contracts that provide for increases in the CPI. Indirectly, the CPI now affects 31 million social security recipients whose benefits are tied to the CPI.

TABLE 11.4

GNP IN CURRENT AND IN 1972 DOLLARS ADJUSTED BY THE IMPLICIT PRICE INDEX

Year	GNP in current dollars	Implicit price index	GNP in 1972 dollars
1950	$ 286.2	53.64	$ 533.5
1955	399.3	60.98	654.8
1960	506.0	68.67	736.8
1965	688.1	74.32	925.9
1970	982.4	91.36	1075.3
1971	1063.4	96.02	1107.5
1972	1171.1	100.00	1171.1
1973	1306.6	105.80	1235.0
1974	1412.9	116.02	1217.8
1975	1528.8	127.18	1202.1
1976	1706.5	133.88	1274.7
1977	1890.4	141.32	1337.6

Source: *Economic Report of the President*, 1978, pp. 257, 258, 260.

Since the last major revision of the Consumer Price Index in 1964, there have been substantial changes in the way Americans live and what they buy. Consequently a new index was introduced in 1978. There are now two published Consumer Price Indexes. One is a revision of the old one and reflects the buying habits of urban wage earners and clerical workers. It represents the items purchased and prices paid by about 40 percent of the population. The new CPI for urban consumers is more comprehensive and reflects the buying habits of *all* urban households. It is based on information about 80 percent of the population including professional workers, the self-employed, the poor, the unemployed, and retired persons.

Under the 1978 revision, prices are now collected in 85 areas, and 250 general items are priced monthly for the CPI for all urban consumers. Under the old system, 56 areas were surveyed for 400 specific items. The commodities whose prices are used represent the kind of goods and services an urban family of four normally buys.

Once the appropriate price index has been constructed, the procedure for correcting—or, as it is called, "deflating"—the GNP for price changes is to divide the GNP by the appropriate price index for that year and multiply by 100. The result will be the GNP restated in constant dollars. For example, if the GNP were to increase from $100 to $200 billion while the price level was increasing from 100 to 125, we would know that in constant dollars, the GNP would have gone from $100 billion to $160 billion. The GNP in constant dollars is said to be the real GNP. That is,

$$\text{Real GNP} = \frac{\text{Money GNP}}{\text{Price index}} \times 100,$$

$$\text{or } \frac{200}{125} \times 100 = 160.$$

Table 11.4 shows the GNP in current dollars and in 1972 dollars, and the implicit price index for selected years.

Figure 11.1 shows graphically how GNP has grown and how money GNP and real GNP differ over time.

Real GNP is a useful measure of total output, but certain qualifications in its interpretation should be made.

The real GNP, or national income, is frequently used as a measure of the total output of an economy. With some reservations, this figure is an accurate measure of a nation's output of goods

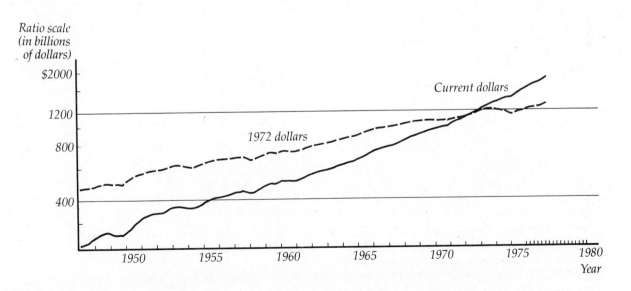

FIG. 11.1 Gross national product in current and 1972 dollars. Source: *Historical Chart Book,* 1977. Board of Governors, Federal Reserve System.

and services. We shall list the most important qualifications:

1. GNP measures only market activity and, therefore, excludes most nonmarket production, such as the work of homemakers, do-it-yourself carpenters, plumbers, and so on.
2. GNP does not measure the increases in leisure, which show up in more holidays, lengthened vacations, and preferred idleness.
3. There tends to be a systematic bias built into the price indexes used to deflate the GNP. As some prices rise, buyers tend to change the combination of products they buy, using less of the higher-priced products and more of the lower-priced products. The price indexes do not reflect the savings arising out of the induced substitution. Also, improvement in the quality of products—particularly those products, such as medical services, that are influenced by scientific developments—is not fully reflected in the price indexes. As a result, the price indexes probably exaggerate the rise in prices and therefore lead to an underestimate of the rise in real GNP.
4. Since GNP is a measure of the market value of goods and services, simple comparisons of GNP among nations or comparison of GNP changes over long periods of time are misleading. For example, as a nation develops, more and more transactions occur in the market-place and hence the GNP of developed countries is overstated, relatively.
5. In recent years especially, GNP has been attacked because it measures both "goods" and "bads" and includes their value in GNP irrespective of the benefit or detriment they generate.

In defense of GNP as a statistic, the statement is made that GNP was never meant to be a measure of welfare or overall happiness; it simply measures the dollar value of output for whatever purpose used.

However, GNP is often used as a measure of welfare and, as such, is perhaps misleading. Economists have tried to devise a new index of overall happiness. Perhaps the most well known is that devised by William Nordhaus and James Tobin called a Measure of Economic Welfare (MEW).* This attempts to correct for increased leisure time, household work, and some of the "bads" associated with economic growth.

Despite these limitations, the real GNP (and the other related measures) is the best measure we have of the output of an industrial economy. We shall turn now to an examination of the factors underlying the growth of the economy over time.

Mini-case 11.1 is provided to clarify your understanding of gross national product.

* William Nordhaus and James Tobin, "Is Growth Obsolete?" *Fiftieth Anniversary Colloquium V*, National Bureau of Economic Research, Columbia University Press, New York, 1972.

MINI-CASE 11.1

Suppose that the women's movement increases the percentage of working wives from about 30 to 90 percent. As a result, the child-care industry becomes a major one and employs almost as many people as the automobile industry. In interpreting the GNP during the time that this important change was taking place, it would be important to realize the following:

a) The changes in real GNP would really understate the growth in the total output.
b) The changes in GNP would have to be corrected for the price changes in order to get an accurate measure of the changes in GNP.
c) The changes in real GNP, which include the entire growth of the child-care industry, would really overstate the growth of total output.
d) The changes in the real GNP should include an additional amount to represent the pleasure working wives get from their jobs.

GROWTH AND THE UNITED STATES ECONOMY

Now that you know how to measure the economy and adjust the important statistical series for inflation, we can examine the performance of the economy in increasing output over time.

Suppose you are a member of the Smith family and that your great-grandfather worked in a typical factory from 1909 until 1939. Further assume your grandfather worked from 1929 to 1959 and your father began his work career in 1949, shortly after World War II, and is still working. Finally, assume you enter the labor force in 1977 and also work in a typical manufacturing enterprise. As you look back on your family's experience, one of the most important developments in their lives as workers has been the increase in wage rates and the reduction in weekly hours worked (see Table 11.5 columns 1, 3, and 5, and Fig. 11.2). You will see that your great-grandfather began work at $0.19 an hour in 1909. He earned about $10.00 per week working slightly more than 51 hours. By the time your great-grandfather quit working in 1939, he was making $0.63 an hour, earning $24.00 per week for 38 hours of work. Your grandfather had the same experience, except that he started at about $0.56 an hour in 1929 and ended up making about $2.19 per hour when he retired in 1959. Finally, your father, who went to work for $1.38 in 1949, is

now making about three times as much per hour and earning about $227 a week.

From 1909 to 1975, weekly earnings in manufacturing increased from about $10 to over $227. But the wage increase, you might object, is mostly inflation. What would wages be if prices had not risen?

To correct for changes in the cost of living, we "deflate" these figures by dividing each year's wage rate and weekly earnings by the consumer

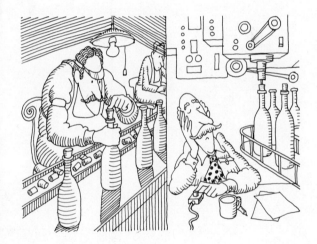

TABLE 11.5

EARNINGS AND HOURS IN MANUFACTURING FOR SELECTED YEARS

	Year	(1) Average weekly hours	(2) Consumer price index	(3) Current dollars	(4) 1967 dollars	(5) Current dollars	(6) 1967 dollars
				Average hourly wage rate		Average weekly earnings	
Great grand-father	1909	51.3	27	$ .19	$ .70	$ 9.74	$ 36.07
	1919	46.5	45	.47	1.04	21.84	48.53
	1929	44.2	51	.56	1.10	24.76	48.55
	1939	37.5	42	.63	1.50	23.64	56.29
Grand-father Father	1949	39.0	71	1.38	1.94	53.88	61.93
	1959	40.0	87	2.19	2.52	88.26	101.45
	1969	43.0	110	3.19	2.73	129.51	117.74
Father	1973	40.7	133	4.08	3.07	166.05	124.95
	1977	40.3	182	5.63	3.09	226.89	124.53

Source: Calculated from *The Economic Report of the President*, January 1978.

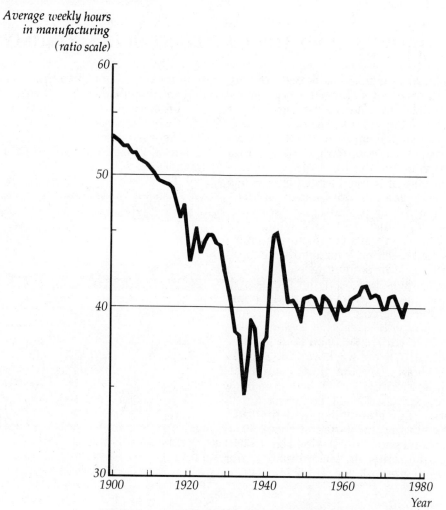

*Average weekly hours
in manufacturing
(ratio scale)*

FIG. 11.2   Average weekly hours in manufacturing. Source:
Historical Chart Book, **1977, Board of Governors, Federal
Reserve System.**

price index for that year. Table 11.5 also shows
these wage rates and average weekly earnings
translated into 1967 prices. You will see that your
great-grandfather's real wage rate doubled during
his working years, from $0.70 to $1.50 an hour,
and his real weekly earnings increased about 56
percent. The same thing happened to your grandfather and to your father. Hence, even after adjusting for inflation, it is clear that the real income
of the average family has risen dramatically over

the last three generations despite the fact that
hours worked have decreased. All of the economic measures of material well-being reflect the
same story. Average family incomes stated in
1967 dollars have more than tripled during the
first seventy years of this century; during this
same time, the average size of the family has decreased from about five at the beginning of the
century to about three and a half, so that per
capita incomes have risen even faster.

It is important to note, however, that in recent years, the rate of growth in real income has been slow. For example, your father's real average weekly earnings increased from $61.93 in 1949 to $117.74 in 1969, an average annual increase of 3.3 percent. During the seven years since 1969, however, the average annual growth rate has been below 1 percent.

The total output of the United States economy has grown enormously during the last 45 years.

When your hypothetical grandfather started working in 1929, the gross national product in 1958 prices was a little more than $200 billion. In 1954, twenty-five years later, it had doubled. In the next nineteen years it doubled again, so that by 1973 the GNP was slightly more than four times as large as it had been in 1929.

Another way of describing the growth in the United States economy would be to say that despite the great depression that plagued your grandfather during the 1930s, the real GNP increased at a rate of over 3 percent during the first 70 years of this century. During the years after World War II, the real GNP increased at an average rate of almost 4 percent a year. Figure 11.3 shows the growth of the real GNP during the years 1900 to 1977.

Growth in the GNP is uneven from year to year.

The saw-tooth appearance of the GNP in Fig. 11.3 reflects the fact that your great-grandfather and your grandfather may have had many slack work periods when the economy was not fully productive. Since World War II, the growth appears to be more steady, but even during this period, year-to-year fluctuations in the growth of the economy indicate that there have been periods of unemployment. For the present, our objective is to explain why growth occurs or why the GNP chart rises at all.

The output of the economy is determined by the input of resources—labor, land, and capital—and the productive efficiency of these resources.

Since it is difficult to measure all of the specialized kinds of land and capital inputs into the

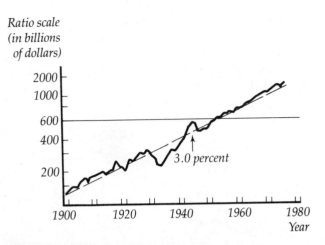

FIG. 11.3   Gross national product in constant dollars. Source: *Historical Chart Book,* **1977, Board of Governors, Federal Reserve System.**

economy, we will simplify the explanation. We will assert that the output of the economy is determined during any period by the input of labor, measured in person hours multiplied by the output per person hour. This is like saying that the distance a car can travel is determined by the input of gasoline multiplied by the number of miles per gallon achieved by the car.

We should be clear about what we are doing when we use this simplified approach. We are not ignoring the inputs of resources other than labor. We are simply saying that we will discuss the importance of these factors, such as the amount of capital used in cooperation with labor, when we discuss productivity. Because a particular car can go further on a tank of gasoline does not prove that the gasoline is better. It may be that better oil is used or that the design of the car is better.

GNP in real terms is equal to the input of labor multiplied by its productivity.

Figure 11.4 illustrates how output per person hour has risen since 1900. The factors underlying the concept of productivity can be illustrated by applying a study recently undertaken by the United States Department of Labor. The study is

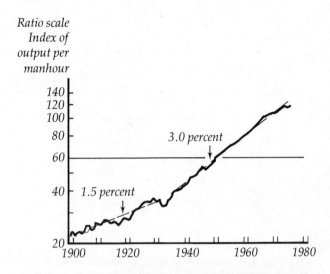

Ratio scale
Index of
output per
manhour

FIG. 11.4   Output per manhour. Source: *Historical Chart Book*, 1977, Board of Governors, Federal Reserve System.

industry as a whole. Then specific innovations will be identified followed by predicted future changes.

Trends in productivity
Between 1958 and 1964, output per hour in the food service industry rose at an average annual rate of only 0.5 percent, reflecting gains below the long-term trend in both output and aggregate hours. Between 1964 and 1968, productivity increases accelerated, averaging 2.3 percent a year, as output grew rapidly and hours advanced moderately. From 1968 forward, productivity improvement again slackened to 0.4 percent a year; however, output continued to expand vigorously, accompanied by relatively large increase in hours.

Factors affecting growth of the industry
1. Increase in income per capita
    The industry's output gains reflect an upward trend in real per capita spending on meals eaten away from home. At $159 per capita in 1976 (constant 1972 dollars), such spending has risen 24 percent since the mid-1960s with all of the rise having occurred since 1973.
2. Increase in number of households headed by unattached individuals
    The long-term trend in food service output was also influenced by the more rapid rise in the number of households headed by unattached individuals (97 percent between 1960 and 1975) than in the number of families (24 percent). Such individuals are more likely to eat out than families: according to the latest Bureau of Labor Statistics consumer expenditure survey, 1-person households, on average, spend 40 percent of their food budgets on meals away from home, compared with 25 percent for families (the proportion diminishes as size of family increases).
3. Increase in number of wives in outside employment
    Another important factor that bolstered output gains in food service was the increase in the number and proportion of wives in outside employment, contributing to family incomes. In 1975, 44 percent of all wives (husband present) held a paid job, compared with 31 percent in 1960. Real income of such families climbed 37 percent over that period; real incomes increased 27 percent for families with wives not in paid employment.

Labor-saving innovations

1. Food preparation
    Food service establishments have been substituting off-premise for on-premise prepared foods in order to reduce labor costs and to control the portions served.

designed to clarify your understanding of productivity as an abstract concept by citing the real-world kinds of events that have influenced productivity in the food service industry.

CASE STUDY OF PRODUCTIVITY IN THE FOOD SERVICE INDUSTRY*

Introduction
Productivity gains cannot be measured without concerning first the environment in which a given industry is operating and second the specific innovations that contribute to more efficient operation. This case study will therefore summarize recent trends in productivity and identify the major economic changes affecting the

---

* Richard B. Carnes and Horst Brand, "Productivity and New Technology in Eating and Drinking Places," *Monthly Labor Review* 100 (July–December 1977): 9–14. U.S. Bureau of Labor Statistics. Reprinted by permission.

Almost three-fifths of the respondents in a 1972 survey gave these two reasons for serving convenience foods. Other respondents cited the broadened menu, as well as reduction in costs per portion made possible by convenience foods. (Although a substantial proportion of off-premise prepared food originates in central kitchens or commissaries classified in the industry, some originates in food processing industries.)

2. Food processing

The major improvement in food service equipment has been the microwave oven. The heat generated in microwave ovens is distributed uniformly throughout the product being cooked (rather than conducted from its surface inward, as in conventional ovens). Moreover, all the energy produced is absorbed by the product, rather than by the oven walls and the surrounding air. Hence, processing time is greatly reduced, although microwave ovens are often supplemented by auxiliary equipment so that an acceptable product texture and surface color is obtained.

Forced convection ovens have been rapidly adopted in the industry. These ovens are reported to reduce cooking time up to 50 percent by using a recirculating loop with a built-in fan to reheat the air within the cooking chamber, thereby increasing the rate of heat transfer to the product. Forced convection ovens are being installed in most new operations, and are replacing free-convection ovens in many existing facilities.

Fat fryers have been refined for more convenient operation and better product quality. Processing control has been improved by more accurate timers and thermostats, and by automatic basket lifts which terminate cooking after a preassigned period. Pressure containers, which increase the heat to the product and thus speed up processing time, have been introduced.

Gas burning broilers are still widely used, but commercial installations are beginning to use infra-red heat to generate high temperatures and shorten cooking time. Operations producing large volumes of processed foods are increasingly using continuous-flow broilers which require only unskilled labor once the temperature and speed of the transfer belt have been set.

3. Food preservation

Important developments have occurred in the quick freezing of fresh foods and in the efficient thawing of frozen foods. Minor but significant changes have also been taking place in other phases of food preservation. Whether or not food service establishments operate their own food processing and preservation equipment, these changes tend to reduce on-premise preparation time, improve the quality, and expand the variety of foods served.

Future improvements

Productivity in the food service industry should continue to improve. The adoption of labor-saving equipment and off-premise prepared foods is likely to be spurred by the expansion of corporate establishments with their focus on efficient management. The continued decline in the number of smaller marginal firms, while perhaps a loss in terms of customer convenience, will nonetheless help raise industry productivity.

1. Food processing and preservation

Developments in food processing and preservation technology will probably make for more widespread off-premise preparation of food, especially insofar as such developments improve quality and help broaden menu choices.

2. Integrated food service systems

Completely integrated food service systems, with precisely timed and mechanized transfer operations, may increasingly mark the spread of contract feeding (they are not likely to prove feasible in smaller retail operations). In such systems, also called a "cooking street," two persons operate five pieces of equipment—a steam cooker, a water cooker, a deep fat fryer, a grill, and a broiler. All pieces are removable without tools, and there is a minimum of complex mechanisms. These "cooking streets" result in a very high ratio of meals served per employee; however, menus are necessarily restricted and there is little if any floor service.

Productivity shows both short- and long-term influences.

In the short run, productivity may change from year to year and even from quarter to quarter. Decreases in short-run productivity are evident in a business slowdown. The fixed costs of production continue and skilled workers are used less effectively. During the recovery stage of a recession, output grows more rapidly than employment and as a result productivity increases.

The long-run factors affecting productivity have been revealed in a path-breaking study by Edward Denison of the sources of economic growth in the United States.* He has demonstrated that from 1929 to 1969 about a quarter of the growth in real national income was due to increases in the input of labor and the other three quarters were due to increases in productivity (see Table 11.6).

TABLE 11.6
SOURCE OF GROWTH OF TOTAL NATIONAL INCOME, 1929–1969.

Source	Percentage share of total growth
1. Growth due to changes in labor input	27
a) Increase in the labor force less allowance for shorter hours, vacations, etc.	27
2. Growth due to changes in productivity	73
a) Education—the amount by which output has increased due to improved educational background of workers	12
b) Increases in the stock of capital	15
c) Technological knowledge—increases in output from incorporation of new knowledge in production	28
d) Economies of scale—increases in output made possible by changes in the size of the markets served	11
e) Other	7

Source: Calculated from Table 9.4, Sources of Growth of Total National Income, p. 127, in *Accounting for the United States Economic Growth 1919–1969*, by Edward Denison, Brookings Institution, 1974.

We will now consider these sources of economic growth in more detail. Keep in mind, however, that the interaction among these underlying factors is as important as each of the factors taken singly.

The input of labor is determined by many factors.

The input of labor is determined by a large variety of factors, including: (1) the individual work-

* Edward F. Denison, *Accounting for the United States Economic Growth, 1929–1969*. Washington, D.C.: Brookings Institution, 1974.

versus-leisure decisions of the more than 92 million people who make up the labor force; (2) the collective decisions embodied in wage-and-hours laws and union contracts; (3) the prejudices that limit female and minority workers' participation in the labor force; (4) the opportunities for education that delay the entry of young people into the labor force; and (5) the effectiveness of the price system as a means of shifting people from areas where they are not needed to areas where there are jobs. During the forty-year span Denison studied, the civilian labor force increased abut 70 percent, but reduction in the hours worked and other factors limited labor's contribution to economic growth to about 27 percent of the total.

The rest of the increase in real national income during this period was due to increases in productivity. Consider the important factors increasing the productivity of the nation's labor force.

Education (quality of labor). A well-educated and experienced labor force working short hours and making effective use of women and minority groups will obviously be more productive than an illiterate, inexperienced labor force working six twelve-hour days a week. Denison assigned about 12 percent of the increase in productivity to improvements in the level of education of labor alone. One of the most common indexes used to describe the quality of the labor force is the median number of years of school completed. For the United States this number increased from 8.6 in 1940 to 12.3 in 1973.

Capital stock of the nation. As we saw in the food service industry study, the tools and equipment that people work with have an important bearing on the output per worker hour. During the last century the investment in capital equipment per worker has increased substantially. The figures in Table 11.7 are illustrative of the amount and growth of capital and equipment in the United States per worker in different manufacturing activities during selected years in the period from 1950 to 1975.

A nation can increase its capital stock only by consuming less than it produces. In the communist countries the central planning agencies accomplish this by making consumers' goods so

TABLE 11.7

CAPITAL INVESTED PER EMPLOYEE FOR SELECTED
INDUSTRIES IN SELECTED YEARS
(In thousands of 1958 dollars)

Industry	1950	1960	1970	1975
Petroleum and Coal	$51.5	$72.6	$97.4	$110.1
Chemicals	19.1	29.6	—	41.3
Primary Metals	18.8	27.5	29.4	30.2
Food	12.3	14.3	16.5	17.9
Textiles	6.0	7.6	9.6	11.2
Apparel	2.7	3.2	3.4	5.4

Source: *Statistical Abstract of the United States, 1977*, Table 906, p. 556.

high priced that people cannot afford to buy them. This releases capacity to produce capital goods.

In the United States and the other mixed market-directed economies of the world, the additions to the capital stock of the nation are largely determined by the willingness of people to save, that is, to consume less than they receive in income. Households do part of the saving. Thus, if you get $200 a week after taxes and spend $150 on consumption, you will release about a quarter of the resources you could command to others who would use these resources to build new capital goods.

Businesses also do a part of the saving. When they hold back some of their earnings as undistributed profits, they too free some of the nation's resources to be used to build additional capital goods. If their earnings were distributed as dividends to stockholders, then the stockholders could use dividend income to buy consumers' goods. Since businesses are controlled by people, we can view business savings as occurring indirectly by the voluntary decisions of households.

Government can also have an enormous effect on the rate of capital accumulation. When it runs a surplus, it can force people to save. The income people use to pay taxes cannot be used to buy consumption goods. And then when the government uses its surplus to pay off government bonds, it pours additional funds into the financial capital market. In this way the government not only forces people to save, it also encourages businesses to invest in new plant and equipment by adding to the supply of loanable funds in the financial capital market.

Government can do the opposite. It can divert some of the nation's savings into the production of consumption goods. Thus when a government runs a deficit in order to make transfer payments to poor people and finances the deficit by selling bonds in the financial capital market, it converts some of the nation's savings into consumption spending.

The stock of capital you see as you look around you—factories, apartment houses, trucks, labor-saving equipment, dormitories—all represent savings people have made in the past. They represent vacations not taken, bottles of beer not drunk, and even the economics books not written. We discussed the process of savings and investment in Chapters 2 and 6 and we will not review it here, except to say that in one way or another every society that would increase its productivity by adding to its stock of capital must find some way to divert resources from the production of consumption goods into the production of capital goods.

Technological knowledge applied to production. About a quarter of the increase in the real national income during the last forty years has come about because of the application of new knowledge to the production process. On the surface, it would appear that the easiest way to increase the productivity of the labor force is to invest in the discovery of new knowledge. But it is not as easy as you might think. There are a number of steps involved in developing new technologies.

The first step is *discovery*, or *scientific development and invention*. Sometimes this is accidental, as the discovery of the process for vulcanizing rubber was supposed to have been. But most of the time, particularly at present, discoveries are the result of deliberate efforts, usually undertaken in a scientific or engineering laboratory, to discover new products and new ways to produce existing goods and services.

The second step may be called *innovation*, the act of introducing a new process or product. The innovation step is a very difficult one in most societies because people become accustomed to doing things in traditional ways. Undertaking the risks involved in change often entails financial risks. There are many examples of innovations that did not work, such as the steam car (as of yet), the helicopter for every garage, or disposable clothing made of nonwoven paper.

The third step in advancing the state of the arts is *diffusion* of knowledge among producers. The diffusion process has been particularly interesting in agriculture. The agriculture extension service of the Department of Agriculture is perhaps the best example of a well-organized program of information diffusion. It sends many teachers into the field to "sell" farmers on the advantages of the new techniques, seeds, fertilizers, and so on. Much of the amazing increase in agricultural productivity is credited to this diffusion approach.

Increase in the size of the market. Denison has indicated that the transformation of local markets into a national market may have been responsible for as much as 11 percent of the increase in income during the 1929 to 1969 period. Certainly the size of the market does have a marked effect on the productivity of labor. For example, when a market is small, as it has been in the local residential construction activities, it does not pay a contractor to introduce factory techniques for producing houses. But as a result of the larger market made accessible by means of transporting factory-made houses, either as mobile homes or as prefabricated houses, new labor-saving techniques, possible only with large-scale production, were introduced that have led to a lower cost per cubic foot of shelter.

Hence, the development of a large national market in the United States or a well-developed international market in the world, with low-cost transportation linking the various parts of the market, leads to specialization and increased efficiency. This is not a new discovery by any means, however. Adam Smith recognized this fact in his famous *Wealth of Nations* (1776); he argued that the key to economic growth and well-being was in reducing impediments to trade and enlarging the market so that individuals and areas could specialize. He argued that specialization, guided by the marketplace, would make a nation's resources more productive and, therefore, increase the real wealth of nations.

We could go on listing other factors that also play a role in increasing the productivity of a nation's labor force. They would include the quality of management, the pride people take in their work, and the effectiveness of the price system in shifting people from the lower-paying jobs to higher-paying jobs. We purposely have omitted discussion of these factors, however, since as economists we do not fully understand the processes of economic growth and to go further will involve us in areas of opinion rather than evidence.

Perhaps by now you are wondering why we have not included in our list the generous supply of natural resources that the United States has within its boundaries. It is not clear that resources must lie within the national boundaries of an economy in order to play a role in the productivity improvement process. During the nineteenth century, Great Britain was able to improve its productivity by relying on imported raw materials;

MINI-CASE 11.2

Suppose as a part of the war against inflation you were appointed productivity czar. Which of these four policies do you think would do most to increase the productivity of the United States labor force?

a) Further reduce the hours per week.
b) Urge people to work harder when they go to work.
c) Use education and other devices to get higher participation among women and other minority groups.
d) Reduce absenteeism.

more recently Japan, with a limited supply of natural resources, has led the world in productivity improvements. In contrast, countries such as Argentina and Chile have abundant natural resources and yet have not been able to increase productivity as rapidly as the United States and Japan.

Mini-case 11.2 is presented to help you clarify your thinking about the factors underlying the somewhat abstract concept of productivity.

COMMENTARY

The following is an excerpt from an article entitled "Effects of Selected Changes in the Institutional and Human Environment upon Output per Unit of Input," by Edward F. Denison. It cites several important factors that have had an impact on overall productivity of the economy during the last decade. Please read the excerpt and answer the questions.

a) Of the three factors cited, which one has had the greatest impact per unit of input (productivity)?

b) From an economic point of view, is this change good or bad? Does your answer differ if you ask the question from an ethical point of view?

EFFECTS OF SELECTED CHANGES IN THE INSTITUTIONAL AND HUMAN ENVIRONMENT UPON OUTPUT PER UNIT OF INPUT

In the last decade, the institutional and human environment within which business must operate has changed in several ways that adversely affect output per unit of input. This article examines the effects of three such changes:
(1) new requirements to protect the physical environment against pollution; (2) increased requirements to protect the safety and health of employed persons; (3) a rise in dishonesty and crime. The common characteristic of these changes is that they have reduced the measured output that is produced by any given amount of input. By "measured" output, I mean national income or net national product as defined by the Bureau of Economic Analysis.

By 1975, the last year for which this article provides estimates, output per unit of input in the nonresidential business sector of the economy was 1.8 percent smaller than it would have been if business had operated under 1967 conditions. Of this amount, 1.0 percent is ascribable to pollution abatement and 0.4 percent each to employee safety and health programs and to the increase in dishonesty and crime. The reductions had been small in 1968–70 but were rising rapidly in the 1970s. The increase in their size cut the annual change in output per unit of input from 1972 to 1973 by 0.2 percentage point, the change from 1973 to 1974 by 0.4 percentage point, and the change from 1974 to 1975 by 0.5 percentage point.

A reduction of 0.5 percentage point in the annual growth rate, the reduction reached by 1975, is equal to a large fraction of the growth rates that have been achieved in the past. For example, it is equal to nearly one-fourth of the annual growth rate of output per-unit of input from 1948 to 1969 (2.1 percent) and nearly one-fifth of the growth rate of output per person employed during that timespan (2.6 percent). The fractions are even larger if comparisons are made with more recent growth rates, which are lower for other reasons besides the impact of pollution abatement, employee safety programs, and crime.

The purpose of this article is to aid analysis of growth and productivity; it is not to judge the wisdom of government programs, which have benefits as well as costs. It must also be stressed that, as the article explains, many of the costs occasioned by pollution abatement, employee safety and health programs, and dishonesty and crime do not reduce output per unit of input and therefore are not included in cost estimates cited. In particular, costs imposed directly upon governmental units and consumers do not have this effect. A major part of the estimating process was the division of costs between those that change output per unit of input and those that do not.

Reprinted with permission of the *Survey of Current Business*, January 1978, Bureau of Economic Analysis, U.S. Dept of Commerce.

ECONOMIC GROWTH: ADVANTAGES AND DISADVANTAGES

In summary, then, gains in productivity, largely stemming from the factors we have discussed, have made a major contribution to economic growth in the United States. Economies change rapidly as the result of economic growth stemming from productivity gains. Economies, such as that of Japan with an 11 percent annual real growth rate during the decade of the 1960s, find themselves immersed in rapid change. We will list the important changes, some perceived as advantages and some as disadvantages. Later in the chapter, after we have considered growth-caused changes in the economy, we will ask the speculative question: Can growth continue during your working life?

1. Economic growth has raised the real income of wage earners.

You will remember that your hypothetical great-grandfather went to work in 1909 for a wage rate in 1967 dollars of $0.70 per hour. Thirty years later, when he retired from the labor force, he was making $1.50 per hour in 1967 dollars. Your grandfather and father have had similar increases in pay. Your father, whom we assumed went to work in 1949, had doubled his average weekly earnings by 1973.

This increase in real wage rates and weekly earnings was financed by increases in productivity. Had there not been increases in productivity, these increases in money earnings would have been lost in price increases as they were from 1973 to 1977.

2. Economic growth substantially reduced poverty, measured in absolute terms.

During the period from 1949 to 1977 economic growth caused family incomes, measured in constant dollars, to double. As we pointed out earlier in the chapter, this is a remarkable achievement for any economy; but whether this rapid economic growth alleviated poverty in the United States depends on how you define poverty.

If poverty is defined in relative terms, economic growth has *not* contributed to the allevia-

tion of poverty. Suppose that we said any person was "poor" who is a member of a family whose income is less than half the median family income of the United States. Using this definition, there could be no decrease in poverty despite rapid economic growth. The distribution of income, as we pointed out in Chapter 10, is remarkably stable, and as a result, the percentages of the total income received by the various quintiles of the population have remained about the same.

But if you define poverty in absolute terms, then economic growth has reduced the number of people living in poverty in the United States since the end of World War II. The federal government defines a "poor" person as one living in a family unit that receives less than three times the amount required to buy a nutritionally adequate diet. In 1959, for example, the average nonfarm family of four was said to be living in poverty if it received less than $2,973. By 1972, this threshold income had moved up to $4,275, and in 1975 it was $5456.

Using this absolute definition of poverty, the number of people living in poverty has been cut from about 39 million in 1959 to about 24 million in 1975. During this same period of time the population of the United States increased by about 40 million. Thus, in this 15-year period the incidence of poverty has been decreased from over 30 percent of the population to 11 percent of the population.

Which of these definitions of poverty is the correct one? If you are concerned with destitution, you would use the absolute definition of poverty. You would say that about an eighth of the population did not have enough money to buy the food, clothing, and shelter they needed compared to about a third of the population a generation ago. However, if you are concerned with the ability of low-income persons to participate in the social and political life of the nation, you would probably use the relative definition of poverty.

Economic growth, then, may be said to have sharply reduced the amount of destitution in the United States, even though it has not made the distribution of income more equal. By shifting the entire distribution upward, economic growth has reduced the number of persons receiving less than enough to take care of their physical needs.

3. Economic growth has also produced what has been called a "growth dividend" for the government.

During the forty-four years from 1929 to 1975, all levels of government increased their expenditures from about $200 per capita to almost $700 (in 1958 dollars). Had there been no increase in per capita real incomes, per capita disposable income would have had to decline by about $500 to finance these additional government expenditures. People would probably have perceived this increase as being very painful to bear. But as it turned out, per capita real income rose enough during these forty-four years so that the necessary increase in taxes was relatively painless compared to what it otherwise would have been. Indeed, per capita income *after taxes* more than doubled from 1929 to 1973. Whether you see this as an advantage or disadvantage depends on how highly you value the additional government services.

Not all of the growth-induced changes in the economy are considered to be advantageous. We shall consider in the following sections some of the negative results that flow from economic growth.

4. Economic growth has made many skills obsolete.

Economic changes have come so rapidly that many people are finding that their skills have become obsolete during their lifetimes. You will recall that most of the transfers of people from one occupation to another came about as a result of the turnover of generations. When farmers' children become computer programmers, the turnover of the generations has in effect onverted a farmer into a programmer. But many people suffer hardships when occupational changes come about so rapidly that they outrun the turnover of populations; midway through their careers they are forced to start over in some occupation where they have few skills. The mechanization of

farming has forced many farmers from the land; while the nation has benefited from cheaper food, the displaced farmers have suffered a loss that has not shown up in the cost of food. If economic progress were to come at a slower pace, these additional real costs would not have to be borne by those whose skills have become obsolete.

5. Economic growth has increased pollution.

Economic growth as well as the increase in population is responsible for a great deal of the pollution we see around us. When the industrial output of the nation was small and the factories farther apart, the environment was not seriously damaged because it could absorb the pollution that was occurring. But with the rapid rate of economic growth, the environment became overtaxed. The rivers became open sewers and smog enveloped our cities.

The automobile is a case in point. When there were few cars and most of them had low horsepower, few people worried about exhaust omissions. But when the population of automobiles reached 100 million in the United States, the problem of emission control became a serious one. Economic growth, as represented by the increase in the population of automobiles, has both pluses and minuses: People are more mobile but our cities have been damaged.

Pollution, then, is a negative output. To get a more accurate measure of economic growth, we should really subtract from real GNP an estimate of

the damage done to the environment by industrialization. Part of the gain in average real income of families is illusory; it should be offset by the deterioration of the environment in which the typical family lives.

Eventually we will devise social institutions to charge producers for the use of the environment, just as we charge them for the use of capital. Pollution-intensive products will then be more costly to produce and higher in price, and real GNP, as we now measure it, will be lower because of the increase in the price level.

However, until we modify the system to charge producers for the use of the environment, we will have to think of pollution as one of the negative aspects of economic growth.

6. Economic growth has used up a large part of the world's resources.

Another negative aspect of economic growth is the depletion of nonreplaceable natural resources. During the last few years the proven reserves of oil in the United States have been declining. More oil is now being pumped out of the ground than is being found, and the annual loss of production in the United States is about a half billion barrels. The same thing is happening to known world reserves of copper, tin, zinc, and some other key metals used by the industrialized countries of the world.

Because of rapid economic growth, the United States and the other developed nations have become heavily dependent on imports of raw materials, largely from the developing nations. Should something happen to the international trading system that supplies these imports, the economies of the developed nations would be disrupted, as they were during the oil crisis of 1973 and 1974. Your attention is directed to Table 11.8 which shows what percentages of the United States' consumption of important minerals must be imported.

7. Economic growth has led to enormous inequalities of per capita income.

Finally, the advantages flowing from economic growth have been concentrated in few countries

TABLE 11.8

SELECTED INDUSTRIAL IMPORTS AS A SHARE OF CONSUMPTION, 1975

Mineral	Percentage imported
Natural Rubber	100
Cobalt	98
Manganese	98
Chromium	91
Tin	84
Aluminum	84
Nickel	72
Zinc	61
Tungsten	55
Iron ore	29
Lead	11

Source: *International Economic Report of the President,* 1974, Table 78, p. 187.

in the world. Figure 11.5 shows world gross national product for 1976 and how it is distributed among the major nations and blocs. The United States comprises almost one-fourth of world GNP followed by the USSR, Japan, West Germany, France, China, the United Kingdom, and Italy in that order.

The disparities in income and living standards among the countries of the world are very wide. Table 11.9 provides an economic profile of the major developed countries of the world and Table 11.10 shows the same statistics for selected less developed countries.

GNP per capita ranges from a high of almost $8000 for the United States to a low of $120 for Zaire. Keep in mind, however, the danger mentioned earlier in this chapter in making international comparisons.

These disparities raise the question of how stable the world can be when a small percentage of the world's population live in rich nations and most of the people in the world live in poor nations.

Consider Mini-case 11.2, which is provided to clarify your thinking about productivity and resources.

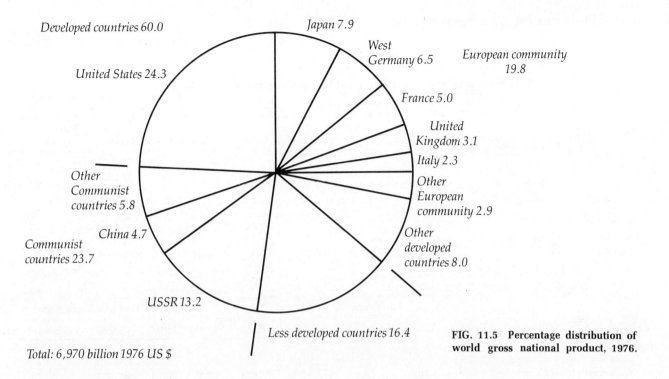

FIG. 11.5 Percentage distribution of world gross national product, 1976.

TABLE 11.9
ECONOMIC PROFILE: DEVELOPED COUNTRIES, 1976

	Developed countries					
	United States	Canada	Japan	European Community	France	Italy
Aggregative data						
Population						
Million persons at midyear	215.1	23.1	112.8	258.8	52.9	56.2
Percentage change from 1975	0.7	1.3	1.1	0.1	0.2	0.7
Gross national product						
Billion 1976 US $	1,691.6	187.8	550.2	1,380	346.2	163.2
Percentage change from 1975	6.1	4.7	6.0	4.5	5.0	4.5
Per capita (1976 US $)	7,860	8,130	4,880	5,330	6,540	2,900

	Developed countries		Communist countries		
	United Kingdom	West Germany	USSR	Eastern Europe	China
Aggregative data					
Population					
Million persons at midyear	56.0	61.5	256.7	107.0	950.7
Percentage change from 1975	0	−0.5	0.9	0.8	1.7
Gross national product					
Billion 1976 US $	216.6	451.7	921.7	316	323.7
Percentage change from 1975	1.0	5.5	3.7	3.9	0.2
Per capita (1976 US $)	3,870	7,340	3,500	2,950	340

TABLE 11.10
ECONOMIC PROFILE: SELECTED LESS DEVELOPED COUNTRIES, 1976

	Sub-Saharan Africa				Asia			
	Ivory Coast	Kenya	Morocco	Zaire	Hong Kong	Malaysia	Philip-pines	South Korea
Aggregative data								
Population								
Million persons at midyear	5.0	13.9	17.8	25.6	4.4	12.3	43.8	3.0
Percentage increase from 1975	2.7	3.4	3.0	2.9	0.2	3.4	3.1	
Gross national product								
Billion 1976 US $	4.4	3.2	8.5	3.2	9.0	10.5	17.0	2.0
Percentage increase from 1975	8.5	5.0	2.4	−3.5	16.0	11.3	6.3	1.0
Per capita (1976 US $)	880	230	480	120	2,000	850	390	71.0

	Latin America					Middle East and South Asia				
	Brazil	Chile	Colombia	Mexico	Peru	Egypt	India	Israel	Pakistan	Syria
Aggregative data										
Population										
Million persons at midyear	109.2	10.4	24.4	62.3	16.1	38.1	627.9	3.5	72.4	7.6
Percentage increase from 1975	2.8	2.0	3.5	3.7	3.0	2.4	2.3	2.4	3.0	3.2
Gross national product										
Billion 1976 US $	111.0	8.3	15.1	78.6	13.5	13.0	84.7	12.2	13.2	2.6
Percentage increase from 1975	8.7	5.5	7.0	2.0	2.8	2.0	2.0	1.5	4.9	8.0
Per capita (1976 US $)	1,020	800	620	1,260	840	340	130	3,490	180	340

Source: *Handbook of Economic Statistics*, 1977, Office of Economic Research, Central Intelligence Agency, Washington D.C.

MINI-CASE 11.3

Suppose a friend of yours argues that productivity will not continue to grow because of the shortage of resources. You, as an economics student, try to restate the argument so that it will have some validity. Which of the restatements below is best?

a) There isn't such a thing as a shortage in a price-directed economy.

b) The government can always use conservation measures to prevent the overuse of scarce resources.

c) It is always possible to develop new rationing schemes to prevent the excess use of scarce raw materials.

d) Resource scarcities divert capital from labor-saving devices and thus limit the rise of productivity.

ECONOMIC GROWTH: CAN IT CONTINUE?

Whether productivity will continue to rise in the United States between now and the year 2000 will be important to you on many counts. As a member of the labor force, your hope of getting increases in your real wage rate will depend largely on whether there are increases in productivity. Or, as a citizen, you will be interested in the size of the annual growth dividend.

Your evaluation of the probability of continued economic growth will depend on whether you listen to the optimists or the pessimists. We will present in analytical form both arguments, leaving it to you to decide between them.

Optimists argue that the knowledge industry will contribute substantially to gains in productivity in the years to come.

The optimists have argued that productivity will continue to rise as it has in the past, thus causing the economy to continue to grow. They base their argument largely on two propositions. First, the knowledge industry, consisting of scientists and engineers, is just reaching its full size. Of all the scientists and engineers who have ever lived in the world, more than half of them are working now. They will produce a flow of new technologies that will lead to continued increases in productivity. To support their case, the optimists cite the important contributions being made by the computer microelectronics industries, which promise to release people from many production activities.

The optimists also point to the continued improvements in the size and quality of the labor force as more and more young people finish high school and go on to college. Furthermore, the percentage of the noninstitutional population actually included in the labor force appears to be rising slowly, hitting almost 62 percent in 1976, as opposed to 60 percent in 1960 and 61 percent in 1970. They point to the fact that a large portion of the female minds have been underutilized by the economy in the past. With the change in the culture, women are just coming into their own as career members of the labor force.

In summary, these products of the knowledge industry—new technological information and more and better-educated people working—will, the optimists argue, contribute to further increases in productivity and, therefore, to economic growth.

Pessimists argue that pollution and natural resource exhaustion will limit economic growth in the future.

The pessimists readily admit that the knowledge industry will make a significant contribution in the future, but, they say, the energy and other natural resources are not available to support continued economic growth. They argue that continued economic growth will produce so much pollution and so deplete the reserves of oil, readily available coal, copper, bauxite, and other raw materials that economic growth will cease.

Before we accept the pessimists' argument as being decisive, we should ask ourselves what would happen if the price system were allowed to mediate between the growing shortages of natural resources and the demand for products. As we said earlier in this chapter, the prices of oil, natural gas, copper, and other natural resources would rise. This cost increase would cause producers and finally households to use energy-intensive products sparingly and might solve the problem in the short run.

But there are some long-run complications. Higher prices for oil, natural gas, copper, bauxite, and other natural resources will cause producers to invest in new facilities for obtaining oil and minerals. Consider oil, for example.

As the shallow oil wells have run dry, wildcat drillers have turned to deep wells. Oil companies have invested large amounts in off-shore exploration and new wells. The Alaskan pipeline will still require a large investment to make the north shore oil available for refining.

The companies producing other raw materials face the same prospect. As deposits of easy-to-mine bauxite in Jamaica and other bauxite-rich nations are either exhausted or become uneconomical because of the imposition of withdrawal taxes, the aluminum companies will require additional investment to convert poorer raw materials into aluminum.

Higher prices for raw materials will also cause the users of these materials to invest in material-saving equipment, much as in the past they have invested in labor-saving equipment. Recycling of paper, aluminum, and many metals will also become economically feasible, and this too will result in new investment or recycling facilities.

Pollution abatement also requires large amounts of capital. Paper mills so clean that they can be located next to city parks are much more expensive to build than the old paper mills, which dumped their untreated effluent into the streams. Sulphur-free coal from the West requires a larger investment in transport equipment than the coal currently being used.

We can now translate the pessimists' argument into a proposition that makes more analytical sense. It would run like this: Efforts to reduce pollution and to compensate for the loss of cheap energy sources will take large amounts of real investment. Some of the saving that has in the past been used to finance the building of labor-displacing equipment will now have to be used to protect the environment and to replace cheap sources of energy. The result is that productivity will not rise as rapidly in the future as it has in the past.

Which of these arguments is correct? Are the optimists right in believing that your real income will continue to rise in the future just as grandfather's and father's did in the past? Or are the pessimists right in believing that the golden age of economic growth lies in the past, and that you should not expect your real wage rate to rise very much in the future?

Only time will tell. What we see here is the classic confrontation between the human spirit and the baleful effects of the Law of Diminishing Marginal Returns as we try to squeeze more out of the earth's limited resources.

This completes our discussion of the factors underlying the total supply of products. We turn in the next four chapters to a discussion of the factors underlying the total demand for products. The interaction of total supply and total demand will determine whether your paycheck will be diminished by unemployment or eroded by inflation.

REVIEW QUESTIONS

1. You are given the following figures that are building blocks in constructing gross national product, the net national product, and national income.

Consumption	$200 billion
Gross private domestic investment	40
Personal income taxes	25
Government expenditures	100
Net foreign expenditure	0
Capital consumption allowances (depreciation)	25
Indirect business taxes	50

The gross national product is:

a) $425 billion   c) 340 billion
b)   275 billion   d) 325 billion

2. The consumer price index cannot always be applied to your personal situation because:

a) the index reflects past prices.

b) the index is computed for the representative budget expenditures for an urban family of four with a moderate income.

c) raw materials and capital goods are included in the index.

d) all the items purchased by consumers are included in the price index.

3. You are given the following figures.

Year	Money GNP	Implicit price index
1972	$1200 billion	100
1978	1800 billion	150

a) From 1972 to 1978, the real GNP rose $300 billion.

b) The real GNP remained the same.

c) The real GNP fell by $300 billion.

d) The real GNP rose by $600 billion.

4. In 1977 the GNP was approximately $1900 billion in current dollars. In 1972 dollars the 1978 GNP was approximately $1300 billion. What is the implicit price index for that year?

a) 125

b) 67

c) 600

d) 146

5. The difference between the GNP in Bangladesh and the GNP in Britain may be overstated because:

a) the GNP is a more workable measure of economic activity than compiling lists of goods and services produced in each country in each year.

b) the GNP measures only market activity.

c) it is calculated by British economists.

d) the GNP measures only nonmarket activity.

6. If depreciation (capital consumption allowance) was exceeded by gross private domestic investment in any given year, it should be concluded that:

a) the economy was at a standstill.

b) net investment is positive.

c) the economy is exporting more than it imports.

d) production efficiency is decreasing.

7. If we observe that U.S. per capita real GNP for 1977 is double the figure for 1941, we may conclude:

a) nothing because the population of the U.S. has changed during the same period.

b) every resident of the U.S. in 1977 possesses twice the goods and services of every resident in 1941.

c) average persons in 1977 are probably better off because they have a greater amount of goods and services than their counterparts in 1941.

d) nothing, since prices have risen substantially in the same period of time.

8. The long-run growth of the American economy has been characterized by:

   a) a smooth pattern of year-to-year growth exceeding 3 percent per year.
   b) a growth rate in money terms exceeding 3 percent per year, but considerably lower when adjusted for inflation.
   c) an up-and-down pattern with periods of rapid growth and rapid decline resulting in little if any real growth.
   d) a rate of increase exceeding 3 percent even after adjusting for inflation.

9. In accounting for the economic growth of the United States since 1929, which of the following factors has been most important?

   a) economies of scale.
   b) increases in technological knowledge.
   c) the availability of natural resources.
   d) improvements in the quality of labor.

10. Productivity in general is defined as:

   a) total output divided by prices.
   b) total output divided by the labor hours or some other resource inputs used in the economy.
   c) total output divided by the national income expressed in real terms.
   d) the addition to output divided by the additional input of resources.

11. Which of the following would have a retarding effect on the rate of GNP growth?

   a) Repeal of all tariffs and import quotas.
   b) The establishment of a maximum tax on earned income.
   c) The repeal of the wage-hour law requiring overtime payment for all hours in excess of 40 hours a week.
   d) The elimination of public support for education, particularly in the central cities.

12. Suppose the government establishes a program that allows welfare mothers to place their children in day-care centers at no cost. Suppose further that the welfare regulations are such that a family head with a job that earns below poverty level (say $5000 a year) can still receive welfare subsidies. The overall effect of these policies would be:

   a) to increase hourly wages.
   b) an increase in potential GNP.
   c) to decrease the labor force.
   d) to insure the blessings of liberty to ourselves and our posterity.

13. Suppose you were asked to design public policies which would substantially reduce the *amount of poverty*—defined in an absolute sense—in the United States in the year 1990. Pick the set of policies from the list below that would be most effective.

   a) Substantially increase the power of labor unions to achieve wage-rate increases.
   b) Increase the minimum wage rates from their present level.
   c) Establish a high tariff on all imported "necessity" products, such as food, clothing, and gasoline.
   d) Encourage through tax incentives and other devices an increase in investment expenditures in research.

ESSAY QUESTIONS

1. Suppose you were running a dry cleaning service for a college dormitory. Your accountant gives you the following figures:

Sales	$10,000
Payments to dry cleaners	7,000
Gasoline and oil for your truck	500
Depreciation of your truck	500
Income taxes which you pay	500

   Using these figures, determine what your contribution to the gross national product is. What is your contribution to the national income? What is your "disposable income"?

2. Suppose that you have a job in a neighboring town. It costs you $1500 a year to drive back and forth to work. You are paid $1000 a month for your work. What is your contribution to the GNP? Should the amount you pay for gasoline and oil be treated as an intermediate product or as a final product? Give your reasons. How is it treated for national income measurement purposes?

3. Why is the value of the goods produced in a society precisely equal to the amount of income created by the production process? Does this mean that those who have produced the GNP would always have enough income to buy back what they have produced?

4. Using what you know about the calculation of a price index, discuss the inherent weaknesses of a price index that purports to measure changes in the cost of living over a fifty-year time span. What does it really mean to say that the cost of living has quadrupled since 1920?

5. Would receipts from the sale of marijuana be included in the GNP? Would the receipts of legal gambling in Las Vegas be included in the GNP? What is the difference?

6. The GNP per capita is much lower in the less-developed countries of the world. Is this entirely due to differences in output per person, ignoring the question of whether the output flows through the market or not?

7. Suppose that a new drug is discovered that makes people prefer leisure to work. As a result, the GNP declines by a third. Does this mean that the welfare of the nation would decline by a third?

8. Suppose real GNP in the United States grew about 1 percent a year. If population increases about 1 percent a year, what would happen to real wage rates? If population increases about 2 percent a year, what would happen to real wage rates? Can you make a generalization about population and real GNP growth rates?

9. "The standard of living a country enjoys depends on the ratio of its population to its natural resources." Criticize and cite examples to support your answer.

10. You find youself debating with a labor-union leader who insists that the high productivity of labor in the United States is due solely to the willingness of people to work hard. How would you answer him?

11. It has been argued that productivity increases in the United States have been largely due to science and technology. Is this true? How important is the innovator's role? Describe it and indicate what types of public policies make the innovator's job more difficult.

12. Suppose you were an economic adviser to a developing country in which poverty, defined as destitution, was widespread. Suppose, too, that ways had been found to keep the population from increasing. What policies would you recommend that would reduce the amount of destitution? Would these policies be inconsistent with the use of taxes to redistribute income? Which would be more important in this situation: economic growth or quality?

13. It has been argued that high rates of economic growth such as those experienced by Japan, Canada, United States, and some countries in Western Europe, will exhaust the resources of the world within a short period of time. How would the price mechanism handle this problem? List some alternative approaches.

14. "If the rest of the world tried to catch up with the average GNP of the United States, Canada, and Western Europe, there probably wouldn't be enough resources to go around." Discuss the implications of this statement. What is the answer to international inequality of income?

ANSWERS TO REVIEW QUESTIONS

1. The gross national product is equal to the sum of consumption, investment, government, and net foreign expenditures. In this case, that is $200 billion + $40 billion + $100 billion equalling $340 billion. Hence, the correct answer is (c).

2. The consumer price index is an index number that measures the change in the prices of a select group of about 400 commodities that comprise the major expenditures of an urban-dwelling family of four.
   a) This is not the correct answer. The fact that past prices are used in its calculation does not mean it cannot be applied to your personal situation.
   b) This is the correct answer. If you, for example, are an unmarried college student, it is unlikely that the kind of expenditures made by an urban-dwelling family of four will represent your expenditures.
   c) This is incorrect. Raw materials and capital goods are *not* included in the CPI and hence, would not be less applicable to you.
   d) This is incorrect. As noted above only certain items are included in the survey of the Bureau of Labor Statistics which provides the data for the CPI.

3. Real GNP (GNP in constant dollars) is equal to money GNP (GNP in current dollars) divided by the implicit price index. Hence, real GNP in 1978 equals $1800 billion divided by 150 times 100, that is, $1200 billion. Therefore,

   a) this is incorrect since *real* GNP did not change from 1972 to 1978. It remained at $600 billion.
   b) this is correct as calculated above.
   c) this is incorrect since real GNP did not change.
   d) this is incorrect since real GNP did not change.

4. Real GNP = (money GNP ÷ the implicit price index) × 100. Hence, money GNP ÷ real GNP = the implicit price index × 100. That is, the IPI = (1900 ÷ 1300) × 100 = 1.46 × 100 = 146. Therefore, (d) is the correct answer.

5. One of the shortcomings of GNP is that one cannot easily make international comparisons. One reason for this is that GNP measures only the market value of output, hence many productive nonmarket activities are excluded. This means that the GNP of developing economies that have a larger share of nonmarket productive activities than developed countries will be understated. Hence,

   a) this is an incorrect choice. Although it is true, it does not explain why the GNP of Britain may be overstated relative to that of Bangladesh.
   b) this is correct as explained above.
   c) this is incorrect. We have no evidence that this might be the case.
   d) this is incorrect. GNP measures market activity.

6. Capital consumption allowance (CCA, or depreciation) refers to the value of equipment worn out in the economy in a year's time as GNP is produced. Gross Private Domestic Investment (GPDI) refers to the value of capital equipment added to the economy in a year. If GPDI exceeds CCA, then net investment is positive. Hence,

   a) this is incorrect since GPDI was greater than CCA.
   b) this is correct as explained above.
   c) this is incorrect. It is irrelevant.
   d) this is incorrect and irrelevant.

7. If real GNP doubles over a 36-year span, we can't really say much about whether the average person in the economy is, or at least could be, better off, since the population may have doubled, tripled, or even been reduced. A change in real GNP per capita, however, tells us that potentially, if not actually, people are better or worse off, depending on the direction of the change. This, of course, is using GNP per capita as a somewhat questionable welfare measure. Hence,

   a) this is not true. Since real per capita GNP has doubled, the people are likely to be better off.
   b) this is not true. We don't know how the increase in GNP has been distributed.
   c) this is correct as explained above.
   d) this is incorrect. *Real* GNP per capita has risen.

8. The GNP of the United States has grown to an average real rate of 3.1 percent per year throughout this century. There have been times, such as during the Great Depression of the 1930s, when the

economy failed to grow at all. But on average there has been growth, albeit not steady.

a) This is incorrect. The rate of growth has been in excess of 3 percent, but the pattern has not been smooth.

b) This is incorrect. The growth rate adjusted for inflation has been in excess of 3 percent per year.

c) This is incorrect. The real growth rate has exceeded 3 percent per year.

d) This is correct as explained above.

9. According to the Denison study, increased technological knowledge accounted for 28 percent of the economic growth of the United States experienced between 1929 and 1969. This was not exceeded in importance by any other factor underlying growth.

a) This is incorrect. This accounted for 11% of the growth.

b) This is correct.

c) This is incorrect. We have no information on this input.

d) This is incorrect. This accounted for 12% of the improvement.

10. Productivity refers to the relationship of output to the labor, materials, and machines (factor inputs) that are used to make the goods and services we consume. The ratio of output to factor inputs is a measure of total factor productivity, or the efficiency with which factor inputs are combined.

a) This is incorrect. Prices are not a factor input.

b) This is correct as defined above.

c) This is incorrect. National income is not a factor input.

d) This is incorrect. This is a measure of marginal productivity.

11. Let us consider each answer separately.

a) The repeal of tariffs and import quotas would stimulate further specialization and division of labor internationally and thereby increase the growth of output. Hence, this is not the correct choice.

b) The establishment of a maximum tax on earned income would ensure that the incentive to innovate in the form of a high-income possibility will exist. This, then, is not the correct choice.

c) Although this might have some socially disruptive effects, economically this would likely stimulate rather than retard growth. So, this is not the correct choice.

d) This is the best answer. Increased productivity, as noted by Denison, is heavily dependent on the level of education, hence, to reduce support for education would retard growth.

12. This program will enable welfare mothers to work by caring for their children and will not penalize them for subpoverty-level earnings. In effect it reduces the opportunity cost of working.

a) This is incorrect. If anything, the increased supply of workers may tend to lower wages.

b) This is correct. The size of the labor force has increased.

c) This is incorrect. Mothers will enter the labor market and work who formerly did not do so.

d) This is incorrect. It is irrelevant.

13. Absolute poverty has been reduced primarily through economic growth. Hence, policies to stimulate economic growth appear to have the best chance of reducing absolute poverty in the United States.

    a) This is incorrect. It would likely cause a redistribution of income but not reduce poverty.

    b) This is incorrect. This would not stimulate growth and might even increase poverty by increasing the rate of unemployment among the unskilled.

    c) This is incorrect. This will redistribute income to protected industries and workers. It will not stimulate growth.

    d) This is correct. This approach is most likely to stimulate growth and if increased growth reduces absolute poverty, this will work.

OBJECTIVES

Upon successful completion of this chapter, you will be able to:

1. Summarize the essence of Keynesian employment theory, identifying the crucial role of investment in the analysis.

2. Explain the effect that the Keynesian interpretation of investment has on the role of the capital market.

3. Explain the relationship that is assumed to exist between consumption and income in the Keynesian approach, defining the marginal propensity to consume (MPC) in the process.

4. Explain the process by which an economy seeks its equilibrium level of national income.

5. Trace the step-by-step adjustment process of national income to changes in investment and government expenditure with a given MPC.

6. Identify and explain the implications that Keynesian analysis has for public policy.

EMPLOYMENT, INFLATION, AND OUTPUT: THE KEYNESIAN VIEW

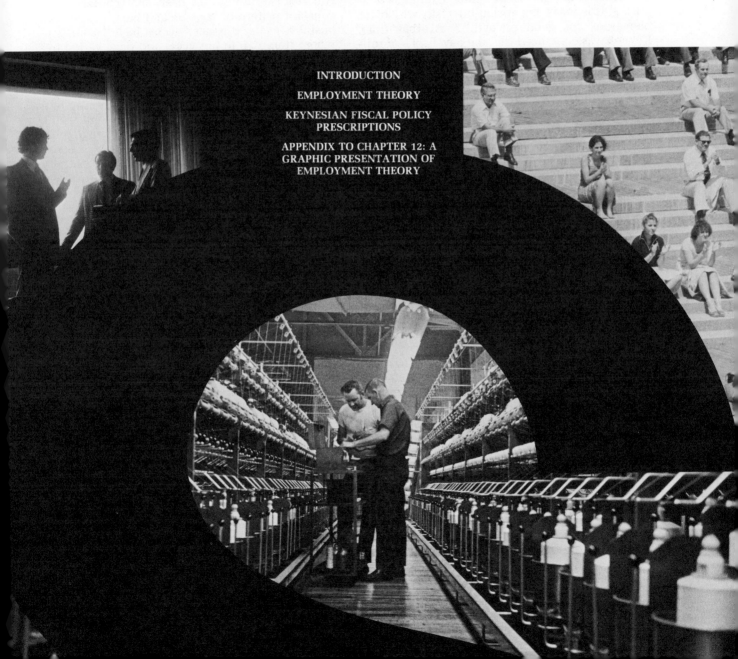

INTRODUCTION

EMPLOYMENT THEORY

KEYNESIAN FISCAL POLICY
PRESCRIPTIONS

APPENDIX TO CHAPTER 12: A
GRAPHIC PRESENTATION OF
EMPLOYMENT THEORY

INTRODUCTION

Almost forty years ago, in the midst of the Great Depression, John Maynard Keynes, an English economist (1883–1946), wrote the following words: "Practical men, who believe themselves to be quite exempt from any intellectual influences, are usually the slaves of some defunct economist. . . It is ideas, not vested interests, which are dangerous for good or evil." * At that time, Keynes was convinced that the paychecks of millions of people all over the world were being threatened by the adherence of practical men of affairs to the ideas of the classical economists who believed that depressions would be self-curing. He wrote *The General Theory of Employment, Interest, and Money* to propose a new way of looking at macroproblems—the problems of unemployment and inflation.

Many things have happened since Keynes advanced the hypothesis proposed in this book. The Employment Act of 1946 made it the national policy of the United States to "use all practicable means . . . for the purposes of creating and maintaining . . . conditions under which there will be afforded useful employment opportunities . . . for those able, willing and seeking to work, and to promote maximum employment, production, and purchasing power." Most economists have accepted the Keynesian hypothesis as a description of the way an economy works. Almost all textbooks have organized their macroeconomics around the Keynesian ideas. On the basis of these ideas, President John Fitzgerald Kennedy proposed a tax cut in 1962, despite a continuing deficit, to "get the economy moving," and President Lyndon B. Johnson used his influence to get the tax cut accepted by Congress and signed the legislation into law in 1964. President Richard M. Nixon, after experimenting with tight money policies to solve the inflationary problems of the late 1960s, declared that he too was a Keynesian and would use deficit financing to resolve the 1970 recession. Keynesian ideas are as widely accepted nowadays by "practical men, who believe themselves to be quite exempt from any intellectual influences" as were the ideas of the classical economists before the Great Depression.

* John Maynard Keynes, *The General Theory of Employment, Interest, and Money*, New York: Harcourt, Brace, 1935.

The Great Depression left an indelible impression on those that lived through it. The fact, however, that this was an exceptionally severe downturn should not hide the reality that both prior to and after the Great Depression, the American economy has been characterized by a constant pattern of "booms and busts" called the business cycle. Business cycles have lasted anywhere from two to ten years and have varied tremendously in both scope and severity. The phases of a typical business cycle include the *peak*, which indicates the end of an expansionary period of economic activity and the beginning of a contraction, and the *trough*, which designates the end of the contraction and the beginning of expansion. The term *recession* is usually used to describe a mild contraction of business activity while a *depression* applies to a more severe downturn lasting longer than one year. Figure 12.1 shows the pattern of a typical business cycle.

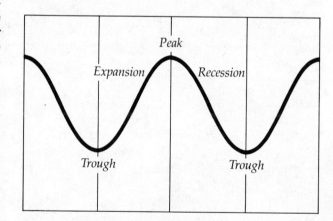

FIG. 12.1   Phases of the business cycle.

The expansion phase of the typical cycle occurs as consumers, government, business firms, or even foreigners increase spending in the economy. In response to this spending, more workers are hired and larger amounts are paid in wages. The forces of expansion then cumulate in strength. Sales to consumers increase, inventories fall, and investment spending increases even more. At some point in the boom, however, the seeds for a recession are already being sown. Any slack that existed in the economy is gone, new capacity is being added to the economy, shortages increase, and bank credit becomes tight. Activity continues to grow but at a slower pace. Costs per unit of output begin to rise. Finally, business eases up on further investment, stock exchange prices begin to fall, new construction decreases, the expansion falters, and the recession begins.

New orders for capital equipment fall off and new workers are no longer sought. In time, workers are laid off. The cumulative effects of lower employment and wages reduce demand and the economy slows down further. Eventually the recession bottoms out as inventories are depleted and small increases in investment expenditure cumulate, spreading to the other sectors.

Economists have been tracking the business cycle for over 120 years, and during that time 29 expansionary periods have been recorded. During the early part of this 120-year period, commercial crises were the focus of economic interest. These crises were characterized by sharply rising interest rates, decreases in prices, and frequent bankruptcies. By the beginning of this century, interest moved toward fluctuations in employment and output with special emphasis on the pattern of investment expenditure.

As noted earlier, however, it was the business cycle that occurred in the 1930s, the Great Depression, that spawned what is known today as *employment theory*.

The economic wisdom of the times had no explanation for The Great Depression.

The economic wisdom of the times—and at the beginning of the depression John Maynard Keynes was a product of that wisdom—argued that there are built-in mechanisms in market economies that will make depressions self-limiting. If a recession occurred because people were not buying all that was being produced, for example, prices would fall. This would increase the ratio of money holdings to money income. With excess money holdings and lower product prices, people would start buying again. Businesspeople, too, seeing that interest rates were low, would borrow to build new factories and buy new equipment. As total spending in-creased, unemployment would disappear and the depression would be over.

But in the 1930s the economic system didn't appear to work this way. From 1929 to 1933 the depression became steadily worse. It persisted and prices did not seem to fall far enough to stimulate people to buy again. The banking system, in place of holding the quantity of money constant, reduced loans and investments and thus destroyed about a quarter of the money that the public had held at the beginning of the depression. Interest rates fell, but investment spending was not stimulated.

Whatever the reason for the severity and persistence of The Great Depression—and there were sharp differences of opinion among economists about these matters—John Maynard Keynes saw a failure of classical monetary theory to explain how the system really worked. He was particularly disturbed by the arguments of the classical economists that were based on flexible prices. In the real world, which he observed as a journalist and financial manager, labor unions and firms with monopoly power tended to resist price cutting. Declines in aggregate demand reduced employment rather than prices. As a result, Keynes developed a theory based largely on the assumption that prices would remain the same and that changes in the level of national income would cause changes in employment. Thus his theory came to be known as an employment theory rather than a monetary theory.

The problems we face today are different from what they were when Keynes wrote *The General Theory*. The Western world is experiencing recurrent inflationary periods in place of a deep depression. There are too few natural resources instead of too many. The question now is how to deal with too much demand rather than too little demand.

Despite these new problems, the ideas proposed by John Maynard Keynes are still widely used. In this chapter we will be concerned with the major ideas proposed by Keynes and their implications for avoiding unemployment and inflation. Later we will compare the monetarists' views with the Keynesian views about what should be done to protect your paycheck from the two economic diseases of unemployment and inflation.

EMPLOYMENT THEORY

The basic elements of employment theory will be shown in a table.

In this section we will present an explanation of Keynes' fundamental ideas. This is necessarily a somewhat simplified version compared to what originally appeared in *The General Theory of Employment, Interest, and Money*, but this version has gained such acceptance that it is now widely used by practical men of affairs.

First, however, the essence of the problem that Keynes grappled with in the thirties can be shown clearly in terms of the notion of potential GNP, the output rate produced when the economy fully utilizes its resources. During any given period of time, there is a rate of economic growth that the economy is capable of achieving. This rate may vary from time to time as demographic factors change. Most economists agree, however, that the potential growth rate of GNP for the

TABLE 12.1
POTENTIAL AND ACTUAL GROWTH RATES OF GNP

Years	Potential*	Actual
1947 through 1952	4.50%	3.85%
1953 through 1962	3.50	3.03
1963 through 1968	3.75	4.45
1969 through 1975	4.00	2.41

* Based on estimates of the Council of Economic Advisers.

United States varied from 3.5 to 4.5 percent per year in the post-World War II era. Table 12.1 shows the potential and actual growth rates for several sub-periods in this era. Figure 12.2 shows the gap between potential and actual GNP for the post-Korean War years.

The graph in Fig. 12.2 shows three major sub-periods of economic growth. From 1956 to 1964 the economy performed below its capability.

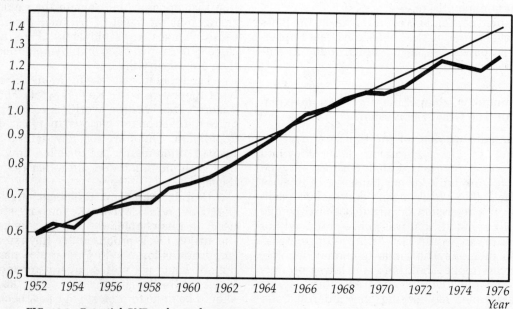

Ratio scale (in trillions of dollars)

FIG. 12.2 Potential GNP and actual output.

From 1965 to 1969 it "overproduced," and, since 1969, especially in 1973, 1974, and 1975, the performance has been far below capacity. We now turn to the task of constructing a framework for analyzing these kinds of growth behaviors.

We will use a series of tables listing GNP and other aggregated statistics to present the basic ideas of employment theory. Those of you who learn more easily from graphs may wish to examine the appendix to this chapter, in which we have presented the same materials in graphic form.

In column 2 of Table 12.2, we have listed a series of alternative quantities of GNP expressed in constant prices, starting with zero and ending with $2 trillion. (The actual GNP of the United States in 1978 as measured in 1972 dollars was almost $1400 billion.) In column 1 we have shown, using hypothetical figures, the number of workers required to produce the various quan-

tities of GNP in column 2. Thus, if GNP were $1500 billion, total employment would be 90 million persons.

In columns 3, 6, and 7 we have shown the amount of planned expenditures associated with each level of GNP by the three major groups in the economy: households, businesses, and government. Households engage in consumption expenditure, businesses engage in investment expenditure, and the government buys productive services. We should point out that these planned expenditures are like the quantities of a demand curve. They tell us how much each group would spend if the GNP in column 2 were given. Thus, if GNP were $500 billion, households would spend $433 billion. Alternatively, if GNP were $600 billion, households would spend $500 billion. In using this table it is important always to look at the GNP figure first. Moving your eye to the left, you can see how much employment will

TABLE 12.2
EMPLOYMENT THEORY—ILLUSTRATIVE TABLE 1 (Dollar figures are expressed in billions.)

(1) Employment (in millions of persons)	(2) Output: GNP in constant prices	(3) Derived demand: Consumption	(4) Withdrawals from income: Taxes plus savings	(5) Total	(6) Autonomous demand: Private investment	(7) Autonomous demand: Government purchases
0	$ 0	$ 100	$−100	$400	$150	$250
10	100	167	−67	400	150	250
20	200	233	−33	400	150	250
30	300	300	0	400	150	250
35	400	367	+33	400	150	250
40	500	433	+67	400	150	250
45	600	500	100	400	150	250
50	700	567	133	400	150	250
55	800	633	167	400	150	250
60	900	700	200	400	150	250
65	1000	767	233	400	150	250
70	1100	833	267	400	150	250
75	1200	900	300	400	150	250
80	1300	967	333	400	150	250
85	1400	1033	367	400	150	250
90	1500	1100	400	400	150	250
95	1600	1167	433	400	150	250
100	1700	1233	467	400	150	250
105	1800	1300	500	400	150	250
110	1900	1367	533	400	150	250
115	2000	1433	567	400	150	250

be generated; moving your eye to the right, you can see how much GNP households, businesses, and government would want to purchase.

We will want, in the explanation that follows, to find that level of GNP where planned purchases of all sectors of the economy combined will be equal to planned output. If all buyers collectively want to buy more than is currently being produced, then there won't be enough to go around. Inventories will decline and businesses will try to expand their output in order to satisfy their customers' demands. As a result, GNP will rise. Or, if all buyers collectively want to buy less than is currently being produced, inventories will rise, businesses will reduce their output, and GNP will fall. Our problem will be to discover the equilibrium level of GNP, that level of GNP at which purchases equal output.

Perhaps an analogy would be helpful.

Suppose the members of your class represent the total economy. Some of you will represent households, some businesses, and still others government. Now suppose you all work to produce goods, which you then place on a table in front of the classroom. As you do this you will receive money income in exchange for your goods that is precisely equal to the aggregate value of all the goods placed on the table. Taxes and capital market transactions may shift some of this income from some of you to others, but the fact remains that the total number of dollars paid out during the production process and available to purchase products will be precisely equal to the total value of everything that is available to be purchased. Now the question is: Will you as representatives of your groups want to buy back everything you have produced? If you do not, and some of it is left over, then it would be sensible during the next period to produce less, and some of you would be unemployed. Or, if you collectively wanted to buy more than was being produced, then there would be a shortage of products, and it would be necessary to find some more workers who could help you produce more goods.

We will first consider what determines planned consumption expenditures by households. After we have done this, we will consider the planned purchases of the other groups. Putting these together we will learn what determines the equilibrium of GNP.

Consumption spending is assumed to be determined by GNP.

The proposition that consumption is income-determined is a keystone in the Keynesian system of thought. Consumption is assumed to be reasonably constant.

The consumption function (as this relationship between GNP or aggregate income and consumption as represented in columns 2 and 3 of Table 12.2 is called) is in turn determined in modern mixed economies by: (1) the structure of the tax system; and (2) decisions by households and businesses to save.

The *consumption function* is the schedule of alternative quantities of national output consumers in the economy would demand at alternative levels of national income.

To see how these two factors work together, consider a hypothetical situation in which you are receiving $1000 a month.

Let us assume that the government takes 20 percent of your monthly income in tax withholdings. This leaves you $800. Now suppose you regularly put aside $100 of savings, some of which you may put into a savings and loan association and some of which you hold in the form of a cash balance. This leaves you $700 to spend out of your $1000 monthly income. Your *average propensity to consume* might be said to be 0.7. That is, you would be spending 70 percent of your monthly income.

Now if you receive a $200 monthly raise from $1000 to $1200, how would you spend your raise? In other words, what would your *marginal propensity to consume* be? To answer this question we will divide the increase in your consumption expenditure by the increase in your income. If the government took $40 of your extra income and you decided to save $60, then your marginal propensity to consume would be 0.5. (The $100 increase in your consumption spending divided by the $200 increase in your income would be 0.5 or ½.)

The *Marginal Propensity to Consume* (MPC) is the ratio of a change in consumption expenditures to a change in income. The ratio is expressed in the equation

$$\text{MPC} = \frac{\Delta C}{\Delta Y},$$

when

MPC = marginal propensity
to consume
ΔC = change in consumption
expenditures
ΔY = change in income.

In the Keynesian system, then, consumption (column 3) is said to be determined by income. Once you know what the GNP (as a measure of income) is, you automatically know what consumption will be; consumption is a predictable dependent variable. The figures in column 3, which are rounded off to the closest billion, are based on the assumption that the marginal propensity to consume for the entire economy is 0.67 or ⅔.

Now looking at column 4 we can see how much of the GNP would be left after households have purchased consumption products. For example, at a GNP level of $500 billion, $67 billion would remain. The difference between GNP and consumption consists of the two types of withdrawals from the income stream: taxes, which are involuntary, and savings, which are voluntary. We have discussed taxes and savings in earlier chapters. They both represent devices for releasing resources for uses other than producing consumption products. Resources released by taxes and savings can be used by either government or businesses depending on their respective plans. Consider your own situation.

If you earn $200 a week working in a factory, that $200 is in some sense a measure of the value of your output. Using the $200, you could buy back what you have produced, although you would probably want to buy a variety of products and not just the products you personally were producing. But now suppose that the government takes $60 in taxes and you decide to save $40 of your take-home pay. This too will mean that you will use only half of your output for consumption purposes. The rest of it is available for businesses and government to use to buy the products you could have bought had taxes and savings not taken half of your total earnings.

We should point out that we have included in the savings reported in column 4 not only those savings made directly by households out of their paychecks, but also those savings made by businesses for their stockholders. These include profits earned for stockholders but not distributed in dividends and depreciation reserves earmarked to replace capital goods as they wear out.

If we were to stop right here in the building of the Keynesian system of thought, we would be involved in circular reasoning. We would be saying that GNP determines planned consumption spending and planned consumption spending determines GNP. To get out of this box, we will need to consider what determines the two other parts of the total demand for products: private investment spending and government spending.

Private investment and government purchases are independent of GNP.

We will think of government spending and planned investment by business as being determined by events outside the system, usually called autonomous expenditures. Later on we will modify this explanation slightly to show that private investment spending is dependent on the rate of interest, which can also be determined by GNP.

To say that investment spending by businesses on such items as new factories, new equipment, additional inventories, or new apartment houses is independent of GNP is a more questionable assumption. But it is an assumption we will make in the interest of simplification. Accordingly, consider Table 12.2 again, where we have shown private investment in column 6 as being $150 billion at all the possible levels of GNP.

The equilibrium level of GNP is the level at which aggregate demand is equal to GNP.

The question we now want to investigate is how large GNP will be when *autonomous demand* (planned investment spending plus government purchases) and *derived demand* (consumption) equal total output or GNP.

The answer is clear when you examine Table 12.2 carefully. It is $1500 billion. If GNP were less than $1500 billion, aggregate demand would be larger than the GNP. Add columns 3 and 5 (and compare the total) to column 2. Suppose, for example, that GNP were $1400 billion. Consumption spending would be $1033 billion and the total of investment and government spending would be $400 billion. The aggregate demand, then—$1433 billion—is larger than the aggregate supply—$1400 billion. Businesses' inventories would shrink and businesses would produce more in order to take care of their customers—GNP would rise.

On the other hand, if GNP were larger than $1500 billion, the aggregate demand would be smaller than the GNP. Suppose that $1600 billion of GNP were produced. Table 12.2 tells us that consumption spending would be $1167 billion and the total of investment and government spending would be $400 billion. Thus aggregate demand would be $1567 billion, which is less than the aggregate production of $1600 billion. The extra output would show up initially as unplanned investment spending because businesses would find that they had accumulated inventories of unsold products; this unintended accumulation of inventories would cause businesses to cut back on their production and, in turn, cause GNP to decline.

It follows that in our example there is only one level of GNP that is consistent with $400 billion of investment and government spending. This is the equilibrium level of GNP.

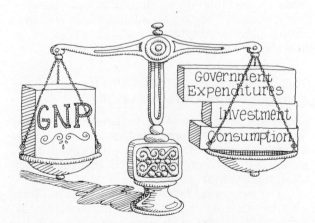

The *equilibrium level of GNP* is that level of output at which aggregate demand—the total amount that consumers, businesses, and government want to spend—is equal to the total supply of products—GNP.

The equilibrium level of GNP can also be viewed as that level at which savings plus taxes are equal to investment plus government purchases.

At the equilibrium level of GNP, $1500 billion in Table 12.2, the amount of resources released by taxes and savings is exactly equal to the amount of autonomous expenditures by businesses and government. To see this, examine columns 4 and 5. We have shown the total amounts of money income withdrawn from the economy by taxes and savings in column 4. We have shown the total amount of autonomous demand in column 5. The economy has achieved equilibrium when the figures in these two columns are equal. At a GNP of $1500 billion, for example, $400 billion of taxes and savings are equal to $400 billion of private investment and government purchases.

At this point, you may be inclined to say, so what? How does this affect my paycheck? Consider the following. If there were 98 million people in the civilian labor force and jobs available for only 90 million, your chances of finding a job if you lost yours would be much lower than if the equilibrium level of GNP were higher. Changes in the components of aggregate demand cause larger changes in the level of GNP.

A change in consumption, investment, or taxes causes a change in total output greater than the original change.

Let us suppose that businesspeople cut back their investment budgets from $150 billion a year to $50 billion. What would this do to the level of output and employment in the economy? You might at first be inclined to think that it would reduce total demand by $100 billion. But upon further reflection, you will conclude that a cutback in investment expenditures—or any other expenditures for that matter—will have an effect that ultimately is much greater than the effect of the initial cut-back. There will be a *multiplier effect* working to change the level of output and employment. The people who lose their jobs in the capital goods industries will not have the income necessary to buy consumption goods. Some of the workers in consumption goods industries will in turn lose their jobs and they will not be able to buy products, and so on.

The *multiplier principle* **is an explanation of how an increase or decrease in investment or government expenditure can cause cumulative effects in the level of national output.**

To see how far this contraction process would go, examine Table 12.3, which is similar to Table 12.2 except that investment spending is $50 billion instead of $150 billion. You will see that the equilibrium level of GNP when investment spending is $50 billion is $1200 billion—$300 billion lower than it was when investment spending was $150 billion. The reduction in GNP, $300 billion, is three times the reduction in investment spending, $100 billion, so the multiplier is three.

The multiplier also works when investment spending is increased rather than decreased. Suppose that businesspeople, impressed by the high prices of oil, gas, coal, and other energy sources, increased their investment budgets from $150 billion to $250 billion. Table 12.4 shows that the equilibrium level of GNP would rise by three times the increase in investment spending, so that the equilibrium level of GNP would be $1800 bil-

lion and employment, if there were enough people to be hired, would be 105 million.

The multiplier is the reciprocal of marginal propensity to tax and save.

There is a simple way to determine how much the equilibrium level of GNP will change whenever there is a change in autonomous expenditures. There are three steps involved in obtaining the multiplier: (1) Measure the marginal propensity to consume. In our case, we assumed that the marginal propensity to consume was 0.67 or $\frac{2}{3}$. (2) Subtract this percentage from 1. This gives us the percentage of extra income that will be withdrawn in taxes and savings. In our case, this would be 0.33 or $\frac{1}{3}$. (3) Invert the fraction. The

TABLE 12.3

EMPLOYMENT THEORY—ILLUSTRATIVE TABLE 2 (Dollar figures are in billions.)

(1) Employment (in millions of persons)	(2) Output GNP in constant prices	(3) Derived demand: Consumption	(4) Withdrawals from income: Taxes plus savings	(5) Total	(6) Autonomous demand: Private investment	(7) Government· purchases
70	$1100	$ 833	$267	$300	$50	$250
75	1200	900	300	300	50	250
80	1300	967	333	300	50	250
85	1400	1033	367	300	50	250
90	1500	1100	400	300	50	250
95	1600	1167	433	300	50	250
100	1700	1233	467	300	50	250
105	1800	1300	500	300	50	250
110	1900	1367	533	300	50	250
115	2000	1433	567	300	50	250

TABLE 12.4

EMPLOYMENT THEORY—ILLUSTRATIVE TABLE 3 (Dollar figures are in billions.)

(1) Employment (in millions of persons)	(2) Output GNP in constant prices	(3) Derived demand: Consumption	(4) Withdrawals from income: Taxes plus savings	(5) Total	(6) Autonomous demand: Private investment	(7) Government purchases
80	$1300	$ 967	$333	$500	$250	$250
85	1400	1033	367	500	250	250
90	1500	1100	400	500	250	250
95	1600	1167	433	500	250	250
100	1700	1233	467	500	250	250
105	1800	1300	500	500	250	250
110	1900	1367	533	500	250	250
115	2000	1433	567	500	250	250

result is the multiplier, which in our case is 3. The arithmetic is as follows:

$$\text{multiplier} = \frac{1}{1 - \tfrac{2}{3}} = 3.$$

The multiplier takes time to work itself out.

The effect of the multiplier is a time-consuming process. Suppose that in period 1 both investment spending and GNP rise by $100 billion and that investment spending continues at this higher rate from that time on. In period 2, consumption spending and GNP will increase by $67 billion as the newly employed workers spend their paychecks. This increase will in turn cause a $44 billion increase in period 3, and so on. The total increase, after the process has run its course, will be equal to the sum of the increases in each of the subsequent time periods. The arithmetic would look like this:

$100 + 66.67 + 44.44 + 29.60 + 19.73
$$+ 13.15 + \cdots = \$300.$$

For every level of autonomous expenditure there is only one equilibrium level of GNP.

The important conclusion is that for every level of investment spending there is one and only one equilibrium level of GNP, however long it might take the economy to get there. If investment spending falls, GNP and the level of employment will also fall and by a predictable amount. Or, if the level of investment spending rises, so too will the GNP and the level of employment.

Investment spending in the Keynesian system is the tail that wags the GNP dog.

This conclusion, that there is a unique equilibrium level of GNP, fascinated economists and led them during the last 40 years to develop a body of theory based on the Keynesian foundations. Philosophically, this was a startling theory because it destroyed the idea that a price-directed economy is self-managing, and that once the government has established a framework of laws that will enable the market to work, it could leave the rest to the marketplace. The long-held belief that the equilibrium level of employment was also the full-employment level could no longer be defended. It is not surprising, then, that the Keynesian economists should have become economic activists who believe that the government should regulate the aggregate demand for products to avoid unemployment and inflation. What are their prescriptions?

KEYNESIAN FISCAL POLICY PRESCRIPTIONS

Suppose you defined your "full employment" target as providing jobs for 100 million workers, and your inflation control target was to avoid price increases of more than 2 percent a year. If you were the president of the United States, how could you, using employment theory, achieve these two goals?

The answer to these questions will depend partly on what the equilibrium level of GNP is when you begin to implement your "full employment" policies. Suppose that initially the equilibrium level of GNP were $1500 billion, and the employment level were 90 million, as it is in Table 12.2. Your job as president would be to create jobs for an additional 10 million workers and increase GNP by $200 billion.

An increase in government purchases or a decrease in taxes will increase employment.

To increase GNP $200 billion you could: (1) increase government expenditures by $67 billion, (2) decrease government taxes enough so that consumption will increase by $67 billion, (3) reduce taxes on business or implement an incentive program to boost investment expenditures by $67 billion, or (4) undertake a combination of these approaches. After the multiplier had its full effect on the economy, the equilibrium GNP would be $1700 billion and total employment would be 100 million persons.

In Table 12.5 you will see that government purchases have been shifted from the $250 billion level to the $317 billion level. These additional expenditures will drive the equilibrium level of GNP up to $1700 billion—your target level.

If you choose to reduce taxes enough so that consumption will be $67 billion higher at all GNP levels instead of increasing government spending by $67 billion, you will also drive GNP up to $1700 billion—your target level (see Table 12.6). In either case, you will create 10 million more jobs, and presumably you will be rewarded appropriately. However, you may object that we are ignoring the fact that the government is now running a deficit. The size of the deficit will depend on whether the budget was balanced when you started your full employment program and whether you increased government expenditures or reduced the taxes. (The two policies do not necessarily create the same-sized deficit.)

Won't the deficit defeat your full employment program? The answer is no. Whatever feedback effect a deficit might have would have to be embodied in these figures, and since consumption,

TABLE 12.5
EMPLOYMENT THEORY—WORKING TABLE 4 (Dollar figures are in billions.)

(1) Employment (in millions of persons)	(2) Output GNP in constant prices	(3) Derived demand: Consumption	(4) Withdrawals from income: Taxes plus savings	(5) Total	(6) Autonomous demand Private investment	(7) Autonomous demand Government purchases
80	$1300	$ 967	$333	$467	$150	$317
85	1400	1033	367	467	150	317
90	1500	1100	400	467	150	317
95	1600	1167	433	467	150	317
100	1700	1233	467	467	150	317
105	1800	1300	500	467	150	317
110	1900	1367	533	467	150	317
115	2000	1433	567	467	150	317

TABLE 12.6
EMPLOYMENT THEORY—WORKING TABLE 5 (Dollar figures are in billions.)

(1) Employment (in millions of persons)	(2) Output GNP in constant prices	(3) Derived demand: Consumption	(4) Withdrawals from income: Taxes plus savings	(5) Total	(6) Autonomous demand: Private investment	(7) Government purchases
80	$1300	$1033	$267	$400	$150	$250
85	1400	1100	300	400	150	250
90	1500	1167	333	400	150	250
95	1600	1233	367	400	150	250
100	1700	1300	400	400	150	250
105	1800	1367	433	400	150	250
110	1900	1433	467	400	150	250
115	2000	1500	500	400	150	250

investment, or government purchases are not affected by the deficit, it can be ignored.

Keynesian employment theory then gives us a rule that we can use to manage the economy. *Whenever the economy is operating at less than the target level of employment, the government should either increase its purchases or reduce taxes enough to induce consumers or businesspersons to increase their purchases.*

A reduction in government purchases or an increase in taxes will reduce the level of output.

Employment theory would also tell you, as president, what to do if prices started to rise faster than, say, 2 percent a year. Suppose investment spending were to rise to $250 billion and, as is indicated in Table 12.4, the equilibrium level of GNP would be $1800 billion. This level would require 105 million workers, but if there are only 100 million workers available, you would be 5 million workers short. Pressures for increased wages and prices will develop. What should you, as president of the United States, do about this?

As president, you should either reduce government purchases or increase taxes enough so that the equilibrium level of GNP will decline by $100 billion. If you chose to reduce government expenditures, you would have to find ways to cut

the budget by $33 billion. Or if you chose to increase taxes, you would have to find ways to increase taxes enough so that consumers would spend $33 billion less. In either case, once the multiplier had its full effect, you would have reduced the equilibrium level of GNP to $1700 billion. At this level the economy would be in balance. There would be a demand for 100 million workers and there would be 100 million workers to respond to the demand.

However, again you may object. In this case the government is running a surplus that will have a feedback effect on the financial capital market; as a consequence, some of the reduction you have achieved in the equilibrium of GNP may be offset. But employment theory tells you that you can safely ignore the effects of the surplus on consumption and investment spending.

Consequently, whenever prices start to rise at an unacceptable rate, either reduce government purchases of goods and services or increase taxes. The Keynesians have an answer to what causes unemployment and inflation. It is that the government is not managing its affairs properly. The government, they argue, should be a balance wheel. Whenever unemployment threatens, the government should increase its purchases or reduce its taxes. Whenever inflation threatens, the government should reduce its expenditures or increase its taxes.

COMMENTARY

The following is excerpted from the Economic Report of the President, 1978. It reflects the fiscal policy steps recommended by the president to deal with the problems of slow growth and unemployment. Please read the excerpt and answer the following questions.

a) What does the president mean when he says, "I propose to rely principally upon growth in the private sector of the economy to reduce unemployment and raise incomes"?
b) What is fiscal drag? How does the president hope to cope with it?

ECONOMIC REPORT OF THE PRESIDENT

To the Congress of the United States:

I will be working closely with the Congress in 1978 to enact a program addressed to the immediate and the long-term needs of our economy. I am proposing tax reductions and reforms to continue our strong economic recovery, to encourage increased investment by American businesses, and to create a simpler and fairer tax system. I am seeking legislation to address the special problems of the disadvantaged and the unemployed. And I am taking new steps to combat inflation.

This report to the Congress on the condition of the economy sets forth the overall framework within which my economic proposals were formulated. It outlines, for you and for the Nation, my economic priorities for the years ahead and my strategies for achieving them. . . .

I propose to rely principally upon growth in the private sector of the economy to reduce unemployment and raise incomes. Special Federal efforts will, of course, be necessary to deal with such problems as structural unemployment, but tax reductions will be the primary means by which Federal budget policy will promote growth. Careful management of budget outlays and a growing economy should permit substantial reductions in the years ahead. Tax reductions will be needed to strengthen consumer purchasing power and expand consumer markets. Stable growth in markets, together with added tax incentives for business, will lead to rising business investment and growing productivity.

As inflation and real economic growth raise the incomes of most Americans, they are pushed into higher income tax brackets. The tax burden on individuals is raised just as if higher rates had been enacted. The payroll taxes levied on workers and business firms for social security and

unemployment insurance will also increase substantially over the years ahead. These are very large increases, but they are needed to keep our social security and unemployment insurance systems soundly financed.

Between 1977 and 1979, taxes on businesses and individuals will rise very sharply as a result of these several factors. Even though our economy is basically healthy, this increasingly heavy tax burden would exert a mounting drag on economic growth. It must, therefore, be counteracted by tax reductions. The magnitude and timing of the reductions should be designed to maintain economic growth at a steady pace, taking into account the effects both of the growing tax burden and of other factors at work in the economy.

Consistent with this strategy, I am proposing a $25 billion program of net tax reductions accompanied by substantial tax reforms.

Individual income taxes will be reduced primarily through across-the-board reductions in personal tax rates, with special emphasis on low- and middle-income taxpayers. Personal taxes also will be simplified by my proposal to replace the existing personal exemption and credit with a tax credit of $240 for each person in the taxpayer's family. . . .

These tax reductions are essential to healthy economic recovery during 1978 and 1979. Prospects for continuation of that recovery in the near term are favorable. Consumers have been spending freely, and many other economic indicators recently have been moving up strongly. Without the tax reductions I have proposed, however, the longer-term prospects for economic growth would become increasingly poor. Because of the fiscal drag imposed by rising payroll taxes and inflation, economic growth would slow substantially in late 1978, and fall to about 3½ percent in 1979. The unemployment rate would stop declining and might begin to rise again, and the growth of investment outlays for new plant and equipment would slow significantly. . . .

Success in keeping a firm rein on spending will permit further tax reductions in years to come. Our ability to foresee the future course of the economy is not good enough, however, to enable us to know when additional reductions will be needed or how large they should be. It would therefore be imprudent to plan specific policy measures now for more than the current and the next fiscal year. But I will make recommendations for budget and tax policies for 1980 and beyond that are in keeping with our objectives of steady growth in the economy, more stable prices, and principal reliance on the private sector to achieve economic expansion.

MINI-CASE 12.1

You believe the Keynesian interpretation of the economy provides a useful framework for formulating fiscal policies. One of your friends claims that the economic problems of inflation and unemployment we now face are caused by government interference in the economy. Which of the following arguments would you use in rebuttal?

a) In an economy as large as that of the United States, some form of control is necessary to maintain stability.
b) Investment spending by businesses is very volatile and must be counterbalanced by the government.
c) Consumers tend to increase their spending when for the good of the overall economy, they should be cutting back, therefore the government must step in.
d) Business savings through undistributed profits and depreciation reserves must be counterbalanced by government spending.

REVIEW QUESTIONS

1. As a generalization it may be said of the Keynesian economists that:
   a) they believe that stock of money, the functioning of the capital market, and price flexibility will achieve a full-employment level of national income.
   b) they believe that the capital market is ineffective in achieving the right level of investment spending and that the government budget must act as the balance wheel.
   c) they believe that the multiplier if left to itself will drive the economy toward full employment.
   d) they believe that the problem of inflation is the most important problem and this will have to be solved through Federal Reserve policy.

Given the following information, answer questions 2 through 8. Dollar figures are in billions.

Employment in millions	GNP	Consumption	Taxes plus savings	Investment	Government spending
50	$1000	$ 900	$100	$100	$200
60	1100	950	150	100	200
70	1200	1000	200	100	200
80	1300	1050	250	100	200
90	1400	1100	300	100	200
100	1500	1150	350	100	200

2. The marginal propensity to consume in this example is:
a) 0.30.   c) 0.67.
b) 0.50.   d) 0.80.

3. The marginal propensity to save and pay taxes would be:
a) 0.70.   c) 0.33.
b) 0.50.   d) 0.20.

4. The equilibrium level of GNP would be:
a) $1100 billion.   c) $1300 billion.
b) $1200 billion.   d) $1400 billion.

5. Now suppose that "full employment" were defined as 85 million people with jobs. This situation would give rise to:
a) depression, prices falling.   c) prosperity, prices stable.
b) depression, prices stable.   d) prosperity, prices rising.

6. Now let us change the situation. Suppose that the federal government decides to cut governmental expenditures sharply, but does not reduce taxes. Using draconian methods, the president manages to slice $100 billion off the federal budget. As a result, this equilibrium level of GNP would be:
a) $1000 billion.
b) $1100 billion.
c) $1200 billion.
d) $1300 billion or more.

7. As a result, the following situation would develop:
a) depression, prices falling.   c) prosperity, prices stable.
b) depression, prices stable.   d) prosperity, prices rising.

8. It is clear from this last example, that the multiplier is:

a) 1, GNP declined $100 billion as a result of the $100 billion reduction in government expenditure.
b) 2, GNP declined twice as much as the reduction in government expenditure.
c) 3, GNP declined three times as much as the reduction in government expenditure.
d) 4, GNP declined four times as much as the reduction in government expenditure.

9. Suppose that the marginal propensity to consume was 0.8. From what you know about Keynesian economics, you would know that the multiplier is:

a) 2.   b) 3.   c) 4.   d) 5.

10. If you were told that every $10 billion change in real GNP would change total employment by 300,000 people, then, assuming that the marginal propensity to consume was 0.8, a $20 billion change in government expenditures would change employment by:

a) 600,000.   b) 1,200,000.   c) 2,000,000.   d) 3,000,000.

11. Suppose, on the other hand, that the economy is involved in persistent double-digit inflation. If you were a Keynesian, which of the following policies would you be most likely to advocate?
a) Increase productivity through eliminating make-work union provisions.
b) Have a tight money policy that would increase the interest rate.
c) Increase both taxes and government expenditures.
d) Increase taxes and reduce government expenditures. Use the surplus to retire the national debt.

ESSAY QUESTIONS

1. State in your own words a capsule summary of employment theory as proposed by John Maynard Keynes. What does this theory do to the proposition advanced by the classical economists that the market, if left to itself, could manage the economy in such a way as to keep all resources employed?

2. During periods of rapid growth in GNP, taxes are said by some to be a "drag" on the economy. How could this be?

3. If the tax system of the United States were progressive, would this make a given set of taxes more of a drag or less of a drag? Would this mean that as the economy grows, tax rates should be cut?

4. Appraise the following policy proposals and indicate what problems, if any, would be involved in implementing them.

   a) The economy is in a recession that is not expected to last more than two years. Unemployment has risen until it is about 8 percent of the labor force. Some members of Congess advocate that income taxes be reduced enough so that unemployment will again be about 4 percent of the labor force.

   b) The economy is in an inventory recession. The same congressional group recommends that the government borrow the money from the banks to put the 4 percent of the labor force to work rebuilding the roadbeds of the eastern railroads.

   c) The aggregate demand for products has failed to grow as rapidly as the aggregate supply of products. As a result, unemployment has been creeping up over an extended period of time. The same group of members of Congress has proposed that all income taxes be taken off families whose income is less than average family income in the United States. They also advocate that the deficit resulting from this action be financed by the sale of government bonds to the public.

5. The economy has sunk into an unexpected depression. Tax revenues have shrunk and the government is starting to run a large deficit. As a Keynesian economist, would you recommend that the government increase tax rates or decrease expenditures in order to eliminate the deficit?

6. A peacetime inflation is well underway. Some members of Congress propose raising taxes and using the proceeds to pay off some of the government debt. However, others argue that when prices are rising people cannot afford to pay higher taxes. How would you answer the members of Congress who do not agree? What is the most feasible way to use the federal budget to fight inflation?

ANSWERS TO REVIEW QUESTIONS

1. The key propositions of Keynesian economics are that the level of consumption is determined by the level of income and that withdrawals from the economy, such as savings, will not automatically be counterbalanced by a financial capital market that will equate investment to it.

   a) This is incorrect. There is no automatic mechanism that will achieve full employment according to the Keynesians.

   b) This is correct as explained above.

   c) This is incorrect. There is no automatic mechanism that will achieve full employment.

   d) This is incorrect. Keynesian economics puts little reliance on monetary policy.

2. The marginal propensity to consume is equal to the ratio of the change in consumption expenditure to the change in income (output). In this example, consumption increases by $50 billion for every $100 billion increase in GNP, and hence the MPC is equal to 0.5. The answer, therefore, is (b).

3. The fourth column shows that taxes plus savings increase by $50 billion for each $100 billion increase in GNP. Hence, the marginal propensity to save and pay taxes is 0.5. This could also be computed simply by subtracting the MPC from 1, that is $(1 - MPC) = 0.5$. The correct answer is (b).

4. The equilibrium level of GNP is that level at which aggregate demand (consumption plus investment plus government spending) equals aggregate supply, that is, GNP. This is true at the GNP level of $1400 billion. Another way of verifying this is to note that withdrawals from the system, taxes plus savings, equal investment plus government spending at this level. Hence, the correct answer is (d).

5. The equilibrium level of GNP is now $1400 billion. But that level of GNP requires a labor force of 90 million. Since there are only 85 million workers available, pressure will tend to bid wages, and in turn prices, up. The result will be full employment or prosperity, with prices rising. The correct answer, then, is (d).

6. If the president reduces government spending by $100 billion, then GNP will fall by a multiple of that amount. In this example the MPC is 0.5. Hence the multiplier will be:

$$\left(\frac{1}{1 - MPC}\right) = \left(\frac{1}{1 - 0.5}\right) = \frac{1}{0.5} = 2.$$

This means GNP will fall to $1200 billion. This can be verified. The new situation is a GNP of $1200 billion, consumption of $1000 billion, taxes plus savings of $200 billion, investment of $100 billion, and government spending of $100 billion. Investment plus government spending equals taxes plus savings at this level of GNP. Also, GNP equals consumption plus investment plus government spending. The correct answer is (c).

7. The size of the labor force required to produce this $1200 billion level of GNP is 70 million workers. Since there are 85 million workers in the labor force, there will be pressure for wages and prices to fall. The correct answer, then, is depression with prices falling, choice (a).

8. In the answer to question 6, we determined that the multiplier was 2. Thus a $100 billion decline in government spending will cause a $200 billion reduction in GNP. The correct answer is (b).

9. If the MPC is 0.8, then the multiplier would be:

$$\left(\frac{1}{1 - MPC}\right) = \left(\frac{1}{1 - 0.8}\right) = \frac{1}{0.2} = 5.$$

The correct answer is (d).

10. A $20 billion change in government expenditures will generate a $100 billion change in GNP if the MPC is 0.8. This is the case since an MPC of 0.8 implies a multiplier of 5. This multiplier will generate a $100 billion increase in GNP from the initial $20 billion change in government spending. Now, if a $10 billion change in GNP will change total employment by 300,000, then a $100 billion change in GNP will cause a 3 million change in employment. Hence, the correct answer is (d).

11. If the economy is experiencing a rate of inflation exceeding 9 percent (double-digit), the Keynesians would urge that the government reduce purchases and/or increase taxes to cut back on aggregate

demand.

a) This is incorrect. This is not a form of Keynesian fiscal policy.
b) This is incorrect. This is a form of monetary policy.
c) This is incorrect. The increase in government expenditures would stimulate the economy.
d) This is correct as explained above.

APPENDIX TO CHAPTER 12

OBJECTIVES

Upon successful completion of this appendix, you will be able to:

1. Identify the level of output at which aggregate demand equals aggregate output using a graph.

2. Represent graphically the change in output stemming from a change in one or more components of aggregate demand.

3. Show conditions of excess demand and supply graphically.

4. Demonstrate graphically the multiplier effect.

A GRAPHIC PRESENTATION OF EMPLOYMENT THEORY

In Fig. 12A.1 we have presented in graphic form the numbers we used in Table 12.2 to determine the equilibrium level of GNP. You may find the use of graphs to be a useful way to think about the level of economic activity in the economy.

The heavy line with a 45-degree slope represents the locus of points at which the total output equals aggregate demand. It is always equal to GNP, which is measured along the horizontal axis. This line has a 45-degree slope so that the length of a vertical line dropped from the aggregate supply line will be precisely equal to the GNP measured along the horizontal axis.

The aggregate demand for products, measured along the vertical axis, is equal to (1) planned consumption, indicated by the bottom line labeled C; plus (2) planned investment spending, I, indicated by the vertical difference between C and $C + I$; plus (3) government spending, G, indicated by the vertical difference between $C + I$, and $C + I + G$. View it this way. If all three groups, households, businesses, and government, spent what they had planned to spend at each level of GNP, then their total spending at each level would be indicated by the line marked $C + I + G$.

The equilibrium level of GNP would be that output at which planned expenditures or aggregate demand would be equal to the aggregate supply of products. Where would this be? The answer is that it is at the intersection of the aggregate demand and the 45-degree lines. In this case the equilibrium level of GNP is $1500 billion. If the GNP were larger, such as $1800 billion, the aggregate demand for products would be too small to take all of the output off the market. The excess output of $100 billion is shown in Fig. 12A.1. Some of the output would be left in inventories, and this output would shrink. Or if the GNP were smaller, such as $1200 billion, then planned purchases would exceed the aggregate supply of products by $100 billion, as shown in Fig. 12A.1. Inventories would shrink and output would expand in the future. The only stable level of GNP would be $1500 billion. This is the only output level where aggregate demand is equal to total supply.

If planned investment spending shrinks by $100 billion, the equilibrium level of GNP would drop from $1500 to $1200 billion. In Fig. 12A.2 a new aggregate demand line, $C + I' + G$, is drawn reflecting a decrease in investment by $100 billion. The new equilibrium level of GNP, $1200 billion, is $300 billion lower than before. Since the MPC is $2/3$, as indicated by the slope of the consumption line, the multiplier is three. Hence, three times the $100 billion decrease in investment yields the $300 decrease in GNP.

The same principle holds when investment spending increases by $100 billion from its original level of $150 billion. In Fig. 12A.3, the new GNP equilibrium will be $1800 billion, or $300 billion higher than the initial equilibrium of $1500 billion.

Instead of influencing investment spending, the more direct action of changes in government spending can also be used and illustrated. If the "full employment" level of GNP is determined to be $1700 billion and the equilibrium level of GNP is $1500 billion, then the government, by increasing its spending by $67 billion, can drive the economy to this level. We show this in Fig. 12A.4, based on Table 12.5. It is important to note that the additional spending must be financed by borrowing and not by taxing. If taxes were levied to finance this additional spending, then the consumption line would have to be lowered to reflect the effect of taxes on consumption spending. Lowering the consumption line would lower the aggregate demand $C + I + G$, thus offsetting or partially offsetting the increase in government spending.

An alternative way for the government to increase the aggregate demand for products is to lower taxes while keeping government expenditures constant. In Fig. 12A.5, based on Table 12.6, we have shown how a tax reduction could accomplish the same result as an expenditure increase (although the tax reduction would have to be larger than $67 billion in order to induce people to increase their spending by $67 billion, and this in turn would make the deficit larger than in the preceding case). The multiplier when applied to the $67 billion increase in consumption spending would increase the aggregate demand for products to the full employment level of $1700 billion.

It is clear, based on Keynesian employment theory, that governmental deficits arising out of increases in government expenditures or reduction in taxes will increase the equilibrium level of GNP. Since the opposite result would follow from a reduction in government spending or an increase in taxes, then fiscal policies can also be used to reduce the aggregate demand when it is too large and the price level starts to rise.

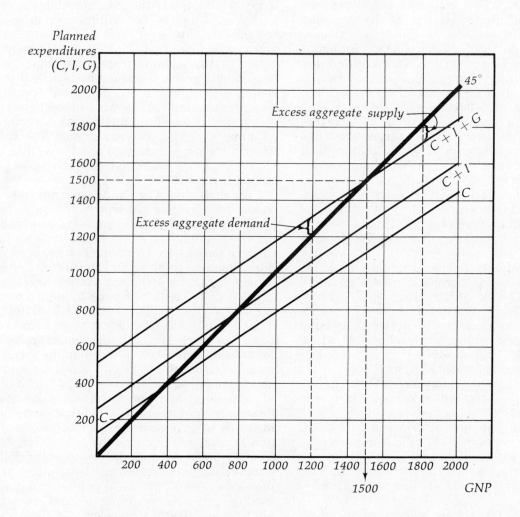

FIG. 12A.1   Employment theory—Working Graph 1 (see Table 12.2).

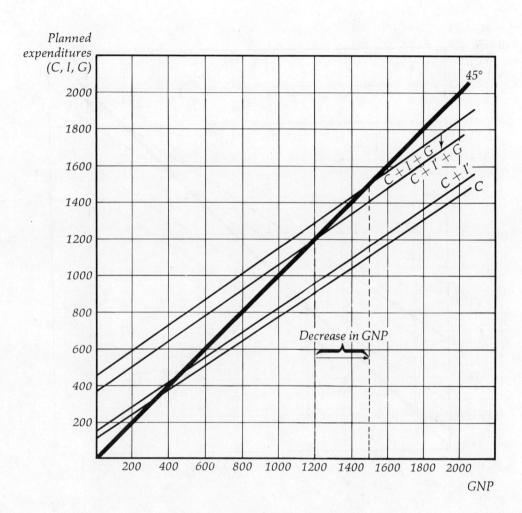

FIG. 12A.2   Employment theory—Working Graph 2 (see Table 12.3).

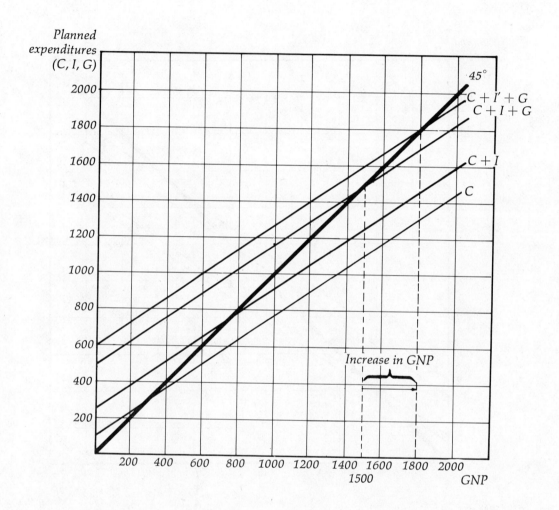

FIG. 12A.3   Employment theory—Working Graph 3 (see Table 12.4).

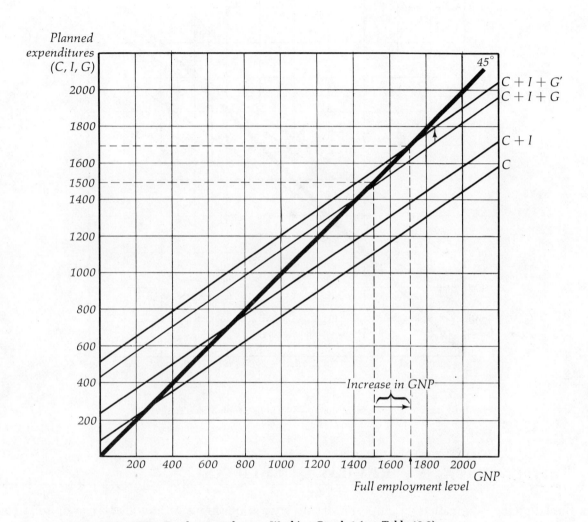

FIG. 12A.4 Employment theory—Working Graph 4 (see Table 12.6).

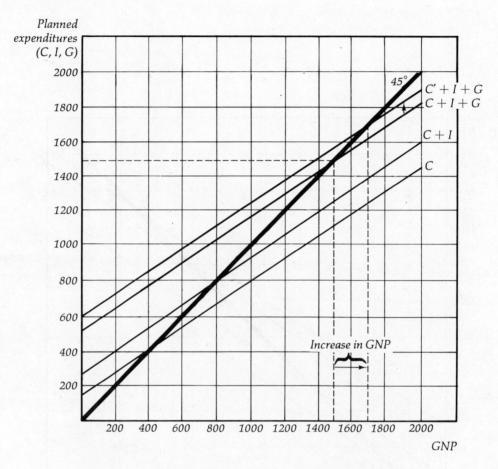

FIG. 12A.5   Employment theory—Working Graph 5 (see Table 12.5).

REVIEW QUESTIONS

Plot the following information on graph paper and answer questions 1 through 8 by examining your graph. Dollar figures are in billions.

Employment in millions	GNP	Consumption	Taxes plus savings	Investment	Government spending
50	$1000	$ 900	$100	$100	$200
60	1100	950	150	100	200
70	1200	1000	200	100	200
80	1300	1050	250	100	200
90	1400	1100	300	100	200
100	1500	1150	350	100	200

1. The marginal propensity to consume in this example is:
   a) 0.30.
   c) 0.67.
   b) 0.50.
   d) 0.80.

2. The marginal propensity to save and pay taxes would be:
   a) 0.70.
   c) 0.33.
   b) 0.50.
   d) 0.20.

3. The equilibrium level of GNP would be:
   a) $1100 billion.
   c) $1300 billion.
   b) $1200 billion.
   d) $1400 billion.

4. Now suppose that "full employment" were defined as 85 million people with jobs. This situation would give rise to:
   a) depression, prices falling.
   c) prosperity, prices stable.
   b) depression, prices stable.
   d) prosperity, prices rising.

5. Now, let us change the situation. Suppose that the federal government decides to cut governmental expenditures sharply, but does not reduce taxes. Using draconian methods, the president manages to slice $100 billion off the federal budget (show this on your graph). As a result, this equilibrium level of GNP would be:
   a) $1000 billion.
   c) $1200 billion.
   b) $1100 billion.
   d) $1300 billion or more.

6. As a result, the following situation would develop:
   a) depression, prices falling.
   c) prosperity, prices stable.
   b) depression, prices stable.
   d) prosperity, prices rising.

7. It is clear from this last example that the multiplier is:
   a) 1, GNP declined $100 billion as a result of the $100 billion reduction in government expenditure.
   b) 2, GNP declined twice as much as the reduction in government expenditure.
   c) 3, GNP declined three times as much as the reduction in government expenditure.
   d) 4, GNP declined four times as much as the reduction in government expenditure.

ESSAY QUESTIONS

1. Assume that the economy is in aggregative equilibrium with withdrawals due to savings and taxes equal to autonomous demand (private investment plus government spending). Now let households choose to save $33.33 billion more. If the marginal propensity to consume is $\frac{2}{3}$, how much will aggregate income fall? Show this graphically. After the decline in income, will the consumers be able to save the extra $33.33 billion? How do you explain the paradox that if consumers want to save more the economy will make this impossible? Why is it impossible for all consumers to do at the same time what any single consumer can do?

2. Suppose that the federal government collects an additional $60 billion in taxes from households. Assuming that the marginal propensity to consume is $\frac{2}{3}$, how much will consumption spending fall as a result of $60 billion in taxes? Show this graphically. Apply the multiplier to the net

reduction in consumption spending. How much will GNP fall? Now suppose that the government increases its total spending by $60 billion, the amount of its extra tax revenue. Once the multiplier has done its work, how much will GNP rise? Explain why the transfer of income to the government increases the GNP. Does this mean that if all income were transferred to the government that GNP would rise to infinity?

3. Would the reverse be true? If the government reduced its taxes and expenditures, would GNP fall? Would this be a way to cure steady but persistent increases in prices during peacetime?

4. It is sometimes said that Keynesian economics ignores financial capital market transactions. Going back to question 2, what would happen to the interest rate if more and more of aggregate income were funnelled through a government that was spending as much as it was taking in? Would there be any feedback effects on investment spending from the financial capital markets?

5. Now suppose that the government simultaneously reduces its taxes and expenditures. Would this have any effect on the interest rate and quantity of investment spending?

ANSWERS TO REVIEW QUESTIONS

1. The marginal propensity to consume is equal to the ratio of the change in consumption expenditure to the change in income (output). It is represented by the slope of the aggregate demand curve. In this example, consumption increases by $50 billion for every $100 billion increase in GNP, hence the MPC is equal to 0.5. The answer therefore is (b).

2. The graph shows that taxes plus savings increase by $50 billion for each $100 billion increase in GNP. Hence, the marginal propensity to save and pay taxes is 0.5. This could also be computed simply by subtracting the MPC from 1, that is $(1 - \text{MPC}) = 0.5$. The correct answer is (b).

3. The equilibrium level of GNP is that level of output at which the aggregate demand curve (consumption plus investment plus government spending) intersects the total supply curve. This is true at the GNP level of $1400 billion. Another way of verifying this is to note that withdrawals from the system, taxes plus savings, equal investment plus government spending at this level. Hence, the correct answer is (d).

4. The equilibrium level of GNP is now $1400 billion. But that level of GNP requires a labor force of 90 million. Since there are only 85 million workers available, pressure will tend to bid wages and in turn prices, up. The result will be full employment or prosperity with prices rising. The correct answer then is (d).

5. If the president reduces government spending by $100 billion, then GNP will fall by a multiple of that amount. In this example the MPC is 0.5, hence the multiplier will be:

$$\left(\frac{1}{1 - \text{MPC}}\right) = \left(\frac{1}{1 - 0.5}\right) = \frac{1}{0.5} = 2.$$

This means GNP will fall to $1200 billion. This can be verified. Examine the horizontal axis. The new situation is a GNP of $1200 billion, consumption of $1000 billion, taxes plus savings of $200 billion, investment of $100 billion, and government spending of $100 billion. Investment plus government spending equals taxes plus savings at this level of GNP. Also, GNP equals consumption plus investment plus government spending. The correct answer is (c).

6. The size of the labor force required to produce this $1200 billion level of GNP is 70 million workers. Since there are 85 million workers in the labor force, there will be pressure for wages and prices to fall. The correct answer, then, is depression with prices falling, choice (a).

7. In the answer to question 5, we determined that the multiplier was 2. Thus a $100 billion decline in government spending will cause a $200 billion reduction in GNP. Compare the change on the vertical axis to that on the horizontal axis. The correct answer is (b).

OBJECTIVES

Upon successful completion of this chapter, you will be able to:

1. Define and give examples of money.
2. Define the money supply.
3. Differentiate between money and near-monies.
4. Differentiate between the financial intermediaries known as savings institutions and those called commercial banks in terms of their functions.
5. Explain how a commercial bank creates money by making a loan.
6. Trace through the effects of a money transaction involving a deposit or withdrawal in a financial intermediary.
7. Identify the three basic tools of the Federal Reserve System and explain how they affect the money supply.
8. Explain the role of the banker in allocating loanable funds.

MONEY AND THE BANKING SYSTEM

INTRODUCTION

Do you know the source of the money in your pocket or in your savings or checking account? The first answer you might be inclined to give is that only the federal government has the power to create money and therefore all the money used in the United States must have been created by the government. If you gave this answer, you are wrong.

In this chapter you will discover that the banking system, including the Federal Reserve System, has created the money that you use to purchase goods and services. You will learn that when commercial banks lend to persons, businesses, or government, they usually add to the amount of money already existing in the economy. This is a simple fact, yet one that is a mystery to most citizens. We will also describe how banks, including the Federal Reserve System, determine the money holdings of the public. It is necessary to understand how money gets created and destroyed in order to ask the important question: "What difference does money make in the way the economy operates?"

MONEY

How much money do you have? This is an ambiguous question. In answering this question some people would estimate the value of all the items they own—their assets—and then subtract the value of their obligations or debts. They would be telling you the value of their wealth. Others would look in their wallets and tell you how much "carrying money" they have.

From the point of view of economics this is also an ambiguous question. The answer to it would depend on how money is defined.

Before we propose a definition of money, let us first dispose of a common misconception. Many people confuse money and wealth. If Nelson D. Rockefeller is said to be worth $400 million, people picture Mr. Rockefeller as having stashed away $400 million in paper money and coins. This of course is not true. Most of his wealth will be invested in real estate, paintings, antique furniture, shares of stock in corporations, corporate bonds, and government securities. Only a very small part of his wealth is in that type of asset we normally regard as *money*.

What is the characteristic that distinguishes "money" from other assets? The answer is its acceptability in payment for goods and services. *Liquidity* is a term used to describe the degree to which an asset is generally acceptable. Money by definition is liquid. Near-liquid assets are those that can easily be converted into cash. Consider the last column in Table 13.1, which is a hypothetical list of your assets arranged in descending order from the most liquid to the least liquid.

Money **is anything that is generally acceptable as a means of payment or in settlement of debts.**

Ignoring, temporarily, the different totals, where should we draw the line between those assets we call money and other assets? Specifically, what comprises the money supply in the United States? Many objects have been generally acceptable in the past or in other cultures that are not now acceptable, including gold and cigarettes from the list above.

Clearly, paper money and coins are generally acceptable in payment of debts. But what about checking accounts? They usually are, although it is quite common for the recipient to make sure that the payor does have a large enough balance in the bank to cover the check. These three items—paper money, coin, and checking accounts—make up a definition of the *money supply* that has been designated as the M_1 definition. Checking accounts or demand deposits, as they are called, should not be confused with savings accounts or time deposits.

TABLE 13.1

HYPOTHETICAL LIST OF YOUR ASSETS

Assets	M_1	M_2	M_3	Wealth
1. Coins	$ 1.45	$ 1.45	$ 1.45	$ 1.45
2. Paper money	30.00	30.00	30.00	30.00
3. Checking account	115.00	115.00	115.00	115.00
Total M_1	$146.45			
4. Savings account in a commercial bank		300.00	300.00	300.00
Total M_2		$446.45		
5. Shares in savings-and-loan associations			250.00	250.00
6. Shares in a credit union			400.00	400.00
Total M_3			$1,096.45	
7. Gold in a safety deposit box				1,655.00
8. Cash surrender value of life insurance				755.00
9. U.S. Government savings bonds				500.00
10. Corporate bonds owed by U.S. Steel Co.				1,000.00
11. International Business Machines stock at current prices				3,000.00
12. Five cartons of cigarettes				40.00
13. One half of the equity in a condominium				10,000.00
14. New car				4,000.00
17. Hk-fi set				500.00
16. Loan to a friend				50.00
Total wealth				$22,596.45

If checking accounts in banks are included, why not include the savings accounts in commercial banks? Commercial banks are banks permitted to have checking accounts. All you have to do to convert a savings to a checking account is to call your bank's bookkeeping department and instruct it to transfer money from your savings account to your checking account and you will have a larger checking account. It is on the basis of this logic that the M_2 definition of the money supply was established. The M_2 definition includes all of the items in the M_1 definition plus savings accounts in commercial banks. In the rest of this chapter, we will use this M_2 definition of the money supply although we realize that it is an arbitrary definition.

Some of you may argue that if savings accounts in commercial banks are to be included among those assets we call money, we should also include the savings accounts in savings-and-loan associations, mutual savings banks, and credit unions. But they are slightly different. These institutions do not have checking accounts and therefore you would physically have to move

your withdrawal from one of these thrift institutions to a commercial bank if you were to use the proceeds to buy a new hi-fi set.* Were we to include deposits in thrift institutions, we would have an even broader definition of the money supply that is designated M_3. Table 13.1 shows the components of M_1, M_2, M_3, and wealth.

As you examine the rest of the items in Table 13.1, you will see some items that you might think should be included in a definition of the money supply. What about gold? It was once the world's premier example of money. At the present time, however, you probably couldn't use gold to buy things. You would first have to sell it and then use the proceeds to buy whatever you wanted.

Not only are the definitions of money somewhat arbitrary, but they are also subject to change

* This is no longer true in certain areas of the country. Mutual savings banks in Massachusetts and New Hampshire have offered Negotiable Order of Withdrawal (NOW) accounts since late 1972. NOW accounts are technically savings accounts that could require 30–90 days notice before funds are withdrawn. Since prior notice is not required in practice and since the negotiable order functions like a check, NOW accounts provide the convenience of a checking account while paying interest like a savings account.

as the payment habits of people change. Should credit cards become even more widely used in place of money, it might be necessary to create a new definition of money to include the maximum credit limits of the credit cards. But for the pres-ent, we will use the M_2 definition of the money supply.

The *money supply* consists of currency outside banks plus deposits in commercial banks.

COMMENTARY

The following excerpt reveals that the definition of money is constantly changing. Please read the excerpt and answer the following questions.

a) Why is money difficult to define?

b) What three approaches to the definition of money are most widely used?

c) List some major changes currently occurring in the payments system.

MONEY—A CHANGING CONCEPT IN A CHANGING WORLD

The money stock has been given increasing attention in recent years. Both the Federal Reserve and the public currently closely observe the rate at which the quantity of money is growing. Accompanying this increased attention to money is a recognition that there is considerable disagreement as to how money should be defined.

In 1974 the Board of Governors of the Federal Reserve System, recognizing the importance of this problem, appointed the Advisory Committee on Monetary Statistics (generally termed the Bach Committee after Professor G. L. Bach, the chairman) to examine some of the issues involved. The Bach Committee's report was released in June 1976,* but given the extent of disagreement on the subject, its conclusions are unlikely to greatly reduce the controversy over the definition of money.

An increasing source of difficulty in defining money is the rapid change taking place in the nation's payments system.†

The final third of the 19th century saw radical changes in the monetary system of the United States, particularly in the domestic payments

* Board of Governors of the Federal Reserve System, *Improving the Monetary Aggregates, Report of the Advisory Committee on Monetary Statistics*, Washington, D.C., June 1976.

† It is probably more accurate to refer to "payments systems,"as there are currently a number of alternative ways of making funds transfers. The term "payments system" is used here to include all systems for making funds transfers, including those which may only be implemented in the future.

system. On the eve of the Civil War (January 1860), the American-money stock—defined to include specie, bank notes, and bank deposits—consisted of $186 million in gold, $184 million in bank notes, and $241 million in bank deposits. During and after the War, the composition changed drastically. Bank deposits increased from 38.6 per cent of money holdings in 1860 to 54.7 per cent in 1867, and to 68.6 per cent in 1875. By 1899, deposits had risen to 81 per cent of all money holdings. While we do not have data on either the quantity of demand deposits or the volume of payments by check during this period, this movement from currency to bank deposits was indicative of the shift that took place in the payments system toward the making of payments by check.

In spite of this shift, there was a general reluctance to include demand deposits in the money supply. It is not clear to what extent late 19th century economists realized that this change was taking place. Since they did not have published figures on the money stock, they were not aware of the precise degree to which changes were occurring. Perhaps the changes taking place were recognized, but a kind of intellectual inertia caused the economists of the day to prefer the traditional definitions which excluded deposits. At any rate, there seems to have been a general reluctance to expand the definition of money to include bank deposits, just as many economists are reluctant to modify today's commonly accepted definitions.

There is at least some reason for believing that changes in the payments system currently taking place will be every bit as significant as the changes of the 19th century. It is widely believed that the United States is in the early stages of movement toward an electronic funds transfer system (EFTS)—a system where many—perhaps most—payments would be made in response to electronic instructions rather than instructions written on a paper check.

While there are very wide differences of opinion as to the likely speed and extent of EFTS development, there seems to be very little reason for doubting that another change in the payments system is well underway. Until recently, with the minor exception of traveler's checks, payments could be made only with currency and commercial bank checking accounts. It is now increasingly possible to make payments from other types of accounts—commercial bank savings accounts, accounts at savings and loan associations (S&L's), mutual savings banks (MSB's), credit unions (CU's), and even certain mutual fund accounts. In addition, an increasing proportion of purchases is being made with credit cards.

In light of these developments, it seems useful to attempt to consider whether these changes, like the changes of the late 19th century, will require modifications in our definitions of money.

Current definitions of money

Three approaches to the definition of money have been widely used. The traditional approach has been to define money as those assets which can be used to purchase goods and services or to pay debts—that is, those assets which serve as media of exchange. A second approach, suggested by Milton Friedman, would define money as those assets which serve as a "temporary abode of purchasing power"—that is, assets which are held during relatively brief periods when an individual or firm has receipts exceeding expenditures. The third approach is not always explicitly stated, but has been widely used in monetary research and seems to have been extremely important to the Bach Committee. This approach would define money as the aggregate or aggregates which are highly correlated with gross national product or some other measure of economic activity. Presumably this approach rests on the belief that the money stock thus defined would be of greater value in the formulation of stabilization policy.

The Federal Reserve System regularly publishes data for five alternative money stock definitions. Multiple measures are published because there are differences of opinion as to what is the appropriate basis for defining money and because there is a good deal of uncertainty as to what empirical definition best fits the various theoretical approaches. Since the Federal Reserve has only limited access to data for many nonmember institutions, the money stock definitions are inadequate in some instances.

M1, which consists of currency and demand deposits other than those held by commercial banks and the U.S. Government, corresponds to the traditional medium of exchange approach to the money supply. It does not, however, include one familiar medium of exchange, traveler's checks.*

M2 is M1 plus time and savings deposits of commercial banks other than large negotiable certificates of deposit (CDs), at weekly reporting banks. M3 is M2 plus deposits at MSBs [mutual savings banks], S&Ls [savings and loan associations], and CUs [credit unions]. M4 is M2 plus large negotiable CDs and M5 is M3 plus large negotiable CDs. These four definitions reflect to some extent the "temporary abode of purchasing power" approach, as well as the belief of many economists that one or another of these magnitudes is more closely related to GNP than is M1.

Major changes in the payments system

The extension of payment accounts to new institutions. Historically, commercial banks have been the only financial institution to provide a deposit account which could be used to pay third parties. From 1933 to 1972 these payments could be made only from noninterest bearing demand deposit accounts. Since 1972, there have been a number of innovations which have allowed other institutions to offer close substitutes for bank checking accounts.

NOW accounts. In 1972, following a favorable court decision, MSB's in Massachusetts began

---

* The largest U.S. issuer of traveler's checks is not a commercial bank and thus does not report to the Federal Reserve (or any other bank regulator). At one time, bank-issued traveler's checks were a part of the money supply. The two major banks in the traveler's check business now use holding company subsidiaries to issue them. Thus, they are not liabilities of the bank and not part of the money supply.

offering NOW accounts to their customers. These accounts are legally savings deposits but allow the customer to withdraw funds by writing a "negotiable order of withdrawal (NOW)." Since a NOW looks, and more importantly, functions like a check, NOW accounts are—from the point of view of the customer—an interest bearing checking account.

Electronic funds transfer. Electronic funds transfer (EFT) developments are probably the most widely discussed innovations in the payments system today. While EFT is likely to have a substantial effect on the demand for money, its impact on the nature of money will likely be confined to facilitating the growth of overdraft accounts and by reducing whatever barriers remain between noninterest bearing checking accounts and interest bearing accounts.

Conclusions

Just as the 19th century changes in the way that payments were made required a broadened definition of the money stock, the changes currently underway will require a broadening of any definition based on which assets can serve as media of exchange. Only the broadest definitions, those which include the deposits of thrift institutions as well as those at commercial banks, are likely to be unaffected. Many policymakers and scholars prefer to use a narrower definition. They are likely to be increasingly faced with a dilemma as it is unlikely that it will be possible to develop any narrow money stock series which can be extended very far into the past and still be conceptually consistent.

CARL M. GAMBS. "Money—A Changing Concept in a Changing World." *Monthly Review*, January 1977, Federal Reserve Bank of Kansas City. Reprinted by permission.

Money is largely supplied by the banking system.

Many people are surprised that the source of the money supply, as we have defined it, is not the federal government. Rather, it is the banking system, which includes a network of over 13,000 commercial banks, and the Federal Reserve System. Except for an insignificant amount of currency supplied by the United States Treasury Department, virtually all of the currency in circulation in the United States consists of Federal Reserve notes. While it is true that the Federal

TABLE 13.2

MONEY SUPPLY MEASURES FOR SELECTED YEARS
(All figures represent billions of dollars)

	Overall measures			Components and related items		
					Deposits at commercial banks	
Year	M_1 (Currency plus demand deposits)	M_2 (M_1 plus time deposits at commercial banks other than large CD's)	M_3 (M_2 + deposits at nonbank thrift)	Currency	Demand deposits	Time and savings deposits
1950	$116.2	—	—	$25.0	$91.2	$36.7
1955	135.2	—	—	27.8	107.4	50.0
1960	144.2	217.1	314.4	29.0	115.2	72.9
1965	171.3	301.4	462.7	36.3	134.9	146.3
1970	219.6	423.5	656.2	49.1	170.5	229.2
1971	233.8	471.7	742.8	52.6	181.3	271.1
1972	255.3	525.3	844.5	56.9	198.4	313.5
1973	270.5	571.4	919.6	61.5	209.0	313.9
1974	283.3	612.4	981.5	67.8	215.3	418.3
1975	294.8	664.3	1092.6	73.7	221.0	451.7
1976	312.4	740.3	1237.1	80.5	231.9	491.1
1977	335.4	806.5	1373.9	88.4	247.0	545.8

Source: Economic Report of the President, 1978.

Reserve notes have been printed by the United States Mint, they are nevertheless obligations of the Federal Reserve banks and not of the Treasury Department of the United States. Bank deposits, which make up the major part of the money used in the United States, are supplied by the approximately 13,000 commercial banks scattered around the country. Table 13.2 shows the magnitudes of the various money supply measures for the United States in selected years from 1950 to 1977.

The M_2 definition of the money supply has increased almost fourfold since 1960, increasing from $217 billion to $807 billion. The banking system, including the twelve Federal Reserve banks, has created that additional $590 billion. We now will explain how this occurs.

Mini-case 13.1 is presented to help you clarify your understanding of the money supply.

MINI-CASE 13.1

Suppose you are living in the year 2000 and that the computer has taken over as the chief financial agent. Whenever you buy anything, you insert your universal credit card into a computer reader that records your payment as a "negative." And suppose that whenever you receive income or sell something, the computer records the receipt as a "positive." At the end of the month, the computer records your net balance—if it is positive, as an addition to your holdings of interest-bearing government bonds, or if it is negative, as a subtraction from your holdings of interest-bearing government bonds. When you get a negative balance, the computer starts charging you interest. You are asked to define money for this economy. It would be:

a) currency plus demand deposits.
b) currency plus demand deposits plus savings accounts in commercial banks.
c) credit limits on credit cards plus government bonds held.
d) currency, demand deposits, credit limits, and government bonds.

HOW BANKS CREATE MONEY

The banking system consists of commercial banks, the twelve Federal Reserve banks, and the Board of Governors.

When you deposit a paycheck or send a check to a friend in some other part of the country, you are involved with the network of banks that make up the banking system of the United States. If you receive a check drawn on some other bank, your own bank is capable of collecting the money for you. If you send a check across the country to a friend, your friend can go to a bank and get the money you want her to have. Without going into detail about how this is accomplished, we can say that your bank, assuming it is a member of the Federal Reserve System, keeps enough on deposit in one of the twelve Federal Reserve banks so that it can transfer money for you or collect money from other banks for you. The 13,000 individual banks, about 6,000 of which are members of the Federal Reserve System, plus the twelve Federal Reserve System banks, supervised by the Board of Governors of the Federal Reserve System in Washington, D.C., make up the banking system of the United States.

The twelve regional banks of the Federal Reserve System, controlled by a board of governors in Washington, D.C., behave in many ways like a branch of the federal government. Although the twelve banks are technically owned by the 6,000 "member" banks, their policies are established by the seven governors who constitute the board appointed by the president of the United States, with the consent of the Senate, for staggered 14-year terms. One of the seven members is designated by the president to serve as chairman for a 4-year term. Because of their long terms, the governors have more independence of the president and the Congress than do many public officials, but this does not change the fact that they are really part of the government.

As a central bank, the Federal Reserve System controls the reserve position of member banks.

The twelve Federal Reserve banks are really the bankers' banks; they do not do business directly with the public. They issue currency to the banks when the public wants to convert its bank deposits into currency and, most importantly, the Fed (as we shall call the twelve banks and the board of governors) creates the reserves that the banks are required to hold against their deposits.

The dictionary defines *reserves* as "something stored up, kept back, or relied upon, for future use or advantage." This general definition gives us a clue to the role of reserves in the banking system. Within the context of our monetary system, reserves consist of (1) vault cash, which is paper money and coins held in the bank in case depositors want currency, and (2) deposits in the Federal Reserve. Bankers would want to keep reserve deposits in the Fed even if they were not required to do so, because their balances in the

Fed serve somewhat the same function as your checking account. They can be used to pay the Fed for Federal Reserve notes should you decide to withdraw some of your deposits from your bank. Or they can be used to pay other banks, should you decide to write a check to a depositor in another bank.

To get a visual picture of the structure of the banking system, your attention is directed to Fig. 13.1. You will see that the chairman of the Board of Governors of the Federal Reserve System and six other governors sit at the top of the banking pyramid. The twelve Federal Reserve banks, each with its own president, make up the second tier of the pyramid. The member banks, all 6000 of them, comprise the third tier. And finally, the nonmember banks and thrift institutions that keep their deposits in the member banks make up the fourth tier. All four tiers, acting together, make up the banking system of the United States.

The Federal Reserve requires banks that are members of the Federal Reserve System (and this includes all of the large banks and all national banks) to maintain reserves equal to a certain percentage of their deposits. This means that banks can make loans only up to the amount of their excess reserves—the amount by which their total reserves exceed their required reserves. We shall assume in the rest of this section that the Fed has set reserve requirements at 15 percent of all bank deposits. (In fact, banks are required to keep a smaller percentage of reserves for savings ac-

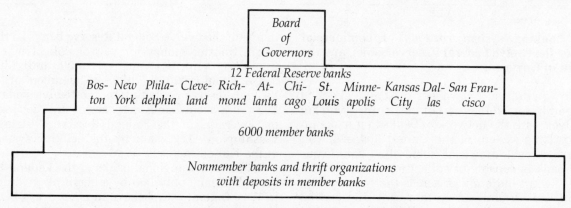

FIG. 13.1   The organization of the Federal Reserve System and United States banking system.

counts than for checking accounts, but we will ignore this limitation for purposes of discussion.)

Reserve requirements are the percentage requirements of their deposits that banks must keep available in the form of cash in their vaults or as deposits in their district Federal Reserve bank.

Required reserves are the dollar amounts banks must hold as reserves.

Excess reserves are the bank's total reserves less required reserves. They consist of extra vault cash and deposits in the Fed not legally required.

Banks create money when they make loans.

Now suppose that your bank has some excess reserves, that is, more vault cash and deposits in the Fed than it is required to keep for its deposits. Suppose, further, that you visit your bank in order to borrow $5000 in the form of a checkbook balance to pay your tuition, dormitory bill, and incidental expenses during the next year. Let us suppose that the loan officer in the bank is satisfied that you will pay off your loan with interest when you have been graduated.

The following transaction will take place: (1) you will be asked to sign a promissory note in which you agree to pay off the loan in, say, two years and, in addition, agree to pay 8 percent interest on the $5000 at the end of each year; (2) the loan officer will then open a checking account for you and credit your account with $5000.

When you exchange your signed note for a deposit slip, something very remarkable happens. The total amount of money in existence increases by $5000 and you have in your possession the new money that has just been created. You have given the bank officer an IOU note that he accepts, but few others would, and in exchange for it, he gives you a checkbook with a balance of $5000 in it. The checks you write on that account will indeed be *generally acceptable*. They are *money*. Furthermore, you are not simply getting the money somebody else has put in the bank. All of the other depositors still have their deposits and, since bank deposits are money, there is as much money in circulation as before, *while you have an additional $5000.* The additional $5000 was added to the existing stock of money. It is just as

if your bank had a mint in the basement. In brief, the amount of money in existence is increased when banks make loans.

Even if you insist on taking the proceeds of your loan in cash rather than checkbook form, the situation will not be changed. We have already said that your bank had some excess reserves, and therefore, if you wish, you may take your new money in the form of cash. Your bank will take $5000 in currency out of the vault and give it to you.

Remember, when we defined money, we said that *currency outside banks* and bank deposits in commercial banks made up the money supply of the nation. Therefore, when the loan officer gives you cash, he is giving you something that was not part of the money supply when it was in the bank but becomes a part of the money supply when you receive it. It follows that when you exchange your note for vault cash, the money supply is increased just as surely as when you exchanged your note for a new bank deposit. The only difference is that in the first case you had a claim against a particular bank, but now you have a claim against the Federal Reserve System—since the new money you have received will be Federal Reserve notes.

You might argue that the only reason you were borrowing from the bank was to pay your

educational expenses and that as soon as you write a check to a college or university the money will disappear. This is not true. You are living in a "closed system." When the university receives your check, it will deposit the check in its bank. This will move the new money to the university's bank. The money does not disappear; it just shows up in another location. In the process, the excess reserves your bank used to make a loan to you will be transferred to the university's bank.

Money is also created when banks buy bonds and other items.

The same result would have occurred if you had sold your bank a government bond. In place of delivering your own IOU to the bank in order to get a new deposit, you would have delivered the government's IOU. In fact, if you were to sell your bank anything, for example, real estate for a new branch location, a corporate bond, or gold, the result would be the same. The money they pay you will be new money. The only time the bank does not create money when it acquires something is when it first sells securities to people and uses the proceeds from a stock or bond sale to buy things. Since this is rarely done, we can say that usually when banks acquire assets, they create new money.

Banks destroy money when they accept repayment of loans and sell claims.

The reverse is also true. When you pay off your loan, the total amount of money in existence is reduced. Suppose you have been graduated, have obtained a good job, and during the first year have managed to save enough to pay off the $5000 plus the interest accrued. During the period you were accumulating these savings, your cash balance would go up and someone else's cash balance would go down; no change would occur in the total. But when you pay off your note, the total amount of money held by the public will go down by $5000 plus interest. Your cash balance will be that much lower and no one else's cash balance will be higher. Money is destroyed, just as surely as it would be if the bank had a shredder in the basement that cut up the money you delivered to them to pay off your note.

To make the story complete, let us suppose that several years later you have accumulated $10,000 to buy some Treasury bills from your bank. Treasury bills are IOUs issued by the Treasury Department for the federal government. When you pay for these securities, total bank deposits will shrink by $10,000. Your $10,000 deposit will be cancelled when you transfer your deposit claim back to the issuer of the claim. Your money holdings will be $10,000 smaller and no one else's money holdings will be larger.

Some people worry about the interest payments people make to the banks on these loans. Do they reduce the money supply? Initially, they might: But most of the interest paid to the banks is used by the bank to pay expenses, such as computer rentals and tellers' salaries. Some of the interest is used to pay dividends to the bank's stockholders. When the bank pays out these funds, it increases the money supply, and so we can think of the banks as recycling the interest payments they receive from the public. Normally, it is only the repayment of principal that reduces the money holdings of the public.

To make sure that you understand this process of money creation and destruction, assume that the persons in your economics class are the only participants in a closed economy. Suppose the class has $8000 in currency and bank deposits. Now, let a member of the class borrow $1000 from the instructor, whom we will assume is managing your class's bank. At the instant the loan is made, your class will have $9000 in currency and bank deposits, $1000 more than the class had initially. Where did the money come from? It resulted from the exchange of debts between the member of the class and the banker. The banker's debt is money and the student's debt is not. Should the borrower spend the proceeds of the loan, the new money would merely go to another member of the class. The reverse would, of course, be true: when the student pays off the note, some of the bank's debt is extinguished and, as a result, the class's holding of money is reduced.

Banks create and destroy money.

Finally, we can answer the question: Where does money come from? It comes from the banking system. Whenever the banking system exchanges its debts for the debts of others, money is created. Whenever the banking system accepts repayment of debts or sells claims against others to non-banks, money is destroyed. In modern industrial nations, money comes from the banks and not from the government. This leads to the question: Who is in charge? Who regulates the creation of money?

THE ROLE OF THE FEDERAL RESERVE SYSTEM

The Federal Reserve System is responsible for regulating the supply of money and credit.

As the central banker for the United States, the Federal Reserve System has three major "levers" it can pull when it wants to encourage or limit the creation of money by banks. To keep our discussion as simple as possible, we will not discuss a series of less important controls and services that can be activated.

The Fed sets reserve requirements.

The first lever for money control is the setting of reserve requirements for the member banks. The reserve requirements determine how much money banks can create from a given quantity of bank reserves. If the Fed wants to encourage the banks to create money, it can reduce the reserve requirements. In place of having to hold reserves equal to 15 percent of its deposits, the Fed can announce that required reserves will have to be only 14 percent of deposits, thus freeing reserves for lending. Thus, if your bank has $100 million of deposits, it will then have an additional $1 million of its reserves available to make loans and purchase securities, that is, to create money.

If the Fed wants to reduce the money-creating power of the banks, it can increase reserve requirements. Suppose your bank has no excess reserves and that the Fed increases reserve requirements from 15 percent to 16 percent. Your hometown bank will either have to borrow $1 million of additional reserves from some bank that does have excess reserves (or, as we shall see

shortly, from the Fed itself) or it will have to sell securities and demand repayment of some of its loans. If you wanted an educational loan at a time when the Fed was raising reserve requirements, you probably would not get it. The loan officer would say the bank did not have the money.

Because this power to change reserve requirements does not have the flexibility of the other two control devices, it is not used as a day-to-day control device by the Fed.

COMMENTARY

The following excerpt from the *Wall Street Journal* indicates how the financial community reports a change in the required reserve rate. Please read the excerpt and answer the following questions.

a) What is the purpose of this action?

b) Why do you suppose the Fed would take this action just when the Treasury Department is about to raise $2 billion through new bond issues?

FED LOWERS SOME RESERVE REQUIREMENTS, ADDING $1.1 BILLION TO MONEY SUPPLY

WASHINGTON—The Federal Reserve Board reduced reserve requirements that its member commercial banks must maintain on net demand, or checking account, deposits—a move that will increase the nation's money supply.

The action will free about $1.1 billion used to support the deposits, the Fed estimated. It said the action was "designed to permit further gradual improvement in bank liquidity and to facilitate moderate growth" in the nation's money supply.

Current reserve requirements will be reduced one-half percentage point on all categories of net demand deposits of up to $400 million and one percentage point on deposits above $400 million. The Fed lowered the rate to 7.5% from 8% on deposits up to $2 million; to 10% from 10.5% on deposits of $2 million to $10 million; to 12% from 12.5% for $10 million to $100 million; to 13% from 13.5% for $100 million to $400 million; and to 16.5% from 17.5% on deposits over $400 million.

The Fed said the new reserve rates will apply to net demand deposits beginning with the week of Jan. 30 to Feb. 5 and will determine the reserves banks must maintain beginning with the week of Feb. 13–19. The Fed financing program to refund maturing debt didn't change current reserve requirements on time and savings deposits.

The Fed action came two days before the Treasury is expected . . . to raise probably about $2 billion to meet its cash needs. By lowering its reserve requirements, the Fed will help accommodate the Treasury's program because it will help increase the amount of cash and private checking accounts, or money supply, in the U.S.

The action also is a further sign of an easing by the Fed in its monetary policy as the U.S. economy continues to stagnate. The move should put pressure on interest rates to continue their downward trend, and it should also prod banks to further lower their prime, or minimum, interest rate on loans to large companies.

The Fed action was unanimous, a spokesman said.

"The immediate impact will probably be a downtrend in money market interest rates," one government securities trader in New York agreed.

One analyst guessed rates on short-term money market instruments could open 0.25 percentage point lower today. "It's pumping money into the system, which has to be constructive in the markets."

Reprinted with permission of *The Wall Street Journal*, © Dow Jones & Company, Inc. (January 21, 1975). All rights reserved.

The Fed sets the discount rate.

The second control device is the power to determine the *discount rate*. The discount rate is the rate of interest that the Fed charges when it lends reserves to member banks. It is called a discount rate because member banks sometimes use loans they have made as collateral, and this process of borrowing against existing loans is called discounting. When the Fed wants to discourage creation of money, it raises the discount rate. This action makes it more expensive for the banks to borrow the additional reserves from the Fed.

When the Fed wants to encourage the creation of money by banks, it reduces the discount rate, thus making it cheaper for banks to acquire the additional reserves they need to make loans and buy securities. The mere fact of the Fed's announcement of a change in the discount rate informs the banking and business community of the Fed's attitude toward making loans.

Changes in the discount rate, like changes in reserve requirements, are not used as a day-to-day control device. Once established, the discount rate is maintained until there has been a significant change in the rate of interest.

COMMENTARY

The following excerpt from the *Wall Street Journal* shows the newsworthy effect of a change in the discount rate. Please read the excerpt and answer the following questions.

a) How does change in the discount rate affect the reserves of member banks?
b) In what way does a reduction in the discount rate ease monetary policy?

FEDERAL RESERVE'S KEY INTEREST RATE IS REDUCED TO 6% CUT FROM 6.25% IN DISCOUNT FEE CONFIRMS EASING IN FED MONETARY POLICY

The Federal Reserve Board approved a slight reduction in its key interest rate, confirming earlier indications of an easing in its monetary policy.

The monetary authorities approved a cut in the discount rate to 6% from 6.25% effective today for 10 of the 12 regional Federal Reserve banks. The two other banks are expected to follow suit.

Although the Fed's move was considered by market analysts to be lagging behind other interest rates rather than leading them, it increases the likelihood of further reductions in the prime, or minimum, interest rate of commercial banks.

This is the fourth cut this year in the discount rate, which is the rate charged by Federal Reserve banks on loans to member commercial banks. The discount rate, which is considered one key monetary tool of the central bank, was 7¾% at the beginning of the year.

Lending Capacity

The Federal Reserve has been supplying reserves, or lending capacity, to the banking system in fairly generous doses in recent weeks, according to market analysts. The purpose is to accommodate an economic upturn, without renewing inflationary pressures.

Reprinted with permission of *The Wall Street Journal*, © Dow Jones & Company, Inc. (May 16, 1975). All rights reserved.

The Fed supplies reserves when it buys government securities.

The third control device, *open-market operations*, is by far the most important tool used by the Fed. To understand it we must first realize that an active market for government securities is maintained by dealers in New York City. These government securities are different from the ones that you and I usually see. You may wish to read the definition of government securities starting in the next column. Securities include long-term bonds that pay a fixed amount of interest every six months and can be bought and sold in the government bond market, just as shares of stock are sold in the stock market. Securities also include short-term bills and notes issued by the federal government for periods from three months to two years. United States government bills are short-term obligations of the federal government. They are sold initially at an auction, where the dealers put in a sealed bid indicating the minimum rate of interest they will accept. Those dealers who make the best bids, that is, offer the lowest interest rates, get the government bills and notes.

Definitions of Securities and Government Obligations

A note of explanation is appropriate when we discuss government bonds and borrowing. There are several kinds of bonds and hence it can be confusing. The following definitions should help eliminate this confusion.

A *security* is any written evidence of debt or equity ownership of a corporation or other financial institution.

A *bond* is a written agreement by which one party (which may be a corporation, governmental unit, other body, or person) promises to pay a stated sum of money at some specified future time (known as the maturity date) and to pay interest at a stated rate at specified dates until the maturity date.

A *Treasury bill* is an obligation of the United States government to pay the bearer a fixed sum after a specified number of days from the date of issue. Treasury bills are the shortest-term government securities issued, with maturities of 91, 182, and 365 days in denominations ranging from $10,000 to $1,000,000.

A *Treasury note* is a longer-term interest-bearing obligation of the United States government with a maturity of more than one year but less than five years.

A *Treasury bond* is a long-term interest-bearing obligation of the United States government with a maturity customarily exceeding five years.

A *savings bond* is a special United States bond issued in two series, E and H. Series E bonds are sold at a discount and mature in 5 years. The interest of H bonds is paid semi-annually, and these bonds mature in 10 years. They can be redeemed early but cannot be sold to others, as the bonds described above can.

Government bond dealers maintain a market for government securities. That is, they are constantly buying and selling these securities to banks, individuals, and so on. When the interest rate rises, government securities go down in price, and when the interest rate falls, they go up in price. This inverse relationship between the price of a bond and the actual interest rate the bond pays can be clarified by an example.

Assume I need some money badly and write an IOU note for $1000 that I will pay back in one year. I then visit my "friends" and try to sell them the note. Friend A offers me $800 for it. This means that at the end of the year A will receive $1000; he has earned $200 for lending me $800. Hence the rate of interest I would pay would be $200/$800 × 100 = 25%. Some friend! Friend B offers me $750 for the IOU note. If I borrowed from him, I would be paying a 33⅓% rate of interest ($250/$750 × 100). An even less friendly friend. You see now, however, that the lower the price of the bond, the higher is the interest rate, and vice versa.

COMMENTARY

The following article from the *Wall Street Journal* indicates how the financial community perceives the effect of open-market operations. Please read the article and answer the following questions.

a) How does a Fed purchase of government securities add to the money supply?
b) Explain in your own words how a build-up of funds in the Treasury's account at the Fed reduces funds from the banking system.

FED ADDS OVER $5.5 BILLION TO HOLDINGS OF GOVERNMENT SECURITIES, AGENCY ISSUES

NEW YORK—The Federal Reserve System, the nation's money manager, added more than $5.5 billion to its holdings of U.S. government securities and federal-agency issues in the week ended Wednesday.

The massive acquisitions were designed to add funds to the banking system where technical operating factors were heavily draining reserves. . . .

Purchases by the Fed add funds to the banking network because sellers place proceeds into their commercial bank accounts. The major Fed operation was necessitated by a large buildup in funds in the Treasury's account at the Fed, which in essence takes funds from the banking system. . . .

In another area, figures released by the Fed showed the nation's money supply declined in the week ended April 23 after registering several weeks of growth. . . .

The money supply is the total of private demand deposits plus cash in the public hands. In the statistical quarter ended April 23, the supply grew at a 7.1% annual rate.

Still other figures showed that loan demand remained slack. The Fed said commercial and industrial loans on the books of the 12 leading New York banks rose $56 million in the week ended Wednesday.

Reprinted with permission of *The Wall Street Journal*, © Dow Jones & Company, Inc. (May 2, 1975). All rights reserved.

When the Fed decides that the banks should have more reserves, it orders the manager of the Federal Reserve Open Market Account in New York City to buy some securities from the government dealers. This is easily accomplished by telephone; but then something very remarkable happens. A delivery service will bring the securities to the Federal Reserve Bank of New York City, which, as a representative of the system, will write a check for these securities. But where does the Fed get the money to pay for these securities? The answer is that it creates the money, just as the banks create money when they buy securities.

How, you may ask, did the Fed get this power to create money and therefore reserves? The answer is that power was given to the Fed by the act creating the Federal Reserve System as the central bank of the United States. Whenever the Fed pays for anything—a government security, a unit of foreign currency, or gold—it writes a check on itself, not on any other bank. This creates the money it uses to pay for these additional assets. The persons receiving checks from the Fed are pleased to receive them. When they deposit these checks in their commercial banks, they will have more bank deposits than they had before and nobody else has less. The bankers receiving the checks are also pleased; they now have additional reserves that they can use to make loans and purchase additional securities. It never occurs to the persons receiving and handling the Fed's checks that they represent only the debt of the Federal Reserve System and not a payment out of an existing cash balance.

When the dealers who buy and sell government bonds deposit their checks from sales to the Fed in their own banks, two things happen. The dealers' bank balances are increased and, more importantly, the reserve balances of their banks are also increased. When the dealers use their new balances to pay off their debts for the securities they have bought from sellers all over the country, the newly created bank reserves are shifted to other banks. In this way, the additional reserves created by the Fed's purchase of government securities get distributed all over the nation.

The important part of this transaction is that the Fed can create reserves whenever it chooses to do so. All it has to do is to buy government securities. When it pays for these securities with new money, the commercial banks get additional reserves. The total amount of United States government securities held by private investors, the banks, and the public and foreign owners in early 1977 was about $345 billion. The Fed also has a $97 billion inventory of bonds from which it operates.

When the Fed sells government securities, it destroys reserves.

The reverse is also true. The Fed can take reserves away from the banks by selling securities. To do so the manager of the open market account would offer the dealers, say, $1 billion of government bills. They would quote a price and the sale would be made. When the bills are delivered, the dealers would write checks for this amount to the Fed. Once the Fed has received these checks, it would deduct that amount from the reserves of the dealers' banks. At this point reserves would be destroyed, just as banks destroy money when they sell securities. The dealers, in turn, would sell these securities to purchasers all over the country, so that the decrease in bank reserves would be spread throughout the nation.

Again the important point is that the Fed can reduce the reserves of the banking system whenever it chooses to do so. All it has to do is sell government securities in the government security market in New York City. When it does so, it destroys reserves, just as surely as if it were shredding a large bundle of $1,000 bills.

When we speak of the Fed as creating reserves and therefore enabling the banking system to create money, we should remember that the Fed, like all governmental institutions, is made up of people. Who are the people who comprise the Federal Open Market Committee and make the decisions whether the economy should have more or less money? They are the Chairman and the other six members of the Board of Governors; the president of the New York Federal Reserve Bank; and four presidents of other Federal Reserve Banks, selected by the Board on a rotating basis. These twelve people acting collectively decide how much money people in the United States should hold.

To see how the Fed, acting through the Open Market Committee, can manipulate the reserves of the banking system, we will use hypothetical balance sheets of the Fed and the member banks (see Table 13.3).

A balance sheet is a simple listing of what an individual or an institution "owns" and "owes." What it "owns"—its assets—are listed on the left side of the balance sheet. What it "owes"—its liabilities and claims against it by owners and others—are on the right side. A balance sheet always "balances" because every item listed among the assets is owned by somebody and therefore shows up in the form of some liability.

The first asset listed in the balance sheet of the Federal Reserve System is $10 billion in *gold certificate reserves*. The Fed may not own gold, but the Treasury is allowed to issue gold certificates for gold held by the government. The Fed credits the account of the Treasury (United States government) in exchange for gold certificates.

United States *government securities* consist of treasury bills, notes, and certificates. Purchases of government securities are the principal means by which the Fed can create reserve bank credit.

Discounts for member banks represent the amount of Fed credit that member banks obtain at their own initiative through borrowing from the Fed.

TABLE 13.3
BALANCE SHEET OF THE
FEDERAL RESERVE SYSTEM
JAN. 1, 1978 (All figures represent billions of dollars)

Assets (owned, in billions)		Liabilities (owed, in billions)	
Gold certificates	$10	Deposits of member banks	$30
Government securities	12	Federal Reserve notes	95
Discounts of member banks	15	U.S. Treasury deposits	10
Other assets	5	Other liabilities	15
Total assets	$150	Total liabilities	$150

CONSOLIDATED BALANCE SHEET OF THE
MEMBER BANKS OF THE FEDERAL RESERVE SYSTEM
JAN. 1, 1978 (All figures represent billions of dollars)

Assets (owned, in billions)		Liabilities (owed, in billions)	
Deposits in Fed	$30	Demand deposits	$250
Vault cash	100	Time deposits	400
Government securities	70	Other liabilities	50
Loans	500	Total liabilities	$700
Total assets	$700		

Looking now at the liabilities, *deposits of member banks* consist of the reserve accounts of member banks. They, along with their vault cash, constitute the operating base of the banking system.

Federal Reserve notes, the principal type of currency in circulation, are the IOU notes of the Fed, which move in and out of circulation in response to public demand. Federal Reserve notes are paid out to member banks on request, and the amount of notes paid is charged to the member bank's reserve account.

United States Treasury deposits represent the checking accounts of the government. The Fed is the United States government's bank.

The consolidated balance sheet of the member banks of the Federal Reserve System contains many items included in the Fed's balance sheet—but on the opposite side of the ledger. Member banks keep deposits or reserve accounts in the Federal Reserve bank of its district. This asset, along with cash (mainly Federal Reserve notes), comprises the reserves of member banks. Government securities comprise an important income-earning asset of member banks. They are easily bought and sold and therefore easily convertible into reserves or cash. The largest asset item is the amount of loans a bank makes. These IOUs are the major source of the bank's income.

On the other side of the ledger, deposits make up the vast majority of the member bank's liabilities.

You will see when you examine these two balance sheets (the figures are hypothetical to make them easier to read) that the member banks and the twelve Federal Reserve banks make up a "closed system." The "deposits of the member banks," shown as a liability item on the Fed's balance sheet, is the asset item "deposits in the Federal Reserve" on the member bank balance sheet. View it this way. You lend your brother $100. Your brother will show this $100 on his personal balance sheet as a liability, something he owes, and you will show it on your balance sheet as an asset. If the two of you make up a closed system, what is an asset to you is a liability to him.

When the Fed buys $1 billion of government securities, say from several insurance companies through bond dealers, it adds $1 billion to its earning assets. The Fed, we will assume, will pay for these securities by writing a check to the insurance companies. When these companies deposit the checks in their banks, they will add to the bank deposits of the member banks. When the member banks deposit these checks in their Federal Reserve banks, they will add $1 billion to their deposits (reserves) in the Federal Reserve and the Fed will recognize this by adding $1 billion to the deposits of member banks. The balance sheet changes are shown in Table 13.4. When all the transactions are completed, both balance sheets will be in balance. The Fed, then, by the purchase of government securities, will have added $1 billion to the reserves of the member banks. Since only $150 million (15 percent of the additional deposits) will be required to "back" the additional deposits (assuming a 15 percent required reserve ratio), the member banks will now have $850 million of excess reserves—all acquired as a result of a simple purchase by the Fed of an additional $1 billion of government securities, and with money the Fed did not have when it started the process.

The Fed can create and destroy high-powered money: the multiplier effect.

The creation and destruction of reserves is particularly important because of the *multiplier effect*

TABLE 13.4
BALANCE SHEETS OF
Federal Reserve banks

Government securities + $1 billion	Deposits of member banks + $1 billion

Member banks

Deposits (reserves) + $1 billion	Deposits of insurance companies + $1 billion

it has on the commercial banking system's ability to create money. You will recall that banks are required to hold only a fraction of their deposits in reserves. Thus, when bank 1 gets an additional $1000 of deposits and reserves, it can lend an additional $850. Why? If reserve requirements are 15 percent, bank 1 has to keep only $150 to support the additional $1000 of deposits. If it then lends the $850 to a borrower, who in turn writes a check to a depositor in another bank, bank 2 will get an additional $850 of deposits *and reserves*. Bank 2 will, in turn, earmark $127.50 as required services, leaving it $722.50 to lend to somebody who would write a check to a depositor in bank 3. This chain reaction could go on until the increase in deposits is several times larger than the original increase in reserves. Thus reserves are called high-powered money.

The multiple relating the initial increases in bank reserves to the ultimate increase in the money holdings of the public varies depending on whether the public chooses to hold currency or bank deposits. When the public chooses to hold currency, the multiple is one. A $1 increase in reserves leads to a $1 increase in the money supply. When the public chooses to hold bank deposits, the multiple is the reciprocal of the required reserve ratio. Thus when the reserve requirement is 15 percent, the multiple would be $1 \div .15$, or $6\frac{2}{3}$. In recent years, because of the public's desire to hold enormous amounts of currency, the multiple has been between two and three.

The important point is a simple one. When the Fed adds $1 of this high-powered money to existing reserves, it enables the commercial banking system to create new money by some multiple of this increase in reserves. This multiplier effect also works in reverse. When the Fed destroys reserves, the banking system must in turn destroy several dollars of bank deposits. Open-market operations, then, may be said to create or destroy high-powered money.

Open-market operations also enable the banks to pay out unlimited amounts of currency without losing reserves.

Open-market operations are also important because they enable the banking system to take care of any of the currency needs of the public. Suppose that the public does not trust the commercial banks and as a result it asks the banks to convert its bank deposits into currency. Wouldn't this bring the banking system to its knees? The answer is no. It is true that banks might be forced to convert their reserve deposits in the Fed into Federal Reserve notes and that this could leave them short of reserves. But the Fed could easily buy government securities to replace the reserves that the banks would lose as a result of the currency drain, leaving the banks with the same capacity to create money that they had before the public converted its bank deposits into currency.

Consider the following fairy tale to illustrate the flexibility of the Federal Reserve System. Sup-

---

TABLE 13.5
THE WITHDRAWAL OF $10 BILLION
Federal Reserve System

(2) Government securities + $10 billion	(1) Deposits of member banks − $10 billion
	(2) Deposits of member banks + $10 billion
	(1) Federal Reserve notes outstanding + $10 billion

Member banks

(1) Deposits (reserves) in Fed − $10 billion	(1) Bank deposits − $10 billion
(2) Deposits (reserves) in Fed + $10 billion	
(2) Government securities − $10 billion	

pose you were the wealthiest person in the world and that you decided to attempt to "break" the banking system of the United States by demanding that your $10 billion of deposits be converted into cash. There might be a little delay in the response of your bank to the unusual demand you've made since banks don't usually keep a large percentage of their deposits in cash. But your withdrawal would not even cause a ripple if the Fed cooperated. To see why, examine the abbreviated balance sheets in Table 13.5.

This massive withdrawal would lead to a temporary reduction in member banks' deposits in the Fed (step 1). The member banks might initially have to use their reserve deposits to acquire Federal Reserve notes from the Fed in order to respond to your currency demands. But this would be a temporary flurry. The Fed could easily replace these reserve losses by buying government securities, as is indicated in the balance

sheet transactions (step 2). Indeed, the Fed could even increase excess reserves to counter such a currency drain. The important point is that the Fed is in complete control, and no withdrawal of funds by an irate depositor need bring the banking system to its knees.

We can now answer the question: Who is in charge here? The answer is that the Federal Reserve System, consisting of the 12 Federal Reserve banks and the board of governors in Washington, D.C., is in charge. It can induce the commercial banks to create money, or it can keep the banks from creating money by using its money supply controls. The responsibility for regulating the money supply of the nation, then, belongs to the Federal Reserve.

Mini-case 13.2 is included here in order to help you clarify how the Fed influences the money supply through changing the commercial banking system's lending capacity.

MINI-CASE 13.2

Suppose that the Fed wants to restrict the commercial banking system's capacity to make loans and buy securities. Which of the following sets of changes would most effectively accomplish this?

a) Lower reserve requirements, raise the discount rate, and purchase government securities in the open market.
b) Raise reserve requirements, lower the discount rate, and sell government securities.
c) Raise reserve requirements, raise the discount rate, and purchase government securities.
d) Raise reserve requirements, raise the discount rate, and sell government securities.

HOW THE BANKING SYSTEM FITS INTO THE ECONOMY

At the microeconomic level, bankers allocate loanable funds.

It should now be clear that it is the Federal Reserve System and the nation's banks rather than the government that provides money in our economy. But what difference does it make?

Consider the role of bankers in the economy. At the microeconomic level, your local banker is constantly seeing people who want to borrow money for different projects. The banker's job is to decide who among the prospective borrowers is most likely to pay the going rate of interest and repay the loan when it is due. The banker will be

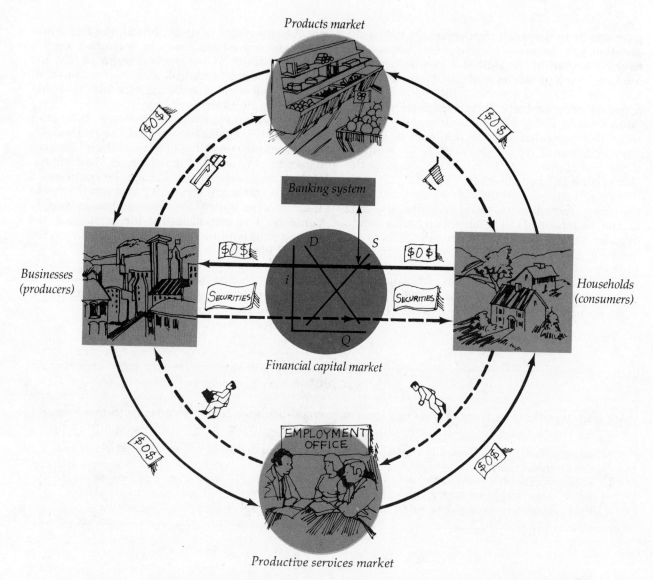

Products market

Banking system

Businesses (producers)

Households (consumers)

D S

i

Q

SECURITIES

SECURITIES

Financial capital market

EMPLOYMENT OFFICE

Productive services market

FIG. 13.2   The circular-flow model incorporating the banking system in the financial capital market.

concerned with questions such as these: Do the borrowers have enough money of their own so that they have a real stake in the outcome of the project and will not be tempted to throw in the sponge when the going gets rough? Do the borrowers have a good track record on previous projects? Are the borrowers morally responsible?

Have they paid off loans in the past?

The banks with officers most successful in distinguishing the reliable borrowers from the bad ones will show the greatest profit, other things being equal. Bankers, then, in their day-to-day decision-making activities determine who will get the nation's credit and what projects will be financed! In a sense, the bankers perform a personnel function. They sort out would-be borrowers and say, these people should get credit and these should not.

At the macroeconomic level, the Fed determines the supply of money.

At the macroeconomic level, the banking system, largely guided by the Federal Reserve, adds to or subtracts from the supply of loanable funds in the capital market. Figure 13.2 shows the circular-flow model of the economy. The supply and demand curves in the financial capital market reflect how the supply of and demand for loanable funds in this market determine the interest rate.

When the banking system (which we have represented as a box above the capital market) increases the money supply, it shifts the supply curve for loanable funds out and to the right. As a result, it decreases the interest rate—at least in the short run. The reverse is also true.

It is this close connection between the interest rate and the supplying of additional money to the economy that presents the Fed with some difficult choices. It can regulate the supply of money in the economy, but when it does this, it must take into account the growth in the economy and determine how much more money is required to keep the economy running smoothly. It can also regulate the interest rate by injecting or withdrawing funds from the capital market, and therefore affect the supply of loanable funds. When it chooses an interest rate target—say a 6 percent rate on short-term government bills—it can easily supply too much or too little money for the economy.

Two potential goals of Fed policy are money supply targets and interest rate stabilization.

These two goals—supply the appropriate amount of money to the economy and maintain the aggregate interest rate—require different money-growth strategies. Therefore, the Fed must decide which of these two goals is most important.

What makes this choice particularly difficult is that the interest rate is a widely publicized price. Borrowers (and the federal government is the largest borrower at the present time) don't like high interest rates. They continually put pressure on the Fed to keep interest rates down, and when the Fed responds to these pressures, it can easily print too much money.

Because of the way Western industrial societies have evolved, the money-creating function has always been linked to private and governmental borrowing. Suppose that it were not this way. Suppose that the Fed could create money only through the financing of educational structures—school buildings, college buildings, and so on. Suppose further that banks were required to keep 100 percent reserves: The only money they could lend would be the money their stockholders had given them. How would the economy work under these conditions, fanciful though they might be?

The answer is that banks would be largely service institutions. They would provide the check system—for a fee, of course. Their lending would be limited to the amounts provided by their stockholders. The amount of money provided by the new Fed would be determined by the amount used to finance new educational structures. The members of the new Board of Governors would still face some difficult choices. How far should the new Fed go in building an elaborate network of educational buildings? There would no doubt be pressure from teachers and parents to build beautiful new structures for learning. But the new Fed would also have to decide how much money it should create through the financing of educational buildings. If it went too far in constructing buildings, it would create too much money. If it didn't go far enough, people would complain that there was not enough money to "grease the wheels of industry."

The important point of this story is that whatever money-creating institution is used—and every society must have social institutions for determining the amount of money people shall have—there will be problems involving the immediate and long-run effects of inserting new money into the economy. The present Fed's interest-rate versus money-growth dilemma is just one aspect of a larger problem.

We turn now to the question: Is money important in determining the three variables: the rates of growth, unemployment, and inflation?

REVIEW QUESTIONS

1. The money supply (M_2) is defined as:

    a) currency in circulation outside of banks plus deposits in commercial banks.
    b) savings accounts, checking accounts, and currency in circulation outside of banks.
    c) currency in circulation outside of commercial banks plus demand deposits.
    d) the sum of coins, federal reserve notes, and checkbook money existing in the economy.

2. When a person cashes a check drawn on her own account, the money supply:

    a) increases.
    b) decreases.
    c) remains the same.
    d) increases because of interest rates.

3. Indicate which of the following transactions would increase the stock of money held by the public. Do not consider secondary effects.

    a) One commercial bank buys a government bond from another commercial bank.
    b) A commercial bank buys a government bond from a student.
    c) A commercial bank sells a government bond to the Federal Reserve.
    d) A commercial bank buys a bond from the Federal Reserve.

4. At the present time,

    a) the money supply is limited by the gold holdings of the nation.
    b) the money supply is limited by Congress.
    c) the money supply can be expanded without limit, if the Fed chooses to supply the reserves.
    d) the money supply is insensitive to the demands for money by the public.

5. * Suppose several persons in your community decide to open a bank to serve the community by offering checking accounts and savings accounts. As a result of establishing this bank, which of the following statements is *false*?

    a) The debts of the bank would be considered money whereas the debts of people in the community would not be money.
    b) The currency held by the bank would not be considered money whereas the currency held by members of the community would be considered money.
    c) When the bank made loans to members of the community, new money would be created, but when private individuals made loans, no new money would be created.
    d) The debt of large corporations are bought and sold on the New York bond market; hence they are generally acceptable and are considered money.

6. Consider now the role of the Federal Reserve System (assuming the newly established bank is a member). What could the Fed do that the commercial bank could not do?

    a) Cash checks for private citizens.
    b) Create additional reserves in the banking system by buying bonds from other commercial banks.
    c) Buy government bonds.
    d) Make loans to the rest of the community.

* Questions 5 through 7 comprise a series of interdependent questions.

7. Suppose that the new bank finds itself with $10,000 of excess reserves and lends that $10,000. If the reserve requirement was 20 percent and if the person who borrowed the $10,000 wrote a check to a depositor in another bank, and this bank in turn used these new reserves to make loans, what would be the size of the money supply increase caused by these two transactions?
   a) $10,000.
   b) $15,000.
   c) $18,000.
   d) $20,000.

8. When the Fed sells securities, other things being equal, either to the banks or to the public, this action tends, in the first instance, to:
   a) increase the interest rate, because it reduces the supply of loanable funds in the capital market.
   b) have no effect on the interest rate, since it does not affect the flow of savings into the capital market.
   c) decrease the interest rate, since some of the government debt is taken off the market.
   d) It is impossible to tell what effect this policy would have on the rate of interest, even in the short run.

ESSAY QUESTIONS

1. Make a list of your total assets. Now list your "money" holdings. What is the difference between those assets you classify as money and those you do not classify as money? Is there a clear line between "money" and "near-monies"?

2. Using your list of total assets, determine your holdings of M_1, M_2, and M_3.

3. Imagine a society in which every person carries a universal credit card. Whenever a person is paid, that person's balance in a bank is increased. Whenever a person pays for something, his or her balance in a bank is reduced. How would you define money in this type of society? Now suppose that everybody would automatically have a credit line with their bank that was equal to one half of a year's pay as determined by last year's income tax return. Define the money supply for this type of economy.

4. Think carefully about the monetary system of the United States and in your own words indicate what is "back of money."

5. When you exchange debts with your bank, what is it that makes the bank's debt money? Why wouldn't your debt be money? What is the difference between these two types of debt?

6. Indicate the effect of the following transactions on the total amount of money held by the public.
   a) John Doe increases his holding of currency by writing a cash check on his account in the bank.
   b) John Doe borrows money from the bank to go on his honeymoon.
   c) Sally Doe, his new wife, cashes a savings bond and pays off the loan that John had obtained from the bank.
   d) Mr. and Mrs. Doe deposit currency they have had under the mattress in a new savings account that they have opened to finance a down payment on a home.
   e) Mr. and Mrs. Doe, who are now doing very well, buy some government bonds that their bank had held as a short-term investment. They pay for their new bonds by writing a check to the bank.

f) John Doe dies and Sally gets $250,000 from an insurance company.

g) Sally Doe, in difficult straits after the death of her husband, sells the government bonds they had owned to her bank.

7. What determines the total amount of reserves that all the banks, taken collectively, have? What determines how these reserves are distributed between banks?

8. When the Fed buys a government security from a dealer, where does the Fed get the high-powered money it uses to pay for this security? What is unique about the Fed as a supplier of reserves?

9. Suppose that you and millions of other people in the United States decide to hold more currency. You ask your bank to convert your bank deposits into currency. Your bank in turn uses its reserves to acquire Federal Reserve notes from the Fed. Won't this necessarily mean that the banking system, will run short of reserves and therefore have to call in loans and sell securities? Wouldn't this mean that you and millions of other depositors can really control the banking system's ability to create money?

10. What do bankers do? Are they merely creators of money? Are they merely suppliers of an elaborate system for clearing checks and facilitating payments between people? Couldn't an elaborate computer be programmed to do everything bankers do?

11. Suppose that the banking system, including the Fed, increases the supply of loanable funds so that those who build capital goods can command more resources than are being released by savers. What effect will this have on the total demand for resources? If there are not unemployed resources when the banking system does this, what will be the effect on the price level?

12. Assume that the banking system, including the Fed, in pursuing a "tight money policy" absorbs some of the loanable funds flowing into the financial capital market. As a result, savers release more resources than those who would buy capital goods will command. What will happen to the aggregate demand for products? If prices were flexible, what would happen? If prices were sticky and did not fall, what would happen?

ANSWERS TO REVIEW QUESTIONS

1. The M_2 money supply definition includes all currency in circulation outside of banks plus the demand and savings deposits of commercial banks. It excludes savings accounts in savings and loan associations, and so on.

   a) This is correct as defined above.
   b) This is incorrect. It includes savings accounts in noncommercial banks.
   c) This is incorrect. It excludes savings accounts in commercial banks.
   d) This is incorrect. It excludes savings accounts in commercial banks and includes currency held by banks.

2. When a person cashes a check drawn on her own account, she exchanges one asset—a claim on her bank—for another asset—a claim on the Federal Reserve bank. Both are included in the definition of the money supply, so there has been no change in the quantity of money—only a change in its composition.

   a) This is incorrect as explained above.   c) This is correct as explained above.
   b) This is incorrect as explained above.   d) This is incorrect. The answer is irrelevant.

3. The stock of money held by the public changes in only certain cases. Consider each of the choices.

   a) If one commercial bank buys a bond from another, the reserves of the purchasing bank will decrease and the reserves of the selling bank will increase. For the banking system there will be no change in reserves and there is no change in the money supply.
   b) This is the correct choice. When a commercial bank buys a bond from a student, the student gives up a nonmonetary asset, the bond, for either cash (Federal Reserve notes) or a check written on that bank. In either case the money supply has increased.
   c) When a commercial bank sells a bond to the Fed, the commercial bank's reserves increase and hence its lending capacity; but until it makes a loan, there is no change in the money supply.
   d) When a commercial bank buys a bond from the Fed, the commercial bank's reserves decrease, and therefore its lending capacity decreases. But at this stage there is no change in the actual money supply.

4. Today, the money supply is not constrained by any artificial or legal limit. The Board of Governors of the Federal Reserve System determines the amount of money in the system.

   a) This is incorrect. There is no relationship between the amount of money and gold.
   b) This is incorrect. Congress established the Fed and only if the Fed were changed by legislation could this be the case.
   c) This is correct as explained above.
   d) This is incorrect. The Fed reacts to the demands of people for money.

5. Money is anything that is generally acceptable. Usually, the debts of a bank are accepted in a community and hence are money whereas your IOU notes and my IOU notes do not enjoy acceptability.

   a) This is *not* the correct answer. The statement is indeed true as explained above.
   b) This is *not* the correct answer. By definition the money supply excludes currency held by commercial banks.
   c) This is *not* the correct answer. The debt of banks is money; the debt of an individual is not money.
   d) This is the correct answer. It is false that corporation debt is generally acceptable. It may be negotiable, but that doesn't make it money.

6. The Fed is a banker's bank and does not transact generally with individuals.

   a) This is incorrect. The Fed will not cash checks for private citizens while banks do.
   b) This is correct. When the Fed buys bonds it creates reserves. When one bank buys bonds from another, reserves are merely transferred.
   c) This is incorrect. Both commercial banks and the Fed can buy bonds.
   d) This is incorrect. The Fed does not make loans to the community. Commercial banks do. The Fed does, however, make loans to commercial banks.

7. If the new bank has excess reserves of $10,000, it can lend $10,000 and thereby increase the money supply by that amount. If it does so, and the borrower spends it and the recipient deposits it in his or her bank, then the recipient's bank now has $10,000 of new reserves, 20 percent of which ($2,000) is required and the rest ($8,000) is excess. Hence, in total, $18,000 could be created up to this step. Therefore, the correct answer is (c).

8. When the Fed sells securities, the supply of securities increases and the price will fall, other things being equal. When the price of a bond falls, the interest rate rises.

   a) This is correct as explained above.
   b) This is incorrect. The interest rate will rise as explained above.
   c) This is incorrect. The interest rate rises, not falls. It would fall if the Fed bought securities.
   d) This is incorrect. We know, as explained above, that the interest rate will rise.

OBJECTIVES

Upon successful completion of this chapter, you will be able to:

1. Explain the Keynesian interpretation of the role of money in the economy.

2. Explain the monetarist interpretation of the role of money in the economy.

3. List the components of the equation of exchange and demonstrate the relationship among them.

4. Compare the Keynesian and monetarist approaches.

5. Discuss the prospects for reconciliation of the differences between Keynesians and monetarists.

CHAPTER 14

THE KEYNESIAN AND MONETARIST APPROACHES TO MONETARY POLICY

INTRODUCTION

THE SUPPLY OF MONEY, INTEREST RATES, AND AGGREGATE DEMAND: THE KEYNESIAN EXPLANATION

THE SUPPLY OF MONEY, INTEREST RATES, AND AGGREGATE DEMAND: THE MONETARIST EXPLANATION

THE MONETARIST AND KEYNESIAN APPROACHES COMPARED

CAN MONETARIST AND KEYNESIAN POLICY PRESCRIPTIONS BE RECONCILED?

INTRODUCTION

Would it make any difference in your spending decisions whether you had $1,000, $10,000, or $100,000 in your checking account? The actions of the Federal Reserve Board, you remember from the last chapter, influence how much money you and everybody else in the economy hold. In this chapter, we will be concerned with the question of how the amount of money created by the Fed and the banking system affects the way the economy operates. Does the amount of M_2 held by people determine only the price level, as the classical economists of the nineteenth century argued, or do increases in M_2 grease the wheels of industry and facilitate economic growth, as many contemporary economists argue?

We should point out at the outset that there are few topics so controversial among economists as monetary theory. Keynesian economists believe that money plays a minor but supporting role in determining the aggregate demand for products. The monetarists believe that money plays the dominant role in determining the aggregate demand for products. We will not try to resolve the differences between these two schools of thought in this chapter. We do want you to understand the position each group takes, with the hope that you will be able to follow the debates that will occur in the forum of public policy about what the Fed's role in the economy should be.

THE SUPPLY OF MONEY, INTEREST RATES, AND AGGREGATE DEMAND: THE KEYNESIAN EXPLANATION

The money supply affects the economy through investment decisions.

As we pointed out in chapter 12, Keynesian economics came into being during the Great Depression of the 1930s, when falling prices, slow economic growth, and unemployment were the major problems. Keynesian economics gained wide acceptance during the 1950s and 1960s, when prices were relatively stable—at least until the increased government expenditure accompanying the Vietnam War affected the economy during the late 1960s. Now most economists, monetarists excepted, accept the Keynesian explanation of the link between money and the aggregate demand for products.

The aggregate demand for products consists of the demand by consumers, producers, government at all levels, and net foreign spending. You will recall from Chapter 11 that these are the four components of the expenditure approach to measuring the economy. Consumer spending is regarded by Keynesians to be positively related to the level of income. Keynesians also believe, however, that the amount of money held by consumers has little, if any, effect on consumer spending. Finally they believe that state and local government spending, as well as federal government spending, are independent of the amount of money held by these entities. This leaves only gross private domestic investment and net exports to be influenced by the stock of money.

Gross private domestic investment has comprised only about 15 percent of total GNP in recent years, while *net* exports comprise less than half of 1 percent of total GNP. The sizes of the components of aggregate demand expenditures are shown in Fig. 14.1 for the post-World War II years. Since net exports make up so insignificant a share of total expenditure, we will concentrate our attention on the relation between gross private domestic investment and the growth in the money supply. We will use the supply and demand for loanable funds model, developed in Chapter 6, to explain the relationship between money and investment.

In Fig. 14.2, the supply curve shows the amount of loanable funds available in the capital

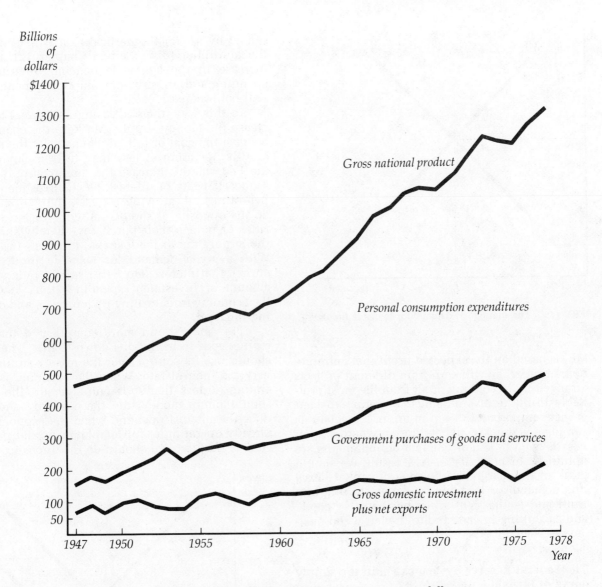

FIG. 14.1   Components of aggregate demand (GNP), 1947–1977, in 1972 dollars.

market at each interest rate as a result of private savings decisions. The demand curve, labeled ME, shows the amount of loanable funds businesses are willing and able to borrow at each interest rate for investment expenditures. We shall use the term investment to refer to those expenditures, such as plant and equipment expenditures, new housing, and so on included in gross private domestic investment. The intersec-

tion of the supply and demand for loanable funds determines the equilibrium price, in this case the equilibrium rate of interest.

The demand curve labeled ME requires comment. In the Keynesian system this curve is called the *marginal efficiency of capital*. This is another name for the marginal productivity of capital we first encountered in Chapter 6, with one modification. The marginal efficiency of capital curve,

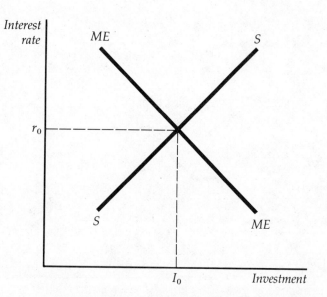

FIG. 14.2   The supply and demand for loanable funds.

ME, is based on the *expected profit* that entrepreneurs think they will earn from different projects arranged in descending order from the most profitable to the least profitable. The term *expected profit* is important to keep in mind. Expectations can change quickly, depending on whether business is good or bad or whether entrepreneurs are optimistic or pessimistic. As a result, we should think of the marginal efficiency of capital curve (the demand for loanable funds) as shifting outward and to the right when business is "good" and as shifting inward and to the left when business is "bad."

The Federal Reserve System can shift the supply curve of loanable funds.

With this simple model in mind, we can easily see how the Federal Reserve can change the amount of investment spending. When the Fed buys government securities, it increases the supply of loanable funds. It shifts the supply curve for loanable funds outward and to the right, as is shown by S_1S_1 in Fig. 14.3. This increase in supply reduces the interest rate and leads, given the marginal efficiency of capital curve, to an increase in the quantity of investment spending. The increased quantity of investment spending repre-

sented by I_0I_1 on the vertical axis will lead, via the multiplier (discussed in Chapter 12), to an increase in the aggregate demand. Investment spending and, in turn, consumption expenditure will both increase.

In this way, the Fed, using its powers to increase the money supply, can help the economy achieve the goal of full employment. If the economy is operating at less than full employment, the Fed should increase the money supply and reduce the rate of interest. Or, if investment expenditures are growing too fast, the Fed should do the opposite. It should sell government securities or reduce their purchases, thereby shifting the supply curve for loanable funds to the left. With a given demand for loanable funds (ME curve), the interest rate will rise and reduce the amount of investment spending—thus keeping the economy from heating up too much and causing inflation.

This may sound more complicated than it really needs to be. It boils down to this: The Fed should use its control over the money supply to vary the interest rate. When the economy is operating at less than full employment, the Fed should pump money into the economy and reduce the interest rate. and when the economy is already operating at full employment and prices start to rise, the Fed should do the opposite.

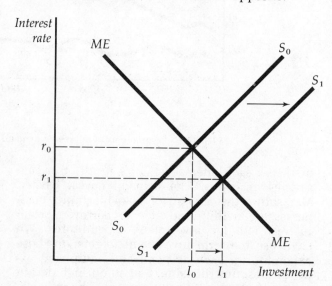

FIG. 14.3   A shift in the supply of loanable funds.

You may ask: "If the Fed has this much control over the economy, why should fiscal policies—government deficits and surpluses—play such an important role in the Keynesian system of thought? Why not rely on the Fed to manage the economy entirely?" The answer to these questions is to be found in the sensitivity of the marginal efficiency of capital schedule to changes in business conditions. When business is good and producers are optimistic, the marginal efficiency of capital curve shifts out and to the right. To keep investment spending from increasing too much (and therefore causing inflation), the Fed would have remained neutral and let interest rates rise to very high levels—never a very popular thing to do.

When the economy slows down, the marginal efficiency of capital schedule may shift so far to the left that the interest rate would fall to very low levels. In Fig. 14.4, the interest rate falls from r_0 to r_1 when the marginal efficiency of capital schedule shifts from ME_0 to ME_1. It is clear that putting more money into the economy in this situation, shifting the SS curve to the right, would not restore investment spending to a reasonable level. It would just drive the interest rate down toward zero.

Because the marginal efficiency schedules are so unstable (based as they are on profit expectations), monetary policies have been assigned a secondary role in the Keynesian system. The Fed should do what it can, but it is unrealistic to expect the Fed to play the major role in managing the aggregate demand for products. Fiscal policies should be used to manage the economy and

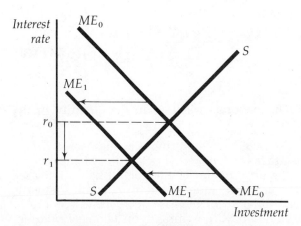

FIG. 14.4   Shift of the marginal efficiency of capital curve.

monetary policies should have a minor but supporting role.

To summarize: The Fed should be concerned with the appropriate interest rate. When investment spending is too low, the Fed should increase the amount of money held by the public; when investment spending is too high, it should do the opposite. In accomplishing these objectives, the Fed need not be concerned with rates of growth of the money supply, except as these rates accomplish their interest rate objectives. Money, taken by itself, will never cause inflation. It is only when increases in the supply of money cause investment spending to be too high that the Fed has to be concerned with the inflationary effects of its policies.

We turn now to the almost opposite arguments advanced by the monetarist school of economists to guide Fed policies.

MINI-CASE 14.1

The unemployment rate is 7 percent and rising while the rate of inflation has been stuck at 7 percent for a year. As a Keynesian economist, what monetary policy should you recommend?

a) Unemployment has far more serious effects on human lives than inflation. Therefore I recommend that we encourage the monetary authorities to reduce the interest rate.

b) Since the rate of inflation has been constant and unemployment is rising, we must reduce interest rates and increase government spending without increases taxes.

c) We must lower the interest rate to encourage investment spending, but reduce the government spending to ensure that inflation will not increase.

d) The effect of the interest rate is inconsequential, so we must reduce unemployment by increasing aggregate demand. We must therefore reduce taxes.

THE SUPPLY OF MONEY, INTEREST RATES, AND AGGREGATE DEMAND: THE MONETARIST EXPLANATION

Early economists believe in the quantity theory of money.

Most economists during the eighteenth, nineteenth, and early part of this century believed that if the government or the central bank increased the quantity of money held by the public, it would lead only to an increase in the level of prices. John Stuart Mill, writing in his famous *Principles of Political Economy* (1848), stated:

> *There cannot, in short, be intrinsically a more insignificant thing in the economy of a society than money; except in the character of a contrivance for sparing time and labour. It is a machine for doing quickly and commodiously what would be done though less quickly and commodiously, without it; and like many other kinds of machinery, it only exerts a distinct and independent influence of its own when it gets out of order. (Mill, J. S.; Principles, 1848. Book III, Ch. 7)*

This belief in the *quantity theory*—as this relationship between money and prices is called—led them to ignore the relationship between money and economic growth.

There were some economists, including Richard Cantillion (1680–1734), David Hume (1711–1776), Henry Thornton (1760–1815), Stanley Jevons (1835–1882), Knut Wicksell (1851–1926), and Irving Fisher (1867–1947), who believed that, in the short run, increases in the quantity of money held by the public could, under certain conditions, lead to increases in total output, and that monetary policies could be used to stabilize the economy. To explain these relationships, they, along with some classical economists, developed the *Equation of Exchange*. The Equation of Exchange, like the $Y = C + I$ equation in the Keynesian system, is a model that can be used to analyze the overall economy. To understand monetarism, it is important to understand what the Equation of Exchange represents and to be able to use the quantity theory to analyze the economy.

The Equation of Exchange is a useful truism.

The equation $MV = PQ$ tells us that M, the total supply of money in an economy, multiplied by its income velocity, V, or the average number of times each year a representative unit of money is spent on *final* products, will be equal to the sum total of all the sales invoices, listing the quantities of final products, Q, sold multiplied by their prices, P. Now this is not a very surprising statement. It merely says that total spending on final products will be equal to the total receipts from the sale of final products.

What is useful about this equation is that it provides a way to organize a discussion of the factors determining the level of output and prices. Before we discuss what underlies each of these symbols, let us make sure that we understand the equation.

MV refers to the flow of money payments represented in the circular-flow model we developed in Chapter 1 of this book. For example, if the stock of money totaled $500 billion in 1979 and on average each dollar is used four times during that year to purchase some kind of final output, the value of the flow of money payments or expenditures will be $2000 billion in 1979. The letter Q represents the real GNP, the number of physical units, flowing in the opposite direction. Assume, for example, that Q is 1 billion units. Then the average price of the 1 billion units would be $2000. Now, if the flow of money payments, MV, rises relative to the flow of final products, Q, then the average level of prices P will rise. For example, if M increased to $600 billion, and V were 4, then the average price P would be $2400. Or, if V increased from 4 to 6, then P would rise from $2000 to $3000. The reverse would also be true.

Using simple algebra, we can manipulate these variables to show the relationships among M, V, P, and Q represented in this identity, $MV = PQ$. Suppose the real GNP (Q) increases and the opposite flow of money payments (MV) does not. Common sense tells us that prices would tend to fall. The Equation of Exchange restated as follows demonstrates this:

$$\frac{MV}{Q} = P.$$

If the denominator, Q, rises and the numerator, MV, does not, then the price level, P, will fall. Or, if the prices are sticky and do not change when there is a reduction in MV, then Q, or the real GNP, will fall, as it does during recessions. This can be most easily seen by restating the Equation of Exchange as follows:

$$\frac{MV}{P} = Q.$$

You may want to continue manipulating this simple equation to see what other propositions you can derive. But, as noted above, the useful aspect of this equation is that it tells us how to organize our search for the factors linking the supply of money to the price level. Consider what determines the value of each of these symbols, beginning with M and concluding with V.

The supply of M depends on the banking system.

In the last chapter we discussed the factors determining the supply of money, M. We saw that commercial banks, operating within the limits established by the Federal Reserve System, determine how much money the economy will have at any time.

The price level as a component of the Equation of Exchange.

Suppose we gave you two Sears, Roebuck catalogs, one for the year 1960 and the second for the year 1979, and asked you to put a dot on the 1960 graph in Fig. 14.5 for each price you observed in the catalog. Some of the prices, such as those for appliances, will appear to be high and some of the prices, such as those for clothes, will seem low. To avoid having all of the dots on top of each other, we spread them along the horizontal scale according to the page in the catalog. The dots from the 1960 catalog would look like the graph on the left in Fig. 14.5.

Now suppose we asked you to put dots on a second and adjoining graph for the 1979 Sears, Roebuck catalog.

The cluster of prices taken from the 1979 catalog is clearly higher than the cluster of prices from the 1960 catalog. Up to now in our study of economics we have been concerned with individ-

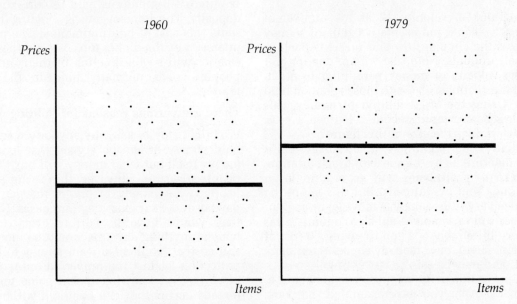

FIG. 14.5   Sears, Roebuck catalog prices.

ual prices and the relationship among them, for example, why the prices of appliances are relatively high and the prices of clothes are relatively low. We shall call each year's concentration *the price level,* and we will be concerned with why the concentration of dots from one year's catalog are higher than the dots from another year's catalog.

The real factors underlying Q are the size of the labor force and its productivity.

In Chapter 11, in which we discussed the factors underlying the aggregate supply of products, Q, we saw that factors such as those underlying the size of the labor force, the average weekly hours of work, and so on, all combine to determine the total input of labor hours. We also saw that factors such as the size of the capital stock, the quality of the labor, the level of technological development, and the size of the market all combine to determine the average productivity of labor. The two sets of factors governing input of labor hours and its productivity jointly determine the real GNP and its rate of growth.

Velocity, V, is determined by the demand for money.

We can think of velocity, V, as the number of times each year a representative unit of money completes the circular flow and presents itself to buy final products. Note that we are dealing not with the velocity of money pertaining to all financial transactions, just with those spent on final output. Using the M_2 definition of money, this figure has been running about 2.4 times a year. What determines the size of this figure?

Initially, you might be tempted to say that it will be determined by the speed of transportation. Money sent by airplanes will go around faster than money sent by railroads. But this is not the case since very little money is moving, or as Dennis Robertson, a famous English economist, has said, very little money is "on the wing." Most of it is being held in somebody's pocket or bank deposit, and may be said to be "sitting."

To prove this point, suppose you are about to buy a book. After you have examined the book, you approach the sales clerk with money in hand. As long as the money is in your possession it may be said to be "sitting." Only in the fraction of a second when the money is being transferred from your hand to the hand of the sales clerk can we say that the money is "on the wing."

It follows, then, that if we want to explain how fast money moves through the economy to complete its circular flow, we will have to explain what determines the length of time money is held unspent in cash balances. Now, as is true of most economic magnitudes, this requires that we pose the question in terms of supply and demand.

The demand for money, like the demand for any asset, can be expressed as a fraction of one's income. Thus some people demand a house equal in value to about three times their annual income. Others drive cars valued at about half of their annual income. Accordingly, we will measure the quantity of money people want to hold in terms of the fraction of their year's income they keep in their pockets and in commercial banks.

When people hold assets in the form of money, a real cost is involved. They give up the opportunity to invest that money in income-earning assets, such as government bonds and common stocks, or in a pleasure-yielding asset, such as a new hi-fi set. Because of this we will think of the cost of holding money as the income that must be forgone if money is held in currency or bank deposits. The interest rate is a figure that represents this cost of holding money. The higher the interest rate, the higher the cost, and therefore the smaller will be the fraction of their income that people would normally hold in the form of money.

There are various reasons for holding money.

We might stop to ask why anybody would like to hold money. It can be argued that it is not the money itself but what money will buy that brings people pleasure. However, this is not sufficient. People want money to bridge the gap between payday and their everyday purchases. Otherwise, they would have to borrow every time they bought anything and this would be inconvenient and costly. People also want money to hold as a protection against the proverbial rainy day. People feel good knowing that if some unexpected tragedy occurs they can handle it without selling assets or borrowing. Some people want to hold money so that they will have it on hand if an unexpected bargain shows up on the used car lot or on the stock exchange. Whatever the reasons, people hold money because it gives them pleasure to do so, just as it gives them pleasure to own an original painting.

The demands for money to hold will differ from individual to individual. Figure 14.6 shows several such demand curves with the interest rate on the vertical axis and the quantity of money held expressed in number of months' salary. Consider the following examples.

A conservative professor—the type that carries an umbrella on a sunny day—would probably want to hold a money balance equal to nine months' income. If, for example, he were earning $24,000 a year, he would want to hold currency and bank deposits amounting to about $18,000 if the interest rate were 6 percent. The slope of his demand curve would probably be rather steep, indicating that his demand for money was not very sensitive to changes in the rate of interest (see the first graph in Fig. 14.6).

In contrast, a student, full of optimism and short on monthly income, might be satisfied to scrape along with an average of about two weeks' income held in the form of money at a 6 percent interest rate. If anything serious happened, the student probably could get more money from home or from student loan funds. And since the typical student is not thinking about investing in securities, he or she tends to ignore the rate of interest. The student's demand curve for money would not only be closer to the origin but also more inelastic. The demand curve in the middle might best

represent an optimistic student's demand for money.

Finally, there are the sophisticated Wall Street investors, who also have demands for money. Their demands stem partly from their needs to have (1) transactions balances for their everyday expenses, (2) precautionary balances against unforeseen events, and (3) speculative balances that they could invest if the market takes an unexpected dip. Their demands for money would probably be much more interest sensitive than those of the other types of individuals. At high rates of interest they would hold small amounts of money, expressed in terms of their annual income, and at low rates of interest they would keep larger amounts of money. See the last graph in Fig. 14.6.

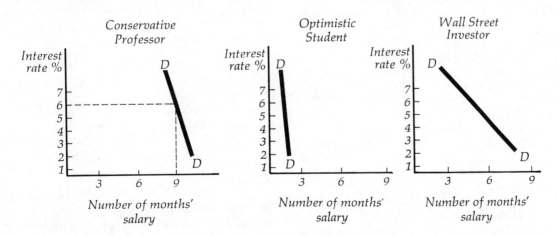

FIG. 14.6 **The demand for money.**

The demand for money determines how long a representative unit of money will "sit" in the various balances before it gets passed on.

Money paid to our conservative professor would stay in his balance nine months before he paid it out to others. On the other hand, money paid to an optimistic student would get passed on to the next transactor within two weeks. If money typically passed through four money balances before it completed the circular flow it would take three years to get around the economy if all the transactors had the same demand for money as our conservative professor. Or, in contrast, if all the transactors had the same demand for money as the optimistic student, money would complete the circular flow in eight weeks, or about seven times a year.

As you might expect, the demand for money is influenced by a wide variety of factors. When real incomes rise, people generally feel they can afford the luxury of holding a larger percentage of their incomes unspent; as a result, velocity tends to decline. Wealth also influences the demand for money. Wealthy people can use other assets to protect their real incomes against unexpected events. The supply of money substitutes, such as credit cards and liquid assets other than money, also determine an individual's demand for money.

Expectations can also be important. During periods of rapid inflation, people tend to hold less money relative to their incomes. In place of holding money they go out and buy anything rather than wait until their money will buy less. It is difficult to make a complete listing of all these factors. *What is important is that velocity is not a random variable or one that adapts easily to changes in the quantity of money.* It is deeply rooted in the economizing decisions of the individuals who make up the economy.

What would happen if the Federal Reserve System permitted the banks to create more money than all of the people, taken together, wanted to hold? If you found yourself with more money than you wanted, you could either spend it or use it to buy securities. But the economy as a whole is a closed system. What one person spends, another person receives. It is impossible, then, for everybody, taken collectively, to dispose of money by spending it or using it to buy securities.

However, as people spend more money, total money incomes rise. (Security prices may also rise, but more of this later.) As people continue playing this game of "hot potato" or passing their excess cash to others, money incomes rise to the point where people are satisfied to hold the amount of cash the Federal Reserve has created. Thus, when the supply of money exceeds the demands for money, or aggregate expenditures, *MV* increases.

Whether the demand for money and, therefore, velocity is a variable or a constant is important.

If year after year the public wanted to hold the same percentage of its money income in the form of money, the velocity of money would be constant. If *V* really were constant, then the problem of avoiding unemployment and inflation would be fairly simple. Just have the Fed undertake studies to determine the annual increase in real GNP and permit the same percentage increases in the money supply. As we noted early in this chapter, the classical economists, writing during the nineteenth century and the early part of this century, believed in what has been called the Quantity Theory of Money, which holds that the demand for money is fixed and, therefore, velocity is constant. Notice that the Quantity Theory differs from the Equation of Exchange. The Quantity Theory makes certain assumptions about how *V*, for example, behaves and then is used to predict the effect on *P*, prices, and *Q*, output, when *M* is changed. The classical economists' prescription for avoiding inflation was simply to manage the quantity of money properly.

More recently, some economists (under the leadership of Professor Milton Friedman), whom we shall call *monetarists*, have argued that while velocity is not a constant, it varies in a systematic manner. They also believe that the proper management of the money supply is the key to avoiding depressions and inflations. We turn now to a discussion of the monetarists' theory about how much money the Fed should allow the banks to create.

The monetarists believe that velocity varies systematically and can therefore be predicted.

Professor Friedman has modified the view of the classical economists that velocity is a constant.

Using historical studies, Professor Friedman has demonstrated that velocity (at least for M_2) varies over time. As people receive more real income and accumulate more wealth, they choose to hold more money relative to their money incomes. From 1880 to about 1950, velocity declined steadily. From 1950 to the present, velocity has risen slightly.

Professor Friedman also asserts that in the short run there is a lag between the introduction of new money and the resulting increase in expenditures. During this lag period, velocity appears to be less stable than it really is.

Once the velocity figures are adjusted for long-term trends and short-term lags, however, the relationship between the GNP and the money holdings of the public is said to be very stable—so stable, in fact, that changes in the money supply will change aggregate demand in a predictable way.

Consider the following example.

Suppose the banking system pumped an additional $10 billion into the economy. Some households, finding themselves with more money than usual, would increase their expenditures on consumption products. Others would invest in new housing. Similarly, some businesses, with more liquidity than they had expected, would invest directly in new plants. These expenditures directly increase aggregate demand.

However, a part of the initial impact of the new money may be channeled through the financial capital market. Security prices would be driven up if some of the recipients of the new money chose to buy securities. As a result, many investors would feel wealthier, and this would induce them to spend more for consumption goods or for direct investment. At the same time, the increased flow of money into the financial capital market would temporarily reduce the rate of interest and induce some businesses to sell securities to finance additional investment projects. Thus aggregate demand is again increased, but indirectly in this case.

Some critics have argued that the decline in the interest rates that follows an increase in the supply of money would cause velocity to decline. People would be content to hold the additional money unspent. Monetarists, however, point to the empirical evidence. They say that velocity, adjusted for long-term trends and short-term lags, is remarkably stable. Evidently the demand for money is quite insensitive to changes in the interest rate, or possibly the wealth effect of reduced interest rates shifts the demand curve for money enough to compensate for interest rate changes. In either case, an increased supply of money will, after a lag, increase the total demand (MV) for products.

While the monetarists do not claim that they know the exact sequence of events for every monetary expansion, they do argue that more money will mean higher expenditures. The stable demand for money will reassert itself and, after an adjustment period, money expenditures will be increased.

Because of the unspecified lags and other considerations, the Fed should increase the money supply at a steady rate.

The Board of Governors of the Federal Reserve System currently uses its discretion in deciding when and by how much to increase the supply of money. Unfortunately the lengths of the adjustment periods vary considerably. If, for example, the rate of growth in the money supply is increased to counteract a threatening recession, it is possible that there will be a turnaround in the economy before the new money has its full effect.

As a result of the uncertainty introduced by lags and other considerations, the monetarists argue that the Fed should not be trusted to use its discretion. Rather, some arrangements should be made for the Fed to increase the reserves of the banking system at a steady rate, say 4 percent a year.

If 4 percent were chosen as the desired rule for the Fed to follow, the increase in the money supply would be large enough for the aggregate demand to grow at about the same rate as the real GNP. The price level, P, would remain about the same.

The monetarists argue that the exact percentage is not as important as the steadiness of the rate. They contend that the economy will adjust to a steady rate and this will reduce the amount of uncertainty in the economy. Thus, the precise rule that the Fed should follow would depend on the predicted changes in velocity and the growth rate of the total output.

MINI-CASE 14.2

You are a monetarist. Which of the following causes for persistent inflation would you accept as being valid?

a) The government is spending too much money and is financing its deficits by selling bonds to the public.

b) The federal budget is balanced, but at such a high level that the economy is dominated by the government.

c) The Federal Reserve has permitted the banks to increase the money supply at a 10 percent annual rate. GNP, in real terms, is rising at a 4 percent rate.

d) The Federal Reserve has adopted a tight money policy and this has increased the interest rate to 15 percent, which has increased the costs of all businesses.

COMMENTARY

The following is a column written by Milton Friedman that appeared in *Newsweek* magazine, February 7, 1972. Please read it and answer the following questions.

a) Why doesn't Milton Friedman feel the Fed should manage the money supply in a discretionary manner?

b) Does he believe the Fed is capable of controlling the money supply?

THE CASE FOR A MONETARY RULE

I and most other monetarists have long favored a policy of a steady and moderate rate of growth of the quantity of money. We have strongly opposed the Fed's trying to fine-tune the economy.

Recent policy conformed to our prescription only in 1970.

Critics ask why we are so modest. Why not use the powerful instrument of monetary policy to offset other forces pushing the economy toward inflation or recession? Why tie the hands of the Fed? Why not trust their discretion in adapting to changing circumstances?

We favor the rule of steady monetary growth for several reasons.

1 The past performance of the Fed. Throughout its history, the Fed has proclaimed that it was using its powers to promote economic stability. But the record does not support the claim. On the contrary, the Fed has been a major source of instability.

The Fed was responsible for converting what would have been a serious recession after 1929 into a major catastrophe by permitting the quantity of money to decline by one-third from 1929 to 1933, even though it had ample power to prevent the decline.

In recent years, the Fed set off the accelerating inflation that Mr. Nixon inherited by expanding the money supply too rapidly in 1967 and 1968, then stepped too hard on the brake in 1969, and too hard on the accelerator in the first seven months of 1971. Federal Reserve officials have often admitted their errors after the fact—as chairman Burns did in july 1971, in testimony before the Joint Economic Committee—and have promised better performance in the future. But then the same forces have produced a repetition of the same errors.

We conclude that the urgent need is to prevent the Fed from being a source of economic disturbance.

2 The limitations of our knowledge. Economic research has established two propositions: (1) there is a close, regular, and predictable relation between the quantity of money, national income, and prices over any considerable period of years; (2) the same relation is much looser from month to month, quarter to quarter, or even year to year. In particular, monetary changes take time to affect the economy, and the time delay is itself highly variable.

The first proposition means that a steady price level over the long pull requires that the quantity of money grow at a fairly steady rate roughly equal to the average rate of growth of output.

The second proposition means that any attempt to use monetary policy for fine-tuning is likely simply to introduce additional instability. And this is indeed what has happened.

3 The promotion of confidence. An announced, and adhered to, policy of steady monetary growth would provide the business community with a firm basis for confidence in monetary stability that no discretionary policy could provide even if it happened to produce roughly steady monetary growth.

4 Neutralization of the Fed. An independent Fed may at times be too insulated from political pressures—as it was in the early '30s—and yet at other times unduly affected by political pressures. If we really knew enough to use monetary policy for finetuning, we would probably experience a four-year cycle, with unemployment reaching its trough in years divisible by four and inflation reaching its peak in the succeeding year.

A monetary rule would insulate monetary policy both from the arbitrary power of a small group of men not subject to control by the electorate and from the short-run pressures of partisan politics.

Is the rule that we have proposed technically feasible? Can the Fed control the quantity of money? No serious student of money—whatever his policy views—denies that the Fed can, if it wishes, control the quantity of money. It cannot, of course, achieve a precise rate of growth from day to day or week to week. But it can come very close from month to month and quarter to quarter.

As I wrote some five years ago, if the monetary rule were followed, "other forces would still affect the economy, require change and adjustment, and distort the even tenor of our ways. But steady monetary growth would provide a monetary climate favorable to the effective operation of those basic forces of enterprise, ingenuity, invention, hard work and thrift that are the true springs of economic growth. That is the most that we can ask from monetary policy at our present stage of knowledge. But that much—and it is a great deal— is clearly within our reach."

MILTON FRIEDMAN, *Newsweek*, February 7, 1972.
Copyright 1972 by Newsweek, Inc. All rights reserved.
Reprinted by permission.

THE MONETARIST AND KEYNESIAN APPROACHES COMPARED

Monetarists and Keynesians differ on how the money supply affects the various components of aggregate demand.

The monetarists argue that the supply of money in the economy will influence investment spending, consumption spending, state and local government spending, and some elements of federal government spending (quasi-government corporations, such as the TVA and the Post Office). Keynesians, however, argue that increases in M_2 will change only the interest rate and therefore investment spending. They argue that consumption spending—spending on new cars, refrigerators, clothes, vacations, and so on—is independent of the amount of money held by consumers. Government spending is determined by public policy and therefore is independent of the money holdings of the various governmental entities.

Keynesians and monetarists differ as to whether the Fed should focus on the interest rate or the supply of money.

The monetarists argue that since M_2 determines the total amount of spending, the Fed should focus its attention on the *quantity* of money it is supplying to the economy. The Fed should *not* be concerned with the *interest rate*. The interest rate has the job of rationing the nation's savings among different projects. When the Fed tries to keep interest rates from rising by feeding more money into the economy, it keeps the interest rate from doing its job of rationing savings among competitive users.

The Keynesian economists argue that the Fed should focus its attention on the interest rate and ignore the rate of growth of M_2. The stock of money can only influence the amount of investment spending. By regulating the interest rate, the Fed can always keep investment spending from getting out of hand and therefore causing inflation. Whenever investment spending is too small to achieve full employment, the Fed can add to the money supply without having to worry about its inflationary implications.

Monetarists and Keynesians differ over the long-run effect the Fed has on the interest rate.

The monetarists argue that it is the demand for and the supply of savings that *normally* determines the interest rate. They would argue as follows. Suppose that the interest rate, in the absence of the Fed's intervention, is 8 percent, but that the Fed thinks that the interest rate should be 7 percent, and to achieve this goal it increases the money supply by 10 percent a year. After a 12- to 18-month lag, the additional money will so increase the aggregate demand that prices will begin to rise. Producers, seeing prices rising, will add to their inventories and initiate new investment projects while prices are still lower than they expect them to be in the future. As a result, the demand for loanable funds rises faster than the supply of loanable funds and this, in turn, causes interest rates to rise. The result is higher interest rates than would have obtained if the Fed had not tried to keep interest rates down in the first place. In Fig. 14.7, for example, the increase in the supply from S_0S_0 to S_1S_1 reduces the interest rate from 8 percent to 7 percent and eventually the increase in demand pushes the rate up to 10 percent.

To support their contention that the Fed cannot keep interest rates down in the long term, monetarists point to the high interest rates in Italy, Great Britain, and some South American countries, where inflation rates of 20 to a 100

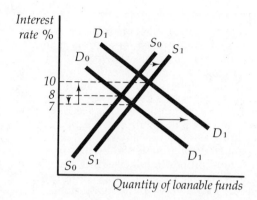

FIG. 14.7   Supply and demand for loanable funds.

percent are common. They point out that in countries such as Germany and Switzerland, where the central banks have maintained tight money and have not tried to keep interest rates down, interest rates tend to be much lower.

Keynesian economists deny that the Fed lacks the power in the long run to keep interest rates down. They say that when investment spending is so high that it will lead to inflation, the Fed can draw money out of the financial capital market, increase interest rates temporarily, and thus shut off investment spending. Once investment spending is under control, interest rates will go down to their previous levels.

Monetarists and Keynesians differ as to how and when to change the money supply.

Monetarists argue that there is a lag between the initiation of a new monetary policy and its full effect that can vary from six months to two years. They argue that economists know very little about the length of this lag and if the Fed is to use its discretion it must always base its actions on predictions of developments in the economy. These predictions tend to be unreliable. As a result, viewed from the needs of the economy 18 months later, the Fed frequently adds or subtracts money from the economy when it should not be doing so. In short, the Fed can, by using its discretion, be adding another random variable to which the economy must adjust.

The monetarists also argue that if the Fed adopts a rule requiring it to increase the money supply at, say, 4 percent a year, Fed policies are likely to be less inflationary than they otherwise would be. The reason is that there is always pressure from farmers, businesspersons, and politicians to keep interest rates down while there is no pressure to keep interest rates up. Consequently, when the Fed uses its own discretion in setting monetary policies, it is likely to be swayed by the pressures from these groups. Thus, in the absence of a rule to govern its behavior, the governors, who determine Fed policies, are likely to increase M_2 too rapidly, and in this way cause inflation.

Keynesian economists argue that while the Fed may not be perfect in predicting the monetary needs of the economy, it will do a better job than it would if it followed a mechanical rule. They also argue that if a monetary rule is adopted, there will be wide variations in the interest rate, which will add another uncertainty to which investors must adjust.

Keynesians and monetarists differ over the effects of government deficits on aggregate demand.

Monetarists argue that government deficits are largely ineffective in adding to the aggregate demand for products and therefore to total employment. They do admit that when a depression sets in, such as the one during the 1930s or at the bottom of the business cycle, government borrowing can take money out of the financial capital market that might not otherwise find its way into investment spending. But after a recovery has begun and velocity returns to its normal level, government deficits merely take money out of capital market that would otherwise have been borrowed to finance private investment spending. They argue that when the government sells its bonds to savers, it tends to "crowd out" private borrowers who are not prepared to pay the higher interest rates caused by government borrowing.

Keynesian economists flatly disagree with the "crowding out" thesis. They say that if investment spending had been high enough, the government would not borrow in order to increase the aggregate demand. They say that when investment spending increases, the government can cut back on its deficit financing and get out of the way of private borrowers. In the short run, the Fed can always accommodate the private sector by increasing the supply of money and in this way keep interest rates down. If investment spending then gets to be too high, the Fed can increase interest rates temporarily while the government cuts back on its spending to give way to the private economy. It is the government's role to stabilize the economy and thus create the basic stability the private sector needs to thrive. Government deficits, properly used, help, not hurt, the private economy.

CAN MONETARIST AND KEYNESIAN POLICY PRESCRIPTIONS BE RECONCILED?

It is unlikely that these two sets of policy prescriptions will be reconciled in the near future. Keynesian economists are largely concerned with combating unemployment. Economists who feel strongly about the injustice of unemployment are attracted to Keynesian economists. It offers an activist approach to solving a serious social problem. Monetarists say "establish the right monetary rule and let the economy solve the problem. If the economy doesn't solve unemployment problems, look carefully at the minimum wage rate or other impediments to the normal functioning of the market." Monetarists are usually more concerned about inflation than are Keynesian economists. Monetarists and Keynesian economists tend to have different social goals—and this makes reconciling their policy prescriptions difficult.

Probably, in the long run, you and the other members of society will decide on which set of economists to rely. You will be concerned with whether countries that depend to a larger extent on monetarist concepts have a better long-run inflation and unemployment record than countries that depend on Keynesian concepts. In making these comparisons, you will have to remember that there are many other differences between countries that may affect their economic outcomes.

You will also make comparisons over time in the same country. Do the political administrations that depend on monetarist concepts have better inflation and unemployment records than political administrations that depend on Keynesian concepts? Again, you will have to adjust for differences in the problems of each administration.

In the end, you and the other members of society will have to decide which set of economic concepts to use. It is unlikely that professional economists who have already debated this issue for well over a decade will resolve this question for you. It is therefore particularly important that you follow the debate going on around you about which policy prescriptions are best.

COMMENTARY

The following is from an article entitled "Toward a 'New' Economics" by Irving Kristol that appeared in the *Wall Street Journal*. In it Kristol describes a "new" economics that he asserts is emerging to replace the Keynesian approach, which has not been able to explain contemporary economic events. Please read the excerpt and answer the following questions.

a) Why is the "new" economics described as "supply-side fiscal policy"?
b) How can the "new" economics expose tax cuts and a balanced budget at the same time?
c) Is this different from the Keynesian approach?

TOWARD A "NEW" ECONOMICS?

"We do not dance even yet to a new tune. But change is in the air. We hear but indistinctly what were once the clearest and most distinguishable voices which have ever instructed political mankind."

So wrote John Maynard Keynes in 1926, in a book called *The End of Laissez-Faire*. He was pointing to the intellectual impotence of the prevailing economic orthodoxy, which seemed less and less capable of explaining what was happening to the economic universe, and quite incapable of providing a coherent set of economic policies which statesmen could look to with confidence. And, of course, he was predicting—with a prescience matched only by his self-assurance—the emergence of a new economics, what we today call Keynesian or neo-Keynesian

economics to replace the old.

It all came to pass as he foretold. During the next 50 years, Keynesianism established itself as the new economic orthodoxy. Even conservative politicians eventually were to be heard saying cheerfully, "we are all Keynesians now."

But the number of politicians saying it has, in the past five years, dwindled remarkably. For the Keynesian orthodoxy itself is showing clear signs of sclerosis, even senility, and is well on the way to suffering the fate of its predecessor. It cannot explain the key economic phenomenon of our time, "stagflation," i.e., the coexistence of inflation and unemployment. And the "stimuli" it recommends mysteriously fail to stimulate, but only enfeeble. . . .

The "monetarist" school

In response to this crisis in the theory of economic policy, a "new" economics is beginning to emerge. Based on the critique of Keynesianism by the "monetarist" school, as further developed (in a rather heterodox way) in the work of such economists as Robert Mundell and Arthur Laffer, and as vigorously publicized by Jude Wanniski of The Wall Street Journal and Congressman Jack Kemp (R., N.Y.), it is still in an embryonic condition and the world has not yet taken much notice of it. To requote Keynes: "We do not dance even yet to a new tune. But change is in the air."

One uses the inverted commas around that term "new" because, in truth, much of the "new" economics is very old—as old as Adam Smith, say. Its focus is on economic growth, rather than on economic equilibrium or disequilibrium, and it sees such growth arising from a free response (e.g., investment, hard work, etc.) to the economic incentives of a free market.

It does retain the Keynesian macroeconomic apparatus for diagnostic purposes, but its inclination is "conservative" rather than "liberal"—i.e., it believes that only the private sector can bring us sustained economic growth, and that whatever tasks one might wish to assign to the public sector, economic growth cannot be one of them.

This "new" economics is sometimes described, rather cumbersomely, as "supply-side fiscal policy." (There is also an international monetary aspect which a critic has called, not inaccurately, "global monetarism"—but that is another story. It arises in opposition to the Keynesian notion that an increase in demand, by itself, will increase supply and therefore accelerate economic growth. The "new" economics asserts that an increase in demand, where the natural incentives to economic growth are stifled, will result simply in inflation. It is only an increase in *productivity*, which converts latent into actual demand by bringing commodities (old and new) to market at prices people can afford, that generates economic growth.

At the moment, and under existing circumstances, the major emphasis by far of the "new" economics is on the need for a substantial, across-the-board cut in tax rates, because it is the high level of tax rates that is stifling incentives to growth. This has caused some concern and confusion among Republican Congressmen, and business executives too, who sense a continuation of the Keynesian unconcern with budget deficits. But the "new" economics is all in favor of balanced budgets—only it believes that, to achieve such a goal, temporary imbalances may be required. Its emphasis on tax-cutting flows from its conviction that this will, through economic growth, eventually lead to a balanced budget.

Substantial Tax Cut

Simply to reduce government expenditures, in a depressed economy, creates too many problems. (And a ruthless dismantling of the welfare state is, in any case, unthinkable.) It is only a substantial tax cut that will, in time, permit us to reduce the *relative* size of the public sector by an expansion of the private sector.

This is a highly simplified and much foreshortened version of a set of economic ideas that is beginning to reshape our thinking on economic policy. Its political appeal to conservatives is obvious (just as the political appeal of Keynesianism to liberals was obvious) and helps explain the recent willingness of congressional Republicans to vote in favor of a permanent tax cut despite the state of the budget. They were not "playing politics," as some critics claimed. They were acting on an economic theory which, if only dimly understood, was nevertheless persuasive. After all, as Congressman Kemp has pointed out, all that Republicans were urging is a tax cut similar to the Kennedy tax program of 1963—also made in the face of a deficit. And it worked: The deficit soon declined, employment went up.

It is hard to overestimate the importance of the fact that, for the first time in half a century, it is the economic philosophy of conservatives that is showing signs of intellectual vigor, while the economic philosophy of liberalism keeps tying itself into ever more elaborate knots. As some sage once observed: You can't beat a horse with no horse. Conservatives, who believe in limited government and a strong private sector, may be in the process of acquiring a horse.

IRVING KRISTOL, *The Wall Street Journal.* May 9, 1977.
Reprinted by permission from *The Wall Street Journal,* ©
Dow Jones & Company, Inc. All rights reserved.

REVIEW QUESTIONS

1. You are a new chairman of the Board of Governors of the Federal Reserve System. You ask your staff to explain how Keynesian monetary theory works. Which of the four explanations given below is the complete Keynesian explanation of the way Federal Reserve can maintain full employment?

   a) Maintain a steady and predictable rate of growth of the money supply.
   b) Whenever unemployment threatens, sell government securities and in this way satisfy the liquidity needs of the economy.
   c) Whenever unemployment threatens, increase the money supply, reducing the rate of interest to stimulate investment spending and eventually consumption spending.
   d) Choose a target rate of interest and maintain whatever the change in employment.

2. In the Keynesian system of thought, fiscal policy rather than monetary policy has the dominant role in the management of aggregate demand. Monetary policy has been assigned the lesser role because:

   a) money is not important.
   b) the rate of interest does not have any effect on total spending. It only influences investment spending.
   c) profit expectations dominate the marginal efficiency schedule, which makes it very difficult for monetary policy to have a decisive role in determining total spending.
   d) Congress likes to reduce taxes and increase government expenditures. As a result, it is easier to get Congress to act than it is to get the Fed to act.

3. Keynesians argue that the Fed can always manipulate the interest rate to accomplish its objectives. The monetarists argue that in the long run—over, say, two or three years—efforts on the part of the Fed to keep interest rates lower than they would otherwise be are bound to fail because:

   a) low interest rates will lead to depression.
   b) efforts to keep the interest rates lower than they would otherwise be will lead to inflation and higher interest rates.
   c) low interest rates will reduce the costs of doing business and therefore make prices fall.
   d) efforts to keep the interest rate lower than it would otherwise be reduces the rate of increase in the money supply to below what it should be to keep the economy moving.

4. The Keynesian economists argue that the "crowding out" hypothesis used by monetarists to demonstrate why deficit financing won't work, except at the bottom of the depression, is wrong because:

   a) funds coming into the capital market are typically not used by private industry.
   b) involuntary unemployment is evidence that people want to save more than private industry wants to invest.
   c) only consumption spending—that is, spending on final products—really keeps the economy going. Businesses will invest only when consumption spending is rising.
   d) All of the above.

5. You have been given the Equation of Exchange $MV = PQ$. Using the following key, indicate what will happen to the price level P, if all other variables are constant apart from the one that will be influenced by the following developments.

a) Price level will rise.
b) Price level will remain constant.
c) Price level will fall.
d) There is no way of knowing what would happen to the price level.

( ) The banking system, together with the Fed, increases the money supply 15 percent in one year.
( ) People become frightened about the future value of their money and, as a result, they decide to hold half as much money, relative to their incomes, as before.
( ) A new cheap energy source is discovered. As a result, the productivity of labor rises 8 percent a year, and there is no reduction in the number of hours of labor input per year.

6. Using the key below, indicate what effect the following changes will have on the velocity of money.

a) Increase velocity.
b) Leave velocity unchanged.
c) Decrease velocity.
d) You can't tell from the data given.

( ) People get to be more affluent and decide that they want the luxury of keeping a larger amount of money in their checking accounts relative to their incomes. They keep six months' income rather than four months' income.
( ) The interest rate rises from 7 percent to 25 percent a year.
( ) Stock prices rise and people feel more affluent. The interest rate does not change.
( ) Credit cards are invented and people no longer feel it is necessary to keep money balances in the bank to take care of unusual expenses or to take advantage of good buys in the stock market.

7. You are a monetarist. Which of the following policies would you ask the Fed to follow in carrying out its monetary responsibilities?

a) The Fed should take care of the nation's need for credit and thus keep the interest rate from rising or falling.
b) The Fed should use its monetary policies to prevent unemployment.
c) The Fed should use its monetary policies to stimulate the growth of the economy.
d) The Fed should ignore the interest rate, unemployment, and growth, and let the money supply grow at a fixed rate per year.

8. There are many explanations for the inflation we are having at the present time. Which one of the following explanations is consistent with monetarism?

a) The United States has allowed the foreign exchange rate to float, which has made imports more expensive.
b) The OPEC countries have increased the price of oil, which has led through a chain reaction to increased prices for all types of energy.
c) The federal government has run a large deficit that it has financed through the sale of bonds to the banking system.

    d) The structure of the Federal Reserve System has contributed to inflation by providing 12 district banks, thereby making it easy for the commercial banking system to obtain loans to increase reserves.

9. If you were a monetarist you would argue that a monetary "rule" to guide the Federal Reserve is better than allowing the Federal Reserve to use its own discretion because:

    a) the Federal Reserve does not know enough about the economy to improve on the effectiveness of the 4–5 percent rate.

    b) the Federal Reserve knows enough about the economy to use its own discretion to guide monetary policy, but it is not good for the economy to be stabilized.

    c) the Federal Reserve does not have to be concerned about lags in the effectiveness of its policies and therefore it can accomplish its goals without relying on mechanical rule.

    d) the Federal Reserve should stabilize the interest rate and not be concerned with the levels of prices and unemployment.

ESSAY QUESTIONS

1. You see the following headline in a newspaper: ECONOMISTS SEE SLOWDOWN IN THE ECONOMY: RECOMMEND LARGE TAX CUT. Comment on this (a) from a monetarist point of view and (b) from a Keynesian point of view.

2. Some critics have said that the Keynesian policy prescriptions are inappropriate for a democracy. Members of Congress can always justify running a deficit because they can say they are "saving the country from a depression." Comment on this.

3. Discretionary policy is likely to be a "one-way street." There are more pressure groups demanding low interest rates and easy money than there are demanding a stable dollar. If this is true, do you think that there is any hope that a democracy can ever have a stable price level? Enlarge on your argument.

4. Monetarists argue that Keynesians are wrong. Running a deficit to cure a recession merely changes the composition of aggregate demand, not the size of aggregate demand. If you were a Keynesian, how would you respond?

5. In recent years the United States has bought a great deal of oil from the OPEC countries. This together with other factors has caused the United States to have a net import balance in excess of $25 billion a year. The Keynesians would say that it is necessary to run a large deficit to offset the depressive effect of this import balance. The monetarists would say that a net import balance is equivalent to additional private saving, and that these additional savings can be used to finance additional plant and equipment to supply energy from nonpetroleum sources. Comment fully.

6. Write out the definitions for each of the variables in the Equation of Exchange, M, V, P, and Q. Then, in your own words indicate what the equation $MV = PQ$ says.

7. What determines the size of M? What effect does the amount of money people want to hold have on it?

8. What underlies the output capacity of the nation related to Q in the Equation of Exchange?

9. List the factors that determine the "demand for money." Of these only one, the interest rate, is explicitly shown on the demand curve relating the "price" of money to the "quantity" of money (measured as a percent of annual income) that people want to hold. How are these other factors expressed when the demand curve is drawn?

10. Suppose that normally your income does not change from year to year, but unexpectedly you receive a bequest of $1 million from a distant relative. The bequest was in the form of a stock that does not pay dividends but is easily sold. Would your demand for money be increased or decreased by this bequest?

11. How would your demand for money to hold be affected by the following circumstances? You are convinced that the prices of most things will be higher next year than they are this year. Interest rates are falling and you are convinced that they will fall further. Your real income increases as a result of a 50 percent decrease in prices.

12. Suppose you are a monetarist. You are told that Argentina is suffering from 100 percent inflation. What would you look for as the cause of this inflation?

13. Again suppose that you are a monetarist. You are told that if the government runs a deficit and finances that deficit by selling bonds to the public, the total demand for product, MV, will rise. Would you agree? If so, why? If not, why not?

14. As a result of the underemployment of construction workers, the Fed injects a substantial amount of new money into the economy in an effort to reduce the interest rate. Do you think that the Fed will succeed in the *long* run?

15. The monetarists argue that the Fed should increase the stock of money by a given percentage each year, regardless of short-run swings in the business cycle. Why do they argue that the Fed should not use its own discretion in deciding how much money to inject into the economy?

16. The Fed has been charged with providing enough money for the economy. As a result, the Fed tries to feed enough money into the economy to keep the interest rate from rising during harvest and tax-paying time. The Fed also tries to keep the interest down when there are unemployed resources. As a monetarist do you agree with this stance? If not, why not?

ANSWERS TO REVIEW QUESTIONS

1. The Keynesian answer is that increases in supply of money will lead to the following: (1) a reduction in the rate of interest; (2) the lower rate of interest will increase investment spending; and (3) this will in turn, via the multiplier, increase *consumption* spending, and thus total spending.
   a) This is incorrect. This is the monetarist answer.
   b) This is incorrect. The Fed should buy government bonds to increase the supply of money.
   c) This is the correct answer for the reason given above.
   d) This is incorrect. The Fed should reduce the rate of interest when unemployment threatens and increase it when inflation threatens.

2. In the Keynesian system of thought, money has a lesser role in the management of aggregate demand because it operates an unstable variable—the marginal efficiency of capital—and because changes in the rate of interest have their effect only on one of the relatively small components of total spending.

   a) This is incorrect. Money does have an effect on the rate of interest.
   b) This is incorrect. Monetary policy does have an effect on total spending via the multiplier.
   c) This is correct as explained above.
   d) This is incorrect. While it is true that Congress does like to reduce taxes and increase spending, the Fed can move more quickly.

3. Monetarists argue that in the long run efforts to keep the interest rate down will lead to an increase in the money supply, which in turn leads to inflation and large increases in the demands for loanable funds and thus higher interest rates.

   a) This is incorrect. Low interest rates will increase rather than decrease aggregate demand.
   b) This is correct as stated above.
   c) This is incorrect. Low interest rates will lead to inflation, which in turn will increase the costs of doing business.
   d) This is incorrect. Lower than normal interest rates will force the Fed to increase the money supply faster than it otherwise would.

4. The Keynesian economists argue that unemployment is evidence that people want to save more than industry wants to invest. Therefore, the government can borrow without interfering with private investment.

   a) This is incorrect. Keynesians would not argue that all funds coming into the capital market are wasted.
   b) This is correct as stated above.
   c) This is incorrect. The Keynesian economists do not argue that investment spending is wholly dependent on consumption spending.
   d) This is incorrect. There is only one correct answer.

5. If the banking system increases the money supply by 15 percent and all other variables in the Equation of Exchange are held constant, then P must increase. The answer is (a).

   If people try to reduce their money holdings, we can expect demand for goods and services to increase, driving up prices. The answer is (a).

   The discovery of a new cheap energy source will increase productivity and presumably increase real GNP, that is, Q, in the Equation of Exchange. While Q rises, P will fall. The answer is (c).

6. If people try to increase their money holdings, they will in effect hold each dollar for a longer period of time. Velocity will decrease. The answer is (c).

   The increase in the interest rate will cause people to reduce their money balances to a lower level. The effect will be an increase in velocity as the period over which they hold money decreases. The answer is (a).

   As people become more affluent, they will wish to increase their money holdings and increase the period of time over which they hold money. As a result velocity will fall. The answer is (c).

   The invention of credit cards will reduce the period of time that people hold money and the velocity will increase. The answer is (a).

7. The monetarists argue for a steady increase in the supply of money.

   a) This is incorrect. The Fed should not use its powers in a discretionary fashion.
   b) This is incorrect for the same reason as (a).

   c) This is incorrect for the same reason as (a).

   d) This is correct as noted above.

8. Monetarists argue that persistent inflation has one major cause: too rapid an increase in the money supply.

   a) This is incorrect. This is not the basic cause of inflation according to monetarists.

   b) This is incorrect. This is not the basic cause of inflation according to monetarists.

   c) This is correct. This increases the money supply.

   d) This is incorrect. The institutional structure providing 12 district banks has nothing to do with inflation.

9. Professor Friedman asserts that the Fed has been a major source of instability by attempting to "fine tune" monetary policy.

   a) This is correct. The lags and leads make it too difficult to know when to "pull the monetary levers."

   b) This is incorrect. It of course is good to stabilize the economy.

   c) This is incorrect. It is precisely the lags that complicate discretionary monetary policy.

   d) This is incorrect. The monetarists are concerned primarily with the supply of money, not the interest rate.

OBJECTIVES

Upon successful completion of this chapter, you will be able to:

1. Define inflation.
2. Describe the behavior of prices and unemployment rates since World War II.
3. Graph the Phillips Curve and demonstrate the inflation-unemployment trade off it is supposed to represent.
4. Provide three explanations for inflation.
5. Describe how the unemployment rates are determined.
6. Identify the structural changes that have occurred in recent decades that affect the rate of unemployment.
7. Describe the costs of unemployment and inflation.
8. Suggest three alternative solutions to the problem of stagflation and cite the criticisms of each approach.

CHAPTER 15

UNEMPLOYMENT AND INFLATION: CAUSES, COSTS, AND SOLUTIONS

INTRODUCTION

Ask anyone what he or she thinks is today's most pressing economic problem and you will receive one of two answers: inflation or unemployment.

Inflation is an increase in the general price level which becomes apparent when the supply of money increases relative to the quantity of goods and services available.

Unemployment is the condition of being unable to find gainful employment when able and willing to work.

These issues affect the lives of every citizen, so it is not surprising that they are the focal point of economic policy makers. Insight into the scope of these problems can be grasped by examining two important indexes of the economy's health, the unemployment rate and the yearly changes in the consumer price index. These indexes are shown

in Fig. 15.1 for the years since 1946. This year has special significance since it was the year in which the Employment Act of 1946 was passed by Congress.*

The colored line shows the year-to-year changes in the consumer price index. It shows for each year the percentage change from the preceding period. The black line represents the annual unemployment rates. Table 15.1 contains the numbers underlying the graphs.

The colored line in Fig. 15.2 represents the fiscal activities of the federal government as re-

* The Employment Act of 1946 states that it is the federal government's responsibility to maintain high levels of employment and production and, to achieve these goals, directs the president to make an annual report to the Congress on the general economic condition of the nation that includes recommendations. To assist the president in preparing his report and to provide him with expert advice on economic conditions, the act set up the Council of Economic Advisers.

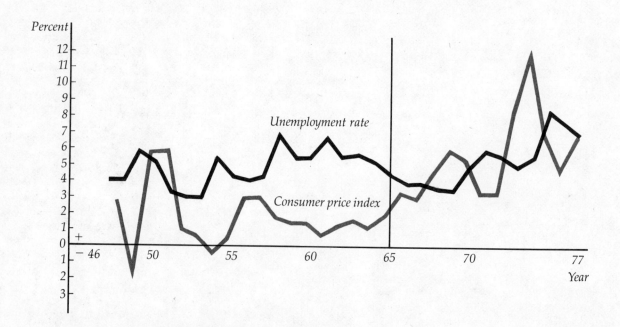

FIG. 15.1 Annual percentage rates of change of the consumer price index and unemployment rate.

TABLE 15.1

THE UNEMPLOYMENT RATE AND THE ANNUAL
PERCENTAGE CHANGE IN THE CONSUMER PRICE INDEX,
1947–1978

Year	Annual percentage change in the consumer price index*	Unemployment rate
1947		3.9
1948	2.7	3.8
1949	−1.8	5.9
1950	5.8	5.3
1951	5.9	3.3
1952	0.9	3.0
1953	0.6	2.9
1954	−0.5	5.5
1955	0.4	4.4
1956	2.9	4.1
1957	3.0	4.3
1958	1.8	6.8
1959	1.5	5.6
1960	1.5	5.5
1961	.7	6.7
1962	1.2	5.5
1963	1.6	5.7
1964	1.2	5.2
1965	1.9	4.5
1966	3.4	3.8
1967	3.0	3.8
1968	4.7	3.6
1969	6.1	3.5
1970	5.5	4.9
1971	3.4	5.9
1972	3.4	5.6
1973	8.8	4.9
1974	12.2	5.6
1975	7.0	8.5
1976	4.8	7.7
1977	6.8	7.0
1978	6.8	7.0

* Percentage change from the preceding period.
Source: *Economic Report of the President, 1978*, U.S. Government Printing Office, Washington, D.C., 1978.

flected in the annual budgetary surpluses and deficits of the federal government as a percent of GNP since 1946. The black line shows the monetary activities of the Federal Reserve System as reflected in the annual percentage changes in the money supply, using M_2. Table 15.2 lists the numbers underlying Fig. 15.2.

Neither the Federal Reserve Board nor the federal government played active roles in seeking to manage aggregate demand during the 1950s and early 1960s.

Figures 15.1 and 15.2 show that despite the passage of the Employment Act of 1946, neither the Federal Reserve Board nor the federal government appear to have taken aggressive action in managing the aggregate demand for products during the period from 1946 to 1965. The vertical line in Figs. 15.1 and 15.2 are drawn to show 1965 as a watershed. The average annual increase in the money supply (M_2) during the pre-1965 period was 6.1 percent, with mild variation from year to year except for the Korean War period. The Federal Reserve Board, with William McChesney Martin as chairman, took no drastic actions to change the rate of growth of the money supply.

The federal government also did little to actively manage aggregate demand for products during the Truman and Eisenhower years. The federal budget showed a surplus for six of the years from 1947 to 1960. The largest deficit years occurred during the Korean War early in the 1950s.

During the period from 1946 to 1965, real GNP grew at an annual average rate of 3.7 percent, almost doubling. Prices rose at an annual rate of 2.6 percent, with little variation from year to year except for the Korean War period. In retrospect, economists now believe that, corrected for product quality improvements, the price level rose very little. Unemployment varied with the business cycle. During the boom period of the Korean War it fell to 2.9 percent, but it rose to 6.8 percent of the labor force in the recession of 1958.

In looking back over these years, it is fair to say that although there were mild business cycles (as indicated by variations in the growth rate of real GNP) by the standards of the 1970s, the economy performed reasonably well. The real GNP doubled, prices did not get out of hand, and unemployment averaged 4.8 percent.

The tax reduction of 1964 proved to be a turning point in national policy.

The beginning of a more active period in terms of fiscal policy actions by the federal government

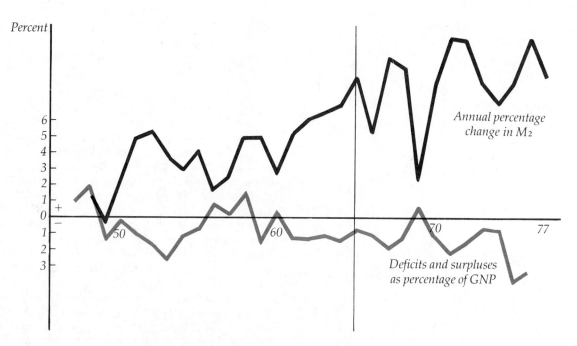

FIG. 15.2   Federal government annual budgetary surpluses and deficits as a percentage of GNP, 1947–1976, and annual percentage changes in the money supply (M₂).

can be traced to the promise of President Kennedy during the political campaign of 1960 "to get the country moving again." He pointed to the 6.8 percent unemployment rate during 1958 and the 5.5 percent rate in 1959 as a serious problem. After the election, he appointed Walter Heller, a Keynesian economist from the University of Minnesota, to head his Council of Economic Advisers. Heller assumed an active role, urging President Kennedy to cut income taxes in order to increase the aggregate demand for products and urging the Federal Reserve Board to adopt easier monetary policies. After President Kennedy's tragic assassination, President Johnson was able to persuade Congress to follow Heller's plan to cut income taxes, despite the fact it would initially increase the deficit, in order to increase the aggregate demand for products. Congress approved the tax reduction in 1964.

The tax reduction of 1964 marks a turning point in the monetary-fiscal policies of the federal government. Up to that time, taxes were viewed primarily as a way of paying for the goods and services purchased by the government. From that time on, however, taxes became an important policy tool in determining aggregate demand. Later, during the the late sixties and seventies, Presidents Nixon, Ford, and Carter all justified changes in taxes as a means of increasing or decreasing aggregate demand.

The governors of the Federal Reserve Board also took a more activist position, increasing M_2 rapidly when they thought that the economy was facing a recession and increasing M_2 less rapidly when they thought inflation was the major problem.

The period after 1965 is characterized by wider swings in GNP and unemployment combined with varying inflation rates.

Examine the period after 1965 in Fig. 15.2. You will see that the percentage changes in M_2 were substantially greater during this period than they had been during the earlier period. You will also see that the government incurred a deficit every year except 1969, and that recently these deficits

TABLE 15.2

FEDERAL GOVERNMENT BUDGETARY SURPLUSES AND DEFICITS AS A PERCENTAGE OF GNP AND ANNUAL SUPPLY
FIGURES AND PERCENTAGE CHANGES
1947–1977

(1) Year	(2) Net budgetary surplus or deficit (−)	(3) GNP (in billions)	(4) = (2)/(3) Surplus or deficit (−) as a percentage of GNP	(5) Money supply (M$_2$) (in billions)	(6) Change as percentage of previous year
1947	$ 2.4 billion	$232.8	1.0	146.0	1.4
1948	5.2	259.1	2.0	148.1	−0.4
1949	−3.6	258.0	−1.4	147.5	2.2
1950	−0.4	286.2	−0.1	150.7	3.9
1951	−3.4	330.2	−1.0	156.5	5.4
1952	−5.8	347.2	−1.7	164.9	3.8
1953	−9.2	366.1	−2.5	171.2	3.0
1954	−4.0	366.3	−1.1	176.3	4.2
1955	−2.8	399.3	−0.7	183.7	1.7
1956	3.9	420.7	0.9	186.9	2.6
1957	0.7	442.8	0.2	191.8	4.9
1958	7.0	448.9	1.6	201.6	4.9
1959	−7.2	486.9	−1.5	210.9	2.9
1960	1.8	506.0	0.4	217.1	5.3
1961	−6.3	523.3	−1.2	228.6	6.2
1962	−7.2	563.8	−1.3	242.8	6.6
1963	−6.6	594.7	−1.1	258.9	7.0
1964	−8.3	635.7	−1.3	277.1	8.8
1965	−4.7	688.1	−0.7	301.4	5.4
1966	−7.3	753.0	−1.0	317.8	10.0
1967	−14.0	796.3	−1.8	349.7	9.4
1968	−10.8	868.5	−1.2	382.4	2.5
1969	7.1	935.1	0.8	392.1	8.4
1970	−10.9	982.4	−1.1	425.2	11.3
1971	−22.8	1063.4	−2.1	473.0	11.1
1972	−16.9	1171.1	−1.4	525.5	8.6
1973	−7.9	1306.6	−0.6	570.7	7.3
1974	−12.0	1412.9	−0.9	612.4	8.5
1975	−59.4	1528.8	−3.9	664.3	11.4
1976	−53.6	1706.5	−3.1	740.3	8.9
1977		1890.4		806.5	

Sources: *Handbook of Basic Economic Statistics*, January 1977; Federal Budgetary Receipts and Expenditures, pp. 214, 215; Economic Statistics Bureau of Washington, D.C.

have become substantially larger as a percentage of GNP than they had been in the earlier period.

During 1965–1977, the annual year-to-year percentage changes in the consumer price index varied from a low of 3.0 in 1967 to a high of 12.2 in 1974.

The variability of the unemployment rate also increased. As the Vietnam War heated up, the unemployment rate went down to 3.5 percent in 1969. But when the Federal Reserve Board reduced the rate of growth of the money supply in 1969, unemployment rose to 5.9 percent in 1971. After that, *both* inflation and unemployment rose to new post-World War II heights, with the inflation rate peaking in 1974 and the unemployment rate peaking in 1975. Instead of varying inversely, as they had done generally during the 1950s and early 1960s, unemployment and inflation seemed to vary together.

What does all this mean? Are we in the midst of a fundamental change in the economy? Will your future be characterized by inflation *and* unemployment? Has steady economic growth come to an end? Did the experiment of reducing taxes to get the economy moving lead to all of this?

These are all hard questions to answer. We will deal with them under the heading of "stagflation."

STAGFLATION: INFLATION AND UNEMPLOYMENT

The normal expectation is for inflation to rise when unemployment is falling and vice versa.

Suppose you were operating a fast food company with a number of outlets, such as MacDonald's, Burger Chef, or Kentucky Fried Chicken, and that for the most part you employed unskilled workers at a wage of $3.50 an hour. Also assume that real GNP is growing at 6 percent a year and that the economy is rapidly approaching full employment. How will this affect your business?

You will find it increasingly difficult to hire qualified people to work for you at the wage you are paying. Up to now you have been able to hire your workers away from other low-paying establishments and part-time jobs. To improve your chances of finding people, however, assume you increase your wage rate to $4.00 an hour, and at the same time increase the price of your food as other outlets have.

Now suppose the economy reverses itself and goes into a slump. You discover that once again there are people willing to work for $3.50 an hour. Since other fast-food chains can also hire low-priced labor, they tend to run specials and find other ways of reducing the price of their food in order to increase their business. You too run specials and reduce the regular price of some of your fast-food items.

What can you learn from this? It seems logical that when prices are rising, as they tend to be during an economic expansion, unemployment would shrink; and that when the economy is in a recession, prices would tend to fall and unemployment increase.

This is what tended to be true during the twenty years following the passage of the Full Employment Act of 1946. Indeed, this inverse relationship between inflation rates and unemployment has a name. It is embodied in the Phillips curve.

The Phillips curve illustrates the expected relation between unemployment and inflation.

Writing in 1958, A. W. Phillips, a professor at the London School of Economics, argued that there was a predictable trade-off between unemployment and inflation rates.* A hypothetical Phillips curve such as those used to illustrate this trade-off is shown in Fig. 15.3. You will note that a Phillips curve resembles a convex production possibilities curve. It shows the various combinations of inflation rates measured along the vertical axis and unemployment rates measured along the horizontal axis.

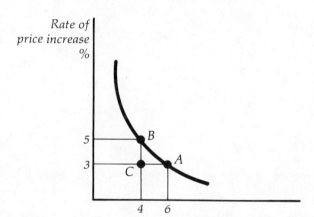

Unemployment as a % of the labor force

FIG. 15.3   The Phillips curve.

The relationship that this curve represents is that low levels of unemployment can be achieved only by accepting certain high rates of inflation.

* A. W. Phillips, "The Relation between Unemployment and the Rate of Change of Money Wage Rates in the United Kingdom, 1862–1957," Economica (November 1958); 283–299.

For example, point *A* shows that a 6 percent unemployment rate is consistent with a 3 percent rate of inflation. If we want to reduce the amount to, say, 4 percent, we will have to accept a 5 percent rate of inflation, point *B*. It also tells us that a very low unemployment rate is inconsistent with a low inflation rate, for example, point *C*.

If the Phillips curve could represent accurately the relationship between rates of unemployment and rates of inflation then the problems of inflation and unemployment could be reduced to a question of social goals. The choice is clear: inflation or unemployment? As economists, our job would be done (except as we could find ways to move this curve closer to the origin) and we could leave the rest to the political process of choosing the best trade-off between these two social goals.

Since 1967 the Phillips curve hasn't represented the real world.

Unfortunately, as Fig. 15.4 shows, the current relationship between unemployment and inflation is not as stable as it appeared to be during the 1950s and 1960s. During the early 1970s, the curve seemed to shift outward and to the right—indicating that higher inflation rates were associated with unemployment rates. The figures are not conclusive for the years 1974 through 1978, but it would appear that the curve for these years, if one exists, is still further out and to the right.

It is clear that the problem the economy now faces is higher inflation rates (than existed during the 1950s and 1960s) *and* higher unemployment rates. What causes this? Has something fundamental happened to the economy to cause high rates of inflation *and* unemployment?

Economists have offered many explanations for this apparent paradox. In the sections that follow we will present these explanations. Twenty years have passed since A. W. Phillips called attention to what appeared to be a trade-off between inflation and unemployment. There is little agreement among economists about which explanation or combination of explanations has caused this apparent change in the economy. After we have discussed these explanations, we will present two different types of policy prescriptions that have been offered to deal with the problem of inflation plus unemployment.

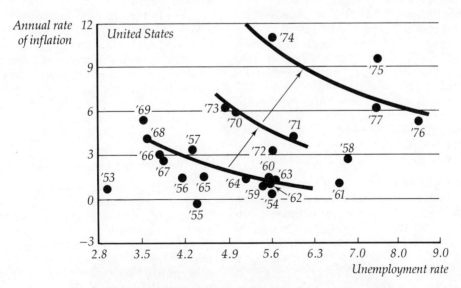

FIG. 15.4 **Changes in the Phillips curve.** Source: "The Phillips Curve; Rainbow with No Pot of Gold," *Monthly Economic Letter,* First National City Bank, New York, June 1975, p. 10. Reprinted by permission. Figures for 1975, 1976, 1977 added.

EXPECTED AND UNEXPECTED INFLATION

Economists over 100 years ago asserted that expected, in contrast to unexpected, inflation is not necessarily associated with low levels of unemployment.

More than a hundred years ago, Thomas Attwood, a monetary activist, testifying before a parliamentary committee, argued that:

> As a general principle, I think unquestionably that as long as any number of industrious honest workmen in the Kingdom are out of employment supposing such deficiency not to be local, but general, I should think it the duty, and certainly the interest of Government, to continue the depreciation of the currency until full employment is obtained and general prosperity is achieved.*

John Stuart Mill, one of the leading economists of the period replied:

> Mr. Attwood opines that the multiplication of circulating medium, and the consequent diminuation in its value, do not merely diminish the pressure of taxes and debts, and other fixed charges but give employment to labor, and that to an indefinite extent . . . Mr. Attwood's error is that of supposing that a depreciation of the currency really increases the demand for all articles, and consequently their production, because under some circumstances, it may create a false opinion of an increase in demand; which false opinion leads, as the reality would do, to an increase of production, followed, however, by a fatal revulsion as soon as the delusion ceases.†

Translated into modern prose, Attwood is saying that printing more money and increasing aggregate demand will reduce unemployment. Mill disagrees, stating that increasing the supply

---

* Report of the Committee on Secrecy in the Bank of England Charter: with the minutes of evidence. Parliamentary Papers, Commons, 1831–1832, p. 467.

† Mill, J. S., "The Currency Juggle"; *Tait's Edinburgh Magazine*; 1833. As reprinted in Volume I of Dissertations and Discussions, Boston: 1865, pp. 68–71.

of money will fool people for a short time into believing that there really is an increase in the real demand for goods, but when they see what really happens they will learn to expect prices to be higher whenever there is an increase in the quantity of money.

What, then, is at issue is: Will *expected* inflation (in contrast to unexpected inflation) reduce unemployment? If the answer is no, then the trade-off represented by Phillips curve just isn't so. Increases in inflation rates, *if they are expected*, will not reduce unemployment.

In a modern setting the argument would run as follows. After a period of stable prices, increasing aggregate demand will increase employment until resources are fully employed. Thereafter, prices will rise. After prices have risen for a number of years, people will learn to expect prices to rise every year. Those persons who have monopoly power will not allow their real incomes to be reduced by inflation. They will increase their prices in anticipation of inflation, and this will prevent real GNP from rising as much as it otherwise would.

In terms of the Equation of Exchange, $MV = PQ$, if the money supply (M) rises, velocity (V) remaining the same, aggregate demand (PQ) will increase. But if prices (P) rise in anticipation of the increase in aggregate demand, then output (Q) will not rise as much as it otherwise would, which will keep employment from rising as much as it otherwise would.

A wide variety of groups have the power to raise prices.

Suppose you were a member of a powerful union—say the steelworkers union or a county medical association—and you meet with your fellow members to discuss your bargaining or pricing strategy for the next year. One of your members argues that inflation is running at the rate of 7 percent a year and that there is no reason why your real incomes should fall during the next year. After a long debate, you finally decide that you will increase your prices enough so that after both price increases and increased income taxes, you will have a little more disposable income than you had last year. With an expected 7 percent inflation rate, this would mean that you would have to increase your prices about 10 to 12 percent, so that your after-tax real income would be slightly higher next year than it was during the preceding year.

Who are the groups that have enough monopoly power to anticipate inflation and raise their prices ahead of time? As we have already pointed out, some trade associations, such as the American Medical Association, have such power, as do some unions. Regulated industries, such as public utilities, railroads, trucking, and maritime transportation between United States ports are largely immune from the threat of entry. They have been successful in getting government support for increasing their prices. Other groups, such as tobacco farmers, peanut farmers, and milk producers have their prices set by the government. Farmers, as a group, have had enough political clout in the past to get the government to establish target prices that will partially protect them from losses of real income. Industries where there are few producers and little threat of entry also have the market power necessary to protect themselves from anticipated inflation.

Anticipatory increases in prices pose a difficult problem for the managers of aggregate demand.

The aggregate demand for goods consists of goods purchased from both competitive and monopolistic producers. Each sector receives a certain number of dollars in exchange for the sale of its goods and services. When the monopolistic sector increases its prices (given no change in aggregate demand), something must give. The same level aggregate demand cannot support a higher price level without causing a reduction in output and employment.

Think about it this way. The monopolistic sector of the economy with higher relative prices cannot sell as much as it sold before, the amount depending on the elasticity of demand. For example, when the trucking industry increases its prices relative to other forms of transportation, some truck drivers will lose their jobs. The ones who lose their jobs will look for work in other areas of the economy.

The competitive sector of the economy could hire these people if the prices of competitively produced products were to fall. Then the price level (including prices in both sectors) would be the same, with competitive prices lower and monopolistic prices higher.

Prices in the competitive sector would have to fall even more if the products sold by the monopolistic sector had an inelastic demand. For example, when the price of oil went up sharply, as it did in 1973, there was less aggregate demand left for the other sectors of the economy.

However, prices are seldom flexible in the short run. It is true that agricultural prices can rise and fall with relative ease. But the prices of brown paper, screw-machine products, and many other industrial products tend to be sticky even though they are produced in competitive industries. What is more, the wage rates in these competitive industries are sticky downward.

As a result, prices in the competitive sectors are not likely, in the short run, to go down fast enough to compensate for the price increases in the monopolistic sectors of the economy. And this is what presents the managers of aggregate demand with a difficult problem.

Should they increase the aggregate demand by, say, issuing more money and incurring a deficit? If they do, they will absorb the unemployment foisted on the competitive sectors of the economy, but the price level will have risen. Or should they maintain the same aggregate demand and depend on price flexibility in the competitive sector to solve the unemployment problem? Their choice is a hard one—either more unemployment or continued inflation.

If the Fed chooses to avoid the unemployment by increasing the money supply, it will have acquiesced to the inflation brought on by anticipatory price increases. In a sense the monopolistic sectors of the economy will be calling the tune, so far as inflation is concerned. The faster they increase their prices the faster the general level of prices will rise. When the Fed and other managers of aggregate demand acquiesce to the price increases brought on by monopolies, the inflation will feed on itself. This is sometimes called cost-push inflation.

Once this process of expected inflation gets under way, it does not reduce the amount of unemployment. In fact, the faster prices rise, the more money the Federal Reserve Board will have to create to keep unemployment from rising. Those who manage the aggregate demand will have run faster and faster in order to stay in the same place.

The point is that once inflation gets started, it feeds on itself. It gives people with market power the excuse to increase their prices and it gives the Federal Reserve Board the difficult choice of the consequences of maintaining or increasing the money supply. Expected inflation, as John Stuart Mill argued more than a century ago, is not very effective in reducing unemployment.

Variable inflation rates also create uncertainty and therefore reduce investment expenditures.

Not only does inflation feed on itself, it also creates an environment in which businesses are hesitant to invest in long-term projects such as building new plants. Investors are hesitant to buy long-term bonds during inflationary periods unless the rate of interest is high enough to compensate them for the loss of purchasing power. The inflation premium built into the long-term rate of interest adds significantly to costs of building plants and buying new equipment and this limits the growth of real GNP in the future.

In addition, inflation creates social tensions. Those citizens without market power become disgruntled. They demand that the inflation be brought under control. When the monetary authorities shut down the printing presses and reduce the amount of money flowing into the capital market in response to these demands, the short-term interest rates rise to high levels, as they did in 1974. Depression follows, as it did in 1975, and this causes unemployment rates to rise.

We turn now to another explanation of the failure of the Phillips curve to work.

GOVERNMENT EFFORTS TO COPE WITH UNEMPLOYMENT

Autonomous price increases combined with increases in aggregate demand also produce inflation without reducing unemployment.

Sometimes there are price increases that seem to come out of nowhere. In 1973, the economy had two sets of these autonomous increases to deal with. The OPEC cartel quadrupled the price of oil and there were crop failures abroad. The exports of feed grains increased the prices of meat and other agricultural products in this country.

In the absence of government intervention, unemployment would have risen until the prices of all other products had fallen. A given aggregate demand can support only one price level. If the prices of some products rise, others will have to fall.

Think of it this way. When the prices of oil and food rise, you spend more of your given income on these products and less on clothing, automobiles, and vacations. Initially, the reduced demand for the goods and services produced by these "other" industries will cause unemployment to increase. Unless the government increases the aggregate demand for products, this unemployment will persist until resource owners are finally willing to accept lower prices for their productive services used in these industries.

To prevent unemployment in these other industries, the government may do whatever is necessary to increase the aggregate demand for products. It may run a larger deficit and borrow from the Federal Reserve. Or the monetary authorities, impressed by growing unemployment, may just make money easier to borrow and in this way add to the aggregate demand. In either case, a larger aggregate demand will be effective in preventing what we shall call adjustment unemployment.

But when the government does this, it *validates* the inflation stemming from these autonomous increases in prices—just as it validated anticipatory price increases. In the absence of such governmental action, the relative prices of products would have adjusted to these autonomous price increases given time, but at the cost of high unemployment. By increasing aggregate demand, however, the government can ease the adjustment process, but at a different cost. The cost is the new higher level of prices.

Autonomous price increases of this type occur continuously. When the coal miners strike for higher wage rates than would be required to maintain their real wages, the result is an autonomous increase in public utility rates. When government regulations and the American Medical Association regulations combined increase hospitalization rates faster than the inflation rate, this too is an autonomous price increase. When the government imposes environmental protection regulations that add significantly to production costs, this too leads to autonomous price increases.

It is sometimes said that autonomous price increases combined with increases in aggregate demand produce a *ratchet* effect. Each price increase not compensated for by price reductions in some other part of the economy produces a higher price level. We turn now to a discussion of structural changes in the economy, which may have increased the unemployment rate independent of changes in aggregate demand.

STRUCTURAL CHANGES IN THE ECONOMY

Unemployment figures are based on the monthly surveys.

Every month, interviewers from the Bureau of the Census contact 47,000 carefully chosen households and ask a series of questions related to the week containing the twelfth day of the month. Those that say they are neither working nor looking for work are said to be outside of the labor force. Those who say they are looking for work are said to be unemployed. The total of those who are employed and those who are unemployed make up the labor force. The unemployment rate, which receives such wide publicity, is the percentage of people who say they would like to work but haven't found a job. The figures for the nation as a whole are derived by the Bureau of Labor Statistics from this sample of 47,000 households. Figure 15.5 shows the civilian labor force and employment from 1948 to 1977. Detailed figures are shown in Table 15.3.

The number of people in the toal civilian labor force has increased substantially in recent

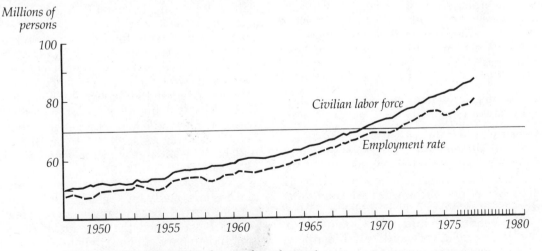

FIG. 15.5   The civilian labor force and employment.

TABLE 15.3
NONINSTITUTIONAL POPULATION AND THE LABOR FORCE, 1958–1977

Year	Total population (in millions)	Noninstitu- tionalized 16 years and over	Armed forces	Total civilian labor force	Total employed	Total unemployed	Unemployment rate (percentage of civilian labor force)
1958	174.9	116.4	2.6	67.6	63.0	4.6	6.8%
1959	177.8	117.9	2.6	68.4	64.6	3.8	5.5
1960	180.7	119.8	2.5	69.6	65.8	3.8	5.5
1961	183.7	121.3	2.6	70.5	65.7	4.8	6.7
1962	186.5	123.0	2.8	70.6	66.7	3.9	5.5
1963	189.2	125.2	2.7	71.8	67.8	4.0	5.7
1964	191.9	127.2	2.7	73.1	69.3	3.8	5.2
1965	194.3	129.2	2.7	74.5	71.1	3.4	4.5
1966	196.6	131.2	3.1	75.8	72.9	2.9	3.8
1967	198.7	133.3	3.4	77.3	74.4	2.9	3.8
1968	200.7	135.6	3.5	78.7	75.9	2.8	3.6
1969	202.7	137.8	3.5	80.7	77.9	2.8	3.5
1970	204.9	140.2	3.2	82.7	78.6	4.1	4.9
1971	207.1	142.6	2.8	84.1	79.1	5.0	5.9
1972	208.8	145.8	2.4	86.5	81.7	4.8	5.6
1973	210.4	148.3	2.3	88.7	84.4	4.3	4.9
1974	211.9	150.8	2.2	91.0	85.9	5.1	5.6
1975	213.6	153.4	2.2	92.6	84.8	7.8	8.5
1976	215.1	156.0	2.1	94.8	87.5	7.3	7.7
1977	216.8	158.6	2.1	97.4	90.5	6.9	7.0

Source: Table B-27, *Economic Report of the President,* 1978, Government Printing Office, p. 288.

years, from 68 million in 1958 to over 97 million in 1977. At the same time the number employed has increased, but the gap between the civilian labor force and employment has widened. In 1975, for example, 7.8 million people were unemployed. Does this mean that something basic has happened to the economy to make unemployment rates permanently higher than they have been in the past?

Full employment is defined as the noninflationary level of unemployment.

To answer this question we have to have a concept of "full employment." Initially you might be inclined to say that "full employment" means the situation in which all persons looking for work could find jobs at prevailing wage rates, and that anybody who is not working is doing so out of choice and therefore should not be included in the labor force. In other words, "full employment" would mean zero unemployment.

Further reflection reveals some difficulties with this definition, however. How would you reconcile the existence of the following groups: college students who would take jobs if they were paid $10 an hour but wouldn't give up their education if they were paid less; the 65-year-old man who is looking for work but won't take one unless it pays well enough for him to give up his social security benefits; a migrant worker who is looking for work but can't find any until he moves to a new location; the steelworker in Youngstown, Ohio, who lost his job because of foreign competition but won't take another one in Youngstown at a lower wage rate; or the worker who has quit her old job and is in the process of looking for another?

There are many gray areas in deciding what persons are really in the labor force and what persons are not. Because of these gray areas, economists have coined the concept of frictional or "noninflationary" unemployment. This is the rate of unemployment that an economy could have without such a shortage of people that wage rates and therefore prices would start to rise.

From 1947 through 1965, the average annual inflation rate was below 2 percent and the rate of unemployment just below 5 percent. On the basis of this experience, a 4 percent unemployment rate was regarded as the "full employment" rate. Today, some economists believe that the noninflationary unemployment rate is at least a half to one percentage point higher.*

The question is: Has anything happened to the economy in recent years to increase this noninflationary unemployment rate? If something has happened, then part of the reason for the additional unemployment may be said to be structural and not related to the aggregate demand for products.

Many changes in the composition of the labor force and social institutions have probably raised the noninflationary level of unemployment.

Some economists believe that there have been structural changes in the economy that should raise the "full employment" rate of unemployment. Consider their arguments.

1. The composition of the labor force has changed. Women comprised 31 percent of the labor force in 1956. They now comprise 40 percent of the labor force. Young people—16 to 24 years old—made up 17 percent of the labor force in 1956. They now make up 24 percent of the labor force. These new entrants to the labor force normally have higher unemployment rates than do prime age men— age 24 to 54— who have labor force experience.

2. Unemployment benefits have been extended to about 80 percent of the labor force compared to about 64 percent in 1956. Unemployment benefits are nontaxable. In the case of a two-worker family, where marginal tax rates are high, unemployment benefits as a percentage of take-home pay are larger than in the 1950s. Unemployment benefits make it possible for workers to take longer in searching for new work and therefore increase reported unemployment.

3. Minimum wage rate legislation has increased the minimum wage relative to the going wage in industrial employments. Most studies show that minimum wage rates increase unemployment among young people, women, blacks, Mexican-Americans, and other minority groups who lack significant labor force experience.

4. In their concerns over the effects of welfare and other income-maintenance programs on work incentives, Congress has required welfare mothers and those getting food stamps to register for work. In many cases, it is really impossible for these people to work. Including them in the unemployment roll inflates the total.

It is difficult to quantify the results of these structural and other changes in the economy. But it is reasonable to believe that these four sets of factors—and the interaction among them—may have added as much as one or two percentage points to the noninflationary unemployment rate.

Exactly how much unemployment—using the current definition of unemployment—should be associated with full employment is very difficult to say. But it does appear that these changes in the economy, however desirable they might be from the point of view of equity, have added to the percentage that would be unemployed under noninflationary conditions.

Economists do not agree about which combination of these explanations—expected inflation, autonomous increases in prices, and structural changes in unemployment—account for what is now called stagflation. They do, however, agree that rising prices combined with higher unemployment rates is a serious problem, perhaps the most serious macroeconomic problem the Western nations are facing.

---

* See Franco Modigliani and Lucas Papademos, "Monetary Policy for the Coming Quarters: The Conflicting Views," *New England Economic Review* (March/April 1976).

COMMENTARY

The following excerpt deals with a peculiar kind of unemployment—unemployment among the highly educated. Please read the excerpt and answer the following questions.
a) Why should there be concern about unemployment among the highly trained when the rates of other subsets of the population are much higher?
b) What are the causes of unemployment among the highly trained?
c) What are some solutions to the problem?

IDLE MINDS

According to government statistics, there is little reason to be concerned about joblessness among society's more highly trained people. For one thing, there is a general tendency for unemployment rates to decline as one moves up the educational ladder. Last March, for example, the jobless rate was only 3.3 percent for workers with at least a college degree, compared with 7.5 percent for high-school graduates and 10.3 percent for primary-school graduates. Again, the unemployment rate for professional and technical workers—generally the most highly educated occupational group—has averaged about 3½ percentage points below the overall unemployment rate for the past two decades.

Unemployment, underemployment

In contrast to this statistical picture, one often hears of the employment difficulties faced by holders of graduate degrees. Actually, the problem among such individuals is probably more of underemployment than of unemployment. Everyone knows (or knows someone who knows) a Ph.D. in History or English who is driving a taxi while awaiting that teaching position to turn up. Anecdotes are more abundant than statistics in this area, but there are a few studies which suggest the dimensions of the problem. For example, a survey by the Modern Language Association found that 39 percent of last year's Ph.D.s in English were unable to find teaching positions. Also, Professor Ernest May of Harvard reports that roughly 90 percent of all new Ph.D.s in the humanities found academic jobs over the past several decades, but that only 10 percent of similar graduates in the next two decades may find academic jobs.

The problem does not seem to affect all disciplines equally, but appears to be concentrated in the humanities and a few social sciences—those fields which traditionally recycle most of their graduates back into the university. The physical sciences are much less troubled by this type of problem, as evidenced by the National Science Foundation finding that the unemployment rate for Ph.D. scientists and engineers was just under 1 percent in the recession year 1975.

With considerably more dramatic unemployment problems faced by other groups, such as the 35–40 percent rate among black teenagers, why should we be concerned with the job problems of such a seemingly privileged group as advanced-degree receivers? For one reason, society has made a sizable investment in this group. Practically all education in the United States involves a substantial subsidy to the student, since tuition at most covers only a fraction of the true cost of the student's education. The further the student treads up the educational hill, the larger is the public investment embodied in his "human capital," and it can average more than $20,000 for the college graduate who decides to go on for a Ph.D. When this individual is found in the unemployment lines, the large public investment is not reaping any social benefits. And when he or she is underemployed, the return on this social investment becomes less than was originally anticipated.

Causes

What are the causes of unemployment among the highly educated? First there is apparently a lack of useful job-market information. When people decide to enter advanced-degree programs, they typically have some impressions concerning future employment opportunities. These impressions are generally based upon information gleaned from newspapers, magazines, and conversations with knowledgeable people. However, such information may not be very helpful, because it is typically based on individual cases rather than on overall surveys of the relevant field. Again, even when the quality of the information is high, it may not be a very good guide to the state of the market three to six years hence, when the student will be completing his or her degree.

Even in cases where there is sufficient information and a relatively stable job market, the graduate may become unemployed because he doesn't give proper weight to the available information. If a student enjoys his field, his decision to remain in graduate school may have a large consumption component and a relatively small investment component. In other words, he may not really care very much whether he gets a job when he graduates, because of his intense interest in French literature or whatever else he may be studying at the time. The pursuit of any sort of knowledge can easily become an end in itself.

Some evidence suggests that those who choose the humanities—the field in which the unemployment/underemployment problem is the greatest—give the least weight to the state of the job market. Thus, between 1971 and 1973, long after the job market had begun to send signals back to the universities, graduate enrollments in physics declined 11 percent while graduate enrollments in the humanities expanded by 15 percent.

Even when the individual does have some interest in post-degree job prospects, the university atmosphere doesn't always promote full disclosure of employment opportunities. University departments, like other bureaucracies, resemble biological organisms—they are interested in growth, or at the very least, in survival. When the market for a particular field is expanding, university departments are happy to grow with the increased student demand for instruction. However, when the market for that field begins to contract, university departments are reluctant to join in the downturn. In order to maintain their jobs, professors need students. And while altruism may lead departments to inform potential students of the dim job prospects at the other end of the educational tunnel, self-preservation may lead them to downplay the employment problem.

Another cause of Ph.D. unemployment involves the values held by new degree-holders. Typically, most Ph.D. graduates desire university research and teaching positions more than anything else. This is understandable, because for several years the student has interacted largely with university professors, who become increasingly important role models. Graduate school is really an apprenticeship program, and like any other apprentice, the graduate student wants someday to become a journeyman like the professor under whom he or she has worked. To accept any sort of nonacademic employment is often considered a second-rate choice.

Solutions?

The immediate problem to be solved is the un- and underemployment of thousands who have already received Ph.D.'s in surplus fields. Many of them have skills (often related to research, administration or communication) which are readily transferable to nonacademic jobs. But prejudices must first be overcome among both potential employees and potential employers. In one such step, the Modern Language Association has assigned a full-time staff member to explore nonacademic job opportunities for its unemployed members. On a larger scale, the Mellon Foundation has developed a 7-week orientation program at the N.Y.U. School of Business, to help provide 50 unemployed humanities Ph.D.'s with a useful introduction to the business world.

But a long-run solution to the problem must concentrate on the entry rather than the exit to graduate education. Most importantly, complete information on the job market must be made available to potential students, especially when it is pessimistic. For example, when a student applies for a graduate program in English, the university could send the applicant a short statement assessing the current and future market for English Ph.D.'s. Such a statement might be updated once a year, simply using information on the placement of that university's recent graduates or information from broader surveys and Department of Labor studies.

As we've seen, not everyone will put much weight on such information—especially those individuals who view education as a consumption good rather than an investment good. Of course, they have every right to do so, but it doesn't automatically follow that taxpayers should heavily subsidize such consumption when it fails to yield any social payoff. Methods of eliminating unprofitable social subsidies can become administrative and political nightmares, but when public funds have other pressing uses, such education subsidies begin to appear rather inequitable.

Some thought should be given to reducing the social subsidy to those fields where the subsidy has contributed to an oversupply of graduates. This could be done by setting quotas on entry (and letting students compete on merit) or raising the tuition in those fields (and having students compete by income and willingness to pay). Both methods improve the survivors' job prospects, their relative salaries, and the social return to the remaining public subsidy. Whatever methods are used, either to employ the currently un- or underemployed or to restructure incentives to deal with the problem in the longer run, it is clear that some creative thinking is necessary to alleviate what could become a serious social and economic problem in the decades ahead.

MICHAEL GORHAM and JOHN NORTON. "Idle Minds," *Weekly Letter*, Federal Reserve Bank of San Francisco, February 3, 1978. Reprinted by permission.

SOCIAL COSTS OF UNEMPLOYMENT AND INFLATION

Unemployment wastes resources and causes unnecessary poverty.

Unemployment brings with it serious economic problems. Unemployment averaged 8.5 percent in 1975. Had the economy been operating at the full employment level, the actual level of GNP would have been $175 billion higher than the actual GNP of $1369 billion revised that year.* In 1976, the unemployment rate decreased to 7.7 percent. The lost production of that year is estimated to be $156 billion.

Wasting potential GNP is only part of the problem. We have already seen in Chapter 10 that unemployment is particularly hard on those who are bogged down in islands of poverty. It is during

periods of high employment, such as those that characterize a war period, that employers are willing to employ those without previous labor force skills. It is also during periods of high employment that employers are willing to spend money on training programs to upgrade employee skills. But the opposite is true during periods of high unemployment.

Inflation destroys the value of the dollar.

Inflationary periods also have their economic and social costs. This is true whether the inflationary rates are 6 or 10 percent a year. The figures in Table 15.4 demonstrate what various inflationary rates would do to the value of the dollar. A 6 percent annual inflation rate would reduce the value of a dollar to $0.75 in five years and to $0.56

* Based on estimates of the President's Council of Economic Advisers.

TABLE 15.4

THE VALUE OF A DOLLAR IN THE FUTURE AT DIFFERENT RATES OF INFLATION

Annual rates of inflation	Value of $1.00 in			
	1 year	5 years	10 years	20 years
2%	$0.98	$0.91	$0.82	$0.67
5	0.95	0.78	0.61	0.38
6	0.94	0.75	0.56	0.31
8	0.93	0.68	0.46	0.21
10	0.91	0.62	0.39	0.15
15	0.87	0.50	0.25	0.06
20	0.83	0.40	0.16	0.03

in another five years. Even what appears to be relatively low rates of inflation given the experience of the 1970s—say, 5 percent per year—constitutes an important threat to fixed dollar values in the future. In 20 years, for example, a dollar will be worth only $0.38 if the rate of inflation is 5 percent.

Given inflation, the structure of the income tax imposes higher taxes without legislation unless indexed.

If somehow all prices, wage rates, interest rates, rents, tax brackets, and so on were to rise proportionally with the price level, it could be argued, inflation would not be a serious problem. When prices rose, you would get more income as salaries also increased, thereby allowing you to pay the higher prices in the marketplace with no real loss. Your savings account and your debts would increase with the price level. Your only problem would be to add the zeros to your annual income and your annual expenditures. Inflation would be largely a bookkeeping problem.

If everything could be *indexed*, as this process of adjusting prices proportionally with the price level is called, then inflation would not be a very serious problem. The only asset that could not be indexed would be hand-to-hand currency, and it would be easy for people to minimize their holdings of currency.

In some countries, such as Brazil, where high rates of inflation have been common for many years, new social institutions have been developed to accomplish this indexing task. But in most of the countries of Western Europe and North America, these social institutions have not been developed. As a result, inflation is a serious problem. Consider some of the costs associated with inflation.

Unless the income brackets for your personal income tax are indexed, the government will get a larger share of your real income whenever your nominal income rises. (Nominal income refers to money income. Real income refers to money income adjusted for prices.)

For example, assume you are earning $200 a week and having $50 (25 percent of your income) deducted from your paycheck for taxes. If prices

rise by 50 percent and your pay goes up proportionately to $300 a week, your real income appears to be unchanged. But the $100 increase in your money income puts you in a higher tax bracket. You now have $100 (33 percent of your income) rather than $50 deducted from your paycheck. As a result, your real income—money income adjusted for prices—has gone down. The government, without changing the tax law, is now taxing you more heavily.

Inflation imposes higher corporate taxes, also without legislation.

The same thing is true of the corporate tax system. When a company buys some new capital equipment, such as a truck, it can depreciate only the actual dollar cost of the truck, not the replacement value of it. As a result, a part of real income associated with buying the truck is transferred to the government in higher corporate taxes. The total amount of accumulated depreciation will not replace the truck when it is worn out. Some of the profits, on which the company has paid taxes, will have to be used to replace the truck and keep the rest of the company's equipment in good condition.

Inflation constitutes a discriminating tax on those without market power.

High inflation rates constitute a tax on those groups in the economy that do not have enough market power to raise their prices as fast as the overall price level is rising.

If you are not a member of a strong union, nor in an industry that is growing rapidly and attracting workers by posting high wage rates, nor an OPEC member, nor a milk producer or peanut farmer whose prices are set by the government, nor a member of any other group with market power, then your income is not likely to go up as fast as the prices you have to pay for the products you buy. Part of your real income is being taken from you for the benefit of those groups in the economy that do have enough market or political power to increase their prices in anticipation of higher prices in the future. In effect, you are being taxed for their benefit. You may regard inflation as a cruel tax and urge its repeal, but it is not an enacted tax and until something is done about inflation it will automatically increase.

Variation in inflation rates creates uncertainty for business decision making.

Because high inflation rates tend to vary substantially, the inflation process adds a great deal of uncertainty to business decision making. This in turn means that a piece of equipment must give promise of producing a high rate of return in order to overcome the uncertainties of the future. This tends to cut down on business investment in new plant and equipment and restrict economic growth.

All things considered, inflation, like unemployment, imposes real economic and social costs on a nation. It destroys, in part, the logic of the price system. It rewards people for doing unproductive things, such as speculating on price increases or participating in political pressure groups. It tends to feed static into the price system and may easily cause the system to waste resources.

What can be done about these twin evils, unemployment and inflation, which have together come to be known as *stagflation*? Economists are not agreed on the best way to quiet the problem, but since you will be involved in the solution, you should understand their proposals for dealing with it.

COMMENTARY

Inflation is often referred to as a tax. It is also described as the cruelest tax because it violates so blatantly the principles of equity and ability to pay. Read the following commentary and answer the questions.

a) How does the existing tax structure make the burden of inflation more onerous?
b) How are low-income people especially affected?

INFLATION: THE TAXMAN'S FAVORITE PICKPOCKET

Today's high inflation is countering the "built-in stabilizer" properties of the progressive income tax. The result is an uneven squeeze on taxpayers' real aftertax incomes. It's time to take a new look at the old saying that inflation is the cruelest tax. The cliché conveys the idea that inflation adds a "tax" to the prices of goods and services that consumers buy. But in today's world of progressive income taxes, inflation does more than increase prices. It also pushes up tax bills, and it does so in ways that conflict with long-standing notions about how a tax system ought to operate. All this goes largely unnoticed because it happens without any explicit changes in the tax laws.

The problem ranges all the way from taxes on corporate profits to those on individual incomes. . . . Equally pernicious is the way inflation increases individual income tax burdens.

The progressive structure of the individual income tax assures that, as incomes rise during a time of inflation, the average rate of tax paid by most taxpayers goes up. In other words, tax bills don't just rise as fast as inflation—they actually rise faster.

The size of the personal exemptions, the standard deduction and the low-income allowance all are fixed in amount. So, as money incomes increase because of inflation, there's a concurrent rise in the taxable percentage of an individual's income. Moreover, the widths of the tax-rate brackets are fixed, so that inflationary increases in income push taxpayers into new tax brackets where higher tax rates apply. Finally, inflation increases the monetary value of property even if it does not increase its real value. If this property is sold, capital-gains taxes are based on the increase in money value, not the smaller increase in real value. Perhaps the last is not systematic enough to be said to affect all taxpayers, but the first two effects are universal and easily demonstrated.

Out goes equity. Computations of the precise magnitude of the impact vary, but the general conclusion is that, when inflation is as high as it is today, the impact is significant. One researcher has calculated that two years of inflation at a 14% rate is the equivalent of increasing each of the tax rates by 3 percentage points in a world without inflation.

Not only does inflation increase the tax burden, but it tends to do so in a way that violates the standards of equity espoused by most tax reformers. Percentage increases in taxes are greatest for taxpayers with low incomes who began the period of inflation with no tax bills or very small ones. Even though much or all of their increase in money incomes represents inflation, it is taxed because the exemptions and standard deduction don't increase. So the percentage of income paid in tax would climb even if purchasing power does not.

The effect is also significant for people in the middle-income ranges where the tax brackets are relatively narrow and the increase in rates between brackets is quite large. When incomes are very large, however, rate brackets are wide and changes in rates from one bracket to the next are slight, so that the percentage of income paid in tax does not increase as much as it does for those with low and medium-sized incomes.

The equity principle underlying the progressive income tax structure is that the percentage of income paid in tax ought to rise as income rises. The increases in the tax burden that accompany inflation, however, are regressive. As a percentage of income, the percentage increase is greatest for those with the lowest amounts of taxable income.

Another tenet of tax equity is that taxpayers with the same income should bear the same tax burden. But inflation can frustrate this goal because it hits people with similar real incomes in differing degrees. Two people whose before-tax incomes will buy equal amounts of goods and services can have differing amounts of actual cash income. Since taxes are based on cash income, the taxpayer with the higher total will pay out more in taxes even though his income before taxes won't buy any more than the income of the taxpayer with less cash income.

Monthly Economic Letter, First National City Bank, New York, January 1975. Reprinted by permission.

SOLUTIONS TO THE STAGFLATION PROBLEM

In this section we will examine two polar positions taken by different groups of economists for solving the stagflation problem. The first, which we shall call the *Heller* position, tends to be the position of many Keynesian economists.* The second, which we shall call the *Friedman* position, tends to be the position of most monetarists.†

Many economists do not agree with either of these polar positions and find that they are most comfortable with an in-between position. We shall consider both polar extremes, as well as one of the in-between positions: that being advocated by Arthur Okun.‡

Heller says: Increase aggregate demand to full employment and impose price and wage rate controls.

The Heller position is easy to characterize. Heller favors discretionary fiscal policies to "fine-tune" the economy so that it will operate at full em-

* Walter Heller is the Regents' Professor of Economics at the University of Minnesota. He served as chairman of the Council of Economic Advisers to the President under John F. Kennedy. Professor Heller is generally regarded as the economist who introduced Keynesian economic policies to the government.

† Milton Friedman recently retired as the Paul Snowden Russell Distinguished Service Professor of Economics at the University of Chicago. He was awarded the Nobel Prize in Economics in 1976. He is widely regarded as one of the early and most forceful proponents of the monetarist position in macroeconomics.

‡ Arthur Okun is a Senior Fellow at the Brookings Institution, a research institution in economics. He was Chairman of the Council of Economic Advisers under President Johnson.

ployment. When it appeared that the economy was slowing down, he would either reduce taxes or increase government expenditures to increase the aggregate demand. At the same time, he would have the monetary authorities increase the money supply to support the anticyclical fiscal policies. When it appeared that the economy was growing too fast, he would either increase taxes or reduce government expenditures to reduce aggregate demand. He would also have the Federal Reserve Board tighten interest rates to support the government's fiscal policies. He would have the government manage the aggregate demand for products in such a way that the economy would be constantly pressured against the full-employment limit—defining full employment as being a situation in which there were no more than 3½ to 4 percent of the labor force unemployed.

What should be done if under these conditions prices should start to rise, as they did in 1967 and again in 1973 when unemployment approached this level? The answer is impose wage and price controls. By holding prices down, the excess demand for products will have to increase the real GNP, and that in turn will increase job opportunities for everybody, especially minority groups.

Suppressed inflation will guarantee opportunities for the poor and prevent the wasting of resources.

Every wage contract would have to fall within the guidelines laid down by the government. These guidelines would be set so that wage rates would not rise faster than productivity—thus preventing the pressure on costs that would otherwise characterize the economy. At the same time, the price control agency would impose price controls on all products and in this way keep the cost of living from rising. This policy of imposing productivity-limited wage guidelines and price controls is sometimes known as an *incomes policy*. It maintains price levels and wage rates in such a way as to protect the real incomes of all participants in the economy.

Another way of characterizing the Heller position is to say that the government should manage the aggregate demand for products in such a way that there will always be as many jobs as

there are people seeking work. If inflation develops, suppress it with price controls. The only way an excess demand for products can express itself is through inducing employers to employ people who would not otherwise be employed.

Critics say: An incomes policy won't work.

Will an *income policy* work? The critics say no. Their arguments are:

1. Nobody has yet learned to "fine-tune" the economy. Predictions are difficult to make and not particularly reliable. There are significant time lags between the recognition that a change in aggregate demand is needed and final effects of an increase in expenditures or decrease in tax. The evidence from 1965 on indicates that discretionary monetary-fiscal policies won't work, except possibly to prevent deep and persistent depressions of the 1930s type.

2. Price controls have never worked for a prolonged period of time during peace time. Unions with political power find ways to exceed the wage guidelines. Businesses will reduce the quality of their products as well as find other ways to avoid the effective control of their prices.

3. If all prices are to be controlled, then the federal government must be prepared to run the economy. It is, the critics argue, almost impossible for a central planning system to make all or most of the decisions for an economy that produces millions of products for millions of buyers.

4. Changes in relative prices are necessary to guide the economy. When changes in relative prices are suppressed by price controls, the economy becomes inefficient.

5. In other countries where an incomes policy has been tried, it hasn't work.

Okun says: Manage aggregate demand and use tax incentives to keep wage rates from rising.

Arthur Okun's middle-ground position would replace price controls with financial incentives to businesses not to grant wage rate increases in excess of the guidelines. A business that was able to keep its wage settlements within the guidelines would get a tax reduction. The employees agreeing to keep their wage rate increases within the guidelines would also get a reduction in their social security taxes. In this way Okun hopes to get the employment advantages of suppressed inflation without having to subject the economy to the consequences of price controls.

Critics of Okun's middle-ground position point out the following:

1. This has never been tried and it is yet to be seen whether financial incentives can do the job of keeping wage rates under control.
2. Differential movements in wages—some wages going up more than others—have a role to play in a price-directed economy. Okun's tax incentives would not make allowances for the fact that when certain types of skilled labor are in short supply, their wage rates should rise by more than the guidelines would permit in order to ration those short-supply skills.

Friedman proposes an approach at the polar extreme from Heller.

At the other polar extreme we find the type of macroeconomic policies recommended by Milton Friedman and other monetarists. Their policy prescriptions can be divided into four parts.

In the first place, government tax revenues and expenditures should be determined independently of demand management considerations. The government should enact taxes that will balance the budget at some agreed upon percentage of the full-employment level of GNP—say 95 percent. In this way, if the GNP falls short of the 95 percent full employment level, the government will run a deficit and will have to borrow funds from the capital market. Or if the GNP exceeds this target, the government will run a surplus, which it can pay into the capital market in retiring part of the national debt. The monetarists argue that this requirement that the government balance its budget at, say, 95 percent of full employment will mean that the government must raise taxes whenever it increases expenditures. At

the same time, it will not require that the government balance its budget on a year-to-year basis.

In the second place, Friedman and the other monetarists would have the Fed abandon its policies of stabilizing interest rates. The Fed should announce that it would increase the money supply at a fixed rate, say 5 percent a year. In some years interest rates would be high and in other years they would be low. But as a general rule, they argue, interest rates would be lower than they are now because they would not include an inflation premium.

There are some differences among the monetarists themselves regarding how rapidly this change in monetary policies should be brought about. Some would advocate immediately reducing the percentage rate of growth of the money supply to the target rate. Others would reduce the growth of the money supply step by step over a three- or four-year period. Both groups admit that the initial effect of reducing the growth of the money supply will be to make money tight, as it was in 1974. They also admit that the most likely effect of reducing the rate of growth of the money supply is to produce a depression and unemployment. But, they argue, this is the price that the country will eventually have to pay to stop the inflation, so why not do it now before prices rise any further?

In the third place, Friedman would replace the present welfare system, with its unemployment benefits, aid for families with dependent children, food stamps, rent subsidies, and other categorical programs, with a single income maintenance program. He would have it designed as a negative income tax. A family would be guaranteed a minimum income, say $5000 a year. If their income fell short of this target, the government would send them monthly checks to bring them up to this level. If they found a better job or worked longer hours, they would keep at least a specific percentage of their additional income. If they could keep 50 percent of their additional income, they would get some help from the government until their income rose to $10,000. In this way, Professor Friedman argues, while people would be automatically protected against unemployment and other risks, they would also be encouraged to seek part-time jobs or other fill-in jobs. And many of the working poor who would otherwise not be eligible for government aid would thus be provided with a minimum income.

In the fourth place, Friedman and many other monetarists would have the government take action to eliminate the causes of structural unemployment. Thus they would have the government abolish minimum wage rates, occupation licensing requirements beyond those required for public safety, educational requirements unnecessary for the job, and other impediments to the employment of the disadvantaged.

Summarized, then, the monetarist proposals include: (1) an indexed federal budget, designed to produce a surplus when business is good and a deficit when it is bad; (2) stable rates of growth of the money supply; (3) an income maintenance program to alleviate poverty and reduce the hardships caused by unemployment; and (4) specific policies designed to reduce structural unemployment.

Critics say: These policies will create a massive unemployment problem: inflation is better than unemployment.

1. The federal budget necessarily has an effect on the aggregate demand for products. It is a waste not to use it to specifically stabilize the growth of the GNP. Even small recessions are unnecessary. While a revenue system designed to balance the budget at some target percentage of full employment would provide some automatic stabilizers, these will not be enough to prevent recurrent depressions and loss of employment.

2. Were the Fed to turn to some monetary growth rule—say, increase the money supply at 5 percent a year—the initial effect would be to produce a monstrous depression. The economy is now accustomed to a 4 to 8 percent inflation rate. If this is not continued, money will get to be very tight. Interest rates will rise and the growth of the economy will be stifled. The result will be massive unemployment. It is better to continue inflating than to go through the pains of the massive depression required to stop it.

3. The negative income tax would be too expensive. It would require the government to pay large amounts to the working poor. It is better to have a welfare system that can be administered for the benefit of specific groups of people, such as mothers with dependent children, than to make these income payments available to all of the poor.

4. The programs designed to reduce structural unemployment won't work. The market system won't help the poor, who constitute an underdeveloped nation within a nation, and it is necessary to have massive aid programs to release them from the cruel cycle of poverty.

MINI-CASE 15.1

This mini-case is designed to help clarify your thinking in terms of relating political realities to economic facts.

Which of the following statements best illustrates the dilemma a president faces if he wants to be reelected on the basis of the performance of the economy during his first term?

a) Full employment and price stability are consistent goals but they are difficult to achieve.
b) Compared to inflation, unemployment is clearly the lesser of the two evils, but no president can say so.
c) Compared to unemployment, inflation is clearly the lesser of the two evils, but no president can say so.
d) Price stability and low levels of unemployment are both ethically important goals, and neither one is necessarily dominant over the other one, but it is impossible for the economy to achieve both at the same time.

There is no easy solution to the problem of stagflation.

This chapter was designed to give you some experience in analyzing a current problem. The stagflation problem is a stubborn one. You are likely to face it all of your life. Many politicians, and even some economists, will argue that some simplistic solution will put everything in order. We hope that you will see that solutions are difficult because there is disagreement about both the causes of stagflation and which goals are most important. If you were certain that inflation was the worst danger the society faced, you could probably solve the problem, even though the cost was a severe and prolonged depression. Or if you were certain that unemployment was the worst danger the society faced, then you could probably develop social institutions that would help you live with high rates of inflation. But because as a nation we do not agree on the appropriate trade-off between these two social goals, we will find it difficult to find a clear-cut solution to this problem.

REVIEW QUESTIONS

1. The year 1964 was a landmark year. It marked the political acceptance of Keynesian ideas for managing the aggregate demand for products. Which of the following statements best states the difference between performance of the economy before and after 1964?
   a) From 1946 to 1964, the economy grew slower than it did after 1964.
   b) From 1946 to 1964, the economy showed wider variations in unemployment than it did after 1964.
   c) From 1946 to 1964 the average inflation rate was higher than it was after the government started managing aggregate demand in 1964.
   d) Average unemployment and inflation rates were lower from 1946 to 1964 than they were after 1964.

2. With respect to the Phillips curve drawn for the United States it may be said that:
   a) the data seem to fit the same curve fairly well during the entire period 1950 to 1977.
   b) during the 1950s and 1960s unemployment rates and inflation rates both went up and down in the same years.
   c) in the 1970s, it appears that the Phillips curve has shifted so that rates of unemployment and inflation are both higher than they were in the 1950s and 1960s.
   d) in the 1970s the data conclusively show that rates of unemployment and inflation vary inversely with each other. (When inflation rates rise, unemployment rates fall and vice versa.)

3. Expected inflation differs from unexpected inflation in the following way:
   a) Expected inflation is associated with lower rates of unemployment. This is not true of unexpected inflation.
   b) Unexpected inflation usually is associated with lower rates of unemployment. Expected inflation does not reduce unemployment rates and may actually increase them.
   c) Expected inflation is not a signal for those with monopolistic power over prices to raise their prices while unexpected inflation is.
   d) Expected inflation causes the velocity of money to rise. The reverse is true of unexpected inflation.

4. When prices rise in one sector of the economy, either because of monopolistic price setting or because of autonomous influences, and there is no change in the aggregate demand for products then:

   a) prices will have to fall in some other sectors of the economy or there will be additional unemployment.
   b) prices will rise in all sectors of the economy, with no change in employment rates.
   c) no matter how high the price level rises because of these factors, rates of unemployment will not change.
   d) the quantity and the velocity of money automatically changes to permit the higher prices to continue regardless of what happens to prices in the other sectors of the economy.

5. Suppose, as happened in the early 1970s, petroleum and food prices rise at the same time. Suppose, further, that these price rises are caused by events external to the United States economy. Those who manage the aggregate demand for products will be faced with the following dilemma(s):

   a) Either maintain aggregate demand at a steady level or face more unemployment.
   b) Either increase aggregate demand or accept the fact that the inflation rate will rise.
   c) Either wait for prices to fall in other parts of the economy or accept the unemployment associated with this process or acquiesce to a substantial rise in the price level.
   d) All of the above.

6. An "incomes policy" rigorously pursued for an extended period of time requires that:

   a) wage rates increase at the same rate as prices.
   b) exports are equal to imports.
   c) the government manage the allocation of resources.
   d) rates of unemployment in the economy rise.

7. The solution to the stagflation problem that employs: (a) balancing the budget at 95 percent of full employment and not using fiscal policies to offset inflations and depressions, and (b) adopting and maintaining a 4 percent rate of growth of the money supply would, if adopted suddenly, probably lead to:

   a) a resolution of the problem. There would be no longer any periods of unemployment and inflation.
   b) a depression and a substantial period of adjustment of the economy to these new policies.
   c) stable interest rates and lower rates of private investment.
   d) steadily increasing prices.

8. Suppose that all productive service prices were indexed. Suppose all debts were indexed. Suppose too that all tax and transfer payments systems were indexed. Then:

   a) relative prices would lose their capacity to guide production.
   b) people would not be as concerned about an inflation or deflation as they are now.
   c) inflation would still be effective as a hidden tax.
   d) there is no index appropriate or available to do the job.

DISCUSSION QUESTIONS

1. You are a member of the Board of Governors of the Federal Reserve Board. OPEC increases the price of oil from $15 to $30 a barrel. Gasoline, heating oil, public utility rates, and all oil-derivative products rise in price. Consumers reduce purchases of nonoil products—unemployment rises. What options do you have? What policies will you support?

2. Continuing with the same question, would it make any difference to you, as a member of the Board of Governors of the Federal Reserve System, whether the OPEC countries used their increased income to increase their deposits in United States banks or used their income to buy war materials?

3. "Every price is somebody's income. During inflation, aggregate incomes to consumers, business, and government go up as fast as prices. Since this is true, why worry about inflation? There will always be enough income to purchase the products that are produced." Criticize this statement.

4. During the Vietnam war the unemployment rate fell to 3.7 percent. Therefore, the "full employment target" should be at least an unemployment rate of 4 percent of the labor force. Discuss.

5. The minimum wage rate is raised from 40 percent to 75 percent of the prevailing factory wage rate. What will this do to the "noninflationary unemployment rate"? Explain.

6. Continuing with this problem, what action should the managers of aggregate demand take when unemployment rises due to increases in the minimum wage rate?

7. Discuss the social institutions that you think would have to be created in order for a society such as the United States to adjust fully to a more or less permanent 10 percent inflation rate.

8. Discuss the social institutions that you think would have to be created in order for a society like the United States to live with a more or less permanent 7 percent unemployment rate.

9. Continuing with questions 7 and 8, which of these two sets of social institutions do you think would be best for the United States?

10. It has been said that the only way to stop inflation after it has been under way for five years is to precipitate (with monetary or fiscal policies) a major depression with unemployment rates in excess of 10 percent. Discuss.

11. What are the by-product results of adopting an "incomes policy" that is strictly enforced?

12. What do you think would happen if Professor Friedman's policies as stated at the end of the chapter were implemented in a short period of time?

13. If the Phillips curve were stable, as it appeared to be during the 1950s and 1960s, who should make macroeconomic policies, the economists or politicians?

14. The two-worker family is apparently here to stay. Discuss the implications of the two-worker family for macroeconomic policies.

15. Unemployment rates among young blacks and inexperienced females are substantially higher than for experienced white male workers. Do you think that macroeconomic policies should be designed to eliminate these pockets of unemployment? If not, what would you do to resolve this problem?

ANSWERS TO REVIEW QUESTIONS

1. It is strange, but nonetheless a fact, that the average rates of unemployment and inflation were higher after 1964 than from 1946 to 1964.
   a) This is incorrect. The real GNP grew faster from 1946 to 1964 than it did in the thirteen years following 1964.
   b) This is incorrect. There were recurrent mild recessions from 1946 to 1964, but unemployment rates showed wider variations after 1946 than before.

c) This is incorrect. Inflation rates were higher after 1964 than before.

d) This is correct. See the explanation above.

2. The Phillips curve appears to fit the data fairly well in the 1950s and 1960s, but in the 1970s the curve either no longer fits the data, or the entire curve has shifted outward and to the right, indicating rates of unemployment and inflation are both higher than they were during the 1950s and 1960s.

a) This is incorrect. The same curve does not fit both periods.

b) This is incorrect. The Phillips indicates that these rates vary inversely.

c) This is correct as explained above.

d) This is incorrect. The data are not conclusive that the curve is still applicable to the data being generated by the economy.

3. Expected inflation does cause those with monopoly power to raise their prices to avoid losing real income. As a result, unexpected inflation usually leads to higher rates of growth of GNP and therefore less unemployment. This is not true of expected inflation. It is not effective in reducing unemployment.

a) This is incorrect. It is inconsistent with the explanation above.

b) This is correct as explained above.

c) Expected inflation is a signal for those with monopoly power to increase their prices in anticipation of more inflation. This is incorrect.

d) There is no necessary relation between expected inflation and the velocity of money. This is incorrect.

4. The same aggregate demand can support only one price level, given no change in total output. Therefore, when prices rise in one sector, they will have to fall in other sectors, or additional unemployment will develop.

a) This is correct for the reason given above.

b) This is incorrect. If all prices rise, given no change in aggregate demand, unemployment levels will fall.

c) This is incorrect for the same reason as in (b) above.

d) There is no reason why M and V should change when oil and food prices rise. This is incorrect.

5. Answers (a), (b), and (c) are all correct and state the dilemma that the Fed and other authorities who manage the aggregate demand face when there are either monopolistic or autonomous increases in prices. Therefore (d) is the correct choice.

6. An "incomes policy" (price and wage rate controls) requires in the long run that the government manage the allocation of resources. In the short run, an incomes policy might work, but over the long run, wage rates and prices do have an important allocation function. If these prices are controlled, the government will have to accept the responsibility for managing the economy.

a) This is incorrect. Wage rates can rise faster than prices if productivity is also increasing.

b) This is incorrect. The answer is irrelevant to the adoption of an incomes policy.

c) This is correct as explained above.

d) This is incorrect. In the short run, unemployment rates would probably fall. It is impossible to say what would happen in the long run.

7. The Friedman solution to the stagflation problem would involve facing some serious problems in the short run. In the long run, the policies could work but there would be no assurance that the economy would be free of unemployment and periods of rising prices. Friedman's argument is that the problems of inflation and unemployment would be minimized but not eliminated.

   a) This is incorrect. In the short run, the economy would face a difficult problem of adjustment.
   b) This is correct. A sudden reduction in the rate of growth of the money supply would probably lead to a depression and unemployment.
   c) This is incorrect. Interest rates would vary depending on the supply and demand of loanable funds.
   d) This is incorrect. A constant or slowly rising aggregate demand would not lead to continued inflation.

8. During inflationary or deflationary periods, it is difficult to write contracts involving future prices. Indexing will provide escalator clauses so that prices stated in the contract will move up or down depending on what is happening to the price level.

   a) This is incorrect. Relative prices would not be affected.
   b) This is correct. If you enter a contract assured that inflation will not wipe out some of your investment, you will be less concerned.
   c) This is incorrect. The hidden tax effects of inflation would be eliminated.
   d) This is incorrect. Admittedly, the price indexes we now have are not perfect, but most agree that they would be effective.

APPENDIX TO
CHAPTER 15: THE NATIONAL DEBT

OBJECTIVES
Upon successful completion of this appendix, you will be able to:

1. Describe the national debt in terms of its size, rate of growth, and ownership.
2. Explain the impact of the debt on saving and consumption patterns.
3. Differentiate between the effect of foreign held and domestically held debt.
4. Cite the major problems of a growing national debt.

INTRODUCTION

The national debt is a topic that puzzles many people. In the fall of 1978, the national debt was almost $800 billion, or about $8500 per employed worker. The interest on the national debt—the third largest item in the federal budget—was running at almost $45 billion, or about $500 per worker. In the first eight years of the 1970s, the size of the national debt more than doubled and the interest on the national debt increased about two and one half times.

If you had borrowed $8500 to buy a luxury car, you might be concerned. You might even worry. Should you be concerned about the $8500 you owe as "your share" of the national debt?

There are two widely different answers to this question. The first is: "Don't be concerned. You owe it to yourself, and the size of the national debt is just a bookkeeping problem." The other is: The national debt, like any other debt, is important, and until the federal government learns how to balance its budget we will have serious inflationary and income distribution problems." In this appendix we will examine this problem and find out what elements of truth are to be found in each position.

THE STATISTICAL FACTS

The Federal Reserve System owns a large share of the national debt.

Before we consider the problems growing out of the national debt, we should look at the facts. Is the growth of the national debt as alarming as it appears to be at first sight?

The answer to this question depends on what figures you use. In column 1 of Table 15A.1, you will see the gross public debt of the United States. It has increased about 50 times, from about $16 billion in 1930, when your grandfather was a young man, to almost $800 billion at the end of 1978. This looks alarming.

But to be fair, we should subtract from this figure the portion of the public debt owned by the Federal Reserve System. The Fed uses the interest from the government securities it owns to pay its

TABLE 15A.1
THE NATIONAL DEBT
(at end of fiscal year)

Year	(1) Gross debt (in billions of dollars)	(2) Less 83% of Federal Reserve holdings (in billions of dollars)	(3) Net debt (in billions of dollars)	(4) Employed workers (in millions)	(5) Net debt per employed worker	(6) Cost of living 1977 = 100	(7) Net debt per employed worker in 1977 dollar
1930	16	—	16	47.6	$ 336	27.1	$ 1240
1940	43	2	41	47.5	864	22.3	3874
1950	257	17	240	58.9	4074	38.2	10,664
1960	286	23	263	65.7	4003	47.1	8499
1965	317	34	283	71.1	3980	50.1	7944
1970	383	52	331	78.6	4211	61.7	6825
1971	410	58	352	79.1	4450	64.4	6910
1972	437	59	378	81.7	4627	66.5	6958
1973	468	67	401	84.4	4751	73.3	6482
1974	486	73	413	85.9	4808	81.3	5914
1975	544	77	467	84.7	5514	88.8	6209
1976	632	83	549	87.5	6274	95.9	6542
1977	709	90	619	90.5	6840	100	6840
1978	786*	97*	689*	94.5*	7238*	106	6828

Source: *Economic Report of the President, 1978.*
* Estimates

expenses. In recent years the Fed has had so much income, largely from the ownership of government securities, that it has returned about 83 percent of the interest it has received to the United States Treasury. Technically, then, 83 percent of the Fed's government bonds are not part of the interest-bearing debt of the nation: These securities are a device used by the federal government to support the monetary system of the United States.

After subtracting 83 percent of the Fed's holding of government securities, we get the "net debt" of the federal government (see column 3). It was almost $100 billion lower than the gross debt in 1978. But $689 billion is still a large figure.

The net debt per employed worker was about $7200 in 1978 and has increased by about $3000 since 1970.

To make the net debt figure meaningful, we have divided it by the number of employed workers in the United States. This yields the net debt per employed worker and is shown in column 5. Your grandfather's share of the public debt, if he had been working in 1930, would have been $336— not enough even in 1930 to buy the lowest-priced automobile. However, twenty years later, after

World War II, your grandfather's share of the national debt would have risen to slightly more than $4000, and this is enough to have bought him a luxury car. From 1950 to 1970, the net debt per worker didn't change very much. But from 1970 to 1978, your mother's or father's share of the national debt, if either had been working, would have risen about $4200 to $7200.

Deflated for price changes, the net debt per worker did not rise very much during the 1970s.

At this stage, you might conclude that the figure is getting rather large. But is it? If you state the net debt per employed worker in constant dollars (as we have done in column 7), you get another impression of the public debt. It is increasing, but the price level is also increasing. In 1977 dollars, the public debt per worker changed only slightly from 1970 to 1978. The net debt per worker was large enough to have bought a large car in 1970 and it would still have bought a large car in 1978.

Viewed in perspective, the public debt is not as alarming as it might seem at first sight. If increases in the public debt inevitably lead to inflation or cause other problems, however, then the size of the public debt could be of major concern to us.

PROBLEMS ASSOCIATED WITH OWNERSHIP OF THE DEBT

Foreign owned debt entails a future cost.

If the federal government borrowed from foreigners, then the national debt would be like any other debt. The United States economy would gain resources when the government borrowed money just as you gain resources when you borrow money. The government would have additional funds to invest in new roads and other forms of social capital or increase consumption spending through social security and other social programs. The government would not have to take funds out of the capital market when it borrowed. It could

leave the nation's savings to be acquired by producers who would build additional machinery, plant, and equipment. When a country borrows abroad, it "can have its cake and eat it too"—at least for awhile.

Where do the additional resources available for investment and consumption come from? The answer is that when a country borrows, it usually imports more than it exports and the additional resources come from net imports.

During the latter part of the 1970s the United States imported enormous quantities of oil. It did not export enough to pay for these oil imports and, as a result, foreign countries, largely members of OPEC, acquired dollar claims against the United States. They have used a large portion of these dollar claims to buy government securities, either directly through outright purchase or indirectly through acquiring bank deposits, which were in turn used to buy government securities. The national debt held by foreigners in 1970 was $20.6 billion, and by 1977 it was $110.0 billion. Figure 15A.1 shows the ownership of the public debt since 1945. The growth in the foreign share since 1970 is obvious.

What difference does it make whether the national debt is owed to foreigners? When there is a net increase in the amount of resources available to a nation, it can consume and invest more than it is producing, just as when you borrow, you can consume and invest more than you are earning. But there is a catch to this. Sometime in the future, foreign lenders may want to be repaid. And when they do the nation must get along with less than it is producing, just as when you

repay your debts you will have to consume and invest less than you are earning.

If the United States had borrowed all of its $800 billion of national debt from foreigners, the national debt would be something to worry about. In order to pay off the debt, and foreigners may insist that it be done, the citizens of the United States would have to reduce their real income either by taxation or by additional savings used to buy government bonds from foreigners. A national debt owed to foreigners can be a burden to future generations. In order to pay off the national debt, future generations would have to do with less just as you would have to do with less if you were to use your current income to pay off your parents' debt.

What about a national debt owed to citizens of the United States? Is that different? We will consider a domestically held national debt under the assumption that it is held by citizens roughly in proportion to the amount of taxes that each pays.

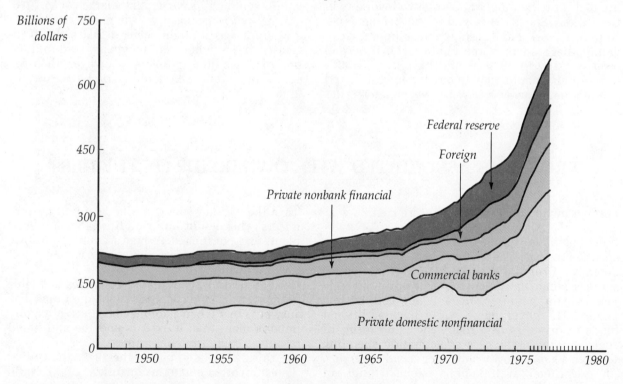

FIG. 15A.1 Ownership of United States Government Securities.

Debt owed by citizens transfers purchasing power within the country.

Suppose that when the federal government goes into debt it borrows from its own citizens in proportion to the taxes they pay. The annual additions to the national debt could be thought of as a less painful way of taxing people. It transfers command over resources from taxpayers to the government.

But it is not quite this simple. When people buy government bonds, they buy them out of their current savings. After all, when you buy a government bond, you have something, unlike a tax receipt, that you can buy or sell in the financial capital market.

When the federal government borrows, it probably reduces the net savings of the nation.

When the government borrows from its citizens, it captures some of the nation's savings. The circular-flow model shown in Fig. 15A.2 demonstrates this.

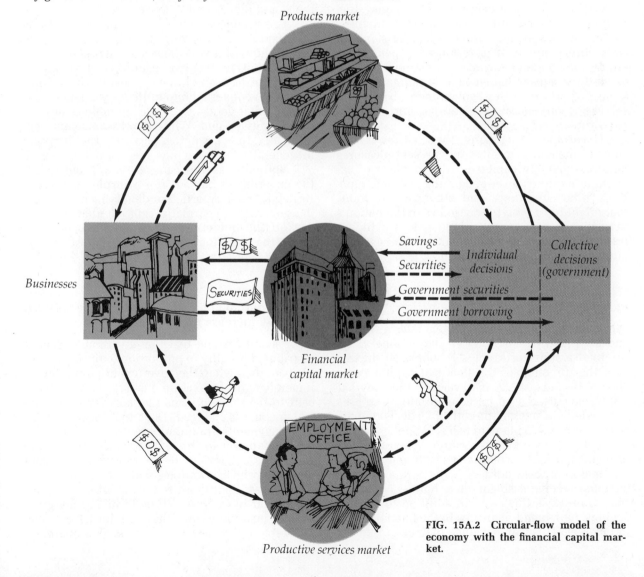

FIG. 15A.2 Circular-flow model of the economy with the financial capital market.

Government borrowing takes some of the money flowing into the financial capital market from savers and returns it to the collective decision box. The government, then, can use these savings for its own purposes. If it uses savings to build new roads or replace worn-out railroad tracks, the government, rather than private businesses will do the investing in capital goods. But if the government uses the savings to finance social security benefits, welfare payments, or national defense expenditures, these savings are converted into consumption uses. An amazing conversion will have occurred: The money that people have saved will be used to buy food, nursing home care, or maintenance for the standing army. Since much of government expenditures are for income maintenance and national defense expenditures (see Chapter 7), it is safe to say that a large portion of the government borrowing serves to convert savings into consumption expenditures.

Government borrowing, then, makes it possible for the nation to substitute present pleasures for investment in capital goods. In place of accumulating new power-generating stations, pipelines, office buildings, and other capital goods that might have been purchased with the nation's savings, the nation as a whole enjoys a higher present standard of living—but at the cost of a lower rate of growth in the future.

When the government repays its debt, it probably increases the net savings of the nation.

When the federal government generates a surplus and uses it to pay off some of the national debt, the total amount of savings is increased. In this case the direction of the financial capital flows shown in Fig. 15A.2 is reversed. Income that might have been used for consumption purposes is diverted via taxes to the collective decision box, so consumers, having paid taxes, cannot consume as much as they otherwise would. When the government uses its surplus to pay off some of the national debt, debt holders (who in this case are citizens) receive cash for their bonds. Normally they would use this cash, in addition to current savings, to demand securities in the financial capital market. This would reduce the rate of interest

and encourage businesses to invest in capital goods. Or if foreigners want to sell their government bonds, citizens can buy these bonds and give foreigners the money to use to buy our exports.

In either case, a government surplus used to pay off the national debt is a way of converting what otherwise would be consumption expenditures into savings. It is a way of converting new automobiles and boats, vacations, new furniture, and other consumption goods into nuclear power plants, new computers, new automobile machine tools, and other capital goods.

You might be inclined to argue that there is no guarantee that savings will be transferred to those who will invest them in capital goods. This is true, but in the two centuries of economic growth in the United States, most of the savings *have* been converted into railroads, airplanes, and other capital goods. Only during depressions are the savings wasted. While depressions come periodically, they are not so pervasive that it is safe to generalize that savings are normally wasted.

Normally, as you can see from Table 15A.1, the government has not run a surplus to pay off its debts. When a particular debt issue comes due, the government normally sells another issue to pay off the holders of the maturing debt. This raises the question of how the interest on the national debt affects the functioning of the economy.

Taxes required to pay the interest on the national debt may increase marginal tax rates.

If we again assume that the government debt is distributed roughly in proportion to the taxes people pay, then when the government pays interest, it merely collects taxes on one day and pays them back to the same citizens the next day. Nobody's real income is reduced. Does that mean that interest payments are unimportant?

The answer to this question depends on the way taxes are levied. If the federal government depends primarily on personal and corporate income taxes, then those recipients of the $50 billion a year in interest will be in higher marginal rates of taxation than if they did not have to pay interest on the national debt. Higher marginal rates can affect the way people make decisions about how people use their time or invest their savings (Appendix to Chapter 7).

National debt owed to foreigners is fundamentally different from debt owed to citizens.

We're now ready to answer the question: Is a national debt owed to citizens fundamentally different from a debt owed to foreigners? The answer is yes. When the federal government borrows from its own citizens, there is no increase in the total amount that could be consumed or invested, although consumption spending may increase relative to investment spending. The reverse is also true. When the federal government pays off its debt, there is no necessary reduction in the total amount of consumption and investment spending, although investment spending may increase relative to consumption spending. Interest payments merely move money from one place to another: They do not add or subtract from the total amount available to be spent.

In contrast, when a government borrows from abroad, it does acquire additional resources. Its citizens can increase their total consumption and investment spending. And when a nation pays back a national debt owed to foreigners, it gives up some of its output to foreigners. Its citizens must pay higher taxes or increase their savings in order to acquire the government securities being sold by foreigners. In other words, a nation that borrows from abroad must expect to pay the piper when the lending nation wants its money back.

Does this mean that a growing national debt largely owned by United States citizens can be ignored or treated as a minor problem? We shall examine three of the problems associated with a large and growing national debt.

National debt owed to foreigners and older people can be a net burden to younger workers.

With respect to ownership of the national debt, the assertion, "Don't worry, we owe it to ourselves" is a questionable statement. In the first place, as we pointed out above, foreigners' lending has increased sharply since 1973. A substantial portion of the increase in foreign dollar hold-ings has been invested either directly or indirectly in federal government securities. In the second place, the persons who buy government securities tend to be a fairly small percentage of the taxpayers.

Young and middle-age workers tend to put their savings into the purchase of homes and other usable assets. When persons get older they tend to acquire securities, as well as a larger vested interest in pension funds, insurance contracts, mutual funds, and other financial intermediaries all of which hold government securities. It is reasonable, then, to think that a large percentage of government securities is owned either directly or indirectly by older people. And even among older people, the ownership of securities tends to be skewed in the direction of those with higher incomes.

As a result, the ownership of the public debt is not distributed even in rough proportion to the amount of taxes people pay. This means that when the government levies taxes to pay the interest on the federal debt, it tends to shift real income from young people to older people, and from lower-income groups to higher-income groups. This would not be a serious matter if the interest on the national debt were small. But when the interest paid on the national debt is roughly $50 billion a year and is more than half as large as social security payments, then it is difficult to say glibly that the public debt is something we owe to ourselves.

It follows that a large public debt is a burden to young people and to people in the lower-income groups. They have to pay their share of the taxes and they get very little interest income in return. The larger the national debt becomes, the larger will be the shift of real income from the young to the old and from the poor to the rich.

The statement, "Don't worry, we owe it to ourselves" can also cause the federal government to get into the habit of running a deficit—even during good times when a deficit is inflationary.

Increases in the national debt do not require the balancing of the benefits and costs of public goods.

People like to receive governmental services, but they don't like to pay for them. Members of Congress like to vote for higher social security benefits, but they don't like to levy higher social security taxes. Government borrowing seems like an easy way out of this dilemma.

When a government consistently runs a deficit, it tends to reduce the net savings of the nation. In the short run, converting savings into consumption seems to be a painless way of financing new governmental services, but it can easily lead to a reduced rate of growth in the future.

Not only does the habit of running a deficit tend to change the ratio of consumption to private investment, it also can waste the nation's resources. If people aren't willing to pay the higher taxes required to balance the budget at, say, 95 percent of full employment, then possibly additional governmental services have too high an opportunity cost. In the absence of the deficit (which appears to be painless), people would choose private goods over public goods.

A large floating debt complicates the Fed's management of the money supply and can lead to inflation.

A large government debt also poses difficult problems for the Federal Reserve Board in the management of the nation's money supply. Of the $344 billion of marketable public debt held by private investors at the end of 1977, approximately $300 billion will mature within five years, and about $175 billion will mature within one year.

This means that even if the budget were balanced, the federal government would have to sell $15 to $20 billion of securities each month just to pay off the debt maturing that month. This is an enormous task, and it is reasonable for the Secretary of the Treasury to expect the Federal Reserve Board to cooperate in helping to sell these securities.

How can the Fed help the Treasury sell securities? If the Fed makes additional reserves available to the banks just at the time when the Treasury is offering these securities, the banks will be eager to buy them. This assures the government bond dealers who buy the government securities and then sells them to customers that they will have a ready market.

But when the Fed cooperates with the Treasury in selling government securities, it tends to add to the rate of growth of the money supply and in the long run to higher prices. Should the Fed be tough and let the Treasury pay whatever interest rate is required to sell its securities, or should the Fed be sympathetic and adapt its money-growth policies to the treasury's needs? This is the dilemma that the Fed faces when there is a large short-term government debt to be "rolled-over" every month. If the Fed responds to the needs of the Treasury, it may easily create too much money and thus have an inflationary effect on the economy.

None of these problems—that the people who own the debt are not the ones who pay the bulk of the taxes, that a government deficit may lead to a waste of resources and lower rate of growth, and that the Fed faces a more difficult problem of managing the growth of the money supply— should automatically rule out federal government deficits. There are times—as during a war or at the bottom of a depression—when a deficit is called for. But a large public debt, even if owed to ourselves, can pose some difficult problems for an economy.

MINI-CASE 15A.1

This mini-case is presented to help clarify your thinking about the impact of the national debt.

Below you will find a series of statements. Which ones would you, as an economist, say are true?

a) The national debt is dangerous. When a nation goes into debt, it means that later generations will have to work harder to pay it off.

b) The national debt is dangerous. Per capita national debt is rising faster than per capita GNP. It is getting to be a crushing burden.

c) The national debt is dangerous. A nation with a large public debt, even though it is held domestically, is not as wealthy as a nation with no national debt.

d) A national debt is dangerous. It can make the management of the nation's money supply more difficult and therefore add to the danger of inflation.

REVIEW QUESTIONS

1. With respect to the size of the national debt, it is correct to say that:

   a) the gross debt of the United States is about three times higher than it was in 1950 and is growing faster during the 1970s than it has any time since the end of World War II.

   b) the net debt of the United States per employed worker has increased, on the average, about $500 a year from 1974 to 1978, inclusive.

   c) adjusted for changes in the value of the dollar, the net debt of the United States per employed worker has shown little change from 1970 to 1978.

   d) All of the above.

2. During the 1970s, the United States tended to run a deficit in its balance of payments. The OPEC nations, particularly, used their dollar balances to purchase United States government securities. In 1978, foreign holdings, including OPEC, of United States government securities totaled about $110 billions. It can be said of these holdings that:

   a) they present no problem. When the United States pays interest to foreigners, they spend the money in the United States; therefore there is no loss of purchasing power.

   b) when interest is paid by the United States government foreign holders of the debt, purchasing power is transferred from United States citizens to citizens of foreign countries.

   c) despite the increase in foreign held debt, the United States is still as well off as it was before because there has been no decrease in the physical assets and wealth of the United States.

   d) this debt, like domestically held debt, is largely a bookkeeping problem. The real wealth of the United States—its educated citizens and its capital in the form of factories, roads, and so on— is still intact and no increase in foreign debt will reduce the real wealth of the United States.

3. Suppose that the national debt is being increased at about $50 billion a year and is being sold to citizens of the United States. Suppose too, that the proceeds of the debt are used to finance (a) unemployment benefits, (b) social security benefits, and (c) welfare payments. It can be said that:

   a) this is just a bookkeeping activity since the debt was sold to citizens of the United States. No effect on the economy.

   b) the people who receive the proceeds from the debt will spend it to buy food, transportation, and other consumption products. No change will occur in the way the economy functions.

   c) even though the economy is in a prosperous period, the savings would probably not have been wasted if the government had not borrowed it.

   d) government borrowing has probably increased consumption spending and reduced investment spending, and thus reduced the growth of the economy in the future.

4. When the government taxes people and uses the proceeds to pay its public debt held by citizens,
   a) the citizens who get the proceeds of debt repayment will probably use the money to buy groceries, transportation, and other consumption projects with no loss of purchasing power.
   b) the citizens who held the debt will probably put the money they receive into the capital market, thus making funds available to businesses to acquire capital goods.
   c) the total savings of the nation will probably be reduced because of the higher taxes the government must levy to pay off the debt.
   d) All of the above.

5. Suppose all of the debt is owed by citizens, but that the government finds it impossible to balance its budget and the debt grows faster than the GNP, finally getting to be as large as the GNP.
   a) The size of the debt is just a bookkeeping problem. We owe it to ourselves.
   b) While the interest on the public debt will be bigger, the government taxes people one day and pays them interest the next, causing no burden on the economy.
   c) The higher the interest payments the higher will have to be marginal tax rates and tax rates can have an effect on the way the economy functions.
   d) As long as the increases in the national debt are used to support the purchasing power of consumers, there is nothing to be concerned about.

6. In appraising the impact of a large national debt on the functioning of the economy it is correct to say that:
   a) the public debt can be a burden on taxpayers because the people who pay the taxes are probably not the people who receive the interest payments.
   b) when governments can freely use public debt rather than taxes, it frees the government from having to balance the benefits and costs of public projects.
   c) when there is a large public debt, the federal reserve may be inclined to help the treasury refinance it by creating additional money to keep the interest rate on the public debt down.
   d) All of the above.

ESSAY QUESTIONS

1. Carefully state the conditions under which increases in the public debt are inflationary. Contrast these conditions with those in which increases in the public debt are not inflationary. Then develop a generalization that will enable you to distinguish between inflationary and noninflationary increases in the public debt.

2. During wartime, governments typically run large deficits rather than tax their citizens to pay for the war. Can you suggest a reason why governments should use deficit financing rather than taxes to pay the costs of war? Is this inconsistent with drafting young people to serve in the armed services?

3. It has been said that a large government debt owed to its citizens is just a bookkeeping problem. If by some magic all the government bonds held by the people were to disappear, the country would be no poorer. The real sources of a nation's wealth are its educated people and its roads, factories, and other types of physical capital. The disappearance of government debt would not destroy these items of capital. Comment on this.

4. During wartime, when governments typically run large deficits, it is the people who go without products they would like to have in order to purchase government bonds who really bear the real costs of the war. And yet many people say that it is unfair to load future generations with the costs of paying for the war by going into debt to finance it. In what sense, if any, do future generations have to bear the costs of a war financed by government debt?

5. Why is the Federal Reserve's task of managing the money supply made more difficult by the presence of large government debt? Would it be impossible for the Fed to adopt monetarist policies while the federal government is running a large deficit?

6. If a large government debt inevitably means that tax rates will have to be higher in the future in order to pay the interest on the government debt, what consequences of a large government debt would you expect in the future?

ANSWERS TO REVIEW QUESTIONS

1. Statements (a), (b), and (c) are all factually correct (see Table 15A.1). Therefore (d) is the only correct answer.

2. When foreigners own our government bonds, they have a claim against the wealth of the United States. When they demand payment, as they do by selling their bonds to United States citizens, they can use the proceeds to acquire our wealth. When they receive interest on the public debt, they can use the proceeds to buy consumption goods that would otherwise have gone to United States citizens.

   a) This is incorrect. There is a problem because they can use their interest payments to acquire some of the real income of the United States.

   b) This is correct for the reason stated above.

   c) This is incorrect. While there has been no decrease in the wealth located in the United States, foreigners now have a claim to the income from some of this wealth.

   d) This is incorrect for the same reason as in (c) above.

3. One of the major effects of government borrowing is that it changes the composition of the total output. Less is probably spent on capital goods and more is spent on consumption goods. Capital goods increase productivity. Consumer goods do not.

   a) This is incorrect as explained above.

   b) This is incorrect as explained above.

   c) This is incorrect. Usually during a prosperous period, the funds coming into the capital market do find their way into the hands of people who spend them on capital goods. Thus savings are not necessarily wasted.

   d) This is correct as explained above.

4. When the government runs a surplus and uses that surplus to pay off the public debt, (1) it adds to the savings of the nation, and (2) by transferring these savings to citizens who will probably use the proceeds to buy other securities, it causes more capital goods and fewer consumption goods to be produced.

a) This is incorrect as explained above.

b) This is correct as explained above.

c) This is incorrect. While private savings may be reduced, the surplus of the government is a form of savings. There will be no reduction in total saving.

d) This is incorrect. Answers (a) and (c) are incorrect. Therefore, this answer cannot be correct.

5. Even though we owe it to ourselves, the size of the national debt can be a problem if it grows faster than the tax base (roughly measured by GNP). Higher tax rates to pay the interest on the national debt can have a significant effect on the economy.

a) This is incorrect. It ignores the tax rates required to pay the interest.

b) This is incorrect. There is no loss of purchasing power, but a larger tax rate is required to pay the interest.

c) This is correct as explained above.

d) This is incorrect. Even though there is no loss of purchasing power, tax rates will have to rise to service the debt.

PART V

THE INTERNATIONAL ECONOMY

OBJECTIVES

Upon successful completion of this chapter, you will be able to:

1. Explain how the Law of Diminishing Marginal Returns is related to interregional and international trade.

2. Illustrate how trade makes the participants "better off" in real terms.

3. Identify the principle of comparative advantage.

4. Explain how a nation's resource endowment affects the goods it exports and imports.

5. Identify ways in which trade is impeded.

6. Explain why various groups seek to impede international trade.

7. Use a graph to illustrate the effects of a tariff on price and on the domestic and the foreign quantity supplied of the good in question.

8. Cite the arguments in favor of tariffs.

9. Explain the effects of trade on resource use.

10. Identify the basic accounts in the balance of payments.

INTERNATIONAL TRADE

INTRODUCTION

The people who plant, raise, and harvest wheat in the Red River Valley of the Dakotas; the people who manufacture integrated circuits in Texas and California; and the people who make computers in New York state are integral parts of a giant complex machine. The people who buy new Datsuns and Volkswagens in dealers' show rooms; those who purchase bananas at the supermarket; and those who buy gasoline at a Massachusetts gas station are also facets of this machine.

What is this remarkable machine, so pervasive that it can be observed all over the country, and, in fact, all over the world? It is the system of interregional and international trade. The people producing wheat in the Dakotas are really, as you will see, supplying gasoline to car owners in Massachusetts. The people producing integrated cir-

cuits and computers in Texas, California, and New York are really, if you view the production and trade process in its entirety, raising bananas in Central America and producing Toyotas in Japan.

Our objectives in this chapter are to understand (1) how this machine, international trade, produces goods and services more cheaply than if produced in a single country; (2) why people, despite the perceived advantages of using this remarkable machine, are constantly trying to impede it; and (3) how the balance of payments statement, which is regularly reported in the newspapers, is used to monitor the performance of this machine. In the next chapter, we will discuss the various social institutions available to a society to control this powerful machine.

THE BASIS FOR TRADE

Specialization and trade can increase total output.

If all the areas of the world were identical, having the same rivers, mountains, rainfall, coastline, and so on; if people were similar, possessing the same skills and abilities; if there were no economies of size; if the ratios of people, capital, and land to each other were identical; and, finally, if people all over the world had the same tastes, that is, demanded the same mix of products, there would be no international trade. The reason is that the cost of producing all goods would be the same no matter where produced and as a result there would be no relative price differences between products. The advantages gained by buying products produced elsewhere would disappear.

International trade is important because resource endowments and consumption tastes are not the same throughout the world. As suggested above, these differences cause different sets of relative prices. This means, for example, that in Mexico, the relationship between the prices of

handmade products and machine-made products will be different from that in the United States.

Whenever relative prices are not the same in different parts of the world, ignoring transportation costs, the total output of the world can be increased by international or interregional trade. This is not as difficult as it might seem to be. Consider some examples.

Norway can produce both fish and beef. Argentina also can produce fish and beef. The price of fish relative to beef, however, is lower in Norway than in Argentina. By the same reasoning, the price of beef relative to fish is lower in Argentina than in Norway. Now suppose that Norway uses its fine fishing waters, labor, and capital to produce fish and Argentina uses its extensive ranges, labor, and capital to produce beef. Norway can trade fish for Argentine beef and Argentina can trade beef for Norwegian fish. The total output of both fish and beef in the two countries taken together will be increased, if Norway specializes in fish and the Argentine in beef. Why?

The Law of Diminishing Marginal Returns underlies trade.

The answer to this question is based on the Law of Diminishing Marginal Returns, which was discussed in Chapter 2. You will recall that as more and more of a variable input, or a fixed combination of variable inputs such as labor and capital, is applied to a given amount of land, the marginal output of the product will diminish. Norway has a small, fixed amount of grazing land. If it uses capital and labor on this small amount of grazing land, at some point, and relatively quickly, marginal output will diminish. Another way of saying this is that the cost of producing beef in Norway will be relatively high because it must use its scarce land so intensively. The reverse is true in Argentina. There is a relatively large amount of good grazing land in Argentina and if the same amount of capital and labor is used as in Norway, the marginal output of beef will be much higher. Figure 16.1 shows the marginal product curves for beef in Norway and Argentina. Diminishing returns occur at a much lower variable input level in Norway than Argentina. This reflects the fact that the amount of fixed input land is smaller in Norway than in Argentina. When the same amount of variable input is used in both countries, Q, the marginal product of Argentina, is greater than the marginal product of Norway.

The reverse is true in the production of fish. If the same amount of labor and capital were used to produce fish in the two countries, the marginal output of fish would be much higher in Norway than in Argentina.

If a way could be found to move some labor and capital from beef production in Norway to beef production in Argentina, then the combined production of beef in the two countries would be increased. Or if some of the labor and capital devoted to fish production in Argentina were moved to Norway, total fish output would increase.

But, you might argue, it is difficult, if not impossible, to move labor and capital from one country to another. People do not willingly leave their native land without some strong incentive. The transfer of capital to foreign nations involves special problems and unfamiliar languages, institutions, and legal systems. Even though labor and

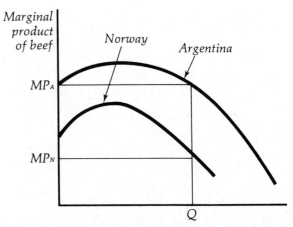

FIG. 16.1   **Marginal output of beef in Norway and Argentina.**

capital are not always very mobile internationally, both fish and beef are easily transportable. If Norway transferred some of its own labor and capital from beef production to specialize in fish production, and if Argentina transferred labor and capital from domestic fish production to specialize in beef production, both countries could end up in different positions on their diminishing return curves. Argentina would be higher in the fish curve and lower on the beef curve than before specialization. The opposite would be true for Norway. If Norway would then trade some of its fish for Argentine beef, that complex machine—international trade—would accomplish the same result as the transfer of labor and capital between the two countries.

This is sensible, you may say, but how does this relate to differences in relative prices in the two countries? Because of the plentiful supply of fishing waters, fish would be cheaper relative to beef in Norway, and beef cheaper relative to fish in the Argentine. Their relative prices, before trade was initiated, reflect the scarcities of certain resources and the penalties associated with substituting labor and capital for scarce resources.

Of course, not all international trade flows from attempts to defeat the Law of Diminishing Marginal Returns. Some is due to the fact that some metals like chromium and tin are only found in some parts of the world. Petroleum is another example of a mineral found only in some parts of the world. Trade is a means of shifting some of these unique resources from their discovery location to their use location.

In the production of some goods the economies of size are important. Countries with a head start in the production of certain goods, such as computers and jet aircraft, are able to achieve the economies of large-scale production and therefore have lower costs than late starters. But there are many products, such as food, textiles, and furniture, that can be produced by resources available in all countries. However, because of the real output advantage of international trade, they tend to be produced in those countries where the diminishing returns penalties are the lightest.

You may not know it, but you use this principle underlying trade when you choose an occupation. Some people are naturally better athletes than others. Others are naturally better students. People can use long hours of hard work to substitute for natural abilities. When they do this, they suffer some "diminishing returns penalties": the further they substitute work for natural ability, the smaller will be the extra return from additional work. To avoid these penalties, most people try to pick an occupation that fits their natural aptitudes. They then trade the products they produce for the products other people produce. Thus, when you decide to become a physician, a lawyer, a plumber, or an accountant, you are engaging in something analogous to international trade, and, as is true in international trade, you will be basing your decision of differences on relative prices.

The benefits of trade can be shown more explicitly with a simple illustration.

Consider the following example.

Assume that I can type fairly well, say 20 pages per day, but know very little about tuning-up automobiles; say, at best, I can tune-up two autos per day. Also, assume that you are skilled at both typing and tuning-up cars so that in one day you can tune-up as many as four autos or type 20 pages. Can I benefit by specializing and trading with you? Or perhaps more importantly, can you, being skilled in both activities, benefit by specialization and trade? At first glance, it may not appear so, since you can type just as well as I can and, in fact, can tune-up cars better. If I decide to spend one day tuning-up cars, I implicitly am giving up 20 pages of typewriting in exchange for the two tune-ups. The real cost to me of a tune-up is the 20 typewritten pages I have forgone. Thus for me:

$$2 \text{ tune-ups} = 20 \text{ pages, or}$$
$$1 \text{ tune-up} = 10 \text{ pages, or}$$
$$1/10 \text{ tune-up} = 1 \text{ page.}$$

Now, let us consider you. Since you can tune-up four autos per day, or type 20 pages, the cost of four tune-ups to you is 20 pages. Hence, for you:

$$4 \text{ tune-ups} = 20 \text{ pages, or}$$
$$1 \text{ tune-up} = 5 \text{ pages, or}$$
$$1/5 \text{ tune-up} = 1 \text{ page.}$$

Given these exchange ratios or prices, would you rather "buy" a tune-up from me or from yourself? My price for one tune-up is ten typewritten pages; your price is five pages. Clearly, you will provide your own tune-up services.

Would you buy typewritten pages from me or type them yourself? Check the prices. I'll sell them to you at the price of one page for 1/10 a tune-up, while your own cost per page is 1/5 of a tune-up, or twice as much. Hence, wouldn't you rather buy typewritten pages from me than type them yourself? By going through the same kind of analysis you can determine that I will buy tune-up services from you. Even though you are more skilled at both typing and tuning-up cars, you are *most* skilled, relatively speaking, at tuning-up cars and I am *most* skilled, in relative terms, at typing. Thus, an exchange decision is determined by the relative exchange ratios or prices of each product.

This example illustrates the concept of comparative advantage, which has become the analytical basis for the justification of trade. It states that a nation should specialize in and export those products in which it has a relative price advantage. In the illustration above, you had a relative price advantage in tuning-up autos and I had a relative price advantage in typing. Note that trade is beneficial even though I was not better at typing and worse at tuning-up cars than you. As long as I can produce typewritten pages *comparatively* more cheaply than you, we can both gain by specialization and trade. Some critics assert that the assumptions underlying this concept are not sufficiently present in the world to justify free trade as being the most efficient policy at all times. In general, however, most economists would opt for free trade based on the principle of comparative advantage.

Another way of illustrating how this machine, international trade, increases the output of a nation follows.

During the middle decades of the twentieth century, an adventurous entrepreneur bought a thousand acres of the Great Dismal Swamp in coastal North Carolina. After draining the land and building a road and rail spur, the mysterious entrepreneur, Mr. X, built a 12-ft. electrified fence around his entire property, posted guards at the gates, and allowed no one to enter except his own trusted employees. He advertised for workers, offering $3 per hour, and hired 5000 workers, all sworn to secrecy. Mr. X announced that he had made several scientific discoveries and inventions that enabled him to transform coal, wheat, tobacco, petroleum, machinery, and other products into a variety of finished products, including textiles, cameras, watches, chemicals, and TV sets. Within a few months, vast quantities of materials were pouring into Mr. X's guarded compound from all parts of the country, and a flood of low-price industrial and consumer goods began to pour out of Mr. X's gates and into the nation's markets, where housewives and industrialists eagerly bought them at prices 20 to 30 percent below the competition. Mr. X's company, Consolidated Alchemy, Inc. (CAI), reported large profits, and was soon listed on the New York Stock Exchange, where it became the growth stock of the century, a favorite of institutional investors.

Meantime, the nation hailed Mr. X as a genius and benefactor of mankind, a man whose inventions greatly increased the productivity of labor and improved the standard of living of the masses. He was favorably compared to both Eli Whitney and Thomas Edison.

It is true that grumbles were heard in some quarters. Several manufacturers of TV sets tried to prevent their dealers from stocking or servicing CAI sets; textile manufacturers tried to persuade Congress to establish production quotas for each firm based on average output in the previous 50 years; a labor union picketed stores carrying CAI merchandise; and three New England legislatures passed laws requiring that stores display "Buy New England" posters. None of these activities had much effect, however. Buyers could not resist the low CAI prices, and many communities were prospering because of their rapidly increasing sales to Con-

solidated Alchemy. The houses of Congress resounded with speeches calling upon the people to accept the necessity for economic adjustment and urging the benefits of the technical change.

As for coastal North Carolina, it was booming as never before. Schools, houses, and roads were constructed; the Great Dismal Swamp was drained and used for truck gardens, its extraordinarily fertile land was selling for $3000 per acre; employment expanded and average wages rose to $5 per hour.

Then one Sunday morning, a small boy, vacationing with his family at a nearby seaside resort, tried out his new skin-diving equipment, penetrated Mr. X's underwater screen, and observed that Consolidated Alchemy's "factories" were nothing but warehouses and that its "secret technical process" was nothing but trade. Mr. X was, in fact, a hoax; his firm was nothing but a giant import-export business. He bought vast quantities of materials from United States producers, loaded them under cover of night onto a fleet of ships, and carried them off to foreign markets where he exchanged them for the variety of goods that he sold through the United States at such low prices.

When the boy told what he had seen, a wire service picked up the story and within 24 hours, Mr. X was denounced as a fraud, his operation was shut down, his thousands of high-paid workers were thrown out of work, and his company was bankrupt. Several members of Congress declared that the American standard of living had been protected from a serious threat of competition from cheap foreign labor and urged higher appropriations for research in industrial technology.*

The resource endowment of a nation helps determine the items it exports and imports.

What products do you think the United States would sell and what products would the United States buy if it fully exploited the international trade machine? Relative to the rest of the world, the United States has abundant supplies of well-watered farmland and abundant supplies of human capital. It has also invested enormous amounts in the development of technological knowledge. It is natural, then, that in the absence of trade, food and high technology products would be cheaper in the United States relative to other products than they would be in other parts

* From *International Economic Problems*, Second Edition, by James C. Ingram, pp. 43–45. Copyright © 1966, 1970 by John Wiley & Sons, Inc. Reprinted by permission.

of the world. It is not surprising, therefore, that the United States tends to export food and high technology products, such as computers, sophisticated electronics, and jet aircraft.

The United States is short of many raw materials such as chromium, zinc, and petroleum. The United States also has less unskilled and skilled labor relative to its other resources than do other parts of the world. It is natural, then, that in the absence of trade, many raw materials and many new materials, as well as handmade products such as soap, sweaters, and shoes, would be more expensive in the United States relative to other products than in the rest of the world.

When the United States fully exploits the international trade machine, it exports food and high technology products and imports raw materials and handmade products. In this way, the United States minimizes the diminishing return

penalties associated with using low-grade ore deposits and deep-drilled oil wells. It also minimizes the costs of labor-saving devices required by high-priced labor in the United States.

BARRIERS TO TRADE

Powerful groups constantly seek to impede free trade.

The importance of international trade has been growing rapidly during the last 35 years. Table 16.1 demonstrates this. Nevertheless, powerful groups continually lobby to establish barriers to trade.

If the international trade machine is so productive, why do some people want to impede it by erecting national barriers to keep foreign-made products out of the country? The United Auto Workers, for example, want tariff barriers to be erected to keep foreign-made cars out of the United States. The shoe companies complain that foreign-made shoes are so cheap that they provide unfair competition for shoes made in the United States.

Many people respond to the international trade machine in the same way. The textile workers in New England have seen their jobs threatened by textiles made in Japan. The shoemakers in St. Louis have lost their jobs because of com-

TABLE 16.1
VALUE AND VOLUME OF WORLD TRADE

Year	Exports (in billions)	Quantity index of exports (1970 = 100)
1938	$ 23.5	21
1948	57.2	22
1958	108.5	38
1969	273.6	93
1970	313.3	100
1971	350.5	106
1972	415.8	117
1973	576.3	131
1974	841.4	137
1975	873.8	132
1976	988.5	N.A.

Source: *Yearbook of International Trade Statistics,* 1976, United Nations: New York, 1974.

petition from foreign countries. The companies producing television sets in the United States have seen their share of the market shrink as a result of competition from Japanese companies. It is natural, then, that people should form groups that would use the government to impede the international trade machine by various devices such as tariffs and import quotas.

At first thought you might think this is self-defeating. International trade like any other productivity-increasing device will increase the real income of a society and therefore the members of that society will in the long run be better off.

However, if you look at the international trade machine from an "income distribution" point of view and not from a "production" point of view, you can understand why people react as they do to foreign competition. The benefits from a tariff, which makes imported products more expensive, are concentrated. The damages are dispersed.

Consider an example.

If you and nine hundred and ninety-nine other people could legally force everybody in the nation to give you one penny, you could argue that the costs were so small that they could be ignored. And yet as a member of this select group you would receive a little less than $2200 a year. And so it is with the shoemakers in St. Louis. If they can rely on a tariff to increase the price of shoes in the United States, they will receive substantial benefits and the damages will be dispersed to the many people buying shoes.

Tariffs are a basic form of trade impediment.

Figure 16.2 shows how a protective tariff works. If the border were closed to all foreign-made shoes, then the equilibrium price of $40 would be at the intersection of the supply and demand curve. But now suppose that an unlimited amount of foreign-made shoes can be imported at $30 a pair. The graph shows that at $30, ignoring transportation costs, 0Q will be the quantity supplied domestically and QF will be the amount supplied by foreigners. Domestic products will get only about half of the market. The rest will be supplied by exporters in other countries.

If the shoemakers can persuade the government to impose a $5 tariff on shoes coming into the country, then shoe companies in the United States will get a larger share of the market, and those already in the market will receive an extra

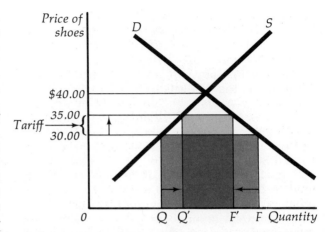

FIG. 16.2   **A tariff on shoes.**

$5 for the shoes they had been producing before. The domestic quantity supplied will increase from 0Q to 0Q', and the foreign quantity supply will fall to Q'F'. The total quantity demanded will fall by F'F. In effect, then, United States shoe companies and the workers employed in them will be in a position to impose a $5-a-pair excise tax on consumers in the United States. Just as in the case of the penny tax example, the benefits will be concentrated and the damages dispersed.

We may be tempted to ask: Should groups of people be permitted to impede the international trade machine in order to get more income? If the only problem is whether those who are displaced by foreign competition will find other jobs, then the answer is probably easy. They should not be permitted to use the power of government to "line their own pockets."

It is possible, however, that international trade will fundamentally change the distribution of income in a nation. Recall our first example. The owners of grazing land in Norway would permanently lose. Trade with the Argentine would, in effect, add the vast grazing lands of pampas to the Norwegian countryside, and the competition from "new" land would permanently reduce the rent of land in Norway.

The same result will occur when the United States imports handmade products from areas where labor is cheap. In effect, the supply of unskilled and manually skilled labor is enormously increased by reliance on international trade. Those workers who can upgrade themselves by becoming more knowledgeable workers will probably gain. They will get higher incomes, and the prices of the products they buy will be lower. But those workers who are unable to upgrade themselves face a new labor market, where, in effect, there are large numbers of people willing to work for less than the usual wage rates in the United States.

Just as "distribution of income" problems tend to dominate the resolution of the inflation problem, so too do distribution of income problems tend to determine the extent to which the international trade machine will be used. Consider the variety of devices used to interfere with international trade.

The most commonly used method of trade restriction is the tariff, the effect of which we have already discussed.

A *tariff* is a tax or a duty imposed by a government on a commodity that is either imported or exported.

Import and export tariffs are both taxes levied on goods involved in international trade. An export tax increases the cost of domestically made goods to foreigners, while an import tax increases the price of foreign goods domestically.

Since the import tax is the most important, people normally regard a tariff as a tax on imported goods. If the tariff is imposed simply to raise money for the taxing body, it is called a *revenue* tariff, whereas if it is imposed to reduce or eliminate imports of the good involved, it is called a *protective* tariff. For example, if the tariff in Fig. 16.2 were $10 rather than $5, no imported shoes would be purchased. The tariff would raise no revenue, but certainly would protect the domestic shoe industry.

This import (or export) tax can be levied in several ways. If the tax is expressed as a percentage of the value of the good, it is called an *ad valorem* tariff. For example, an *ad valorem* tariff of 10 percent on an imported automobile priced at $3000 would be $300. In contrast, a *specific* tariff is simply a tax levied according to the physical quantity of the import, such as a tax of $1 per gallon of imported molasses.

A *quota*, like a tariff imposed by the government, is levied to limit the amount of a good that may be imported or exported. In the United States, quotas have been used to restrict the importation of a number of commodities, for example, meat and oil. In general, economists oppose quotas more than tariffs because the quota that limits imports may protect the domestic selling price of the good considerably above its import cost and, hence, provide abnormal profits for the distributor. The license that must be obtained to deal in the restricted commodity can be very valuable. From the point of view of the people, it would be best for the government to auction off such licenses so that the "monopoly" revenues associated with their ownership would flow to the government rather than to some privately owned firm. In the case of tariffs, we noted that the government automatically received the revenues. This is not so with quotas.

To help clarify your thinking about the effects of trade barriers, consider Mini-case 16.1.

MINI-CASE 16.1

Your member of Congress is a strong protectionist. He believes that whenever any product is imported that could be produced in the United States, "good" American workers lose their jobs to workers abroad who are paid sweat-shop wage rates. You are a free trader and get a chance to spend an hour with him. Which, if any, of the arguments below will you use to support your argument that free trade is good for the United States? Indicate the one you think will be most effective.

a) Trade between nations does not change the distribution of income within a nation and it does add to the total output. Therefore, trade helps everybody in the nation.

b) International trade shifts employment from the import-competitive industries to the export industries. Therefore, your member of Congress should be careful. He may be limiting the employment possibilities for good American workers in the export industries—which are usually high wage-rate industries.

c) International trade increases the total output of the nations participating in it. Some nations may gain more than others, but the productivity of the resources in all of the participating nations will be higher.

d) All of the resources—labor, land, or specialized types of capital—temporarily displaced by free trade will find new and higher-paying employment in the long run. Don't worry about them. The owners of all resources will be better off if there are no impediments to trade.

There are many other forms of trade barriers.

In general, a nontariff barrier is regarded as any measure other than a tariff, public or private, that distorts international trade. Some of the most important barriers, in addition to quotas, are:

1. Aid to domestic firms.
   a) Many governments subsidize industries producing goods for abroad, often through special tax advantages.
   b) Governments may provide procurement policies by which domestic producers are favored over foreign producers, even if the price is higher.
2. Customs administration.
   a) Imported goods that are subject to duties must be classified and valued in order to place the appropriate amount of tax on them. These procedures can add delays, uncertainties, and costs.
3. Technical regulations.
   a) Regulations requiring that imported goods meet special health, safety, labeling, and packaging standards may serve to restrict imports. For example, the United States now requires that foreign automobiles meet certain safety and pollution emission standards. Some foreign countries have complained that this constitutes a form of nontariff barrier.

Many reasons are advanced for using tariffs, quotas, and these devices to protect domestic producers from foreign competition. The two most commonly used are the national defense argument and the infant industry argument.

The *national defense argument* asserts that even though a country may not have a comparative advantage in the production of, say, steel, the possibility that the nation's steel supply will be cut off in the case of war is sufficient justification for nurturing its own steel industry at a cost of wasted scarce resources. Even Adam Smith said "defence . . . is of much more importance than opulence." This argument can be carried to extremes; lacemakers are reported to have once sought increased protection based on the grounds that they could modify their equipment to manufacture mosquito netting in case of a tropical war.

The other case is the *infant industry* argument. It is based on the reasoning that a country might possibly have a comparative advantage in a certain industry if it were given temporary protection until it was large enough to exploit the economics of large-scale production. These industries, however, never seem to succeed in "growing up."

In the end these two arguments, and others like them, can be reduced to one argument: "We don't like the distribution of income arising out of international trade." This leaves us with the question: How far should a society go to protect the incomes of particular groups in that society? We can't answer this question, but we can get a better grasp of the way international trade fits into a market-directed economy.

COMMENTARY

The following article discusses whether the United States steel industry can compete with foreign producers. Please read the article and answer the following questions.

a) How were the Japanese able to increase their penetration into the United States Market?
b) How has the United States steel industry lost its comparative advantage?

CAN STEEL COMPETE?

U.S. steel consumption has risen only 15 percent over the past decade because of intermittent recessions, the loss of markets to substitute materials, and the recent slack in demand for capital goods. But to add to the domestic industry's problems, foreign imports in the past decade have siphoned off a major portion of this modest market growth.

The Administration acknowledges the seriousness of the import problem, but tends to disapprove of the use of mandatory quotas or formal marketing agreements to restrict the flow of low-cost steel into the U.S. market. Administration spokesmen argue that such restrictions would only raise the price of foreign and domestic steel without attacking the basic causes of the import threat, namely, excess worldwide production and relatively high domestic production costs. Consequently the Administration is likely to put less emphasis on import barriers than on tax benefits and other measures to encourage plant modernization and cost reduction.

Meanwhile, several producers have petitioned the Treasury for relief under laws which call for the imposition of duties on foreign products found to be in violation of anti-dumping statutes—that is foreign products sold in the U.S. market at less than cost or home-market prices. This raises the question as to whether the domestic steel industry is in fact a relatively high-cost producer and, if so, whether these cost differentials are sufficient to account for the wide disparity between foreign and domestic steel prices in the U.S. market.

Import upsurge

Since the Second World War, the U.S. steel industry has watched its position in the world steel market steadily decline. In 1950, the United States was the largest steel producer in the non-

Communist world, accounting for 56 percent of total production. In 1976, it was still the largest single producer, but its share of the total had dwindled to 25 percent, just slightly larger than that of Japan and somewhat less than the share of the European Economic Community. Domestic production moved irregularly upward over the 1950–65 period from 97 to 132 million tons, remained at approximately that level until the 1973 boom—but is presently running at an annual rate of only around 125 million tons, approximately the 1964 level.

Steel imports gained their first real foothold in the U.S. market in 1959, when a prolonged strike turned the United States into a net importer of steel. The foreign share of the market continued to rise as the dollar became increasingly overvalued under the then-prevailing system of fixed exchange rates, with imports reaching 18 million tons by 1971, equivalent to 18 percent of total U.S. apparent consumption. Imports then receded after the 1971–73 dollar devaluations, but another import upsurge began in the mid-1970's, with foreign steel reaching 16 percent of total U.S. apparent consumption in January-July 1977—and 20 percent of the total market in August, when the flow reached an annual rate of 22 million tons. As a consequence of the increase in imports over the 1964–76 period, foreign producers captured nearly all of the growth of the U.S. market. In 1976, about 56 percent of U.S. steel imports came from Japan and another 22 percent from the European Economic Community.

Comparative costs

Comparative steel-production costs, as developed recently by the Council on Wage and Price Stability (COWPS), help to explain how Japanese producers were able to increase their penetration of the U.S. market in recent decades. Historical cost data are scantier for European producers, but the available data suggest that U.S.-European cost differentials alone cannot explain their inroads into the U.S. market. Indeed, the data show that total production costs per ton of raw steel are roughly comparable in Europe and the U.S., and that the costs of transporting steel from Europe to the U.S. raise their delivered costs far above those of domestic producers.

Raw-material cost data show that the U.S. steel industry has gradually lost its earlier comparative advantage over Japanese producers. According to COWPS estimates, the costs of purchased raw materials per ton of raw steel currently are about $5 less in Japan than in the U.S. The Japanese advantage is somewhat less if both purchased and company-produced materials are included, since the largest U.S. firms produce most of their own raw materials.

Unit labor-cost data show that the traditional labor-cost advantage held by Japanese producers has narrowed over time, but remains large nonetheless. Output per man-hour more than doubled in the Japanese steel industry over the 1964–76 period, while the productivity gain in the U.S. industry amounted to only about 18 percent due to a much slower growth of output. In contrast, hourly compensation rose nearly six-fold in the Japanese steel industry over that same period, while it increased about 142 percent in the U.S. industry. Yet despite the narrowing differential, unit labor costs are still about $36 less in the Japanese steel industry than in the U.S. industry, per ton of raw steel. This advantage is due mainly to the fact that wage rates in Japan are still only about one-half American rates. Output per manhour is only slightly higher in Japan than in the U.S., despite the more rapid gains made in Japan over the 1964-76 period.

Combining these raw-material and labor-cost differentials—and converting them from a raw-steel to a finished-product basis—results in about a $73 per ton (25 percent) comparative advantage for Japanese over domestic producers. However, the Japanese advantage is narrowed somewhat when capital costs and other expenses are added.

The overall cost advantage held by Japanese producers is further reduced when their inbound raw-material transportation costs and outbound finished-steel transportation costs are included. The Japanese import most of their raw materials, while U.S. firms obtain most of their raw material inputs from domestic sources. Japanese inbound transportation costs are therefore about $2 per ton higher than for U.S. producers, while freight, loading, insurance and duty charges incurred by Japanese producers in U.S. marketing activities range between $44 and $54 per ton. Indeed, subtracting all these transportation costs from the Japanese production-cost advantage, suggests that Japanese producers can sell steel in the U.S. at only a modest overall discount below U.S. producer costs and still make a profit.

Counterattack

Domestic producers argue, however, that foreign producers have been selling steel in the United States at prices that are much lower than would be warranted on the basis of their comparative advantage—in fact, have been selling steel at a loss in order to raise their operating rates and employment above levels that would otherwise prevail. They claim, furthermore, that foreign steelmakers are able to do this because deficits sustained during periods of weak demand are offset by stiff premiums during periods of strong U.S. demand, and also because Japanese firms are subsidized by their non-steel subsidiaries.

These charges are still being investigated, but the fact that the Treasury recently ruled tentatively in favor of a small Pacific Northwest producer, suggests that domestic steel companies may have a good chance of winning their legal case against foreign producers. Whatever the outcome, it is clear that domestic firms will be operating in an intensely competitive environment for several years to come. Consumption of steel in the non-Communist world is expected to grow at an annual rate of around 4 percent over the 1976–80 period. World capacity is expected to grow at an even slower rate as financially-distressed European and other producers sharply modify their expansion plans. Still, this slowdown in the growth of capacity may not be sufficient to raise overall operating rates substantially above current depressed levels. Thus, given their comparative cost advantage, Japanese producers may well continue to focus on the U.S. market as an important outlet for increased exports.

YVONNE LEVY. "Can Steel Compete?" *Business and Financial Letter*, November 4, 1977, Federal Reserve Bank of San Francisco. Reprinted by permission.

THE INTERNATIONAL TRADE MACHINE AND A MARKET-DIRECTED ECONOMY

Resources are used differently when trade occurs.

When we think of international trade, we tend to think of it as separated from the domestic economy—possibly occurring on an island off the coast of the mainland. But this is not the way the international trade machine works. International trade is just another way of using the economy's resources.

When you buy a new Datsun, for example, you are in effect demanding an additional computer from the IBM company. The dollars you pay for the Datsun will be transferred (in the foreign exchange market, which we will discuss in the following chapter) to the buyer of the new computer. The dollars do not really leave the country. They are merely recycled. In place of going to one of the domestic automobile producers, they go to the computer industry.

It is accurate to say that our demand for imports creates a demand for our exports to foreign countries. This is something that those who argue for protective tariffs sometimes forget. If such high tariffs were imposed on the purchase of foreign automobiles that you would choose not to buy one, then the chances are that the Japanese business could not get the dollars to buy a computer in this country.

Looking at the same proposition from another point of view, we could say that the farmers who are raising wheat in the Red River Valley of the Dakotas are, in effect, pumping oil out of the ground in Nigeria. When they sell their wheat in the world market, the United States gets the foreign currency it needs to buy oil from Nigeria. If the United States did not sell products abroad, it could not afford, in the long run, to pay for its imports. In this sense, it would also be fair to say that exports from the United States create a demand for imports from abroad.

Financial capital movements are an important part of international transactions.

When households and businesses find that interest rates are higher abroad than they are in the

United States, they can buy securities from people and businesses in other countries. When businesses believe that profit-making opportunities are greater in other countries than they are in the United States, they can shift their funds to other countries and use the foreign money balances they acquire to build new factories abroad. In either case, the shift of financial capital from the United States to other countries will give other countries the dollars they need to buy more from the United States than they are selling to the United States.

The opposite is also true. When OPEC countries transfer loanable funds to the United States, that is, loan money to the United States, they make it possible for households and businesses to buy more imports than they would otherwise be able to do. In this way, the OPEC countries can finance the sale of oil to the United States. In effect, they accept claims against United States institutions in return for their oil.

International trade expands the resource base of participating countries.

The United States has very little tin and chromium, but the United States does have a highly productive agricultural establishment. By exporting agricultural products and using the foreign currencies we acquire to buy tin and chromium, we are, in effect, converting farmland into tin and chromium mines. In this way the exports from business can be used to acquire resource imports that would otherwise not be available.

International trade increases the real income of participating nations.

The prices of imported products will be lower than the prices of the competitive products produced in the United States. If they weren't, people would not buy them. The prices of some export products, such as agricultural products, may be higher because of foreign sales. The prices of

other export products, such as computers and aircraft, may not change as a result of export sales. In fact, some may even be lower because of economies of scale. Putting all of these export prices together, if the average price level is lower, then given the same flow of money payments, the real income of the nation would have been increased by international trade.

Now we will examine how the balance of payments serves as a device for monitoring international trade transactions. To help clarify your thinking about the effects of trade on a market economy, consider the following situation.

MINI-CASE 16.2

There is a crop failure in Russia. As a result, the Russians are buying wheat and corn again. Since this tends to increase the price of bread and meat in this country, your member of Congress has consistently advocated placing an embargo on the export of feed grains to Russia and the rest of the world. You are thinking of writing a letter to him and you are searching in your own mind for the most effective argument to convince him that this is a short-sighted policy. Which of the following arguments would you use? Select the best one.

a) The Russians need the wheat. It is up to us as citizens of the world to help feed the hungry Russians.
b) When the Russians buy wheat at the world price, they pay for it by giving the United States the foreign currencies it needs to buy oil and scarce raw materials from the rest of the world.
c) When the Russians buy wheat at the world price, they must borrow the money from our banks. This adds to the money supply and therefore adds to the total demand for goods. As a result, employment will rise.
d) If we don't sell wheat to the Russians, they will buy it from other wheat-exporting countries. This will increase the world price of wheat as certainly as if they buy it from the United States. If the Russians are buying wheat, the United States might as well get the foreign credits it needs to buy oil and scarce raw materials.

THE BALANCE OF PAYMENTS ACCOUNTS AS A MEASURE OF INTERNATIONAL TRANSACTIONS

Everyone has his or her own personal balance of payments account.

At some times in your life you will be paying out more than you are taking in and at other times you will be receiving more than you are paying

out. To monitor these flows of receipts and expenditures you could construct a simple balance of payments statement for yourself. It would show the amounts you are earning from selling your productive services and the amounts you are borrowing. It would also show how much you had

TABLE 16.2

HYPOTHETICAL BALANCE OF PAYMENTS FOR JANE DOE.

	(1)	(2)	(3)
1. Income earned	+$3,900		
2. Interest received	+ 100		
3. Grant from a relative	+ 1,000		
Received on current account		+$5,000	
4. Tuition, books, and living expenses	−$6,000		
5. Interest paid on debt	− 500		
Paid on current account		−$6,500	
6. *Balance on current account*			−$1,500
7. Borrowed from a student loan fund		+$1,000	
8. *Basic balance: current account plus long-term capital*			− 500
9. Short-term borrowing from home town bank		+ 400	
10. *Liquidity balance*			− 100
11. Balancing item: additional debt to the book store		+ 100	
		$ 0	

spent on goods and services or lent to others. Any difference between the amounts you had taken in and the amount you paid out would show up either as an increase in your claims against others (including the change in your cash balance) or as an increase in the claims others have against you.

To see how an individual balance of payments statement might look, examine Table 16.2, which is a hypothetical balance of payments statement for a student whom we shall name Jane Doe.

You will note that the first three items measure the income and gifts flowing to Jane Doe. The $1000 grant from a relative, when added to her wage and interest earnings, would give Jane $5000 for her educational expenses. However, Jane's tuition, books, and living expenditures total $6000, and the interest she has to pay on money she has borrowed in the past will add another $500 to her expenditures. Altogether, then, her expenditures exceed her receipts by $1500. The balance in the three accounts listed will be defined as her "balance on current account." It is a negative $1500.

To cover this negative balance, let us suppose that Jane borrows $1000 from a student loan fund that does not require repayment until she is graduated. The addition of this long-term loan to the

previous balance still leaves her $500 short, or in balance of payments terminology, her "basic balance" is −$500, as is indicated in column 3. To give her enough money to get through the year, let us suppose that she is able to borrow $400 from her hometown bank for the three-month period until she starts earning money in the summer. This still leaves her $100 short. Her "liquidity balance," which includes a short-term loan, is then −$100. We shall suppose that this $100 is covered by an unpaid debt to the bookstore for her last semester's books.

It is interesting to note that Jane Doe's balance of payments statement balances. The figures in column 2 will total zero at the bottom line. This is necessary because if Jane spends more than she is taking in she will have to go into debt, while if she spends less she will accumulate claims against others, including money.

The fact that Jane's balance of payments statement balances does not mean that her accounts are in "equilibrium." Indeed, the bookstore may be very anxious to get its money, so that Jane could really be said to be having a "balance of payments" problem (as many of us do). What her statement does show is how she has managed her receipts and expenditures.

TABLE 16.3
UNITED STATES BALANCE OF PAYMENTS STATEMENT 1977 (in billions of dollars)

	(1)	(2)	(3)
1. United States exports			
a) goods	+$120.5		
b) services	+ 31.2		
c) income from U.S. investments abroad	+ 24.9		
Exports		+$176.6	
2. United States imports			
a) goods	− 151.7		
b) services	− 11.9		
c) income paid on foreign investment in U.S.	− 13.0		
Imports		−$192.0	
Balance on goods + services		− 15.4	
3. Remittance, pensions, and other transfers, net		− 1.9	
4. United States government grants		− 3.1	
5. *Balance on current account*			−$20.4
6. Long-term capital movements			
a) United States government		− 3.7	
b) foreign private investment in U.S.		+ 4.5	
c) United States private investment abroad		− 10.8	
Total long-term capital		− 10.0	
7. Basic balance: *current account plus long-term capital net*			− 30.4
8. Short-term capital movements		− 4.6	
9. Errors and omissions		+ 3.0	
Total		− 7.6	
10. *Net liquidity balance*		− 38.0	
11. Balancing items		+ 38.0	
		$0	

Source: Calculated from *Survey of Current Business*, March 1978, U.S. Dept. of Commerce
+ indicates receipt
− indicates expenditure

The nation's balance of payments is divided into several basic sub-accounts.

A nation's balance of payments statement also shows how it has managed its receipts and expenditures. It cannot by itself show whether a nation is having a balance of payments problem. It is a history of a nation's international transactions for a period of time.

Examine the United States balance of payments statement for the year 1977 in Table 16.3. You will note that we have arranged it in a format similar to Jane Doe's balance of payments statement. Because these figures are widely reported in newspapers and magazines, you should examine it carefully.

You will note that in 1977, residents of the United States sold $120.5 billion of goods and $31.2 billion of services to the rest of the world. Americans also received $24.9 billion from investments in foreign countries. But you will also see that people in the United States spent more than its income from these sales and from investments and services from the rest of the world, leaving it with a deficit of goods and services expenditures of $15.4 billion. Private remittances and pensions to people living abroad and United States government grants added to this negative balance, leaving a net balance on current account of −$20.4 billion.

This figure is important because it tells us how effective a nation is in earning its way. Over an extended period of time, most nations and most people have to earn as much as they are spending. Figure 16.3 shows how the United States current balance has varied since 1950. You will see that, except for the early 1970s, the United States has tended to earn more from the sale of goods and services than it was spending to buy goods and services. In 1977, the account fell to −$20.4 billion.

Just as Jane Doe borrowed money for educational expenses, so too people participating in an international economy borrow funds or lend funds for extended periods of time. They also buy securities and make direct investments in foreign countries, as, for example, when General Motors adds to its Opel plant in Germany. Foreigners also buy securities in our stock market and make direct investments in new factories in the United States. These transactions are summarized as long-term capital movements. You will note in Table 16.3 that in 1977 the United States government paid $3.7 billion to foreigners. Foreigners made private investments of $4.5 billion in the United States. However, residents of the United States paid out a total of $10.8 billion to build new factories abroad and to buy securities from foreigners. Altogether, then, the long-term capital account resulted in a new outpayment of $10.0 billion.

This brings us to another important figure, the United States basic balance, which combines the current accounts and the long-term capital accounts. This figure indicates whether a nation is purchasing and investing more abroad than it is earning and borrowing in the long-term capital market. In the long run, a nation cannot invest more abroad than its *net* earnings from the sale of goods and services—unless, of course, other nations are continually willing to finance these deficits. Because businesses in the United States have invested large amounts abroad, the United States basic balance has tended to be negative since 1950.

Finally, some people put money in foreign countries for short periods of time to obtain higher rates of interest and to speculate on changes in exchange rates (this will be discussed

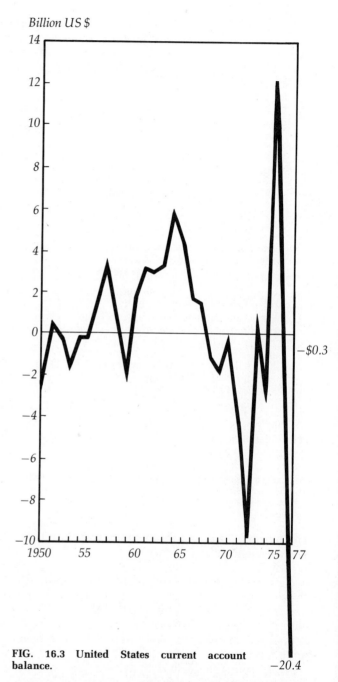

FIG. 16.3 United States current account balance.

in the following chapter). When they do this, loanable funds either come into the country (+) or they leave the country (−). In this way, short-term capital movements either add to a country's claim against other countries or they do the reverse. You will note that in 1977, $4.6 billion of short-term capital left the country. Some transactions are hard to find and are missed in the calculation. These are lumped into a catch-all term, "errors and omissions," line 9.

Altogether, then, the net liquidity balance of −$38.0 billion indicates that foreign countries acquired additional claims of this amount against the United States. Some of these claims took the form of additional holdings of deposits in United States banks, some were debts of United States corporations, and some were settled by transactions between the central banks of the various countries. Because of the complicated nature of

these "balancing transactions" we will leave them for later courses in economics.

It is interesting to note that a nation's balance of payments balances, just as Jane Doe's statement balanced. The sum of all the figures in column 2 will equal zero. Just as it was impossible to tell whether Jane Doe had a "balance of payments" problem by examining her statement, so too is it impossible to tell whether a nation has a balance of payments problem from examining its statement. The answer to this question depends on whether, given the foreign exchange rates and the interest rates, foreigners and foreign central banks want to hold the additional claims they are receiving.

REVIEW QUESTIONS

1. Suppose that land in Florida could be used to raise citrus fruit or cattle. Suppose that because of the moderating influence of the Gulf Stream, the land at the tip of Long Island could also be used to raise citrus fruit or cattle. If interregional trade were not permitted, the following regional exchange ratios would exist.

Long Island

5 bu of citrus fruit
would be exchanged for
100 lb of beef

Florida

10 bu of citrus fruit
would be exchanged for
100 lb of beef

If interregional trade were permitted,

a) Long Island should raise citrus fruit.
b) Florida should raise beef.
c) Long Island should raise beef and exchange it for citrus fruit.
d) Unless you know the dollar cost of each it is impossible to say what should be done.

2. Given the following pretrade information concerning France and the United States, who will buy and sell what, if international trade is opened up?

Goods	France Price in francs	United States Price in dollars
Wine	20 fr per gallon	$4 per gallon
Wheat	40 fr per bushel	$4 per bushel

After looking at these data, it is clear that:

a) France will sell wheat and buy wine.
b) France will want to sell wine but the United States will not buy wine.
c) the United States will sell wheat and buy wine from France.
d) the United States will sell wine and buy wheat from France.

3. Suppose that the supply of beef in the United States includes low-cost beef from Argentina as well as high-cost beef from the United States. Now suppose a quarantine is imposed on beef from Argentina. Pick the answer below that best describes the situation.

    a) The price of beef in the United States will be lower because it will achieve the economies of scale.
    b) The price of beef in the United States will be higher with no effect on United States exports.
    c) The price of beef in the United States will rise and the demand for United States exports will fall.
    d) The price of beef in the United States will stay the same and there will be no change in the demand for United States exports.

4. Suppose that the United States does not have a comparative advantage in producing automobiles and tends to import more and more foreign cars. But suppose that the United Auto Workers and the auto manufacturers have enough political clout to get a high tariff imposed on foreign-made cars. This would:

    a) increase the demand by foreigners for agricultural products.
    b) decrease the demand for workers in the automobile industry.
    c) shift resources from agriculture to automobile production.
    d) shift resources from automobile production to agriculture.

5. Below you will find a series of transactions. Using the following key, indicate what effect each transaction will have on the balance of payments of the United States.

    a) It will increase foreign claims against the United States.
    b) It will have no effect on the amount of foreign claims on the United States.
    c) It will decrease the amount of foreign claims against the United States.
    d) It is impossible to say from the information given what the effect will be on the amount of foreign claims against the United States.
    ( ) You trade in your United States-made car for a Volvo made in Sweden.
    ( ) The United States government decides to strengthen NATO and sends two additional divisions to Europe.
    ( ) You decide to take a vacation in Greece.
    ( ) Multinational corporations have large profits abroad and because of new tax legislation bring all of their profits back to the United States.
    ( ) The United States stock market rallies. As a result, the middle eastern nations shift their funds to the United States and buy large amounts of General Motors stock.
    ( ) The OPEC countries decide not to leave their net earnings from the sale of oil in Europe. They shift them to the United States.
    ( ) Multinational corporations in the United States build new plants in Western Europe.

ESSAY QUESTIONS

1. Suppose the Law of Diminishing Marginal Returns were "repealed" and that with appropriate applications of fertilizers and the use of capital and labor, enormous amounts of food could be raised on a minimum amount of land. Suppose, too, that there were no cost penalties associated with drilling deeper oil wells or with drilling offshore oil wells. How would this development influence the amount of international trade?

2. Suppose that there were no economies of size, so that small steel mills were as efficient as large ones. How would this affect the amount of trade between nations or between regions? Are the economies of scale an important reason for international and interregional trade?

3. Demonstrate that if all relative prices in two regions are the same, there will be no trade between the regions.

4. It has been said that as the world runs short of important metals and energy sources, international trade will become more and more important. Do you agree or not? Give reasons for the position you take.

5. Assume that if the market forces were allowed to work out a solution, only machine-made shoes would be produced in the United States. You are a member of the AFL-CIO policy council. The shoe workers' union asks you to support a high tariff on shoes. In deciding which way you should vote, what factors should you take into account? Remember, you also have union members employed in the export industries.

6. Suppose a quota system were used to limit the imports of crude oil produced abroad. Under this system, each oil company would be issued a quota entitling it to buy foreign oil up to one quarter of its needs. If there were no price controls on domestic oil and if the total amount of oil demanded in the nation was more than the total supply of oil at the then existing prices, what would happen to the price of oil in the United States? If the price of domestic oil was then higher than the price of the imported oil, what would happen to the price of quota entitlements, those with large supplies of domestic oil or those with large supplies of foreign oil? Which companies would get the benefits of such a quota entitlement system? Can you think of a better way to distribute the quotas?

7. Suppose that a quarantine is established on imports of frozen and canned beef from Argentina. Argentine beef typically sells for less than beef produced in the United States. Trace the effects of such a quarantine on the price of beef in the United States, on the price of grazing land in the West, and on the demand "export" products produced in the United States. Do you think that such a quarantine will increase or decrease the incomes of all farmers considered collectively? Do you think such a quarantine will increase or decrease the real income of consumers?

8. The Jones Act requires that all shipments from one United States port to another United States port be made in United States-owned ships. The cost of shipping in United States bottoms is much higher than it is in ships of foreign registry. If you worked for a lumber company in the United States that would have to pay a higher price to gets its lumber from the West Coast to the East Coast than a similar lumber company located in British Columbia, Canada, what position would you take on the Jones Act? What effect will the Jones Act have on the cost of homes in the United States? If you were a member of the policy council of the AFL-CIO, would you lobby for the continuation of the Jones Act?

9. When there is a large foreign demand for soybeans, their price rises, which causes beef and other protein-supplying products to be higher in the United States than they would otherwise be. Labor unions and consumer groups have demanded that the United States impose an embargo on soybeans. What will be the effect of this embargo on the cost of living in the United States, taking into account the costs of imports as well as other products?

10. Because of certain monetary and fiscal policies, United States exports carry a higher price in the world markets than do the competitive exports from Western Europe. As a result, the United States has a negative balance on current account. United States manufacturers, in an effort to become competitive, embark on a program to establish production facilities in Western Europe. What effect will this have on the balance of payments position of the United States? If other countries are willing to accumulate short-term claims against the United States, will there necessarily be a problem?

11. The price of crude oil from the OPEC countries has been tripled. They expect to accumulate about $45 billion of additional short-term claims against the rest of the world. However, suppose that the OPEC countries are unwilling to accumulate claims against countries in proportion to their sales of crude oil to those countries. Specifically, let us suppose that they are unwilling to accumulate claims against Great Britain but are anxious to accumulate additional claims against the United States. How would this show up on our balance of payments statement? What effect would this have on the British balance of payments statement?

ANSWERS TO REVIEW QUESTIONS

1. The analysis underlying regional trade is no different from that for international trade. In this question the pretrade exchange ratio on Long Island between fruit and beef is 5 bu of fruit equal 100 lb of beef. This can be restated in two ways, 1 bu of fruit exchanges for 20 lb of beef and 1 lb of beef exchanges for 1/20 bu of fruit.

   In Florida, 10 bu of fruit exchange for 100 lb of beef. This can be restated as 1 bu of fruit exchanges for 10 lb of beef or 1 lb of beef exchanges for 1/10 bu of fruit. Now, it is easy to see that the price of fruit is cheapest in Florida, since it exchanges for only 10 lb of beef, whereas in Long Island this bushel of fruit would cost you 20 lb of beef. Therefore, Florida should specialize in the production of fruit. By the same approach, a pound of beef would cost you 1/10 bushel of fruit in Florida, while in Long Island it would be cheaper, costing you only 1/20 bushel of fruit.

   a) This is incorrect. As explained above, Long Island should specialize in beef.
   b) This is incorrect. As explained above, Florida should specialize in fruit.
   c) This is correct. Long Island should raise beef and exchange it for fruit raised in Florida.
   d) This is incorrect. We can determine what area should specialize in what as long as we know relative prices.

2. In France, a bushel of wheat costs twice as much as a gallon of wine. In the United States, a bushel of wheat costs the same as a gallon of wine. This means that in France, 1 bushel of wheat equals 2 gallons of wine and in the United States, 1 bushel of wheat equals 1 gallon of wine. Hence, wheat is cheaper in the United States and wine is cheaper in France.

   a) This is incorrect. France will sell wine and buy wheat.
   b) This is incorrect. The United States will in fact want to buy wine.
   c) This is correct as explained above.
   d) This is incorrect. The United States will buy wine and sell wheat.

3. A quarantine on Argentine beef will reduce the supply of beef available in the United States. Other things being equal, the price of beef will rise in the United States and the price of beef will fall in Argentina.

a) This is incorrect. The price will rise in the United States.

b) This is incorrect. The price will indeed rise, but the quarantine means that Argentina will have fewer American dollars, and hence their imports from the United States (our exports) will fall.

c) This is correct as explained in (b).

d) This is incorrect. The price will rise, not stay the same.

4. A tariff imposed on foreign-made automobiles will of course increase the price of foreign cars. Demand for domestically made cars will increase since, relatively speaking, their prices have fallen compared to foreign automobiles.

a) This is incorrect. Agriculture is an important export industry. If we eliminate a major source of foreign countries' foreign exchange by reducing their sales of automobiles in the United States, in time it is quite likely that they will demand less United States products.

b) This is incorrect. The increase in demand for domestic automobiles will increase the demand for automobile workers.

c) This is correct. Resources will be bid away from other industries into the automobile industry. Since we can expect some of our export industries to suffer in time, and agriculture is an important export industry, these workers may well shift into automobile production.

d) This is incorrect. There will not be a shift out of domestic automobile production.

5. If you purchase a new foreign-made automobile, the demand for foreign exchange increases. This will increase foreign claims against the United States. The correct answer is (a).

The decision to send a larger military force to Europe will increase expenditures by the United States in foreign countries. This will increase foreign claims against the United States. The correct answer is (a).

If you decide to vacation in Greece, you will be spending money in a foreign country. The effect will be to increase foreign claims against the United States. The correct answer is (a).

If multinational corporations "bring home" the profits made on foreign investment, there will be an inflow of foreign currency into the United States. The result will be a decrease in the amount of foreign claims against the United States. The correct answer is (c).

If the stock market rallies and stimulates foreign financial investment in the United States, there will be a decrease in the amount of foreign claims against the United States. The correct answer is (c).

If the OPEC countries decide to invest in the United States, there will be a decrease in the amount of foreign claims against the United States. The correct answer in this case is (c).

If multinational corporations in the United States build new plants in foreign countries, there will be an outflow of dollars. This will increase the amount of foreign claims against the United States. The correct answer is (a).

OBJECTIVES

Upon successful completion of this chapter, you will be able to:

1. Explain the process by which foreign currencies are made available for international transactions.

2. State the two basic tasks that the set of institutions known as the international monetary system must perform.

3. Describe the three basic types of economic systems and the variants on these systems, indicating in each case how the adjustment problem is resolved.

4. Define the exchange rate and express the value of any currency in terms of another.

5. Use supply and demand curves to explain how the foreign exchange market determines exchange rates.

6. Explain how the temporary imbalance in a country's accounts caused by a change in supply or demand will be resolved through the exchange market process.

7. Relate, historically, the world's experiences with the gold standard and the Bretton Woods System.

8. Describe the "managed" floating exchange rate system that now prevails.

9. Identify the lessons we have learned through the demise of Bretton Woods and the introduction of flexible exchange rates.

10. Describe the choices available to us for the international monetary system.

CHAPTER 17

THE INTERNATIONAL MONETARY SYSTEM

INTRODUCTION

International financial transactions involve exchanging one nation's currency for another.

If you were a camera buff living in the United States and saw the following advertisement in the American edition of the London *Times*, you might become very interested.

> *Hasselblad Camera. Model 500 EL with a planar F2.8 lens. For sale by executor to settle an estate. Price £400. To purchase send a bank draft drawn in pounds on a London bank.*

The Hasselblad camera is recognized as the world's finest camera and you might think that this is a good buy. But the price is quoted in a strange currency. How would you find out what the camera would cost in dollars and how would you go about buying and paying for it? First, you could look up the current dollar price of a British pound in the financial section of a number of publications such as *The Wall Street Journal*. Finding that the British pound is selling for about $2, you would then know that the Hasselblad camera would cost you about $800 exclusive of mailing costs.

Let us assume you decide, after puzzling about the matter for a few days, to use your savings to buy the camera. Your next problem would be to convert your dollars into pounds. Specifically, the ad says the seller wants payment by means of a bank draft drawn in pounds. How would you go about doing this?

You decide to go to your local bank to see what your banker can do for you. Your banker offers to sell you the draft for $808, including a 1 percent service charge. (A draft is simply a check written by one bank on another.) In this case we assume your local bank has an account with Barclay's Bank in London. With this draft drawn on Barclay's Bank in London, you are in a position to buy your Hasselblad. You mail the draft to the seller and anxiously await its arrival at the local post office, where you will have to

pay an import tax before you can actually take possession of the camera.

Meanwhile, let us suppose that this transaction stimulates your interest in how international payments such as the one you made are organized. How are these transactions organized?

Most local banks keep accounts with a correspondent bank in New York City or Chicago that specializes in international business. When your banker sells you a draft, he or she asks the correspondent bank to write a check or draft, as it is called, on the correspondent's account that it maintains in a bank in London and charge the cost of the draft to your bank's account. Your banker in turn charges you what the correspondent bank has charged plus a small service charge. In this way, you are able to convert your bank deposit into a draft drawn on a London bank.

This is fine, you might say, but where does the correspondent bank get the pounds it has on deposit in Barclay's Bank in London? The answer is that some United States exporter who has received a check drawn on Barclay's Bank for, say, a used computer sold in Great Britain, is anxious to convert the check into dollars. He, in effect, sells the check to the correspondent bank and receives dollars in return. Therefore the pounds you use to pay for your camera actually came from a British importer of computers. Or, looking at it another way, the dollars you use to buy your draft are really used to help pay for the computer.

But this still leaves some unanswered questions. What determines the rate of exchange—the $2.00 price for pounds? The answer to this is that there is a network of banks in New York, London, and other financial centers who specialize in buying and selling foreign currencies for customers. Whenever the New York banks find that they are not selling drafts on their deposits in London as rapidly as they are acquiring deposits, they offer these deposits for sale to other banks who participate in this market. If at a given price there is a larger quantity of pounds being offered for sale than the quantity demanded for pounds, then the price of pounds will fall, like any other commodity in a free market. If it fell to $1.50, your Hasselblad would cost you $600 rather than $800.

You might be inclined to think that this explanation of the international payments system seems to be too simple. There are many international banks in all of the financial centers of the world. They sell dollar balances as well as pound, franc, mark, and peseta balances. Couldn't the exchange rates in these various centers get out of line with each other, so that the cost of a pound might be $2.00 in New York and $1.98 in Frankfurt, West Germany? The answer to this is that there are employees in each of these banks who simultaneously buy pounds where they are cheaper and sell them where they are more expensive. This process is called *arbitrage*. In this way the exchange rate between any two currencies is the same in all of the foreign exchange markets of the world.

Foreign exchange is defined as whatever serves as a medium of exchange in making payments to nonresidents of the United States.

The *foreign exchange rate* is the price you would have to pay for one unit of a specific foreign currency. Thus, if the exchange rate for the West German mark were $0.50, you would have to pay $50.00 for 100 marks.

International trade requires institutions, such as the type we have just described, to facilitate it. Whenever international trade has become an important way of using resources, in the history of the world, institutions have been developed to facilitate it.

In this chapter we will (1) describe the tasks international economic institutions must accomplish if the international trade machine is to be used effectively; (2) examine three general types of economic institutions that have been used in various combinations to manage international trade; (3) review the way these institutions have been used in the past; and (4) discuss the choices available to the world in selecting new social institutions for managing international trade.

THE FUNCTIONS OF THE INTERNATIONAL MONETARY SYSTEM

Any set of international monetary institutions must achieve two important tasks.

The gains from that complex machine, international trade, will never be fully realized unless international monetary institutions help a country decide what products it will export and what products it will import. To a person living in a market-directed economy, this sounds easy. Just import the products that are cheaper abroad than at home and export those products that are cheaper at home than abroad. But in many centrally planned economies the market is not used to guide the economy. In these countries, a special set of economic institutions must be set up to choose what should be exported and what should be imported. If these institutions do not work properly, the world would waste some of its resources.

The second important task of the international economic institutions is to ensure that over the long run the flow of foreign currencies into the country is equal to the outflow of domestic currency. This is called the adjustment problem. Consider two countries.

Country A is a spendthrift. It tends to adopt inflationary policies and it usually tries to buy or invest more abroad than it is selling or borrowing in the long-term capital market. In the short run, other nations are willing to advance credits to the spendthrift nation, but in the long run they become fed up and begin to look for a way to discipline it.

In contrast, Country B has miserly instincts. Its goal is to sell more than it is buying. This would be alright if it were willing to make long-term loans to the rest of the world. But let us suppose that it is reluctant to enter into long-term lending arrangements. As a result,

Country B becomes a problem to the international community. Its perennial balance of payments surplus makes it more difficult for other nations to manage their affairs.

An important aspect of the second question then becomes: How can the nations participating in international trade design a system that will discipline those nations who continually run balance of payments deficits or surpluses?

Perhaps it will help you to view it this way.

You are a member of a stamp collectors club. The members of your club are constantly exchanging stamps. Whenever a person wants a stamp from another member, but doesn't have a good stamp to trade for it, the buyer gives a generally recognized chit to the seller. The creditors can then use these chits to acquire stamps from other members. Now suppose that your club is bothered by two types of members: those that acquire too many stamps by issuing chits and those who acquire too many chits.

The community of nations faces the same problem: What to do about the perennial debtors and the perennial creditors.

If the international trade machine is to be used effectively, international economic institutions must be designed to facilitate it. We turn now to a description of three different devices that could be used to facilitate international trade and financial flows.

DIFFERENT APPROACHES TO THE REGULATION OF INTERNATIONAL EXCHANGE FLOWS

The use of direct controls is one approach to the regulation of international exchange flows.

In the communist countries, for example, a government agency that is responsible for all international transactions decides what to export and what to import. This agency collects whatever currencies or credits are used to pay for the exports it is selling. In turn, it uses these currencies or credits to pay for the imports that it is purchasing.

Communist countries frequently negotiate bilateral trade agreements. Country A will agree to sell to Country B a certain quantity of machine tools, receiving credits it can use to purchase a certain quantity of raw materials or other products from Country B. Communist countries also sell agricultural products, wood pulp, gold, and other commodities in the world markets. The accumulated short-term capital claims can, in turn, be used to buy other commodities in the world markets. In this way, the countries are not limited to trade arising exclusively out of bilateral agreements. They can engage in multilateral trade, selling to countries D, E, and F and buying from countries G, H, and I. In this sense they resemble any market economy except, of course, that the government rather than private citizens makes the foreign-trade decisions.

If the agencies responsible for foreign trade in the communist countries were told that it was their job to use international trade transactions to maximize the productivity of their resources, they would export the products in which they had a comparative advantage and import the products in which they did not have a comparative advantage. But internal prices in a communist country do not necessarily reflect their relative opportunity costs. Indeed, other considerations, such as international prestige and military advantage, may be of overriding importance. It is particularly easy for governments of the communist countries to maximize noneconomic goals, since they can subsidize their international trade through internal price adjustments. In any case, direct controls serve as a device for determining what commodities to export and import, and for ensuring that in the long run the outflow of domestic currency equals the inflow of foreign currency.

Market-oriented economies also use controls to effect international currency flows.

The Western or noncommunist nations have also used many direct controls together with market institutions to perform these tasks. During the 1950s, for example, the United States had a *quota system* for limiting the import of petroleum products. *Protective tariffs*, too, are used by many countries to protect home industries and to improve their balance of payments position. Laws that prevent the use of foreign ships in coastwise shipping make it impossible for other nations to exploit fully their comparative advantage in the provision of transportation services. *Embargoes*, which make it illegal for a country to export such products as military supplies or feed grains, also change the composition and quantity of trade. *Quarantines* are sometimes used ostensibly to protect the health of a nation's livestock population, but in fact are used to prevent foreign competition for the domestic market for beef.

On the other side, nations use a large variety of subsidies and grants to encourage purchasers in other nations to import their products. Common Market countries reimburse exporters for the taxes that are included in the domestic prices of the products they are selling outside the country. The United States has in the past subsidized agricultural exports, that is, paid exporters the difference between the domestic and world market price of wheat and other agricultural products. The United States has also required the countries receiving military and domestic aid to apply the credits thus earned to the purchase of United States products. The British and French governments have subsidized the development of supersonic aircraft with the hope that this will help their balance of payments in the future.

Some countries have used various forms of foreign exchange controls to solve their balance of payments problems. They have required that all foreign currencies received by exporters be sold to the government. The government then allocates this foreign exchange to the purchase of certain imports, usually those that do not compete with domestic producers.

Direct controls, then, whether tariffs, quotas, quarantines of export subsidies, exchange controls, or a myriad of other regulatory devices, are usually used to determine what products shall be exported and imported and to resolve the adjustment problem.

A single world monetary system is another device that could be used to manage international trade and payments.

A single world currency system has never been tried on a worldwide scale in its pure form. Two variants of this system—the gold standard as it was practiced for almost a century before World War I, and the dollar standard as it was practiced for 25 years after World War II—have been used.

To illustrate how a world currency system might work, we will set up an imaginary system, using the symbol $\mathcal{C}$ to refer to the "world currency." At the outset, the world currency system could be created by establishing conversion rates that permit each country to convert its currency—dollars, pounds, francs, lira, pesetas, pesos, and so on—into the world currency. Thus, if $2 = $\mathcal{C}$1$, everybody in the United States would receive one unit of world currency for every two dollars, and if 50 pesos = $\mathcal{C}$1.00$, Mexicans would receive one unit of world currency for every 50 pesos. The same conversion would be applicable to each of the other currencies and countries.

Once the conversion was complete, all prices in the world would be quoted in terms of world currency. It would no longer be necessary for a United States tourist to use exchange rates to translate a 400 peso price for a Mexican hotel room into its corresponding dollar price. But this is a small part of the conversion.

The most important part of the conversion to a world currency system would be the creation of a central bank for the world. Let us assume that the world central bank, to be called the World Reserve System, would be located in some neutral part of the world and that its board of governors would supply reserves to the commercial banks of the world. We shall also assume that the World Reserve System could take care of the currency needs of the world—just as the Federal Reserve System does in the United States. Hence, each nation would relinquish its right to issue domestic currency.

A single world currency system has built-in disciplinary devices to resolve the adjustment problem.

Now suppose that Country A gets out of line and starts to buy more from the rest of the world than the rest of the world wants to buy from it. Initially, this deficit in its balance of payments would be financed by (1) a loss of world currency reserves, and (2) an accumulation of debts to the rest of the world. This process of overspending could not persist, however, and two feedback mechanisms would force Country A back into line.

First, the excess purchase of foreign products will reduce demand for domestic products in Country A and cause money income and employment to fall. In time Country A will reduce its imports since a decline in income will reduce total expenditures, including expenditure for imports. Meanwhile, the rest of the world will initially be experiencing a boom. Their money incomes and employment will have been increased by the additional orders received from Country A and will tend to increase their imports from Country A. Both of these developments will help Country A get its international accounts into balance.

Second, Country A will lose bank reserves to banks in other countries. This loss will force Country A's banks to call loans and sell securities, thus reducing the supply of world currency in Country A. At the same time, commercial banks in other countries, having acquired additional reserves, will make additional loans and buy more securities, thus increasing the supply of world currency in the rest of the world. The fact that money will be tight in Country A and easy in other countries will tend to decrease money incomes and prices in Country A and to increase money incomes and prices in the other countries of the world.

Thus a single world monetary system would serve as a disciplinary device. It would force localized depressions on those "deficit" countries that wanted to buy or lend more than other countries were willing to either buy or borrow from them. The depressions would reduce outpayments from the "deficit" countries. Concurrently, the "surplus" countries would suffer from "overfull" employment and inflation; boom conditions in these countries would increase the outpayments from the "surplus" countries.

It is interesting that within a given country this system works very well. If California residents persist in buying more from the rest of the United States than they are selling to the rest of the United States, or more than the rest of the country is willing to buy from or lend to California, California banks lose reserves, and money becomes tight on the West Coast. Unemployment and falling prices force California back in line.

The same consequence would be true of the world if a single world currency were used. The nations of the world would move in lock step. No country could independently adopt a different monetary and fiscal stance; it would have to accept the discipline inherent in a single world currency.

The gold standard is a variant of the single world monetary system, and left alone it would work the same way.

The gold standard is a modified form of the single world currency system. When nations adopted the gold standard, they announced the price at which they would buy and sell gold, thus tying all of the currencies of the world together. If the United States, for example, set a $42.00 price for an ounce of gold and West Germany set an 84 marks price per ounce of gold, the mark would be worth $0.50. Gold is also allowed to circulate as a form of domestic currency and is part of the money supply used as a reserve for the banking system. As a consequence, a country loses gold when it spends more than it is taking in. This reduces monetary reserves and income. The reverse will be true for the country that runs a surplus because the gold standard ties all of the currencies of the world into a single system. It penalizes the countries that spend and invest too much abroad by depressing their economies, and it causes the countries that spend and invest too little to experience inflationary developments.

The dollar standard was another form of a single world currency standard.

From the end of World War II until August 1971, a dollar standard prevailed in the world. This system, which was created at a conference held in Bretton Woods, New Hampshire, is called the Bretton Woods System. The currencies were defined in terms of the dollar and the dollar was tied to gold at $35 per ounce. The United States was obligated to buy and sell gold to the other nations at that price. Rather than hold gold reserves, however, most countries chose to hold dollars. After all, they could always be converted into gold, hence dollars were as good as gold and more convenient. Countries running deficits lost dollar reserves, and countries running surpluses gained dollar reserves. Had the economies of the world played the game according to the simple rules stated above, both of these systems would have worked—particularly if there had been an effective way to limit the total number of dollars to be used as monetary reserves.

For a single monetary system to work, nations must give up some of their sovereignty.

A key feature of the world currency system is that participating nations must give up some of their sovereignty; they must agree to expose their economies to the discipline of a world system. Thus, countries will experience depressions if they consistently spend more than they are earning or than other countries are willing to lend to them. Those that consistently run balance of payments surpluses and are unwilling to lend to other nations will experience inflation. If instead, nation states use fiscal and monetary policies to insulate their economies from these income and monetary effects, a single monetary system will not work.

This point leads us to a discussion of a third control system: flexible exchange rates.

Flexible exchange rates are a regulator of international trade.

This control system, as the name implies, resolves the adjustment problem through changes in foreign exchange rates. Since the exchange rates themselves are so important in this system, we will explain the concept of foreign exchange in greater detail.

If you were going to travel to Europe for three months next summer, you would need a collection of pounds, marks, francs, lira, and pesetas—the foreign currencies of Great Britain, West Germany, France, Italy, and Spain. We refer to all of these currencies as "foreign exchange."

Table 17.1 is a copy of the daily foreign exchange rate quotations that appear in *The Wall Street Journal* and many other newspapers. The numbers in this list are the prices quoted in dollars or fractions of dollars that you would pay for one unit of a foreign currency deposited in a foreign bank.

Looking down this list, you will see a British pound would cost you $1.8880, so that if you were buying an antique that was listed at £1000, it would cost you $1,888. Or, if you were traveling in West Germany and needed 2000 West German marks they would cost you about $975.00 (2000 × $0.4875).

It is also interesting to see that there is a futures market for some currencies. If you were running a shoe company and had ordered a shipment of English shoes that would have to be paid for in 90 days, you could assure yourself of the price by buying 90-day pounds, that is, pounds that will be delivered to you in 90 days. Thus, if your bill, quoted in pounds, was 5000, then by purchasing this number of pounds today in the futures market you could be sure that bill would be $9,377.50 (5000 × 1.8755). In this way, you can protect yourself against a loss because of an increase in the price of pounds.

The demand for foreign exchange is derived from the demand for foreign goods, services, and securities.

If you have never been to Europe or even Canada, you may think you have never purchased foreign

TABLE 17.1
FOREIGN EXCHANGE RATES

Wednesday, July 12, 1978

Selling prices for bank transfers in the U.S. for payment abroad, as quoted at 3 p.m. Eastern Time (in dollars).

Country	Wed.	Yr. ago
Argentina (Peso) Finc'l	.00127	.00260
Australia (Dollar)	1.1480	1.1250
Austria (Schilling)	.0675	.061850
Belgium (Franc)		
Commercial rate	.030885	.028160
Financial rate	.030530	.028130
Brazil (Cruzeiro)	.0558	.0700
Britain (Pound)	1.8880	1.7207
30-Day Futures	1.8832	1.7157
90-Day Futures	1.8755	1.7026
180-Day Futures	1.8622	1.6827
Canada (Dollar)	.8903	.9439
30-Day Futures	.8900	z
90-Day Futures	.8904	z
180-Day Futures	.8908	z
China-Taiwan (Dollar)	.0265	.0265
Colombia (Peso)	.0290	.0275
Denmark (Krone)	.1782	.1678
Ecuador (Sucre)	.0404	.03750
Finland (Markka)	.2376	.2494
France (Franc)	.2248	.2058
30-Day Futures	.2246	.2050
90-Day Futures	.2242	.2034
180-Day Futures	.2235	.2010
Greece (Drachma)	.0270	.0280
Hong Kong (Dollar)	.2148	.2153
India (Rupee)	.1235	.1145
Indonesia (Rupiah)	.002590	.002590
Iran (Rial)	.0144	.0142
Iraq (Dinar)	3.43	3.44
Israel (Pound)	.05653	.1068
Italy (Lira)	.001178	.001134
Japan (Yen)	.004924	.003785
30-Day Futures	.004947	.003786
90-Day Futures	.004994	.003786
180-Day Futures	.005060	.003785
Lebanon (Pound)	.3435	.3235
Malaysia (Dollar)	.4236	.4037
Mexico (Peso)	.04377	.0436
Netherlands (Guilder)	.4506	.4085
New Zealand (Dollar)	1.0415	.9781
Norway (Krone)	.1853	.1899
Pakistan (Rupee)	.1020	.1025
Peru (Sol)	.0067	.01240
Philippines (Peso)	.1365	.1355
Portugal (Escudo)	0220	.02600

TABLE 17.1 (continued)

Saudi Arabia (Riyal)	.2910	.2845
Singapore (Dollar)	.4330	.4060
South Africa (Rand)	1.1522	1.1522
South Korea (Won)	.0021	.0021
Spain (Peseta)	.01290	.01153
Sweden (Krona)	.2199	.2298
Switzerland (Franc)	.5512	.4150
30-Day Futures	.5542	.4161
90-Day Futures	.5608	.4178
180-Day Futures	.5707	.4207
Thailand (Baht)	.05	.05
Uruguay (New Peso) Finc'l	.1660	.2120
Venezuela (Bolivar)	.2331	.2331
West Germany (Mark)	.4875	.4385
30-Day Futures	.4893	.4391
90-Day Futures	.4836	.4405
180-Day Futures	.5004	.4432
Supplied by Bankers Trust Co., New York.		

Source: *The Wall Street Journal*, July 12, 1978. Reprinted with permission of *The Wall Street Journal*, © Dow Jones & Company, Inc. (1978). All rights reserved.

exchange. In reality, every time you have purchased a foreign-made commodity, you have indirectly bought foreign exchange.

Whenever a person wants to pay for a purchase from outside the country, there is a demand for foreign exchange. Thus, if you buy a new Volkswagen produced in West Germany, you are actually demanding foreign exchange.

Similarly, whenever you sell something outside the country, the transaction creates a supply of foreign exchange. Suppose, for example, that you sell a herd of prize cows to a French farmer. When he sends you a check drawn on a French bank, he is supplying you with foreign exchange, whether the check is drawn in francs or dollars. The same effect is created when you sell a security to a resident of a foreign country. When she pays you, she is really supplying foreign exchange.

The supply and demand for foreign exchange determine its rate under a flexible system.

The foreign exchange rate, which is actually a price, serves as a control mechanism. It determines the mix of products entering into international trade, and it solves the adjustment problems. The demand for foreign currency, like the demand for any normal good, is downward sloping to the right, indicating that the quantity demanded increases with decreases in the price of the foreign currency. For example, in Fig. 17.1, if D_0D_0 is the demand curve for German marks (DMs) and if the price of a DM is $0.50, the quantity demanded is 5000 DMs per week. Alternatively, if the price of DMs is $0.25, the quantity demanded is 8000 DMs per week. The supply of foreign exchange can be represented in Fig. 17.1 as the supply curve, SS. The supply schedule is upward sloping to the right, reflecting the fact that larger quantities will be supplied at higher prices. The supply and demand for foreign currency determine, under competitive conditions, the equilibrium price or exchange rate, and the quantity. In Fig. 17.1, for example, the equilibrium price is $0.40 and the quantity supplied and demanded at this price is 6000 DMs per week.

To see how a freely fluctuating foreign exchange market works, suppose that initially the mark was selling for $0.40 or two and a half marks to the dollar and that the foreign exchange market was in equilibrium. Now let us suppose that two events occur that change the basic situation. In the first place, let us assume that multinational companies with home offices in New York City decide to build new plants in West Germany in order to sell their products in the Common Market. Let us also suppose that fiscal and monetary policies in the United States increase prices in the United States at a faster rate than they are increasing in West Germany. Both of these events would increase the demand for German marks. The financial officers of multinational companies would ask their banks to convert their dollar balances into mark balances in order to finance the building of new plants in West Germany. The rising prices in the United States would cause purchasers to increase their purchases of Volkswagens, machine tools, and other industrial products from West Germany.

This increase in the demand for West German marks is shown in Fig. 17.1 as a shift of the demand curve from D_0D_0 to D_1D_1. This shift would produce an excess demand of 2000 marks, at the old price of $0.40. If the foreign exchange rate were permitted to fluctuate, it would rise to $0.50. At this price, the quantity of marks supplied

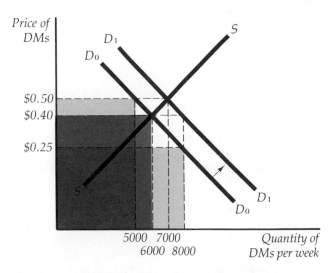

FIG. 17.1 **The demand and supply for German marks.**

would equal the quantity of marks demanded (7000).

How would this change in the foreign exchange rate resolve the situation? The answer is that imports from West Germany would rise in price. It would cost 25 percent more to get the marks to pay for the imports, such as Volkswagens, machine tools, and other products imported from Germany. The increase would ration some buyers out of the market because this feedback mechanism would tell residents of the United States that they should buy less from Germany. At the same time, the devaluation of the dollar, as this process is sometimes called, would make United States products more attractive to buyers in West Germany. What had cost Germans 2½ marks before would now cost them only 2 marks. Travel by Germans in the United States would be cheaper, agricultural products would be less expensive, and securities in the New York Stock Exchange would be better buys. The feedback mechanism would tell West Germans to buy or invest more in the United States. The combination of these two feedback effects would bring a new equilibrium in the foreign exchange market.

In the process—and it takes time for the feedback mechanism to work itself out—there would be a new list of exports and imports. Some machine tools that previously had been produced in

West Germany would now cost less in the United States. Some agricultural products such as beef, which had previously cost less in New Zealand, will now be exported from the United States to West Germany. The exchange rate, then, serves as a control mechanism that not only keeps the totals in balance but also determines what products will be exported and imported.

The reverse would be true if prices rose faster in West Germany than they did in the United States. Our exports to West Germany would rise. Some West Germans would invest in the United States in an effort to protect the value of their savings. These developments would increase the supply of marks. As a result, the mark would fall in the foreign exchange market and the dollar would rise.

We can think of the foreign exchange rate as a regulator, something like a thermostat, that controls the flow of money payments into and out of the country. When nations tend to be spendthrifts, the price to them of foreign currencies rises, making it more costly for them to buy products abroad. When nations are miserly, the cost of foreign exchange falls, making it cheaper to buy products from abroad.

Exchange rates serve as buffers between a country and the rest of the world.

When flexible exchange rates—many times called floating, or freely fluctuating, rates—are used to regulate trade, they serve as a buffer between a country and the rest of the world. Suppose Country A is determined to maintain a steady price level and manages its monetary and fiscal affairs accordingly. And suppose, at the same time, the rest of the world is experiencing a persistent inflation averaging about 10 percent a year. Other countries would tend to buy more from Country A than Country A would buy from them. If other countries succeeded in buying more from A than A was buying from them, then the inflation would spread to A, despite A's conservative monetary and fiscal policies. But it is at this point that a floating exchange rate intervenes.

Because of the excess demand for A's currency, A's currency would go up in price relative to other currencies. It would appreciate in value. This would limit A's exports. Meanwhile the price of other currencies would go down relative to Country A's currency. The other currencies would be said to depreciate. This would make it cheaper (than it would otherwise be) for A to buy from abroad and thus encourage imports.

Of course the reverse is also true. If a country follows policies that lead to rapid inflation, then its currency will depreciate rapidly. In place of spreading to the rest of the world, the inflation is, in a sense, quarantined by changes in the exchange rate.

This completes our explanation of the three basic ways to regulate international trade. All three of these control devices or modifications of them have been used, sometimes simultaneously, by the community of nations as they seek the optimum mix of regulatory devices. Before we turn to the different choices the world faces, let us review briefly the way in which these regulatory devices have been used in the past.

COMMENTARY

The following excerpt is from *The Wall Street Journal* and reflects the impact of international economic events on the value of the dollar. Please read the excerpt and answer the following questions.

a) What factors have caused the dollar to drop in value relative to the yen?
b) What is the impact on consumers of a dollar with a lower value relative to the yen?

DOLLAR PLUNGES TO NEW DEPTHS AGAINST THE YEN

Post-World War II low set in Tokyo; value declines against most currencies
The U.S. dollar plunged to new depths against the Japanese yen in hectic Tokyo trading. In slower dealings elsewhere, the dollar tumbled against most other major currencies as well.

In Tokyo Tuesday, the dollar plummeted to 211.58 yen, a post-World War II low for the

Japanese market. Later in New York, it dropped further to 210.88 yen from 213.26 yen Monday.

Tuesday's Tokyo rate reflected a drop of 2.7% in the dollar's value against the yen in the past week in Tokyo, and it was 3.8 yen below the previous low of 215.38 yen set last Thursday.

All in all, the dollar has dropped 11% against the yen since the beginning of the year. Traders in Tokyo Tuesday said they thought the dollar might recover a bit on profit taking in the next few days, but they expect even lower rates in the near future.

Two important factors in the dollar's drop against the yen had been inflation in the U.S. which tends to reduce the competitiveness of U.S. goods on foreign markets, and the massive size of Japan's trade surplus with the U.S. which swells the amount of dollars overseas.

As a result of the dollar's drop against the yen, a Japanese car that would have cost a U.S customer

$5,000 on Jan. 1 currently would have to be priced at about $5,550 to yield the same number of yen for the exporter. And because of U.S. inflation, Japanese auto makers have been able to raise their prices, without losing too much of their market shares.

On European and American markets, trading was dominated by the dollar's drop against the yen and activity was generally quiet, dealers said.

In Zurich, the dollar fell to 1.8760 Swiss francs; in New York, it dropped to 1.8668 francs from 1.8921 francs Monday. The dollar declined to 4.5938 French francs in Paris and moved down to 4,5863 francs from 4.6041 francs in New York.

Reprinted with permission of *The Wall Street Journal*, © Dow Jones & Company, Inc. (June 21, 1978). All rights reserved.

HISTORICAL EXPERIENCES WITH DIFFERENT INTERNATIONAL MONETARY SYSTEMS

The gold-standard system acts as a single world currency.

During most of the nineteenth century and during the first part of this century, the nations of the world relied on a modified version of the gold standard to manage international trade.

Each nation defined its currency as being the equivalent of a certain amount of gold. The United States, for example, defined the dollar as equal to one-twentieth of an ounce of gold (1 ounce of gold = $20.67), and other nations defined their currencies in terms of gold. This made it possible during the early part of this century to fix the exchange rates among all currencies.

All the nations that joined the "gold standard club," and this included most of the industrially advanced nations, kept their monetary reserves in gold. When they spent and lent too much, they would lose gold, depressing their economies in accordance with the single world currency process we described above. Or when they were too

miserly, they would acquire gold and this would increase their money supply and cause their prices to rise.

This system worked reasonably well until World War I. It disciplined the spendthrift nations, prevented peacetime inflations, and maintained an effective world market for many products.

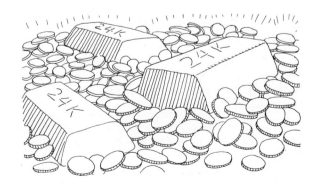

But after World War I, the gold standard ran into difficulties. Great Britain tried to return to the prewar relationship between the pound and gold although its prices had risen during the war. Then with the coming of the Great Depression, the nations of the world tried to increase their exports in order to reduce their unemployment rates. At the same time they were anxious to keep imports out. To do this, they experimented with devaluations of their currencies. First one country would reduce the amount of gold behind its currency in an effort to make the price of its currency cheaper and therefore expand its exports and reduce its imports. Then, not to be outdone, other countries would follow suit. These competitive devaluations undermined the confidence the world had in the gold standard as a protection against inflation.

In addition, the nations of the world experimented with a variety of direct controls to solve their unemployment problems. They erected high tariffs to keep foreign products out. In the United States the Hawley-Smoot Tariff of 1930 imposed high taxes on a long list of imported products. Other countries followed suit and the volume of international trade became substantially reduced. Thus, prior to World War II, many nations had imposed foreign exchange controls that crippled the foreign trade machine.

By the end of World War II it was painfully clear that a gold standard combined with a large number of direct controls would hobble the international trade machine. To solve this problem an international monetary conference was held in Bretton Woods, New Hampshire. It was attended by many economists and government officials from the world's leading economic powers. They designed a new international monetary system to replace the gold standard as it had functioned during the nineteenth century.

The Bretton Woods System, as it was called, contained elements of all three regulatory systems we discussed earlier.

The Bretton Woods System was partly a gold standard and partly a flexible exchange rate standard, and it made provision for the use of direct controls under certain conditions.

Two new international institutions were created: the World Bank, which was to facilitate long-term lending between nations, and the International Monetary Fund (IMF), which was to provide the framework for postwar trade among nations.

Each member nation was supposed to define its currency in terms of gold so that there would be fixed rates of exchange among all currencies. Each nation then was required to keep a portion of its gold and other foreign exchange reserves, largely dollars, in the International Monetary Fund. If a nation's currency tended to go down in price in the foreign exchange markets, the nation was obligated to use its reserves of gold and foreign currencies to support its own currency. If it ran short, it could borrow reserves from the IMF. If, however, the weakness in its currency persisted, the nation was permitted to lower the price of its currency relative to other currencies, that is, devalue by reducing the amount of gold exchanged for each unit of its currency up to 10 percent. If a nation felt it should devalue by even more, it was supposed to seek approval from the International Monetary Fund. In this way the Bretton Woods System provided for fixed rates of exchange, as under the gold standard, and at the same time it also provided for adjustments in these fixed rates when they proved to be wrong, as under the flexible exchange rates regime.

Finally, the Bretton Woods System provided for a limited use of direct controls. If a nation ran a persistent balance of payments surplus, then other nations could declare that nation's currency to be a "scarce currency" and increase tariffs against that nation's exports.

Did this mix of (1) fixed exchange rates, (2) controlled changes in foreign exchange rates, and (3) limited use of direct controls successfully manage international trade in the postwar period? The answer is that it did, although not wholly as had been planned.

During the 1950s and early 1960s, the Bretton Woods monetary system began to reveal some weaknesses. In place of keeping their monetary reserves in gold or as claims against the IMF, the major trading countries kept their reserves in New York City, either as dollar balances or as short-term investments that would easily be converted into dollar balances. Thus, when France took in more than it paid out, it acquired dollar claims. The same thing was true of other countries. As a result, the nations of the world may be said to have gone on a "dollar standard."

When a major trading nation decided that its currency was too high priced, it reduced the gold content without going through the consultation process with the IMF. As a result, the influence of the IMF in establishing exchange rates was seriously undermined. Possibly in a world of nation states, each jealously guarding its sovereignty, this result could have been predicted. In that event, long-term international agreements to establish new settlement systems may be of limited value.

Finally, the "scarce currency" clause was not used. During the Bretton Woods conference, it was generally believed that the United States would be the culprit that would take in more money than it would pay out and would have to be disciplined. But it worked the other way. The United States turned out to be the nation that consistently paid out more than it took in, and in the end this is what caused the downfall of the Bretton Woods System.

During the 1950s and the 1960s the dollar claims of other countries against the United States increased substantially.

Although in each of the 25 years following World War II the United States sold more goods and services than it bought from the rest of the world, it usually paid out more dollars than it took in. You might ask, "How could this happen?" The answer is that during this period the dollar was the dominant currency in the world and other nations wanted to hold dollars as part of their international reserves. These reserves comprise the pool of foreign currencies and gold that nations hold to cover short-term balance of payment problems.

This made it possible for Americans to buy factories, and invest in banks and income-producing securities in Western Europe and other parts of the noncommunist world. The value of United States assets abroad increased from about $55 billion in 1950 to about $181 billion in 1971. As a result, foreign nations acquired dollar claims against the United States in almost every year during this period. By 1971, foreign nations held about $100 billion dollars as part of their monetary reserves.

Except for the communist countries, we could think of the world's money supply as being an inverted pyramid, with the United States' $10 billion of gold at the bottom of the pyramid supporting more than 100 billions of dollar equivalents in the various currencies of the world. Many economists were concerned that there were not enough monetary reserves to support the whole system.

As a new form of international reserves, SDRs were created in 1970.

In recognition of the shortage of reserves the members of the IMF developed a new plan in the late 1960s to create *Special Drawing Rights*, or SDRs as they are called, to serve along with gold and key currencies as international reserves. Unless vetoed by 15 percent of the membership of IMF, the director, in consultation with the membership, could give credit to each of the countries for its proportionate share (depending on its contributions to the IMF) of these new SDRs—or paper gold as they are sometimes called. The new reserves are created out of thin air by the simple act of crediting the nation's account in the IMF. A nation that was spending more than it was taking in could, in support of its currency, use these accounting credits to buy back its currency from other countries. Other member countries are obligated to accept SDRs, or paper gold, up to a limit. Thereafter they could demand that the spendthrift country pay them in gold and good currencies.

MINI-CASE 17.1

You are convinced that world-wide inflation will lead to a world-wide collapse of the 1930's variety. Since you think this will be followed by revolution and chaos, you believe that stopping inflation has the highest priority. Which of the following settlement systems would you choose?

a) A freely flexible exchange rate system with no central bank intervention.
b) A managed float—flexible exchange rates with a substantial amount of intervention by the central banks to maintain the stability of foreign exchange rates.
c) A modernized Bretton Woods System based on a new set of foreign exchange rates.
d) A nineteenth century type gold standard with gold valued at $225 an ounce and a new set of exchange rates reflecting the higher price of gold and other factors entering into international trade.

THE EMERGENCE OF A NEW INTERNATIONAL MONETARY SYSTEM

By 1971 the dollar was no longer acceptable as the world's basic currency.

Despite the creation of additional reserves, the international monetary system proved to be top-heavy by the end of the 1960s. Speculators, who could see what was going on, began to sell dollars and buy other currencies. Central bankers in Western Europe began to worry about whether their dollar holdings could be redeemed for gold and other international reserves.

By 1971 it was clear that the United States had a serious balance of payments problem. Partly as a result of the inflation accompanying the Vietnam War, prices had risen more rapidly in the United States than they had in many other countries. Products made in the United States began to be priced out of the world market. For the first time in 25 years, the United States in 1971 bought more goods and services from other countries than it sold to other countries—and at the same time, investors in the United States continued to buy assets abroad. By August 1971 the dollar was no longer generally acceptable to the rest of the world. Tourists in Europe found they could not use their dollars to buy francs, marks, guilders, and other foreign currencies. Central bankers in Western Europe demanded gold and other international reserves for the dollars they were holding.

The era of floating exchange rates began.

To stop the "run on the dollar," President Richard M. Nixon announced on August 15, 1971 that the United States would no longer pay out gold to foreign central banks when they presented their dollar claims to the Federal Reserve. With this unilateral act, the Bretton Woods system, which had served the free world well for a quarter of a century, was largely demolished and the dollar was allowed to "float." Other nations followed and the free world entered the era of floating exchange rates.

Did this act mean that the system of freely flexible exchange rates would now regulate the flow of trade between nations? The answer is a qualified yes.

Whenever a nation, such as the United States, persistently buys more goods and services than it is selling and other nations are not prepared to accept that nation's currency claims, then the price of the currency, in this case the dollar, will fall. The top half of Figure 17.2 shows the relationship between the value of the dollar and the currencies of major trading partners after it was allowed to float in 1971. Figure 17.2B shows the effective exchange rate of the dollar compared to all other countries weighted according to trade importance. These changes in exchange rates serve as "corrective" devices to solve the balance of payments problem.

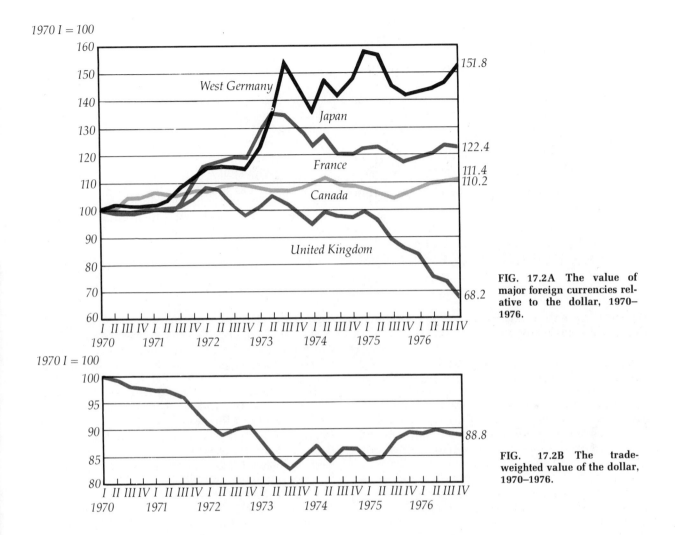

1970 I = 100

FIG. 17.2A The value of major foreign currencies relative to the dollar, 1970–1976.

1970 I = 100

FIG. 17.2B The trade-weighted value of the dollar, 1970–1976.

The "managed float" has tended to be the rule rather than the exception in the operation of the flexible exchange rate system.

There are, however, some modifications to the textbook explanations of the flexible exchange rate system that we should take into account. The central banks of the world are constantly in touch with each other. They buy and sell foreign currencies to smooth out the day-to-day fluctuations. They sometimes go further and try to influence the long-run price of a nation's currency as they did under the Bretton Woods system. Suppose the

price of the dollar tends to fall and the price of the West German mark tends to rise in the foreign exchange markets of the world. The West German central bank, in an effort to keep its exports from rising in price in the United States market, may use marks to buy dollars. At the same time, the Federal Reserve, in an effort to keep its import prices down, may borrow West German marks to buy up some of the excess dollars in the foreign exchange markets. Both central banks, then, use their resources or borrowing capacity to thwart the forces that would otherwise establish a new price for the dollar or the West German mark. In the short run, these expedients seem to be attractive. But they seldom work in the long run. Speculators, seeing what is going on, tend to buy marks and sell dollars—in a sense they "bet" against the central banks. This forces the central banks to go even further in their efforts to maintain the former prices of their currencies. Eventually, if the long-run forces are persistent, the central banks will be forced to yield and the speculators will obtain extraordinary gains.

The new system has elements of the Bretton Woods system left in it.

The system that replaced the Bretton Woods system is a mixed bag. It is predominantly a flexible exchange rate system with a little of the Bretton Woods concept of central bank management of exchange rates left in it. Whenever the International Monetary Fund is called in to keep a nation's currency from sinking to too low a level (as was the case of Great Britain in 1977), the Bretton Woods system shows itself again as standing in the wings waiting to help the flexible exchange rate system.

The new system has worked. It survived the oil price explosion of the early seventies and the marked changes in agricultural prices. The question that the world must face in the future is this: Is there a better set of social institutions for managing the international trade machine in the years ahead?

THE CHOICES OF SOCIAL INSTITUTIONS FOR MANAGING THE INTERNATIONAL ECONOMY

It is impossible for any economy to manage its resources effectively without some set of social institutions to answer the following questions: What should be produced? What technologies should be used? Who should do which jobs? And to whom should the output go?

The same thing is true of international trade. Some set of social institutions has to evolve or be created to decide what products shall be exchanged and how the "adjustment" problem will be resolved. The international trade machine cannot be used effectively to increase the productivity of the world's resources, unless there is an effective set of social institutions to manage it.

Direct controls usually restrict trade between nations.

When nations turn to some set of direct controls in the management of international trade, such as exchange controls, tariffs, export subsidies, quarantines, embargoes, or import or export quotas, the international trade machine usually suffers.

Why, it is interesting to ask, should direct controls necessarily tend to throttle international trade? Shouldn't the nations of the world want to regulate their trade so as to increase the productivity of their resources?

The answer is that while the consuming public has much to gain from the enlargement of international trade, consumers as a group seldom have much to say about what set of social institutions shall be adopted to manage international trade. Individual industries such as steel, bicycles, shoes, and many other producer groups, as well as labor unions in certain industries, have much to gain from tariffs and nontariff devices that will keep cheaper foreign products out of the country. These groups stand to lose a great deal if their markets are invaded by producers in other countries. They therefore are inclined to make strong appeals to their government to protect them against foreign competition. Consumers, meanwhile, seldom realize how much they stand to lose if all these special interest groups, taken together, are successful in limiting international trade.

Some economists advocate closing international boundaries to trade as a means of achieving full employment and equality.

Usually these limitations on international trade creep into the economy through a series of little-noticed changes in governmental policies. Sometimes they masquerade as a special protection for low-wage industries. At other times they are sold as a means of protecting the environment from oil spills due to the use of cheap foreign ships or as a means of making automobiles safe.

In recent years, with an increased emphasis on job security and full employment, some British economists have advocated the closing of national boundaries to all trade except that managed by the government. The so-called siege economy, they argue, will better achieve the national goals of full employment and equality of incomes than an open economy that encourages economic growth and increased productivity.

The trade-off between different social goals also is important in deciding between fixed and flexible exchange rates.

The trade-off between different social goals is also important in determining whether some form of fixed exchange rates or flexible exchange rates should be adopted as the appropriate adjustment mechanism. Fixed exchange rates do have a disciplinary effect on the national economies of the world. When a country inflates to the point that it runs short of reserves, the country must do something about it. It must either reverse its inflation policies or devalue its currency. Devaluation—letting its currency depreciate relative to other currencies—is a warning signal. It tells the electorate that its government has adopted inflationary policies.

Flexible exchange rates, in contrast, allow a country to inflate without having to face the sudden devaluation of its currency. The day-to-day small declines of its currency in the foreign exchange markets do not present the nation with such a dramatic choice—either stop inflation or face devaluation.

Flexible exchange rates, do, on the other hand, permit a country to adopt its own set of macroeconomic policies rather than stay in lock step with the other nations of the world. West Germany, for example, was able to resist adopting inflationary policies during the latter part of the 1970s by allowing its currency to appreciate. Had its economy been tied by fixed exchange rates to the rest of the world, it would have had much less chance of avoiding the worldwide inflationary developments of the 1970s.

In the end, the choice of social institutions for managing international trade turns on what national goals are to be served.

If the productivity of the world's resources is perceived to be of paramount importance, then free trade and appropriate adjustment devices will be selected. On the other hand, if each country perceives itself as being primarily interested in job security and full employment, then some set of direct controls plus government management of the foreign exchange rate will no doubt be chosen.

As has always been true, economics is largely concerned with explaining how each set of social institutions will work. The choice of social institutions for managing international trade (or for managing the entire economy, for that matter) hangs on what you and the other people in the nation want your economy to achieve. As economists, we can't tell you what to do, but as choice makers, you will need economics to make intelligent choices about what set of economic institutions will best achieve your goals.

REVIEW QUESTIONS

1. Assume you are considering taking a trip around the world. You can buy your foreign exchange now or three months later. What would you do, given the situations below, assuming flexible rates?

Case I: The United States is running a substantial surplus in its basic balance (current account plus net investment abroad).

Case II: The United States is engaged in a military build-up in the Middle East. This build-up requires more foreign exchange than is being earned on current account.

a) You should buy foreign currency now.

b) You should buy foreign currency three months from now.

2. Assume the world is operating under a Bretton Woods System. The United States has persistent deficit in its basic balance (current account plus net investment abroad). After a period of time you would expect:

a) other countries would buy up the surplus dollars in order to keep their currencies from depreciating relative to the dollar. In time this will become too expensive.

b) other countries would buy up the surplus dollars in order to keep their currencies from appreciating relative to the dollar. In time this will become too expensive.

c) other countries would run out of gold and other foreign exchange reserves.

d) other countries would invoke the scarce currency clause against the United States.

3. Assume the world is operating under the nineteenth-century gold standard. The United States persistently runs a surplus in its basic balance (current account plus net foreign investment). You would expect the following:

a) the United States would eventually be forced to devalue its currency.

b) the United States would have a depression and this would cure the surplus.

c) the United States would gain reserves and this, in time, would lead to a rise in prices in the United States.

d) other countries would experience a depression and this would cause the United States to buy less from them.

4. Suppose the countries of the world are using freely flexible exchange rates—without intervention by the central banks—to manage their international trade. A major country, say West Germany, persistently runs a surplus in its foreign accounts. You would expect:

a) the German mark would become overvalued.

b) the German mark would rise in price relative to other currencies.

c) the other currencies of the world would rise in price relative to the German mark.

d) the central bank of West Germany would acquire additional foreign exchange reserves consisting of dollars, pounds, francs, and other currencies.

5. The interest rates in the major money markets of the world tend to move up and down together. When interest rates are higher in one country than they are in others, funds tend to move to that country and this keeps that country's interest rate in line with the interest rates in other countries. However, you notice that interest rates are rising in the United States and funds are not moving to the United States. You would suspect that:

a) the system is not working.

b) prices are rising faster in the United States than they are in other countries.

c) prices are rising faster in other countries than they are in the United States.

d) foreign exchange rates are not serving as an equilibrating mechanism.

6. The OPEC countries raise the price of oil again. They sell the bulk of their oil to Europe. The demand for oil is inelastic. The OPEC countries use all of their additional revenues to purchase United States Treasury bills in the New York money market. You would expect that:

a) the price of the dollar would rise relative to other currencies.
b) the price of the dollar would be unaffected since there has been no change in the exports and imports of the United States.
c) the price of the dollar would fall relative to other currencies.
d) the price of all other currencies would rise relative to the dollar.

7. You are an advocate of flexible exchange rates as a device for managing international trade. Which of the following arguments would you use to convince your opponents that flexible exchange rates were best?
a) Flexible exchange rates will be managed by the central banks of the world.
b) Flexible exchange rates will make it possible for a country to follow its own monetary and fiscal policies without fear that they will be upset by what is happening abroad.
c) Flexible exchange rates will encourage countries to adopt inflationary policies.
d) Flexible exchange rates work all right during normal times, but when something like an oil or food price crisis hits the world, they must be helped by the central banks to do their job.

8. You are an advocate of fixed exchange rates, under a revived Bretton Woods System or under a new gold standard. Your best argument is:
a) the major trading nations can exert heavy pressure on other nations to avoid inflationary monetary policies.
b) fixed exchange rates as they worked from 1948 to 1971 solved the basic balance of payments problem of the world.
c) fixed exchange rates are easy to implement. They do not require substantial central bank intervention.
d) fixed exchange rates make it possible for smart people to put their money in safe currencies. This is impossible under a flexible exchange rate system.

ESSAY QUESTIONS

1. Suppose in an effort to be fair to all industries, a random method of selecting products to be exported and imported was used. For example, if an industry's representative picked a blue number out of a hat, then the industry would be called on to sell abroad as much as a quarter of its total output. Similarly, if an industry's representative picked a red number out of a hat, then as much as a quarter of that industry's output would be supplied from products produced abroad. Indicate what effect such a method of selecting exports and imports would have on the productivity of resources in the United States.

2. Suppose there were no system for keeping a country's balance of payments in equilibrium. What type of problems would the world then face? Suggest some alternative solutions for the balance of payments problem.

3. Why do "direct controls" tend to reduce the volume of international trade and thus impede the international trade machine?

4. The United States uses a single currency system. Now suppose that the state of Florida continually buys more from the rest of the United States than it sells, so that there is a net outflow of dollars. Trace out the steps by which this balance of payments problem will be resolved. If this system works so well within a country, why can't it be used between nations?

5. Suppose that the United States and other major countries are on a gold standard and that the United States tends to buy more from and lend more to the rest of the world than other countries buy from or lend to the United States. Explain how the gold standard system would correct this situation. What political problems could arise in the United States and in the other major countries of the world because of the way the gold standard works?

6. Given the same fact situation as in question 5, how would a flexible exchange rate system solve the problem? What type of political problems would arise because of this solution to the problem?

7. Define the types of assets which would be used as international reserves if a gold standard system is used to settle balances between countries. Would the same assets be used if a freely flexible system is used to settle international balance of payments problems between countries? How could international reserves be used by central banks in a flexible rate system to "manage a country's foreign exchange rate"?

8. Indicate how a "managed float" differs from a truly flexible exchange rate system. Suppose that countries with "surplus" problems buy foreign exchange to keep their currencies from appreciating. Will doing this add to the probability of world-wide inflation? How?

9. The dollar is falling in value relative to other major currencies. Which industries will gain from this and which industries will lose? What political problems will arise because of the fall in the value of the dollar?

10. The dollar is rising in value relative to the other major industries. Which industries will gain and which industries will lose by this development? Again what political problems will arise because of the appreciation of the dollar?

11. You are thinking of buying a foreign car. You notice that recently the dollar has been very strong in the foreign exchange markets. After examining the evidence you come to the conclusion that the dollar will continue to gain in strength relative to other currencies. Should you buy your car now or wait six months? Explain reasons for the decision you make.

12. Will flexible exchange rates make it possible for a country to avoid the same inflationary developments that are simultaneously occurring in the rest of the world? Won't the prices of raw materials rise so rapidly that inflation will spread to a country that is following conservative monetary and fiscal policies, despite its reliance on flexible exchange rates?

13. Suppose that the oil-exporting countries raise the price of oil again, but this time they are reluctant to accept pounds, francs, marks, and dollars in exchange for their oil. They insist on being paid in their own currencies. What would happen to the value of the currencies of the oil-importing countries relative to the currencies of the oil-exporting countries? What would this change in the values of currencies do to the price of gasoline in the oil-importing countries?

14. You are convinced that tariffs, quotas, quarantines, and other impediments to international trade will substantially diminish the effectiveness of the international trade machine. Which should you favor, freely flexible exchange rates or fixed exchange rates? Explain your answer.

15. Because the United States imports many of its raw materials, it will be very expensive for the country to allow the dollar to fall in the foreign exchange markets of the world. Therefore, it is the policy of the Federal Reserve System to use its supply of foreign currencies and gold to support the dollar in the foreign exchange markets of the world. Discuss the implications of this policy on the price levels of other countries. What action could they take to counter this policy? What action could they take to support it? Which set of actions do you think they will take, and why?

ANSWERS TO REVIEW QUESTIONS

1. Obviously you are interested in purchasing your foreign exchange at as low a rate as possible. By analyzing each given situation we should be able to draw some conclusions about the supply and demand pressures being put on the dollar and therefore its potential price movements.

   If the U.S. is running a surplus in its basic balance, this implies we are importing less than we are exporting and/or finding on balance more foreign investment in the U.S. than U.S. investment overseas. This means the supply of foreign currency is greater than demand. This may well change so you should buy now before the price rises. The correct answer is (a).

   If the U.S. is engaging in a military build-up in the Middle East, this will increase the demand and therefore the price of foreign exchange. You should buy now. The correct answer is (a).

2. If the United States has a persistent deficit in its basic balance and we assume the Bretton Woods System prevails, then there will be pressures for the United States to devalue, take measures to increase interest rates, or devalue the domestic economy.

   a) This is incorrect. Other countries would buy up U.S. dollars, but would do so to keep their currency from appreciating, rather than depreciating relative to the dollar. The pressure is there for the dollar to fall in value relative to other currencies but under the Bretton Woods System, the other countries are obligated to keep the pegged relationships intact.
   b) This is correct. They would buy dollars to keep their currencies from appreciating.
   c) This is incorrect. The United States might run out of gold, not the other way around. Gold and dollars would be flowing into these countries.
   d) This is incorrect. The scarce currency clause is invoked against a nation when that nation is running a surplus, not a deficit.

3. Under the gold standard, a nation running a surplus would find its monetary base increasing as gold flows into the country. This would increase the prices of that country and ultimately eliminate its surplus.

a) This is incorrect. Adjustment occurs through influencing the money supply, interest rates, and the level of income in the surplus country, not by devaluation.

b) This is incorrect. Prices and employment would be high with the surplus.

c) This is correct. The increase in reserves would overstimulate the domestic economy and turn around the inward-bound flows as prices rise.

d) This is incorrect. As other countries' prices become cheaper, relatively, the United States would buy more from them.

4. Under a flexible exchange rate system, supply and demand forces determine the exchange rate.

a) This is incorrect. If West Germany runs a surplus, the price of the mark will rise. It will not become overvalued since it is free to move about, upward in this case.

b) This is correct. Other nations are demanding a larger quantity than the quantity supplied at the current price. This will drive up the price of the mark relative to other currencies.

c) This is incorrect. Other currencies of the world will fall.

d) This is incorrect. Under Bretton Woods this would have happened, but under flexible rates, the price of the mark rises instead.

5. When a nation experiences persistent inflation, that fact will soon be incorporated in its interest rate structure.

a) This is incorrect. If interest rate differentials exist for extended periods, some other event is occurring which is having an influence.

b) This is correct. Inflation tends to increase interest rates and therefore an interest rate differential will persist between nations if the country with the high interest rates is experiencing a relatively large inflation.

c) This is incorrect. If this were so, funds would flow into the United States, reducing the rate.

d) This is incorrect. The mechanism is working, taking note of the rate of inflation.

6. If OPEC countries sell most of their oil to Europe and spend their receipts in the United States for Treasury bills, the demand for dollars will rise and this will increase the price of the dollar relative to other currencies.

a) This is correct as explained above.

b) This is incorrect. The price of the dollar will rise due to the increased demand for dollars to buy Treasury bills.

c) This is incorrect. The price of the dollar will *rise*, not fall.

d) This is incorrect. The price of other currencies will *fall* relative to the dollar.

7. A major benefit of flexible exchange rates is that nations can pursue independent monetary and fiscal policies in spite of the international monetary system pressures.

a) This is incorrect. Flexible exchange rates like any free market price are determined by supply and demand.

b) This is correct as explained above.

c) This is incorrect. The adjustment occurs through the exchange rate and the price of imports and exports, not through discretionary monetary and fiscal policies, be they inflationary or deflationary.

d) This is incorrect. They will allocate foreign exchange, if the price is allowed to move freely.

8. A major benefit of a fixed exchange rate system is the relative stability of exchange rates. When you make a contract to buy or bill foreign exchange, you don't have to worry about daily fluctuations in the value of the foreign exchange.

a) This is incorrect. This was a failure of the Bretton Woods System.

b) This is incorrect. During the late 1960s and early 1970s, the system did not work well.

c) This is incorrect. Central banks are obligated to keep the exchange rates close to the pegged value.

d) This is correct as explained above.

STATISTICAL APPENDIX*

These statistical tables comprise the most frequently used data employed in economic analysis. The information falls under the following categories of economic concern.

National income or expenditure

Table A.1   Gross National Product or Expenditure, 1929–1977

Table A.2   Gross National Product or Expenditure in 1972 dollars, 1929–1977

Table A.3   National Income by Type of Income, 1929–1977

Population, employment, wages, and productivity

Table A.4   Population by Age Groups, 1929–1977

Table A.5   Selected Unemployment Rates, 1948–1977

Prices

Table A.6   Consumer Price Indexes by Expenditure Classes, 1929–1977

Money stock, credit, and finance

Table A.7   Money Stock Measures, 1947–1977

Government finance

Table A.8   Federal Budget Receipts, Outlays, and Debt, Fiscal Years 1969–1979

Table A.9   Net Public and Private Debt, 1929–1976

International statistics

Table A.10   U.S. Balance of Payments, 1946–1977

* Source of the statistical appendix is the *Economic Report of the President*, 1978. Washington, D.C.: U.S. Government Printing Office.

General Notes

Detail in these tables may not add to totals because of rounding.
Unless otherwise noted, all dollar figures are in current dollars.

Symbols used:
ᵖ Preliminary.
_ _ Not available (also, not applicable).

Table A.1   Gross national product or expenditure, 1929–1977

| Year or quarter | Gross national product | Personal consumption expenditures | Gross private domestic investment | Net exports of goods and services | | | Government purchases of goods and services | | | | | Percent change from preceding period, gross national product |
| | | | | Net exports | Exports | Imports | Total | Federal | | | State and local | |
								Total	National defense	Nondefense		
1929	103.4	77.3	16.2	1.1	7.0	5.9	8.8	1.4	-------	-------	7.4	-------
1933	55.8	45.8	1.4	.4	2.4	2.0	8.2	2.1	-------	-------	6.1	−4.2
1939	90.8	67.0	9.3	1.1	4.4	3.4	13.5	5.2	1.2	3.9	8.3	6.9
1940	100.0	71.0	13.1	1.7	5.4	3.6	14.2	6.1	2.2	3.9	8.1	10.1
1941	124.9	80.8	17.9	1.3	5.9	4.6	24.9	16.9	13.7	3.2	8.0	24.9
1942	158.3	88.6	9.9	.0	4.8	4.8	59.8	52.0	49.4	2.6	7.8	26.8
1943	192.0	99.4	5.8	−2.0	4.4	6.5	88.9	81.3	79.7	1.6	7.5	21.3
1944	210.5	108.2	7.2	−1.8	5.3	7.1	97.0	89.4	87.4	2.0	7.6	9.6
1945	212.3	119.5	10.6	−.6	7.2	7.8	82.8	74.6	73.5	1.1	8.2	.9
1946	209.6	143.8	30.7	7.6	14.8	7.2	27.5	17.6	14.8	2.8	9.9	−1.3
1947	232.8	161.7	34.0	11.6	19.8	8.2	25.5	12.7	9.0	3.7	12.8	11.1
1948	259.1	174.7	45.9	6.5	16.9	10.4	32.0	16.7	10.7	6.0	15.3	11.3
1949	258.0	178.1	35.3	6.2	15.9	9.6	38.4	20.4	13.2	7.2	18.0	−.4
1950	286.2	192.0	53.8	1.9	13.9	12.0	38.5	18.7	14.0	4.7	19.8	10.9
1951	330.2	207.1	59.2	3.8	18.9	15.1	60.1	38.3	33.5	4.8	21.8	15.4
1952	347.2	217.1	52.1	2.4	18.2	15.8	75.6	52.4	45.8	6.5	23.2	5.1
1953	366.1	229.7	53.3	.6	17.1	16.6	82.5	57.5	48.6	8.9	25.0	5.5
1954	366.3	235.8	52.7	2.0	18.0	16.0	75.8	47.9	41.1	6.8	27.8	.0
1955	399.3	253.7	68.4	2.2	20.0	17.8	75.0	44.5	38.4	6.0	30.6	9.0
1956	420.7	266.0	71.0	4.3	23.9	19.6	79.4	45.9	40.2	5.7	33.5	5.4
1957	442.8	280.4	69.2	6.1	26.7	20.7	87.1	50.0	44.0	5.9	37.1	5.2
1958	448.9	289.5	61.9	2.5	23.3	20.8	95.0	53.9	45.6	8.3	41.1	1.4
1959	486.5	310.8	77.6	.6	23.7	23.2	97.6	53.9	45.6	8.3	43.7	8.4
1960	506.0	324.9	76.4	4.4	27.6	23.2	100.3	53.7	44.5	9.3	46.5	4.0
1961	523.3	335.0	74.3	5.8	28.9	23.1	108.2	57.4	47.0	10.4	50.8	3.4
1962	563.8	355.2	85.2	5.4	30.6	25.2	118.0	63.7	51.1	12.7	54.3	7.7
1963	594.7	374.6	90.2	6.3	32.7	26.4	123.7	64.6	50.3	14.3	59.0	5.5
1964	635.7	400.4	96.6	8.9	37.4	28.4	129.8	65.2	49.0	16.2	64.6	6.9
1965	688.1	430.2	112.0	7.6	39.5	32.0	138.4	67.3	49.4	17.8	71.1	8.2
1966	753.0	464.8	124.5	5.1	42.8	37.7	158.7	78.8	60.3	18.5	79.8	9.4
1967	796.3	490.4	120.8	4.9	45.6	40.6	180.2	90.9	71.5	19.5	89.3	5.8
1968	868.5	535.9	131.5	2.3	49.9	47.7	198.7	98.0	76.9	21.2	100.7	9.1
1969	935.5	579.7	146.2	1.8	54.7	52.9	207.9	97.5	76.3	21.2	110.4	7.7
1970	982.4	618.8	140.8	3.9	62.5	58.5	218.9	95.6	73.5	22.1	123.2	5.0
1971	1,063.4	668.2	160.0	1.6	65.6	64.0	233.7	96.2	70.2	26.0	137.5	8.2
1972	1,171.1	733.0	188.3	−3.3	72.7	75.9	253.1	102.1	73.5	28.6	151.0	10.1
1973	1,306.6	809.9	220.0	7.1	101.6	94.4	269.5	102.2	73.5	28.7	167.3	11.6
1974	1,412.9	889.6	214.6	6.0	137.9	131.9	302.7	111.1	77.0	34.1	191.5	8.1
1975	1,528.8	980.4	189.1	20.4	147.3	126.9	338.9	123.3	83.9	39.4	215.6	8.2
1976	1,706.5	1,094.0	243.3	7.8	162.9	155.1	361.4	130.1	86.8	43.3	231.2	11.6
1977 ᵖ	1,890.4	1,210.1	294.3	−9.0	175.6	184.7	395.0	145.4	94.3	51.1	249.5	10.8

Source: Department of Commerce, Bureau of Economic Analysis.

Table A.2 Gross national product or expenditure in 1972 dollars, 1929–1977

Year or quarter	Gross national product	Personal consumption expenditures				Gross private domestic investment				
						Total	Fixed investment	Nonresidential		
		Total	Durable goods	Non-durable goods	Services		Total	Total	Structures	Producers' durable equipment
1929	314.7	215.6	21.5	98.1	96.1	55.9	51.3	37.0	20.6	16.4
1933	222.1	170.7	10.9	82.9	76.8	8.4	13.3	10.4	4.9	5.5
1939	319.7	220.3	19.1	115.1	86.1	33.6	32.0	20.7	8.6	12.1
1940	343.6	230.4	21.8	119.9	88.7	44.6	38.4	25.7	9.9	15.8
1941	396.6	244.1	24.7	127.6	91.8	55.8	43.8	30.3	11.9	18.5
1942	454.6	241.7	16.3	129.9	95.5	29.6	24.4	17.6	6.7	10.9
1943	527.3	248.7	14.5	134.0	100.1	18.1	18.0	14.0	4.2	9.8
1944	567.0	255.7	13.5	139.4	102.7	19.8	22.1	18.7	5.5	13.2
1945	559.0	271.4	14.8	150.3	106.3	27.8	31.4	27.6	8.3	19.2
1946	477.0	301.4	25.8	158.9	116.7	71.0	58.8	42.0	18.8	23.2
1947	468.3	306.2	30.6	154.8	120.8	70.1	70.4	48.9	17.3	31.6
1948	487.7	312.8	33.1	155.0	124.6	82.3	76.8	51.0	18.4	32.7
1949	490.7	320.0	36.3	157.4	126.4	65.6	70.0	46.0	17.8	28.2
1950	533.5	338.1	43.4	161.8	132.8	93.7	83.2	50.0	19.1	30.9
1951	576.5	342.3	39.9	165.3	137.1	94.1	80.4	52.9	20.6	32.3
1952	598.5	350.9	38.9	171.2	140.8	83.2	78.9	52.1	20.6	31.5
1953	621.8	364.2	43.1	175.7	145.5	85.6	84.1	56.3	22.5	33.8
1954	613.7	370.9	43.5	177.0	150.4	83.4	85.6	55.4	23.5	31.8
1955	654.8	395.1	52.2	185.4	157.5	104.1	96.3	61.2	25.3	35.9
1956	668.8	406.3	49.8	191.6	164.9	102.9	97.1	65.2	28.1	37.1
1957	680.9	414.7	49.7	194.9	170.2	97.2	95.7	66.0	28.1	37.9
1958	679.5	419.0	46.4	196.8	175.8	87.7	89.6	58.9	26.4	32.5
1959	720.4	441.5	51.8	205.0	184.7	107.4	101.0	62.9	26.8	36.1
1960	736.8	453.0	52.5	208.2	192.3	105.4	101.0	66.0	28.8	37.2
1961	755.3	462.2	50.3	211.9	200.0	103.6	100.7	65.6	29.3	36.3
1962	799.1	482.9	55.7	218.5	208.7	117.4	109.3	70.9	30.8	40.1
1963	830.7	501.4	60.7	223.0	217.6	124.5	116.8	73.5	30.8	42.7
1964	874.4	528.7	65.7	233.3	229.7	132.1	124.8	81.0	33.3	47.7
1965	925.9	558.1	73.4	244.0	240.7	150.1	138.8	95.6	39.6	56.0
1966	981.0	586.1	79.0	255.5	251.6	161.3	144.6	106.1	42.5	63.6
1967	1,007.7	603.2	79.7	259.5	264.0	152.7	140.7	103.5	41.1	62.4
1968	1,051.8	633.4	88.2	270.2	275.0	159.5	150.8	108.0	42.0	66.1
1969	1,078.8	655.4	91.9	276.4	287.2	168.0	157.5	114.3	44.0	70.3
1970	1,075.3	668.9	88.9	282.7	297.3	154.7	150.4	110.0	42.8	67.2
1971	1,107.5	691.9	98.1	287.5	306.3	166.8	160.2	108.0	41.7	66.3
1972	1,171.1	733.0	111.2	299.3	322.4	188.3	178.8	116.8	42.5	74.3
1973	1,235.0	767.7	121.8	309.3	336.5	207.2	190.7	131.0	45.5	85.5
1974	1,217.8	760.7	112.5	303.9	344.3	183.6	175.6	130.6	42.5	88.1
1975	1,202.1	775.1	112.7	307.6	354.8	141.6	151.5	112.7	36.3	76.5
1976	1,274.7	821.3	127.5	321.6	372.2	173.0	164.5	116.8	37.1	79.7
1977	1,337.6	860.3	138.0	333.3	389.0	195.6	184.0	127.1	38.4	88.7

Table A.2 (continued)

[Billions of 1972 dollars, except as noted; quarterly data at seasonally adjusted annual rates]

Year or quarter	Gross private domestic investment—continued				Change in business inventories	Net exports of goods and services			Government purchases of goods and services			Percent change from preceding period, gross national product
	Fixed investment—continued											
	Residential			Producers' durable equipment		Net exports	Exports	Imports	Total	Federal	State and local	
	Total	Nonfarm structures	Farm structures									
1929	14.3	13.6	0.6	0.1	4.6	2.2	15.6	13.4	40.9	6.9	33.9	------
1933	2.9	2.6	.2	.1	−4.9	.2	9.4	9.3	42.8	10.8	32.0	−2.1
1939	11.3	10.6	.6	.1	1.6	2.0	13.3	11.4	63.8	22.6	41.2	7.6
1940	12.8	11.8	.8	.1	6.2	3.0	14.6	11.5	65.5	26.3	39.2	7.5
1941	13.5	12.5	.9	.2	12.0	.8	14.7	14.0	95.9	58.6	37.3	15.4
1942	6.8	6.1	.6	.1	5.2	−2.5	10.3	12.8	185.8	151.5	34.3	14.6
1943	4.0	3.5	.4	.0	.1	−7.3	9.0	16.3	267.9	236.3	31.6	16.0
1944	3.4	3.0	.4	.0	−2.3	−7.2	10.0	17.3	298.8	268.2	30.6	7.5
1945	3.8	3.5	.3	.1	−3.6	−4.5	13.5	18.0	264.3	232.7	31.6	−1.4
1946	16.8	15.5	1.1	.2	12.2	11.6	26.1	14.6	93.1	58.4	34.8	−14.7
1947	21.5	19.8	1.3	.3	−.2	16.6	30.2	13.6	75.4	36.1	39.3	−1.8
1948	25.8	23.9	1.5	.3	5.5	8.5	24.2	15.7	84.1	42.4	41.8	4.1
1949	24.0	22.3	1.4	.3	−4.4	8.8	24.2	15.4	96.2	48.9	47.4	.6
1950	33.2	31.5	1.3	.3	10.6	4.0	21.7	17.7	97.7	47.0	50.7	8.7
1951	27.5	25.9	1.3	.3	13.7	7.4	25.9	18.5	132.7	81.3	51.3	8.1
1952	26.8	25.3	1.2	.3	4.3	4.9	24.9	20.0	159.5	107.0	52.5	3.8
1953	27.8	26.3	1.2	.3	1.5	2.0	23.8	21.8	170.0	114.6	55.4	3.9
1954	30.2	28.8	1.1	.3	−2.2	4.5	25.3	20.8	154.9	95.2	59.7	−1.3
1955	35.1	33.8	.9	.4	7.7	4.7	27.9	23.2	150.9	86.9	64.0	6.7
1956	31.9	30.4	1.0	.4	5.8	7.3	32.3	25.0	152.4	85.9	66.5	2.1
1957	29.7	28.3	1.0	.4	1.5	8.9	34.8	26.0	160.1	89.8	70.3	1.8
1958	30.6	29.2	.9	.5	−1.8	3.5	30.7	27.2	169.3	92.8	76.4	−.2
1959	38.1	36.5	1.0	.6	6.5	.9	31.5	30.6	170.7	91.8	78.9	6.0
1960	35.0	33.7	.8	.5	4.4	5.5	35.8	30.3	172.9	90.8	82.0	2.3
1961	35.1	33.6	1.0	.5	2.9	6.7	37.0	30.3	182.8	95.6	87.1	2.5
1962	38.4	36.9	.9	.6	8.1	5.8	39.6	33.9	193.1	103.1	90.0	5.8
1963	43.2	41.7	.9	.6	7.8	7.3	42.2	35.0	197.6	102.2	95.4	4.0
1964	43.8	42.2	.9	.7	7.3	10.9	47.8	36.9	202.7	100.6	102.1	5.3
1965	43.2	41.6	.8	.7	11.3	8.2	49.1	41.0	209.6	100.5	109.1	5.9
1966	38.5	36.9	.9	.8	16.7	4.3	51.6	47.3	229.3	112.5	116.8	5.9
1967	37.2	35.5	.9	.8	12.0	3.5	54.2	50.7	248.3	125.3	123.1	2.7
1968	42.8	41.1	.8	.9	8.7	−.4	58.5	58.9	259.2	128.3	130.9	4.4
1969	43.2	41.5	.9	.9	10.6	−1.3	62.2	63.5	256.7	121.8	134.9	2.6
1970	40.4	38.9	.6	.9	4.3	1.4	67.1	65.7	250.2	110.7	139.5	−.3
1971	52.2	50.5	.7	1.0	6.6	−.6	67.9	68.5	249.4	103.9	145.5	3.0
1972	62.0	60.3	.7	1.1	9.4	−3.3	72.7	75.9	253.1	102.1	151.0	5.7
1973	59.7	57.9	.5	1.2	16.5	7.6	87.4	79.9	252.5	96.6	155.9	5.5
1974	45.0	43.0	.9	1.1	8.0	15.9	93.0	77.1	257.7	95.8	161.8	−1.4
1975	38.8	37.1	.7	.9	−9.9	22.5	89.9	67.4	263.0	96.7	166.3	−1.3
1976	47.7	46.0	.7	1.0	8.5	16.0	95.8	79.8	264.4	96.5	167.9	6.0
1977 P	56.9	55.1	.7	1.1	11.6	10.7	98.0	87.3	271.1	101.4	169.7	4.9

Source: Department of Commerce, Bureau of Economic Analysis.

Table A.3 National income by type of income, 1929–1977

Year or quarter	National income	Compensation of employees			Proprietors' income		
		Total	Wages and salaries	Supplements to wages and salaries	Total	Farm Total	Nonfarm Total
1929	84.8	51.1	50.5	0.6	14.9	6.2	8.8
1933	39.9	29.5	29.0	.5	5.8	2.6	3.2
1939	71.3	48.1	46.0	2.1	11.7	4.4	7.3
1940	79.7	52.1	49.9	2.3	12.9	4.5	8.4
1941	102.6	64.8	62.1	2.7	17.4	6.4	10.9
1942	135.7	85.3	82.1	3.2	24.0	9.8	14.3
1943	169.1	109.5	105.8	3.8	29.0	11.7	17.3
1944	181.9	121.2	116.7	4.5	30.2	11.6	18.6
1945	180.6	123.1	117.5	5.6	31.7	12.2	19.4
1946	178.3	118.1	112.0	6.0	36.6	14.9	21.6
1947	194.6	129.2	123.1	6.1	35.8	15.2	20.6
1948	219.0	141.4	135.5	5.9	40.7	17.5	23.2
1949	212.7	141.3	134.7	6.6	36.1	12.7	23.5
1950	236.2	154.8	147.0	7.8	38.4	13.5	24.9
1951	272.3	181.0	171.3	9.7	42.8	15.8	27.0
1952	285.8	195.7	185.3	10.4	42.9	14.9	28.0
1953	299.7	209.6	198.5	11.0	41.3	12.9	28.4
1954	299.1	208.4	196.8	11.6	40.8	12.3	28.5
1955	328.0	224.9	211.7	13.2	42.5	11.3	31.2
1956	346.9	243.5	228.3	15.2	43.6	11.2	32.4
1957	362.3	256.5	239.3	17.2	45.0	11.0	33.9
1958	364.0	258.2	240.5	17.7	47.4	13.1	34.3
1959	397.1	279.6	258.9	20.6	47.2	10.7	36.6
1960	412.0	294.9	271.9	23.0	47.0	11.4	35.6
1961	424.2	303.6	279.5	24.1	48.3	11.8	36.4
1962	457.4	325.1	298.0	27.1	49.6	11.9	37.7
1963	482.8	342.9	313.4	29.5	50.3	11.6	38.7
1964	519.2	368.0	336.1	31.8	52.2	10.3	42.0
1965	566.0	396.5	362.0	34.5	56.7	12.6	44.1
1966	622.2	439.3	398.4	40.9	60.3	13.6	46.7
1967	655.8	471.9	427.5	44.4	61.0	12.1	48.9
1968	714.4	519.8	469.5	50.3	63.4	12.0	51.4
1969	767.9	571.4	514.6	56.8	66.2	13.9	52.3
1970	798.4	609.2	546.5	62.7	65.1	13.9	51.2
1971	858.1	650.3	580.0	70.3	67.7	14.3	53.4
1972	951.9	715.1	633.8	81.4	76.1	18.0	58.1
1973	1,064.6	799.2	701.2	98.0	92.4	32.0	60.4
1974	1,136.0	875.8	764.1	111.7	86.2	25.4	60.9
1975	1,217.0	930.3	805.7	124.6	86.0	23.2	62.8
1976	1,364.1	1,036.3	891.8	144.5	88.0	18.6	69.4
1977 ᴾ	1,520.3	1,155.8	989.5	166.3	97.9	19.5	78.4

Year or quarter	Rental income of persons Total	Corporate profits					Net interest
		Total	Profits before tax Total	Profits tax liability	Profits after tax Total	Dividends	Undistributed profits	
1929	4.9	10.0	1.4	8.6	5.8	2.8	4.7
1933	2.2	1.0	.5	.4	2.0	−1.6	4.1
1939	2.6	7.0	1.4	5.6	3.8	1.8	3.6
1940	2.7	10.0	2.8	7.2	4.0	3.2	3.3
1941	3.1	17.7	7.6	10.1	4.4	5.7	3.3
1942	4.0	21.5	11.4	10.1	4.3	5.9	3.1
1943	4.4	25.1	14.1	11.1	4.4	6.6	2.7
1944	4.5	24.1	12.9	11.2	4.6	6.5	2.4
1945	4.6	19.7	10.7	9.0	4.6	4.4	2.2
1946	5.5	24.6	9.1	15.5	5.6	9.9	1.6
1947	5.3	31.5	11.3	20.2	6.3	13.9	2.1
1948	5.7	35.2	12.4	22.7	7.0	15.7	2.1
1949	6.1	28.9	10.2	18.7	7.2	11.5	2.2
1950	7.1	42.6	17.9	24.7	8.8	15.9	2.3
1951	7.7	43.9	22.6	21.3	8.5	12.8	2.7
1952	8.8	38.9	19.4	19.5	8.5	11.0	3.0
1953	10.0	40.5	20.3	20.2	8.8	11.5	3.4
1954	11.0	38.1	17.6	20.5	9.1	11.4	4.3
1955	11.3	48.4	22.0	26.4	10.3	16.1	4.8
1956	11.6	48.6	22.0	26.6	11.1	15.5	5.2
1957	12.2	46.9	21.4	25.5	11.5	14.0	6.5
1958	12.9	41.1	19.0	22.1	11.3	10.8	8.0
1959	13.2	51.6	23.6	28.0	12.2	15.8	8.8
1960	13.8	48.5	22.7	25.8	12.9	13.0	9.8
1961	14.3	48.6	22.8	25.8	13.3	12.5	11.2
1962	15.0	53.6	24.0	29.6	14.4	15.2	12.8
1963	15.7	57.7	26.2	31.5	15.5	16.0	14.3
1964	16.1	64.7	28.0	36.7	17.3	19.4	15.9
1965	17.1	75.2	30.9	44.3	19.1	25.2	18.5
1966	18.2	80.7	33.7	47.1	19.4	27.6	21.9
1967	19.4	77.3	32.5	44.9	20.1	24.7	24.3
1968	18.6	85.6	39.4	46.2	22.0	24.2	26.8
1969	18.1	83.4	39.7	43.8	22.6	21.2	30.8
1970	18.6	71.5	34.5	37.0	22.9	14.1	37.5
1971	20.1	82.0	37.7	44.3	23.0	21.3	42.8
1972	21.5	96.2	41.5	54.6	24.6	30.0	47.0
1973	21.6	115.8	48.7	67.1	27.8	39.3	52.3
1974	21.4	126.9	52.4	74.5	31.0	43.6	69.0
1975	22.3	123.5	50.2	73.4	32.4	41.0	79.1
1976	23.3	156.9	64.7	92.1	35.8	56.4	88.4
1977 ᴾ	25.3	172.1	69.2	102.9	41.2	61.7	100.9
1975: I	22.1	101.5	40.8	60.8	32.0	28.8	76.4
II	22.3	113.9	45.7	68.2	32.2	36.0	77.6
III	22.2	137.7	56.3	81.4	32.9	48.5	79.9
IV	22.6	141.0	57.9	83.1	32.5	50.6	82.3
1976: I	23.0	153.5	63.1	90.4	33.6	56.8	85.0
II	22.9	159.2	66.1	93.1	35.0	58.1	86.5
III	23.3	159.9	65.9	94.0	36.0	58.0	90.1
IV	24.1	154.8	63.9	90.9	38.4	52.5	92.0
1977: I	24.5	161.7	64.4	97.2	38.5	58.8	95.3
II	24.9	174.0	69.7	104.3	40.3	64.1	98.9
III	25.5	172.3	69.3	103.6	42.3	61.2	103.1
IV ᴾ	26.4	-------	-------	-------	43.6	-------	106.4

Source: Department of Commerce, Bureau of Economic Analysis.

Table A.4 Population by age groups, 1929–1977

[Thousands of persons]

July 1	Total	Age (years)						
		Under 5	5–15	16–19	20–24	25–44	45–64	65 and over
1929	121,767	11,734	26,800	9,127	10,694	35,862	21,076	6,474
1933	125,579	10,612	26,897	9,302	11,152	37,319	22,933	7,363
1939	130,880	10,418	25,179	9,822	11,519	39,354	25,823	8,764
1940	132,122	10,579	24,811	9,895	11,690	39,868	26,249	9,031
1941	133,402	10,850	24,516	9,840	11,807	40,383	26,718	9,288
1942	134,860	11,301	24,231	9,730	11,955	40,861	27,196	9,584
1943	136,739	12,016	24,093	9,607	12,064	41,420	27,671	9,867
1944	138,397	12,524	23,949	9,561	12,062	42,016	28,138	10,147
1945	139,928	12,979	23,907	9,361	12,036	42,521	28,630	10,494
1946	141,389	13,244	24,103	9,119	12,004	43,027	29,064	10,828
1947	144,126	14,406	24,468	9,097	11,814	43,657	29,498	11,185
1948	146,631	14,919	25,209	8,952	11,794	44,288	29,931	11,538
1949	149,188	15,607	25,852	8,788	11,700	44,916	30,405	11,921
1950	152,271	16,410	26,721	8,542	11,680	45,672	30,849	12,397
1951	154,878	17,333	27,279	8,446	11,552	46,103	31,362	12,803
1952	157,553	17,312	28,894	8,414	11,350	46,495	31,884	13,203
1953	160,184	17,638	30,227	8,460	11,062	46,786	32,394	13,617
1954	163,026	18,057	31,480	8,637	10,832	47,001	32,942	14,076
1955	165,931	18,566	32,682	8,744	10,714	47,194	33,506	14,525
1956	168,903	19,003	33,994	8,916	10,616	47,379	34,057	14,938
1957	171,984	19,494	35,272	9,195	10,603	47,440	34,591	15,388
1958	174,882	19,887	36,445	9,543	10,756	47,337	35,109	15,806
1959	177,830	20,175	37,368	10,215	10,969	47,192	35,663	16,248
1960	180,671	20,341	38,494	10,683	11,134	47,140	36,203	16,675
1961	183,691	20,522	39,765	11,025	11,483	47,084	36,722	17,089
1962	186,538	20,469	41,205	11,180	11,959	47,013	37,255	17,457
1963	189,242	20,342	41,626	12,007	12,714	46,994	37,782	17,778
1964	191,889	20,165	42,297	12,736	13,269	46,958	38,338	18,127
1965	194,303	19,824	42,938	13,516	13,746	46,912	38,916	18,451
1966	196,560	19,208	43,702	14,311	14,050	47,001	39,534	18,755
1967	198,712	18,563	44,244	14,200	15,248	47,194	40,193	19,071
1968	200,706	17,913	44,622	14,452	15,786	47,721	40,846	19,365
1969	202,677	17,376	44,840	14,800	16,480	48,064	41,437	19,680
1970	204,878	17,148	44,774	15,275	17,184	48,435	41,975	20,087
1971	207,053	17,177	44,441	15,635	18,089	48,811	42,413	20,488
1972	208,846	16,990	43,948	15,946	18,032	50,254	42,785	20,892
1973	210,410	16,694	43,227	16,310	18,345	51,411	43,077	21,346
1974	211,901	16,288	42,538	16,590	18,741	52,593	43,319	21,833
1975	213,559	15,879	41,956	16,793	19,229	53,735	43,546	22,420
1976	215,142	15,343	41,459	16,928	19,629	55,130	43,705	22,947
1977	216,817	15,236	40,572	16,966	20,073	56,692	43,784	23,494

Source: Department of Commerce, Bureau of the Census.

Table A.5   Selected unemployment rates, 1948–1977

[Percent]

| Year or month | Unemployment rate [1] | | | | | | | | | Employment as percent of population [5] | | |
| | All workers | By sex and age | | | By selected groups | | | | | | | |
		Both sexes 16-19 years	Males 20 years and over	Females 20 years and over	Experienced wage and salary workers	Household heads	Married men [2]	Full-time workers [3]	Blue-collar workers [4]	Total	White	Black and other
1948	3.8	9.2	3.2	3.6	4.3	----	----	----	4.2	55.8	----	----
1949	5.9	13.4	5.4	5.3	6.8	----	3.5	5.4	8.0	54.6	----	----
1950	5.3	12.2	4.7	5.1	6.0	----	4.6	5.0	7.2	55.2	----	----
1951	3.3	8.2	2.5	4.0	3.7	----	1.5	2.6	3.9	55.7	----	----
1952	3.0	8.5	2.4	3.2	3.3	----	1.4	2.5	3.6	55.4	----	----
1953	2.9	7.6	2.5	2.9	3.2	----	1.7	----	3.4	55.3	----	----
1954	5.5	12.6	4.9	5.5	6.2	----	4.0	5.2	7.2	53.8	----	----
1955	4.4	11.0	3.8	4.4	4.8	----	2.8	3.8	5.8	55.1	----	----
1956	4.1	11.1	3.4	4.2	4.4	----	2.6	3.7	5.1	56.1	----	----
1957	4.3	11.6	3.6	4.1	4.6	----	2.8	4.0	6.2	55.7	----	----
1958	6.8	15.9	6.2	6.1	7.2	----	5.1	7.2	10.2	54.2	----	----
1959	5.5	14.6	4.7	5.2	5.7	----	3.6	----	7.6	54.8	----	----
1960	5.5	14.7	4.7	5.1	5.7	----	3.7	----	7.8	54.9	----	----
1961	6.7	16.8	5.7	6.3	6.8	----	4.6	6.7	9.2	54.2	----	----
1962	5.5	14.7	4.6	5.4	5.6	----	3.6	----	7.4	54.2	----	----
1963	5.7	17.2	4.5	5.4	5.5	3.7	3.4	5.5	7.3	54.1	54.0	55.2
1964	5.2	16.2	3.9	5.2	5.0	3.2	2.8	4.9	6.3	54.5	54.3	56.1
1965	4.5	14.8	3.2	4.5	4.3	2.7	2.4	4.2	5.3	55.0	54.8	56.8
1966	3.8	12.8	2.5	3.8	3.5	2.2	1.9	3.5	4.2	55.6	55.4	57.2
1967	3.8	12.8	2.3	4.2	3.6	2.1	1.8	3.4	4.4	55.8	55.7	56.9
1968	3.6	12.7	2.2	3.8	3.4	1.9	1.6	3.1	4.1	56.0	55.9	56.6
1969	3.5	12.2	2.1	3.7	3.3	1.8	1.5	3.1	3.9	56.5	56.5	56.7
1970	4.9	15.2	3.5	4.8	4.8	2.9	2.6	4.5	6.2	56.1	56.2	55.5
1971	5.9	16.9	4.4	5.7	5.7	3.6	3.2	5.5	7.4	55.5	55.7	53.7
1972	5.6	16.2	4.0	5.4	5.3	3.3	2.8	5.1	6.5	56.0	56.4	53.0
1973	4.9	14.5	3.2	4.8	4.5	2.9	2.3	4.3	5.3	56.9	57.3	53.9
1974	5.6	16.0	3.8	5.5	5.3	3.3	2.7	5.1	6.7	57.0	57.5	53.0
1975	8.5	19.9	6.7	8.0	8.2	5.8	5.1	8.1	11.7	55.3	55.9	50.0
1976	7.7	19.0	5.9	7.4	7.3	5.1	4.2	7.3	9.4	56.1	56.8	50.5
1977	7.0	17.7	5.2	7.0	6.6	4.5	3.6	6.5	8.1	57.1	57.9	51.1

[1] Unemployment as percent of civilian labor force in group specified.
[2] Married men living with their wives. Data for 1949 and 1951–54 are for April; 1950, for March.
[3] Data for 1949–61 are for May.
[4] Includes craft and kindred workers, operatives, and nonfarm laborers. Data for 1948–57 are based on data for January, April, July, and October.
[5] Civilian employment as percent of total noninstitutional population.

Source: Department of Labor, Bureau of Labor Statistics.

Table A.6   Consumer price indexes by expenditure classes, 1929–1977, for
urban wage earners and clerical workers

[1967 = 100]

Year or month	All items	Food	Housing		Apparel and upkeep	Trans-porta-tion	Medical care	Personal care	Reading and recrea-tion	Other goods and services
			Total	Rent						
1929	51.3	48.3	....	76.0	48.5	....	....	....	....	....
1933	38.8	30.6	....	54.1	36.9	....	....	....	....	....
1939	41.6	34.6	52.2	56.0	42.4	43.0	36.7	40.3	45.3	46.9
1940	42.0	35.2	52.4	56.2	42.8	42.7	36.8	40.2	46.1	48.3
1941	44.1	38.4	53.7	57.2	44.8	44.2	37.0	41.2	47.7	49.2
1942	48.8	45.1	56.2	58.5	52.3	48.1	38.0	45.2	50.0	50.7
1943	51.8	50.3	56.8	58.5	54.6	47.9	39.9	49.9	54.1	53.3
1944	52.7	49.6	58.1	58.6	58.5	47.9	41.1	53.4	60.0	54.7
1945	53.9	50.7	59.1	58.8	61.5	47.8	42.1	55.1	62.4	56.9
1946	58.5	58.1	60.6	59.2	67.5	50.3	44.4	59.0	64.5	58.8
1947	66.9	70.6	65.2	61.1	78.2	55.5	48.1	66.0	68.7	63.8
1948	72.1	76.6	69.8	65.1	83.3	61.8	51.1	68.5	72.2	66.8
1949	71.4	73.5	70.9	68.0	80.1	66.4	52.7	68.3	74.9	68.7
1950	72.1	74.5	72.8	70.4	79.0	68.2	53.7	68.3	74.4	69.9
1951	77.8	82.8	77.2	73.2	86.1	72.5	56.3	74.7	76.6	72.8
1952	79.5	84.3	78.7	76.2	85.3	77.3	59.3	75.6	76.9	76.6
1953	80.1	83.0	80.8	80.3	84.6	79.5	61.4	76.3	77.7	78.5
1954	80.5	82.8	81.7	83.2	84.5	78.3	63.4	76.6	76.9	79.8
1955	80.2	81.6	82.3	84.3	84.1	77.4	64.8	77.9	76.7	79.8
1956	81.4	82.2	83.6	85.9	85.8	78.8	67.2	81.1	77.8	81.0
1957	84.3	84.9	86.2	87.5	87.3	83.3	69.9	84.1	80.7	83.3
1958	86.6	88.5	87.7	89.1	87.5	86.0	73.2	86.9	83.9	84.4
1959	87.3	87.1	88.6	90.4	88.2	89.6	76.4	88.7	85.3	86.1
1960	88.7	88.0	90.2	91.7	89.6	89.6	79.1	90.1	87.3	87.8
1961	89.6	89.1	90.9	92.9	90.4	90.6	81.4	90.6	89.3	88.5
1962	90.6	89.9	91.7	94.0	90.9	92.5	83.5	92.2	91.3	89.1
1963	91.7	91.2	92.7	95.0	91.9	93.0	85.6	93.4	92.8	90.6
1964	92.9	92.4	93.8	95.9	92.7	94.3	87.3	94.5	95.0	92.0
1965	94.5	94.4	94.9	96.9	93.7	95.9	89.5	95.2	95.9	94.2
1966	97.2	99.1	97.2	98.2	96.1	97.2	93.4	97.1	97.5	97.2
1967	100.0	100.0	100.0	100.0	100.0	100.0	100.0	100.0	100.0	100.0
1968	104.2	103.6	104.2	102.4	105.4	103.2	106.1	104.2	104.7	104.6
1969	109.8	108.9	110.8	105.7	111.5	107.2	113.4	109.3	108.7	109.1
1970	116.3	114.9	118.9	110.1	116.1	112.7	120.6	113.2	113.4	116.0
1971	121.3	118.4	124.3	115.2	119.8	118.6	128.4	116.8	119.3	120.9
1972	125.3	123.5	129.2	119.2	122.3	119.9	132.5	119.8	122.8	125.5
1973	133.1	141.4	135.0	124.3	126.8	123.8	137.7	125.2	125.9	129.0
1974	147.7	161.7	150.6	130.6	136.2	137.7	150.5	137.3	133.8	137.2
1975	161.2	175.4	166.8	137.3	142.3	150.6	168.6	150.7	144.4	147.4
1976	170.5	180.8	177.2	144.7	147.6	165.5	184.7	160.5	151.2	153.3
1977	181.5	192.2	189.6	153.5	154.2	177.2	202.4	170.9	157.9	159.2

Source: Department of Labor, Bureau of Labor Statistics.

Table A.7 Money stock measures, 1947–1977

[Averages of daily figures; billions of dollars, seasonally adjusted, except as noted]

Year and month	Overall measures			Components and related items						
	M_1 (Currency plus demand deposits)	M_2 (M_1 plus time deposits at commercial banks other than large CDs)	M_3 (M_2 plus deposits at non-bank thrift institutions)	Currency [1]	Deposits at commercial banks				Deposits at non-bank thrift institutions [5]	U.S. Government demand deposits (unadjusted) [6]
					Demand [2]	Time and savings [3]				
						Total	Large CDs [4]	Other		
1947: Dec	113.1			26.4	86.7	35.4				1.0
1948: Dec	111.5			25.8	85.8	36.0				1.8
1949: Dec	111.2			25.1	86.0	36.4				2.8
1950: Dec	116.2			25.0	91.2	36.7				2.4
1951: Dec	122.7			26.1	96.5	38.2				2.7
1952: Dec	127.4			27.3	·100.1	41.1				4.9
1953: Dec	128.8			27.7	101.1	44.5				3.8
1954: Dec	132.3			27.4	104.9	48.3				5.0
1955: Dec	135.2			27.8	107.4	50.0				3.4
1956: Dec	136.9			28.2	108.7	51.9				3.4
1957: Dec	135.9			28.3	107.6	57.4				3.5
1958: Dec	141.1			28.6	112.6	65.4				3.9
1959: Dec	143.4	210.9	303.8	28.9	114.5	67.4		67.4	92.9	4.9
1960: Dec	144.2	217.1	319.3	29.0	115.2	72.9		72.9	102.3	4.7
1961: Dec	148.7	228.6	342.1	29.6	119.1	82.7	2.8	79.9	113.4	4.9
1962: Dec	150.9	242.9	369.2	30.6	120.3	97.6	5.7	92.0	126.4	5.6
1963: Dec	156.5	258.9	400.3	32.5	124.1	112.0	9.6	102.3	141.4	5.1
1964: Dec	163.7	277.1	434.4	34.3	129.5	126.2	12.8	113.4	157.3	5.5
1965: Dec	171.3	301.3	471.7	36.3	134.9	146.4	16.4	130.0	170.4	4.6
1966: Dec	175.7	318.1	495.4	38.3	137.3	157.9	15.5	142.4	177.3	3.4
1967: Dec	187.3	349.9	543.9	40.4	146.9	183.3	20.6	162.6	194.0	5.0
1968: Dec	202.2	382.9	589.6	43.4	158.7	204.3	23.5	180.8	206.7	5.0
1969: Dec	208.8	392.3	607.3	46.1	162.8	194.4	10.9	183.5	214.9	5.6
1970: Dec	219.6	423.5	656.2	49.1	170.5	229.2	25.3	204.0	232.7	7.3
1971: Dec	233.8	471.7	742.8	52.6	181.3	271.1	33.3	237.8	271.1	6.9
1972: Dec	255.3	525.3	844.5	56.9	198.4	313.5	43.5	270.0	319.3	7.4
1973: Dec	270.5	571.4	919.6	61.5	209.0	363.9	63.0	300.9	348.1	6.3
1974: Dec	283.1	612.4	981.5	67.8	215.3	418.3	89.0	329.3	369.1	4.9
1975: Dec	294.8	664.3	1,092.6	73.7	221.0	451.7	82.1	369.6	428.3	4.1
1976: Dec	312.4	740.3	1,237.1	80.5	231.9	491.1	63.3	427.9	496.8	4.7
1977: Dec [p]	335.4	806.5	1,373.9	88.4	247.0	545.8	74.7	471.1	567.4	5.5

[1] Currency outside the Treasury, the Federal Reserve Banks, and the vaults of all commercial banks.

[2] Demand deposits other than those due to domestic commercial banks and the U.S. Government, less cash items in process of collection and Federal Reserve float, plus foreign balances at Federal Reserve Banks.

[3] Time and savings deposits other than those due to domestic commercial banks and the U.S. Government. Effective June 1966, excludes balances accumulated for payment of personal loans (about $1.1 billion).

[4] Negotiable time certificates of deposit (CDs) issued in denominations of $100,000 or more by large weekly reporting commercial banks.

[5] Average of the beginning- and end-of-month deposits of mutual savings banks, savings capital at savings and loan associations, and credit union shares.

[6] Deposits at all commercial banks.

Source: Board of Governors of the Federal Reserve System.

Table A.8 Federal budget receipts, outlays, and debt, fiscal years 1969–1979

[Millions of dollars; fiscal years]

Description	Actual					
	1969	1970	1971	1972	1973	1974
BUDGET RECEIPTS AND OUTLAYS:						
Total receipts	187,784	193,743	188,392	208,649	232,225	264,932
Federal funds	143,321	143,158	133,785	148,846	161,357	181,219
Trust funds	52,009	59,362	66,193	72,959	92,193	104,846
Interfund transactions	−7,547	−8,778	−11,586	−13,156	−21,325	−21,133
Total outlays	184,548	196,588	211,425	232,021	247,074	269,620
Federal funds	148,811	156,301	163,651	178,104	186,951	199,920
Trust funds	43,284	49,065	59,361	67,073	81,447	90,833
Interfund transactions	−7,547	−8,778	−11,586	−13,156	−21,325	−21,133
Total surplus or deficit (−)	3,236	−2,845	−23,033	−23,373	−14,849	−4,688
Federal funds	−5,490	−13,143	−29,866	−29,259	−25,594	−18,701
Trust funds	8,725	10,297	6,832	5,886	10,746	14,013
OUTSTANDING DEBT, END OF PERIOD:						
Gross Federal debt	367,144	382,603	409,467	437,329	468,426	486,247
Held by Government agencies	87,661	97,723	105,140	113,559	125,381	140,194
Held by the public	279,483	284,880	304,328	323,770	343,045	346,053
Federal Reserve System	54,095	57,714	65,518	71,426	75,182	80,649
Other	225,388	227,166	238,810	252,344	267,863	265,404
BUDGET RECEIPTS	187,784	193,743	188,392	208,649	232,225	264,932
Individual income taxes	87,249	90,412	86,230	94,737	103,246	118,952
Corporation income taxes	36,678	32,829	26,785	32,166	36,153	38,620
Social insurance taxes and contributions	39,918	45,298	48,578	53,914	64,542	76,780
Excise taxes	15,222	15,705	16,614	15,477	16,260	16,844
Estate and gift taxes	3,491	3,644	3,735	5,436	4,917	5,035
Customs duties	2,319	2,430	2,591	3,287	3,188	3,334
Miscellaneous receipts:						
Deposits of earnings by Federal Reserve System	2,662	3,266	3,533	3,252	3,495	4,845
All other	247	158	325	381	426	524
BUDGET OUTLAYS	184,548	196,588	211,425	232,021	247,074	269,620
National defense	79,418	78,553	75,808	76,550	74,541	77,750
International affairs	4,573	4,295	4,092	4,674	4,036	5,640
General science, space, and technology	5,016	4,508	4,180	4,174	4,030	3,977
Energy	1,001	990	1,031	1,270	1,180	843
Natural resources and environment	2,848	3,003	3,855	4,195	4,714	5,664
Agriculture	5,779	5,164	4,288	5,279	4,855	2,230
Commerce and housing credit	533	2,077	2,339	2,206	860	3,920
Transportation	6,531	7,013	8,057	8,395	9,070	9,176
Community and regional development	1,545	2,395	2,846	3,413	4,593	4,084
Education, training, employment, and social services	7,538	8,624	9,839	12,519	12,735	12,344
Health	11,758	13,051	14,716	17,471	18,832	22,074
Income security	37,281	43,066	55,423	63,911	72,958	84,431
Veterans benefits and services	7,640	8,677	9,776	10,730	12,013	13,386
Administration of justice	761	952	1,299	1,650	2,131	2,462
General government	1,649	1,940	2,159	2,466	2,682	3,327
General purpose fiscal assistance	430	536	535	673	7,351	6,890
Interest	15,793	18,312	19,609	20,582	22,813	28,072
Allowances						
Undistributed offsetting receipts	−5,545	−6,567	−8,427	−8,137	−12,318	−16,651
Composition of undistributed offsetting receipts:						
Employer share, employee retirement	−2,018	−2,444	−2,611	−2,768	−2,927	−3,319
Interest received by trust funds	−3,099	−3,936	−4,765	−5,089	−5,436	−6,583
Rents and royalties on the Outer Continental Shelf	−428	−187	−1,051	−279	−3,956	−6,748

See next page for continuation of table and for footnotes.

Table A.8 (continued)

[Millions of dollars; fiscal years]

Description	Actual				Estimate	
	1975	1976	Transition quarter	1977	1978	1979
BUDGET RECEIPTS AND OUTLAYS:						
Total receipts	280,997	299,197	81,687	356,861	400,387	439,588
Federal funds	187,505	200,291	53,999	240,412	267,889	289,095
Trust funds	118,590	133,695	32,071	152,763	168,490	187,991
Interfund transactions	−25,098	−34,789	−4,383	−36,313	−35,992	−37,497
Total outlays	326,092	365,643	94,657	401,902	462,234	500,174
Federal funds	240,018	269,146	65,017	294,948	340,036	363,580
Trust funds	111,171	131,286	34,023	143,267	158,190	174,092
Interfund transactions	−25,098	−34,789	−4,383	−36,313	−35,992	−37,497
Total surplus or deficit (−)	−45,095	−66,446	−12,970	−45,040	−61,847	−60,586
Federal funds	−52,514	−68,855	−11,018	−54,536	−72,147	−74,485
Trust funds	7,419	2,410	−1,952	9,496	10,300	13,899
OUTSTANDING DEBT, END OF PERIOD:						
Gross Federal debt	544,131	631,866	646,379	709,138	785,583	873,668
Held by Government agencies	147,225	151,566	148,052	157,295	167,740	182,826
Held by the public	396,906	480,300	498,327	551,843	617,843	690,843
Federal Reserve System	84,993	94,714	96,702	105,004	---------	---------
Other	311,913	385,586	401,625	446,839	---------	---------
BUDGET RECEIPTS	280,997	299,197	81,687	356,861	400,387	439,588
Individual income taxes	122,386	130,794	38,715	156,725	178,828	190,077
Corporation income taxes	40,621	41,409	8,460	54,892	58,949	62,487
Social insurance taxes and contributions	86,441	92,714	25,760	108,638	124,122	141,889
Excise taxes	16,551	16,963	4,473	17,548	20,150	25,475
Estate and gift taxes	4,611	5,216	1,455	7,327	5,618	6,067
Customs duties	3,676	4,074	1,212	5,150	5,792	6,390
Miscellaneous receipts:						
Deposits of earnings by Federal Reserve System	5,777	5,451	1,500	5,908	6,200	6,300
All other	934	2,575	112	622	728	902
BUDGET OUTLAYS	326,092	365,643	94,657	401,902	462,234	500,174
National defense	85,550	89,430	22,307	97,501	107,626	117,779
International affairs	6,861	5,567	2,180	4,831	6,747	7,691
General science, space, and technology	3,989	4,370	1,161	4,677	4,757	5,077
Energy	2,179	3,127	794	4,172	7,837	9,634
Natural resources and environment	7,329	8,124	2,532	10,000	12,125	12,222
Agriculture	1,660	2,502	584	5,526	9,106	5,433
Commerce and housing credit	5,604	3,795	1,391	−31	3,523	2,969
Transportation	10,392	13,438	3,306	14,636	16,310	17,399
Community and regional development	3,692	4,709	1,340	6,283	9,694	8,669
Education, training, employment, and social services	15,870	18,737	5,162	20,985	27,471	30,421
Health	27,647	33,448	8,720	38,785	44,261	49,677
Income security	108,605	126,598	32,710	137,004	147,640	160,024
Veterans benefits and services	16,597	18,432	3,962	18,038	18,916	19,257
Administration of justice	2,942	3,320	859	3,600	4,019	4,211
General government	3,089	2,927	878	3,357	4,119	4,304
General purpose fiscal assistance	7,187	7,235	2,092	9,499	9,860	9,636
Interest	30,974	34,589	7,246	38,092	43,841	48,991
Allowances						2,800
Undistributed offsetting receipts	−14,075	−14,704	−2,567	−15,053	−15,619	−16,021
Composition of undistributed offsetting receipts:						
Employer share, employee retirement	−3,980	−4,242	−985	−4,548	−5,024	−5,157
Interest received by trust funds	−7,667	−7,800	−270	−8,131	−8,595	−9,064
Rents and royalties on the Outer Continental Shelf	−2,428	−2,662	−1,311	−2,374	−2,000	−1,800

Note.—Through fiscal year 1976, the fiscal year runs from July 1 through June 30; starting in October 1976 (fiscal year 1977), the fiscal year runs from October 1 through September 30. The period July 1, 1976 through September 30, 1976 is a separate fiscal period known as the transition quarter.
Earned income credit payments in excess of an individual's taxable liability are classified as income tax refunds beginning 1976 and as outlays prior to 1976.

Sources: Department of the Treasury and Office of Management and Budget.

Table A.9 Net public and private debt, 1929–1976[1]

[Billions of dollars]

| | | Public | | | Private | | Individual and unincorporated enterprise | | | | | |
| | | | | | | | | | Nonfarm | | | |
End of year	Total	Federal Government [2]	Federally sponsored credit agencies [3]	State and local governments	Total	Corporate	Total	Farm [4]	Total	Mortgage	Commercial and financial [5]	Consumer
1929	191.9	16.5	....	13.6	161.8	88.9	72.9	12.2	60.7	31.2	22.4	7.1
1933	168.5	24.3	....	16.3	127.9	76.9	51.0	9.1	41.9	26.3	11.7	3.9
1939	183.3	42.6	....	16.4	124.3	73.5	50.8	8.8	42.0	25.0	9.8	7.2
1940	189.8	44.8	....	16.4	128.6	75.6	53.0	9.1	43.9	26.1	9.5	8.3
1941	211.4	56.3	....	16.1	139.0	83.4	55.6	9.3	46.3	27.1	10.0	9.2
1942	258.6	101.7	....	15.4	141.5	91.6	49.9	9.0	40.9	26.8	8.1	6.0
1943	313.2	154.4	....	14.5	144.3	95.5	48.8	8.2	40.5	26.1	9.5	4.9
1944	370.6	211.9	....	13.9	144.8	94.1	50.7	7.7	42.9	26.0	11.8	5.1
1945	405.9	252.5	....	13.4	140.0	85.3	54.7	7.3	47.4	27.0	14.7	5.7
1946	396.6	229.5	....	13.7	153.4	93.5	59.9	7.6	52.3	31.8	12.1	8.4
1947	415.7	221.7	0.7	15.0	178.3	108.9	69.4	8.6	60.7	37.2	11.9	11.6
1948	431.3	215.3	.6	17.0	198.4	117.8	80.6	10.8	69.7	42.4	12.9	14.4
1949	445.8	217.6	.7	19.1	208.4	118.0	90.4	12.0	78.4	47.1	13.9	17.4
1950	486.2	217.4	.7	21.7	246.4	142.1	104.3	12.3	92.0	54.8	15.8	21.5
1951	519.2	216.9	1.3	24.2	276.8	162.5	114.3	13.7	100.6	61.7	16.2	22.7
1952	550.2	221.5	1.3	27.0	300.4	171.0	129.4	15.2	114.2	68.9	17.8	27.5
1953	581.6	226.8	1.4	30.7	322.7	179.5	143.2	16.8	126.4	76.7	18.4	31.4
1954	605.9	229.1	1.3	35.5	340.0	182.8	157.2	17.5	139.7	86.4	20.8	32.5
1955	665.8	229.6	2.9	41.1	392.2	212.1	180.1	18.7	161.4	98.7	24.0	38.8
1956	698.4	224.3	2.4	44.5	427.2	231.7	195.5	19.4	176.1	109.4	24.4	42.3
1957	728.3	223.0	2.4	48.6	454.3	246.7	207.6	20.2	187.4	118.1	24.3	45.0
1958	769.6	231.0	2.5	53.7	482.4	259.5	222.9	23.2	199.7	128.1	26.5	45.1
1959	833.0	241.4	3.7	59.6	528.3	283.3	245.0	23.8	221.2	141.0	28.7	51.5
1960	874.2	239.8	3.5	64.9	566.1	302.8	263.3	25.1	238.2	151.3	30.8	56.1
1961	930.3	246.7	4.0	70.5	609.1	324.3	284.8	27.5	257.3	164.5	34.8	58.0
1962	996.0	253.6	5.3	77.0	660.1	348.2	311.9	30.2	281.7	180.3	37.6	63.8
1963	1,070.9	257.5	7.2	83.9	722.3	376.4	345.8	33.2	312.6	198.6	42.3	71.7
1964	1,151.6	264.0	7.5	90.4	789.7	409.6	380.1	36.0	344.1	218.9	45.0	80.3
1965	1,252.5	266.4	8.9	98.3	878.9	454.3	424.6	39.3	385.3	244.3	51.1	89.9
1966	1,349.1	271.8	11.2	104.7	961.3	506.6	454.7	42.2	412.5	260.9	55.4	96.2
1967	1,450.8	286.4	9.0	112.8	1,042.7	553.6	489.1	47.9	441.1	278.2	62.2	100.8
1968	1,596.8	291.9	21.5	122.7	1,160.9	631.5	529.3	51.7	477.6	298.4	68.5	110.8
1969	1,753.4	289.3	30.6	133.3	1,300.2	734.1	566.2	55.2	511.0	319.8	70.0	121.1
1970	1,881.9	301.1	38.8	144.8	1,397.2	797.3	600.0	57.8	542.1	344.9	70.3	127.0
1971	2,067.3	325.9	39.9	162.7	1,538.8	871.3	667.5	62.5	604.9	389.3	77.0	138.6
1972	2,299.8	341.2	41.4	178.0	1,739.2	975.3	763.9	68.2	695.8	448.7	89.8	157.2
1973	2,562.3	349.1	59.8	192.3	1,961.1	1,106.7	854.4	79.0	775.5	510.4	86.1	179.0
1974	2,793.5	360.8	75.4	211.2	2,145.1	1,223.0	922.1	89.2	832.9	561.0	83.1	188.7
1975	3,028.8	446.3	78.8	222.7	2,281.0	1,286.6	994.4	98.2	896.2	612.8	86.2	197.3
1976	3,354.9	515.8	81.4	236.3	2,521.5	1,414.7	1,106.8	108.5	998.3	684.1	96.4	217.8

[1] Net public and private debt is a comprehensive aggregate of the indebtedness of borrowers after eliminating certain types of duplicating government and corporate debt.

[2] Net Federal Government debt is the outstanding debt held by the public, as defined in "The Budget of the United States Government, Fiscal Year 1979."

[3] Debt of agencies in which there is no longer any Federal proprietary interest. The obligations of the Federal land banks are included beginning with 1947, the debt of the Federal home loan banks is included beginning with 1951, and the debts of the Federal National Mortgage Association, Federal intermediate credit banks, and banks for cooperatives are included beginning with 1968.

[4] Farm mortgages and farm production loans. Farmers' financial and consumer debt is included in the nonfarm categories.

[5] Debt to banks (other than consumer credit), security credit, policy loans, and some single-payments loans.

Source: Department of Commerce (Bureau of Economic Analysis), based on data from various Federal agencies and ther sources.

Table A.10 United States balance of payments, 1946–1977

[Millions of dollars; quarterly data seasonally adjusted, except as noted]

Year or quarter	Merchandise [1][2]			Investment income [3]			Net military transactions	Net travel and transportation receipts	Other services, net [3]	Balance on goods and services [1][4]	Remittances, pensions, and other unilateral transfers [1]	Balance on current account
	Exports	Imports	Net balance	Receipts	Payments	Net						
1946	11,764	−5,067	6,697	772	−212	560	−493	733	310	7,807	−2,922	4,885
1947	16,097	−5,973	10,124	1,102	−245	857	−455	946	145	11,617	−2,625	8,992
1948	13,265	−7,557	5,708	1,340	−280	1,060	−799	374	175	6,518	−4,525	1,993
1949	12,213	−6,874	5,339	1,395	−333	1,062	−621	230	208	6,218	−5,638	580
1950	10,203	−9,081	1,122	1,593	−369	1,224	−576	−120	242	1,892	−4,017	−2,125
1951	14,243	−11,176	3,067	1,882	−414	1,468	−1,270	298	254	3,817	−3,515	302
1952	13,449	−10,838	2,611	1,828	−421	1,407	−2,054	83	309	2,356	−2,531	−175
1953	12,412	−10,975	1,437	1,910	−461	1,449	−2,423	−238	307	532	−2,481	−1,949
1954	12,929	−10,353	2,576	2,227	−420	1,807	−2,460	−269	305	1,959	−2,280	−321
1955	14,424	−11,527	2,897	2,444	−489	1,955	−2,701	−297	299	2,153	−2,498	−345
1956	17,556	−12,803	4,753	2,662	−568	2,094	−2,788	−361	447	4,145	−2,423	1,722
1957	19,562	−13,291	6,271	2,817	−639	2,178	−2,841	−189	482	5,901	−2,345	3,556
1958	16,414	−12,952	3,462	2,845	−669	2,176	−3,135	−633	486	2,356	−2,361	−5
1959	16,458	−15,310	1,148	3,043	−828	2,215	−2,805	−821	573	310	−2,448	−2,138
1960	19,650	−14,758	4,892	3,350	−1,063	2,287	−2,752	−964	579	4,040	−2,308	1,732
1961	20,108	−14,537	5,571	3,944	−1,007	2,937	−2,596	−978	594	5,529	−2,524	3,005
1962	20,781	−16,260	4,521	4,421	−1,110	3,311	−2,449	−1,152	809	5,042	−2,638	2,404
1963	22,272	−17,048	5,224	4,650	−1,325	3,325	−2,304	−1,309	960	5,897	−2,754	3,143
1964	25,501	−18,700	6,801	5,392	−1,457	3,935	−2,133	−1,146	1,041	8,499	−2,781	5,718
1965	26,461	−21,510	4,951	5,899	−1,730	4,169	−2,122	−1,280	1,387	7,105	−2,854	4,251
1966	29,310	−25,493	3,817	5,740	−2,142	3,598	−2,935	−1,331	1,365	4,514	−2,932	1,582
1967	30,666	−26,866	3,800	6,267	−2,307	3,960	−3,226	−1,750	1,612	4,395	−3,125	1,270
1968	33,626	−32,991	635	6,937	−2,890	4,047	−3,143	−1,548	1,630	1,621	−2,952	−1,331
1969	36,414	−35,807	607	8,090	−4,438	3,652	−3,328	−1,763	1,833	1,002	−2,994	−1,993
1970	42,469	−39,866	2,603	8,575	−5,082	3,493	−3,354	−2,023	2,190	2,912	−3,294	−382
1971	43,319	−45,579	−2,260	9,512	−4,893	4,619	−2,893	−2,315	2,509	−340	−3,701	−4,041
1972	49,381	−55,797	−6,416	10,161	−5,975	4,186	−3,621	−3,028	2,789	−6,088	−3,854	−9,942
1973	71,410	−70,499	911	13,540	−8,744	4,796	−2,287	−3,086	3,185	3,520	−3,887	−367
1974	98,306	−103,673	−5,367	19,763	−11,019	8,744	−2,083	−3,105	3,970	2,160	−7,188 [5]	−5,028
1975	107,088	−98,043	9,045	17,330	−11,376	5,954	−876	−2,552	4,594	16,164	−4,612	11,552
1976	114,694	−124,014	−9,320	21,369	−11,561	9,808	366	−2,145	4,888	3,596	−5,023	−1,427
1975: I	27,018	−25,563	1,455	4,283	−3,052	1,231	−393	−685	1,100	2,708	−1,195	1,513
II	25,851	−22,566	3,285	4,306	−2,799	1,507	−311	−579	1,129	5,031	−1,110	3,921
III	26,562	−24,483	2,079	4,403	−2,784	1,619	−139	−604	1,180	4,135	−1,070	3,065
IV	27,657	−25,431	2,226	4,338	−2,741	1,597	−34	−684	1,184	4,289	−1,238	3,051
1976: I	27,000	−28,343	−1,343	5,298	−2,861	2,437	−65	−669	1,192	1,552	−1,029	523
II	28,380	−29,955	−1,575	5,167	−2,887	2,280	−39	−337	1,176	1,505	−1,015	490
III	29,603	−32,411	−2,808	5,483	−2,816	2,667	235	−458	1,239	875	−1,936	−1,061
IV	29,711	−33,305	−3,594	5,421	−2,997	2,424	235	−681	1,279	−337	−1,045	−1,382
1977: I	29,458	−36,561	−7,103	6,133	−2,881	3,252	516	−953	1,293	−2,995	−1,163	−4,158
II	30,590	−38,347	−7,757	6,660	−3,156	3,504	311	−785	1,338	−3,389	−1,215	−4,604
III p	30,869	−38,378	−7,509	6,430	−3,215	3,215	577	−727	1,494	−2,950	−1,352	−4,302

[1] Excludes military grants.
[2] Adjusted from Census data for differences in valuation, coverage, and timing.
[3] Fees and royalties from U.S. direct investments abroad or from foreign direct investments in the United States are excluded from investment income and included in other services, net.
[4] In concept, the sum of balance on current account and allocations of special drawing rights is equal to net foreign investment in the national income and product accounts, although the two may differ because of revisions, special handling of certain items, etc.

(Footnotes continued on following page.)

Table A.10 (continued)

[Millions of dollars; quarterly data seasonally adjusted, except as noted]

Year or quarter	U.S. assets abroad, net [increase/capital outflow (−)]				Foreign assets in the U.S., net [increase/capital inflow (+)]				Allocations of special drawing rights (SDR)	Statistical discrepancy	
						Foreign official assets					
	Total	U.S. official reserve assets⁶	Other U.S. Government assets	U.S. private assets	Total	Total	Assets of foreign official reserve agencies	Other foreign assets		Total (sum of the items with sign reversed)	Of which Seasonal adjustment discrepancy
1946		−623									
1947		−3,315									
1948		−1,736									
1949		−266									
1950		1,758									
1951		−33									
1952		−415									
1953		1,256									
1954		480									
1955		182									
1956		−869									
1957		−1,165									
1958		2,292									
1959		1,035									
1960	−2,833	2,145	−1,100	−3,878	2,120	1,473	1,258	647		−1,019	
1961	−4,484	606	−910	−4,180	2,467	765	741	1,701		−988	
1962	−2,979	1,533	−1,085	−3,426	1,697	1,270	1,118	427		−1,122	
1963	−5,764	377	−1,662	−4,479	2,981	1,986	1,558	995		−360	
1964	−8,128	171	−1,680	−6,618	3,317	1,661	1,363	1,656		−907	
1965	−4,176	1,222	−1,605	−3,793	382	132	67	249		−457	
1966	−5,530	568	−1,543	−4,554	3,320	−674	−787	3,994		628	
1967	−8,002	52	−2,423	−5,630	6,938	3,450	3,367	3,488		−206	
1968	−8,547	−880	−2,274	−5,393	9,439	−776	−761	10,215		439	
1969	−8,763	−1,187	−2,200	−5,376	12,270	−1,301	−1,552	13,571		−1,515	
1970	−6,164	2,477	−1,589	−7,052	5,923	6,907	7,362	−984	867	−244	
1971	−9,299	2,348	−1,884	−9,763	22,445	26,895	27,405	−4,450	717	−9,822	
1972	−9,929	32	−1,568	−8,392	21,127	10,705	10,322	10,422	710	−1,966	
1973	−14,666	209	−2,645	−12,230	17,753	6,299	5,145	11,454		−2,720	
1974	−27,029	−1,434	⁵365	−25,960	33,612	10,981	10,257	22,631		−1,555	
1975	−31,548	−607	−3,463	−27,478	14,336	6,960	5,259	7,376		5,660	
1976	−42,959	−2,530	−4,213	−36,216	34,520	17,945	13,007	16,575		9,866	
1975: I	−8,749	−325	−874	−7,550	2,443	3,452	3,024	−1,009		4,793	1,121
II	−7,881	−29	−867	−6,985	3,663	2,279	1,884	1,384		297	38
III	−3,081	−342	−745	−1,994	2,416	−1,603	−1,977	4,019		−2,400	−2,475
IV	−11,836	89	−977	−10,948	5,814	2,832	2,328	2,982		2,971	1,316
1976: I	−10,751	−773	−723	−9,254	6,856	3,847	2,323	3,009		3,372	717
II	−9,779	−1,578	−944	−7,257	7,385	4,051	3,308	3,333		1,905	129
III	−8,409	−407	−1,405	−6,597	8,201	3,070	1,251	5,131		1,268	−2,622
IV	−14,022	228	−1,142	−13,108	12,079	6,977	6,125	5,102		3,325	1,780
1977: I	331	−388	−909	1,627	2,510	5,719	5,007	−3,209		1,317	524
II	−10,283	6	−825	−9,464	13,781	7,908	7,452	5,873		1,106	−215
IIIᵖ	−3,396	151	−1,175	−2,372	12,923	8,243	7,924	4,680		−5,225	−2,506

⁵ Includes extraordinary U.S. Government transactions with India.

⁶ Consists of gold, special drawing rights, convertible currencies, and the U.S. reserve position in the International Monetary Fund (IMF).

Note.—Quarterly data for changes in U.S. official reserve assets, U.S. private assets abroad, and foreign assets in the U.S. are not seasonally adjusted.

Source: Department of Commerce, Bureau of Economic Analysis.

GLOSSARY

Aggregate Demand The total demand or expenditure for goods and services by consumers, businesses (investment expenditure), governments, and foreigners (after subtracting domestic expenditures for foreign commodities) in a given year.

Arbitrage The activity of dealing in two or more markets in order to take advantage of differences in prices for the same commodities.

Asset Something of value that one owns.

Autonomous Expenditures Expenditures that come about independently of any economic factors.

Average Propensity to Consume The ratio of consumption expenditure to national income.

Balance of Payments A record of a nation's international transactions giving rise to an inflow (credit) of foreign currency and an outflow (debit) of domestic currency. The balance of payments is normally divided into a number of subaccounts.

Balance Sheet An account of assets and liabilities showing net worth at a given point in time.

Breton Woods System The international monetary system created in 1944 at Bretton Woods, New Hampshire, which prevailed until August 15, 1971. It was a form of the gold-exchange standard in which the dollar was defined in terms of gold and all other currencies were defined in terms of the dollar.

Built-in Stabilizers Features of an economy which tend to dampen fluctuations in employment and output. For example, unemployment benefits are designed or "built-in" the economy so that they modify the decrease in consumption expenditure that would normally follow an increase in unemployment.

Capital The man-made resources used in the production of goods and services, including plants, tools, and machinery.

Capital Consumption Allowance The value of capital equipment used up during production in the economy over a given period of time. It is the deduction made from gross national product to determine net national product.

Cartel An association formed for the purpose of regulating the purchase, production, or marketing of goods by its members.

Classical School of Economics A school of thought in economics represented by a group of writers in the late eighteenth and early nineteenth centuries. They include Adam Smith, Thomas Malthus, David Ricardo, and John Stuart Mill. They formulated a systematic body of economic principles generally supporting the philosophy of laissez-faire.

Commercial Bank A financial situation which accepts demand deposits and consequently can affect the supply of money by its lending activities.

Comparative Advantage A situation which exists when a nation can produce two products, both at a cost below that of another nation, but in relative terms, can produce one of the two commodities at less cost than the other.

Competitive Market A market characterized by the absence of any restrictions limiting exit or entry, apart from the usual requirement that the participants be prepared to pay for the tools and knowledge required to succeed in that activity.

Consumption Function The relationship between the level of consumption expenditure and the level of national income. John Maynard Keynes identified this relationship, stating that the level of consumption spending increases as national income increases but not as rapidly.

Corporation A legal entity chartered by the government created for the purpose of doing business. Its chief advantage is that it offers limited liability to its owners. It can engage in contractual relationships, own property, incur debts, be sued, and pay taxes.

Cost Cost in economics refers to a choice between alternatives or the sacrifice involved in accomplishing something.

Cost-Benefit Analysis A systematic comparison between the cost of producing a service or good and the value of that good or service, specifying the comparison in quantitative terms where possible.

Creeping Inflation A constant, slow, annual increase in the rate of inflation of approximately 2–3 percent per year.

Demand A schedule of alternative quantities of a good or service that a person (individual demand) or a group of people (market demand) is willing and able to purchase at each alternative price during a specified period of time, other things remaining unchanged.

Demand Deposit A deposit in a commercial bank which can be withdrawn by the depositor without previously notifying the bank. A check is the vehicle for this withdrawal and it is an order by the depositor to the bank to pay the person to whom the check is addressed a given amount of money. Demand deposits do not usually bear interest.

Derived Demand The demand for a productive service that stems from the demand for a final product. The demand for corn, for example, may be derived from the demand for beef.

Discount Rate The interest rate that a Federal Reserve bank charges when it lends to a member bank. It is also called the rediscount rate.

Disintermediation The shift of savings from accounts in financial institutions such as savings banks and savings and loan associations to higher yielding short-term securities such as treasury certificates.

Disposable Personal Income The income of individuals after allowing for personal tax payments to the government.

Economic Growth The increase in an economy's real output, usually measured in per capita terms, e.g., GNP per capita.

Economic Indicator A statistic which is sensitive to changes in the state of economic conditions, e.g., the unemployment rate, consumer prices, wholesale prices, wage rates, etc. Those indicators which precede the general level of economic activity are called leading indicators while those that follow the general trend are called lagging indicators.

Economic Rent That part of the amount paid for the use of a resource which is in excess of its supply price.

Economics The science which deals with the decisions involved in the creation and allocation of goods and services for the satisfaction of human wants under conditions of scarcity.

Elasticity, Price A measure of the responsiveness of the quantity demanded to a change in price. The coefficient of elasticity is calculated by the ratio:

$$\frac{\%\ \text{in quantity demanded}}{\%\ \text{change in price}}.$$

If the coefficient is greater than 1, *demand* is elastic; if it equals 1, it is unitary elastic; and if it is less than 1, it is inelastic.

Employment Act of 1946 An act of Congress that assigns the federal government the responsibility for maintaining full employment, stable prices, and a high rate of economic growth. It also established the Joint Economic Committee and the President's Council of Economic Advisors.

Entrepreneur A person who assumes the responsibilities of organization, management, and risk in a productive enterprise.

Equation of Exchange A mathematical expression of the relationships among the quantity of money (M), the velocity of money (V), the price level (P), and the value of real output (Q). It is a truism stating that total demand equals total supply and is expressed as $MV \ominus PQ$.

Equilibrium A state of rest or balance due to the equal action of opposing forces. In a market situation, equilibrium is characterized by a balance between quantity supplied and quantity demanded.

Equilibrium, General A term referring to a situation in which all the markets of an economy are in equilibrium. Consequently, partial equilibrium refers to a subset of the markets in an economy that are in equilibrium.

Excess Reserves A bank's total reserves minus its required reserves.

Federal Open Market Committee (FOMC) A subcommittee of the Board of Governors of the Federal Reserve System whose function is to facilitate the achievement of economic goals through monetary policy in which government securities are bought and sold.

Fine Tuning The exercise of economic policy to the degree of achieving narrowly defined goals.

Flexible Exchange Rate System An international monetary system in which exchange rates are freely determined by supply and demand.

Free Market Economy An economy characterized by a market system in which buyers and sellers are allowed to engage in production and exchange without restrictions as to prices, quantities, or commodities involved.

Full Employment That condition which prevails in the economy when anyone who is willing and able to find employment at the prevailing wage rates can do so.

Gold Standard A monetary system which uses gold as the standard of value for its currency. The monetary unit is defined in terms of gold and gold coins are allowed to circulate freely in the economy.

Gross National Product The market value of all the final goods and services produced in an economy in a given period of time.

Gross Private Domestic Expenditure Expenditures over a given period of time by businesses for new buildings, equipment, and inventories and by individuals for residential construction.

Implicit Price Index A measure revealing changes in the price level based on a broad collection of goods and services. It is used to convert the money value of GNP into real GNP.

Income Statement An account of the operations of a business or institution over a given period of time usually reflecting sales or receipts, the cost of sales or expenditures, and profit or loss. It is also called a profit and loss statement.

Incomes Policy   A program which exercises restraint on increases in personal income and/or prices in order to reduce inflation. Wage-price guidelines are an example of one form of incomes policy. A more extreme example is a wage-price freeze.

Indexation   The idea of inflation-proofing the economy by tying monetary contracts to a general price index.

Inflation   A relatively large increase in the general price level.

Innovation   The process by which new products and processes are introduced into production.

Interest Rate   The price at which loanable funds are bought and sold is determined by the interaction of supply and demand.

Keynesian Economics   The body of economic thought espoused by John Maynard Keynes (1883–1946), an English economist, and his followers. It states that the level of economic activity depends on the level of aggregate demand—investment and consumption expenditure.

Liability   A debt or obligation owed by an individual or institution.

Liquidity   The ease with which an asset can be converted into money. Hence, money is the essence of liquidity.

Lorenz Curve   A graph that illustrates the distribution of income by plotting the relationship between the percentage of income received cumulated from lowest to highest against the percentage of families cumulated from poorest to richest.

Macroeconomics   That branch of economics that deals with the behavior of aggregated variables.

Marginal Cost   The change in total cost resulting from one unit change in output.

Marginal Efficiency of Capital   The relationship between the expected yield of an additional unit of capital equipment and the cost of producing that unit.

Marginal Product (Output)   The increase in total product stemming from the use of an additional unit of a variable input.

Marginal Prospensity to Consume   The ratio of the rate of change of consumption expenditure to the rate of change of national income.

Marginal Revenue   The change in total revenue resulting from a one-unit change in quantity sold.

Market   A situation which exists when buyers and sellers are in communication with one another for the purpose of exchange.

Measure of Economic Welfare   A measure of national welfare which is broader than GNP in that it attempts to adjust for the disamenities of production.

Microeconomics   That branch of economics that deals with particular individuals, single commodities, or single markets.

Mixed Economy   An economy which has the characteristics of both a market economy and a centralized economy with some measures of control and regulation by the central government.

Model   A simplified representation of reality, including only those aspects necessary to observe the essence of the issue under consideration.

Monetarism   A school of thought in economics led by Professor Milton Friedman of the University of Chicago which places emphasis on the money supply as the chief determinant of the level of economic activity.

Money   Anything generally acceptable in exchange for goods or services or as a means of paying debt.

Money GNP   The value of GNP as measured in terms of the dollar used in the year in which the measurement was made. It is also called GNP as measured in current dollars.

Money Supply   The amount of money existing in an economy at any point in time. There is no single universally accepted definition. Three of the most common are:

M_1 — currency in circulation outside of commercial banks plus demand deposits,

M_2 — M_1 plus time deposits in commercial banks,

M_3 — M_2 plus time deposits in financial institutions other than commercial banks, such as savings banks and savings and loan associations.

Monopoly Power   The economic power secured by a single seller or a small number of sellers when there are restrictions of one type or another on entry into an industry or occupation.

Multiplier Principle   In Keynesian economics this principle describes the relationship of a change in a component of aggregate demand on the level of economic activity. The concept of the investment multiplier, for example, asserts that an increase in investment expenditure will increase the level of national income by a multiple of the original increase in investment.

National Income   The value of the earnings of the factors of production in an economy over a given period of time such as one year.

Net National Product   The market value of all the final goods and services produced in an economy in a given period of time after allowing for the capital equipment used up in the process of production.

Normative Economics   The part of economics which concerns value judgments, the "ought" or "should" of any solution to a given problem.

Open-Market Operations   The buying or selling of government securities by the Federal Reserve System for the purpose of regulating the supply of money in circulation. These activities comprise one of the most important policy "tools" of the Federal Reserve System.

Opportunity Cost   The value of the best alternative given up when a decision is made. In production, the amount that must be paid to purchase materials or the amount that producers must pay to keep multiple-use resources from being used to produce other products.

Partnership   A joint proprietorship by two or more individuals.

Patent   The right of exclusive proprietorship of an invention granted by a government to a person or organization for a limited period of time.

Personal Income   The total current income received by persons and other institutions, such as unincorporated businesses and nonprofit institutions, in an economy.

Phillips Curve   The graphical representation of the relationship between the annual percentage change in prices and the unemployment rate. This relationship, developed by A. W. Phillips of the London School of Economics, suggests that a reduction in unemployment will be accompanied by an increase in prices.

Positive Economics   The aspect of economics which deals with the economic effects of individual, institutional, or governmental actions.

Poverty   A situation which exists when a person's (family's) income is inadequate to satisfy basic needs.

Present Value   The current value of a payment or series of payments due sometime in the future. It is calculated by discounting this payment at a specified rate of interest.

Price, Equilibrium   The price at which the quantity demanded is equal to the quantity supplied. It is also called the market clearing prices.

Production   The process of increasing the capacity of goods to satisfy human desires or of rendering services capable of satisfying human desires.

Productivity   The term used to refer to output per man-hour. Or, more generally, the ratio of output to the input of resources.

Profit   Ordinarily the difference between the selling price of a product and the cost of producing the product. In economics, it is the difference between the selling price of a product and the opportunity costs of producing it.

Proprietorship   A term describing a business operated by and for an individual.

Quantity Theory of Money   A theory which states that in the equation of exchange, $MV \ominus PQ$, M, or the quantity of money, is the dominant variable which determines the level of price P.

Quasi-Rent   Payment made for a good or service which is temporarily limited in supply.

Real GNP   The value of GNP adjusted for the change in the general level of prices as reflected by the Implicit Price Index. It is also called GNP measured in constant dollars.

Required Reserves   The amount a commercial bank must hold in the form of cash in its vault or as a deposit in its district Federal Reserve bank. This amount is a prescribed percentage of the bank's demand deposits.

Reserves   The amount of cash a bank has in its vault plus its deposits in the Federal Reserve bank of its district.

Resources   The factors of production used to produce goods and services. They are usually classified into land, labor, and capital representing natural, human, and man-made resources.

Scarcity   The condition which exists when wants exceed the resources available to satisfy wants.

Social Institution   An established pattern of social interaction. It may be enacted into law and administered by the courts, and/or be embedded in custom and tradition.

Special Drawing Rights (S.D.R.s)   An instrument created by the International Monetary Fund for financing international trade, to be used in place of gold or reserve currencies.

Subsidy   Financial assistance, or its equivalent, given for a service which, though uneconomic from a profit-making standpoint, is considered essential to the public welfare.

Supply   A schedule listing the alternative quantities of a good or service that sellers are willing and able to provide at each alternative price during a specified period of time, other things remaining unchanged.

Tariff   A tax or a duty imposed by a government on a commodity that is either imported or exported.

Tax   A tax is a compulsory payment made to the government.

Tax, Ad Valorem   A tax which is expressed as a proportion of the price of the good.

Tax, Corporate Profits   A tax levied on the earnings of a corporation.

Tax, Incidence   The person or persons on whom the burden of a tax eventually rests regardless of on whom it is levied.

Tax, Progressive   A tax whose rate increases as the base on which the tax is levied increases.

Tax, Property   A tax levied on real (e.g., buildings) or personal (e.g., stocks and bonds) property.

Tax, Proportional   A tax whose rate is constant regardless of the base on which it is calculated.

Tax Rate   That proportion of the monetary value of a tax base which is collected by the government.

Tax, Regressive   A tax whose rate decreases as the base on which it is levied increases.

Tax, Sales   A tax levied on the sales of goods or services at one or more points in the process of distribution.

Tax, Social Security   A tax usually levied on employers and employees to finance public insurance programs.

Tax, Specific   A tax which is expressed as a given amount per unit of the good.

Taxation, Ability to Pay Principle   The principle that tax payments should be related to the individual's ability to pay.

Taxation, Benefit Principle   The principle that tax payments should be related to the benefits received from government services.

Technology   The body of knowledge applied to the production of goods and services.

Time Deposit   A deposit in a financial institution which need not be paid to the depositor without prior notice of a stipulated time period. Time deposits bear interest.

Transaction Costs   The costs involved in reimbursing owners of private property for injuries incurred by third parties.

Transfer Payment   A transfer payment is a payment made to an individual by government or business for which no services are rendered. The requirements for eligibility are only that a person meet the qualifications specified for receiving the payment.

Value of Marginal Product   The selling price of a product multiplied by the marginal product of a variable resource used in the production of the product. It determines the amount of a variable resource that will be employed by a firm.

Velocity of Money   The average number of times that each unit of the money supply is exchanged in a year for a final product. It depends on the length of time people hold their money.

Wealth   The market value of goods and services in existence at any point in time.

INDEX